THE OLYMPUS OM WAY

The latest OM Models

OLYMPUS OM-1N, OM-2N, T-20

A month or so after publication of this book, Olympus announced modified versions of the OM-1 and OM-2 cameras, to be known temporarily as the OM-1N and OM-2N (= New).

The Olympus OM-1N differs from the OM-1 described in the chapter starting on page 17 by having a small LED built into the finder at the left of the frame for operation with the T-20 flash unit (see below).

The Olympus OM-2N has a similar LED in the finder just above the shutter speed scale (visible in AUTO mode). It also has a brighter LED for the battery check, a longest automatic exposure time of 120 seconds (instead of 60) and an indicator in the viewfinder when the exposure override dial is set to any exposure correction figure.

The mirror lockup and reset procedure (page 27) is changed: if the mirror locks up you can bring it down again (after replacing exhausted batteries if necessary) by moving the meter switch to the CHECK/RESET (previously only CHECK) position. The reset button below the lens mount now only unlocks the B setting.

The T-20 flash unit is a simplified (and less powerful) version of the 310 with additional interaction features with the OM-1N and OM-2N. It fits onto these cameras via the accessory shoe 4. With the OM-1N the T-20 permits manual or normal automatic operation with the flash duration controlled by a sensor cell on the flash unit. When the T-20 is fully charged for flashing, the LED in the OM-1N finder lights up. In the automatic mode, the LED also blinks after a flash to signify that the exposure was within the range of correct exposures of the unit.

On the OM-2N the T-20 has the same operating modes plus through-the-lens flash control similar to the QA 310 (page 206). The T-20 can also be used on the previous OM-2 with the accessory shoe 3 and then permits through-the-lens exposure control but without signals in the finder.

The new 1-14 focusing screen is similar to the 1-13 screen (page 89) but has a 45° split in the wedge rangefinder area (instead of a horizontal split).

THE OLYMPUS OM WAY

The Olympus OM Photographer's Companion

L. ANDREW MANNHEIM

With photographs by DON MORLEY, ALL-SPORT

Focal Press · London

Focal/Hastings House · New York

BL British Library Cataloguing in Publication Data
Mannheim, Ladislaus Andrew
The Olympus OM way.—(Camera way books).
1. Olympus camera
I. Title II. Morley, Don
77.1.3'1 TR263.04

ISBN (excl USA) 0 240 50985 4
ISBN (USA only) 0 8038 5390 4

ALL ENQUIRIES
relating to this book or to any photographic problem are answered by post by the Focal Press without charge if a stamped addressed envelope is enclosed for reply.

Printed and bound in Great Britain by
A. Wheaton & Co. Ltd., Exeter

CONTENTS

THE REFLEX SYSTEM CAMERA

The most accurate way of assessing what you get on a picture taken in the camera is to look at the image projected by the lens into the film plane. The standard way of doing this is via a focusing screen located in the place of the film, as used on studio and technical cameras where exact image control is vital. By introducing a movable mirror, the reflex camera reflects the image projected by the lens onto a screen located in an optically equivalent focal plane and makes it unnecessary to replace the screen by the film before taking a picture. In the modern reflex camera you thus see the image projected by the lens right up to, and immediately after, the instant of exposure.

You see just what you are going to photograph, irrespective of the lens used, and of subject distance or special optical systems (macro, photomicro, endoscopic or other attachments). With the help of further elements that form part of the finder optics (pentaprism and magnifying eyepiece) the finder image always appears upright and right-reading (laterally correct) whichever way you hold the camera. Also, with the standard lens, the image in the finder appears in nearly full natural size.

A further vital feature of the reflex system is that you also see the image as sharply as it will appear on the film. A focusing screen in the finder accurately shows the change of sharpness as you focus the lens on nearer or further objects in the view.

Finally, the image appears at optimum brightness most of the time irrespective of the lens aperture used for the exposure. During viewing and focusing the lens remains set to its maximum opening and closes down to a selected working aperture only during the instant of the exposure itself.

The compact camera

The Olympus OM cameras are 35 mm single-lens reflexes (SLRs) using the 24 × 36 mm format introduced more than half a century ago, but the Olympus OM-1 was the first SLR to be deliberately tailored to pack its features into the smallest possible space. With an overall size (including 50 mm f1.8 lens and lens cap) of 86 × 86 × 139 mm (about 3.4 × 3.4 × 5.5 inches) the Olympus OM-2 and OM-1—the dimensions are the same—are still among the compactest 24 × 36 mm reflex cameras.

The rest of the equipment system largely matches the bulk and weight ratio of the camera bodies. Zuiko lenses for the OM cameras tend to be 10 to 20% lighter and smaller than comparable lenses of other makes. (But lens carrying cases with Olympus tend to be bulky.) And Olympus from the outset designed its lens range to provide somewhat slower but especially compact optical units in the main focal lengths as an alternative to faster and slightly bigger ones. Among other equipment, the Olympus motor drive is to date one of the smallest on the market, without sacrificing framing rate.

The universal system camera

The accessories that turn the Olympus OM cameras into different specific cameras for general to specialised applications form the Olympus equipment system. Thus with appropriate supplementary or extension units the OM-1 or OM-2 becomes a sports or action camera, a photomicrographic recording unit, a medical or endoscopic camera and so on. The majority of these accessory units are optical systems of various kinds, adapted to fit them to the camera. But they equally include alternative units that might carry out some of the camera functions better for a specific subject field (for instance alternative focusing screens) or that modify film capacity (the 250 exposure film back) and supplement the equipment involved in using these units (film loader, remote control systems and so on).

The system camera idea is also some 40 years old, as the designers of the first 35 mm miniature cameras soon realised that a small basic camera body could be converted to different specific uses by successive adapting accessories. What has subtly changed in this time is the basic system approach. Where designers a generation or two ago gradually kept adding bits and pieces to adapt an already existing camera, such systems nowadays tend to

SINGLE LENS REFLEX PRINCIPLE

In the Olympus OM models the pentaprism finder shows an upright and right-reading image (6) of the subject (1) projected by the lens (2) via mirror (3) on to focusing screen (4). The pentaprism (5) reverses the laterally reversed image formed on the screen, for upright viewing through the eyepiece.

During the exposure the mirror (3) swings up so that the lens (2) projects the upside down image on the film.

For automatic operation, the mirror is coupled to the lens aperture, exposure metering and shutter.

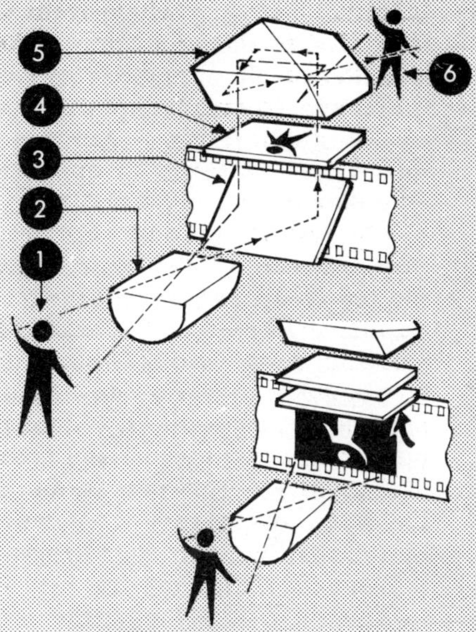

On pressing the release, the mirror swings up and the lens closes to its preset working aperture *(left)*. The shutter then begins to open and expose the film *(right)* while—in the OM-2—silicon cells in the camera front measure the light reflected from a specially patterned shutter blind and the film.

When the cells have registered enough light for a correct exposure, the shutter begins to close; as soon as it is closed the mirror returns to its viewing position and the lens iris re-opens to full aperture.

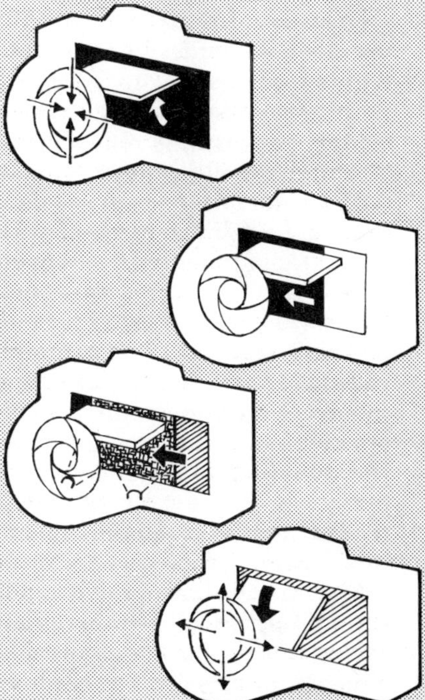

be envisaged as a whole from the outset. For it is as important to plan accessories to fit a camera as it is to plan a camera to fit accessories and conversion or extending units. The whole Olympus OM system with around 250 or so components was envisaged and announced from the start.

OM models

The Olympus OM-1 appeared in 1972 as a compact single-lens reflex camera for 24 × 36 mm images taking standard 36-exposure 35 mm film cartridges. It has an eyelevel pentaprism viewing system with interchangeable focusing screens and takes interchangeable lenses in a bayonet mount with internal aperture coupling to permit viewing and focusing at the full lens aperture, stopping down automatically to a preselected working aperture at the moment of exposure. A pair of cadmium sulphide cells built into the finder system measures the brightness of the screen image (through-the-lens exposure measurement). Lens apertures and exposure times are set manually by a cross-coupled zero balancing system of a meter needle visible in the finder. The camera has a focal plane shutter with speeds from 1 to 1/1000 second and B, X and FP flash synchronisation and a built-in self-timer. The camera back is fully removable. The rapid winding lever advances the film and tensions the shutter.

Current OM-1 models (since about early 1974) are designed for direct attachment of the Olympus OM motor drive; these models are designated OM-1 MD. The first OM-1 models need conversion by Olympus workshops or local agencies to take the motor drive.

The Olympus OM-2 was first shown in 1974 and reached the market in late 1975. It differs from the OM-1 mainly in having a fully automatic exposure control option with a pair of silicon cells measuring the light reflected from the front of the shutter curtain and/or the film during the exposure. The focal plane shutter is electronically controlled and with automatic operation covers a timing range from 1/1000 second up to around 60 seconds. All OM-2 models have provision for fitting the motor drive; the MD designation is therefore dropped in this case.

Both Olympus models are available either in a chrome or in a black version. The chrome model has a matt chrome baseplate and top cover with lettering (e.g. meter switch positions) engraved in black. The black version has a black finished baseplate and top cover as well as shutter speed ring; the settings (other than blue shutter speeds) are in this case engraved white.

The Olympus OM-10, first shown in 1978, is a simplified automatic camera with an exposure time range from 1 to 1/1000 second and shutter speed indication in the viewfinder (but not on the top of the camera). It further provides electronic battery checking with acoustic and optical signals, and electronic self-timer and interactive flash control with the T 20 flash unit. The OM-10 is primarily an amateur camera as it does not have directly user-settable shutter speeds but is integral to the OM system and takes all OM lenses and the winder. It does not work with the motor drive, nor does it take any special camera back since the OM-10 back is not removable.

The lenses are largely finished in black with scales engraved in white, orange and green. There are no alternative lens finishes.

OM system grouping

The equipment system built up around the camera bodies can for convenience be considered as a number of more or less self-contained application groups. They comprise:

The interchangeable lens group—the series of lenses covering focal lengths from 8 mm to 1000 mm ranging from fisheye, through ultrawide-angle, wide-angle, standard, tele to zoom and macro lenses.

The finder group—finder attachments, eyepiece correction lenses and alternative focusing screens.

The motor drive group—the motor drive 1, Winder 1, battery packs and control box, relay cords and also the 250 exposure film back with its accessories.

The close-up and macro group—including extension tubes, bellows, copying stands and a comprehensive range of lighting units.

The photomicrography group—with various adapters to fit different microscopes, exposure units etc.

A photo-technical group—covering adapters for endoscopic and astrophotography and other optical systems.

The flash group—with special flash units, brackets and especially a link with the OM-2 for automatic exposure

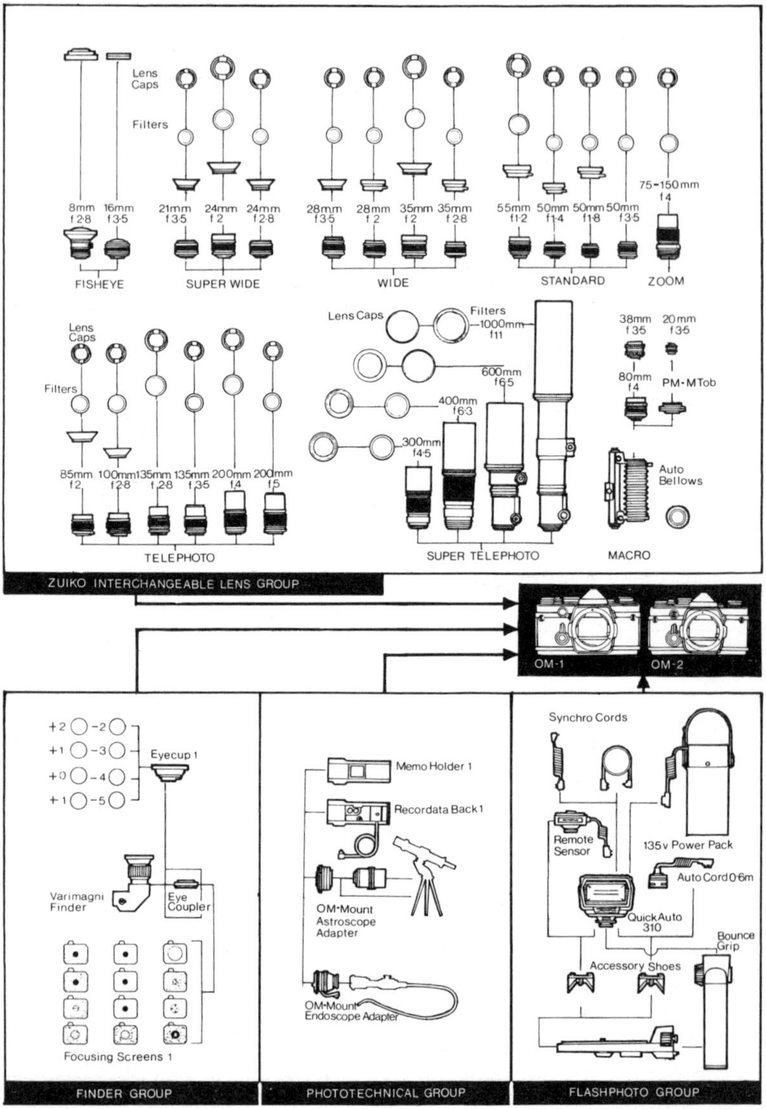

BIRD'S EYE VIEW OF THE OM SYSTEM

The OM equipment system is developed in groups covering various functional aspects of the camera and its accessories. Thus we can in general consider the system in terms of lenses, macro equipment, photomicrographic equipment, flash equipment, the motor drive system and so on. There are also specific accessory groups (e.g. the finder groups and camera cases) and a miscellaneous group of adapters for various purposes—the phototechnical group. In general, OM equipment is described in detail in chapters that reflect these system groupings.

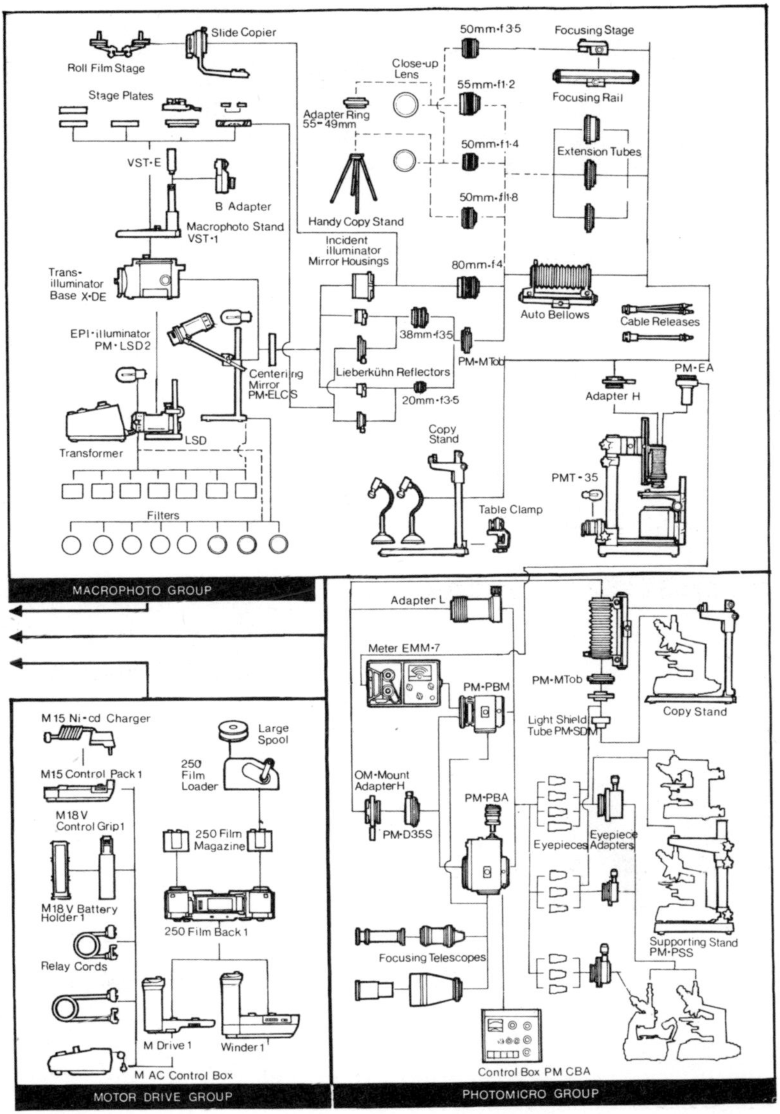

Equipment groupings and applications are inclusive rather than exclusive and elements of different groups can usually be combined freely for special applications. The grouping scheme is thus convenient for description.

The chart is typical rather than comprehensive. Although the OM system was conceived as a unified whole from the outset in largely the form it has now, details constantly change. Hence this chart does not, for instance, necessarily include every latest lens. In its initial publicity, Olympus laid claim to a system of some 250 components.

control via the silicon cells built into the camera.

The groups are not of course mutually exclusive. Items from one can be combined with set-ups from another, for instance motor drive elements or the 250-exposure film back can be used with close-up, macro etc. equipment.

FURTHER OM MODELS

Since the publication of this book Olympus has announced slightly modified versions of the OM-1 and OM-2 cameras–temporarily designated the OM-1N and OM-2N, and the simplified OM-10.

The OM-1N and OM-2N

The OM-1 and OM-2 introduce the interactive flash signalling when the cameras are used with the TE 20 flash unit (see below). Both cameras have a small LED built into the finder at the left of the frame, just above the meter needle markers or the shutter speed scale (on the OM-2). The interaction with the flash unit requires the use of the accessory shoe 4.

There are several further changes of the new OM-2: The longest automatic exposure time is 120 seconds (instead of 60). When the exposure override dial is set to any exposure correction figure, a small flag with a +/− mark appears in the bottom left-hand corner of the finder screen.

The meter switch has a CHECK/RESET position, which brings down again a locked-up mirror (page 27) if the camera contains serviceable batteries. The reset button below the lens mount is now used exclusively to set the shutter to B. The LED for the battery check is slightly larger and brighter. Also, the take-up spool and camera back are slightly redesigned but these points do not affect handling.

The OM-10

The OM-10 differs from the OM-1 and OM-2 in the following respects:

(a) The shutter is electronically controlled and the meter selects exposure times from 1 to 1/1000 which are indicated by a row of LEDs in the finder. A screw-in accessory adapter can provide manual operation.

(b) The meter system uses a single silicon cell in the bottom of the camera, reading the light reflected from a patterned first shutter curtain–or from the film–and a CdS cell reading the light from the image in the finder. This determines the shutter speed signal seen in the finder.

(c) The focusing screens are not interchangeable.

(d) The camera has an electronic instead of a mechanical self-timer. An LED and a buzzer signal the running down of the self-timer; the same LED and buzzer are used for battery testing.

(e) The camera back is not removable. The OM-10 has a fixed accessory shoe. The base-plate carries the coupling elements for the winder 1 (but is not usable with the motor drive) and does not require removal of a cap before fitting the winder.

In the pages that follow, items identical to the OM-1 or OM-2, e.g. lens control features, lens changing, loading, etc., are not described in detail.

OM-10 shutter controls

The OM-10 shutter has three operating modes: AUTO B (for time exposures) and a special mode for flash and the manual adapter. To select the mode, move the small collar at the rear of the film speed setting dial–next to the winding lever. In the AUTO (automatic) mode the shutter speed is set by the silicon cell inside the camera. In the B mode the shutter opens on pressing the release button and closes again when you let go of the button. When set to MANUAL ADAPTER, the shutter operates at a fixed 1/60 second (for flash) without the manual adapter, or at the speed set on the adapter.

In any mode the OM-10 shutter can only operate when the camera contains a pair of appropriate batteries. Pressing the release without them, or if they are exhausted starts the release cycle but stops it before the shutter opens. To get the camera operative again, load it with batteries (or replace exhausted ones). On refitting the battery compartment cover, the shutter concludes its operating cycle, i.e. it opens and closes again and is then ready once more for a next exposure.

The OM-10 exposure meter system

The OM-10 has a single metering system that corresponds to the automatic system of the OM-2. A centre-weighted

OM-10 FEATURES

1. Frame counter.
2. Film transport and shutter tensioning lever.
3. Release button and cable release socket.
4. Mode selector.
5. ASA setting and exposure override ring.
6. Finder eyepiece.
7. Fixed hot shoe.
8. Meter, selftimer and battery test switch.
9. Rewind knob and back lock release.
10. Display cut-in switch.
11. Mode index.
12. Distance scale.
13. Depth of field scale.
14. Aperture ring.
15. Focusing mount.
16. Lens release key.
17. Locating stud for manual adapter.
18. Rewind release.
19. Socket for manual adapter.
20. Plug of manual adapter.
21. Shutter speed setting index.
22. Shutter speed dial of manual adapter.
23. Selftimer LED.
24. Battery compartment cover.
25. Guide pin hole for winder.
26. Winder coupling shaft.
27. CV sound signal (selftimer and battery check).
28. Depth of field preview key.
29. Lens.
30. Tripod bush.
31. Motor drive contacts.

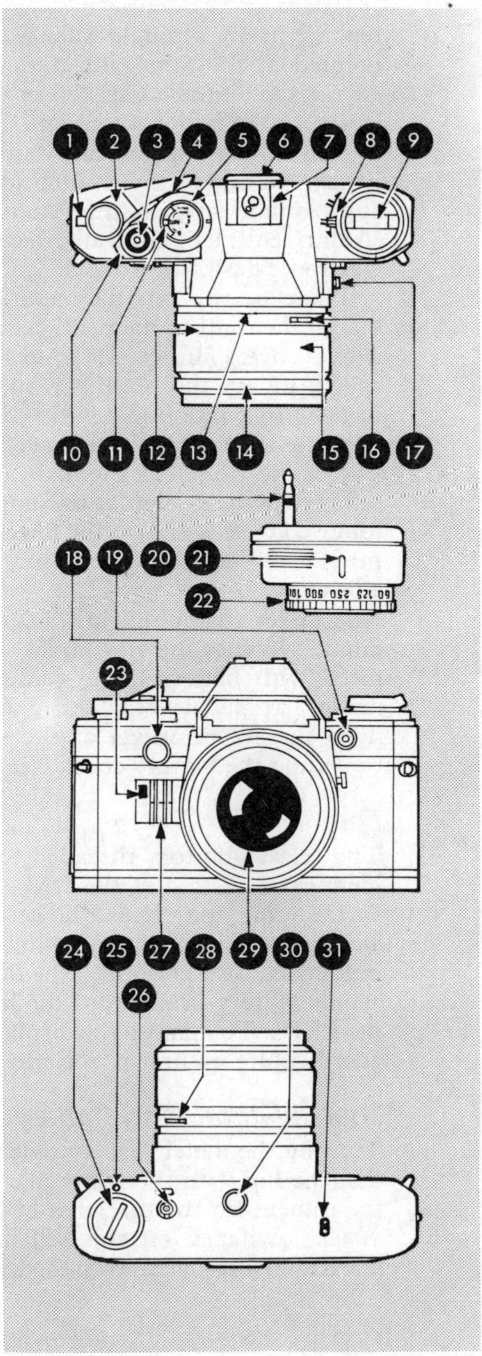

reading from a single silicon cell inside the camera, pointed at the film gate, directly controls the shutter. At the same time a Cds cell in the pentaprism reads the image on the finder screen and controls a set of 12 LEDs next to a shutter speed scale visible in the finder. An LED lit next to one of the shutter speed values indicates the approximate exposure the automatic control will produce. (A thirteenth LED operates in conjunction with the T-20 electronic flash.)

There are two external meter controls. The film speed dial to the right of the pentaprism housing (as seen from above) covers film speeds from 25–1600 ASA. To set the speed, lift up the black rim of the dial, and turn it to bring the white index line–between two figures 1–opposite the required film speed you are using. To each side of the white bar the dial carries red figures 1 and 2 followed by a + sign at the upper end and blue figures followed by a – sign at the lower end of this scale. These provide deliberate overexposure or underexposure by 1, 2 or more stops.

The meter switching ring, below the rewind knob and crank, switches the viewfinder display on and off. When fitted with batteries, the camera operates in all three modes irrespective of whether this switch is at ON or OFF. Two further positions of the switch operate the self-timer and the battery check (see below).

The release

The release button, threaded to take a cable release, is identical with that of the OM-1 and OM-2. The guard surrounding the release however is shaped differently and also acts as a display switch. If you leave the guard untouched for $1\frac{1}{2}$ minutes, the display extinguishes. This avoids battery drain from the heavy current needed by the LEDs. To light up the display again, simply touch the guard–quite natural if you are about to take a picture.

The self-timer and battery check

Turning the meter display switch clockwise from OFF so that the lug with the white marker points to the rear of the camera (in the direction of the arrow labelled SELF-TIMER) switches on the self-timer or delayed action release. (It also switches on the LED display in the finder.)

OM-10 EXPOSURE MODES

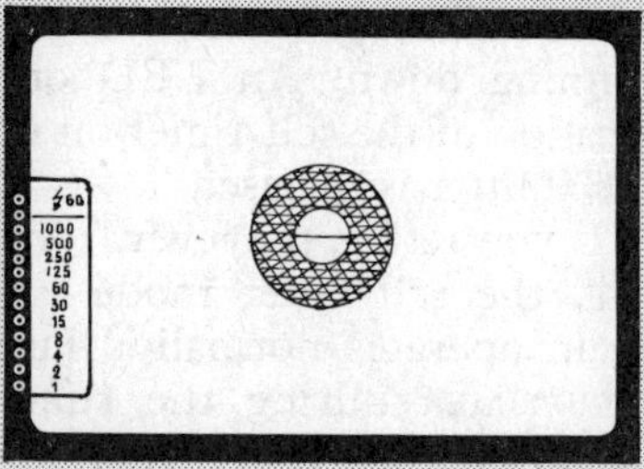

LEDs in the OM-10 finder indicate the shutter speed set by the automatic system. The topmost LED is used in the flash mode, the one below it is the overexposure signal.

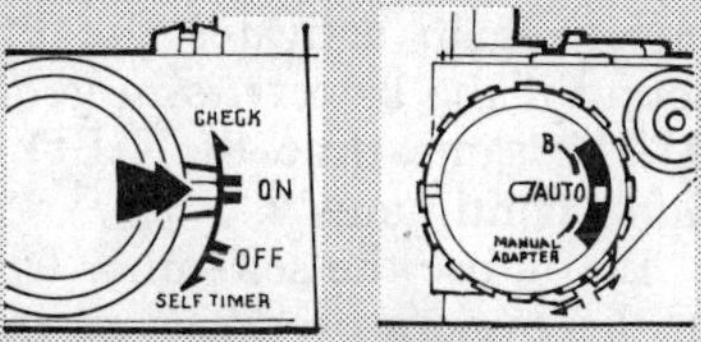

For automatic operation and finder display set the meter switch to ON (*left*) and the mode selector to AUTO (*right*).

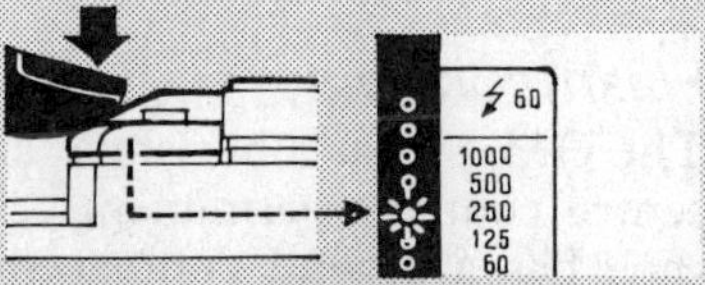

The finder display, automatically switched off after $1\frac{1}{2}$ minutes, is reactivated by pressing the guard around the release.

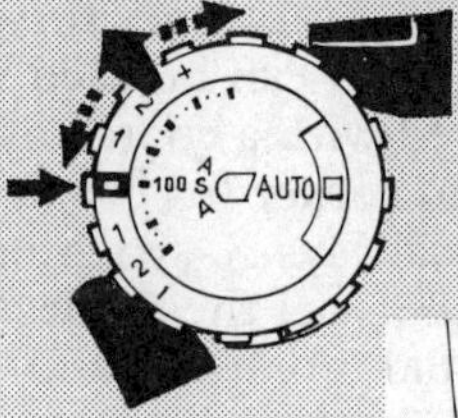

To set the film speed lift the dial rim and move the index (or one of the override values) opposite the required ASA value.

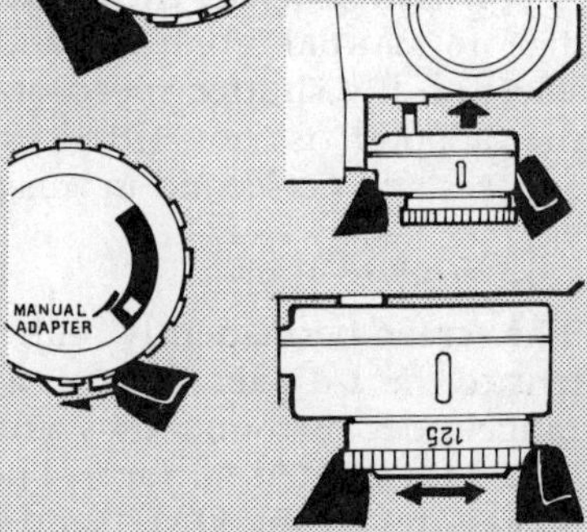

To use the manual adapter, plug it into the camera by its 2.5 mm jack, set the mode selector to MANUAL ADAPTER and set the shutter speed on the dial of the adapter (*right*).

In this mode, pressing the release button delays the release of the shutter by about 12 seconds. During this time a piezo-electric ceramic vibrator (PCV) generates an electronic bleep sound to signal that the delayed action is running down. An LED on the camera front–in the location of the self-timer on the OM-2–also flashes until the shutter is released.

If you return the lever from the SELF-TIMER position to OFF, the self-timer mode is cancelled and the release again operates normally. Turning the lever away from SELF-TIMER during the run-down (of the bleeps and flashing LED) immediately releases the shutter.

Moving the lever in the opposite direction towards CHECK again activates the PCV to emit a continuous sound if the battery is in good condition or still usable. At the same time the LED on the camera front also lights continuously.

If you use the self-timer with the mode selector set to B, the camera produces an instantaneous exposure of a not necessarily consistent 1/60 second.

Flash controls

The OM-10 has a hot shoe (accessory shoe with built-in centre contact) permanently fitted on the camera. The shoe has a second contact slightly forward and to the right of the centre contact for operation with the T-20 electronic flash. It can be used with any other electronic flash unit fitted with a contact in its foot.

There is no socket for coaxial plugs, nor any switch–the camera is always X-synchronized.

For flash shots set the mode selector (in the film speed dial) to MANUAL ADAPTER, and–if the adapter is fitted–select on it a shutter speed of 1/60 second or slower. (If the adapter is not fitted, the camera automatically exposes at 1/60 second in this position.)

The finder system

The screen permanently built in to the OM-10 is equivalent to the 1-13 screen with a central split-image wedge rangefinder surrounded by a microprism ring in a Fresnel area with matted surface. The eyepiece takes the same accessories as the OM-1 and OM-2 (eyecup, correction lenses and Varimagni finder).

There is no provision for locking up the mirror, nor does any mirror lock-up occur if the camera is released without a battery. In that case the mirror is triggered but remains halfway up.

Apart from the fact that the camera back is not removable (there is no release pin in the hinge) the operations of opening the back, loading and unloading are all the same as for the OM-1 and the OM-2. The tip of the arrow just above the SELF-TIMER mark on the camera top indicates the approximate location of the film plane. The OM-10 back has no memo holder.

Inserting and testing batteries

The OM-10 takes a pair of silver oxide batteries of the same type as the OM-2. The camera has a similar battery compartment and screw-on cover. To test the batteries move the meter switch to CHECK–the PCV bleep and LED signals a serviceable battery.

Automatic shooting sequence

Turn the meter switch from OFF to ON and preselect the lens aperture you want to use. The position of the red LED to the left of the finder now indicates the approxi-exposure time the automatic system will select. The actual exposure is always governed by the silicon cell reading the light reflected from the special patterned shutter or from the film. If you want to use a slower or a faster shutter speed, adjust the aperture ring on the lens until the LED display indicates the required speed. Focus the image on the screen and press the release button to take the picture.

Exposure control points

As in the OM-2, the exposure is measured at the full lens aperture; except with extension tubes, the shift lens etc., where the reading is a working-aperture one.

The end positions of the LED display indicate a long exposure time when the lowermost LED is lit and over-exposure when the second-last LED from the top (between the figure 1000 and the flash symbol) lights up. The topmost LED is concerned only with flash exposures. When two LEDs light up together, the exposure time is between the two marked speeds. The actual speed selection by the meter system is continuous.

The metering range of the OM-10 extends from about 1 second at $f1.2$ to 1/1000 second at $f16$ with a 100 ASA film speed setting. At a smaller aperture the long-time limit becomes correspondingly longer up to about 5 or 6 seconds. The low light limit in terms of subject luminance is around 0.15 cd/m². The longest exposure time depends on the film speed setting and can run to around 10–30 seconds at 25 ASA. At 1600 ASA it is little under ½ second.

For exposure compensation turn the rim–after lifting it–of the film speed dial and bring the appropriate figure– −1, −2, or +1, +2 etc. opposite the film speed you are using. This engages in 1/3 stop intervals and is the same as the film speed setting. The override limit is given by the position of the ring and the film speed. Thus with the ring set to 1600 ASA, no underexposure compensation is possibly simply because the film speed cannot be set beyond 1600 to bring the figure 1 or figure 2 on the minus side opposite 1600 ASA. Similarly no over-exposure compensation is possible at 25 ASA. In between these limits the available compensating range grows–it is a maximum at 200 ASA when you have three stops or EV values in either direction (the + and the − signs are equivalent to 3-stop compensation). The criteria for applying the compensation are the same as with the OM-1 and OM-2.

The manual adapter

The manual adapter plugged into the camera, provides a range of fixed shutter speeds from 1 to 1/1000 second–the same range as, for instance, the OM-1.

To use the manual adapter, set the mode selector to bring the index opposite the MANUAL ADAPTER position. Plug the accessory into the camera so that the 2.5 mm jack fits into the socket next to the reflex housing and the groove in the adapter fits over the undercut stud mounted in the side of the reflex housing.

Now set the required shutter speed by turning the dial to bring that speed opposite the white index mark on top. Shutter speeds from 60 to 1000 (1/60 to 1/1000 second) are marked in white as speeds suitable for handheld shots (at least with the standard lens); settings from 1/30 to 1 second are marked in blue as slow speeds requiring tripod mounting of the camera. Set the dial only to the marked speeds (it engages at those points); intermediate positions do not give intermediate times.

The shutter speeds of the manual adapter are operative irrespective of the position of the camera switch (ON, OFF, SELF-TIMER etc.) as long as the mode selector is set to MANUAL ADAPTER.

If the mode selector is set to AUTO, the manual adapter is inoperative. With the mode selector at the B setting, pressing the release opens the shutter and keeps it open until you let go of the release again. If however the manual adapter is set to a long exposure time, for instance 1 second, and you press the release at the B setting and immediately let go again, the shutter only closes after 1 second. The manual adapter socket can also be used for remotely release time exposures through a lead connecting an on/off switch to a 2·5 mm coaxial plug. Select B, or MANUAL ADAPTER, set the self timer; and switch the remote cord off. Press the shutter release, and the shutter will open after the usual delay. To close it again after a suitable interval, turn on the remote cord.

Do not close the remote switch until you want to close the shutter. If you expose with the remote control switch plugged in and closed at the B or MANUAL ADAPTER settings of the camera, the shutter runs down at its top 1/1000 second speed.

Winder operation

The procedure for fitting and detaching the Winder 1 is the same as for the OM-1 or OM-2. The OM-10 has no motor drive socket cap–the transport coupling is open in the camera base and the release is linked through a rubber-sheathed slot–you have no worry over where to park the cap.

Flash photography with the T-20

The T-20 is a smaller and simpler flash unit than the QA 310 with a more restricted range. It permits automatic and manual operation with the OM-10 and OM-1, and automatic, manual or TTL automatic operation with the OM-2. With the OM-1N and OM-2N it also signals flash readiness in the viewfinder. The lighting angle roughly covers the angle of view of the 35 mm wide-angle lenses. The T-20 fits the accessory shoe of the OM cameras but not the bounce flash grip. With 100 ASA film speed the metric guide number is 20 (55 for feet).

T-20 features and controls

A sensor cell in the front of the unit (the centre of the O of the Olympus name-plate) controls the flash duration in automatic operation. The foot fits the camera's accessory shoe and is attached in the same way as for the QA 310. The foot carries four contacts: one at the side and one in the centre which have the same function as on the QA 310; the other two contacts slightly forward of the main contact serve for TTL exposure control with the OM-2 and the viewfinder indicator.

The external power socket at the front of the foot takes the supply plug of the AC adapter or of the 315 volt power pack in the same way as the equivalent socket on the QA 310.

The charge indicator (CHARGE lamp) just above the foot at the back lights up when the unit is ready for flashing.

The AUTO CHECK lamp to the left of the charge lamp also has the same function as the QA 310. The ON/OFF switch to the right of the ready charge lamp switches on the unit. If you switch off when the unit is fully charged and on again a few seconds later, the T-20 is usually still ready to flash if not too much of the capacitor charge has leaked away.

The mode selector just above the ready charge lamp is a three-position sliding bar with a white index line. The left-hand setting is for manual operation, the centre setting and right-hand setting for automatic with the OM-10 or other cameras.

Above the switch is an aperture scale, a distance scale and an ASA scale. The latter is controlled by a sliding bar at the top; this moves ASA figures from 25 to 800 into a small window, opposite an arrowhead index. At the same time the aperture scale also shifts relative to the distance scale and the AUTO index marks. This sliding adjustment functions purely as a calculator and has no effect on the flash operation itself. For automatic mode it shows the aperture to be set for a given film speed. For instance when 100 ASA is in the centre of the upper

THE T 20 FLASH

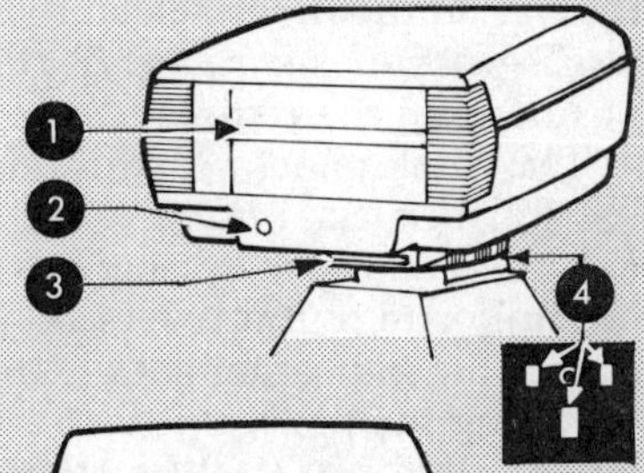

1. Reflector.
2. Sensor cell.
3. External power socket.
4. Control contacts.

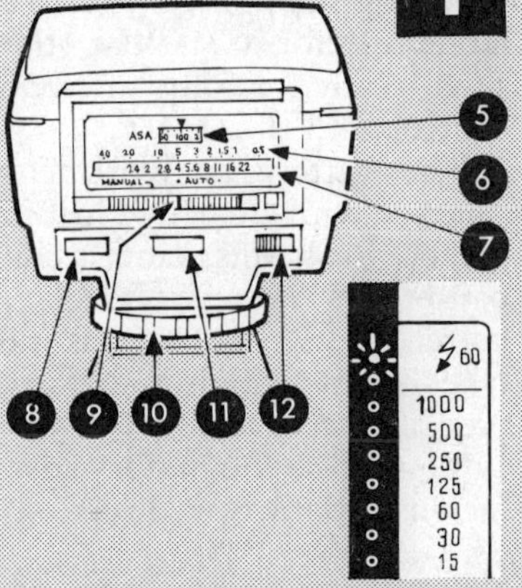

5. ASA scale.
6. Distance scale.
7. Aperture scale.
8. AUTO CHECK lamp.
9. Manual/auto switch.
10. Foot with locking screw.
11. CHARGE lamp.
12. ON/OFF switch.

The LED next to the flash symbol lights up when the flash is ready to fire OM-10, latest OM-1, OM-2). The LED also flickers after correct automatic (sensor cell controlled) flash exposure.

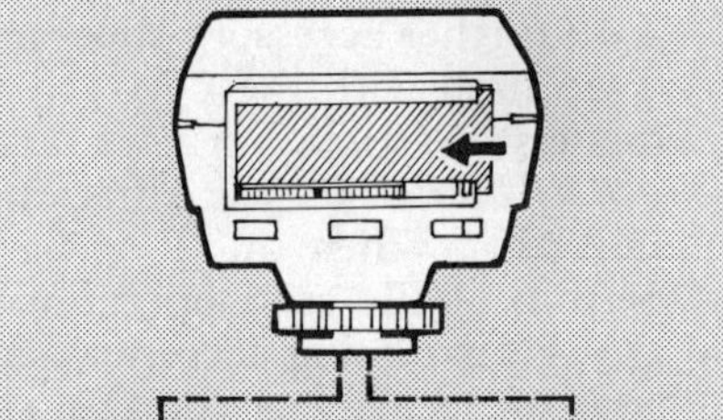

For use with the OM-2 reverse the calculator panel on the T 20 or set flash mode to manual.

Mount the T 20 on earlier OM-2 models via the accessory shoe 3 (*left*), on later OM-2 and OM-1 models (OM-2N OM-1N) with the shoe 4 (*right*).

window, the aperture scale will show 2 (*f*2) opposite 10 m, 4 opposite 5 m and so on. These are the apertures required for the appropriate flash distances. In AUTO mode the bar on the mode selector at the bottom is opposite *f*4 or *f*8 – so you set *f*4 or *f*8 (depending on the selector position) on the camera lens.

The whole panel with this calculator is removable: press the square black button to the right of the mode selector and the panel will spring out sideways. You can pull it out fully and refit it reversed. The back of the panel then carries the indication FULL AUTOMATIC CONTROL BY OM-2. Inserting the panel this way at the same time pushes the mode selector to MANUAL (though this is not indicated as such) ready for fully automatic TTL metering and flash control with the OM-2.

The battery compartment is underneath the panel (marked with an arrow) just in front of the external power socket. Push this panel aside and remove it to insert a pair of size AA 1.5 volt cells (preferably alkali manganese batteries) with polarity as indicated. The T-20 can also take nickel cadmium batteries; the restriction on this type of battery for the QA 310 does not apply in the T-20.

To replace the battery case lid slide it in from the side (against the arrow direction) until it clicks into place.

Accessory shoes and camera matching

Two further accessory shoes are available for linking the T-20 flash with the OM-1N, OM-2N and older OM-2 models.

The accessory shoe 3 fits only the earlier OM-2 (not OM-2N). When the T-20 flash is fitted in this shoe, it permits TTL auto operation in the same way as the QA 310 with the accessory shoe 2. (The T-20 and the accessory shoe 2 or the QA 310 in the accessory shoe 3 only permit normal automatic operation – with the flash's own sensor cell – or manual operation.)

The accessory shoe 4 fits the latest OM-1 and OM-2 models (OM-1N, OM-2N) but not the previous versions. This shoe has a right-handed securing screw (the screw of accessory shoes 1, 2 and 3 is left-handed) and two contacts forward of the main centre synchronizing contact.

The accessory shoe 4 with the T-20 flash on the OM-1N permits normal manual and normal automatic operation (with the sensor of the flash) and also provides flash signalling in the camera's finder. With the OM-2N the T-20 flash in addition permits TTL auto operation.

When the T-20 is mounted in the accessory shoe 1 or 2 (or in the hot shoe of any other camera) the two supplementary contacts of the flash unit are withdrawn and the unit then functions only in normal manual and auto mode without camera interaction.

As there is no synchronizing cord socket on the T-20, this unit can only be used on cameras with a hot shoe. A flash cord is in preparation to link the T-20 flash with the accessory shoes 3, 4 and the shoe of the OM-10 cameras for off-camera flash exposures.

The camera flash signal

The T-20 couples through the accessory shoe 4 to the OM-1N and OM-2N and through the fixed accessory shoe to the OM-10. When the flash is switched on and charged ready to fire, an LED in the left-hand side of the finder lights, whether or not the camera's meter is switched on. On the OM-1N and OM-2N this LED is located above the shutter speed scale or the meter needle markers, on the OM-10 it is the topmost LED at the left of the finder, opposite a flash symbol with '60' next to it.

After a flash this LED flickers in the automatic mode (see below) and then goes out; it comes on again when the flash is recharged ready for the next shot, in parallel with the CHARGE signal on the back of the T-20 itself. For flash shots with the T-20 be sure to set the OM cameras to a shutter speed of 1/60 second or slower (1/30 second or slower when used on earlier OM-2 cameras with the accessory shoe 3). With the OM-10 set the mode selector to MANUAL ADAPTER. If the manual adapter itself is fitted, set this to 1/60 second or a slower speed.

Manual flash with the T-20

For manual flash photography turn the calculator panel in the back of the T-20 so that the scales are showing. Move the index on the selector switch bar to MANUAL. Set the upper bar of the calculator to the ASA speed of the film you are using. Check the subject distance (by focusing on the subject and reading the distance scale on the lens) and look up the white *f*-number opposite the required distance on the orange distance scale. Set this *f*-number on the lens aperture ring. You are now ready to shoot. After the exposure, the red LED in the finder goes out and comes on again when the flash unit has recycled.

This manual mode applies to the OM-1 and the OM-10; it also operates with the earlier OM-2 and the accessory shoe 3 if the camera selector switch is set to MANUAL. In this case however there is no ready/charge signal in the finder, nor is there in the OM-1 with accessory shoe 1 or with any other camera.

Normal automatic operation

This mode is possible with the OM-1N and OM-10. select the film speed on the calculator of the flash unit as before. Set the mode selector of the OM-10 to MANUAL ADAPTER. On the flash slide the mode selector bar so that its white line is opposite one of the two AUTO positions. Check the film speed setting, and read off the lens aperture (white figures) above the position of the flash mode selector. Set this aperture value on the lens. The orange figure above the lens aperture is the maximum distance at which you can work. If your subject is within range, shoot. If the exposure was correct, the flash LED in the finder will now flicker after the flash and then relight continuously as soon as the unit is recharged. At the same time the AUTO CHECK lamp in the back of the flash unit also flickers. If the exposure was insufficient (subject distance too great) the LED will not flash but goes out and comes on again once the unit is recharged.

The same procedure applies for automatic flash with the OM-2 and the accessory shoe 1 or 2, or with any other camera. However there is in that case no finder indication either of the charge condition or of correct exposure. For these signals you have to look at the CHARGE and AUTO CHECK lamps at the back of the flash unit itself.

TTL auto operation with the OM-2

The T-20 with the OM-2 offers the same automatic control features as the QA 310 but with less confusing settings. For such TTL automation the OM-2 (earlier models) must be fitted with the accessory shoe 3 as indicated above, and the OM-2N with the accessory shoe 4. In the latter case you again have the LED in the finder to signal readiness for flashing and correct exposure afterwards. For this mode with the OM-2 models (fitted with appropriate accessory shoe) there are just four preparatory steps: 1. Set the OM-2 to AUTO; 2. Mount the T-20 in the accessory shoe; 3. Set the T-20 to MANUAL–or better still reverse the calculator panel for OM-2 operation; and switch on the unit.

From here on you can leave the rest to the OM-2 controls. Keep a check on the shutter speed in the finder. (The indication should be 1/30 second or slower–otherwise the flash may not fire at all.) Apart from that, simply expose shot after shot. The AUTO CHECK lamp (and the LED in the OM-2N finder) should flicker after every flash if the subject was within the available distance range for automatic control. You need not worry over aperture settings or film speed–for the latter only the film speed setting on the camera is relevant. You can use any lens aperture, the sensor cells in TTL automatic mode take care of that and compensate.

This mode corresponds to the TTL AUTO mode of the OM-2 with the QA 310 flash. It is, as mentioned before, particularly useful for close-up and macrophotography, since the SBC metering cells directly control the flash duration.

The 1–14 focusing screen

This is a new interchangeable screen for all OM-1 and OM-2 models. It is similar to the 1–13 screen. However instead of the horizontal split of the latter screen it has a 45° split in the wedge-range finder area.

THE OM-1
MODELS

The elements and controls c
be broadly grouped as refer
shutter and exposure control
guide and advance system a
So let us look at the OM-1 an

Unless otherwise stated, t
and camera features apply equ
'Left' and 'right' description
held for shooting and viewed

Lens control features

These are part of the interc
described in more detail later, l
here are the main controls tha
all the time:

The aperture ring preselects t
for the exposure. This controls
passing through the lens and
field—how much of the subject

The focusing ring sets the lens
shown approximately on two di
white (metres) and orange (fee
ring adjusts the sharpness of
finder screen.

The depth of field scale also s
extent of the zone of acceptab
distances at various lens apertu

The rearmost ring of the lens c
the top (with serrated surface) r
for removing the lens from the
(near the bottom) stops down t
aperture preselected on the aper
visual observation on the screen
at the working aperture.

O.W. B

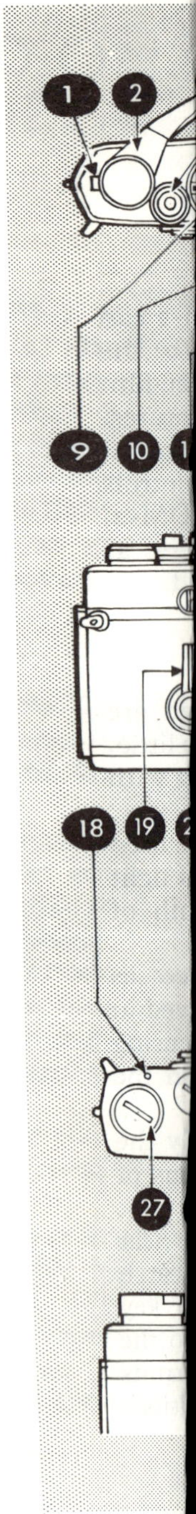

OM-1 FEATURES

1. Frame counter.
2. Film transport and shutter tensioning lever.
3. Film speed dial release button.
4. Release button and cable release socket.
5. ASA film speed dial.
6. Hot shoe socket.
7. Meter switch.
8. Rewind crank.
9. Rewind knob and back lock release.
10. Rewind release.
11. Mirror lock-up.
12. Distance scale.
13. Focusing mount.
14. Depth of field scale.
15. Aperture ring.
16. Lens release key.
17. Flash socket and X/FP selector lever.
18. Guide pin hole for motor drive.
19. Self-timer.
20. Motor drive socket cap.
21. Depth of field preview (stop-down) key.
22. Lens.
23. Tripod bush.
24. Shutter speed ring.
25. Motor drive coupling contacts.
26. Carrying strap eyelet.
27. Rewind shaft.
28. Battery compartment cover.
29. Cartridge camber.
30. Shutter behind film aperture.
31. Finder eyepiece.
32. Transport sprocket.
33. Take-up spool.
34. Camera back.
35. Hinge release pin for removing back.

The interior features of the camera (27 to 35) are also the same as on the OM-2.

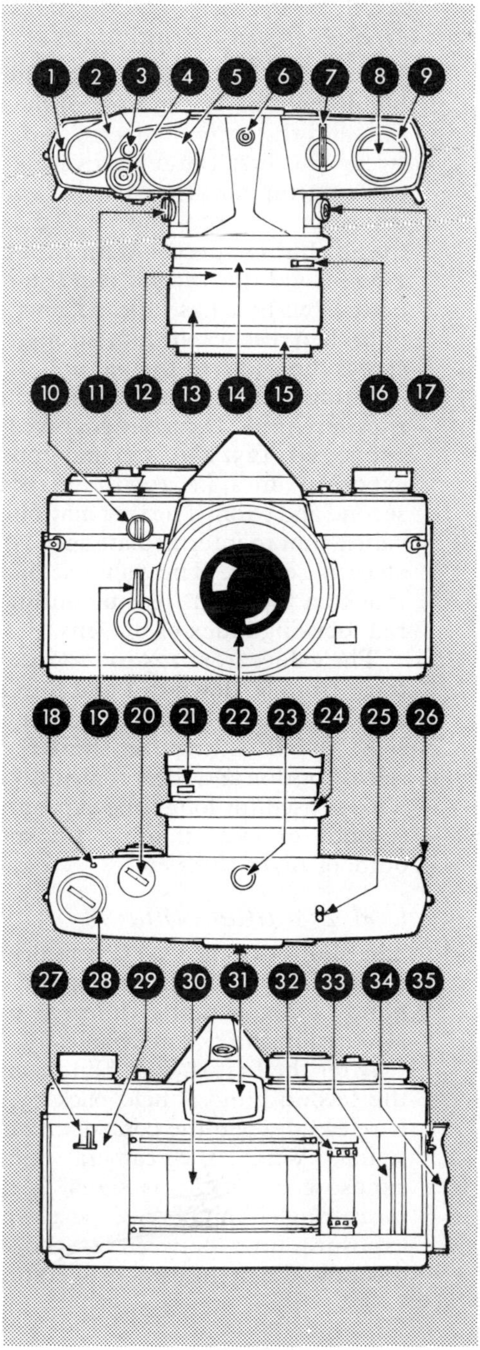

OM-1 shutter controls

The OM-1 has a focal plane shutter consisting of two blinds running just in front of the film. One uncovers the film and the second covers it up again. The interval between the first blind uncovering and the second blind covering the film is adjustable and controls the effective exposure. The run-down speed of the blind is the same for all shutter speeds. With exposure times shorter than 1/60 second, the second blind starts covering up the film before the first has finished uncovering it. In effect the light then reaches the film through a moving slit travelling across the width of the picture.

A ring surrounding the lens changing mount selects the exposure time. It carries engraved figures of B, 1, 2, 4, 8, 15, 30, 60, 125, 250, 500 and 1000. These are reciprocal exposure times, i.e. 1000 = 1/1000 second, 500 = 1/500 second and so on. The ring may only be set to the engraved values (not to intermediate speeds) and it clicks into place at each setting. The value set is that opposite the red index on top of the lens mounting ring—in line with the red focusing index of the lens.

The values from 125 to 1000 are engraved in black, and those from 60 down to 1 and B in blue as shutter settings suitable for synchronisation with electronic flash.

At the B setting the shutter opens on pressing the release button and stays open until you let go of the button. This is used for long time exposures running into several seconds or even minutes for special subjects such as outdoor night shots etc.

OM-2 shutter controls

The shutter of the OM-2 is in principle similar to that of the OM-1 but the timing of the delay between the two blinds for generating different exposures is controlled electrically and not mechanically.

After the first shutter blind starts to uncover the film, the second blind is held back by a solenoid whose hold is released when the control circuit receives an electrical signal. When the camera operates with automatic exposure control, this signal is derived from the light measuring circuit of the exposure meter and can form any exposure time between 1/1000 second and about 60 seconds. When the camera operates with manual exposure

OM CAMERA CONTROLS

For the ASA speed setting on the OM-1 rotate the dial after pressing the button *(left)*; on the OM-2 raise the dial rim to bring speed value into window *(right)*.

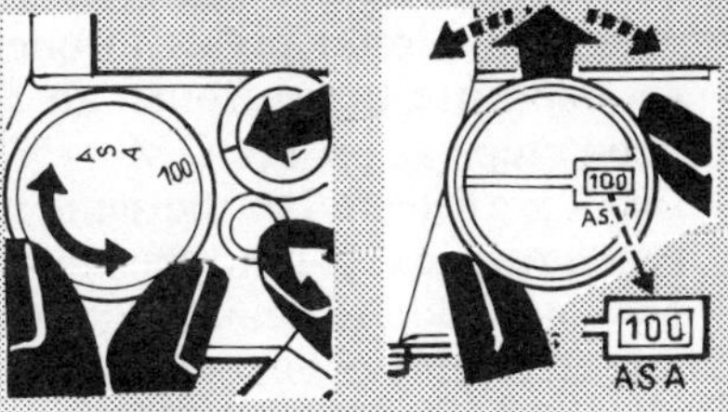

After tensioning the self-timer, operate by pressing the small starting lever *(left)*. Select flash synchronisation by turning the ring surrounding the socket *(right)* to FP or X.

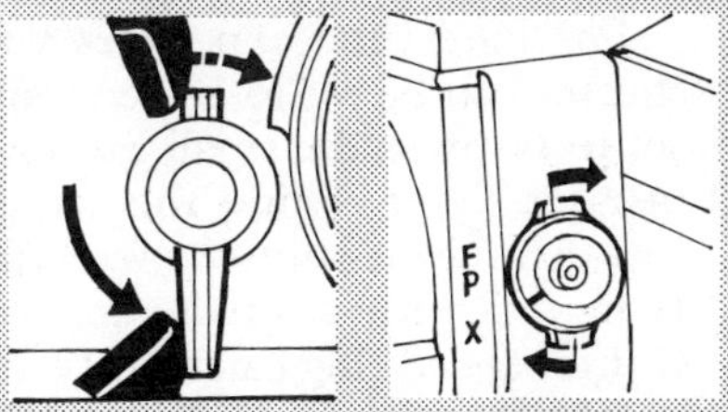

For the reset procedure and B setting on the OM-2, press the reset button and turn the shutter speed ring to bring the asterisk opposite the button *(left)*. The OM-1 mirror locks up by turning the lever/knob in the side (right).

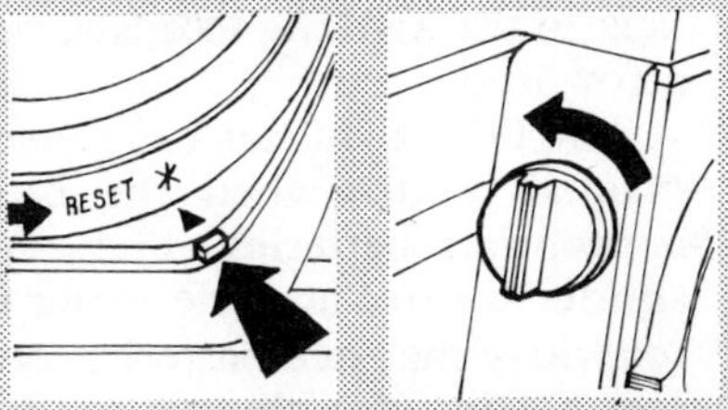

To remove the camera back depress the hinge release pin *(left)*. The OM-1 cell fits in the battery compartment in the base; '+' must face upwards *(right)*.

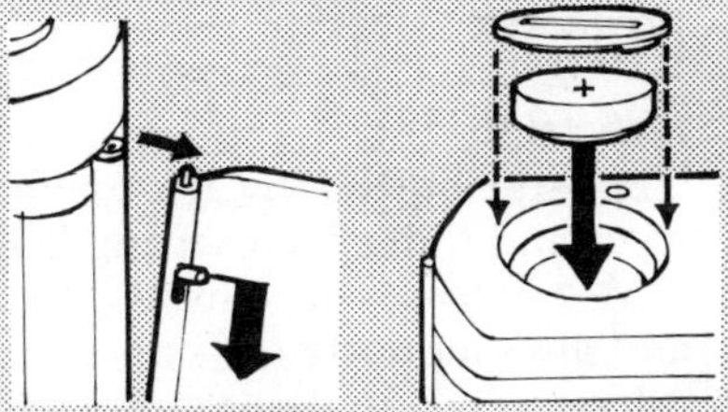

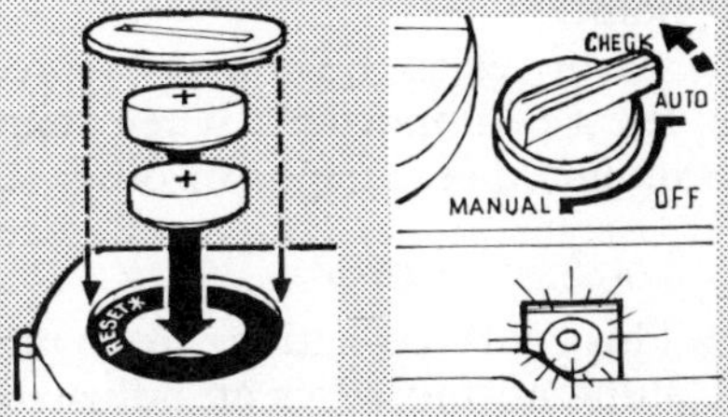

For the OM-2, fit two cells, '+' facing up *(left)*. To test the OM-2 battery move the switch lever to CHECK; check LED should light *(right)*.

control, the signals controlling the shutter come from an electronic circuit preset to one of 11 states. These form set exposure times from 1 to 1/1000 second in the same fixed steps as on the OM-1. With manual operation the times are selected in the same way by turning the shutter speed ring just behind the lens mounting ring. The values from 1 to 60 are again engraved in blue (speeds suitable for electronic flash synchronisation) and from 125 to 1000 in black.

For long time exposures with manual operation the shutter can be set to B—engraved in red on the ring. To set to B, press the small button at the bottom left corner (as seen from behind the camera) of the mirror body—just behind the shutter speed ring. This button is marked B in red with a small red arrowhead next to it. The shutter speed ring can only be turned to B when the small button is depressed; on turning the ring a red asterisk, next to the marking RESET, appears opposite the little red arrowhead.

The OM-2 shutter can only operate—in automatic or manual mode—when the camera contains a pair of appropriate batteries. These power both the electronic shutter control and the meter circuit. Without batteries (or with exhausted batteries) only the B setting is operative. Setting the shutter to B is also part of the reset procedure.

The release

The large button in the camera top, between the winding lever and film speed setting knob on both the OM-1 and OM-2, releases the shutter. A guard surrounds the button and also supports the finger for smoother releasing. The release travel is about 2 mm and there is no first pressure point.

The release button has a threaded socket to take a cable release—important when exposing with the camera mounted on a tripod or other stand.

The self-timer

This delayed-action mechanism releases the shutter automatically after an adjustable delay of about 4 to 12 seconds after triggering. It can be used for exposing without having to press on any part of the camera, to include yourself in your own pictures etc.

The self-timer construction is virtually the same in the OM-1 and OM-2 and consists of a large tensioning lever with a small triggering lever underneath. To use the self-timer, tension the shutter first with the camera's film transport/winding lever. Then pull down the large black lever (with central chrome strip) until it engages with a faint but audible click. This click is important; it occurs just before the horizontal position of the lever. To be on the safe side, pull the lever down fully horizontally. This is the minimum delay setting of about 3–4 seconds.

To make the exposure, then move the short black lever (with white strip)—revealed underneath the large tensioning lever—upwards. The mechanism now begins to run and the large lever returns to its vertical position. When the lever is at about 45° pointing at the carrying strap eyelet on the camera front, it triggers the shutter. The lever still continues to run until it is fully vertical.

For longer delays pull the lever down further. The maximum, with the tensioning lever pointing vertically downwards, is 12 seconds.

If you haven't tensioned the shutter, the self-timer lever comes to a halt when it nears the triggering position. If you then tension the shutter, the self-timer will resume running and almost immediately release the shutter. Once you have started the self-timer running, you can stop it by pulling the short triggering lever outwards. With the self-timer tensioned but not triggered, you can operate the shutter (releasing and tensioning) in the normal way—i.e. use the self-timer at whatever future occasion you feel like it.

The self-timer works equally with flash and with all shutter speeds—on manual or automatic operation with the OM-2. On manual operation and with the OM-1 the self-timer also gives you an additional slow speed by using the B setting. For as the mechanism runs down, there is an interval between depressing the release to triggering point and letting go at the very end of the self-timer run. A shutter set to B thus remains open during this period. Its length depends on the individual camera; on models I have tried out the shortest was just under 2 seconds and the longest just over 3. The interval is however fairly consistent for any one camera.

The OM-1 exposure meter system

To indicate the correct exposure required, the OM-1 measures the light coming through the lens and reaching the finder screen. The brightness of the screen is actually measured by a pair of cadmium sulphide (CdS) cells located in the pentaprism finder unit. The light reading appears as the movement of a needle between two markers in the viewfinder. The needle movement is also coupled mechanically with the shutter speed setting, the aperture presetting of whatever lens is mounted on the camera and the film speed setting. Centering the needle between its markers (a so-called zero-balancing system) by adjustment of the aperture and/or shutter speed sets the correct exposure.

The controls on the camera are:

The ON/OFF *switch* in the camera top to the left of the pentaprism, next to the rewind knob, switches the meter circuit off or on. For maximum battery life keep the meter switched off when not actually in use.

The ASA film speed dial to the right of the pentaprism housing presets the meter system to the sensitivity of the film in the camera. The dial carries ASA film speed values from 25 to 1600. Most values are marked in white, but every third film speed (25, 50, 100, 200, 400, 800, 1600 ASA) is marked in yellow. To set the film speed, pull the winding lever slightly away from the body, press the small button next to the speed dial (just behind the release button) and turn the dial to bring the appropriate ASA value opposite the index mark in the shutter release guard. The film speed dial engages at every setting and is locked in position when you let go of the small button. With the button depressed, the dial rotates freely all round.

The OM-2 exposure meter system

The OM-2 has two metering systems. One serves for manual exposure settings and is virtually identical with the OM-1 meter. The only difference is that the shutter speed is controlled electrically, but the link between the speed setting and the meter needle indication is mechanical.

The second system is automatic. You select the film speed and the lens aperture you want to use; the meter then sets the shutter speed required for a correct exposure under prevailing light conditions.

The automatic exposure system is controlled by a pair of silicon cells mounted inside the camera and pointed at the film gate to measure the light reflected from the film or—at fast shutter speeds—the light reflected from a specially patterned first shutter blind. A pointer reading—essentially the manual metering system which still operates simultaneously—indicates the approximate exposure that automatic control will produce.

The external meter controls on the OM-2 are again a meter switch with a selector lever and a film speed dial.

The meter switch has four positions: MANUAL—OFF—AUTO—CHECK. When set to MANUAL the OM-2 operates in the same way as the OM-1 with its meter switched on. At both the OFF and the AUTO settings the OM-2 yields automatic exposures; in the OFF position these are limited in their maximum duration, while in the AUTO position exposures may reach 1 minute or longer. The CHECK position is for the battery test. The LED indicating the battery state is in the back of the camera just below the meter switch.

The film speed dial to the right of the pentaprism housing (as seen from above) covers film speeds from 12 to 1600 ASA. These speeds appear in a small window in the dial top. To set the film speed lift the top of the dial by its serrated rim and rotate to bring the required film speed value into the window. Then let the top of the dial drop into place to engage in the bottom section.

In some positions of the dial it may not be possible to set the speed you want. Thus if you cannot set a high enough speed, set the highest speed possible, let the dial drop into position, rotate the whole dial clockwise through half a turn, then lift up the top again and finally set the required film speed. Conversely, if you cannot set the low film speed you want, set the lowest speed possible, let the dial engage and turn the whole dial anti-clockwise through half a turn—then finally set the required speed.

After setting the film speed, turn the dial so that the long white line across it is horizontal and points at the index mark in the side of the pentaprism housing. The whole dial may be turned to different positions to bring the markings +1, +2 (and intermediates) opposite the index mark for deliberate overexposure with the automatic control, or to −1, −2 etc. for deliberate underexposure. The film speed dial thus acts also as an exposure compensation or override.

Flash controls

The OM-1 and OM-2 have a coaxial flash socket (standard 3 mm type) in the left-hand side of the reflex body section. The socket takes standard 3 mm coaxial plugs. A switch surrounds the socket in the form of a rotating collar. When the red index line on the collar is opposite the blue X marking, the shutter is set for X-synchronisation (electronic flash); when set to FP, the synchronisation is switched to flash bulbs.

The OM-1 takes a screw-in accessory shoe for flash units with centre contact in the foot. The OM-2 takes a different shoe with additional contact for automatic flash exposures controlled by the camera's silicon cells. The switch surrounding the coaxial flash socket also switches the hot-shoe contact of the accessory shoe.

Electronic flash requires X-synchronisation which is feasible only up to 1/60 second. On the OM-2 an automatic system disconnects the flash contact (in automatic or manual exposure mode) at shutter speeds faster than 1/60 second.

The finder system

The reflex finder consists of the hinged mirror, the focusing screen, pentaprism housing and eyepiece. A lever linked with the mirror movement also acts on an iris control lever in the lens, stopping down the latter to the preselected working aperture.

The focusing screen is located in a hinged frame below the pentaprism housing. The pentaprism is fixed but the screens are interchangeable. Olympus supplies a wide range of alternative screens for different applications.

The eyepiece shows an upright and right-reading (laterally correct) view of the screen image via the pentaprism. The finder eyepiece also takes an eyecup, eyepiece correction lenses and the Varimagni finder unit.

The finder further shows the exposure meter needle for manual or automatic (OM-2) exposure monitoring. In the OM-1 the meter needle and its centering marks are permanently visible. In the OM-2 the markings are brought into view by operation of the meter selector switch. When set to MANUAL, needle centering markers appear similar to those of the OM-1; when the switch is set to AUTO, a shutter speed scale becomes visible.

OM-2 mirror lock-up and reset

When the OM-2 batteries are exhausted—or no batteries fitted—pressing the release at any shutter setting other than B starts the mechanical exposure sequence. The mirror flies up but stays there; the shutter does not run down. You can continue pressing the release button but you cannot operate the winding lever. If you remove the lens from the camera, you see the characteristic checkerboard pattern on the front of the first shutter blind.

The run-down sequence stops there because the rest of it is triggered electrically: with the mirror up, a contact closes to release the first shutter blind and initiate the exposure control operation. This cannot take place without batteries in the camera. Mirror lock-up occurs in that case irrespective of the position of the meter switch lever.

To bring the mirror down again, press the small key at the base of the front plate while turning the shutter speed ring to the red B setting as for time exposures. The mirror then swings down again and the shutter opens for about 1/1000 second. (If this happens while you have a film in the camera, you lose that exposure.)

If the mirror has locked up due to battery failure, use this mirror reset procedure before inserting fresh batteries in the camera to avoid excessive current drain. A reminder inside the battery compartment is a red asterisk and the word RESET.

The same applies if you accidentally press the shutter release during battery changing or insertion even without a film in the camera. So always set the shutter to B when changing batteries.

Do not try to reset the mirror by pulling down the small lever at the right just inside the lens mount. While this does in fact bring the mirror down, it does not complete the reset cycle. If you then start shooting again with new batteries in the camera, pressing the release button simply triggers the mirror again but nothing else. The camera is reset for proper operation only after the complete mirror reset procedure with the shutter set to B. If you do this after bringing the mirror down manually, you still risk some light on the film as the shutter again runs down during the reset procedure. (Fingering the lever inside the lens mount also risks getting finger marks on the mirror—very difficult to remove properly.)

If the mirror locks up due to an exhausted battery and you have no replacement battery at hand, reset the mirror immediately by the normal reset procedure and wait for 5 to 10 minutes. The batteries may recover sufficiently in that time to allow you to go on shooting—at least to finish a few odd exposures. But this is cutting it fine—and shouldn't happen with sensible battery testing and management.

Locking up the OM-1 mirror

The mirror of the OM-1 can be locked up manually—a provision intended for photomicrography, high-magnification macrophotography and where the pre-raised mirror reduces vibration risks during the exposure. The finder image naturally disappears as well, but this is not a major drawback with a macro set-up where you pre-arrange the subject at leisure. Many microscopes have a separate viewing eyepiece, anyway.

To raise the mirror turn the button at the right of the mirror housing so that its black bar is vertical. To bring the mirror down again, turn the button so that the black bar is horizontal. Turn it down fully to make sure that the mirror comes down into its correct focusing position after every shot.

You can move the mirror up or down at any time whether the camera is tensioned or not. Operation of this mirror lock affects no other camera function. But do not leave the camera standing in bright sun with the mirror locked up and the lens uncovered. The lens could in that case act as a burning glass and damage the shutter curtains.

Olympus also suggests that keeping the mirror locked up is convenient for sequence shooting with the motor drive. The fastest sequencing speed is in fact increased by around 10% but this means little against the inconvenience of not seeing the image through the finder.

To reduce vibration to a minimum, the mirror system of the OM-1 and OM-2 incorporates a pneumatic damping mechanism that arrests the mirror and slows down its movement without jar as it reaches its swing-up position. This also reduces shutter noise—a nuisance in sport and certain other types of photography.

Film transport, frame counter, rewind

The winding lever at the right-hand end of the camera top advances the film after every exposure and also retensions the shutter. The lever folds back flush against the top of the body or swings out to a start position of about 30°—convenient for keeping the thumb under the tip of the winding lever for quick action. The complete winding swing is another 150° from this point. You can also work the lever in a number of short strokes instead of one long one: which you prefer is a matter of taste.

The lever advances the film and at the same time tensions the shutter, which in normal use prevents inadvertent double exposures and also blank frames (unless you have pressed the release with the lens cap on the lens). Intentional double exposures are possible by tensioning the shutter without advancing the film (see below, *Multiple exposures*).

Each full swing (whether in one or several strokes) of the lever advances the frame counter next to it by one division. On opening the camera back, the frame counter returns to a position S marked in yellow. As the film advances, the S is followed by two white dots, figures 1 and 2 in white, then figures for every even number and dots for every odd number. The figures 12, 20 and 36 (usual numbers of exposures in which 35 mm film cartridges are sold) are marked in yellow. After 36 there is another white dot followed by E to indicate the end of the film.

The knob with fold-out crank at the left-hand end of the camera top rewinds an exposed or partly exposed film back into its cartridge. To permit rewinding, a rewind release lever on the camera front disengages the transport sprocket. The rewind knob also operates the back lock: to open the camera back pull up the rewind knob, then pull further against spring pressure to release the catch—the camera back then swings open.

Multiple exposures

To superimpose more than one exposure on the same frame of the film, make one exposure, then proceed as follows:

Take up any slack of the film on the spool by gently turning the rewind knob/crank. But do not actually tighten the film. Then switch the rewind release lever to the rewind position. Hold the lever in this position while working the winding lever as when advancing the film. As the rewind release lever has disengaged the film transport, the winding lever only retensions the shutter. Then make the second exposure. With luck—if you have just taken up the film slack and not tensioned the film with the rewind knob—the two exposures should be superimposed within about 1 to 2 mm. By repeating the procedure but without touching the rewind knob/crank, you can make any number of exposures on the same film. Finally, return the rewind release lever to the normal position by hand (red dot pointing upwards) and advance the film for the next frame.

During such a multiple exposure sequence the frame counter advances with every actual exposure, even if the film is not advanced. So if you have for instance taken two exposures on frame No. 19 and finally advanced to the next picture, the frame counter will show 21 when you are actually ready to expose on frame No. 20.

This procedure differs slightly from that recommended by Olympus—namely to hold both the rewind release lever and the rewind knob while retensioning the shutter. Actually that tends to yield poorer registration or superimposition of the two or more exposures. It is the effect of film tensioning that is tricky; tension too little and the film shifts forward when you retension the shutter; tighten it too much and the film shifts back when you operate the rewind release lever.

Accurate superimposition appears to be most reliable if the film was tensioned before the previous exposure. That means planning a little ahead: take up the slack in the film *before* advancing to the first of the multiple exposures planned. Then, after the first exposure, retension the shutter while holding the rewind release lever in the rewind position but do not tighten or at all touch the rewind knob/crank. That way the film usually remains completely stationary between the exposures.

To avoid overlapping, Olympus also recommends making a blank exposure with the lens cap on the lens after the multiple exposures. If you return the rewind release lever to the forward position by hand (instead of letting it click back on its own by operating the winding lever) there is no need for this blank exposure; there is unlikely to be any overlap unless you have really tightened the film with the rewind knob before the second of the double exposures.

Multiple exposures are additive on the film, so reduce the exposure—next smaller stop or faster shutter speed, or set the OM-2 override control to $-\frac{2}{3}$ for each component exposure.

The camera back

To open the back, fully pull up the rewind knob against spring pressure. This releases the latch and the back swings open through about 215°. It is also removable to permit use of the 250 exposure back, Recordata backs and other units. To remove the open camera back, press downwards the small release pin in the hinge, thus freeing the upper end of the hinge, then lift off. To fit the back (or an alternative back), engage the bottom hinge shaft in the bottom eyelet on the camera body, press down the hinge release pin and line up the top of the hinge with the upper eyelet. Then let go of the hinge release pin so that the upper end of the hinge engages in the eyelet.

The back contains a 38 × 60 mm black pressure plate and, near the hook of the lock, a leaf spring that holds the film cartridge in place.

Inside the open camera, the compartment at the left is the cartridge chamber with the rewind shaft protruding into it. Next to it is the film track and film window, then past the film track the transport sprocket and the built-in take-up spool.

The film runs across the film track and past the film window over a pair of precision-ground shiny rails. These border the upper and lower edge of the film window and define the position of the film plane. The outer rails are slightly higher and act as lateral guides for the film, together with the two film guide pins next to the cartridge chamber. Closing the camera back pushes the pressure plate against the outer rails so that the film moves in a very narrow channel between the inner rails and the pressure plate.

The transport sprocket has eight teeth on each side. One complete revolution advances the film by one image frame. This ensures even spacing of the frames on the film. A friction coupling links the take-up spool to the winding lever.

The exact film plane

The subject distances on the lens focusing scales generally refer to the distance from the film plane. But as you focus by observing the image sharpness on the screen, the distance scale is meant to be little more than a guide.

The OM-1 and OM-2 have no film plane mark. If you need a reasonably accurate indication of the film plane, this is located—within a mm or so—at the tip of the OM-2 exposure meter switch set to MANUAL (or the base line of the MANUAL marking) or at the tip of the OM-1 meter switch set to OFF.

The memo holder

The back of the OM-2 carries a memo holder compartment serving also as a film type indicator or reminder. This takes the end flap of most 35 mm film boxes which usually carries main film data (name, speed, number of exposures). Tear off the flap and push it into the memo holder frame from below.

If you buy films in professional multi-packs rather than single boxes, you can cut suitable 4 × 4 cm or $1\frac{1}{2} \times 1\frac{1}{2}$ inch memo panels from thin filing cards and letter them yourself.

The OM-1 has no memo holder (nor other film type indication), but the memo holder back is available separately and can replace the standard back of the OM-1.

With early OM-1 models adaptation of the camera and/or back may be necessary (see below, *Early OM-1 models*).

Other body features

The camera front carries a pair of carrying strap eyelets at the corners. The eyelets take split rings for attachment of one of several kinds of strap.

The camera base contains a $\frac{1}{4}$ inch tripod bush, the battery compartment, the motor drive socket cap and the motor coupling terminal. There is also a guide or location hole for motor fitting next to the battery chamber. The motor drive socket cap is removable and exposes the coupling elements for the film transport and shutter release by the motor.

Main operating steps

Having discussed the camera controls, let us briefly run through the main operations involved in picture taking with the OM-2 and OM-1.

It is worth practising these operations with the camera and a dummy film cartridge, i.e. one with a spoilt film. It is even worth sacrificing a film for this—you can load, unload and reload it repeatedly—to get really familiar with the handling. Using the camera should be as instinctive as driving a car: you know where you want to go, but your response to the varying traffic situation is almost subconscious. With the camera you know what you want to photograph and how you want to shoot it—if you learn to control your camera thoroughly beforehand you won't be held up with having to recapitulate all the time just how you are going to go about it.

Inserting and testing batteries: OM-2

The OM-2 takes a pair of silver oxide Ray-o-Vac RW 42, S-76 or equivalent cells which power the exposure meter circuit and the electronic shutter.

Unscrew the battery compartment cover near the right-hand end of the camera base with a coin and put in two cells, both with the side carrying the + sign and lettering up—i.e. facing you when you look down on the inverted camera base. Replace the cover and screw down. If one or both batteries are inserted the wrong way round, the camera will not work: you get no signal with the battery test and the mirror locks up if you try to make an exposure.

O.W. C

This does not damage the metering circuit; replace the batteries the right way round.

Before inserting the batteries:

(a) Wipe them carefully with a clean handkerchief to remove any deposits and especially grease that may inhibit good contact—then handle the batteries only with a handkerchief. (This is vital with the OM-2 and its two cells but important also when inserting the single battery in the OM-1).

(b) Check that the OM-2 mirror is reset. Inserting batteries with the OM-2 mirror locked up causes an immediate current drain. As a reminder the inside of the battery compartment carries the lettering RESET and a red asterisk, visible as you take off the cover (see above, *OM-2 mirror lock-up and reset*).

To test the batteries move the meter switch to CHECK; the red LED in the camera back below the switch lever lights up if the batteries are in good condition. If the LED flashes, the batteries are near exhaustion and if it does not light up they are exhausted or wrongly inserted.

Inserting batteries: OM-1

Fit the battery in the OM-1 in the same way; this camera takes only one slightly larger mercury cell. The battery is correctly located if the + mark on it faces up. Inserting the battery the wrong way round again yields no meter reading but has no other adverse effect on the camera.

The battery compartment covers of the OM-1 and OM-2 are very similar but not identical. So don't mix them up if you happen to have both camera models. The inside of the OM-2 battery compartment cover has an engraved figure 2 to distinguish it. The OM-2 cover does not screw down fully on the OM-1 battery compartment and the OM-1 cover cannot be properly screwed into the OM-2 baseplate, either.

The OM-1 shows up battery exhaustion by sluggish or no meter needle movement in the finder.

Loading the film

The OM-1 and OM-2 cameras take 35 mm film in standard cartridges.

LOADING

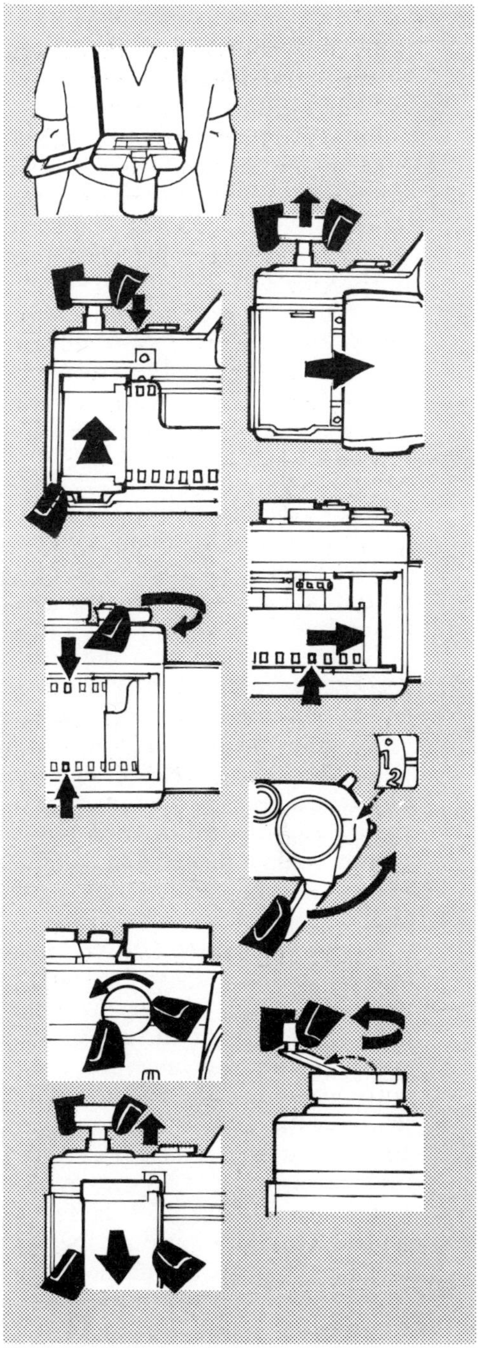

You can load the camera while carrying it round your neck by running the right-hand straps under the right-hand camera end.

Open the back by pulling up the rewind knob *(right)*.

Insert the film cartridge in the chamber *(left)*, tighten the film and thread the end into the take-up spool *(right)*.

Advance the film with the back open until both perforation rows engage the film sprocket *(left)*, then close the back and advance to frame No. 1 *(right)*.

UNLOADING

Turn the rewind release lever horizontal *(left)* and rewind film with the crank *(right)*.

After this, open the camera and let the cartridge drop out.

Load in subdued light, not direct sunlight. Set the shutter speed to 1/30 second or faster and turn the meter switch of the OM-2 to MANUAL.

Pull up the rewind knob and open the camera back fully. Place the film cartridge in the chamber at the left, spool knob in the bottom recess and film pointing to the right across the film window. Pull the whole of the narrow trimmed section of the film from the cartridge mouth. Push back the rewind knob and rotate it slightly if necessary to engage the cartridge spool. Unfold the crank and gently turn it clockwise until it just starts pulling the film leader back into the cartridge. Don't allow more than a few mm of film to run back. Fold up the rewind crank.

Draw the film leader across the film track and push the beginning into one of the slots of the take-up spool. (You will be pulling more film out of the cartridge during this operation.) Push about 15 to 20 mm or $\frac{3}{4}$ inch of film into the spool slot—there is no need for more.

The perforated edge of the film must lie against the bottom edge slot and the film perforations run over the lower sprocket wheel of the transport sprocket.

Keep one finger over the film where it runs over the sprocket, press the shutter release and operate the winding lever. This winds the film inside out on the take-up spool as the transport sprocket pulls it out from the cartridge. Press the shutter release and wind again until the full film width reaches the upper sprocket wheel. Check that the film lies flat in the track and the slot of the cartridge is snug against the left-hand end of the film track. At this point close the camera back, pushing it well against the latch to lock.

Now watch the top of the camera. The frame counter at the left shows a letter S (start) next to the white index mark. Continue winding with the lever until it locks—or if it has already locked, press the release button and wind. During this operation the rewind knob must turn anti-clockwise. The frame counter now advances to the white dot after S. Release and wind again—the counter advances to the second dot—and release and wind once more to bring No. 1 on the counter opposite its index.

You are now ready for the first exposure. Remember to set the ASA speed as described earlier and push the film box flap into the memo holder back (if you have one).

Switch the meter of the OM-2 back to OFF or AUTO, unless you want to shoot in the manual mode. (Switching to MANUAL with a fast shutter speed during the blind exposures at the beginning saves battery power.)

Don't be tempted to skimp the blind exposures before the first frame. They make sure that any beginning of the film light-struck during loading is well out of the way before you begin to record valuable exposures. Don't be misled, either, by having apparently up to 3 inches of blank film between the fogged beginning and the first frame once the film is processed. That blank film is not always blank but sometimes carries slight fog marks—a little light may very occasionally get in through the cartridge slot, especially if you haven't been able to find a reasonably shady spot for loading (or unloading) the film.

Advancing the film—before you close the camera back—until the sprocket engages both sides of the perforation is another safety insurance, in this case against a perforation tearing on the single perforated edge of the film once you have closed the camera back. A torn perforation could leave the film at its beginning while you kid yourself that you are exposing frame after frame. Failure of the rewind knob to turn should of course warn you that the film is not advancing.

Unloading

At the end of the film, you have to rewind it into its light-tight cartridge before removal from the camera. Usually you know that the film is finished by the fact that the winding lever stops halfway when you try to advance to the next frame. Do not force the lever at that point.

To rewind the film, turn the rewind release lever on the camera front (above the self-timer lever) so that the red dot points to the red index next to the letter R on the OM-1 or to the OM-2 lettering on that model. Unfold the rewind crank and turn it (clockwise as shown by its arrow) to wind the film back. Watch for any change in the resistance of the film. You should be able to feel quite clearly when the film end comes off the take-up spool (and you can also hear it): three or four more turns winds up the film end fully in the cartridge. Then pull up the rewind knob, open the camera and extract the cartridge from its chamber—just turn the camera over and let the cartridge drop into your hand.

Some people prefer to stop rewinding when they hear the film end detaching itself from the take-up spool. That way the trimmed leader still protrudes when you take out the film and you can for instance write some identifying data on it in pencil. Also you have to keep the film leader outside if you have unloaded a part exposed film and want to reload it again.

Don't use force

Forcing the winding lever when it blocks at the end of the film is most likely to tear perforations where the transport sprocket engages the film perforation. This can give rise to further troubles.

The small shreds of film torn out between neighbouring perforations can get into parts of the camera mechanism, for instance between the shutter curtains and the film window and interfere with shutter operation.

If you are unlucky, you may tear the film off the cartridge spool in the camera. That would make rewinding impossible—you then have to unload the camera in a darkroom.

While this is rare, another mishap is more likely: in forcing the transport you tear not just the film between perforations but between the perforation and the film edge. When you rewind, this torn film edge may not re-enter the cartridge slot but jam outside. If you then try to rewind by force, the film simply tears right across. Once this has happened, rewinding appears to be easy and straightforward, though in fact the whole of the film stays outside the cartridge and gets fogged when you open the camera back.

Quite a catalogue of horrors—so don't use force.

Manual shooting sequence

The OM-1 has only a manual operating mode. The meter is switched on when you move the exposure meter switch next to the rewind knob from OFF to ON. The OM-2 has a manual mode as one of its alternatives. In this case turn the meter selector switch to MANUAL.

Preselect the lens aperture you want to use on the aperture ring and focus the image on the screen. Watch

OM SHOOTING

Focus the image on the screen *(left)* and preselect the lens aperture *(right)*.

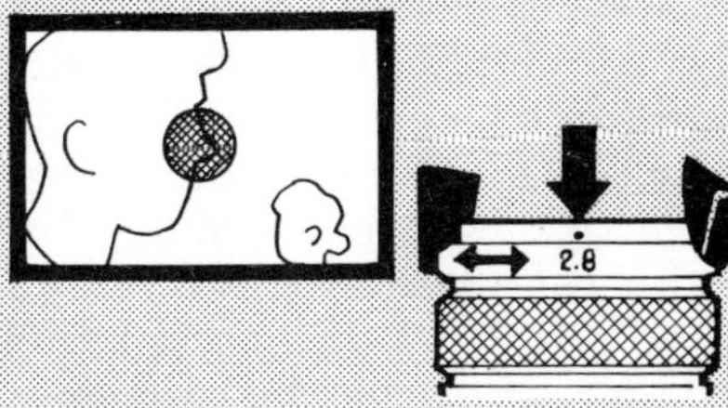

For manual exposures switch the OM-1 meter switch to ON *(left)* or on the OM-2 switch to MANUAL *(right)*.

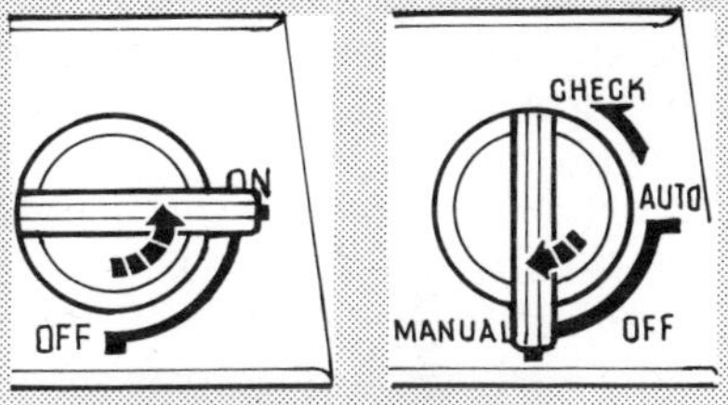

Rotate the shutter speed ring *(left)* to centre the meter needle between its index marks *(right)*; or preselect the shutter speed and centre by the aperture control.

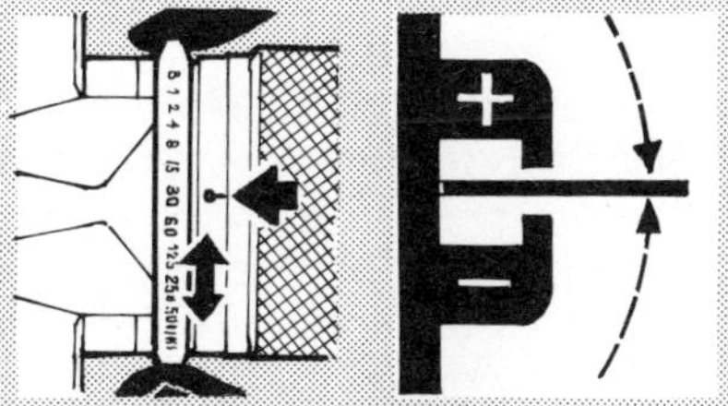

For automatic exposures with the OM-2 set the meter switch to AUTO *(left)*; the needle then shows the approximate speed selected by the camera *(right)*.

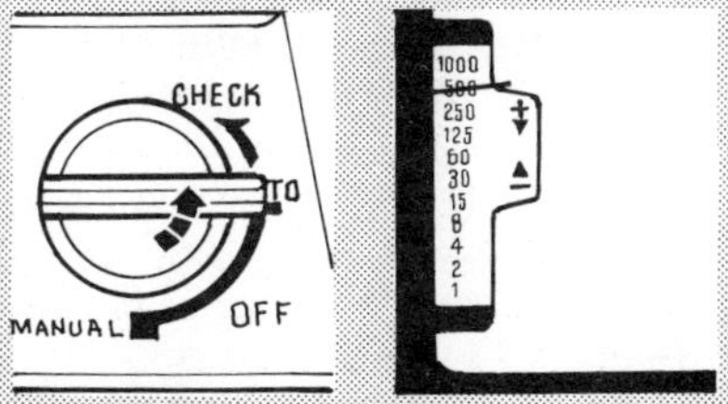

Press the release button to take the picture *(left)*, then advance the film by one or more strokes of the winding lever *(right)*; the frame counter shows the number of exposures made.

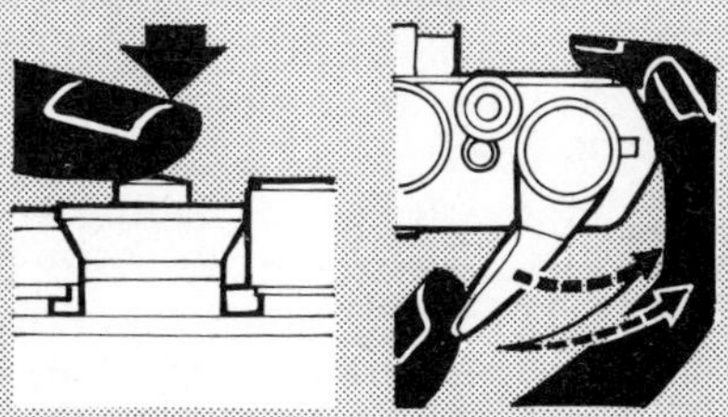

the meter needle in the finder and adjust the shutter speed ring to centre the needle between the two prongs or arrow heads. Provided you have set the correct ASA speed beforehand, this adjustment of the shutter speed selects the correct exposure for the subject conditions. If you want to work with a given shutter speed, preset that and centre the needle by adjusting the aperture ring.

Then press the release button to take the picture. The image in the finder disappears instantaneously as the mirror swings out of the way for the exposure, and re-appears again immediately afterwards. With the winding lever, advance the film and retension the shutter for the next shot.

Automatic shooting sequence

Set the meter switch of the OM-2 to AUTO; the camera now measures and adjusts the exposure automatically for the prevailing lighting level and the previously set ASA film speed value.

Preset the lens aperture to be used on the aperture ring and focus the image. At the left of the finder you now see a shutter speed scale and the meter needle moving across it. The position of the needle indicates the approximate shutter speed selected by the automatic exposure system. The camera automatically exposes at that speed when you press the release button. This automatic system thus also takes care of changing light conditions from shot to shot—you don't have to re-adjust anything.

If you want to use a specific minimum shutter speed, preselect a different lens aperture so that the needle points to about the speed you want to use.

Early OM-1 models

The first models of the OM-1 differed slightly from the later versions. The points of difference—most of which do not affect operation—are:

The camera base does not have provision for coupling the motor drive, i.e. neither the contacts nor the socket cap for access to the drive coupling. These models do not have the designation MD on the front. Pre-MD models can be converted to motor drive coupling by Olympus servicing agencies.

The pressure plate in the camera back is slightly smaller

(38 × 52 mm) and the back itself is a shade less rigid than that of later models.

The film track of early OM-1 models has four screwed-in film guide pins, and it is the location of the second pair of pins near the transport sprocket which makes the shorter pressure plate in the camera back necessary. This needs adaptation to make the camera usable with the memo holder back in place of the standard back: the two extra locating studs prevent the longer pressure plate from lying flat in the film track, though the back appears to fit on the camera without trouble. Get an Olympus agency or servicing to do that. In a few cases the hinge may not fit correctly which also needs a slight adjustment of the memo holder back by Olympus servicing.

The viewfinder eyepiece on the early OM-1 models has its rear lens located very near the outside of the eyepiece frame—instead of being recessed as on later models. This makes the early eyepiece more liable to get dirty—but also more accessible for cleaning.

SMALL-CAMERA PHILOSOPHY

One of the earliest and longest lasting arguments on the photographic scene has been the controversy over camera size and picture format. While the earliest cameras nearly 150 years ago yielded direct pictures larger than the page of this book, there were already then minute camera and image formats that soon had to deal with serious questions of concentrated information storage. The controversy reached a peak when the 24 × 36 mm miniature camera format began to spread in earnest nearly 50 years ago, because then this camera format established the principle of recording pictures on small-size negatives and making enlarged prints afterwards. As might be expected, this approach presented the most serious test of image quality and challenge to optical designers and to photochemical and emulsion research.

While the resulting improvements in lenses and films have made much of the quality argument academic, the 24 × 36 mm format is again under challenge from two sides. The first is the still ultraminiature format—nowadays typically 13 × 17 mm or about a quarter of the 24 × 36 mm area, with its attraction of a small and truly pocketable camera. The other is the considerably more bulky roll film reflex. With a 6 × 6 cm frame, this is again roughly four times larger than 24 × 36 mm and so claims to offer better image quality on enlargements, especially for professional requirements. (We will disregard here the still larger view camera formats as their use is associated with a different level of camera manipulation.)

Information content and image size

The classic image format comparison test is to photograph a view of appreciable detail, for instance an outdoor landscape, in turn with a 13 × 17 mm pocket camera, with a 24 × 36 mm miniature camera and with a 6 × 6 cm

HOW MUCH INFORMATION?

A modern colour television screen image contains 120,000–250,000 individual picture elements—i.e. colour triplets that the additive screen picture is made up of. (The variation is due both to different television systems and different ways of counting basic colour elements.) The 24×36 mm image frame was originally devised for about a million picture elements. The size to which the picture is enlarged does not affect this consideration, provided the viewing distance is in proportion to the picture format.

FILM AND INFORMATION CAPACITY

The 24×36 mm frame is more than large enough to hold 1 million picture elements even with the fastest coarse-grained films. A half-frame 18×24 mm picture (or a cropped 24×36 mm image) is still adequate. With smaller formats the information capacity becomes critical with coarser grained films; the 57×57 mm roll film format on the other hand offers vast—and frequently unused—surplus capacity.

"Fine" here implies a high-resolving colour slide film or fine grain black-and-white material, "Medium" applies to modern fine-resolving colour print (colour negative) and black-and-white films, "Coarse" to ultra-speed colour and black-and-white materials. Document films are finer still.

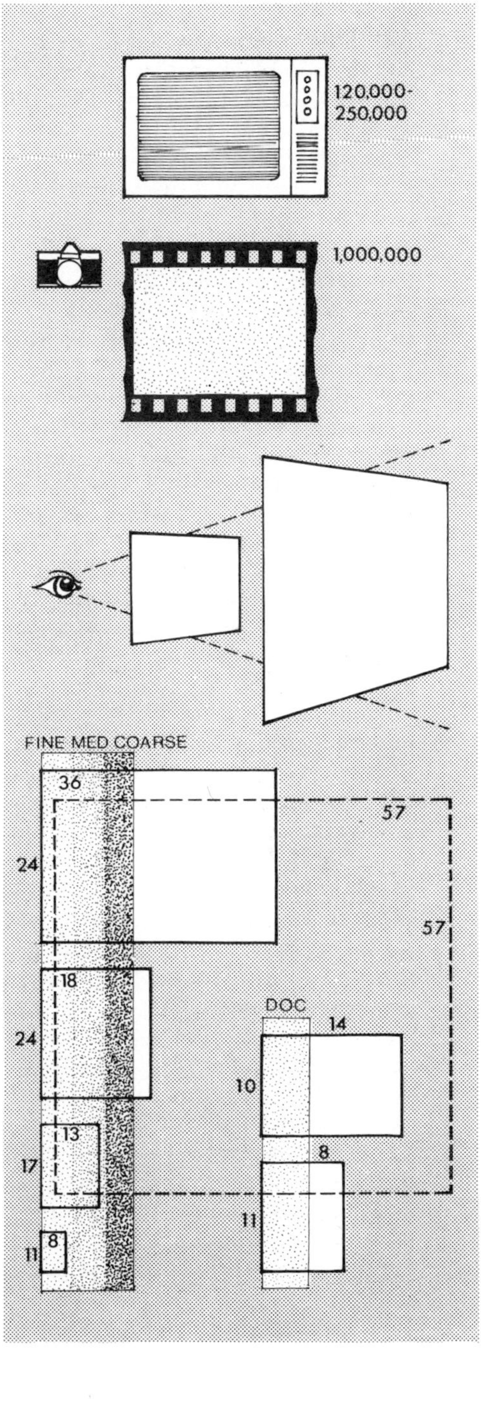

roll film model, using in each case a medium-speed colour or black-and-white film and assuming high-quality lens equipment. Big enlargements from these negatives, say to about 25 × 30 or 30 × 40 cm, would on reasonably close examination show obvious differences in detail quality. This is inevitable, as the 13 × 17 mm negative would need twice as high a linear magnification as 24 × 36 mm and about four times as high linear as 6 × 6 cm. To put the question in its proper perspective we should however consider how much quality and definition we need or are able to appreciate.

We can consider this in terms of a standard viewed enlargement—an enlargement of a negative photographed with a lens of normal focal length and viewed at a distance that recreates the visual perspective of the objects as originally seen. With a 35 mm camera this implies a 5× enlarged print viewed at 25 cm—or bigger prints at correspondingly larger distances. The visual limit of discrimination of the eye is around $1\frac{1}{2}$ to 2 minutes of arc; anything subtending a smaller angle at the eye is indistinguishable from a point. At a viewing distance of 25 cm this corresponds roughly to detail 0.15 mm large or an area of 0.02 mm^2.

In an approximately 13 × 18 cm or 5 × 7 inch print (enlarged about 5× linear from 24 × 36 mm) there are a little over 1 million such minimum picture elements of 0.02 mm^2. However, a million picture elements resolvable by the eye is a convenient and standard round figure and preserves all the visible detail of an image, in other words the information we can perceive by looking at it under normal conditions. Today, with the resolving power of even a high-speed film and good quality lens, a 24 × 36 mm frame can record around 3 to 4 million picture elements. That means that you still have some reserve, for instance to cope with loss of definition through very slight camera shake, not quite correct exposure, sharpness loss through less than ideal processing and so on. In virtually every case an enlargement from the 24 × 36 mm negative shows all the information visible to the eye when it observed the original scene.

With a still smaller image format such as 13 × 17 mm of a pocket camera, a 10× linear magnification could yield a standard viewed enlargement of similar information content, but only with a film of fine grain and high resolution and a lens of highest optical quality. This format—and even more so the still smaller 8 × 11 mm ultra-miniature size—thus operates very near the limits of acceptable information content. Look at an enlargement from such a negative from slightly closer than the normal distance and you become very aware of the lack of fine detail.

In fact, an information content of less than our stipulated 1 million picture elements can still be acceptable. Thus a picture on a television screen—at any rate in colour—barely reaches one quarter of this figure. (That is connected in part with the additive raster structure of the image.) Yet, to a large extent, because the image is moving, and no doubt, due to force of habit we quite readily accept the limited information content when sitting in front of the box.

Logically, a bigger format offers still more information reserve and latitude in technique. That is certainly one reason why roll film and larger cameras are preferred for certain professional applications. (The other reason is a pride of eliminating as much evidence as possible of visible quality limitations, even when these do not affect information in the image.)

Camera size and compromises

The arguments concerning image format and camera use depend also on the compromise between final picture quality and equipment convenience. The pocket and ultra-miniature camera user sacrifices virtually all tolerances of the photographic process and often some visual quality as well. The gain is extreme pocketability, for most No. 110 pocket cameras really go conveniently into a small pocket. (The few designs that sacrifice pocketability for greater versatility tend also to lose the justification for their existence.)

At the other extreme a large film format can in principle record more information and offers much more quality tolerance but needs a correspondingly bulky camera.

The 24 × 36 mm format is thus a favourable compromise for most applications of general photography and in certain specialised fields extensively covered by the Olympus OM system. The OM cameras are not strictly speaking pocketable (unless you have big pockets) but their compactness tells when it comes to carrying accessories of the system. For up to a point (as long as the camera is comfortable to hold), the more compact the equipment the less of a weight it is to lug around in a holdall case. Or conversely, the more equipment you can accommodate within a given case and weight limit.

While the 35 mm camera yields all the quality we need when used with sufficiently precise technique, the margin of error is not generous. Photography with the Olympus OM thus calls for a certain precision in image framing—where the interchangeable lenses are useful—as well as in focusing (served by the reflex screen), exposure (through-the-lens metering looks after that) and processing. There is nothing new about that; similar demands were made on 35 mm photography 50 years ago. Materials and equipment have since improved in quality—but our standards have become higher, too.

Image size is incidentally subordinate to image scale in fields such as macrophotography, photomicrography and even endoscopic photography. The detail revealed in the final picture there depends much more on the optical system than on the film format. In quite a few cases you gain very little by making the image bigger on the film (e.g. by increasing the camera extension) compared with greater enlargement of a smaller negative. This is akin to the microscopist's concept of 'empty magnification' and a powerful reason why the 35 mm camera in these fields is considerably more convenient than larger-format equipment.

HOLDING AND RELEASING

A steady hold and smooth releasing need a comfortable grip on the camera. And that depends to some extent on the size and proportions of your hand: there is no one ideal camera hold that suits everybody.

The basic point of a steady hold is to grip the camera firmly, but not cramped so that your hand trembles. And you have to keep it steady while you press the release button. That instant decides whether the result will be sharp or not. If the camera trembles during the exposure, so will the image on the film, which can make the picture blurred even in a fraction of a second. Camera shake unsharpness may not be obvious on the film unless you look for it with a powerful magnifying glass. But enlarging a negative or projecting a slide is like looking at it through a magnifier.

The degree of camera shake unsharpness depends on how steady you hold the camera and on the actual exposure time. If the time is short—with a fast shutter speed—you can get away with a much less steady hold than if you are obliged to use a slow speed—or if the automatic camera selects a slow shutter speed for you. If you have any control over matters, select therefore a fast shutter speed or adjust the lens aperture to yield a fast speed in the automatic system.

The following pages describe various ways of holding the camera. In the descriptions, the ends of the camera are again related to the hand that holds them: the right-hand end of the camera is that carrying the winding lever and release button which you would normally grip with the right hand when shooting—and similarly for the left hand.

Try out the holds yourself and select the ones that suit your hands and comfort best. Practise holding and releasing the camera in your preferred way until you can do it instinctively, quickly and without camera shake.

The camera strap

The strap supplied with the camera is not only a carrying aid but should also be part of the structure that steadies the camera in your hand and against your head.

Adjust the strap length so that you can loop the strap comfortably round both wrists while holding the camera and pressing it against your face for shooting. Looping round the wrists is necessary to keep the strap long enough so that you can remove the camera over your head without undoing the strap.

Alternatively, the camera can hang round your right shoulder and down to your left side—under your jacket if you wish. But getting the camera up to the eye for shooting is not so quick. The best way of holding the camera depends also on the lens. Front-heavy long lenses need support under the lens barrel—which as a matter of fact often permits more convenient holds. For the purposes of camera holds, lenses are here grouped into short, long and extra long. Short lenses in this context means all wide angle, standard and short tele lenses up to 100 mm focal length; long lenses are all other tele lenses and zooms without a tripod mounting ring while extra long lenses are the long tele and zoom units with tripod mounting ring.

Horizontal holds—short lenses

With the right hand grip the right-hand end of the camera, at the same time wrapping one turn of the strap around your right wrist. The right hand, strap and your head then virtually support the camera. The left hand can operate the focusing and aperture rings and, where necessary, the shutter speed ring.

If the camera is on a long strap around your shoulder, bringing it up to eye level will take up enough of the strap length (either around the left shoulder or round your back) to tension the strap again and push the camera against your face.

The hold is similar if the strap is not attached to the camera (or it is not convenient to hang the strap round your neck). But here the left hand has to play more of a part in supporting the camera and pressing—together with the right hand—against your forehead.

The index finger of the right hand operates the release button and the right thumb the film winding lever.

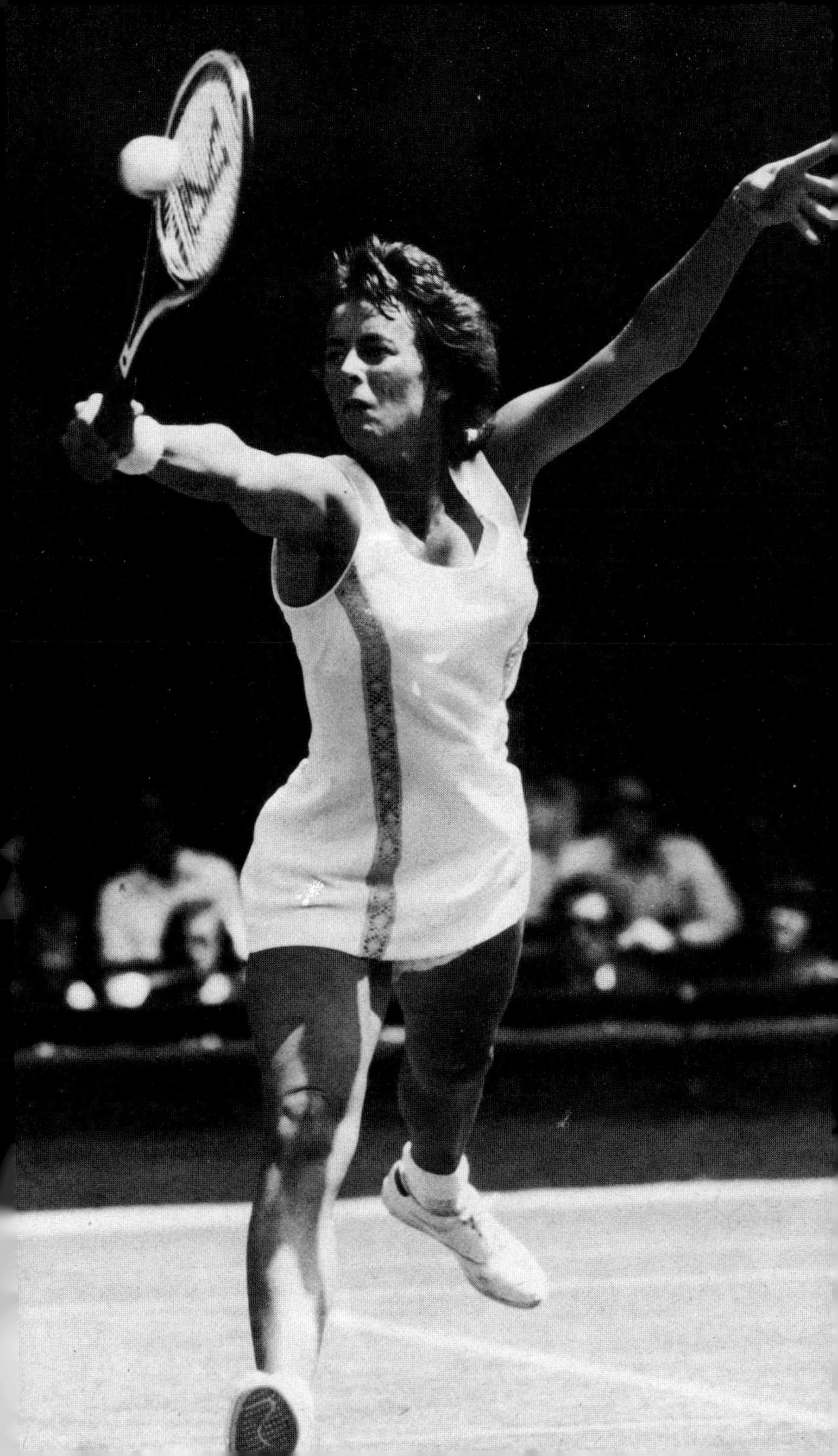

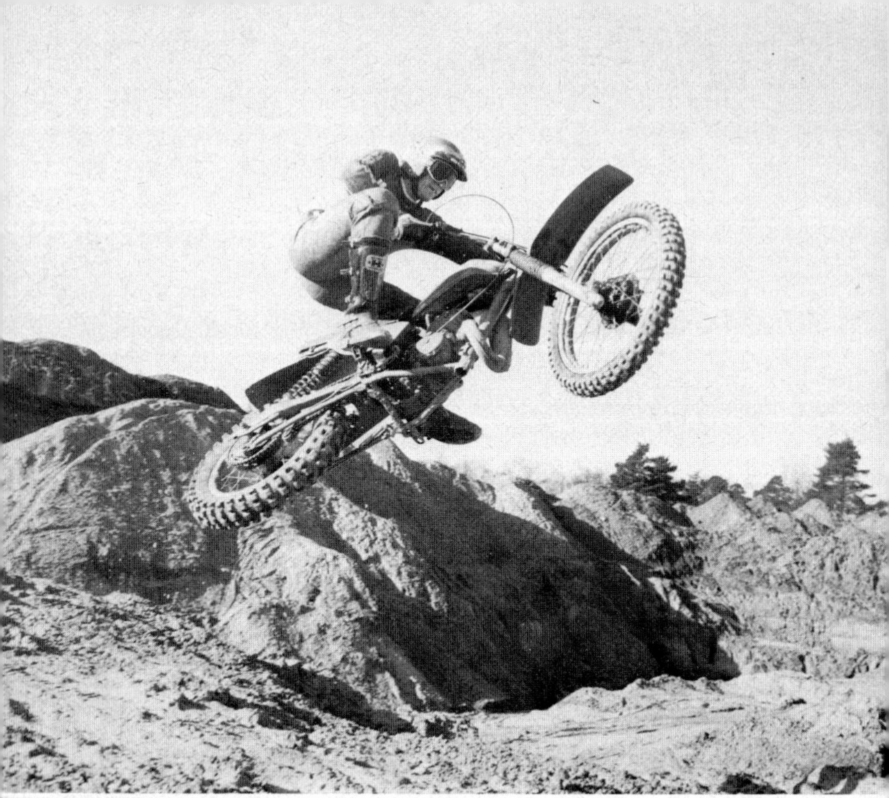

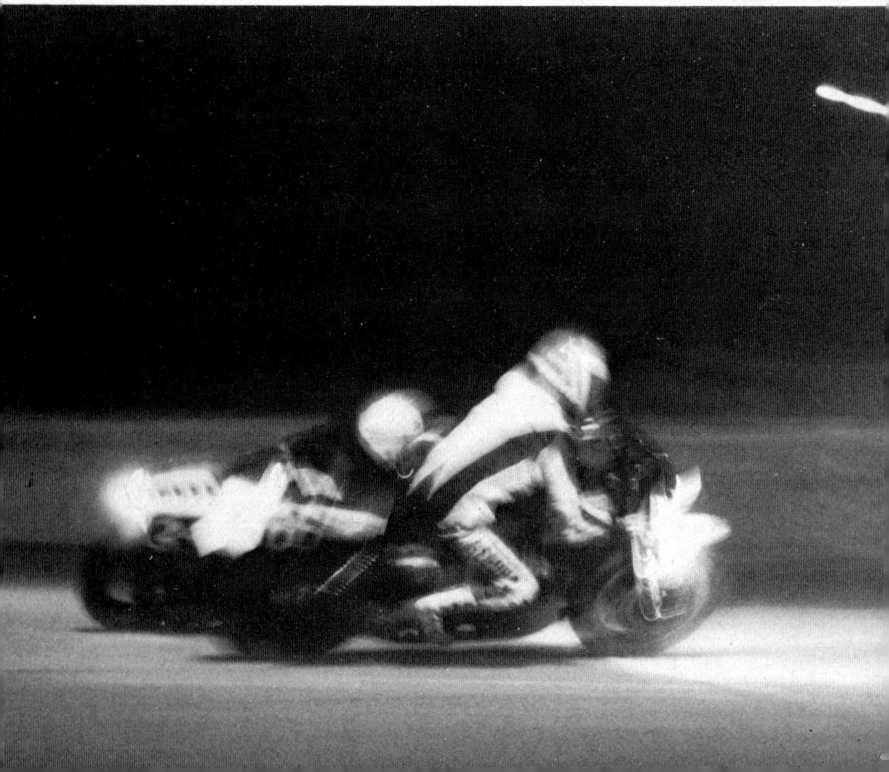

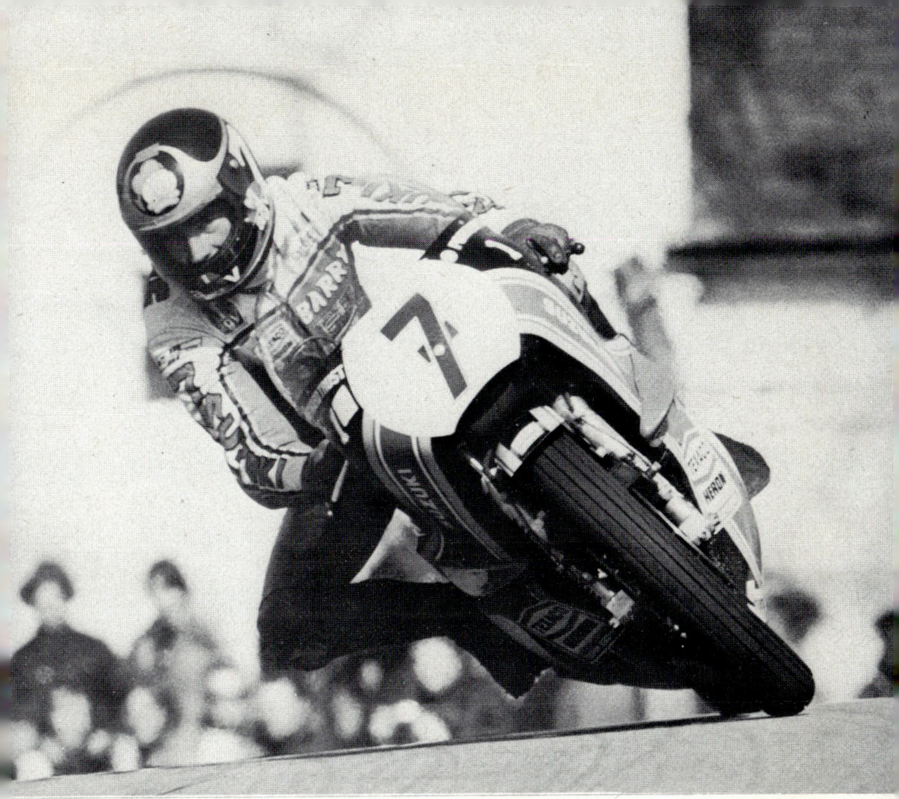

MOTOR CYCLE SPORT

Above. Taken with the 600 mm *f*6.5D world champion Barry Sheene fills the frame even though he was 100 ft away. Fast and accurate focusing is vital, too, for depth of field is limited.

Opposite, top. With the 18 mm *f*3.5 you have to be really near for a big image. But you get dramatic angles and have no focusing worries.

Opposite, bottom. Night riders, lit just by the headlights behind presented no problems to the OM-2 auto exposure system. Panning at the enforced slow shutter gives strong sense of movement.

SPORT IN THE SUN

Plate I. From the side of the tennis court the 85 mm lens showed Mrs. Harris large enough to fill the frame. The bright sun allowed a high shutter speed with a reasonable aperture on medium-speed transparency film.

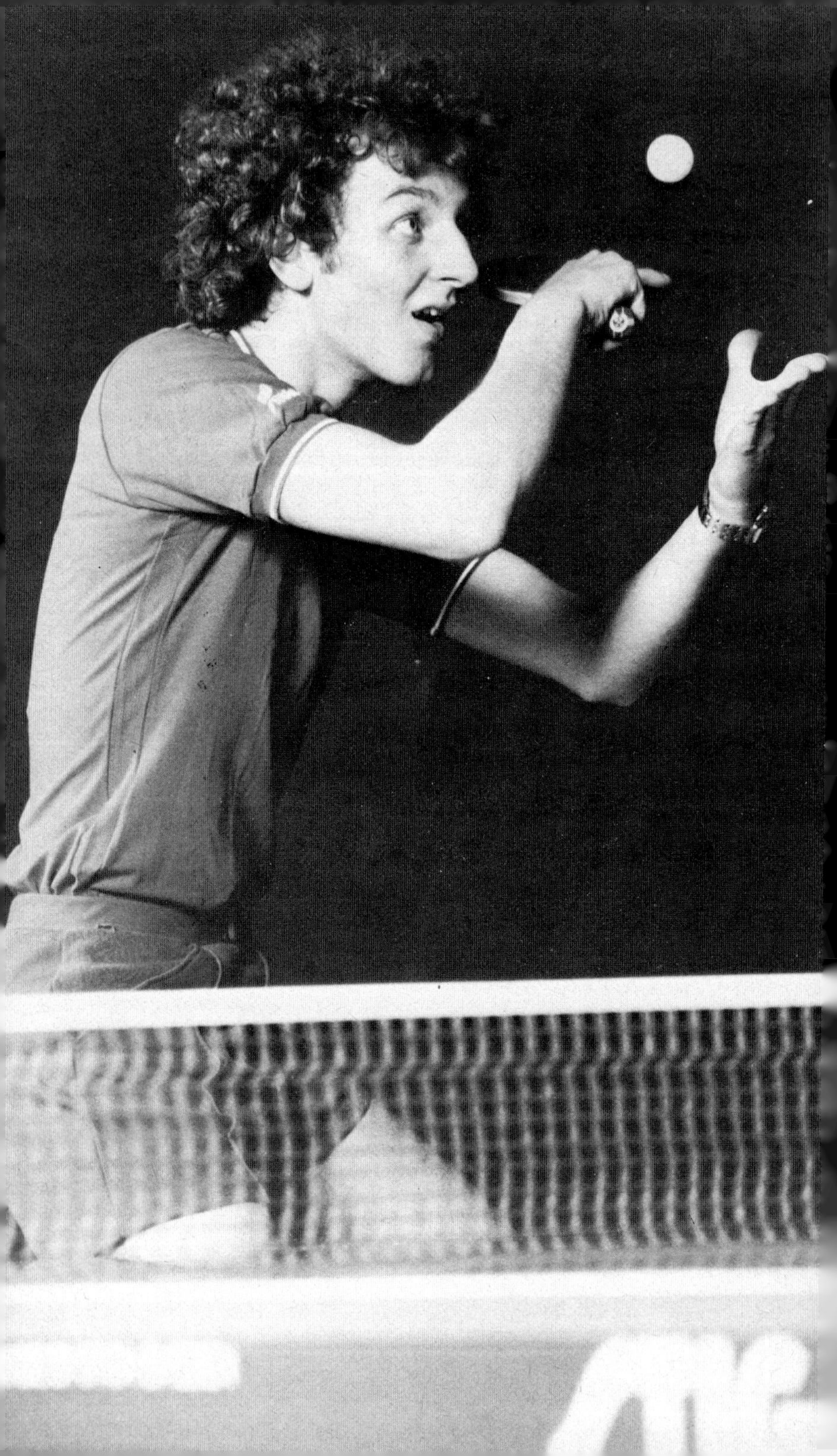

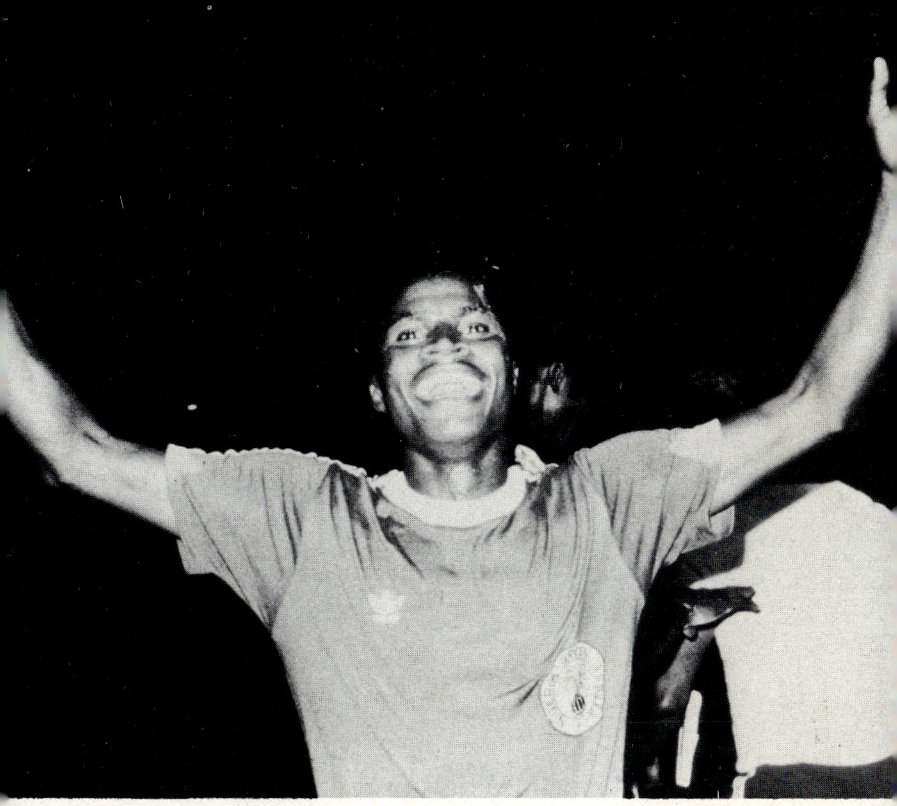

FLASH ACTION

Above. Here flash on camera was the only way of technique. Picturing the winner, however unartistically is more important than the lighting. (From a colour transparency).

Opposite. If you can set up electronic flashes carefully beforehand, you have better control over lighting and modelling. The short flash virtually froze all movement.

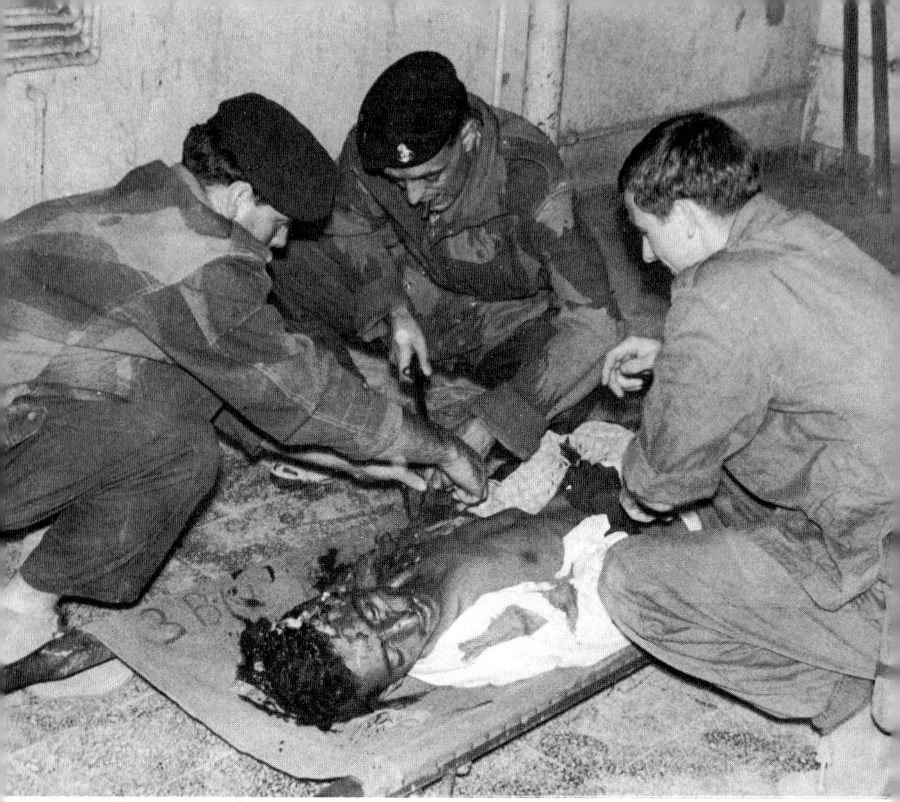

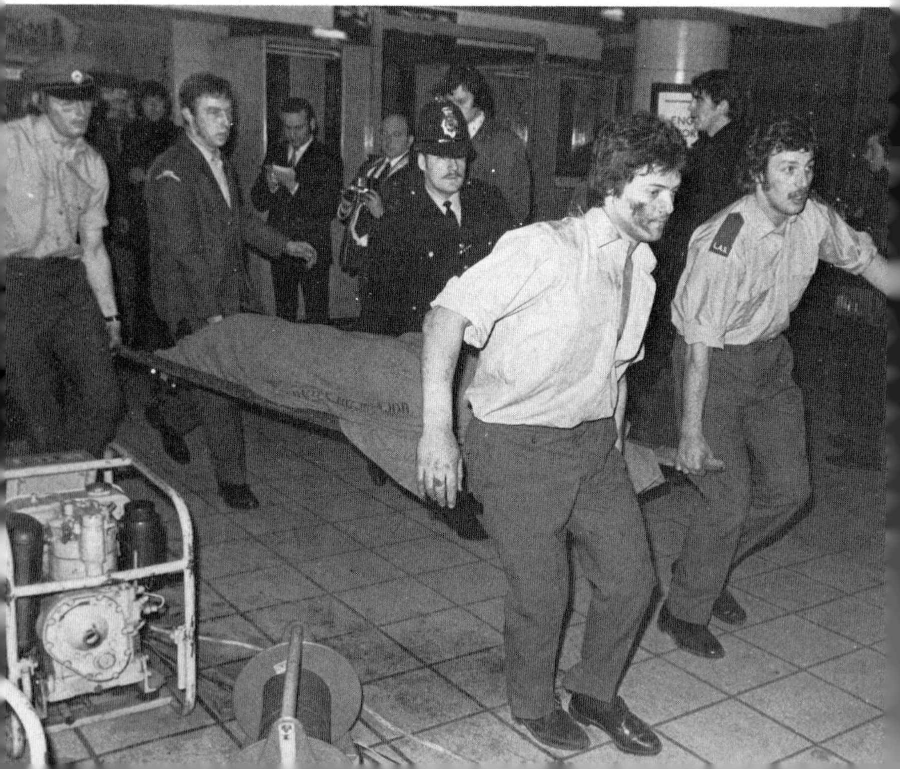

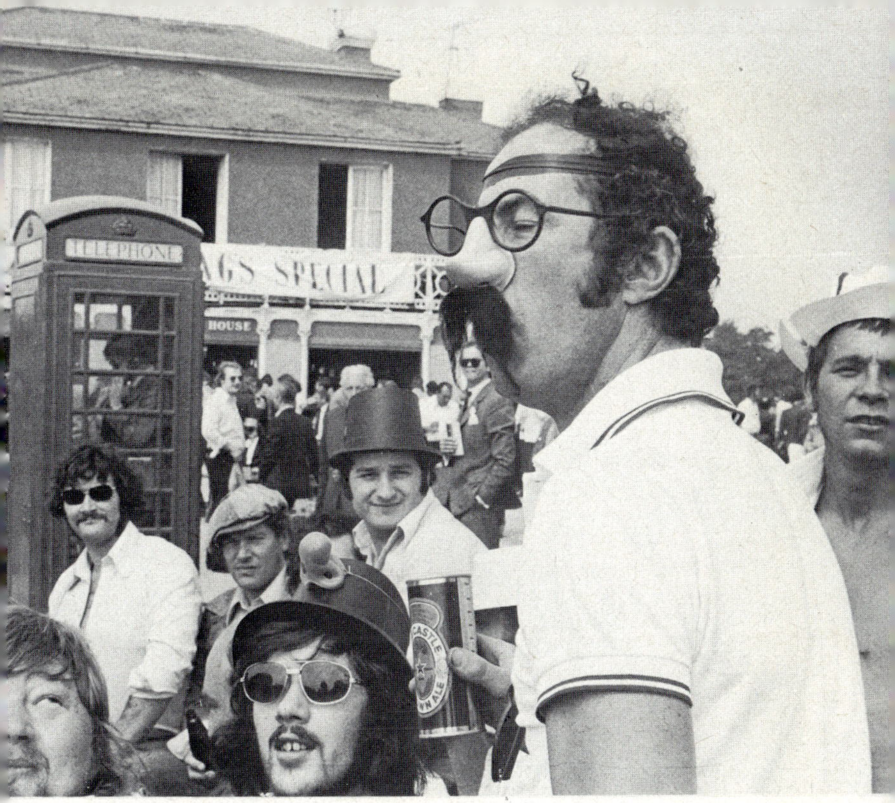

PHOTOJOURNALISM
Above. Derby Day clowing—a typical action shot with a 35 mm lens.

Opposite, top. The first aid personnel will be in close contact with the injured man so the photographer should stand far away, an 85 mm lens gives this shot.

Opposite, bottom. To cover civilian emergencies, for instance, the underground train crash in March, 1975 at Moorgate, London, news photographers can only be on the spot with portable equipment—here camera-mounted flash.

MONTAGE
Plate 8. A number of shots put together may illustrate a point better than a single picture.

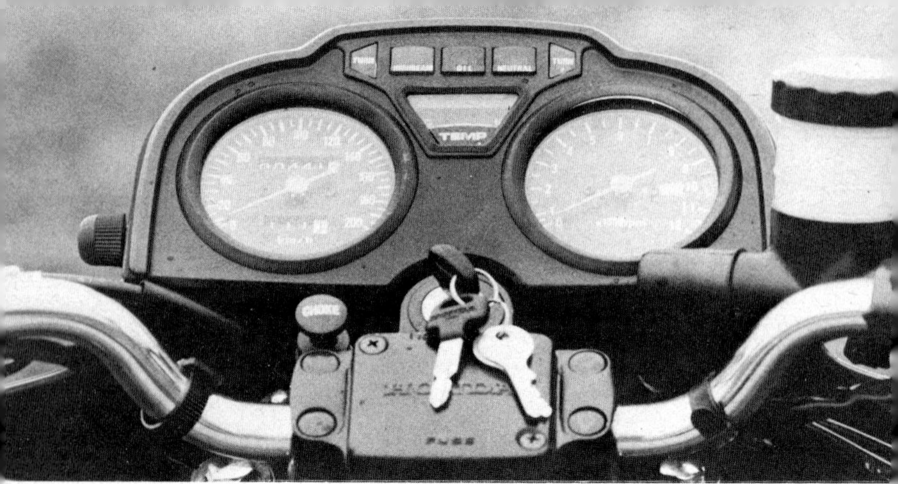
TEMP
CHOKE

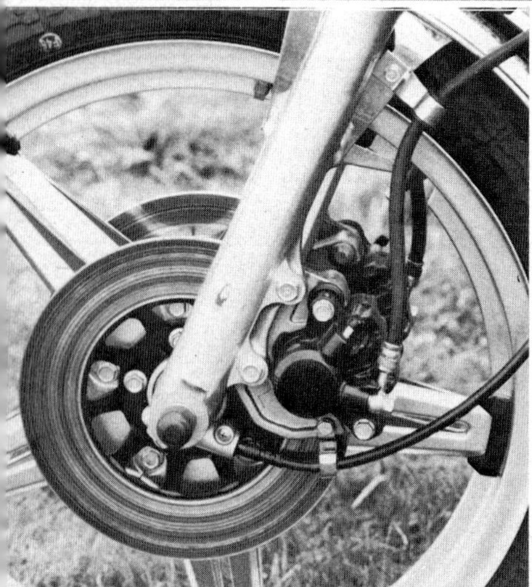

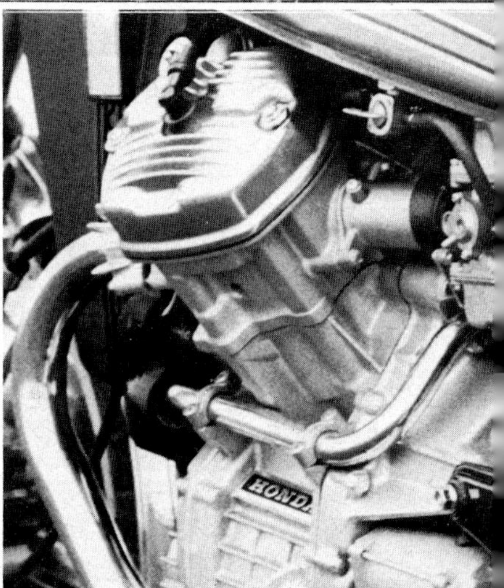
HONDA

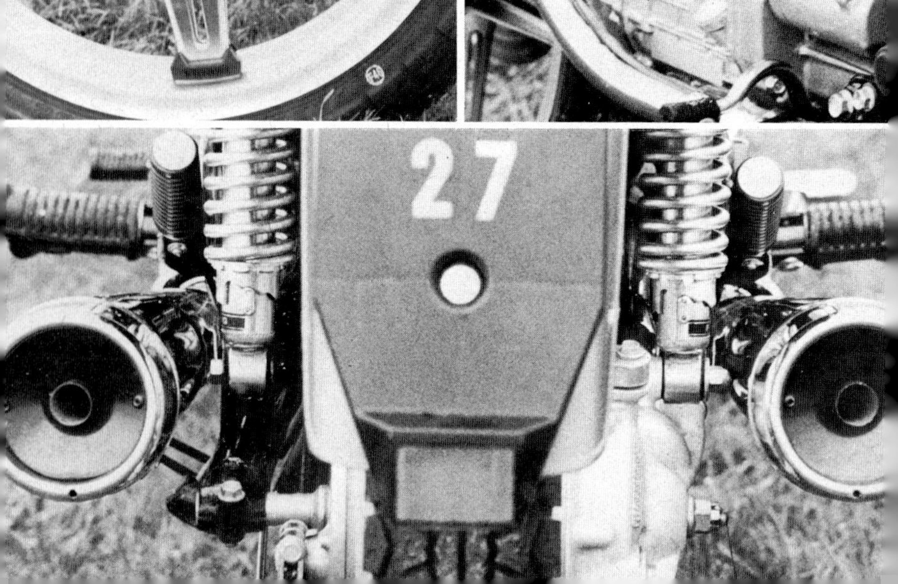
27

OM CAMERA HOLDS

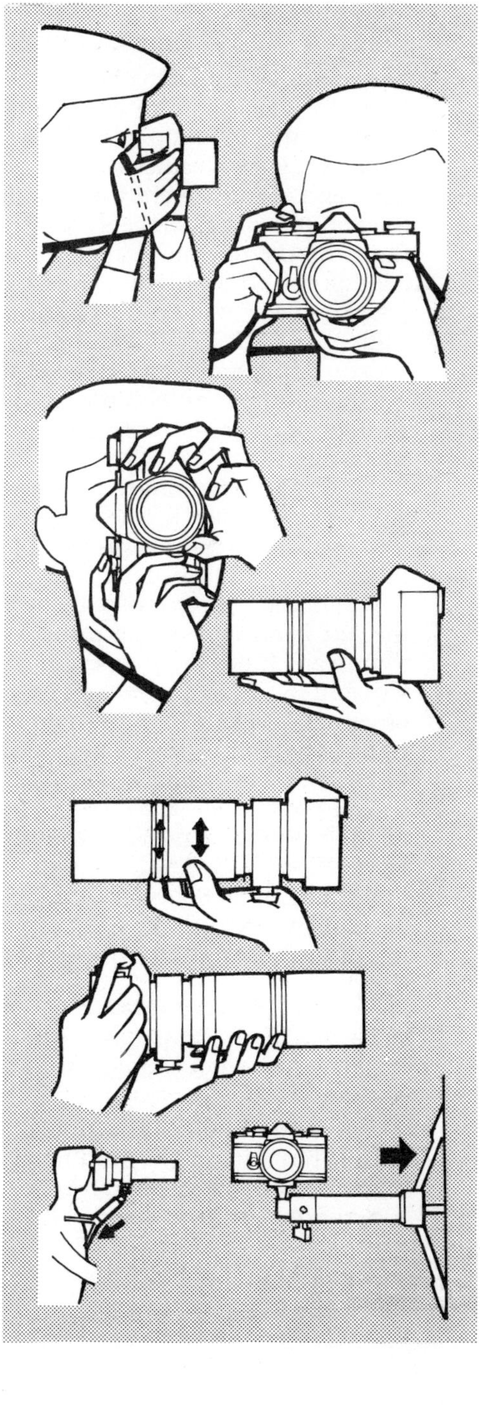

The camera strap, tightened round the neck and wound round the wrist, provides additional camera steadiness with all holds *(left)*. With short lenses, the left hand supports the camera and also operates the lens controls while the right releases *(right)*.

For vertical shots support the camera with the right hand and use the left to press the camera back against your forehead *(left)*.

With long lenses the left hand grips the lens further forward *(right)*.

With longer tele lenses fitted with a tripod mounting ring, support the tripod platform in the palm of your left hand.

A solid table tripod can provide a firm camera support against the chest or shoulder *(left)*. In interiors, push the table tripod against a wall, column etc. for a firm support permitting even short time exposures *(right)*.

Vertical holds—short lenses

There are two ways of holding the camera for upright shots as you can have either the left-hand end or the right-hand end on top.

Probably the steadier hold involves gripping the right-hand end of the camera with the thumb against the back, the middle and ring fingers against the front and the index finger on the release button. The index finger of the left hand presses the left-hand end of the camera front against your forehead while you look through the finder with the right eye. The left-hand operates the focusing ring, aperture ring and shutter speed if necessary. This hold is useful without or with the strap; in the latter case have the left index finger resting against the left-hand edge of the camera.

The right index finger presses the release button and also switches over to the winding lever to advance the film in several short strokes. This is the one slight inconvenience of this hold.

An alternative vertical hold has the left hand supporting the left-hand end of the camera in the palm, with the thumb and index finger operating the focusing ring of the lens and the other fingers pressed against the camera base or camera back. The right hand grips the now topmost right-hand end of the camera and presses it against the forehead. The right-hand index finger operates the release button. To advance the film you lift the camera off the eye to allow the right thumb to operate the winding lever.

With all these holds avoid getting any finger of the left hand anywhere near the front of the lens—especially with the ultrawide-angle and fisheye lenses.

Holds with long lenses

With longer focal lengths the camera hold must be steadier, so use the strap for additional support whenever possible.

The horizontal hold is similar to that with the short lenses, but extend the lens hood and let the left index finger rest on the barrel in front of the aperture ring. The palm of the left hand effectively supports the camera and lens.

For upright shots use only the hold where the right hand

supports the camera while the left index finger presses the other end of the camera against your forehead and the other fingers of the left hand operate the lens controls.

Holds with extra-long lenses

Some of the long tele lenses (e.g. 300 and 400 mm) with tripod mounting ring are still compact and light enough for hand-held shooting. While the tripod mounting ring is removable it does provide an extra support for the lens when holding it. With these extra long lenses use any additional aid available—support for the elbows, table tripod, etc. Also, use the strap.

For a horizontal hold, slack off the clamping knob of the tripod mounting ring and turn the ring so that the tripod mounting platform is underneath. Clamp the ring in this position. Hold the camera so that the tripod platform rests in the palm of your left hand, with the left thumb and middle finger on the focusing mount. The left index finger can if necessary adjust apertures; otherwise it is stretched out underneath the lens barrel. Extend the lens hood. The left hand thus provides most of the camera support. The right hand grips the right-hand end, with the index finger on the release and the thumb operating the winding lever.

For upright shots slack off the clamping knob of the tripod mounting ring and turn the whole camera and lens assembly through 90° so that the winding lever end of the camera is now on top. The hold of the left hand remains unchanged—i.e. the assembly is still resting in the palm of the hand with the platform of the tripod mounting ring. The right index finger rests on the release button, the right thumb operates the winding lever—but you have to take your eye away from the finder for that.

Stance and steadiness

How steadily you can hold the camera depends a great deal also on how much additional support you can find. As already mentioned, the camera strap is one useful aid. Here, in decreasing order of effectiveness, are further ones:

(a) Support your elbows on something solid—a wall, railing, table, the arms of an arm chair or whatever else may be available. If you are sitting on the ground, even your knees can provide additional elbow support. This makes an enormous difference to camera steadiness during the exposure, especially with the long-focus lenses.

Check however that the support is really solid and not subject to vibration. Supporting yourself on the roof or bonnet of a car with its engine running, the window ledge of a moving train or other vehicle simply transmits vibrations through your elbows to the camera.

(b) Jam the camera or lens against something solid where you can still aim at the subject—for instance a tree trunk, wall etc. Usually the hold will be uncomfortable, but the camera may be much steadier. Again avoid possibly vibrating supports.

(c) If none of these aids is available, tuck your elbows well into your sides, stand with the legs apart and use the fastest possible shutter speed that you can for the subject and light conditions.

Smooth releasing

The purpose of a steady camera hold is to allow shake-free releasing. That involves pressing the release button without moving anything else. Pressure must thus be on the release button alone and no other part of the camera. And it must be smooth pressure, not careless pushing, jabbing or thrusting which are the main sources of camera shake.

The OM release mechanism is very soft in operation, so smooth releasing should be no problem. With virtually all camera holds it is the right index finger that operates the release. The easiest way of pressing smoothly is to have the finger resting on top of the film winding lever shaft (this provides a large support surface). Let the tip of the finger overhang onto the centre of the release button. To release the shutter then gradually flex the fingertip to press down on the button itself. The travel of the button is barely 2 mm and there is no first pressure point or resistance on the way.

Practise releasing smoothly with the different camera holds—it pays.

To hold or not to hold your breath? If you have the camera pressed against your face, it will of course move slightly as you breathe. So hold your breath for the instant you are releasing. But don't hold your breath and then wait a few seconds—that causes worse trembling than ever. If you cannot seem to manage it that way, release while breathing out slowly.

Heavy breathing is not good for a steady camera hold. So avoid taking pictures immediately after heavy exertion—for instance climbing or running—relax for half a minute first.

Special releasing aids

There are still some ways of making releasing smoother. The most obvious one is with the motor drive or winder, which has a switch to trigger the release sequence. Less effort and less movement means less risk of shake.

You can use the self-timer when your camera hold is so precarious that any pressure or shifting of pressure is liable to move or shake the set-up. That may for instance be the case if you are pressing the camera with the table tripod and a heavy lens against a column inside a church.

To expose in such a situation, partly tension the self-timer to its minimum tensioning point (halfway down), check that the film is advanced and release the self-timer. You then have about 4 seconds to resume and steady your grip on the camera.

Left-eye viewing

If you view with your left eye, you have to move the camera or your head to advance the film. The most sensible hold in this case is to fold the winder right back into the camera body, pressing the right thumb joint into your right cheek while squeezing your nose against the camera back. Release in this position, while getting whatever purchase you can on the strap to steady the camera. Then pull your head back after the shot while advancing the film with the right thumb, fold the winding lever back against the body again and take the next shot.

Another camera hold that some left-eyed photographers have found useful is to hold the camera upside down, pressing the camera back against the forehead as you look through the eyepiece with the left eye. But operating the lens controls and shutter speed ring (on the OM-1) is less convenient.

For vertical shots use the second alternative hold above, i.e. with the left hand end of the camera resting in the left palm and the right hand pressing the camera back against your forehead while the left eye looks through the eyepiece. You can release in this position, but you have to take the camera off the eye for advancing the film.

Steadying with winder or motor

One problem with modern cameras—especially single lens reflexes—is that they are a compromise between opposing forces of holding convenience and carrying convenience. Making cameras more compact has made them easier to carry but not easier to hold for shooting if you have big hands.

While we wait for possible ergonomic inspirations to propel camera designs to the opposite extreme, an aid much nearer to hand is the motor drive and the winder of the OM system. Apart from their shooting speed and convenience, these units not only provide something more solid by which to grip the camera but also help to steady the support. This is specially valuable with medium to longer tele and zoom lenses where the further grip on the motor or winder with the right hand keeps the left more free for operating focusing and (where applicable) zooming rings. Usually you get the best support from the winder or the motor drive with the M.15V control pack. If the base of the latter or of the winder rests on the palm of the left hand, the fingers can reach up more comfortably to the lens controls. This may even be a help with standard and wide angle lenses—again by providing more for the left hand to support and for the right hand to grip. If you have either motor or winder unit, it is worth using it in this way even for normal single-exposure shooting. But with shorter-focus lenses taking the winder or motor adds proportionally more bulk to the camera outfit—especially if you had planned to take just the camera in its case with one lens.

Tripod mounting

For exposure times longer than about $\frac{1}{8}$ second with the standard lens—or considerably shorter with tele lenses—a hand-held camera is practically never steady enough for sharp pictures and you need a rigid support. The classic though not necessarily the most convenient way is to mount the camera on a tripod. The camera carries a tripod bush in the centre of the base to take the screw of the tripod; long tele lenses have a separate tripod bush in a tripod mounting ring which balances the camera/lens assembly better. A firm tripod is also the best camera support for remote-controlled operation with the motor drive or winder.

A tripod is incomplete without a ball-and-socket or pan-and-tilt head. You have to set up the tripod as firmly as possible, but on uneven ground that means placing the legs in a way incompatible with the direction in which you want to point the camera. The ball-and-socket or pan/tilt head allows independent adjustment of the camera direction.

The tripod must be sturdy. For a really steady stand you need a heavy-duty type, even with a small camera. Lightweight tripods are generally worse than useless for they tend to vibrate with every step you walk on the ground and with every breeze in the air. That applies especially to the thin-legged telescopic tripods with legs about as rigid as a fishing rod.

Outdoors, a string or net shopping bag is a useful accessory. If you have to set up the tripod in windy or otherwise precarious conditions, fill the bag with stones or earth and suspend it from the centre of the tripod. It can make a great deal of difference to steadiness. Ball-and-socket or pan/tilt heads should also be heavy duty ones that can be locked firmly enough not to budge when you touch the camera.

I am not fond of carrying a heavy tripod with a compact miniature camera and for many jobs requiring longer indoor exposures I prefer a table tripod or other aid. But you must have a sturdy tripod with the long tele lenses.

Cable releases

Once the camera is mounted on a tripod or other stand, pressing on the release button is likely to jar it again, so use a cable release screwed into the release button. When making the exposure keep the cable slack to avoid transmitting any vibration to the camera. Press the release plunger gently. Many cable releases incorporate a lock to clamp the plunger when depressed so that you can keep the shutter open for manually timed exposures. The lock may be a clamping screw in the side of the release housing or a small plate surrounding the plunger shaft: as you press the plunger, the plate automatically holds it depressed—and you release the plunger by depressing the plate. The Olympus SR-II cable release is of this kind, but there is a wide range of similar ones of different makes on the market.

If you have no cable release handy, use the self-timer as described below, but set it to its longest delay (12 seconds) to allow enough time for all vibration to die down.

If you have a camera mounted with the winder or motor drive, you can of course release electrically.

Self-timer exposures

The self-timer has somehow survived in cameras from an era when people liked not only to take group photographs but also to include themselves in their groups. A 35 mm camera is not the ideal instrument for formal large-group photography but the self-timer has remained because it is comparatively simple to fit in the camera and is a sales point even for photographers who are never likely to use it.

To include yourself in a group, or even as foreground human interest in outdoor setting, set up the camera on a tripod or other self-contained support. Frame the view and/or arrange the other members of the group. Prepare your own place in it and check that you can reach it without undue hurrying in not more than 8 to 10 seconds.

Tension the camera, set the self-timer and trigger the latter. Move to your place and wait for the camera shutter to be released.

The self-timer could also be used for self-portraiture, but there a remote-released motor drive is far better as you have the instant of releasing completely under control. That means less risk of freezing into a strained expression while waiting for the self-timer to run down.

Table tripods and other aids

One of the most useful accessories for supporting the camera for slow shutter speeds is a table tripod with ball-and-socket head. Select one that folds up yet is solid when open and get a heavy-duty ball-and-socket head with it. Such a unit conveniently fits into a hold-all or compartment case yet does many of the jobs of a full-size tripod at a fraction of the bulk.

It is particularly helpful for three purposes:

(a) Wherever you have a solid surface—flat or otherwise—the table tripod and head combination can support the camera as firmly as a full-scale tripod. Often it's just a matter of finding a surface at the right height. Nor need it be level—with the ball-and-socket head you can compensate for inclined, uneven and innumerable other surfaces—far better than trying to put down the camera directly on a wall, bench etc.

On a table, this set-up is ideal for close-up photography with the 50 mm macro lens and other low-power close-up gear.

(b) You can press the table tripod against a vertical wall, doorpost, a column in a church etc.—whenever in fact three legs spaced 10 to 20 cm apart can be jammed against something. If the table tripod is solid enough, that will support the OM camera with a medium or medium long tele lens for exposures running into seconds. I have used this successfully in dark churches, museums and historical buildings. Release with the self-timer.

(c) Finally, the table tripod provides a first rate chest support for the camera. Mount the camera on the table tripod via the ball-and-socket head, leaving the latter slack for the moment. Brace the tripod legs against your chest or chest and shoulder at a convenient height. Then adjust the camera so that you can conveniently look through the finder. In that position tighten the ball-and-socket head. As a further refinement, you can also tighten the camera strap, so that the camera virtually supports itself against you by the tripod and strap. Steadying it with the hands then needs little effort and the hands are free for focusing, releasing etc.

Two other support ideas are a unipod and a chestpod. The unipod is a single tripod leg—almost as helpful as a wall or railing on which you can lean your elbows. It gives vertical support but you still have to steady the camera laterally.

Chestpods are short unipods that steady the camera against your chest; they may fit into a cup fixed to a leather strap that you hang round your neck. I have found the table tripod as a chest or shoulder support steadier and more efficient.

Level surfaces

With most of its wide angle to medium tele lenses the OM camera can stand almost level and firm on a truly flat surface such as a table. Actually, with lenses of 59 to 61 mm maximum diameter the camera tips very slightly forward to rest on the baseplate and the lens focusing ring. If you place the camera with its baseplate on the flat surface and press down on the accessory shoe (or the camera top near the rear edge) the camera body sits flat with the lens focusing mount just clear of the supporting surface. After focusing you can then push a coin under the focusing ring to support the camera level.

With lenses of 62 to 65 mm maximum diameter the camera rests on a flat surface tipped very slightly backwards, supported at the front by the focusing mount. For levelling, place a pair of identical coins under each end of the baseplate. The coins should generally be thin low-denomination ones, e.g. 2p in Britain, a dime in the US etc. (This rarely has to be an ultra-precision job.)

When supporting the camera in this way, bring the lens forward as near to the edge of the surface as possible. With wide angle and even standard lenses you otherwise include a very unsharp area of supporting surface in the picture.

Carrying and cases

With the camera strap you can carry the OM camera round your neck or shoulder. When not actually taking pictures and when putting the camera away you may also want additional protection by a camera case. I prefer a soft case which buttons around the camera like a glove; you can also pull it off like a glove and stuff it in a pocket.

Ever-ready cases are popular because of the greater protection they provide against knocks and the possibility of dropping the camera. On the other hand they make the camera bulkier. The ever-ready case derives its name from the fact that the unbuttoned top and front hang down and you can shoot with the camera in the case. The hanging-down front is, however, greatly in the way when holding the camera in shooting position. You could unclip it altogether—but then you have nowhere to put it. It is too bulky (especially with the larger models) to go conveniently in a pocket.

If you have a larger outfit comprising the camera with more than a couple of lenses a holdall or compartment case is useful. These exist in innumerable sizes, shapes and types, including several models from Olympus. Their purpose is to take every item of the camera outfit that you carry and hold it easily accessible for instant use.

BATTERIES AND CASES

The exposure meter and—with automatic models—shutter circuit of the OM cameras is powered by batteries. So are various other items of equipment including motor drives, flash units etc. Batteries are thus an essential and consumable camera accessory. Selection of correct batteries and battery care are important to proper operation.

The battery specifications for Olympus equipment are listed in the *Facts and figures* chapter.

Exposure meter batteries

For reliable operation the metering systems need a power source of constant voltage, provided by silver oxide or mercury button cells.

Silver oxide button cells of 1.5 volts each (11.5 mm diameter, 5 mm high) are used in pairs in the OM-2 and OM-10 cameras to yield altogether 3 volts for the meter circuit and electronic shutter. (This same type is also used in the Recordata backs.)

A mercury cell of 1.3 volts is used in the OM-1. This is a standard button cell of 15.3 mm diameter and about 6 mm high.

There are also 1.3 volt mercury cells of the same size as the silver oxide cells (designations: National H-C, Mallory etc. PX 675, Varta 8001 etc.). Do not use these instead of silver oxide as they do not deliver a sufficient voltage. In an emergency only—if you cannot get hold of the correct silver oxide cells—you can temporarily use the mercury type (i.e. PX 675 etc.). You will of course not get anything like normal life of silver oxide batteries out of them and the battery test signal of the OM-2 will blink even with fresh mercury batteries. But they will at least last a few films before their voltage drops below the cut-off point and the camera mirror locks up. So mercury cells behave at all times like nearly exhausted silver oxide cells and give you no sensible warning of impending exhaustion.

Battery life and battery testing

Normally the meter battery or battery set lasts about one year. (Your first batteries won't, if you play about trying out the camera when you first get it.)

To check the batteries on the OM-2, turn the meter switch to AUTO and then push towards the CHECK position. A small light-emitting diode (LED) in the back of the camera, to the left of the finder eyepiece, should then light up. If it lights steadily, the batteries are still good for some time; if the LED blinks on and off, they are nearing exhaustion (or you have put wrong batteries into the camera such as PX 675 mercury batteries). The faster the LED blinks on and off, the nearer is the end of the useful battery life.

But the LED may blink even with reasonably good batteries if (a) you are checking immediately after shooting a number of exposures or (b) you are checking in very cold weather.

When the LED first begins to blink you have probably still enough power reserve for up to about half a dozen 36-exposure films. This is not fully reliable—it might be less if you make a lot of long exposures (the shutter draws current while open). It also might be less if you test after you had left the meter switch on for a long time. You *can* go on shooting if you have a spare set of batteries with you and don't mind stopping to change batteries when the mirror locks up. But it is safer not to have that worry and to change the batteries when the testing LED starts to flicker. If you are using the camera with the motor drive or winder it is much more inconvenient if the mirror locks up during a shooting sequence and you have to detach the motor drive to get at the battery compartment.

When the blinking gets very rapid, change the batteries immediately. If the LED fails to light up at all, the batteries are nearly exhausted and you may without warning (that's what the LED is for) find the mirror locking up during an exposure. When changing batteries after the mirror has locked up, remember to reset the mirror first—with the mirror raised you are also using current as soon as the battery is inserted.

The battery check circuit does consume some current, so avoid keeping the meter switch lever in the CHECK position for too long. One or two seconds is quite enough.

On the OM-10 the bleep and LED signal—with the meter switch at CHECK—indicates a good battery. Change the battery as soon as the signal becomes faint or fails.

The OM-1 has no battery test. To check the battery cell condition, set the shutter to a slow speed (1 second or ½ second), point the camera (without lens) at the sky and—while looking through the finder—turn the meter switch from OFF to ON. The meter needle should swing up from its bottom rest position to at least the centre zeroing mark or higher (depending on the film speed set). If the needle fails to move at all, the battery is either fully exhausted or you have no battery in the camera. Very sluggish movement indicates a nearly exhausted cell. To be on the safe side, it is good practice to change the mercury cell at least once a year.

A sensible test routine is to check the battery briefly every time you load a new film, and also if a camera has been out of use for more than a few days. By all means check it also if you find that you have put the OM-1 or OM-2 away with the meter switched on.

Another useful habit is to open the battery compartment every few weeks and have a look at the cells. Clean away any crystal formation around the sealing ring of the button cell and carefully brush out any solid matter from the camera's battery compartment. Silver oxide and mercury batteries don't leak corrosive liquid like familiar torch batteries, but traces of chemicals do ooze out in time, especially with considerable ambient temperature fluctuations. Removing these deposits protects the camera and also prevents premature battery exhaustion.

Better still, if the camera is likely to be out of use for weeks, take out the batteries. (Whatever battery makers may claim, no battery type appears to be absolutely leak-proof under all conditions.)

Since the battery test does not give much advance warning of battery failure, always carry a spare battery or set. The hard camera case has a compartment for the spare cell inside the top of the front cap. When storing a pair of batteries (silver oxide) keep them separate to avoid short circuits with rapid discharge. When replacing OM-2 cells, replace both together. Also avoid mixing cells of different makes.

Battery saving hints

In the OM-2 the batteries power both the shutter operation and the exposure metering. The former takes around 50 times as much current as the latter as the batteries have to energise a solenoid that holds the second shutter curtain until the end of the exposure. To make the most of battery life therefore avoid excessive shutter operation and shutter open times when not actually required for an exposure. Thus:

(a) Once you have thoroughly tried out the camera to get an idea of how it works, avoid making unnecessary blind exposures—especially with the camera switched to AUTO and the lens cap over the lens. (This can produce exposure times running into many seconds.)

(b) If you have to make blind exposures—for instance during film loading—do them with the meter switch set to MANUAL and at 1/30 to 1/1000 second.

(c) Avoid unnecessary and especially prolonged battery tests—this consumes almost as much current as the shutter.

(d) After a shooting session and before putting the camera away, check that the meter switch is at OFF. But as the CdS meter circuit takes very little current in the dark, forgetting to switch off the meter circuit wastes least current. (If the meter is left switched on and the camera put away in the dark—e.g. lens cap on lens in a camera case—it would take 2 to 3 months to exhaust a fresh set of batteries by the switched-on meter circuit alone.) So it's good practice to switch off the meter every time you stop using the camera, especially if you are likely to put it away for days or weeks. But keeping the meter on a few minutes (or even hours) longer makes very little difference.

Much the same applies to the OM-1. But here the mercury cell powers only the meter circuit; the purely mechanical shutter operation draws no current. By all means switch off the meter switch whenever you are not using the camera, but current drain with the camera in total darkness is again negligible.

Batteries for other equipment

The Recordata 1 back uses the same silver oxide cells as the OM-2 meter but needs three cells; the No. 2 back uses two. Mercury cells of the same size will not do. The same remarks apply concerning care and designations.

Most of the other units are powered by size AA cells of 1.5 volts each. Preferably use alkali (also known as alkaline-manganese) batteries which have the greatest current capacity—about 1.8 ampere-hours—for their size. Ordinary zinc-carbon or Leclanché cells (sometimes referred to as 'manganese'—not to be confused with the alkali type) of the same size can also be used. They are not recommended as their voltage drops fairly rapidly in use and the expected service life is unpredictable. In particular with the motor drive such batteries cannot provide the high current drain needed unless they are very fresh. If you have to use ordinary dry cells of this type in an emergency (for instance in a flash unit) be sure to get leak-proof cells and remove them from the equipment when the latter is not in use.

The bounce flash grip takes size C cells. Again, leak-proof carbon-zinc or Leclanché type cells of the same size can be used in an emergency, but the current capacity is about one-third of the alkaline type. The latter is typically around 5 ampere-hours.

Rechargeable nickel-cadmium cells in the AA size can be used in the motor drives but not in the Quick Auto flash units (where they can damage the circuit). NC cells have a lower capacity—around 0.5 ampere-hour—and cost four to six times as much as alkali cells. Their advantage is that they are rechargeable and a set of cells can generally be recharged several hundred times. But you have to have a charger and a mains supply, so they are more useful at home or in the studio. On location take a set of spare cells or replaceable alkali batteries if you don't want to be stuck in the middle of a picture series. The voltage of NC cells is slightly lower (about 1.25 volts against 1.5 of fresh alkali cells) but stays constant through most of the discharge time. So NC cells give you little or no warning of failure. NC cell manufacturers market various chargers that recharge the cells from an AC mains supply in 4 to 14 hours, depending on the charger type.

Battery care

Different equipment items give their own indication of battery condition: motor drives become sluggish with decreasing battery power and stop altogether when the current drops below a minimum level. A droning sound indicates this state. With flash units the recycling times become increasingly long. When the maximum recycling time (on manual operation with automatic flash units) exceeds about 30 seconds, change the batteries.

When renewing batteries, always change the whole set even if one or two cells still appear to be workable. Otherwise the new set will not last as long—and this loss in effective life is greater than what you appear to save by trying to carry on with one or two apparently serviceable cells of an otherwise exhausted set. Also as some part-used cells become exhausted, the others may force a charging current through them which can cause electrolyte leakage.

A voltmeter (if it is reasonably accurate) can indicate the exhaustion state of an alkaline cell: if the voltage per cell drops below about 1 volt, replace the cells. Such a test is useless with both NC and zinc-carbon cells. NC cells drop from 1.25 volts to 1.1 volt during discharge, but go below 1.1 quite abruptly and only at the very end will you know that the cell is exhausted. Ordinary zinc-carbon dry cells on the other hand can read 1.5 volts in the open voltmeter circuit (because of a limited recovery effect) when the actual current they yield is no longer sufficient to power anything.

Alkali cells are claimed to be leak-proof. Despite manufacturers' guarantees (sometimes covering repair of equipment damaged by leaking cells) such cells do occasionally leak, either when exposed to appreciable temperature changes or—more likely—due to manufacturing faults. That can sometimes also happen with so-called leak-proof ordinary (zinc-carbon) cells. To avoid damage do not leave such cells in equipment that you put away for any length of time. Even when a unit is in fairly constant use, regularly check batteries and remove any crystal deposits showing up around terminals.

Generally I have found that leakage due to faulty alkali cells shows up early on. I try to keep a six months' stock of alkali batteries—partly not to be caught without—and if a cell is going to leak, it shows signs of it during these six months. (Even after a year's storage alkali batteries lose less than 10% of their capacity.)

NC cells are less likely to leak, but even here an occasional check is safe. Ordinary torch batteries (non-leakproof types) invariably leak when they get near exhaustion—a good reason for avoiding them in photo equipment.

Most batteries give less current in very cold weather. If you have to operate motor drive equipment outdoors in the winter, keep battery cases and battery units in a warm pocket and attach to the drive unit only when actually needed.

Camera straps

The OM cameras are supplied with a carrying strap. The standard strap is a comparatively narrow plastic one approx. 130 cm or 51 inches long. It threads through the split rings attached to the carrying strap eyelet on the camera. Thread the strap through the shoulder pad first before attaching it to the camera. Fix the strap by joining the end—after threading through the split ring—to the rest of the strap with the double headed rivet fixed through the slotted holes in the strap. There are several such slotted holes at different points to permit some adjustment in length. If no split rings are fitted on the camera fit these first—even a key ring of 15–17 mm diameter ($\frac{5}{8}$ inch) will serve. The length adjustment primarily allows you to carry the camera either hanging down the middle of your chest or—with the strap longer—around your shoulder.

Place two of the strap loops near the split ring when threading the strap through the latter; the loops there go round both runs of the strap. The third loop holds the two parts of the strap together along the doubled-up stretch when you have shortened the strap.

All the Olympus camera cases are designed so that the strap always remains attached to the camera itself.

The leather strap, available as an alternative, is similar and also comes with a shoulder pad.

The flat braid strap is similar to the standard camera strap in length but lighter yet tougher. It is thus more difficult to cut through—should someone take a liking to your camera and try to snatch it while you are carrying it. (For that reason avoid having the camera hanging loosely around the back of your shoulder.) The flat braid strap is again threaded through the split ring fixed to the carrying strap eyelets. A sliding buckle here secures the strap and three loops keep the attachment tight. With the sliding buckles the length adjustment is infinitely variable and not dependent on the location of punched slots.

The round braid strap is about 102 cm (40 inches) long and not adjustable. It is thus exclusively a neck strap. The ends of the attachment hook are plastic covered and the whole fitting sheathed in rubber to avoid scraping against the camera body. The round braid strap is also fixed to the split rings in the strap eyelets.

Camera straps are also produced by numerous accessory manufacturers. Of interest are extra-wide straps—often in fancy patterns—that are very comfortable because of their width around your neck. But even with the normal strap the shoulder pad, located at the back of the neck, improves comfort.

Camera cases

There is a range of camera cases for the OM models covering different types as well as sizes. In every case there are two sizes: 1.4/1.8 and 1.2. The former takes the OM body with standard *f*1.4 or slower lenses or with most wide-angle lenses other than some ultra-speed types. This includes lenses of overall (not focal) length up to about 40 mm.

The 1.2 cases take the camera with the 55 mm *f*1.2 lens or with any other lens up to about 48 mm long. This covers also the 85 and 100 mm lenses and the ultra-speed wide angle units.

In both cases the lenses are often accommodated together with the clip-on lens hood (where applicable) clipped inverted over the lens or with the screw-in or rubber lens hood just placed over the lens back to front. (This does not apply to the wide hoods of certain ultra-wide-angle lenses.)

The following types of camera case are available—in each instance in the two sizes:

Soft cases are light-weight velvet lined plastic cases that protect the camera against scratches when being carried round the neck or loosely in a soft hold-all case. To fit a soft case, pull it over the camera lens like a glove and button with the press studs around the back of the camera. The soft cases are quick to fit or remove and stuff easily into any pocket. They take the OM body with the appropriate lens and, if required, with the Recordata backs.

Semi-hard cases are ever-ready cases. The top and front section is hinged and drops down to allow photography with the camera still in the case. The front and top is detachable by a press stud—it is otherwise rather in the way when holding the camera.

To fit the camera, insert it in the stiff cradle-like section and secure by screwing in the tripod screw on the case. (The camera with case can in turn be mounted on a tripod.) Close the front over the lens and top and secure with the two press studs. Two gaps near the ends clear the carrying strap eyelet and strap of the camera.

Hard cases are similar to the semi-hard cases but slightly stiffer and more luxurious. The hard cases have no tripod screw; instead the camera is held in place by small flaps at the sides which button down onto press studs around the carrying strap eyelets.

The hard cases have a small pocket in the lid to take a spare exposure meter battery. If you need two spare cells, e.g. for the OM-2, wrap one in a little polyethylene or similar plastic before putting the two cells into the pocket. That avoids contact between the cells with risk of short-circuiting.

Neither hard case takes the camera with Recordata back. And in both cases the memo holder back is obscured—you have to take the camera out to check the film type loaded. But you can tuck in a film box end, a piece of card etc. indicating the film type, underneath the side of the case cradling the camera, for instance next to the self-timer.

The camera cases—hard, semi-hard or soft—also take the appropriate lens hoods for the standard and the 85 mm and 100 mm lenses. Invert the clip-on hoods over the front lens mount and put on the lens cap. In the case of the 85 and 100 mm lenses put on the lens cap first and loosely push the inverted hood over that.

But do not keep the hood inverted on the lens when packing the camera in one of the compartment cases. There it is quicker to seize the camera and appropriate hood when you want it than fiddle with removing the hood from the lens before shooting.

Lens cases

Most lenses come complete with a protective but somewhat bulky leather case that often also holds the lens hood. The cases can serve for carrying a lens on its own; lenses in holdall or compartment cases may be housed in soft lens pouches for protection without the weight of the regular lens case.

Holdall and compartment cases

Once a camera begins to be a camera outfit, the most sensible way of carrying everything with you is in a holdall or compartment case where the different items are easily accessible for immediate use.

Accessibility means being able to get hold of any one item without greatly disturbing the rest. This is easiest in cases sub-divided into compartments or pockets. For adaptability—making one compartment case serve for alternative outfits on different occasions—the compartments should also be capable of re-arrangement.

Adjustable compartments are important to allow you to tailor a case precisely to your own outfit. As outfits vary, holdall cases exist in numerous different sizes and styles. Olympus produces several cases of widely different style and capacity, to meet different requirements of outfit size and versatility.

Olympus compartment cases

The smallest case of the Olympus range is the Compartment case S—a rigid case with hinged lid and outside dimensions (excluding strap loops or lock) 248 × 170 × 100 mm (9.8 × 6.7 × 3.8 inches). It has a lock (and key) and an adjustable plastic strap with shoulder pad allows the case to be carried over one shoulder. Two adjustable partitions divide up a total interior space of some 235 ×

150 × 90 mm (9.2 × 6 × 3.5 inches) into three compartments. One of the partitions carries a stiff foam pad to support the lens of the camera when inserted in the case. The camera goes in upright complete with strap. Although the case is comparatively small, it can cope with a number of quite different outfits with extra lenses or Winder 1 or Quick Auto 310 flash unit etc.

The medium-size Compartment case M has overall dimensions of approximately 160 × 210 × 280 mm (6.3 × 8.3 × 11 inches) with shoulder strap and pad, zip-fastened main compartment, zip-fastened side pockets, a padded insert for three lenses, an internal camera cradle and straps for external attachment of a tripod.

The insert is a padded soft plastic unit of three compartments that can hold lenses (anything up to 200 mm in focal length), the Quick Auto 310 (or 300) flash unit, motor drive or winder etc. Even longer lenses—up to the 300 mm *f*4.5 or the 85–250 mm zoom— can be tied inside the case by the Velcro-lined straps.

The plastic insert clips into the case by press button grips.

The Compartment case L is more of a take-all case—a piece of luggage to carry the largest amount of OM equipment in the smallest space. Discounting straps, buckles and locks, the outside dimensions are approximately 210 × 230 × 380 mm (8.3 × 9.1 × 15 inches) with closing latches, a lockable closing strap, a pair of hand grips that can be clipped together to form a single grip and a detachable shoulder strap. The effective storage space is provided by a rigid box insert 275 × 185 mm large and 195 mm high (10.8 × 7.3 × 7.7 inches) which is sub-dividable by a number of adjustable partitions. These are velvet-lined pieces of card that jam crosswise into the insert; flaps held by rubber bands sub-divide the compartments so formed. There is also a camera holder in velvet-covered plyboard to hold two OM cameras. The square or rectangular compartments formed by the partitions accommodate lenses (up to 300 mm focal length), flash units, bounce flash grip, motor drive—in fact anything that can stand upright and is not more than about 195 mm tall. The L case can even hold two different camera outfits, for instance an OM with a few lenses and motor drive plus a large format camera and one or two lenses for that.

An accessory item for the compartment case L is the partitioned motor drive insert. This allows the case to accommodate a camera with motor drive and 250-exposure film back, spare 250-exposure magazines, hand grip, up to two further cameras with motor drive or winder, various lenses etc.

THE IMAGE IN THE FINDER

One of the most prominent features of a single-lens reflex camera is its through-the-lens viewfinder system. Through the eyepiece at the back we see the image on a screen which provides much important information about optical and other characteristics of the picture being recorded on the film. We shall be spending a lot of our picture taking time looking at this image on the screen. So let's consider its optical characteristics more closely.

Image scale and brightness

The Olympus OM finder is among the brightest SLR viewing systems, due in part to the use of silvered (rather than anodised) prism reflecting surfaces and hence less light loss in the finder. The absolute image brightness also depends on the maximum lens aperture: if you look through two OM cameras side by side fitted with standard *f*1.4 and *f*3.5 lenses, the finder of the former will of course appear brighter.

The OM focusing screens also incorporate a Fresnel pattern which acts somewhat like a condenser lens to redirect light from the outer screen areas to the eyepiece and so make the screen appear more or less evenly bright all over. The ring pattern is sufficiently fine (some 20 rings per mm) to be invisible under all normal viewing and focusing conditions. It doesn't eliminate the darkening of the screen corners when you view with the more extreme ultrawide-angle lenses, but that is due to natural lens vignetting which you cannot help in any case.

With the standard 50 mm lenses the image on the screen appears at about 0.9 × natural size. 'Natural size' in this context means that when you look through the finder with one eye and directly at the scene with the other, the subject appears at a similar scale to both eyes.

The scale changes the moment you switch lenses. With wide-angle lenses the finder magnification necessarily drops—to about 0.5 × with the 28 mm lens and to barely $\frac{1}{3}$ natural size with the 18 mm ultrawide-angle. Conversely, with tele lenses the image magnification in the finder increases: up to $2\frac{1}{2}$ times with the 135 mm, or to some 18 times with the 1000 mm lens. That is as if you were seeing the subject through a telescope—which effectively you are.

The screen format

The actual size of the finder screen frame is about 23.2 × 35 mm—roughly 97% each way of the full 24 × 36 mm frame normally recorded on the film. Area-wise the screen covers 94% of what the film takes in.

This is not just a safety margin against losing anything on the film that was visible in the finder. For the frames used for mounting colour transparencies are also slightly smaller than the full picture area and on the average even a shade smaller—23 × 34.5 mm—than the Olympus OM finder area.

The screen format is occasionally subject to a limitation by vignetting, due in turn to inevitable compromises in the mirror size. With a lens of comparatively short focal length the reflex mirror can be reasonably short to deflect the lens's light path for an image over the whole screen. With a lens of long focal length (and in certain special circumstances) you need a longer mirror to project the image over the whole screen. With a shorter mirror part of the upper screen area may receive no light, and so no image. It makes sense in a compact camera to limit the mirror size to a reasonable compromise that with the long tele lenses yields a slight image loss. It shows itself as a darker strip with the 600 and 1000 mm lenses, but barely noticeable with the 400 mm. It is hardly disturbing in practice and above all the dark strip does *not* appear on the film.

Eyepiece focus

When you look through the eyepiece, the finder image does not appear at visual infinity, but at an optical viewing distance of 2 metres or $6\frac{1}{2}$ feet. This refers to the eye adaptation, not to the subject distance, and is the result of giving the viewing system an inherent −0.5 dioptre correction. The meter needle and other measuring indications in the finder appear at a similar distance. You therefore see the image and the meter needle etc. perfectly with normal or corrected eyesight. You see it even better if you are very slightly short-sighted. But for anything more than the slightest eyesight defects you must either wear spectacles or fit an eyesight correction lens over the eyepiece.

The idea of these lenses is to give you a sharp view of the finder screen and its focusing aids (otherwise you cannot focus on it) without having to wear spectacles. For with the latter you may just marginally fail to take in the whole screen area without having to move your eye slightly to and fro behind the eyepiece. With the dioptric correction lenses you can put the eye close enough to the eyepiece (without hindrance by the spectacles) to cover the entire screen. Also, that way you reduce the amount of stray light likely to enter the eyepiece—and hence erroneous manual or monitoring exposure readings.

But correction lenses are not that convenient: if you have fitted one and wear glasses, you have to take the glasses off to look through the finder and put them on again to look at the subject directly. And if you are long-sighted, you have to put the glasses on to look at the camera controls. I have found it more convenient to look through the camera finder while wearing glasses and without correction lenses, putting up with the very slight viewing difficulty.

The optical design problem involved in all this is in principle quite easy to solve—but at the cost of a bigger finder and hence bulkier camera.

The interchangeable screen system

One criterion of single-lens reflex system versatility is the provision of interchangeable finder units. Some advanced cameras offer alternative eye-level, waist-level and special finder attachments for different ways of viewing the focusing screen. This is associated with interchangeable screens themselves for alternative lenses and applications. One problem with this adaptability is that it again produces a bulky camera.

The OM-1 and 2 offer a compromise: the pentaprism part of the finder is fixed, but the screens are interchangeable through the camera's lens-mounting ring once you have taken off the lens. For occasions where a finder view from the top is preferable—low-level or round the corner shooting, macrophotography etc. with the camera on a stand—you can use the Varimagni finder with its additional high-precision focusing features.

The screens themselves provide a considerable range, consisting broadly of matt screens with a central focusing aid (microprism or wedge rangefinder), matt screens without central focusing spot, clear screens with central focusing aid and clear-centre screens. The latter are intended for aerial-image focusing in macrophotography and photomicrography.

So what screen to choose from this range?

The common sense rule is to stick to a screen that covers most of your needs most of the time. This usually means the 1–1 or 1–13 screen. Changing screens is not difficult but is a comparatively meticulous operation not amenable to the same grab-and-switch handling as lens changing. Certainly, Olympus's wide range of over a dozen interchangeable screens includes a number that in certain fields are better than more universal screens which however remain usable. That for instance is the case with low-profile microprism screens for longer-focus lenses: switch to one of these screens if you are going to use long tele lenses for an extended session or assignment—but don't bother to change from the still acceptable standard screen for just an occasional tele shot. In the tabular listing (see Chpt. *Facts and figures*) of preferred and usable screens for different lenses, this means that if a screen is rated 'A' most of the time you are using it, it's less trouble to put up with its occasional drop to a 'B' rating than to keep changing screens all the time.

In some fields of course you must have the right screen: in high power macrophotography and photomicrography only the 1–12 or 1–11 screens are usable. But when you set up the camera for this kind of photography you also have conditions for screen changing at leisure.

For the rest your choice will depend on whether you prefer a clear or a matted screen and whether you are happier with microprism or rangefinder wedge focusing.

The matted screens—the majority in the range—give an overall ground glass effect that shows the picture sharp or unsharp as you focus the lens. The centre carries an aid to enhanced sharpness assessment. If you find this centre focusing spot disturbing, you can have screens that are evenly all matt for more uniform image appraisal, especially if you compose your picture on the screen. There are also extra-fine grained matt screens for macro and extreme tele work where the normal screen graininess becomes too prominent.

The main advantages of matt screens are:

(a) The screen image brightness is also consistently related to the image brightness on the film—so you can use light measurement on the screen for exposure metering;

(b) The image on the matt surface is equally focusable with large- and small-aperture lenses.

Against that, clear screens yield a much brighter overall image—useful if you do a lot of your photography in poor light, for instance indoor feature photography, theatre and nightclub work etc. This field of what used to be called available-light photography is now much easier with modern ultra-fast films, but such films don't make the finder image in the camera any brighter. Clear screens not only permit no focusing outside the central spot, but no reliable exposure metering by screen image brightness measurement, either. (But with the focal plane metering of the OM-2 camera automatic exposures are still correct—only the pre-shot monitoring is not.)

Rangefinder wedge or microprism

The function of the original ground glass screen from the earliest cameras to the present day was to create a strictly defined plane for the location of the image formed by the lens. When you look at the matt surface, the image only appears sharp if it is exactly in the plane of that surface, and unsharp if it is formed in front of or behind that plane.

However, at its best the eye is not the most efficient judge of absolute sharpness. Unsharpness has to exceed a certain degree before it becomes disturbing or even noticeable. The eye is much better at detecting image discontinuities such as double, broken or displaced outlines. That's why early reflex cameras with a plain matt screen image could not compete with the focusing rapidity of rangefinder models. Modern reflexes use the rangefinder effect of image discontinuity as a more sensitive way of detecting whether the focused image is in exactly the screen plane or not. There are two ways for that.

The original—and simpler—device consists of a pair of opposed wedges in the screen. They are arranged in such a way that their inclined surfaces cross in exactly the focusing plane of the screen. In the area of this wedge, any outline running across the dividing line between the wedges is continuous if the image is in the correct plane (i.e. sharply focused) but becomes discontinuous if it is not. An out-of-focus image thus does not necessarily look unsharp, but appears split with the two halves displaced relative to each other. This discontinuity and its change to a continuous outline are clearly observable even in comparatively poor light when the difference between a sharp and fuzzy ground glass image becomes quite uncertain.

A further development of the wedge or prism idea is a minute pattern of microprisms, which act as pairs of rangefinder wedges. They look like microscopic four-sided pyramids and a typical microprism spot may have about 800 such micropyramids. An out-of-focus image in this microprism spot appears not so much unsharp as broken up with regularly ragged outlines like a kind of mosaic. When the image is focused in the correct screen plane the mosaic pattern disappears abruptly as all the microscopic part images become continuous.

Which type of focusing aid you prefer is to some extent a matter of taste. Olympus has screens with either kind and normally supplies the cameras with a screen having both a central rangefinder wedge and surrounding microprism ring. In general the split-image wedge shows the discontinuity clearest with prominent vertical or nearly vertical outlines. The microprism is particularly successful for focusing on textured surfaces whose pattern interacts optically with the microprism pattern to produce a shimmering moire effect when the image is not absolutely sharp. But on balance the microprism is equally reliable with outlines in any direction while the split image wedge is less efficient with low-contrast and textured subjects without prominent vertical contours.

Aperture limits

One drawback shared by both the wedge and the microprism spot in this arrangement is their dependence on a large lens aperture. For when the aperture is too small, part of the wedge or microprism pattern goes dark. You can get one of the wedge areas (or correspondingly oriented microprism faces) to appear bright by shifting the eye sideways behind the finder eyepiece, but it becomes difficult to see both bright together. That means that the microprism pattern never disappears during focusing and the main advantage of the microprism spot is lost.

It is possible to reduce the problem, i.e. make the microprism suitable for use with slower lenses, by making the microprism or pyramid structure flatter. But then the sharp/unsharp transition becomes less distinct, especially with lenses of shorter focal length. With the OM cameras you normally focus at the maximum lens aperture even when you have preselected a smaller working aperture; but with some longer tele lenses the maximum aperture is low enough to make use of the normal microprism spot difficult.

The OM system therefore offers several alternative screens that differ only in the steepness of the microprism profile: high profile for high-speed standard and wide-angle lenses, lower profile for smaller-aperture tele systems. With the extreme tele lenses it is more efficient to get back to focusing on the matt screen—or even better on a fine grain matt screen.

The darkening effect also shows itself in macrophotography: the increased lens/image distance there increases the effective *f*-number and so reduces the real maximum aperture in the same proportion.

Focusing techniques

To focus the image on a microprism screen, point the camera to bring the main subject detail you are concerned with into the central microprism spot. Rotate the focusing ring on the lens until that subject portion is fully sharp.

The most sensitive indication of the change between sharp and unsharp is a kind of shimmer in image portions with fine detail (texture etc.). This becomes specially apparent on slight movement of the camera. Even the slight inherent unsteadiness of your camera hold is sufficient to make this shimmer visible. At the point where it disappears into a clear image you have the point of maximum sharpness. The shimmer effect is so distinct that you may for instance focus sharply a person's eyes in a portrait, yet see this shimmering incipient unsharpness in the frame of spectacles a cm or two nearer.

With the split-image wedge of rangefinder screens, select a prominent subject outline running across the horizontal split of the rangefinder wedge. Then adjust the focusing ring to get the outline continuous across the split. The displacement and subsequent alignment of the outline is clear enough even if it runs at an angle more than around 45°. For flatter angles, switch the camera hold from horizontal to upright (or vice versa) just for focusing to re-align the outline more distinctly across the split. Choose a single outline that is as sharp and as contrasty as possible; split-image focusing is more difficult on low-contrast or otherwise less distinct contours. Also it is difficult if you have too many confusing outlines, for instance the fine tracery of a tree in winter when you have to pick a sufficiently distinct branch from the confusing mass of thick and thin ones.

When focusing on a matted screen area you may have to turn the focusing ring to and fro a few times, going just past the sharpest appearance of the image to find a point of maximum sharpness. With this so-called bracketing technique you progressively reduce the amount by which you go past the sharpest point.

If you are focusing on the matt portion of a microprism or split-image wedge screen (because the central area is not usable with a particular lens) select still a portion as near the centre as possible. Focusing is less reliable in the outer screen areas, partly because of the less convenient viewing and partly because the viewfinder optics yields best visual sharpness in the centre of the field.

Particularly important when focusing on a matt screen portion (or on an all-matt screen) is accurate visual focus of the eyepiece. If your vision is defective therefore be sure to wear correct spectacles or fit an appropriate eyepiece correction lens (see above, *Eyepiece focus*).

Look straight into the eyepiece with the eye centred behind it, rather than obliquely. With lenses that are near the aperture limit for the screen employed, oblique viewing makes focusing almost impossible. For the microprism spot then takes on a uniform halftone pattern that does not disappear during focusing until the eye is correctly centered behind the eyepiece. This does not happen with all lenses—for instance with the 1–1 and 1–13 screens the microprism pattern remains clear (and disappears on sharp focusing) with the *f*1.8 or *f*1.4 standard lenses, however you look into the finder. With the *f*3.5 macro lens, oblique viewing does bring out the obscuring halftone screen pattern—as it does with *f*3.5 and *f*4 tele lenses. With some of these the sighting direction through the eyepiece is so critical that only part of the microprism spot ever clears sufficiently for focusing. In constant use that is a nuisance—and a good reason for changing to a screen with lower-profile microprism.

Scale focusing

The distance scale on the lens focusing ring indicates the distance, from the camera's film plane, of the subject detail you have sharply focused on the screen. Normally we are only interested in getting the image sharp on the screen, and not in the distance itself—so most of the time the distance scale is comparatively irrelevant. The scale is in fact useful for three purposes: assessing depth of field, focusing in very poor light and infrared focusing (see below).

In poor light, at night etc. the image on the screen becomes so dark that you cannot reliably assess whether it is sharply focused. (The split-image wedge remains the best focusing aid under these circumstances.) Your best bet is then to estimate the distance of the main subject and set the lens to that distance by the white metres or orange feet scale.

Infrared focusing

The colour correction of photographic lenses—essential to ensure sharp images of multi-coloured objects in the same film plane—covers the visible spectrum but does not normally extend into the infrared range. There the effective focal length of the lens very slightly increases, so that for optimum sharpness you have to set the lens to a slightly greater lens/image plane distance.

Infrared photographs are nearly always taken through an infrared but visually almost opaque filter. This makes focusing by screen observation impossible. The usual procedure in infrared photography is to focus the camera by normal light, fit the infrared filter over the lens and adjust the distance setting of the lens by a predetermined amount. Nearly all Olympus lenses carry an infrared focusing index for this purpose. This is a red mark, always to the right of the normal focusing index. It may either be one of the depth of field indicating lines (engraved in red instead of the usually black or white of the other depth indexes) or it may be a red dot between two of the index lines.

To make the adjustment after screen focusing, note the setting on the distance scale opposite the normal focusing index. Then turn the focusing mount to bring that same distance figure (or an appropriate imagined point between two distance figures) opposite the infrared index. For example on the 100 mm *f*2.8 lens, the infrared focusing mark is the right-hand *f*11 depth of field index line. So if on normal focusing the white figure 5 (5 metres) on the distance scale is opposite the central red focusing index, adjust for infrared by moving this white 5 opposite the right-hand *f*11 depth index line. The lens would then be effectively focused (for white light) on about 4.5 metres. Remember to refocus when returning to photography on normal film.

FOCUSING SCREENS AND FINDER ACCESSORIES

The interchangeable focusing screens of the OM-1 and 2 are held in a hinged screen frame underneath the pentaprism and changed through the opening of the lens mount. The screens themselves are each supplied in a plastic box complete with a pair of special tweezers and a cleaning brush. Always use the tweezers for changing the screen. While the operation can in an emergency be done by hand, this risks finger marks or even scratches on the screen and/or the camera mirror—which are virtually unremovable. Never touch the surface of either side of the screen with the fingers and clean only by dusting with the brush supplied.

Changing the screen

To change the screen, remove the lens from the camera and place the latter on its back on a table in front of you. Have the alternative screen in its box ready alongside. Remove the tweezers by pressing down on the front end in the screen case and lift up the tweezers by the handles.

With the inverted tip of the tweezers press up the small spring catch at the front of the screen frame, just inside of the camera's lens mount. This releases the screen frame which drops down together with the screen. With the special tweezers grip the tab protruding at the front of the screen and lift the latter carefully out of the camera. The tab also carries the number of the screen which is the second number of the screen designation—e.g. 4 for the screen 1–4. Place this screen standing up on its side in the groove to the right of the screen compartment in the screen case; this is a convenient parking place while handling the alternative screen.

Pick up the screen to be installed from its compartment in the screen case, again with the tweezers, by pressing the screen lightly against the spring at the back of its compartment and lifting out of the case. Holding the

SCREEN CHANGING

Each alternative screen comes in its own plastic box complete with handling tweezers and cleaning brush.

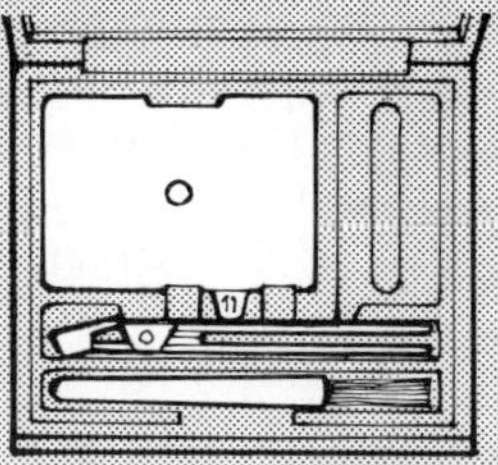

To remove the tweezers *(left)* press down the tip, then grip by the handle. Release the screen frame in the camera by pressing the tweezers against the catch at the top *(right)*.

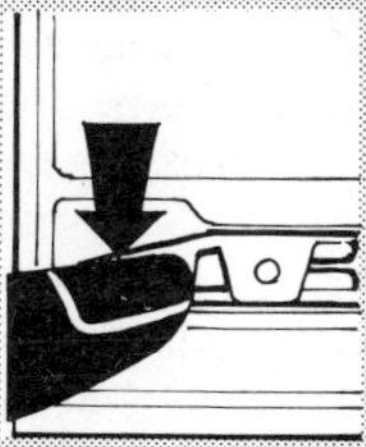

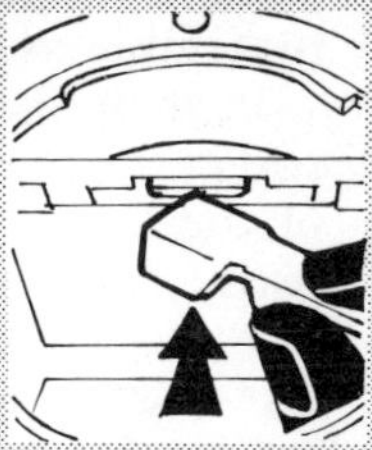

Grip the tab of the screen with the tweezers *(left)*, remove and place temporarily in the parking groove of the screen box *(right)*.

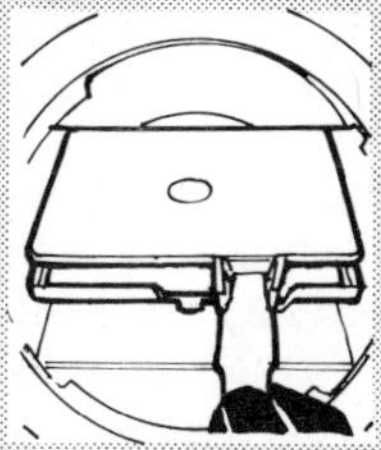

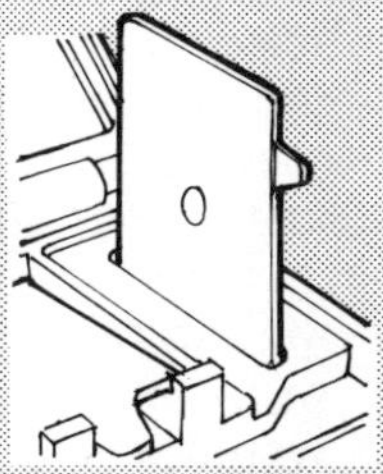

Grip the alternative screen in the box by the tab with the tweezers.

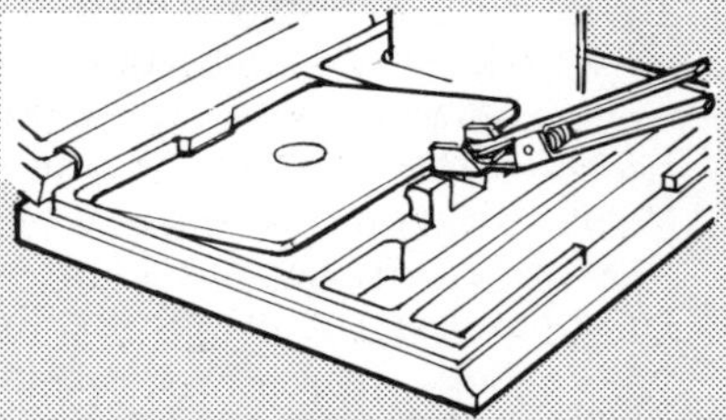

Locate it with the tab at the right in the camera's screen frame, *(left)*. Push up the screen frame in the camera with the tweezer handle *(right)* pressing against the tongue of the frame.

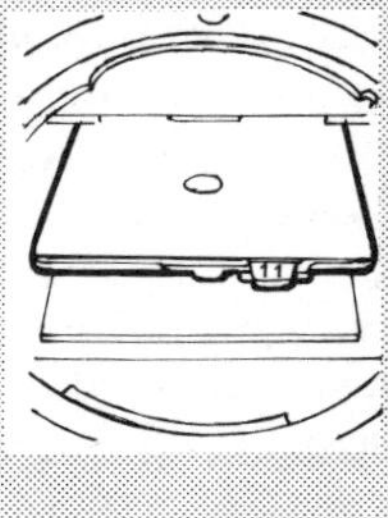

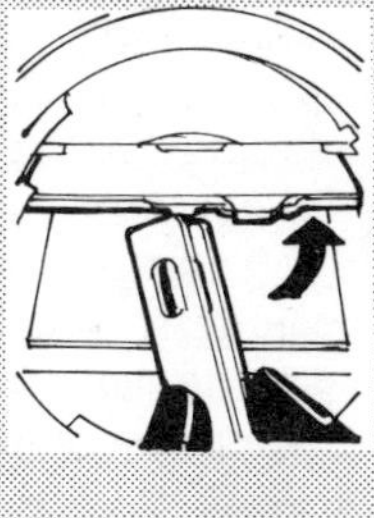

screen by the tweezers, carefully dust the front and back with the cleaning brush. (Don't do this over the camera lens opening to avoid any dust dropping into the camera interior.) Carefully introduce the screen into the lens mount opening and drop it into the screen frame. The tab of the screen must lie centrally on the wide metal tongue just to the right of the screen frame catch.

If the screen is not correctly placed in the screen frame, it will usually drop into the right position if you gently shake the camera while still keeping it lying flat. This is preferable to shifting the screen about by hand.

Push up the screen frame in the camera with the handle end of the tweezers, pressing from underneath the tongue of the frame until it clicks into place below the pentaprism. Take care not to touch the mirror surface. Look at the underside of the screen frame to check that the screen lies flat against it all round. (If not, release the catch again to drop the screen frame and rearrange the screen.) If necessary carefully brush off any dust from the camera mirror—but do not touch it with anything other than the brush. Better still, blow out dust from inside the camera with a rubber ball air blower.

As the screen frame closes, the tongue of the frame and the tab of the screen move into a cut-out in the mount just below the pentaprism. The tab ensures that the screen can only be inserted the right way round—the frame will not close if you have put the screen in reversed. Then replace the lens on the camera.

Finally, again with the tweezers, pick up the first screen from its parking groove in the screen case and place it in the normal compartment, pressing it slightly back against the spring. For easy access the screen tab should be at the right between the two protruding black rectangular studs of the case. That way the number of the screen is also easily readable through the clear plastic top of the closed case. Replace the tweezers in the compartment just below the screen in the case, preferably with the tips facing to the left and handle to the right, so that the tweezers are easier to remove. The cleaning brush fits in the compartment just in front of the tweezers, handle to the left. The closed case protects the screen against dust and is easy to take with you if you anticipate having to change screens away from home.

The 1–9 screen with its large protruding lens surface must be placed in the case upside down, i.e. tab to the left, so that the convex surface faces up. The screen goes into the camera of course with the tab to the right in the usual way.

You can also release the screen catch and push up the frame again with the handle end of the cleaning brush. This involves less danger of scratching the screen or mirror, but more risk of soiling the bristles.

Keep the cleaning brush clean, too, and avoid touching the bristles with your fingers. Otherwise the brush can also put grease marks on the screen or mirror. Always keep the brush in the screen case when not actually used for cleaning the screen.

Screen types

Currently there are over a dozen screens with various combinations of centre focusing aid and outer screen texture to provide optimum image observation and focusing accuracy with different lenses and for different applications. The screens are all moulded in plastic and (except for the special endoscopic screen 1–9) all carry a Fresnel lens pattern embossed into the underside to make the image brightness seen through the finder as even as possible. The Fresnel lens pattern is sufficiently fine (about 20 rings/mm) to be virtually invisible; it may be faintly noticeable with the clear (non-matt) screens.

The 1–1 screen is a normal matt screen with a central 4 mm microprism focusing spot. It is a universal screen for wide-angle, standard and medium long focus lenses up to about 135 mm and maximum aperture *f*4. The microprism profile ensures a crisp change from sharp to unsharp especially with the wide-angle and standard lenses; with tele lenses and maximum apertures smaller than about *f*4.5 the microprism area goes dark and cannot be used for focusing. Meter readings on the screen image indicate correct exposure settings.

The 1–2 screen is similar to the 1–1 but has a lower microprism profile which does not go dark until about *f*5.6 to *f*8. This screen is thus better for tele lenses and is usable even with the 400 and 600 mm units. It is also the ideal screen for the 85–250 mm zoom lens. Meter readings on the screen image indicate correct exposures.

The 1–3 screen is a normal matt screen like the 1–1, but instead of the microprism has a 4 mm diameter split-image wedge rangefinder. It is suitable for the same lenses and applications as the 1–1 screen, and remains usable up to the 300 mm tele lens. The split prism goes dark with lenses of aperture smaller than *f*5.6. Meter readings on the screen image indicate correct exposure settings.

The 1–4 screen is an all-matt screen without central focusing aid. The screen has a centre spot of 8 mm diameter not backed by the Fresnel pattern; this circle is clearly visible and can serve for instance for measuring magnification scales in close-up photography by observing how much of a ruler or other graduated scale appears within the limits of this centre circle. The screen is usable with wide-angle, standard and medium tele lenses if you prefer matt screen focusing to a microprism or split-image wedge; it can also be used with the longer tele lenses and for low-magnification macrophotography. Meter readings on the screen image indicate correct exposure settings.

The 1–5 screen is a clear screen to yield a specially bright finder image which is however not suitable for focusing except in the central microprism spot. The latter is a high-profile microprism for wide-angle and standard lenses; the microprism spot is not usable with lenses of *f*4 or slower. With the *f*3.5 wide-angle lenses the screen is less convenient to use.

As the screen has no matt area, it cannot be used for depth of field previewing. Further, the screen brightness falsifies exposure readings made on the screen image. This applies for instance to OM-1 metering and to the manual or the monitoring indication with the OM-2. Automatic exposures with the OM-2, being controlled by the internal camera cells, are correct even though the needle indication is not.

The 1–6 screen is similar to the 1–5 but has a lower-profile microprism spot more suitable for medium long focus lenses and the zoom lenses. The microprism remains bright down to about *f*5.6 or *f*6.3 and is similar to the spot of the 1–2 screen. The same depth of field preview and exposure metering limitations apply as with the 1–5 screen.

The 1–7 screen is similar to the 1–5 and 1–6, but with a

OM SCREEN TYPES

The 1-1 screen *(left)* is matt with microprism centre spot. Screen 1-2 is similar. Screen 1-3 *(right)* has a rangefinder wedge instead of the microprism.

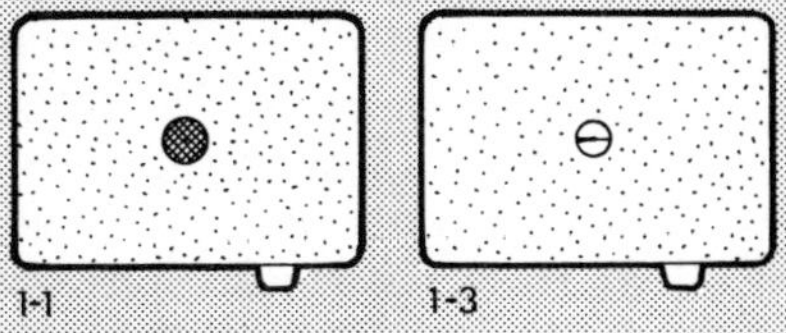

Screen 1-4 *(left)* is all-matt with 8 mm centre circle. Screen 1-5 *(right)* has a microprism spot and is clear outside. Screens 1-6 and 1-7 are similar.

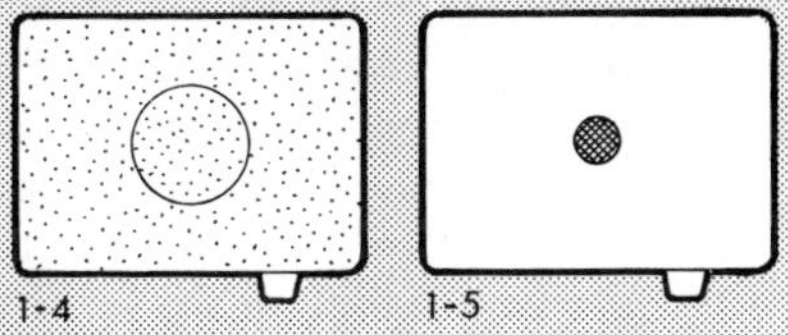

Screen 1-8 is similar to 1-4 but with extra fine matted surface *(left)*. Screen 1-9 is clear with a condenser lens for endoscopic photography *(right)*.

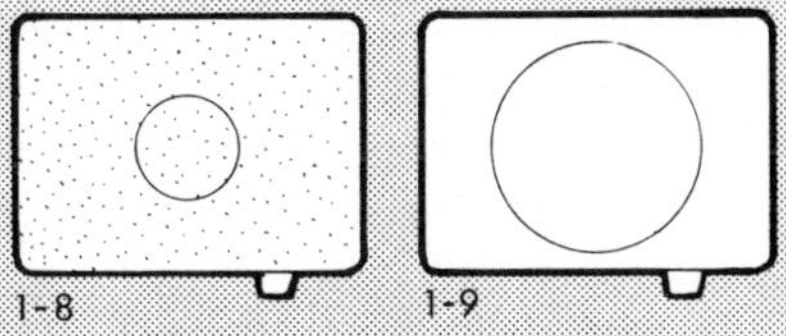

Screen 1-10 is similar to 1-4 but with a line grid *(left)*. Screen 1-11 has extra fine matting with clear centre and hairline graticule *(right)*.

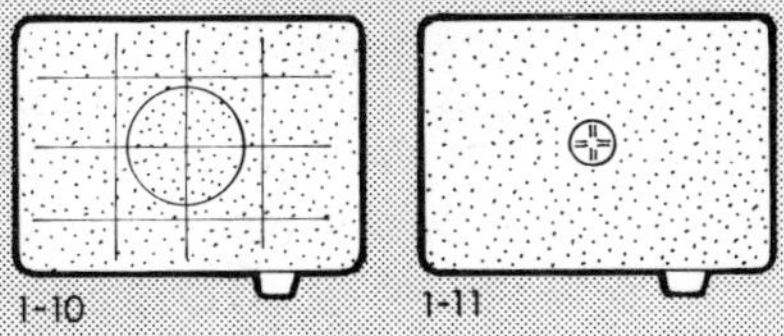

Screen 1-12 is clear with centre circle and hairline graticule for macrophotography and photomicrography *(left)*. Screen 1-13 combines the wedge of 1-3 and microprism of 1-1 *(right)*.

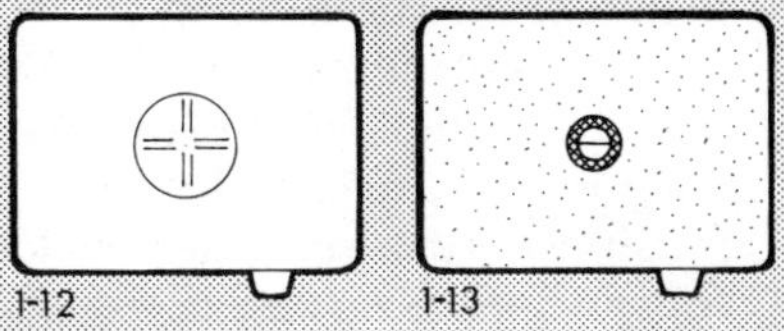

still lower microprism profile which does not go dark with lenses of maximum aperture down to *f*8 to *f*11. This screen is thus useful with tele and extreme tele lenses. The same depth of field preview and exposure metering limitations apply as with the 1–5 screen.

The 1–8 screen looks similar to the 1–4 screen, but the matted surface is extra fine and the central Fresnel-free circle has a 9 mm diameter. Out-of-focus image details appear with a luminous soft-focus effect due to light scatter by the Fresnel pattern. This screen is specially designed for astrophotography and for the longer tele lenses, but is also fine for the medium long focus lenses and usable even with standard and wide-angle lenses down to 35 mm. It is also suitable for macrophotography and the fine screen grain facilitates precise focusing with the Varimagni finder. Meter readings on the screen indicate correct exposure settings.

The 1–9 screen is a clear screen (the only one without a Fresnel pattern altogether) with a central 23 mm diameter condenser lens moulded into the underside. It is used exclusively for endoscopic photography; it is not suitable for use with any of the other lenses.

The 1–10 screen is an all-matt screen with 8 mm Fresnel-free area identical with the 1–4 screen, but carries in addition a line grid of 7 mm line spacing. The centre grid lines go through the middle of the centre spot. The screen is intended for the 35 mm shift lens to permit accurate levelling of the camera—especially vertical subject lines—when using the shift adjustment. It is equally useful for this purpose with the other wide angle lenses and can also be used with long focus and tele lenses.

The 1–11 screen is a matt screen of extra fine grain (similar to the 1–8) but with a 4 mm clear central spot carrying crosshair graticule marks. It is intended for low-magnification macrophotography with the 80 mm macro lens; the clear centre spot is ideal also for aerial focusing in high-magnification macrophotography. The centre graticule area is further useful as an aiming point with long focus tele lenses where the fine screen grain facilitates focusing (but the clear spot cannot be used for this purpose). As on the 1–8 screen, unsharp image detail appears with a luminous soft-focus effect. Meter readings on the screen indicate correct exposure settings.

The 1–12 screen is a clear screen with an 8 mm Fresnel-free centre circle carrying a crosshair graticule for aerial focusing. This is a special screen for high-magnification macrophotography and photomicrography where an image on a matt screen is usually too dark for accurate focusing.

The 1–13 screen combines the characteristics of the 1–1 and 1–3 screens, with a central wedge rangefinder area of 2.5 mm diameter surrounded by a microprism ring of 5 mm outside diameter. It is thus suitable for the standard and wide-angle lenses, medium and tele zoom lenses. The microprism and wedge prism areas go dark with lenses of maximum aperture smaller than *f*4.5. The outer area is a standard matt surface. Meter readings on the screen image yield correct exposure settings.

The Varimagni finder

The Varimagni is a right-angle finder attachment fitting over the camera eyepiece mount, with built-in eyepiece focusing and variable magnification. It is useful for all shots calling for waist-level viewing. That covers low-angle photography, close-ups and macrophotography with the camera mounted on a stand and pointing vertically downwards—and unobtrusive sideways shots with the camera pointing in one direction while you sight in another. The eyepiece part of the Varimagni finder can swivel round through 360°.

The optical system consists of an eyepiece section of 4 lenses in 3 components, a surface silvered mirror and a 2-element single-component relay lens plus a swing-in magnifier group of 3 lenses. Unusual for right-angle finders of this kind is the magnification, including a 2.5 × setting—very useful for precise macro focusing.

To mount the Varimagni finder on the camera, push the rectangular chrome frame at the front down over the protruding eyepiece frame in the back of the camera. The Varimagni should slide easily over the eyepiece frame. Do not touch any of the lens surfaces with the fingers.

Adjust the eyepiece tube; it engages with a click stop in each 90° position. The tube can point upwards for a downward view of the screen (or for horizontal viewing when the camera points down). Swing the eyepiece to either side for 'round the corner' shooting at eye level

VARIMAGNI FINDER

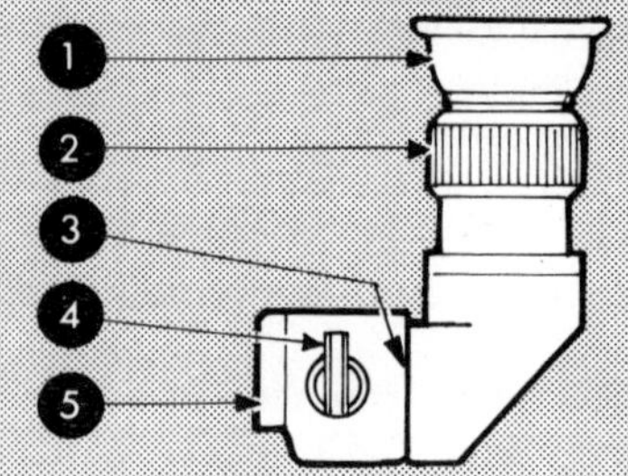

The controls of the Varimagni finder are:

1. Eyecup.
2. Eyepiece focusing ring.
3. Swivelling joint.
4. Magnification selector.
5. Rectangular mounting frame.

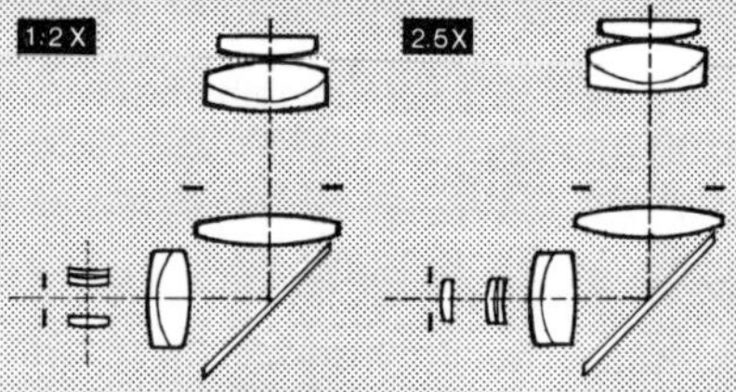

Optical system of the Varimagni finder when set to 1.2× *(left)* and 2.5× *(right)*. The three elements swung into position in front of the large lower lens provide the extra magnification.

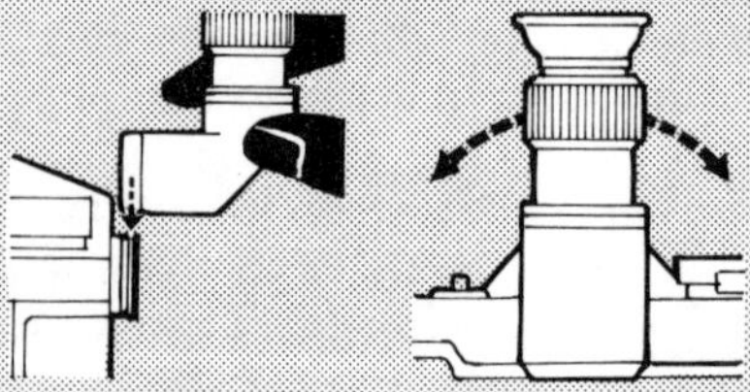

To mount the Varimagni on the camera, push its rectangular frame over the eyepiece *(left)*. The eyepiece tube can swing down in either direction *(right)*.

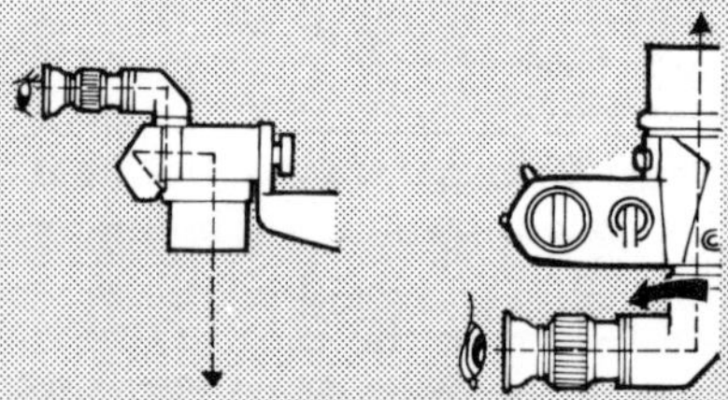

Typical Varimagni applications: camera on stand pointing down for macrophotography *(left)*; right-angle viewing *(right)*.

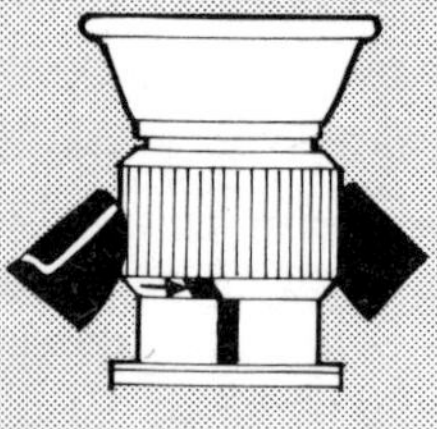

Focus the Varimagni eyepiece to your eyesight. Two self-adhesive markers applied to the focusing ring and eyepiece tube permit quick return to your setting on future occasions.

VARIMAGNI HOLDS

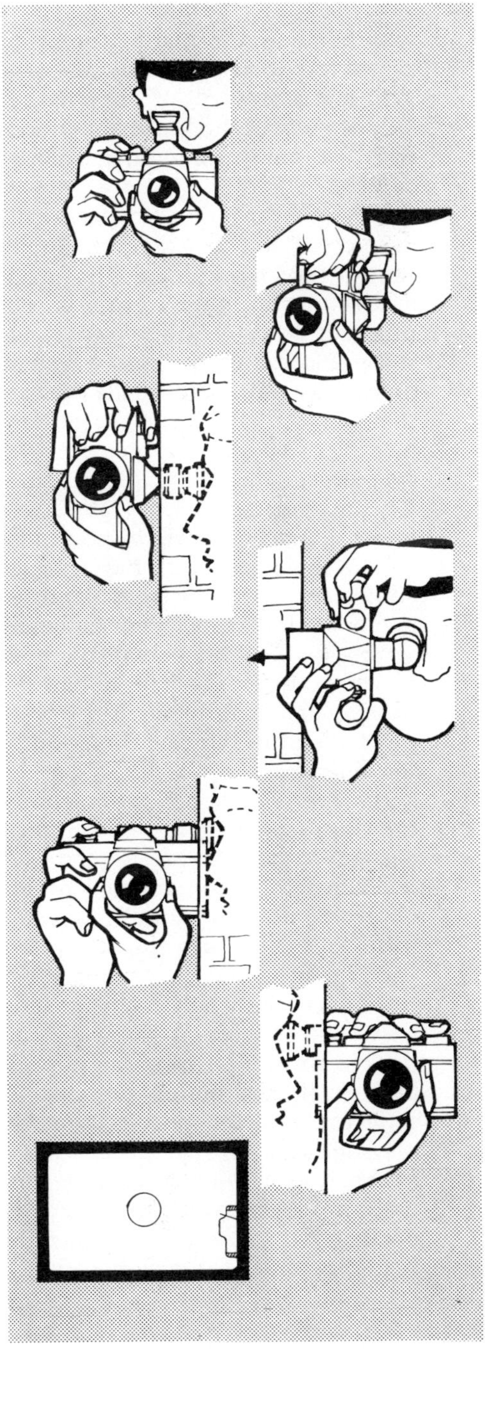

For low-angle waist-level viewing with the Varimagni finder the left hand supports the camera, thumb and index finger on focusing mount while the right hand grips the right-hand end.

For upright shots the left hand supports the left-hand end of the camera while the Varimagni finder tube is swung towards the winding lever end.

For round-the-corner shots with upright format and shooting to the left, the left hand supports the left-hand end of the camera, Varimagni finder tube pointing away from the top *(left)*. For shooting towards the right swing the Varimagni eyepiece tube towards the camera base *(right)* and support the camera in the right hand.

For horizontal round-the-corner shots to the left, the left hand supports the camera while you view through the eyepiece with the right eye *(left)*.

For shooting towards the right, support the camera in the right hand and grip the Varimagni finder with the left which also operates the release and winding controls *(right)*.

The view through the Varimagni finder shows the image reversed left to right, meter needle and shutter speed scale appear at the right.

with horizontal format pictures; swing the eyepiece right down for upright round-the-corner shots. To remove, gently pull upwards off the eyepiece mount.

The body of the Varimagni finder obstructs the camera back, so remove the finder when you load or unload the camera.

To view through the Varimagni finder, first focus the eyepiece. Point the camera at the sky or a bright surface, remove the lens (or defocus its image on the camera screen) and rotate the milled eyepiece mount until the microprism or other central viewing aid of the finder appears sharp. Place your eye closely against the rubber eyecup on the eyepiece. If you normally wear spectacles, view through the eyepiece and focus the latter without spectacles, if possible. (You cannot get the eye close enough to the eyepiece to see the whole screen area with spectacles.) The magnification lever at the side of the Varimagni finder should be upright, pointing to the 1.2× position.

The finder eyepiece has a visual focusing adjustment equivalent to a range from −7 to +3 dioptres but carries no indicating scale. You can mark your own eyepiece setting by sticking a small piece of self-adhesive film or paper on the fixed eyepiece barrel and a second piece on the movable ring in the right position opposite the first piece. For future refocusing you only then have to turn the ring to line up with the markers. (Simpler still—but permanently disfiguring—is scratching a pair of marks in the appropriate positions on the milled ring and the barrel.)

Then focus the camera lens in the usual way while observing the image on the screen. This eyepiece adjustment is particularly important when the Varimagni is used for aerial focusing in macrophotography.

To view the whole focusing screen, set the magnification control lever at the 1.2× position (white bar on lever vertical). Turning the lever down so that the bar is horizontal and points to 2.5× magnifies the central screen section for more accurate focusing at double the magnification.

When you look down into the Varimagni eyepiece with the camera pointing horizontally, the image appears upright but laterally reversed. The same applies if you hold the camera for upright format pictures and swing the eyepiece round to the left or right so as to look down into it. The image also appears upright but laterally reversed if the camera points down and you look horizontally into the eyepiece. The exposure meter needles and centering marks and/or shutter speed scale also appear reversed left to right and are seen at the right instead of the left of the finder screen.

If you point the camera horizontally to the left or right while looking horizontally into the Varimagni, the image appears laterally reversed and upside down. This applies equally when the camera is held upright and the eyepiece protrudes straight towards the top or bottom, or if you hold the camera for horizontal shots with the eyepiece swung down horizontally to either side. The meter needle and centering marks or shutter speed scale then appear at the left but upside down near the top of the finder field.

The Varimagni finder is supplied complete with a leather case.

Eyepiece accessories

The Eyecup 1 is a rubber shell on a rectangular mount that fits over the camera eyepiece. It shields the finder eyepiece against stray light—especially in strong lighting from the side or from behind you. Such stray light entering the finder eyepiece can falsify exposure meter readings from the screen image. The eyecup (and if necessary dioptric correction lenses) are also desirable when you check exposure indications in macrophotography and other subjects where the lighting level around the camera is higher than that of the subject itself. There stray light, reaching the focusing screen through the finder eyepiece, may if not shielded by the eyecup also produce misleading manual exposure readings. The eyecup helps to screen out such light.

The eyecup slightly increases the distance between the eye and the eyepiece and so protects the rear eyepiece lens from steaming up or smudging by your eyelashes. That applies especially to early models of the OM-1; later OM-1 and OM-2 cameras have the rear eyepiece lens further recessed from the back of the eyepiece mount.

You cannot use the eyecup if you wear spectacles as you would then not see the whole of the finder field. However the eyecup takes correction lenses to allow spectacle wearers to view through the finder without glasses.

The eyecup obstructs the opening of the camera back, so remove it before loading or unloading the camera.

The dioptric correction lenses are converging or diverging lens elements of 19 mm diameter and various powers: +2, +1 and +0.5 dioptres to correct presbyopia (long-sightedness) and −1, −2, −3, −4 and −5 dioptres to correct myopia or shortsightedness. The camera viewfinder has an inherent −0.5 dioptre correction, i.e. the finder image is seen at an apparent visual distance of 2 metres.

The dioptric correction lenses are coated and the dioptric power is indicated by a number coated onto the lens near the edge of the glass. This is visible if you hold the glass at an angle below a strong light source so that the light is reflected from the surface. This figure is the effective dioptric correction of the lens plus the camera's finder: a lens marked −3 is in fact a −2.5 dioptre lens to give an overall −3 dioptre correction with the camera's 0.5 dioptre finder.

The correction lenses can be used only in the eyecup. To fit a lens fold back the soft rubber shell of the eyecup and unscrew the black ring with the milled rim just inside. Drop the glass into the recess and screw in the black ring again.

The eyecoupler is a small frame that fits over the camera eyepiece and in turn takes the eyecup or Varimagni finder. The eyecup or finder is thus spaced slightly away from the camera eyepiece. You need the eyecoupler if you use the eyecup with the 250 film back as the top edge of the latter is flush with the bottom edge of the camera eyepiece while the eyecup protrudes below. With the eyecoupler in place, the eyecup can protrude below the rear of the 250 film back.

The eyecoupler may also be more convenient in some applications of the Varimagni finder, for instance in photomicrography, by extending the finder slightly away from the camera.

TECHNIQUE OF DEFINITION

The primary function of the focusing controls in conjunction with the viewing screen is to ensure that the picture will be sharp on the film. Beyond that we are however also concerned with how sharp things shall be, what parts of the image may be sharper or less sharp than others and how to use selective unsharpness for deliberate pictorial effects.

Once the image of a selected subject point is sharp on the screen, these other aspects of creative definition are controlled by the lens aperture and the shutter speed. It so happens that these factors also control exposure, as we shall see in the next chapter. Here we are concerned with the fact that they may modify sharpness in two totally different ways: optical sharpness distribution in terms of depth of field and dynamic sharpness control when dealing with movement.

Depth of field

A camera lens differs from the eye in numerous respects. Two of them are particularly relevant to viewing pictures that the camera has taken. When we look at an original scene the eye scans it, and constantly and automatically refocuses on every detail, whatever (within certain limits) its distance. So we build up an essentially sharp but composite visual picture of our surroundings.

The camera lens takes in the whole scene with a stationary gaze and it does not adapt its focus setting during the exposure. So in the picture only the subject the camera was originally focused on appears really sharp. When we look at the resulting picture we see not only those sharp portions but also that the rest of the view may be more or less unsharp. And no amount of visual refocusing makes such unsharp parts appear sharp again.

The sharpest part of the image—whether in the print

or still on the camera's focusing screen—corresponds to the object on which we focus the lens. That is, any object in a plane at a specific distance from the camera. We might call this the sharpest subject plane. The rest of the image is not all equally unsharp: items just a little nearer or just a little further from the camera than the sharpest-subject plane are only slightly unsharp, but foreground very much nearer than the sharpest-subject plane is liable to be very blurred.

It follows that there must be a zone where the unsharpness in the image is too slight to be noticeable. In effect, the sharpest-image plane gains a depth within which we cannot yet tell the difference between completely sharp and slightly unsharp. The image looks noticeably blurred only when this degree of unsharpness exceeds our visual resolution limit.

The distance range in front of and behind the sharpest-subject plane where things still look acceptably sharp is known as the depth of field.

It is a somewhat uncertain quantity and a variable one. We can however pin it down to some extent by specifying the factors that control it. These are:

(a) Our standard of sharpness;
(b) The lens settings—aperture and distance;
(c) The focal length of the lens.

Factors (b) and (c) provide considerable scope for deliberately controlling the way sharpness is distributed in the picture—rendering everything sharp from near to far or selecting a subject plane to record it sharply against an unsharp foreground or background.

Sharpness standards

Sharpness is to some extent in the eye of the beholder. But we need some standard to define depth of field zones. An accepted standard is based on the detail we can visually resolve in a print or transparency seen under conditions of natural perspective.

In terms of actual dimensions this is equivalent to a print seen about 250 mm or 10 inches away, if the print is an enlargement of the negative such that the focal length multiplied by the degree of enlargement also comes to 250 mm. With the standard 50 mm lens that means a 5 × magnification.

DEPTH INDICATOR

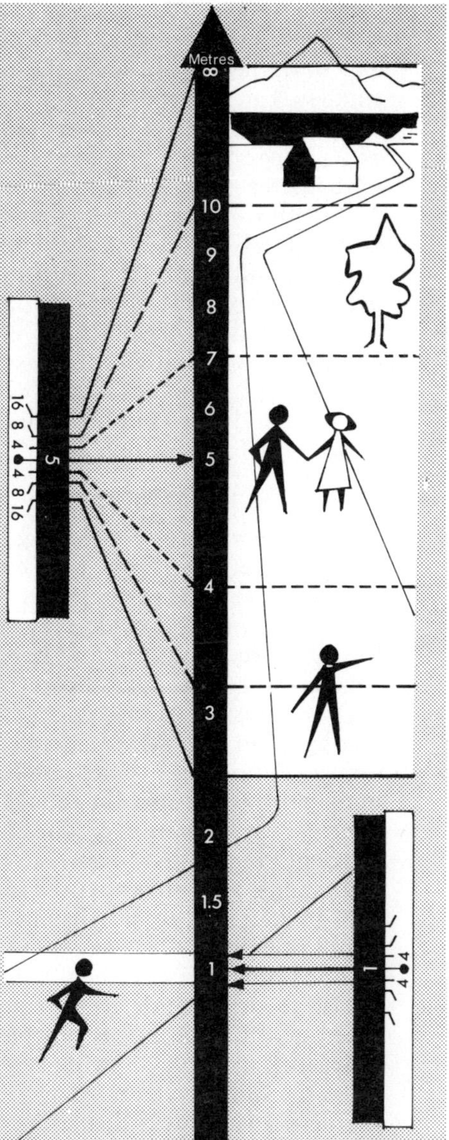

Apart from objects at the distance on which the lens is focused, items nearer and further away also appear acceptably sharp. The depth of this sharp zone is shown on the depth of field scale of each lens and can be controlled by varying the aperture. Thus with the camera focused on 5 metres, the depth indicator shows that at *f*4 you have a sharp zone from 4 to 7 metres. At *f*8 this extends from 3.2 to 10 metres. At *f*16, anything more than 2.5 metres away is sharp.

The zone shrinks at nearer distances: at 1 metre and *f*8 the depth only covers from 0.9 to 1.1 metres.

Finally, the standard of sharpness assumes that at 250 mm viewing distance the eye can resolve no detail smaller than about 0.15 mm. What this means is that an image begins to look unsharp if in such a print every one of its image points becomes a blur larger than 0.15 mm in diameter—and still appears acceptably sharp if image points blur to less than 0.15 mm. This limiting blur size is commonly known as the limiting circle of confusion (COC). And if the COC is 0.15 mm in a 5 × enlarged print, it has to be 0.03 mm on the film.

Any standard of sharpness is of course arbitrary and conditions for ideal viewing distance are rarely achieved. But it gives us something to work with—especially for calculating the extent of the sharp zone and for designing depth of field indicating aids.

Aperture and distance

The primary factor controlling depth of field is the lens aperture setting. You can observe this visually by focusing the camera on say an item in the middle of a table carrying various objects at different distances. Set the aperture ring to the full lens aperture, then press the preview key on the lens and keep it depressed while turning the aperture ring step by step to higher *f*-number settings. On the table nearer and more distant objects appear increasingly sharp as the image becomes darker in the finder. So to obtain great depth, use a small working aperture (if exposure conditions allow) and to restrict the depth of the sharp zone use a large lens aperture.

Distance also affects depth: the further away an object, the greater the actual distance range covered by the depth of field.

The visual check on the screen with the preview button is also a rough guide to the aperture needed to cover a given depth zone. Focus on the main subject, select the aperture you think you will need for correct exposure and press the stop-down or preview key on the lens to observe the actual sharpness distribution on the screen. Repeat that with different aperture settings; finally select one aperture step smaller than the one at which you think the screen showed sharply everything you want sharp. This allows for the fact that the visual sharpness of a dim image is less certain than the actual sharpness on the film.

The depth of field indicator

The visual preview is a convenient rapid check of limited reliability. More reliable is the lens's depth of field indicator. This is the set of index lines to the left and right of the main focusing index. The latter is the point against which you read off the distance on the focusing scale.

To each side of this index there are usually three thin lines, marked in pairs with aperture or *f*-numbers. Thus on the standard 50 mm lenses there are a couple of lines 1.5 mm to the left and to the right of the focusing index, marked with the figure 4. Then, 3 mm to the left and to the right of the index are two further lines marked '8' and 6 mm away another pair marked '16'. When the lens is set to a given distance opposite the central focusing index, other distance figures or notional points on the distance scale line themselves up with these short numbered index lines. These distances define the depth of field zone at the indicated apertures.

For instance if the lens is set so that the white distance figure of 5 metres is opposite the red index, the two *f*4 index lines of the depth scale are opposite positions corresponding roughly to 4 and 7 metres respectively. The *f*8 index lines point to about 3.2 and 10 metres, and the *f*16 index lines to some 2.5 metres at the left and the infinity (∞) sign at the right. So with the lens set to 5 metres you get a sharp zone from 4 to 7 metres at *f*4, from 3.2 to 10 metres at *f*8 and from 2.5 metres to infinity (in other words everything farther than 2.5 metres away is sharp) at *f*16.

For straightforward checking of a sharp zone that is all there is to the use of the depth indicator. However, estimating distance points on the focusing scale needs a little practice.

Practical depth indicator applications

There are a few other ways of getting depth of field information from the indicator—and especially for selecting conditions for a given sharp zone.

If you want a given zone sharp, adjust the focusing mount so that the distance figures for the near and far limits of that sharp zone come opposite index lines of similar *f*-number. For instance to get everything sharp between 6 and 12 feet, adjustment of the focusing ring can bring the orange 6 feet mark halfway between the *f*8 and *f*16 depth lines, while the 12 feet mark is opposite a point between the right-hand *f*8 and *f*16 lines. If you then stop down to *f*11, you automatically have the sharp zone wanted.

The focused distance—read off the distance scale opposite the focus index—is 8 feet and you use that setting even if the main subject is 9 or 10 feet away.

If you don't know the distances of the near and far limits, find suitable objects at those points and focus the camera on them in turn. Then read off the appropriate distances on the focusing scale and continue as above.

A table of focusing zones (see Chpt. *Facts and figures*) lists the selection of near, medium and distant zones with various lens, *f*-number and distance combinations. This zone table is meant for sampling typical subject conditions. Select one or two (not more) that suit you and memorise them for instant zone shooting whenever you have to use them.

You can also use the depth indicator together with the depth preview key. Focus the main subject sharply, then decide what else you want to have sharp nearer and further away. Check a likely lens aperture to give you that depth from the depth of field indicator. Preselect the stop on the aperture ring and stop down the lens by the preview key to see whether the additional detail you want comes up sharp enough or not.

With all aperture-coupled lenses use the stop-down key only for depth previewing, never for exposure metering on the camera's screen. For the results would invariably be wrong.

Depth of field economics

The main factor of depth of field control—the lens aperture—is also a main element of exposure control. The requirements of the two are not always compatible: we may need extended depth of field where light conditions and subject movement call for a large aperture or we may want restricted depth in conditions where a large aperture is not convenient. We can here utilise the two other factors controlling depth, namely the subject distance and lens's focal length. Changing either of these also alters the image scale on the film. To obtain a print showing the subject at a given size we may then also have to alter the degree of enlargement and if necessary crop the print. So print magnification, too, enters into this relationship.

To see how this works, let us assume a 'standard' picture of a standing human figure that in an upright 18 × 24 cm print is 180 mm high. Assuming the figure to be 180 cm tall, this is a 10:1 reduction in the print. This reduction is however a product of a scale reduction on the negative and the print enlargement. This is where we get our additional scope of depth control—but this is only feasible with prints made from negatives, and not with transparencies where we cannot normally vary the magnification on projection from one transparency to the next. Also, for these considerations we will ignore the natural-size viewing distance question for prints.

A fairly normal condition for obtaining the 180 mm tall image of the figure in the print is to reduce the person 1:60 in the negative and enlarge the latter 6× linear. This would be the case for a shot taken with a 50 mm lens at about 3 metres which yields a 30 mm tall image on the film. The depth of field under these conditions at *f*4 would extend from about 2.6 to 3.6 metres, or 1 metre overall in the subject space, given a viewing distance of 6 × 50 mm = 30 cm.

Now here is how you can gain depth of field while remaining at *f*4:

(a) Use a shorter-focus lens from the same subject distance and increase the degree to which you enlarge the print. For shorter-focus lenses yield more depth of field. In practical terms: with the 35 mm lens also at 3 metres and *f*4, the depth of field extends from 2.3 to 4.4 metres—a total depth of 2.1 metres or over twice what it was before. The image of the person on the film is now 21 mm tall and to get it to 180 mm on the print you have to enlarge the negative 8.57×. That gives an identical viewing distance of 8.57 × 35 mm = 30 cm. With the greater enlargement, you have to put up with a slight loss in comparative quality because that depends on the print magnification, but not with any drop in depth of field sharpness standards.

(b) You also gain depth by going further away from the subject and enlarging more afterwards. Thus, instead of taking the shot with the 50 mm lens at 3 metres, you could go back to 5 metres. This yields an image 18 mm high on the film. To get back to 180 mm on the print, you have to enlarge it 10×. At 5 metres, however, the depth of field extends from 4 to 6.8 metres, or 2.8 metres overall.

This time, however, you have to allow for the extra enlargement, because your viewing distance should be 50 cm. By viewing from 30 cm you make the net depth $3/5 \times 2.8 = 1.68$ metres. On the other hand, you have a different picture, because the perspective has changed. That could affect the apparent depth of field by changing the scale of the background.

The depth zones quoted in these examples are not easy to read off the depth of field scale: the figures given are calculated values.

(c) Conversely (and with the same provisos) you can decrease depth by using a longer focus lens or going nearer. In this particular example, you won't necessarily get the whole figure into the picture, but the same principles apply.

(d) You don't normally gain much depth by trading distance against focal length. If, instead of shooting at 3 metres with the 50 mm lens, you go to 6 metres away and use the 100 mm lens, the depth extends from about 5.5 to 6.5 metres—again one metre overall and you have gained nothing. (The image of the main subject is 30 mm high on the film in both cases, although the perspective is not the same.)

In certain cases you may gain some depth this way if you start with a longish subject distance and switch to a wide-angle lens while going closer. But perspective changes then become far too radical to make this a valid method of controlling just depth of field.

Finally, remember that sharpness standards even depend on the subject. Unsharpness is disturbing if it blurs fine high-contrast detail. But it goes largely unnoticed if you only have outlines of detailless shape. A pure black-on-white silhouette suffers little from a blurring of its outline that would kill the impact of a texture subject. And a formless shape emerging from swirling mist is at best hard to define in terms of sharpness. By all means focus with normal care—but don't waste time there over depth of field worries.

Shutter speed and movement

We have already discussed pictures blurred by camera shake. The shorter the exposure time, the less the effect of any residual camera movement that could cause blur.

With no firm camera support available, use an exposure time no longer than 1/60 second, and preferably 1/125 second with the standard 50 mm lens, if conditions allow. Longer-focus lenses need a shorter exposure time as they magnify the effect of any blur. And if 1/60 second is adequate with the 50 mm lens, then—other things being equal—the 200 mm lens would need at least 1/250 second.

Camera movement or camera shake blurs the whole image. Subject movement blurs only the image of the subject on the film. To counteract that we also need fast shutter speeds, but the choice of the correct speed is somewhat more involved.

As in the case of depth of field, we can stipulate a limiting size of blur for each image point as 0·03 mm on the negative. A movement-freezing shutter speed must then be short enough so that the amount of movement on the film during the open period of the shutter is less than this limiting blur. Suppose a car is travelling at about 35 km/hour across the field of view. This is nearly 10 metres/second. During an exposure time of 1/1000 second, the car will shift 10 mm. To reduce a 10 mm movement of the subject to a 0.03 mm shift in the image, the car must be reproduced on an image scale of about 1:300. If the car is about 300 focal lengths away from the camera (at this kind of reproduction scale the subject distance is proportional to the focal length) the image will not appear visibly unsharp in a normal enlargement from the negative. With the 50 mm lens this is a subject distance of about 15 metres.

If the car—or any other object—travels at only half this speed, twice as long an exposure time (1/500 second) yields an acceptably sharp image. The same applies if the car is twice as far away (double the scale of reduction) or photographed with a lens of half the focal length (again double the reduction scale).

This means that to reproduce an object at a given scale (size on the film) the shutter speed needed to arrest movement is the same with a short focus lens from a nearer distance or a long focus lens from further away. Nor is there any point in shooting from further away and enlarging only part of the negative to a higher magnification—the blur gets enlarged up again.

When you are shooting moving subjects you rarely have time to look up tables in a book. But it is useful to memorise a set of standard conditions and then modify them as needed.

Here is a simple one for the 50 mm standard lens: an object moving at 25 km/hour and approx. 25 metres away needs 1/250 second exposure. Increase the speed and the shutter speed increases in proportion. Double the distance and the shutter speed is halved. And double the focal length and the shutter speed is doubled. All other adjustments follow the same scheme. A speed of 25 km/hour (15 mph) is quite convenient as it corresponds to slow town traffic, fast cyclists etc.

Other movement approaches

As the shutter speed controls not only movement sharpness but also exposure, you may on occasion have to use a longer exposure time (slower speed) than you would like for movement stopping. There are several ways of 'cheating':

(a) Instead of photographing the moving subject broadside on, shoot it at an angle or even approaching or receding directly. When an object moves at an angle to the camera axis, the shift of the image on the film is reduced compared with when it moves across the axis.

Subjects that directly approach or recede hardly shift the image across the film at all; it only gets larger (or smaller). The accepted rule of thumb is to allow 2 shutter speed intervals slower for movement stopping than with broadside-on movement.

(b) Where subjects move as a whole—for instance vehicles—without much individual part movement, you can compensate the movement to a large extent by following it with the camera. This panning or swinging is a standard technique of sports photographers covering motor races etc.; it blurs the background and makes the subject appear sharp against it, enhancing the impact of speed. The panning movement must however be smooth; centre the subject in the finder and keep it there.

(c) Some types of movement reciprocate, periodically

reversing the direction. At such a reversal point the moving body—for instance a child on a swing—is stationary for an instant and can then be caught sharply with a comparatively slow shutter speed. This 'dead point' technique needs a little anticipation but is otherwise straightforward.

Finally, sharpness standards are arbitrary in movement, too. How unsharp movement looks depends also on the size of the object relative to its movement speed. For instance if the car travelling at 10 metres/second is 5 metres long, it moves 20 mm (1/250 of its length) in 1/500 second. Such a blur has little effect on the recognisable outline and main details. But a 10 mm thick radio aerial sticking up from the wing moves through twice its thickness during 1/500 second—and so becomes a totally unrecognisable blur. This is also why spokes in wheels, arms and legs of runners etc. appear more blurred than the rest of the subject. They not only move faster but also faster relative to their size.

TECHNIQUE OF EXPOSURE

Subjects usually consist of lighter and darker parts, i.e. tones reflecting (or producing) different light intensities. The action of light records the tones on the film as an image. In the developed film these intensities are reproduced as different densities. In a negative material, a dark shadow in the image projected by the lens on the film yields a low developed density (almost clear film). Bright highlights yield high densities (nearly black film) and intermediate tones intermediate densities. Only if the film records these subject densities in a representatively graded manner can it yield a print that in turn acceptably reproduces the brightness gradations of the original subject. With colour film, corresponding colour shades are recorded at the same time. In a reversal film the principle is similar, but the negative and positive image are produced in the same film in succession.

Subjects in nature can range in brightness (luminance) over a scale of some 10,000,000:1—ranging from brilliant sunlit snow on Alpine peaks to furtive shapes in the night lit by a distant street lamp.

The film's ability to record different luminances of the image formed by the lens is much more restricted. It needs a minimum light intensity to record some density (and detail) in the shadows; too much light however completely exposes the film to detailless black. The furtive shadows in the night need a great deal of exposure to make their mark on the emulsion; the snowy peaks must be restricted to very little.

Recording an image on the film is thus a quantitative process: it needs the right amount of light, depending in the first place on the speed or sensitivity of the film. The required light action is obtained by taking the available light intensity of the subject, modifying it on its passage through the lens by the lens aperture and controlling the length for which it acts on the film by the shutter setting.

The aperture and shutter are thus the two means of controlling the exposure in the camera and provide between them a wide adjustment range. We have already seen how these settings influence image sharpness in terms of depth of field and movement blur. Here we are concerned with their effect on light control.

Setting ranges and combinations

The speed setting ring of the OM-1 and 2 shutter with its range from 1/1000 second to 1 second covers 10 double-or-half speeds. The lens aperture settings also cover a range of double-or-half steps. Going from one aperture or stop value to the next higher value halves the intensity of the light coming through the lens (also known as stopping down by one stop). Going to the next lower *f*-number—e.g. from *f*5.6 to *f*4—doubles the light intensity passing through (1 stop more exposure).

The 50 mm *f*1.4 lens covers 7 stop intervals. Some lenses may have a lowest *f*-number not quite in this double-or-half range, e.g. *f*3.5 or *f*1.2. The aperture ring of the OM lenses engages at each *f*-number interval; with largest apertures (lowest *f*-numbers) outside the range, the first click stop in fact covers roughly 1½ lens stops—e.g. from *f*3.5 to *f*5.6. The smallest aperture also varies but most OM lenses cover at least six double-or-half or stop intervals.

Adjustment of the aperture ring preselects the setting, as the lens iris remains fully open during viewing and focusing. It automatically stops down to the preselected value for the exposure—or when operating the depth preview key.

The OM lenses thus have neither ½ stop nor ⅓ stop engagement clicks. The drawback of this is that accurate aperture settings at these intervals become more difficult. The distance between the clicks is however adequate (about 4 mm on the ring) to permit intermediate setting.

The big advantage of full-stop clicks is however that you can set the lens aperture by touch, for instance in the dark or if you haven't time to take the camera off your eye to look at the aperture scale.

The exposure control range of the 10 shutter speed and 6 lens aperture steps is thus nearly 66,000:1 (2 to the power 16)—even without the long exposure times that can arise with automatic operation. Over most of this range the lens aperture and shutter speed adjustments can overlap in part. For instance if the prevailing light calls for an exposure of 1/1000 second at *f* 2.8, the film would get the same light with 1/500 second at *f* 4 or with other combinations down to 1/30 second at *f* 16.

Through-the-lens light metering

To know how much exposure to apply, we must measure the luminance of the image. Single-lens reflex cameras provide an observable viewfinder image actually formed by the lens. So it is logical to measure the brightness of that image to derive the required exposure information. There are various ways of doing that. The OM cameras employ two methods: premetering on the screen and integrated film plane measurement. The former serves for manual exposure control on both the OM-1 and OM-2 cameras. The latter is an automatic metering method on the OM-2 only.

Screen image metering

Inside the pentaprism housing a pair of cadmium sulphide (CdS) photo-resistor cells—located to each side of the eyepiece—point towards the viewing and focusing screen. The cells form part of an electric circuit which includes a battery (in a compartment in the camera base) and a moving coil galvanometer with an indicating pointer. In the dark, the CdS cells have a high resistance and little or no current flows in the circuit. As light falls on the cells they become more conducting; the circuit carries more current and the galvanometer shows this. The current in the circuit is thus a measure of the light intensity reaching the CdS cells.

The light that reaches the cells is light from the focusing screen, reflected via the pentaprism of the viewing system. Thus the CdS cells in effect read the luminance of the image formed by the lens.

The reading—the movement of the galvanometer needle—still has to be translated into an exposure setting, taking into account the three factors on which the exposure depends: film speed, lens aperture and shutter speed. The camera does this by a zeroing method: as the galvanometer needle moves, the whole galvanometer is rotated

THROUGH-THE-LENS METERING

In the manual mode (OM-1 and OM-2) and for OM-2 monitoring two CdS cells alongside the eye-piece measure light on the screen with the lens at full aperture.

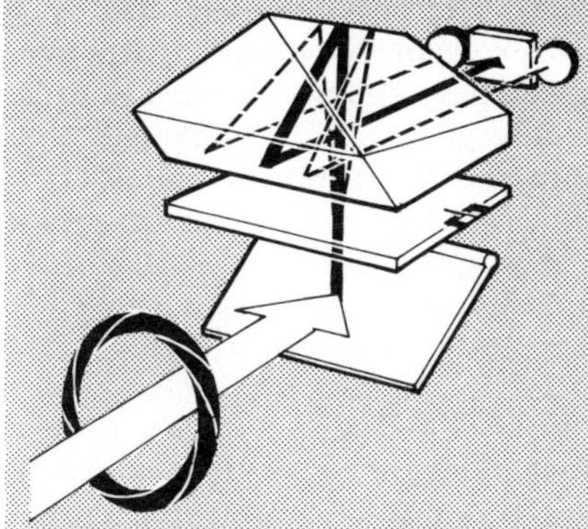

The meter needle is centred between two markers for correct exposure. Off-centre needle positions indicate ½ or 1 stop over (+) or under (−) exposure. The marker arrangement differs slightly in the OM-1 and OM-2 but the principle is the same.

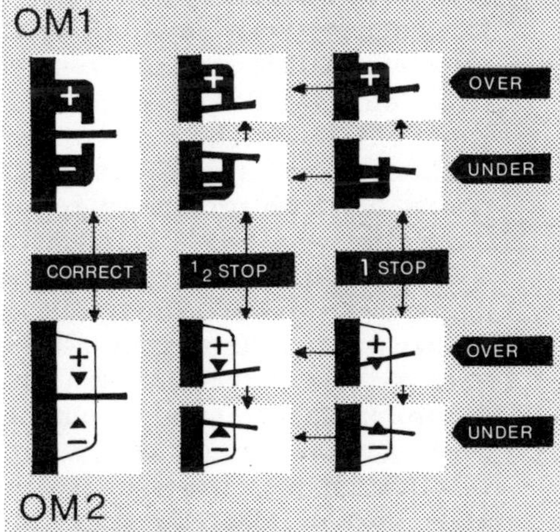

The first shutter blind of the OM-2 simulates average film reflectivity. Silicon cells measure the light reflected from this shutter—and from the film as it is uncovered—at the lens's working aperture. After registering the right amount of light, they trigger the release of the closing shutter blind. The needle and speed scale in the finder *(right)* show beforehand the approximate exposure to be selected by the automatic system.

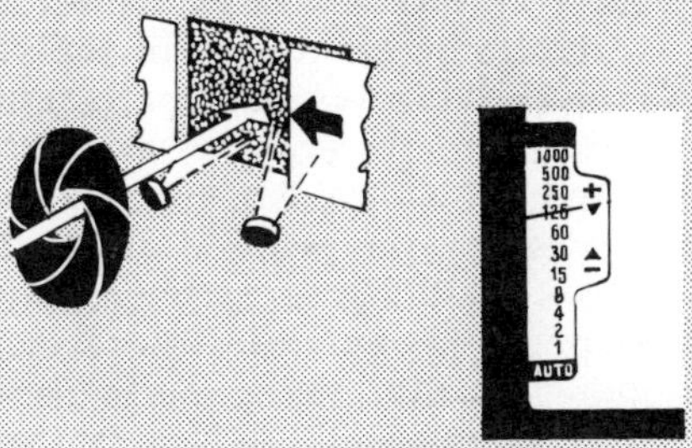

to bring the needle back to a defined zero point. This mechanical galvanometer movement is in turn linked by various cables and gears to the film speed dial, the shutter speed ring and an aperture simulator.

The role of the film speed and shutter speed adjustments is plain enough. Doubling the ASA value on the film speed adjustment acts in the opposite way to doubling the shutter speed (halving the exposure time). The galvanometer needle in the end remains in the same position in both cases.

Aperture input

The aperture control is a somewhat different story. The light coming through the lens also affects the brightness of the screen image and hence the exposure reading. However, the lens is used at full aperture for viewing and focusing; to have to stop it down to the working aperture for the exposure reading would be inconvenient. The OM-1 and OM-2 therefore have a built-in aperture simulator. This is a small lever protruding inside the camera's lens mount, very near the red locating dot for lens insertion. This lever protrudes from a ring rotating concentrically with the lens mount. On fitting a lens, the aperture coupling lever protruding from the rear of the lens engages this aperture input lever in the camera and pushes it into a start position for aperture control. This start position is the same for all lenses, irrespective of maximum aperture and so automatically allows for the effect of the maximum lens aperture on exposure.

When you preselect a smaller aperture, this moves the lens's aperture coupling lever (directly linked with the aperture setting ring) and in turn moves the camera's aperture input lever. This again is mechanically linked with the galvanometer in the same way as the shutter speed setting and film speed setting.

This aperture input system is independent of the automatic stop-down mechanism of the lens. The only link is that the position of the lens aperture ring determines the degree to which the lens is automatically stopped down during the exposure via a second lever linked to the mirror mechanism. That lever engages a stop-down lever at the rear of the lens; the depth preview key is linked with the same stop-down lever.

WEIGHING AND COMPENSATION

The through-the-lens metering of the OM cameras is centre-weighted primarily to cover the area shown clear on the screen. The screen areas outside this contribute less and less to the measurement.

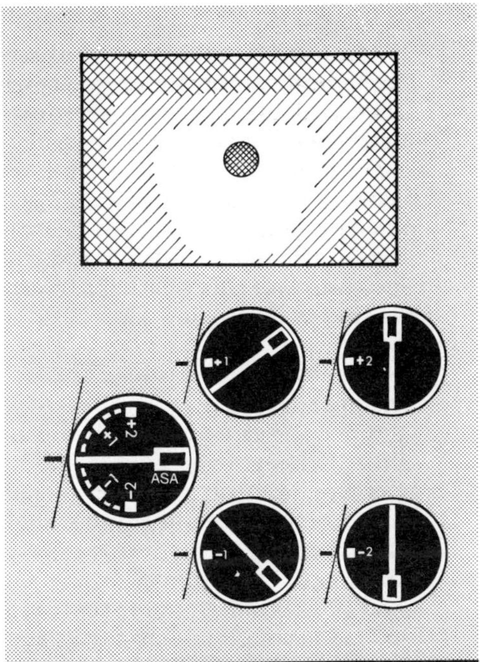

To adapt the automatic exposure to non-standard subject conditions, the exposure compensating dial has various marked positions covering from +2 stops over to −2 stops underexposure.

APERTURE INPUT

An aperture simulator ring inside the camera's lens mount *(left)* is moved up to a start position *(centre)* on fitting the lens. The simulator ring moves the galvanometer housing. This start position defines the full aperture of whatever lens is used—with a faster lens more light affects the meter needle *(left)*.

On stopping down the lens, the aperture coupling lever moves the aperture simulator and hence the galvanometer housing with the needle—even though the light on the screen remains the same *(left)*. If in addition you press the preview key *(right)* the needle also moves giving erroneous readings—the OM system is based on full-aperture metering.

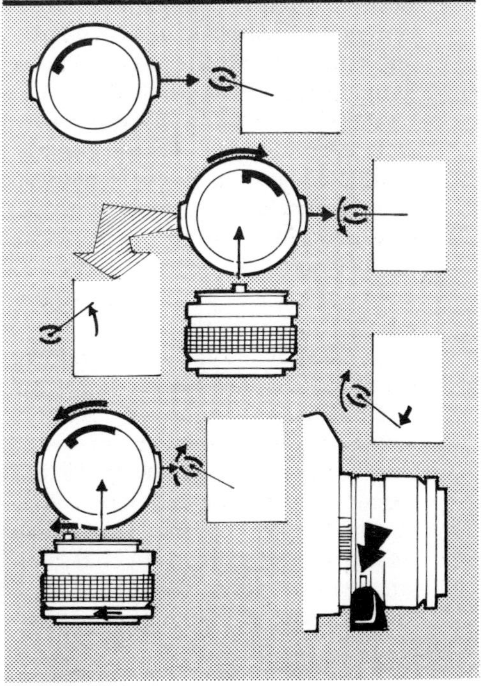

The lens's coupling lever thus transmits to the camera's aperture input only the degree to which the lens is stopped down from its maximum opening. That is also the only additional information the camera needs for exposure metering on the screen at full aperture. However, this system is not usable for working-aperture measurements when a Zuiko Auto lens is mounted directly on the camera. For if you stop down the lens to the working aperture by the preview key, the camera's metering system gets the stopping-down information twice—once through the aperture simulator and once through the manually stopped-down aperture. The result is an erroneous reading.

When the camera is used with any device that does not directly link it with a lens's aperture coupling lever, the aperture input system is out of action. To permit correct exposure readings under those conditions, such devices—extension tubes, the camera body mount of the Auto-bellows, the OM mount H adapter etc.—all have a fixed lever protruding from the rear in the position of the lens's aperture coupling lever in the maximum aperture position. When the lens is mounted via an extension tube, its own aperture ring no longer relays the stop-down information to the camera's aperture simulator—the latter is permanently set to the maximum aperture position. Instead, stopping down the lens directly—and now correctly—affects the exposure reading. (The extension tubes have a second internal fitting that engages the stop-down lever equivalent to permanent pushing in of the preview key.) With these intermediate devices the exposure is thus measured at the lens's working aperture. The same applies to non-auto lenses, for instance the 35 mm Zuiko Shift.

Manual metering procedure

Here then, in detail, is the full procedure of manual exposure measurement. This is the same on the OM-1 and OM-2, though in the latter case the manual mode needs specific selection.

On the OM-1 turn the exposure meter switch from OFF to ON; on the OM-2 turn the switch from OFF to MANUAL to move the exposure meter indexes into the finder field at the left (on the OM-1 the indexes are permanently in view); on both cameras this operation switches on the galvanometer and CdS cell circuit. Check that the ASA dial has been set to the speed of the film in the camera.

Select a shutter speed appropriate to the conditions and observe the meter needle at the left of the finder screen. Then adjust the lens aperture ring to centre the meter needle exactly between the prongs of the index on the OM-1 or between the tips of the triangle marks in the OM-2. The aperture ring can be set to intermediate positions between click stops—sometimes you need that for accurate centering of the needle.

If the needle stays up above the centering position even with the lens aperture fully stopped down, select a faster shutter speed on the ring. If the needle stays down even with the aperture ring fully to the left (full aperture) select a slower shutter speed (longer exposure) and try again.

To work at a specific aperture—for instance for depth of field reasons—preselect that on the lens aperture ring. Then adjust the shutter speed ring to centre the meter needle between its index marks. If you cannot centre the needle at either extreme of the shutter speed setting range, select a different aperture. The B setting on the OM-1 in this context is equivalent to an exposure time of 2 seconds (timed manually). On the OM-2 the B setting can only be engaged if you also press the small reset key at the bottom of the panel just behind the shutter ring. Setting B here however switches off the meter indication.

You cannot set intermediate shutter speeds. If the zero position of the meter would be between two speed settings, set the shutter to the next higher or lower speed and reach the final balance point by an intermediate setting of the aperture ring.

Under and over settings

When the needle is not exactly centred between its index marks, the needle position indicates not only varying but predictable degrees of over or underexposure. This is useful when you want to increase or decrease the exposure deliberately to allow for specific subject conditions.

When the meter needle just touches the tip of the upper index mark (the protruding prong below the + mark) the camera is set to ½ stop overexposure. When the meter needle reaches the upper end of the cut-out below the sign on the OM-1 or is lined up with the top edge of the upper triangle mark on the OM-2, the camera is set to 1 stop overexposure (larger aperture or slower shutter speed).

Corresponding needle positions against the lower marker provide ½ or 1 stop underexposure.

You can take this further to 2 stops over or underexposure, though this is less easy to define accurately. With the OM-1 the needle drops to just below the bottom – for 2 stops under, or goes through the upper half of the + for 2 stops over. On the OM-2 the needle goes just past the – sign and just past the + sign for 2 stops under or over respectively.

The 2 stops and even 1 stop under position on the OM-1 may however also be the result of maximum galvanometer rotation with a high film speed. At 200 ASA this will arise if you use the 1 second or B settings of the shutter speed ring, at 400 ASA with anything longer than 1/4 second, and at 800 and 1600 ASA with settings longer than 1/8 and 1/15 second respectively—in every case with the lens at full aperture. So avoid these shutter speed/film speed/aperture combinations.

Finally, when taking exposure readings through the finder, keep out any stray light that might enter the finder eyepiece and falsify the readings.

Film plane measurement

The exposure metering system described so far by measurement of the screen image is common to the OM-1 and OM-2 cameras—at the MANUAL setting of the latter. The OM-2 in addition has a completely separate metering system based on the image projected by the lens into the film plane.

The measuring elements in this case are a pair of silicon blue cells (SBCs) located just inside the camera's lens mount and pointing at the shutter. The measuring circuit to the cells is switched on by the mirror as it swings up just before the exposure. The lens then projects its image on the first shutter blind which carries an unusual irregular checker board type pattern. Its purpose is to simulate the reflectance of an average unexposed film surface in the camera.

The silicon cells record the light reflected from the checkerboard shutter blind as it runs down. During the run-down the blind uncovers the film and the cells continue to measure the light reflected from the film surface. The cell output, suitably amplified, goes through various electronic circuits that also control the release of the second shutter blind to terminate the exposure. The SBCs thus directly control the exposure time of the OM-2's electronic shutter. If the light is strong enough for short exposure times, the SBCs read the light mostly from the first shutter blind, as the second blind is released before the first blind has moved very far across the film. At an exposure of 1/60 second, half the light is read off the running-down shutter blind and half off the film; at longer exposures the reading from the film predominates.

The exposure meter system only has to be programmed to allow for the film speed and for a standard film reflectivity. Various tests by Olympus, by other camera manufacturers studying film reflection metering and by independent reviewers suggest that the reflection characteristics of most films likely to be used in the OM cameras are remarkably consistent. The source of error contributed by film variations thus appears to be rarely more than $\pm \frac{1}{3}$ lens stop and often much less.

The monitoring scale

The OM-2's auto-exposure system is what is known as aperture-preferred: you preselect the lens aperture and the automatic system controls the exposure time or shutter speed and displays it in the viewfinder when the meter switch is turned to AUTO. This moves a scale into the finder field at the left, showing exposure times from 1000 (1/1000 second) to 1 second by a meter needle moving across the scale. The needle position indicates the approximate shutter speed that the automatic system with the SBCs will select. If this speed appears too slow, preselect a larger lens aperture. If the speed is too fast set a small aperture.

The shutter speed figures from 30 downwards are marked blue in the finder to indicate that they are usable with flash. Actually, exposure times from 1/60 second and longer can be synchronised with electronic flash, but the needle indication in the finder is approximate; if it showed 1/60 second and the actual exposure were slightly shorter, a flash would not fire.

The shutter speed scale in the finder carries three further indications:

(a) The +/− markings for manual metering (see above)—of no significance with automatic metering.

(b) A red field above the '1000' mark. If the needle is in this red area, you have reached the shutter speed limit and the light may be too bright even for the fastest speed, leading to overexposure. So select a smaller lens aperture to bring the needle back into the number range of the scale.

(c) A blue field at the bottom of the scale labelled AUTO. If the needle is in this area, the camera automatically selects an exposure time longer than 1 second—it can under certain circumstances run into minutes.

The shutter speed monitoring system with finder indication is based on the CdS cells measuring the image brightness on the viewing/focusing screen, as with manual metering (see above). The manual CdS and automatic SBC are completely separate indicating and measuring systems that happen to be calibrated to show and to produce the same exposure. But they operate with different circuits and at different times. The CdS system measures screen brightness at the full lens aperture before you take the picture. The SBC system measures and controls the exposure at the working aperture (once the mirror has swung up, the lens is also stopped down to its preselected stop) and it does so while you take the picture.

Further, the two systems can be switched on and off independently. With the meter switch set to MANUAL you have only the CdS system in action; the SBC metering circuits are switched off. With the meter switch at AUTO, the SBC metering circuit is switched on and the CdS cell circuit is also switched on for shutter speed monitoring. Finally, with the meter switch set to OFF, the CdS circuit is out of action—hence the meter needle cannot operate—but the SBC circuits are operative. They come into action as soon as the mirror flies up during an exposure cycle.

So the only operating differences between the AUTO and OFF positions of the meter switch are that in the OFF position you have no shutter speed monitoring in the finder and the longest exposure that the shutter can give is limited to 1 second or less. (See *OM-2 metering range*, below.)

If you feel sure that the exposure time is likely to be shorter than 1/30 second and you are not interested in what it is, you can shoot with correct exposures even when the meter switch is OFF. But it is better to have the extra information by switching to AUTO.

OM-2 metering range

The lowest subject lighting level that the OM-2 can measure depends on the amount of light the lens lets through. It is thus lower with the faster lenses which can at full aperture utilise more of the available subject lighting. With the *f* 1.2 standard lens the metering limit—thanks to the extreme sensitivity of the silicon cells—is as little as 0.003 candela per sq. metre (cd/m^2)—equivalent to very weak candle light indeed. With a medium-speed colour film of say 64 to 100 ASA this is equivalent to an exposure of around 80 seconds at *f* 1.2 and on automatic operation the shutter of the Olympus OM-2 would indeed stay open for this time. In fact, the exposure would be inaccurate because reciprocity failure becomes very prominent at these low light levels (see below).

With the *f* 1.8 standard lens the low-light limit is 0.008 cd/m^2—i.e. again over a minute with medium speed colour film.

The longest exposure time that the OM-2 can yield on automatic operation basically depends on the film speed setting—as modified by the exposure compensation dial where applicable. At 100 ASA Olympus quote a long-exposure limit of about 60 seconds. At 12 ASA this runs up to 8 minutes, and at the other end—1600 ASA—it drops to about 4 seconds. These are approximate values and are controlled not so much by the low-light reading ability of the silicon cells as by limiting circuitry built into the camera electronics. Without such a limit you could otherwise drain the batteries very fast if you carry the camera with the lens cap on the lens and accidentally release the shutter—or if you try to make an automatic long exposure in light conditions where automatic exposure becomes completely meaningless. The shutter draws battery current all the time it is open.

The exact cut-off is to some extent determined by tolerances in the electronic circuit and may thus not be the same on all OM-2 cameras. Further it depends also on the battery voltage: it tends to become shorter as the battery nears exhaustion (rapid flashing of the LED when you test the battery).

With the meter switch at OFF, the cut-off limit of the longest exposure time is greatly reduced—mainly to prevent battery drain should you accidentally press the release button while carrying the camera—for instance with its lens in place. This cut-off point again depends on the film speed setting: it is 1 second with 12 ASA and drops to 1/125 second at 1600 ASA.

At the other extreme the maximum brightness (luminance level) of the subject that you can measure is limited only by the fastest shutter speed available. This limit is imposed by the shutter—the cells themselves can react still faster, as they do with electronic flash. The practical top measuring limit is thus a lighting level that needs 1/1000 second with the smallest lens aperture and slowest film. With the standard and wide-angle lenses stopping down to *f* 16 the limit with 12 ASA setting is an astronomical 256,000 cd/m^2. In fact the highest reflected light intensity of a subject lit anywhere in the world by brilliant sunlight is about 16,000 cd/m^2. This is also the top measuring limit with 200 ASA film. At still higher film speed settings the upper limit drops further, for instance to 2000 cd/m^2 at 1600 ASA. What this means in practice is that with the OM-2 you simply could not avoid overexposure if you wanted to photograph a brighter subject with a film of that speed. But then few people use extreme speed films for extremely bright subject conditions.

OM-1 metering range and manual OM-2 range

The measuring range here is limited on the one hand by the aperture/speed combinations at the lowest and highest exposure levels—1 second at *f* 1.2 and 1/1000 second at *f* 16 with the *f* 1.2 standard lens—and the film speed setting. The shutter cannot expose the film for longer than 1 second and the reading on the viewing screen image takes place at the full lens aperture (and not at the working aperture as in the case of automatic operation). Hence the maximum range is more restricted.

The lower limit with the standard $f1.2$ lens is about 0.36 cd/m² and with the $f1.4$ lens it is 0.5 cd/m². The upper limit is about 16,000 cd/m² for a lens stopping down to $f16$. The metering range further depends on the film speed; the above figures are valid for medium-speed films. With the slowest speed setting of 12 ASA on the OM-2 a lighting level of 0.36 cd/m² would require an exposure of 4 seconds. As the shutter can only go to 1 second, the effective lower metering limit is in this case 1.44 cd/m². You can utilise the full sensitivity only at film speed settings from 50 ASA up. (The same applies to lenses of lower maximum aperture since the lowest measurable lighting level also increases with decreasing lens speed.)

At the other end of the range the 16,000 cd/m² limit applies also to the slowest films since stopping down the lens does not reduce the amount of light reaching the CdS cells via the viewing screen during the actual reading. But at high film speed settings the top limit again comes down for the same reasons as described before with automatic operation.

Weighting the reading

The photocells—CdS above the screen or SBC in front of the shutter or film plane—measure the average light from these areas. Such readings yield reliable exposures if the subject contains its bright and dark parts reasonably evenly distributed in relative areas and in importance. Surprisingly, that is the case with about 90% of the subjects you normally photograph. The main problems arising with the other 10% are situations where less important subject parts contribute excessively to a misleading light reading: a prominent brilliant sky area that makes the overall reading too high and so leads to underexposure of the foreground detail that you are really interested in; bright subjects against large dark background areas or vice versa where the surroundings similarly falsify the exposure for the significant parts, and so on.

To overcome such problems, the photocells are so

arranged that they preferentially measure an approximately central portion of less than one-quarter of the subject field. This area then contributes more than half to the light-reading meter cell output. On early OM-2 models a centrally emphasised checkerboard pattern of the first shutter blind aided this selective or weighted measurement.

On current OM-2 models the measuring angle of the silicon cells provides this selectivity all the time and the shutter blind pattern is uniform.

The OM metering system is thus centre-weighted. Strictly speaking, the weighting area extends vertically from a little above the centre of the screen to nearly the bottom, and horizontally from over half the image width near the centre to virtually nothing at the bottom—broadly a rounded triangular shape. The centre weighting especially excludes the effect of brilliant sky in the upper half of the picture and also subdues the effect of variable background brightness surrounding a main subject assumed to be more or less centred in the field.

Exposure compensation

With some non-standard subject conditions incorrect meter readings can be allowed for by a corresponding exposure compensation—i.e. giving more or less exposure than the meter indicates or the automatic OM-2 control provides. This is particularly important with automatic exposures and the OM-2 has an exposure compensating or override dial as part of the ASA film speed setting dial for such corrections. This carries a thick white line extending from the ASA window to the opposite edge of the dial. When that line appears horizontal, i.e. lined up with an index line on the side of the OM-2 pentaprism housing, the meter is set for normal exposures. The meter system gives or indicates (for monitoring or in manual mode) the right exposure according to the average meter calibration.

Turning the dial in either direction modifies this exposure according to the indications on the dial. Thus if you turn the +1 mark to the index on the pentaprism housing, the meter system in effect gives or shows one stop more exposure than would be correct for a calibrated average reading. In automatic mode this means that the exposure time is doubled. Similarly at the −1 setting the exposure given is reduced by one stop or the exposure time halved. The dial settings extend up to +2 and −2 and the dial clicks into position at $\frac{1}{3}$ stop intervals, shown by small index marks without numbering.

The OM-1 has no separate exposure compensation setting, but you could obtain the same result by temporarily changing the ASA speed dial setting—e.g. halve the ASA setting for +1 stop overexposure and so on. In practice, it is more convenient to line up the meter needle with the $\frac{1}{2}$ stop or 1 stop over or underexposure marks rather than reset the ASA speed. If you do change the film speed setting or use the exposure compensation settings on the OM-2 remember to reset the dial. With the OM-2 dial the very prominent compensation markings are a ready reminder; with the OM-1 there is more risk of forgetting.

Override limits

When the film speed dial is set to 1600 ASA, you obviously cannot compensate by −1 stop through a dial adjustment as there is no faster settable speed. Similarly, no overexposure compensation is possible at the slowest film speed setting.

Corresponding limitations apply to the available settings of the OM-2 exposure compensating dial. Thus at 12 ASA there is no + compensation at all, at 25 ASA the maximum overexposure is +1 stop and you can utilise +2 stops only from 50 ASA onwards. Similarly the minus override begins to be limited above 400 ASA: you can only go to −1 at 800 ASA and there is no correction at 1600 ASA.

Never try to force the exposure compensation dial past such a limit.

Although not marked on the dial, the compensation at film speeds above 50 ASA extends beyond the +2 limit: at 100 ASA and above you can set up to +3 stops overexposure (3 clicks of the dial beyond the +2 setting). Similarly at film speeds lower than 400 ASA you can set more than −2 stops underexposure—up to −3 stops at 200 ASA and below.

In practice however you would rarely need that amount of exposure compensation.

Allowing for lenses

Through-the-lens metering means that exposure measurement and control is based on the image formed by the lens and so automatically allows for any peculiarities of light transmission, exposure factors etc. In a few cases however the exposure reading on the screen is unreliable or even impossible, though automatic exposures with the OM-2 are largely unaffected. Here is a run-down:

The 8 mm fisheye lens leaves the screen dark outside a central 23 mm circle—you don't see the meter needle for manual exposure settings or monitoring. If you are confident that the light is good enough for a reasonably fast shake-free shutter speed with the OM-2, just go ahead—the SBC reading is sufficiently centre weighted not to be significantly affected by the external dark area for negative films. With reversal film decrease the exposure by one-third of a stop.

With the OM-1 the only way of getting an exposure indication is to measure the screen with the standard lens on the camera, set the exposure, then switch to the fisheye. This applies irrespective of the focusing screen used.

With the 35 mm Zuiko Shift lens exposure measurement takes place at the working aperture, so remember to stop down the lens by the manual stop-down key both for metering and for the exposure. While automatic exposures with the OM-2 are accurate, the screen measurement is subject to an error when the lens is shifted. The error varies according to the shift and the aperture and is due to a combination of vignetting and off-centering of the lens axis. The best way of allowing for this is to take the reading—at the working aperture—with the lens centred, then increase the exposure by half to one stop. (When you need one stop more with extreme shift, select the next slower shutter speed rather than a larger aperture which could re-introduce vignetting.)

Other lenses: The centre weighting in the measurement tends to ignore light fall-off at the edges of ultrawide-angle lenses. Increase the exposure if edge shadow detail is important: by half a stop with the 24 mm lens or by one stop with the 21 or 18 mm lenses. The slight vignetting with tele lenses and in macrophotography (darkening at the top of the screen) is too small to have any effect on the centre-weighted meter readings.

Allowing for focusing screens

In measuring screen brightness, the CdS circuits of the OM cameras allow for a standard focusing screen light transmission. The indicated exposure is correct for all screens with a normal surface over most of their area. The other screens need an exposure correction with manual exposure readings, but not of course with automatic control on the OM-2 where the screen image is not involved. The following corrections apply:

Fine grain matted screens (1–8 and 1–11) transmit slightly more light and so indicate less exposure than the subject needs. Here give one-third to half a stop more.

Clear screens, i.e. without a matted area (1–5, 1–6, 1–7, 1–9), do not yield a correct meter indication and cannot be used for manual through-the-lens metering. (Correction factors could be worked out, but depend on so many variables that they are quite impractical in use.)

The clear 1–12 screen can be used with a special metering technique in macrophotography and photomicrography (see Chapt. *Close-up and macro technique*).

Beware of stray light

The screen is primarily illuminated by the image from the lens, but in certain conditions can receive light through the eyepiece that also affects the CdS cells. A manual measurement or the monitoring of the OM-2 then indicates too short an exposure.

This is most likely to arise when you have strong light behind you or from the side and do not have the eye close enough to the eyepiece. Stray light can also be reflected from spectacles. The effect is greatest when the subject is comparatively dark but the camera position well lit—for instance indoors when you are near the window shooting into the room. To avoid possible misreadings, measure with the eye as close to the eyepiece as possible. Use the eyecup if you don't wear spectacles.

In practice the deviation due to stray light rarely exceeds $\frac{1}{2}$ stop. For pre-shot monitoring on the OM-2 screen in the automatic mode this is irrelevant and it is not too serious in most normal cases. The error may become greater with readings where the camera is mounted on a tripod—there it is often less convenient to get the eye really close to the eyepiece. The remedy is to shield the eye and eyepiece with a hand cupped over the top of the camera.

Long time exposures with the OM-2

In automatic mode the electronic shutter of the OM-2 can yield exposures up to about 60 seconds. With subjects requiring such long times—for instance outdoor views at night, floodlit buildings, interiors in dark churches etc. —the meter exposure may not necessarily be the best for the subject. This is because of reciprocity failure on the one hand (see below) and misleading readings (bright light sources) on the other; hence manual long time exposures may be desirable.

For such exposures set the shutter to B and the meter switch to MANUAL, mount the camera on a tripod or firm support and release with a cable release screwed into the shutter release button. Pressing the release then opens the shutter and keeps it open until you let go.

The shutter drains the battery current as during any other exposure even at the B setting. But the B setting can also operate without batteries. So if you expect to take many long time exposures in this way, you can remove the batteries first.

Do not make manual long time exposures on B with the meter switch set to AUTO. In this case, with very dim subjects, the shutter may remain open after you have let go of the release since the metering circuit of the SBC cells overrides the B function even though the visual indication of the CdS cell circuit is inoperative. The shutter can in this case be closed only by switching the meter off (turning the meter switch away from AUTO).

However, at the B setting the mirror will not lock up even if the batteries are exhausted.

Long time exposures with the OM-1

The longest exposure time of the OM-1 is 1 second and for anything longer a time exposure must be used with the shutter set to B. On the OM-1 the shutter speed ring can be turned to B without operation of any reset lock.

The procedure is the same as for manual time exposures with the OM-2 (camera mounted on tripod, shutter released by cable release—with lock if for long time exposures) and the meter switch remains at OFF. Even if you have set it to ON, the current consumption at such low lighting levels is negligible. But the battery on this camera is not involved in shutter operation, anyway.

Reciprocity failure

Exposures using aperture/speed combinations with long exposure times tend to yield underexposed pictures. In the normal exposure range between 1 and 1/1000 second, each increase of the exposure time by one step is equivalent in its action on the film to a reduction by one lens stop of the light coming through the lens. This reciprocal relationship between aperture and exposure time breaks down with longer times and the exposure must be increased beyond the time indicated by the meter reading. The film behaves as if it had lost speed. With colour films you may also get a shift in colour balance.

The leading film manufacturers have investigated the reciprocity behaviour of their own films and have released data. If you use a selected range of such films, find out the respective reciprocity characteristics by asking the makers. Then apply an appropriate exposure compensation—up to three stops extra on the OM-2 by operation of the exposure compensation dial, or by assuming a correspondingly lower film speed when working with the OM-1. A reciprocity failure table (see Chpt. *Facts and figures*) lists more general corrections. With colour films appropriate colour correction filters may also be needed—these are again specified by the film manufacturer.

Subject factors

The automatic exposure control can do no more than measure light intensity and light quantity with the assumption that this reasonably reflects the brightness characteristics of the scene. Some subjects can fool the meter system. We have to allow for that with the compensation dial (automatic operation) or by lining up the needle with an under or over marking (manual) instead of dead centre.

Snow, light sand and other predominantly light subjects are seen as medium tone subjects, leading to underexposure. Give about one stop more exposure.

Large sky areas with little foreground similarly need half to one stop more exposure—but not if the sky is limited to the upper third screen area, where centre weighting takes care of it.

Dark subjects against a light background where you want the subject correctly exposed—for instance people against the sky, whitewashed walls, snow etc.—need no allowance if the main subject fills more than the central quarter of the image area. Allow half to one stop extra if a dark subject is very small in a light background or near the picture edge.

Alternatively, go near the subject so that it fills the finder view (or zoom in with a zoom lens), take a manual reading, go back to the original view and set the values obtained for the exposure.

Strong side and back lighting creates high image contrast which with a normal exposure yields too dark shadows. Give one to two stops extra exposure with negative-positive materials (black-and-white or colour) but not with reversal colour (slide) materials.

For light subjects against large dark backgrounds, for instance a sunlit figure in a dark doorway, decrease the exposure by half to one stop, depending on relative size of subject and background area. (The background modifies the subject reading, leading to overexposure.) This also includes spotlit subjects at night, theatre and stage photography etc. Ignore the correction if the subject covers more than the central quarter of the picture area. Alternatively, take close-up readings as with dark subjects against light background, above.

Sunsets, brilliant highlights and similar scenes where you want the *brightest parts correct* also need less than normal exposure to avoid highlight overexposure. So give half to two stops less, especially with small brilliant highlights. The same goes for backlit scenes where you want the halo rim effect rather than shadow detail.

If in sunsets, night scenes and other dark subjects the *shadows are important*, give half to two stops more, depending on whether the light spots are the centre of the view (greatest correction) or near the edges.

Outdoor scenes in dull flat lighting—mist, fog, dull weather views etc.—record fairly dark on colour slide and other reversal films. For a brighter and more ethereal effect increase the exposure by one stop. Do not use this correction for negative-positive materials.

Predominantly dark and low-key subjects where you want shadows to remain dark, need half to one stop less exposure.

Telephoto landscapes with long tele lenses tend to be overexposed in colour transparencies due to atmospheric light scatter. If there is no significant sky area, give half to one stop less exposure. No correction is needed if the sky occupies up to half the picture area; if more than half, give half to one stop more exposure.

Aim at getting exposures as nearly correct as possible. In the beginning, when you use the above compensations, it helps to keep notes on when you have compensated the meter reading. Then check against the pictures to see how nearly correct you were—you will know better next time. If in doubt, allow up to half a stop more exposure with negative films (colour or black and white) and up to half a stop less with colour slide film.

LENS HANDLING AND TECHNIQUES

The first step of almost any camera—especially a single-lens reflex—towards becoming a camera system is the use of interchangeable lenses. Lens interchangeability provides multiple options of:

(a) Recording an image of a subject at a given distance at different scales on the film;

(b) Recording different amounts of a view from a given viewpoint;

(c) Controlling perspective effects by interaction of (a) and (b);

(d) Lenses of more modest and more extreme speeds for different compromises of poor-light versatility and portability;

(e) Special optical systems for specific applications.

The Olympus OM system comprises some 30-odd different lenses to cover all the above applications.

Lenses are often broadly grouped by their functional focal length as far as that deviates from the standard focal length—i.e. the 50 or 55 mm lenses. In the most generalised terms there are wide-angle lenses on the one hand and long-focus or tele lenses on the other—quite apart from the zoom lenses of variable focal length (with further subdivision into normal and tele zoom) and the special optical systems such as macro lenses.

A wide-angle lens is one that covers on the film a wider angle of view than a standard lens—in the Olympus range focal lengths from 35 mm downwards. You can subdivide further into ultrawide-angle, fisheye etc. A wide-angle lens has to be designed for wide-angle coverage; a short focal length is not enough. For instance the 20 and 38 mm macro lenses are short-focus units but cover only a narrow angle of view.

The nomenclature is a little confused nowadays with long-focus and tele lenses. Strictly speaking a long-focus lens is any lens of a focal length longer than the standard

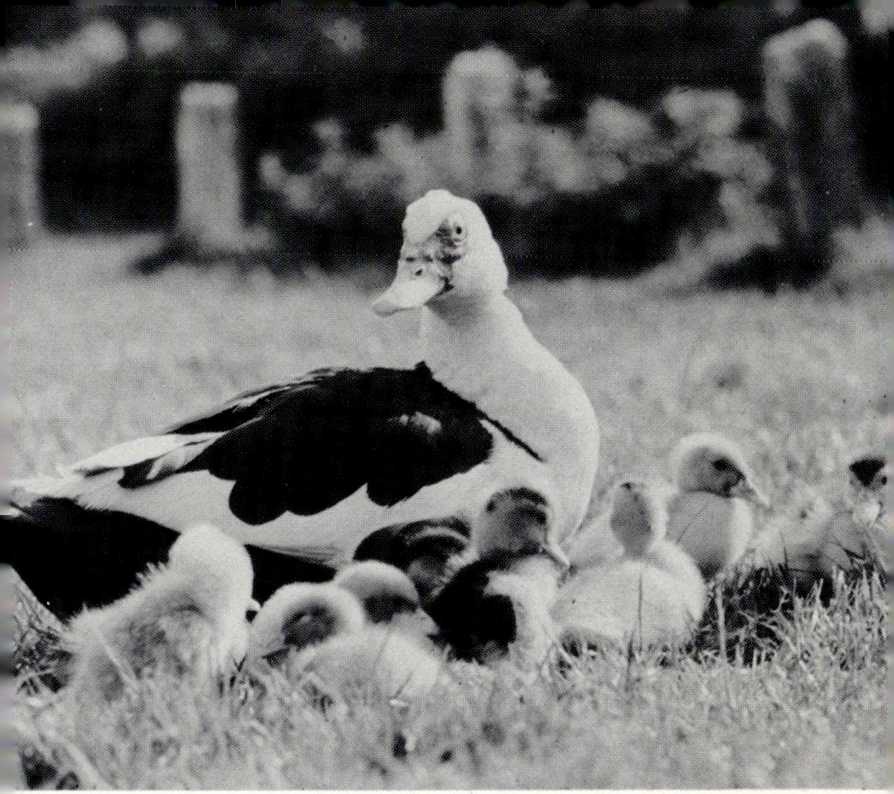

GETTING IN RANGE
Above. With the 200 mm lens the camera was within range before the feathered family got too startled. The restricted depth of field isolates the group from the background.

SPECTATOR
Plate 2. He is actually an Ethiopian football supporter but the outfit has more to do with tradition than with the battles on the sidelines. With the 300 mm lens the photographer can stand well back from the melee.

JAWS
Plate 3. A 35 mm lens was needed to cover this monster model. The two youngsters confirm the enormous size.

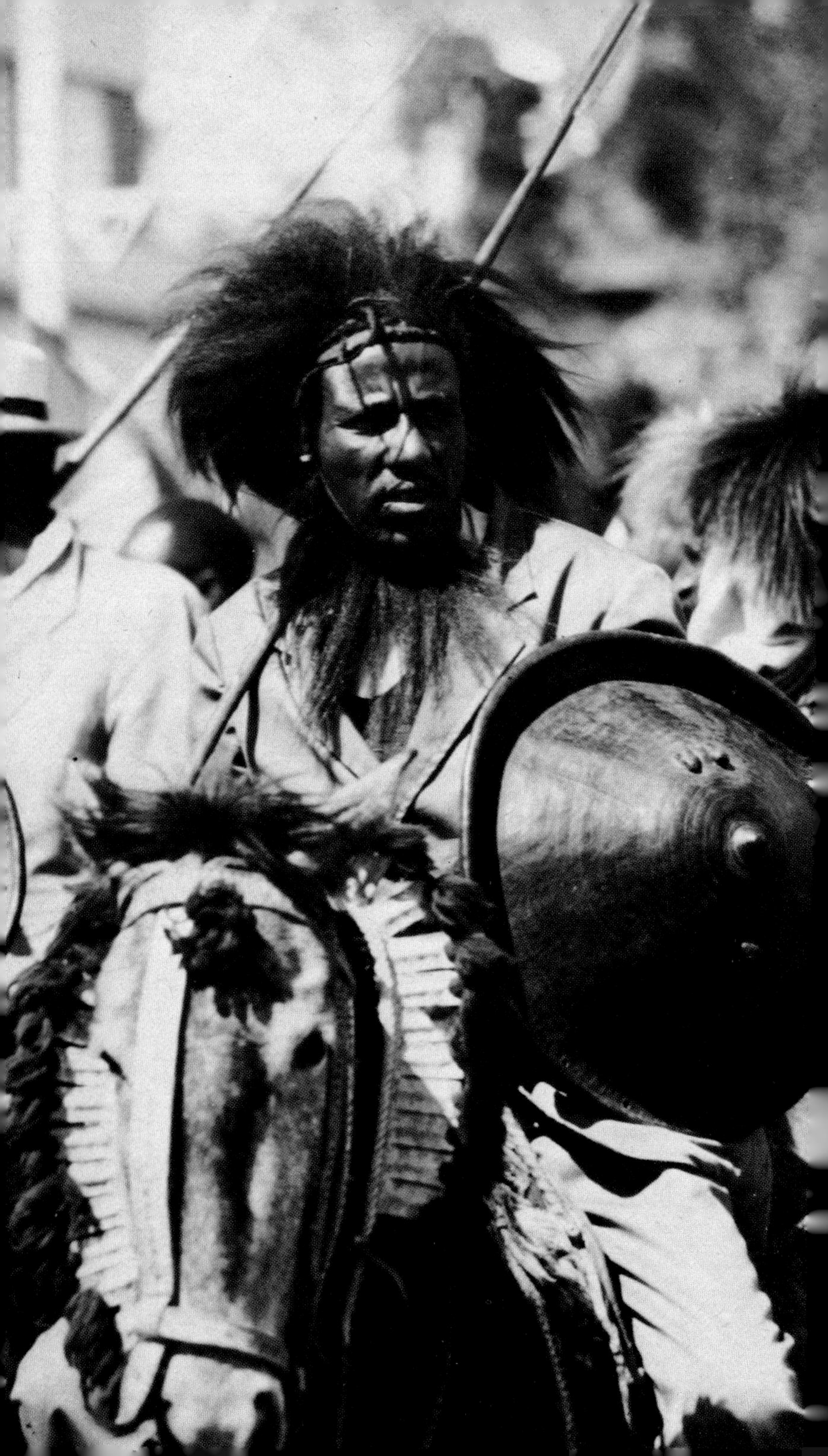

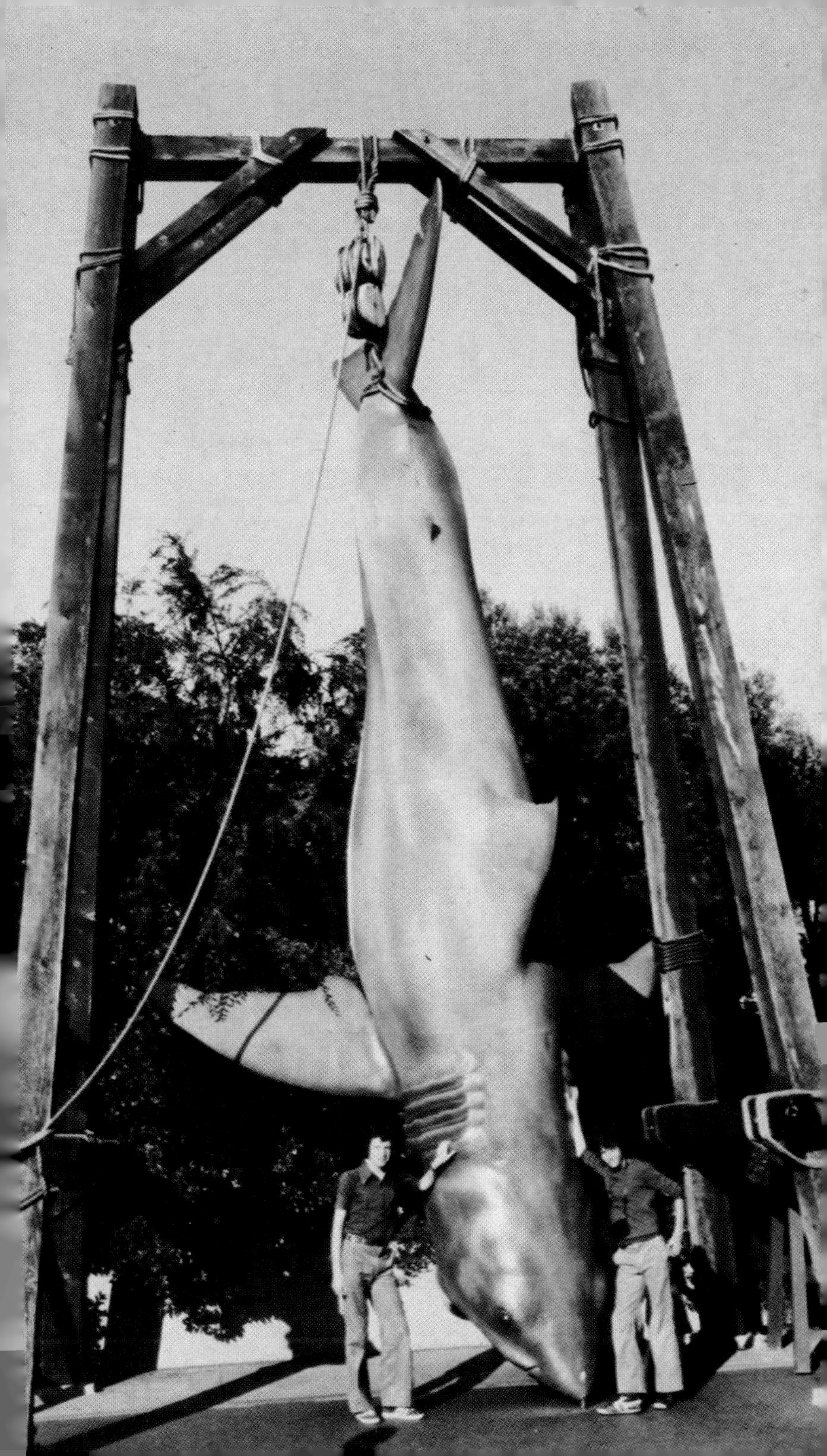

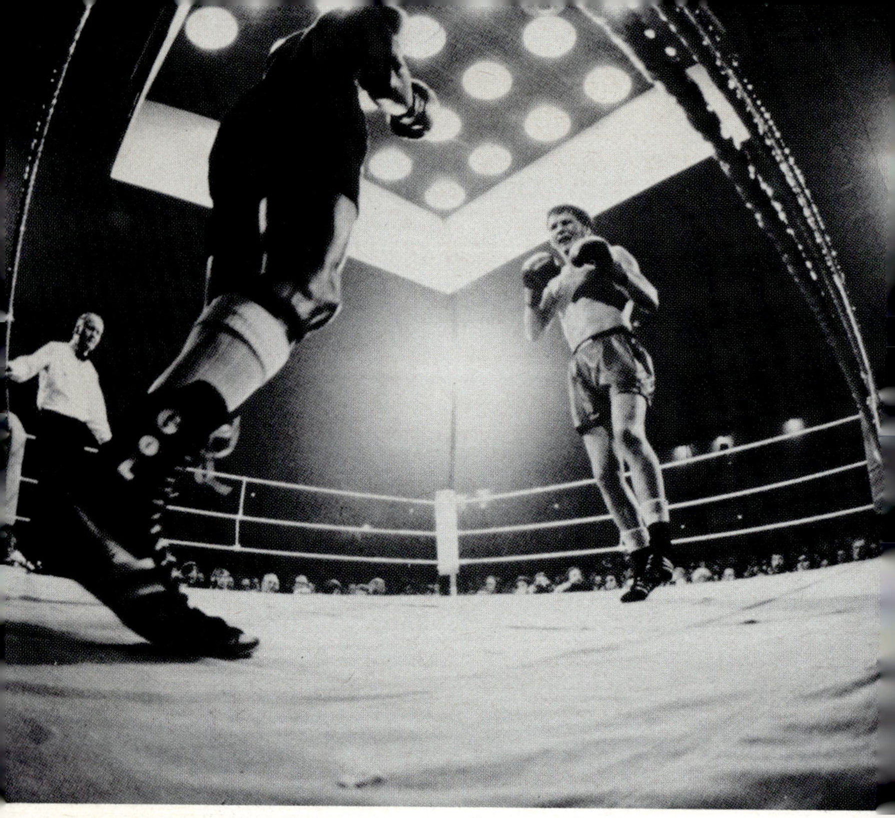

BOXERS FROM BELOW
If you have ever felt like seeing a boxing ring as a fish tank, the 17 mm fisheye lens completes the association of ideas, enhanced by the enclosing curves.

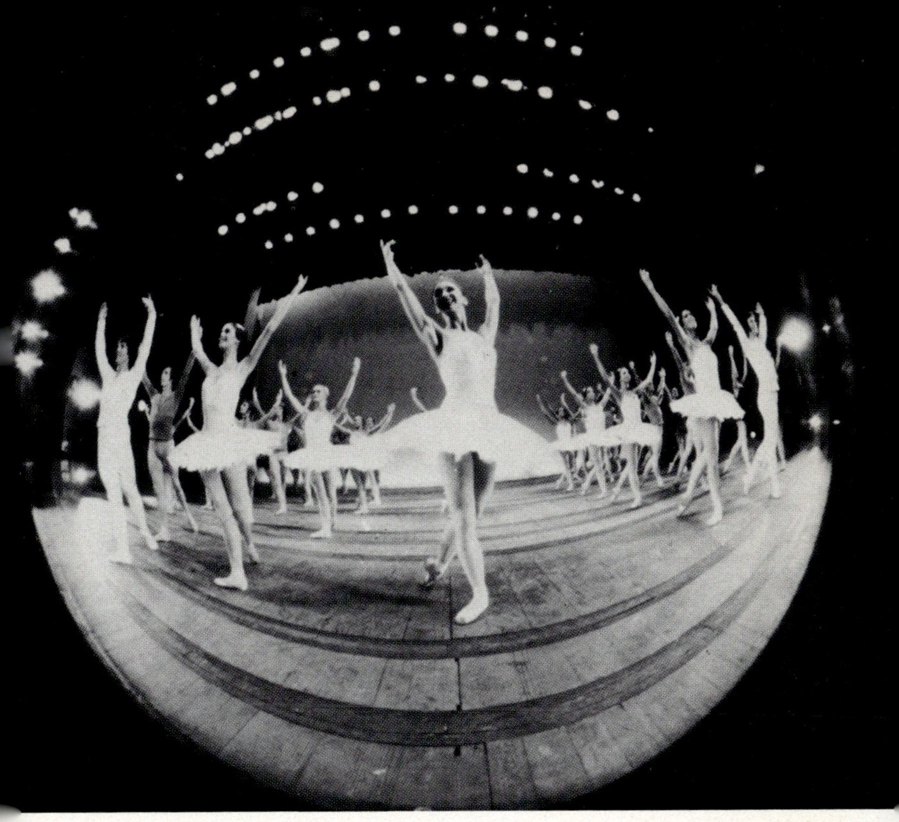

BALLET IN THE ROUND
With the 8 mm fisheye the stage seems enclosed in a crystal ball. The circular image enhances the pattern of the dance—*John Starr*.

THE CAPITOL
Plate 6. Winter backlighting can fool the exposure control and you may need a +1 stop override. This 24 mm shot used the OM-2 automatic exposure system without compensation.

Plate 7. Back in London the OM-2 auto exposure control can still cope with such a night view, taken with a fast 50 mm lens. But as the exposure may run into one or two seconds, support the camera firmly.

TREES
Plate 8. Backlit against the snow, trees and shadows form complex patterns—captured here with a 24 mm lens. This also is on automatic OM-2 exposure.

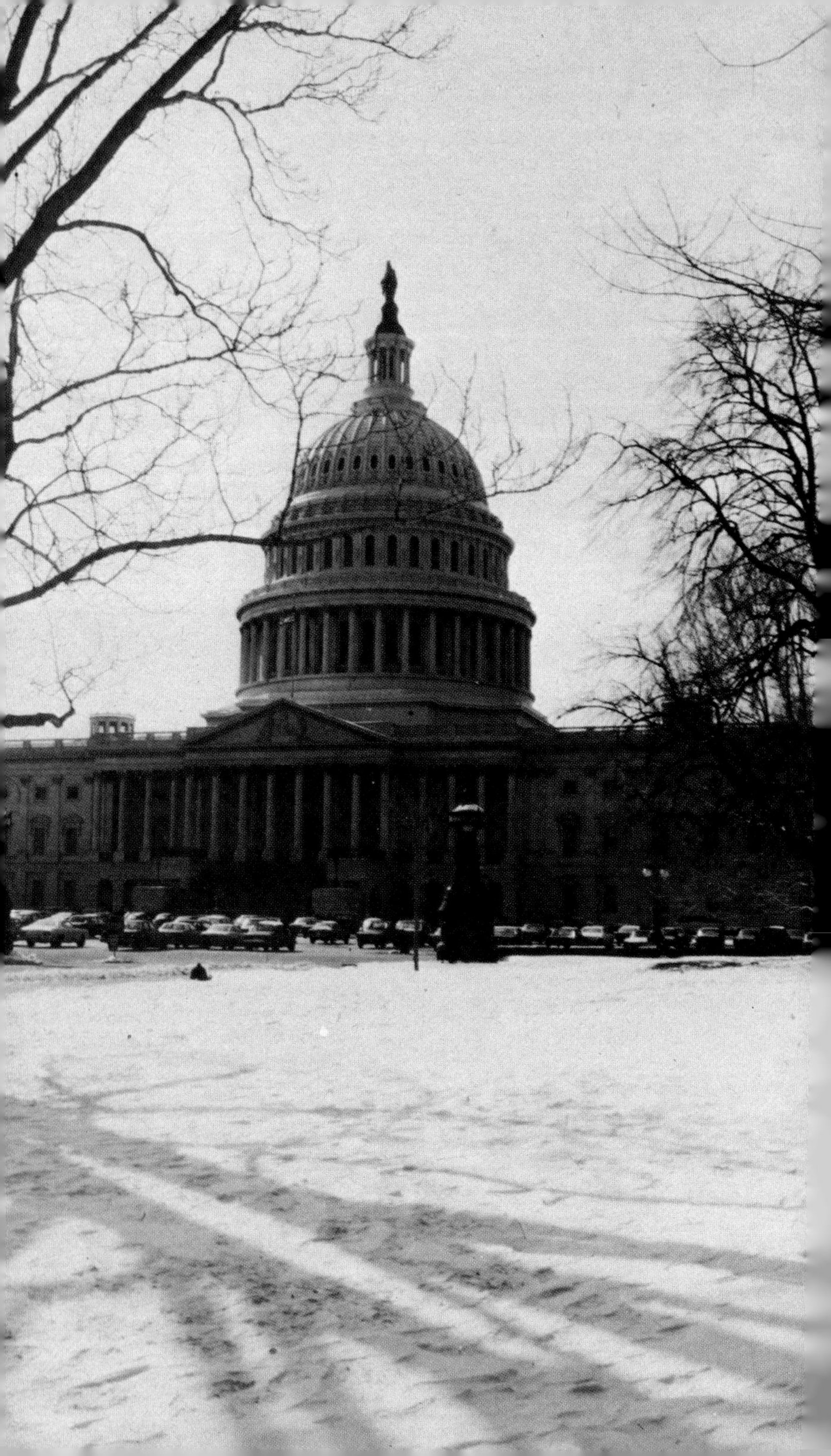

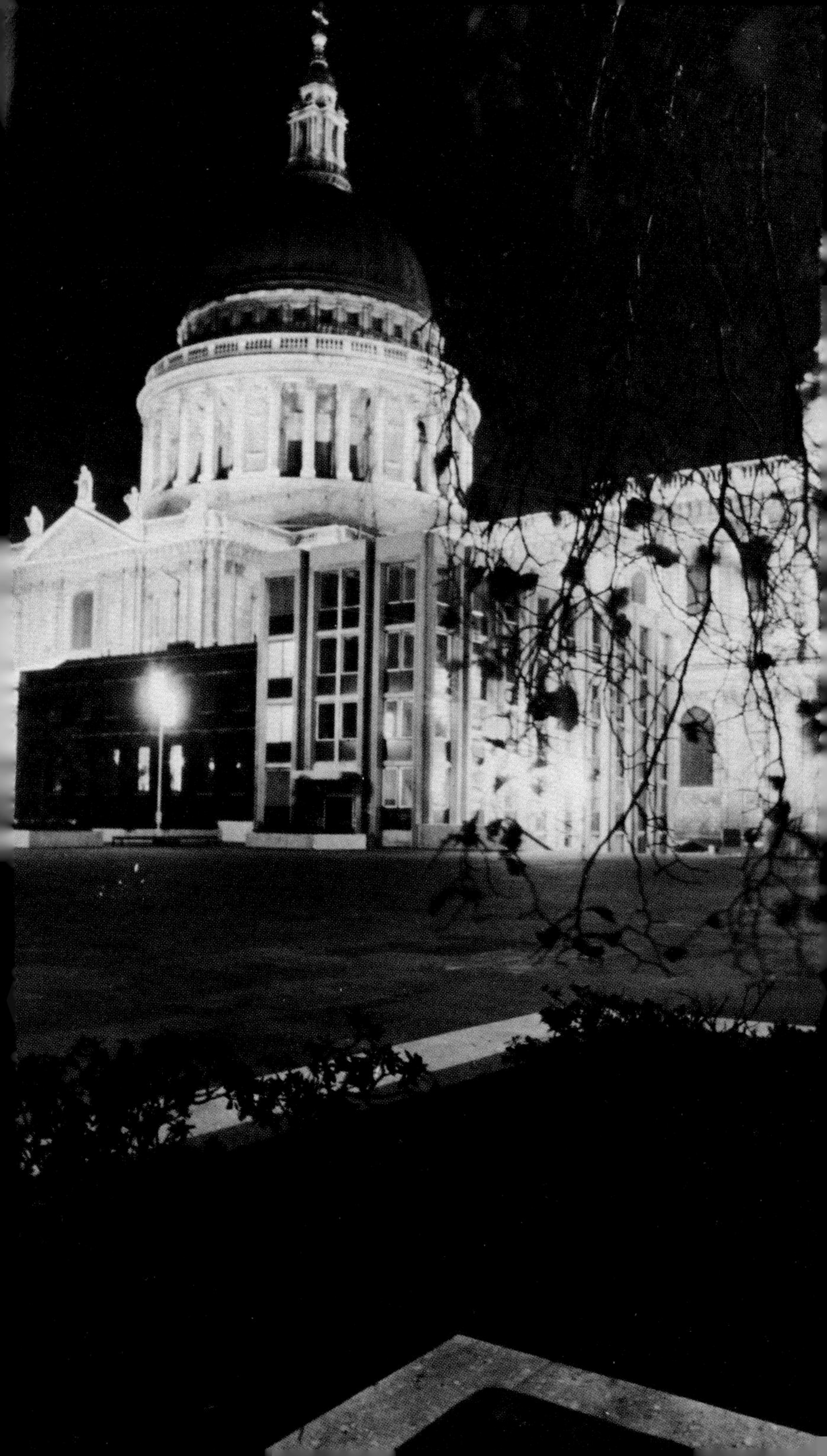

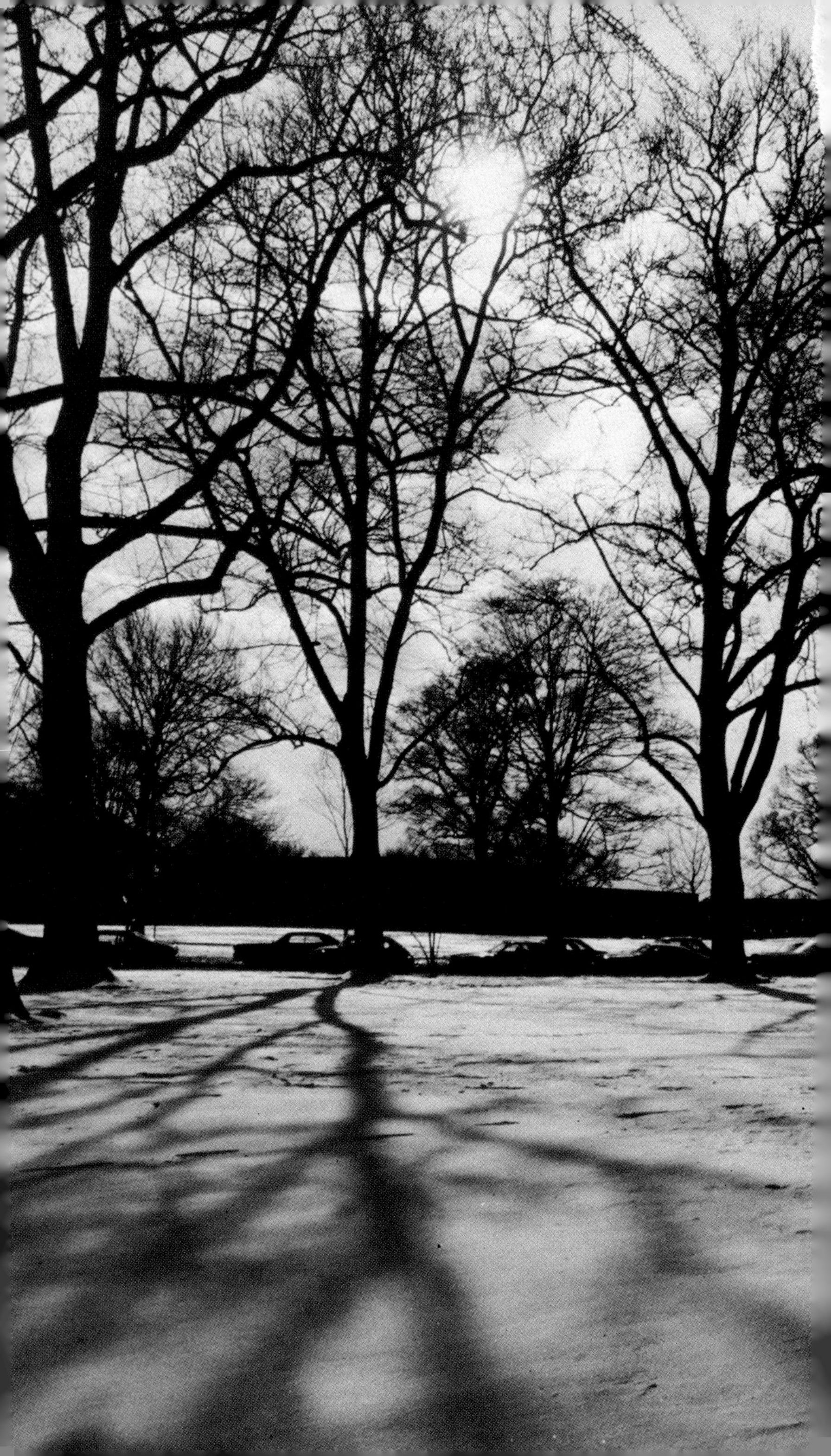

(50 or 55 mm) system. So that covers everything up to 1000 mm. By certain tricks of optical design such lenses can be made shorter in physical length than in focal length; they are then known as telephoto lenses. From that has come the imprecise habit of calling all long-focus lenses tele lenses (T designation in the Olympus range). To save hair splitting, we will stick to that in this book irrespective of whether the lens is a true telephoto construction or not. The difference for general photography is only in handling convenience and not in the appearance or geometry of the image on the film.

Normal lens controls

To maintain system consistency, the manipulative details and layout of controls is fairly similar for most OM lenses. So let us look at the features of a typical lens.

From front to back, the lenses usually have:

(a) A front screw mount to take screw-in filters and—with some lenses—a screw-in lens hood. Lens hoods may screw in or clip on; tele lenses from about 135 mm onwards have a built-in extending hood.

(b) The aperture preselecting ring. This carries a scale of white aperture figures and the ring engages in click stops when any one of the aperture figures is opposite a white index mark just in front of the ring. The click stops are full *f*-stop values apart—to select an intermediate aperture you have to set the ring between two clicks. This adjustment only preselects the aperture that will be used during the exposure; the lens remains fully open during viewing and focusing. The diaphragm may be stopped down manually by the stop-down (preview) key or by the camera mechanism during the release/exposure cycle.

Nearly all Olympus OM lenses, including the long tele lenses, have this auto-aperture coupling feature.

The aperture ring also carries engraved in green the nominal focal length of the lens in mm. (Actual focal lengths vary slightly but are within ± 4% of the nominal value.)

(c) The focusing ring. Rotating this ring adjusts the distance setting of the lens, usually by moving the whole lens in and out of its mounting. Generally the amount of physical movement in and out is greater the longer the

focal length. (The near-focusing macro lens is an exception.) The focusing ring is covered with a coarsely textured (diamond pattern) rubber band to provide an easier grip during operation. It also helps you to tell by touch when you are holding the focusing ring.

(d) The distance scale. The focusing mount also carries two sets of distance figures in metres and in feet, engraved in white and in orange (really a light orange-yellow) respectively. When you have sharply focused the image, the distance figure opposite the red distance setting index (see below) indicates the approximate distance of the object on which you have focused. Conversely, if for any reason it is not convenient to focus on the reflex screen, you can set the lens to the estimated subject distance to be sure of sharp pictures.

The white distance scale also includes an infinity mark (∞), indicating a setting for 'infinitely far' subjects. In practice that means anything more distant than 1000 times the focal length of the lens. With a 50 mm lens, for example, everything beyond about 50 metres counts as infinity.

(e) The distance index and depth of field scale. Usually the rearmost ring of the lens carries a red line ending in a red dot, and a series of black lines with aperture numbers to each side. The red line and dot is the distance setting index against which you read distances on the scale of the focusing mount. The red dot is also a locating mark when fitting the lens on the camera (see below, *Lens changing*).

(f) The depth of field indicator is the set of black index lines spaced to each side of the red distance index. The lines carry aperture numbers (e.g. 4, 8, 16 for *f*4, *f*8, *f*16) and indicate the depth of the sharp zone against the distance scale for different distance settings. Usually there are only three depth indexes so as not to clutter up the scale; estimate intermediate positions.

(g) The infrared focusing index. Generally one of the right-hand index lines of the depth of field scale is engraved in red, or there may be a red dot between two black index lines. This is the infrared focusing index.

(h) The lens release key is the small serrated chrome key to the left of the depth of field scale. It unlocks the bayonet mounting of the lens for removing it from the camera.

LENS CONTROLS

Operating controls and features of a typical lens:

1. Aperture index.
2. Filter thread.
3. Filter (screws into filter thread 2).
4. Aperture scale, with green focal length value.
5. Focusing mount.
6. Distance scale (usually in feet and metres, engraved yellow and white respectively).
7. Focusing index, surrounded by depth of field scale.
8. Clip-on lens hood, fits over lens rim (some hoods screw into filter thread 2).
9. Lens release catch.
10. Infrared focusing index.
11. Rear lens cap.
12. Stop-down control lever.
13. Aperture simulator lever for aperture input.
14. Depth of field preview key.

The control layout is similar on longer-focus lenses, though the focusing mount may be wider and the extension greater. Some longer-focus lenses also have a built-in extending lens hood *(right)*.

For infrared focusing note the distance opposite the normal focusing index *(left)*, then turn the focusing ring to set that distance opposite the infrared index *(right)*.

To remove a lens, press the lens release catch, turn the lens anti-clockwise on the camera *(left)* and lift off. To fit a lens *(right)* line up the red dot with the red dot on the camera mount, push the lens in position and turn clockwise to lock.

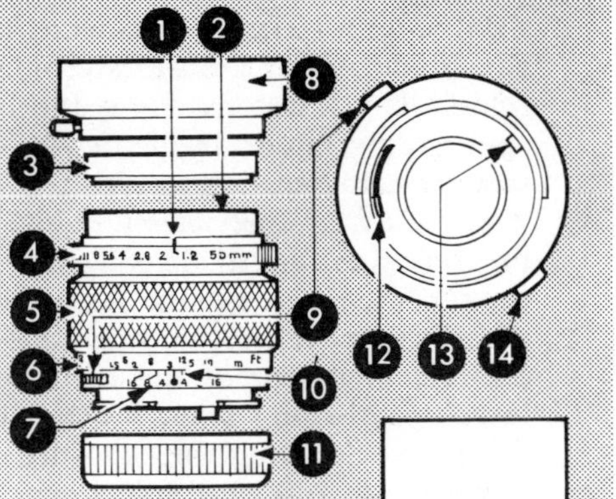

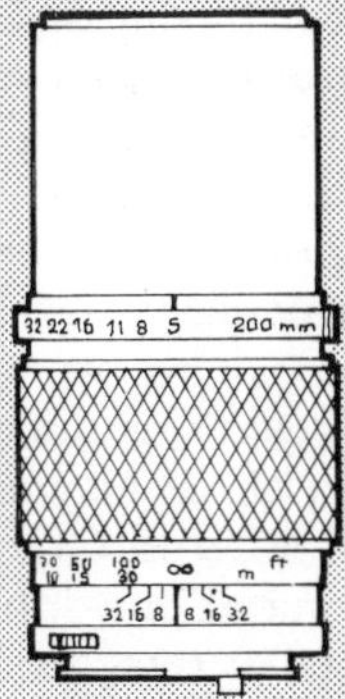

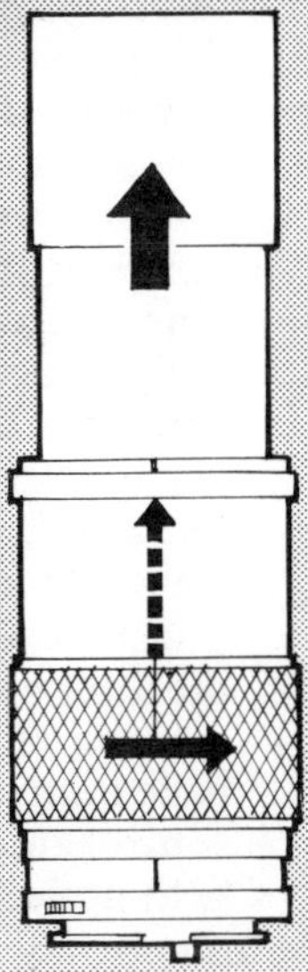

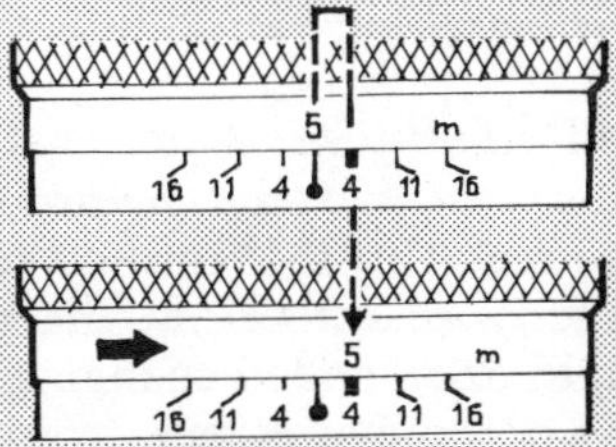

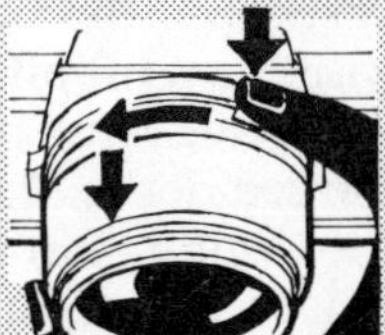

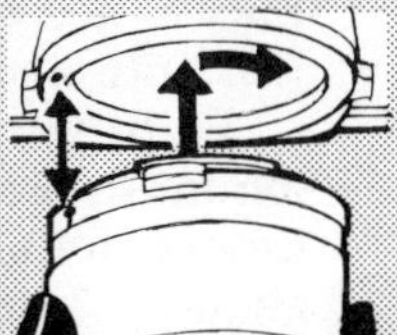

(j) The preview or stop-down key is a smooth chrome key in the same ring, located almost opposite the lens release key. It stops down the lens to the preselected aperture for checking the depth of field on the camera's viewing and focusing screen.

(k) The bayonet mount. This 3-claw bayonet fitting protrudes behind the lens flange—i.e. the rear surface of the chrome ring carrying the red dot and lens release key. The bayonet mount engages the bayonet fitting on the camera. The rear of the mount also carries two more levers protruding from it. One is the automatic stop-down lever: during the exposure an internal lever in the camera side hits this stop-down lever to stop the lens down to the preselected aperture. (You can see the stop-down lever move if you look at the back of the lens—removed from the camera—and press the preview key.) The second is the meter coupling lever which rotates as you turn the aperture ring. This feeds information into the camera's exposure meter of the aperture preselected on the lens—necessary because you are viewing and measuring the exposure at full aperture but generally expose at a small working aperture.

The above scheme and layout applies largely to most of the Zuiko lenses for the Olympus OM cameras. There are individual variations—for instance fisheye lenses have built-in filter turrets, zoom lenses have an additional control ring for focal length adjustment but no depth of field scale, most of the macro lenses have no focusing mount and no aperture coupling with the camera, long tele lenses have an additional tripod mounting and so on.

Lens changing

The OM bayonet mount not only locates every lens precisely at the correct register (i.e. with the flange exactly 46 mm from the film plane) but also permits rapid one-handed changing.

To remove a lens from the camera, press the lens release key to disengage the bayonet lock and turn the lens anti-clockwise, then lift off.

To fit the alternative lens, bring it up to the camera mount so that the red dot on the chrome ring is opposite the red dot on the front mounting flange of the camera—about 70° anti-clockwise from the top. Push the lens with its rear flange flush against the camera mounting flange. The two will only mate in contact if the red dots are correctly aligned. Then turn the whole lens clockwise (but without pressing the release key) until the bayonet catch engages. The red dot on the chrome ring is now opposite the red shutter speed index line on the camera.

That is all there is to it. But take care not to scrape possibly protruding rear lens elements against any part of the camera. The guard rings or segments partly surrounding such protruding elements offer some, but not complete, protection. Above all don't try to force a lens on the camera without first lining up the red dots, or you may damage the lens mounting.

Practical handling

Lens changing is easy if you can do it at leisure and have space to park all the bits and pieces. There is also a way of doing it efficiently and safely on the run. Start by checking that the lens on the camera and the 'new' lens to replace it both carry their front lens caps and the 'new' lens also its rear cap.

Have the camera hanging on its strap round your neck. Hold the 'new' lens in your left hand. With the right, remove the 'old' lens from the camera, holding it with the thumb and index finger. With the ring finger and palm of the same hand remove the rear cap from the new lens (still in your left hand) and fit this lens to the camera. Finally use your free left hand to attach the rear lens cap to the back of the lens you have just removed. With a little practice, such a lens switch need take no longer than 5 to 10 seconds. Get used to keeping both lenses in your hand; that's much safer than putting them down and risking dust or grit on the ground outdoors.

OM system lenses

The interchangeable lenses for the Olympus OM cameras —the main basis of the optical system versatility—are still growing in number and diversity. They can be classified in eight main groups:

(a) Fisheye lenses: Extreme wide-angle lenses with deliberately distorted 180° coverage.

(b) Ultrawide-angle lenses: Generally lenses with a

diagonal angle of view greater than 80°, or in practice focal lengths from 18 to 24 mm.

(c) Wide-angle lenses: Lenses with image angles between the standard focal length (47°) and about 80°—in practice the 28 and 35 mm lenses.

(d) Standard lenses: The 50 and 55 mm lenses for the OM cameras.

(e) Medium tele lenses: Focal lengths up to 200 mm, usually intended for hand-held shooting.

(f) Long tele lenses: Focal lengths from 300 mm upwards for more extreme long-range photography.

(g) Zoom lenses: OM lenses of variable focal length.

(h) Macro lenses: Systems specially designed for close-up photography.

The complete list of lenses appears in the *Facts and figures* chapter at the end of the book.

Nomenclature

All the Olympus OM lenses are named Zuiko. The lens type and other characteristics are expressed by various additions as follows:

Single letters preceding the Zuiko designation are an alphabetical code to indicate the number of lens elements in the system. Thus an E. Zuiko lens contains five elements, F. Zuiko six elements, G. Zuiko seven elements, H. Zuiko eight elements, I. Zuiko nine elements and J. Zuiko ten elements. This letter designation is not used with lenses of larger numbers of elements such as fisheye or zoom lenses, nor for macro lenses. The code for number of elements is also dropped with multi-coated lenses which are labelled Zuiko MC. Occasionally single-coated earlier versions of current multi-coated lenses exist with the letter code.

Auto indicates a lens with internal stop-down aperture coupling with the camera mechanism and an aperture simulator input to the camera's exposure meter. All these lenses therefore operate with semi-automatic or automatic exposure control and full-aperture metering. This applies to nearly all OM lenses; main exceptions are the shift and some of the macro lenses. The *Auto* tag is linked with a designation of the lens type: Auto-Fisheye, Auto-W (wide angle), Auto-S (standard), Auto-Zoom, Auto-Macro or Auto-T (tele).

Fisheye lenses

This special group of ultrawide-angle lenses covers an angle of view up to 180° by introducing deliberate image distortion so that the scale of reproduction decreases the further away an image point is from the centre of the field. Vertical and horizontal straight lines away from the centre of the picture curve more or less strongly about the image centre. Only lines actually going through the centre are straight. This distortion is the only way of covering a 180° image angle within the finite film frame; it also makes more or less uniform image illumination possible without the limitations of light fall-off at extreme angles.

When shooting with these lenses take care not to include accidentally your feet, hands etc. in the 180° view.

To be able to take in a 180° view, the front lens element must protrude in front of the lens rim. This bulging out, like the bulging eye of a fish (which needs this shape to take in a reasonable angle of view under water), is responsible for the name of this lens type. It also makes the front surface of the lens vulnerable and prevents attachment of filters. Those lenses therefore have built-in filter turrets.

The main difference between the two Zuiko fisheye lenses is that the 8 mm provides a circular 23 mm image on the film while the 16 mm image is 44 mm in diameter and the 24 × 36 mm frame crops out a section.

Ultrawide-angle lenses

The distinction between ultrawide and wide-angle lenses is somewhat arbitrary. We have here drawn an imaginary line at about 26 mm focal length or 80° diagonal angle. Within that range Olympus offer 18, 21 and 24 mm lenses. Ultrawide-angle lenses are primarily for special effects; in the results you have to allow for both wide-angle distortion and light fall-off towards the corners. Despite the very great angle of the shortest focal lengths, the images are however virtually free from geometric lens distortion.

In this section Olympus also largely follows its policy of providing alternatives of a very compact if slow lens and a high-speed lens of more bulk in the same focal length. This permits different compromises of choice between versatility and transport convenience.

Wide-angle lenses

The medium wide-angle field, covering diagonal image angles between 75° and 55°, is less subject to light fall-off and wide-angle distortion problems, but still permits the camera to cover a bigger view than with the standard lens. Wide-angle lenses in this range are particularly useful in conveying the breadth of outdoor landscapes, but also in feature photography, in crowds, interiors, etc. With these lenses Olympus again presents a dual range of slower but compact units on the one hand and large-aperture lenses of slightly greater bulk on the other. These are the 28 and 35 mm lenses, including the special shift lens.

The shift mechanism of the 35 mm Zuiko Shift lens consists of three circular plates between the camera mount and the lens itself, sliding across each other in a vertical and a horizontal set of dovetail guides. To use the shift movement, push the forward section of the lens (the fixed ring carrying the depth of field scale) in the direction in which you want to include additional subject detail. Thus for including the top of a building in the picture, push the sliding section upwards. You can combine the vertical and horizontal shift for oblique displacements; an inter-coupling of the displacements keeps the lens always within its limiting circle of displacement. (On pushing the lens sideways when it is in the top position, it automatically returns towards its vertical centre the more you push it to the side.)

Preferably focus while the shift is centred in both directions (the movements engage in click stops in their zero positions) and shift afterwards—especially when using a microprism or wedge rangefinder screen. As subjects requiring a shift lens are often taken with the camera mounted on a tripod, this is no problem.

In view of the shift displacement, the diaphragm mechanism of the lens moves with the optical system and the lens iris is not coupled with the camera. For manual exposure metering and for the exposure the lens must therefore be stopped down by hand.

Preselect the aperture in the usual way. For metering or for the exposure then press in the stop-down key (in more or less the same position as the depth of field preview key on other lenses); this stays pushed in. To

FISHEYE LENSES

The 8 mm *f*2.8 lens *(left)* has 11 elements in 8 groups, the 16 mm *(right)* has 11 elements in 8 groups. (Optical sections are not to scale.)

The controls on the barrel of the 8 mm fisheye lens are:

1. Focusing mount and distance scale.
2. Filter selector wheel.
3. Regular and infrared focusing indexes; no depth of field scale.
4. Aperture ring and scale.

Always screw the special lens cap into the front of the 8 mm fisheye when not actually shooting.

The 16 mm fisheye lens controls are standard; an extra is the frontmost rim which rotates for selecting the filters of the built-in turret.

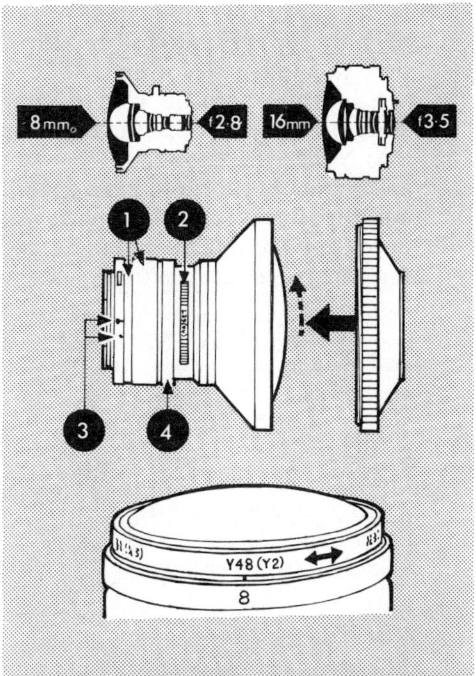

ULTRA WIDE-ANGLE LENSES

The lens sections (not to scale) show the optical construction of the 18, 21 and 24 mm lenses—the latter two in two alternative maximum apertures. In the 21 and 24 mm *f*2 lenses (and also in the 18 mm lens) some of the elements (floating elements) move independently during focusing.

The 18 mm *f*3.5 lens is used with a special 49-72 mm adapter ring to fit filters without touching the protruding front of the lens. The same ring also serves as a lens hood. Always use the specially deep lens cap *(left)* on this lens.

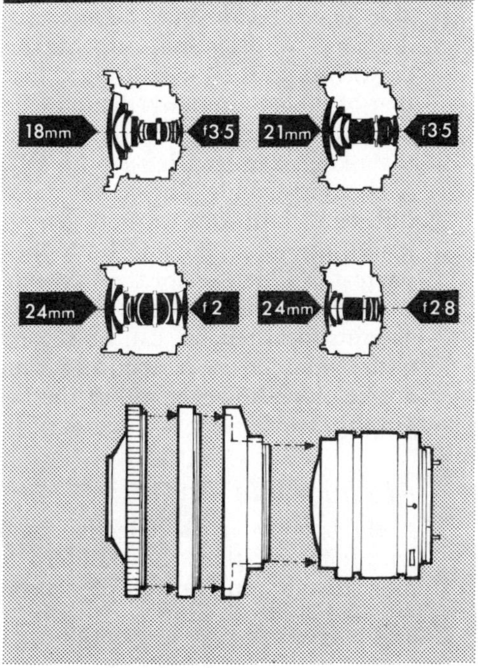

open the lens again to full aperture, press the key a second time to allow it to spring out.

Exposures with the OM-2 on automatic operation are correct in any case; in manual mode with the OM-2 and OM-1 measure the exposure with the lens stopped down and remember to stop down again if you have opened the aperture for a recheck of image sharpness. With the stop-down key *not* depressed, the exposure takes place at the *f*2.8 aperture irrespective of the setting of the aperture ring.

The shift displacement also causes some vignetting and hence light loss in the image corners at larger apertures. So stop down the lens for shifts greater than 5 mm in either direction: expose at *f*4 with horizontal shifts of 5 to 7 mm and *f*5.6 between 7 and 10 mm. Stop down to *f*4 with vertical shifts between 5 and 9 mm and to *f*5.6 beyond 9 mm. For oblique shifts adjust the aperture according to the larger of the two (horizontal or vertical) displacements.

Standard lenses

The standard focal length for a camera with interchangeable lens is reckoned to be one reasonably near the image diagonal. With 35 mm cameras the standard focal length of 50 mm is somewhat longer than the image diagonal; that of the 55 mm lens (the longer focal length was partly chosen to facilitate an extreme-speed design) is longer still.

Among standard lenses the Olympus system offers a particularly wide choice of maximum apertures with different compromises between speed and bulk. These lenses therefore include both the fastest and the compactest of all lenses for the OM cameras.

Also included is one of the macro lenses which, with a 50 mm focal length, can be regarded as a standard lens with extended near focusing capability. Many of the applications however are in the field of close-up photography.

Medium tele lenses

'Tele' is nowadays a collective tag for all lenses of a focal length longer than the standard lens. They thus show more distant (and nearer) objects on a larger scale making

WIDE ANGLE LENSES

The optical sections show the construction of the 28 mm *(top)* and 35 mm *(bottom)* wide angle lenses.

The controls of the 35 mm shift lens are:

1. Aperture ring.
2. Focusing ring with distance scale.
3. Depth of field ring.
4. Horizontal shift scale and index. (A similar vertical scale and index are at the side.)
5. Bayonet release catch.
6. Stop-down key.

During a shift the front section of the lens is displaced relative to the mount *(right)*.

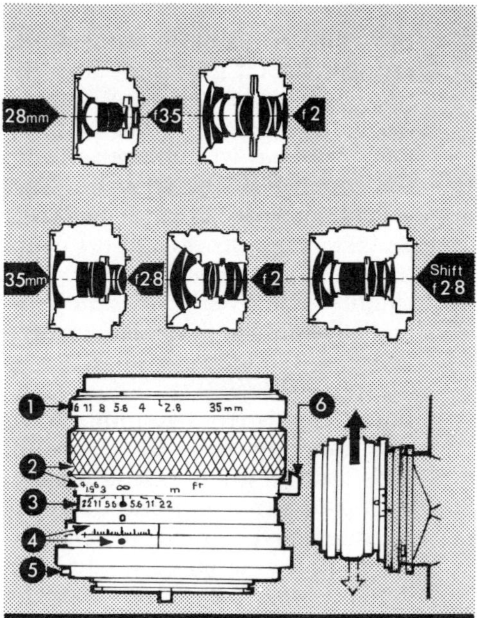

STANDARD AND MEDIUM TELE LENSES

Standard lenses are the 50 mm *f*1.8 *(left)*, *f*1.4 *(centre)* and 55 mm *f*1.2 *(right)*.

The 50 mm Macro *f*3.5 *(left)* is also effectively a standard lens. The 85 mm *f*2 *(centre)* and 100 mm *f*2.8 *(right)* are coupled semi-long focus units.

Further medium tele lenses are the 135 mm *f*3.5 and 135 mm *f*2.8, the 180 mm *f*2.8 and the 200 mm *f*5 and 200 mm *f*4. (The various lens sections are not to scale.)

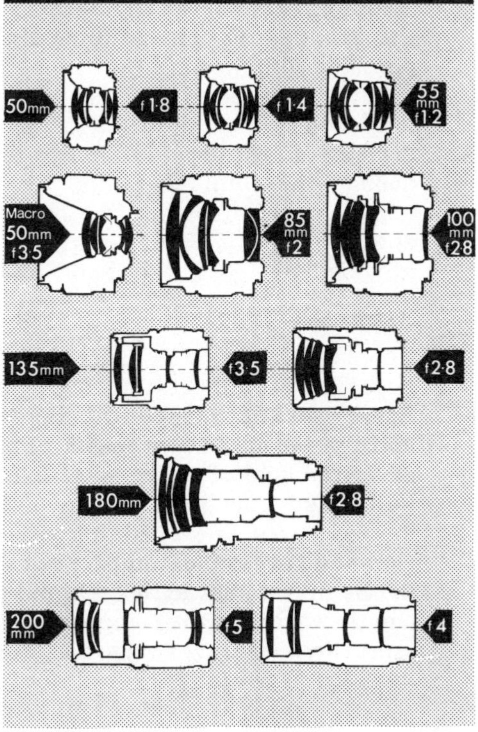

them appear nearer in the picture. True telephoto lenses are also shorter physically than their focal length.

The medium tele lens range for the OM cameras covers mostly lenses that permit reasonably easy hand-held shooting, with image scales magnified up to 4 times compared with the standard lens. Also, the range still covers alternatives with different trade-offs of speed against compactness. The Olympus range of medium tele lenses includes 85, 100, 135, 180 and 200 mm focal lengths. The 85 and 100 mm lenses are compact enough on the camera to fit the larger soft and hard camera cases.

Long tele lenses

Focal lengths from 300 mm upwards are to the camera what more powerful binoculars and telescopes are to the eye. Thus a 300 mm lens shows the image on the film with a 6 × magnification compared with the standard 50 mm lens; with a 1000 mm lens the comparative magnification is 20 ×. While hand-held shooting is still possible with the shorter focal lengths in this range—assuming suitable steadying aids—tripod mounting of the camera and lens is preferable. It becomes indispensable with the longer focal lengths.

The lenses are all true telephoto systems, i.e. with the lens mounted on the camera the lens front/film plane distance is significantly shorter than the focal length, making the equipment more compact. Typically, the telephoto ratio (roughly the ratio of physical length to optical length) is about 0.7 to 0.75 ×. The focal lengths provided are 300, 400, 600 and 1000 mm.

Zoom lenses

Zoom systems offer a greater choice of focal lengths with fewer lenses and are thus a particularly flexible aid to image scale and angle control. For instance the 35–70 mm and 75–150 mm zoom lenses between them more than cover the field of view of five fixed focal lengths in the OM range. Inevitably this involves some compromises in size, speed and operating ease—a 75–150 mm lens cannot be as fast, as compact or as easy to handle as say the 85 or 100 mm lenses that fall within the same focal length range. But the compromises are often worthwhile, especially as you are able to vary continuously the field of

LONG TELE LENSES

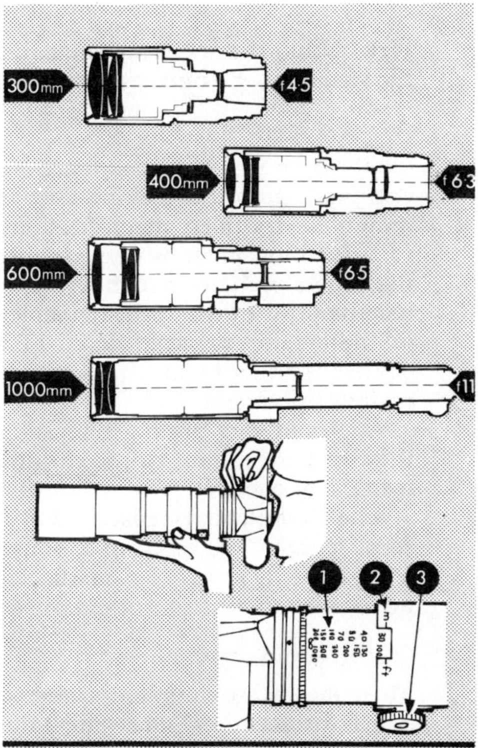

The lens sections show the optical construction of the 300 mm *f*4.5, 400 mm *f*6.3, 600 mm *f*6.5 and 1000 mm *f*11 tele lenses.

For hand-held shooting with the 300 and 400 mm lenses support the lens barrel with tripod mounting ring in the palm of the left hand.

Rear controls of the 600 and 1000 mm lenses:

1. Distance scales on extending lens barrel.
2. Focusing and infrared index marks.
3. Rack-and-pinion drive knob.

ZOOM LENSES

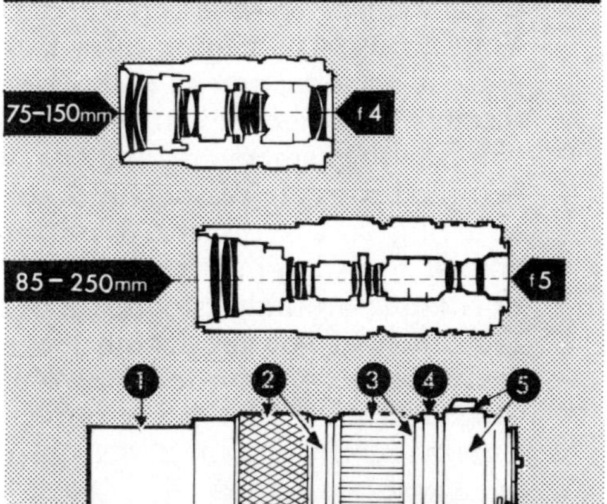

Optical layout of the 75-150 and 85-250 mm Zuiko Zoom lenses.

The elements and controls of a typical zoom lens (85-250 mm) are:

1. Extending lens hood.
2. Focusing mount with distance scale.
3. Zooming ring with focal length scale.
4. Aperture ring.
5. Tripod mounting ring.

MACRO LENSES

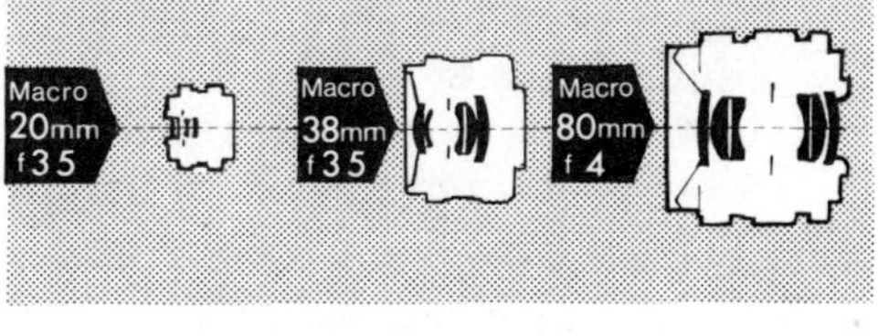

The lens sections are those of the 20, 38 and 80 mm macro lenses—all used on the Auto-Bellows.

view within the zooming range. The Zuiko zooms cover the ranges 35–70 mm, 75–150 mm and 85–250 mm.

Macro lenses

The lenses in this group are specially corrected for optimum performance in close-ups and macrophotography at specified magnifications. Also, they have no focusing movement as they are intended to be used with the variable extension of the Auto-bellows or the PMT-35 macro outfit. Further, the macro lenses have no provision for automatic stopping down of the aperture; the iris control is either by manual preselection or by completely manual operation.

Angles of view are not relevant in the macro range, as they vary according to the magnification—which is the factor that counts.

The Zuiko macro lenses are of 20, 38, 50 and 80 mm focal length. The 50 mm has its own focusing system and can be regarded as a standard lens with special close-up correction.

Carrying lenses

Most lenses are supplied complete with a leather lens case to protect each lens against dust. Often the case also holds the lens hood. Keep lenses in these cases at home. You can also use them to carry lenses—a convenient way is to fit a short strap to each case and thread the straps through your belt (if you wear one). This is handy when you take the camera and one or two spare lenses. On the belt the lenses are reasonably accessible in their cases for changing on the camera. With more than two lenses a holdall bag or compartment case is however preferable to running around festooned like a Christmas tree. But even then, if you are taking longer lenses that you are likely to use a lot, these are often more conveniently carried in their lens case around your belt. That saves lengthy rummaging in a well-filled holdall or compartment case.

Lenses usually fit in their cases rear end (with rear lens cap) first. So you get hold of the front end of the lens when lifting it out of its case. Get used to returning the lens that way, too, otherwise the cases may not close. For the same reason reset lenses to infinity before placing them in their cases. Exceptions to this orientation are certain long tele and zoom lenses with the tripod mounting ring. These lenses are designed to fit front down into the case and you hold the lens by the tripod mounting ring when lifting it out or putting it back. The longest tele lenses (e.g. 600 and 1000 mm) use foam plastic lined aluminium cases for better transport protection. These are pieces of luggage in their own right.

If you are carrying one not too bulky extra lens, a jacket or trouser pocket will also do. First thoroughly clean out all fluff, dust and dirt. Then remember always to put the lens in the pocket with front and rear caps in place. This is not just for protection against residual pocketed debris but to protect the glasses against fingerprints when you fumble in your pocket for the lens.

There are also soft lens pouches to protect lenses in a soft holdall or compartment case. They weigh little, yet protect lenses against knocking into each other in the case. Olympus makes a couple of versions in soft leather—a model 100 for lenses up to 100 mm focal length and a model 200 for longer lenses—with drawstring closure. But numerous other suppliers provide similar soft lens containers in leather or soft cloth. Such pouches are again intended more for long term storage even in the holdall case; while you are shooting it is handier to take all lenses out of their pouches beforehand than to extract each lens laboriously when needed.

Tripod mounting of long lenses

In view of the greater risk of camera shake with long focus and tele lenses, mount such lens/camera assemblies on a tripod whenever feasible. As the longer lenses protrude appreciably in front of the camera, they often carry a tripod mounting ring to permit more balanced mounting. This is attached to the lens barrel some distance in front of the camera mount. It does not normally support the camera/lens assembly at its centre of gravity (usually the front end of the lens is still heavier than the rear end with the camera unless the latter also carries the motor drive and/or 250-exposure back) but it avoids putting excessive strain on the camera's tripod bush. The tripod mounting ring is sufficiently solidly made to bear the weight of its lens under all shooting conditions.

The tripod should of course be as firm as possible and preferably equipped with an easy-locking pan-and-tilt head for rapid but precise adjustment of the camera aiming direction. Obviously the heaviest lenses such as the 1000 mm also need a correspondingly heavy tripod and pan/tilt head.

The tripod mounting rings of the lighter long tele lenses (also for instance the 85–250 mm zoom) are removable as these lenses also permit hand-held shooting. To remove a tripod mounting ring, detach the lens from the camera. Slack off the clamping knob and rotate the mounting ring so that the tripod bush is in line with the red locating dot on the rear chrome lens ring (the same dot as used for aligning the lens when fitting it to the camera). Now withdraw the mounting ring over the rear of the lens. This prepositioning of the ring is important, as a small locating pin inside the ring clears a channel in the fixed rear serrated ring on the lens barrel.

To fit the tripod mounting ring locate it over the back of the lens so that the tripod bush is again in line with the red dot; the locating pin is then lined up with the break in the serrated ring. Push the mounting ring over the rear of the lens so that this pin once more slides through the channel formed by the break in the serrated ring. The extended part of the platform must face forward—otherwise the ring cannot be located correctly over the lens. Once the ring is in position, you can rotate it in any direction for appropriate orientation of the camera format and screw tight.

All lenses with tripod mounting ring allow the lens to be rotated together with the camera for switching from horizontal to upright format pictures. To change over, slack off the clamping knob of the tripod mounting ring, rotate the lens and camera assembly to re-orient it and tighten the clamping knob again.

Lens performance features

A camera lens should yield an undistorted image of ideal sharpness, resolution, colour correction and even illumination. Further, it should do so at all subject distances, over a wide image angle and with a large lens aperture. For reasons of geometric optics, satisfying all these requirements to a reasonable degree involves complex lens design of numerous elements of different glass types. In particular, the wider the angle and the larger the aperture, the more complex the design becomes. Modern lenses, even of modest specifications, thus have at least 4 to 5 separate elements; wide-angle, large-aperture and zoom lenses may run from 8 to 15 or more elements.

One major compromise involved especially with short-focus and large-aperture lenses is that the lens yields its optimum image quality at an aperture somewhat smaller than the full opening. So if subject conditions allow, stop down high-speed lenses of *f* 1.2 to *f* 2.8 to around *f* 4. Lenses of maximum aperture *f* 3.5 to *f* 4 generally yield their best performance at about *f* 5.6. On the other hand you still have the full lens speed available when you need it, with only a slight sacrifice in definition and image brilliance. You generally have to stop down appreciably when using normal lenses (other than special macro types) in an extreme close-up range.

Large-aperture lenses are particularly difficult to correct for even definition over an extended focusing range from very distant to very near subjects. To overcome this, some lenses incorporate so-called floating elements: during focusing the lens not only moves nearer to, or further away from, the image plane but selected elements or groups within the lens shift with respect to the rest. This optimises the lens performance at each distance setting.

Various other performance problems arise not so much from inadequate lens correction as from the nature of image formation:

Distortion is a failure of the lens to register straight lines near the image edges straight. Instead, such lines appear curved towards or away from the centre. Distortion is introduced deliberately in fisheye lenses because otherwise it would be impossible to cover a 180° view on a finite piece of film. With nearly all other OM lenses distortion is either absent or negligible.

Wide-angle distortion (see below) is a different kind of distortion associated with the wide angle of view and oblique projection during image formation.

Uneven illumination is another problem associated with wide angles of view. The image is less bright near the edges as the light there reaches the film at an acute angle. And the lens aperture is also seen obliquely and hence reduced in area. The retrofocus type of wide-angle lens design required in single-lens reflex cameras tends to compensate this to a limited extent but the image at the edges of for instance the 18 mm lens is only about 35% as bright as in the centre. With the 21, 24 and 28 mm lenses the relative edge brightness under optimum conditions reaches around 44, 50 and 60% respectively. This fall-off is most noticeable in colour slides—partly because colour film has a more limited exposure latitude and partly because uneven image brightness becomes more obvious on projection on a screen than in an enlarged print. In addition the lens may also be subject to mechanical vignetting (obstruction of light rays by the lens mount) which generally disappears at the optimum aperture but may get worse when you screw a filter in the front of an ultra-wide-angle lens. (That is one reason for the special filter arrangement of certain such lenses.)

Diffraction destroys sharp definition if you stop down the lens too far. The mathematics of it involves the wavelength of light, actual diameter of the lens opening and the image scale. At normal subject distances and with the wide-angle, standard and medium tele lenses the smallest available aperture still falls short of the point where diffraction begins seriously to affect image definition. With the longer tele lenses preferably avoid stopping down beyond *f* 22 unless essential for exposure control purposes. In macrophotography at certain magnifications diffraction may become significant. The table (see Chpt. *Facts and figures*) indicates limiting apertures to avoid such diffraction problems.

Flare is light reflected between glass surfaces inside the lens, eventually reaching the film as scattered light. This reduces image brilliance and hence also visual sharpness. Nearly all modern lenses carry reflection-absorbing coatings on the glass/air interfaces and some OM lenses—the ones designated Zuiko MC—have multilayer coatings for still greater reflection-killing efficiency. Coating also increases the effective light transmission of the lens. However all non-image-forming light reaching the front of the lens causes some slight flare. Light from strong sources, especially if included in the picture, can cause *ghost images*, generally as bright hexagonal or octagonal spots which are reproductions of the lens diaphragm. Flare from light sources not in the picture area is usually greater reduced by using a lens hood—always advisable, anyway.

Focal length, image scale and angle of view

Let's get back to the functions of lenses of different focal length. We can choose different focal lengths to control the image scale of the film, to select a suitable angle of view and also—a little more involved—control the perspective rendering in a picture.

Primarily the focal length of the lens controls the size of the image of an object that the lens forms on the film. At a given (not too near) distance this size is proportional to the lens's focal length. The other factor controlling the size of an image (for instance with a given lens) is the distance: we get a larger image of an object on the film by going closer. Using a longer focal length from a given viewpoint (for instance when you cannot get closer) also makes things look larger. The longer focus lens does so by narrowing the angle of view and magnifying the image scale accordingly. This is different from actually going closer; the difference is the perspective rendering.

Conversely, the narrower angle makes a greater subject distance essential. That consideration is sometimes important in close-up photography and in close-up telephotography. But to take in a wider view or to cover the whole of the subject from close range you need a lens of shorter focal length covering a wider angle.

So we have the classical application of tele and wide-angle lenses: the former show enlarged detail of distant items, for instance inaccessible architecture, while wide-angle lenses cover the whole of an object from closer up when you cannot get far enough away from it for a normal angle lens.

Controlling perspective

Perspective for our purposes is the size relationship in the image of nearer and more distant objects. It is these size differences that give a clue to depth and hence an illusion of three-dimensionality to a flat picture. Such size relationships cover various aspects; most straightforward are proportions of near and distant objects of similar actual size, for instance the appearance of diminishing size in a row of trees along the roadside. And if we take the tops and bottoms of this row of trees, they form two converging lines apparently meeting at a point on the horizon. This line convergence is familiar also from numerous other structures with parallel lines extending away from us: parallel lines of a building when we look at it at an angle, the sides of a road or a railway line etc.

The degree of such convergence and the size difference between near and distant items determines our impression of perspective. If parallel lines converge strongly and near items appear very much bigger than distant ones, we see enhanced or even violent perspective. If receding parallels hardly appear to converge at all and similar nearer and more distant items appear virtually identical in size, we regard the perspective effect as subdued.

The first effect is associated with enhanced depth—and with wide-angle lenses. The second effect conveys little depth and is associated with pictures taken by tele lenses.

Why?

Take for instance a view of a building seen at an angle receding from nearby to far away. The very top and bottom of the building converge most to a distant vanishing point on the horizon. The centre horizontals converge less (their vertical distance is less). Also near regularly spaced elements (e.g. windows) decrease dramatically in size and spacing. More distant detail on the other hand appears closely spaced together and varies less in size.

This relationship is characteristic of any image formed by a lens that takes in the whole building from near to far from a near viewpoint. However, only a wide-angle lens has a wide enough view to take in the most violently converging top and bottom lines. A normal lens will not cover the lines of maximum convergence, nor can it take in the distant detail together with the very near. And a tele lens with its still more reduced angle can take in only size graduation.

All this is present in the one view from the same viewpoint. If you enlarge the small distant section of the wide-angle view, it looks exactly the same as the tele lens view. But the characteristic of wide-angle perspective

PERSPECTIVE

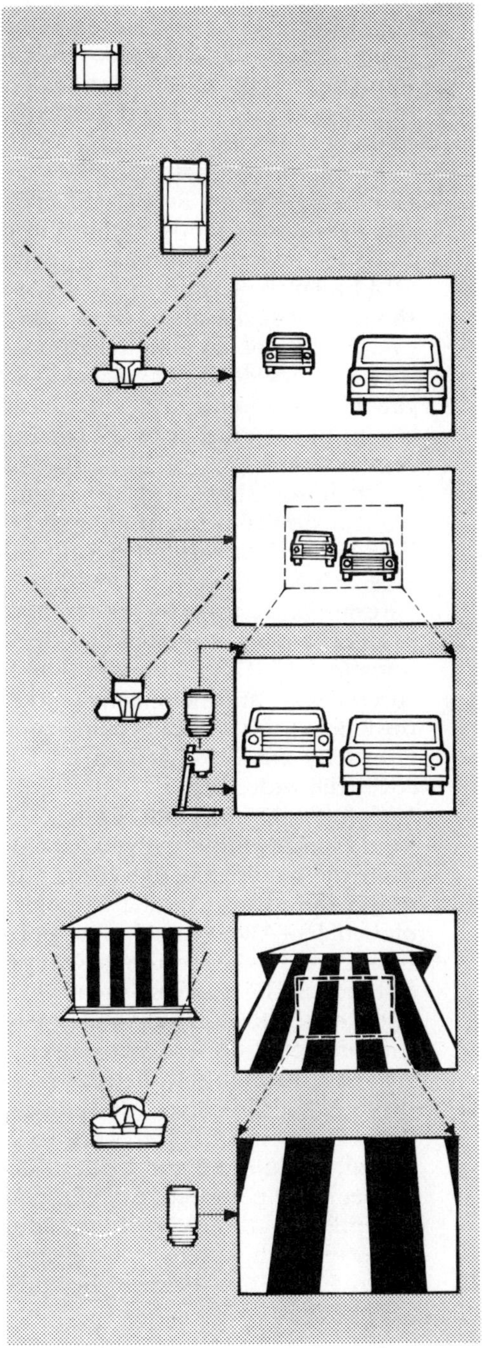

Distance determines the relative size of objects in a picture. From a near viewpoint a car may look twice as big as one further away. From a more distant viewpoint the relative separation between the cars is less significant and both look equally tiny. Perspective thus depends only on viewpoint.

But with a tele lens—or in a big cropped enlargement—the two cars from the distant viewpoint appear large again though still in their same relative size.

The effect of a camera tilt appears very pronounced in a wide-angle view but much less so in a tele view even from the same viewpoint. For the wide angle or even normal lens covers the whole subject and the overall convergence of verticals appears quite violent. The overall convergence is less in the smaller image angle taken in by the tele lens, hence the distortion appears less pronounced.

is its near-to-far coverage and of tele perspective its limited coverage in a far range. The relative distances in the first case are greatly different, giving more depth, and in the second case much less so giving much less depth.

Familiarity of scale also plays a part. The view we can take in by looking at a scene *without roving over it* with our eyes corresponds roughly to the angle of view of a 35 or 40 mm lens with a 24 × 36 mm image format. In the OM finder the 50 mm lens also shows an image of roughly the same visual scale as we see directly with the unaided eye. And if you assume that you will make a 13 × 18 cm or 5 × 7 inch enlargement and look at it from 25 cm away, you again see items in the picture with a similar perspective to the original scene. That is our familiar scale and perspective.

But if you shoot with a 24 mm wide-angle lens, and make a similar print, the perspective looks exaggerated. The scale is unfamiliar because the picture appears to take in more than you would see. You can restore the natural impression by either making twice as large a print or looking at it from half the distance (possibly with a magnifier). But while you then see individual items in correct scale and perspective, you can no longer take in the whole print without roving your eyes over it. And that is exactly what you would do in the original scene to cover the wider angle.

Conversely, the scale of a tele shot with a 200 mm lens would look right only if you looked at a 13 × 18 cm print from the whole negative from 1 metre away. From any nearer the effect is similar to looking at the scene through binoculars—the typical tele perspective compression. Incidentally, the argument of print size and viewing distance can be scaled up in proportion—it applies equally for instance for a transparency taken with a 50 mm lens and projected on a 3 metre or 10 feet wide screen and viewed from about 4¼ metres or 14 feet away.

Note that the perspective effects change as you change your viewpoint. If you were to go further away from the whole building and bring it back larger again with a tele lens, the perspective would be flat as from the distant viewpoint. Conversely, if you approach the far end and use a wide-angle lens you regain the more violent perspective of the nearer viewpoint. Perspective thus depends on the viewpoint, not on the lens used—but the choice of lens determines how much the picture takes in and to what extent you can record the perspectively more enhanced parts of the scene.

Using the shift lens

One problem in using a wide-angle or ultrawide-angle lens to include the whole of tall buildings is that the building usually extends from about the middle of the picture to the top. The lower half is often unwanted and unattractive foreground. To get a picture of just the building you have to crop the negative on enlarging or mask down a colour slide—hardly satisfactory.

A solution to this problem is the Zuiko Shift lens. Although this is a moderate wide-angle lens, it has a considerably larger angle of coverage than you need for the 24 × 36 mm image format. In effect the lens covers a circle of some 64 mm diameter and you can decentre the lens to select any part of it. This is similar to the use of the rising front movement on a view camera; with the shift lens you can crop off the unwanted foreground before you take the picture instead of having to sacrifice enlargeability by cropping afterwards.

To use the shift for photographing for instance a tall building, point the camera at the building so that the verticals are straight. Check this with the grid lines of the 1–10 focusing screen. (Use this screen with the shift lens whenever possible.) Then push the lens upwards in the direction of the top of the building until the image on the finder screen takes in as much as you want. As the top comes into view, so the bottom or foreground disappears from the image—the field of view in the finder appears to slide downwards. For maximum effect with high buildings of course turn the camera for upright format views. This procedure is easiest with the camera mounted on a tripod—even a table tripod will do on a suitable flat surface. That also facilitates manual stop-down checks for exposure readings.

Equally, the lens can be shifted sideways or downwards. A lateral shift is useful to avoid reflections of the camera and photographer when the camera points at glass panels or even mirrors. Similarly, when photographing paintings in a gallery, a viewpoint straight in front of the painting may show glare or unwanted reflections that can be avoided by standing slightly to one side. But if you shoot from the side, the picture is no longer square in the finder. To get it square, point the camera at the wall next to the picture and shift the lens in the direction of the picture until the latter appears in the finder view. Downward shifts similarly avoid converging verticals that you would get when pointing the camera directly down to take in something just outside the lens's field of view with the camera held level.

The amount of additional subject field included by a given shift depends on the subject distance. With the 35 mm focal length it amounts to 1/35 of the distance per mm of shift. So a maximum shift in the direction of the short frame side (up or down with the camera in landscape orientation) brings in a subject extension equivalent of $\frac{1}{3}$ of the distance. Or, with a shift along the long side of the image, the subject frame shifts by 2/7 of the distance. So if you are 70 feet from a subject, the maximum lengthways shift brings in an extra 20 feet of subject.

Note two further points with shift lens operation. First, at the maximum shift some light fall-off of the image becomes visible near the edge of the field towards which the lens moves. (For instance the upper part of the image darkens in the finder when you displace the lens upwards.) With the all-matt screens (1–10 and 1–4) a manual meter reading in the shift position used also indicates an acceptable average exposure. The light fall-off and off-centre location may also make a microprism spot or split-image wedge (of focusing screens equipped with them) go dark, interfering with focusing. You can correct that by moving your eye behind the finder eyepiece in the same direction as you have shifted the lens. That is for focusing only, for you don't see the full finder view with such oblique viewing.

Secondly, when using the shift lens indoors, watch especially the edges and corners of the image in the direction in which you have shifted the lens. Surfaces or objects not parallel with the camera back (for instance table tops, circular horizontal or inclined surfaces etc.) will appear distorted. This is straightforward wide angle distortion due to the angle of view and not to the lens

RISING FRONT EFFECT

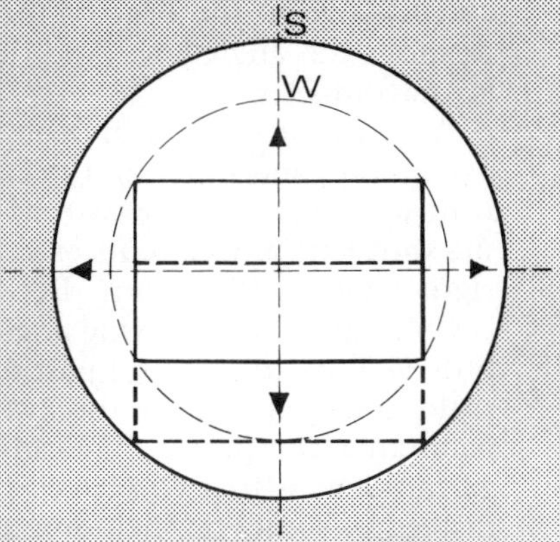

The shift lens has a wider coverage (S) than other wide-angle lenses (W) of the same focal length. The displacement moves the image frame relative to the lens in any of the arrowed directions.

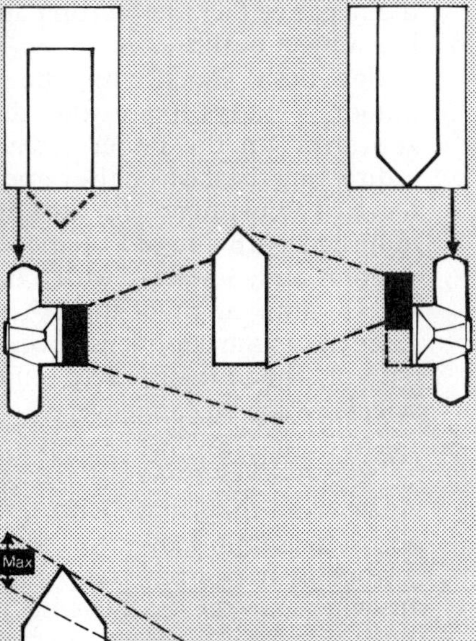

When taking in a near building without a camera tilt *(left)* the field of view may not include the top. With the vertical lens shift *(right)* you get more of the top but less of the foreground in the picture.

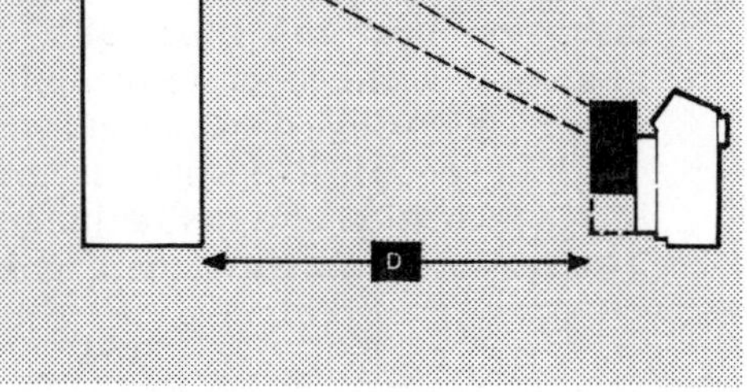

The extra subject field included by the maximum displacement is about one-third of the subject distance for every mm of shift.

(see below). For at the limit of the shift, the image edge corresponds to the edge of the field similar to that of a 24 mm wide-angle lens. And there this kind of distortion is unavoidable.

Another off-beat shift lens application is wide-angle panorama panels. Set up the camera on a tripod or other firm support and make two exposures in succession, with the shift lens moved to its extreme left-hand and extreme right-hand shift in turn. Between them the two shots cover a horizontal viewing angle of nearly 78° and with a little skill in cutting and pasting, you can join up equal-scale enlargements of the two negatives to a kind of panorama composite. The advantage over using say a 24 mm lens is that you cover a vertical angle of only 38° instead of some 53° including unwanted foreground and sky. The considerable central overlap of some 26 mm on the negative facilities cutting an unobtrusive join following subject outlines.

For flash shots with the shift lens—for instance indoors—always point the flash at the subject field appearing on the finder screen. That generally means redirecting the flash on the camera—a reasonably straightforward adjustment with the Quick Auto 310 or 300 when mounted with the aid of the camera bracket. Such reorientation is less easy with a flash in the accessory shoe. The lighting angle of the QA models is quite adequate, since the 35 mm shift lens never takes in more than around 63° of the subject field—the shift movement only selects which 63° are covered.

Wide-angle distortion

Apart from the fisheye lenses, the Zuiko ultrawide-angle and wide-angle lenses for the OM cameras are largely distortion-free: they render straight lines as straight anywhere in the image with only negligible deviation even at extreme angles. Yet pictures taken with wide-angle lenses of 24 mm and shorter often do show a curious distortion near the edges and corners of the image: heads and faces become fatter and in a corner of the image may even look like distorted ellipses or egg shapes.

This special distortion is peculiar to wide-angle image formation and has nothing to do with lens design. The reason is that the camera lens projects an image of a solid object onto a flat film. A more or less spherical shape such as a ball or an orange forms a circle in the centre of the film where the light rays from the lens reach the film at more or less a right angle. Near the edges or corners where the angle of incidence can be 50° or less, the circle becomes distorted towards an oval—the same effect as when you project a circular light spot vertically on a surface and then tilt the latter. This distortion arises only with three-dimensional objects at the edge of the subject field—not only oranges but also human heads—but not with flat surfaces parallel to the film. (There the oblique image-forming rays from the subject compensate the obliqueness of the film plane).

You can do two things about this kind of distortion: accept it or avoid it. Accepting means putting up with these peculiar shapes and possibly locating them deliberately to enhance the picture impact. To avoid it, keep solid objects of recognisable proportions away from the edges and corners of the image field. If they are within the angle of view of say the 28 mm lens you are unlikely to have serious trouble.

Avoid also regular-shaped areas located at an angle to the film plane near the image edges or corners. For instance a square table top there becomes a very distorted trapezoid and a round table no longer looks oval (which is natural) but again oblique egg-shaped. This is, of course, perspective distortion caused by viewpoint, and happens whether you hold the camera straight or not. In such views some surfaces are always at an angle to the film plane. The greater the angle and the nearer the shape to the image edge or corner, the more pronounced this distortion.

Increased distance for a given scale

Portraiture is the main use of this tele lens application, namely to control perspective. Pictures of people show faces and features in more natural proportions when photographed from about 2–3 metres or 7–10 feet away. From nearer, the head tends to look foreshortened (except in profile) with the nose, eyes and mouth large in a comparatively small face and head. Yet with the standard 50 mm lens you have to go down to a metre or $3\frac{1}{2}$ feet to fill the picture with a head-and-shoulders view. This effect looks more prominent in a photograph than when you face a person.

With a medium tele lens you can go farther away for the better perspective rendering and still get no more than the head and shoulders on the film. The 100–135 mm lenses are best for this; with anything longer (and correspondingly greater shooting distance) faces tend to look too flat again. If you have no medium tele lens handy, still keep at least 2 metres from the person you are photographing and enlarge and crop the picture afterwards.

Zoom lens technique

From the point of view of selecting a camera outfit zoom lenses have the advantage of covering a greater focal length range with fewer actual lenses. Against that you have the drawback of greater individual lens bulk—a zoom lens is generally bigger and heavier than a lens of any one of the focal lengths it covers—and slower speed, for design compromises can rarely be stretched to large apertures with variable focal length.

The practical approach to working with zoom lenses differs a little from normal lenses in several respects.

To start with, you select a zoom lens—if you have a choice of several—with less worry over precise focal length. Thus the 35–70 mm lens will cover everything you normally and vaguely regard as medium wide-angle to longish normal-focus subjects. Or for portraits you may use a 75–150 mm zoom without worrying whether the particular occasion demands a 100 mm or 135 mm lens.

Following from the above, generally select the viewpoint first and then, by the focal length adjustment, the framing. With a zoom you can frame the view really precisely with minute adjustment of the zooming control. Naturally you will end up with focal length settings in-between fixed values, e.g. 95, 117 or 142 mm. The focal length scale on the zooming ring indicates focal length only approximately—which doesn't matter, for what counts is that you include in the picture exactly what you want, neither more nor less. And provided you remain within the zooming range of one lens, even greater focal length changes are almost instantaneous, certainly far quicker than physically switching lenses.

A practical handling point: focus the image with the lens set to its tele limit, for instance at 150 mm with the 75–150 mm lens. For the larger image permits more accurate focusing. Then you can reduce the focal length and increase the angle as necessary; the image remains in sharp focus over most of the zooming range. At some focal length settings you may need some refocusing (depending on the lens) but this is slight and normally within the depth of field range. Generally one of the microprism screens is best with the zoom lenses—1–1 with the shorter-focus and 1–2 with the long-focus models.

A special application of zoom lens photography is close-up zooming (sometimes referred to incorrectly as macro-zooming) with extension tubes. If you mount an extension tube between the zoom lens and the camera, the lens is set to a variable close-up range with two unexpected characteristics:

(a) You focus most easily by adjusting the focal length or zooming control, and

(b) With this adjustment the scale of reproduction does not vary dramatically over the available distance range. A practical example: with the 85–250 mm zoom lens and a 14 mm extension tube, you can range from about 0.5 to 1.5 metres in distance with hardly a change in reproduction scale (it remains at around 0.2 ×).

The only drawback with extension tubes is that you have to stop down the lens by hand to the working aperture, for the tubes do not transmit the auto-aperture coupling. You can get over that by shooting at full aperture —the shutter speed you need to cope with the subject movement usually demands that anyway.

Lens hoods

To keep out stray light for maximum image brilliance most Olympus OM lenses are supplied complete with lens hood. Exceptions are the fisheye lenses where any hood would reduce the angle of view. Lenses of focal lengths from 135 mm upwards have a built-in extending lens hood, as the lens dimensions there provide sufficient space for it. The shorter lenses use hoods of several different kinds and for each kind often also in two alternative sizes to fit lenses with 49 mm or 55 mm front screw mounts, or for 51 mm and 57 mm clip-on fittings respectively. The kinds are:

(a) Shallow dished collapsible rubber screw-in hoods. These are provided for the 21 mm *f*3.5 (49 mm thread) and 24 mm *f*2 (55 mm screw thread) lenses.

(b) Shallow screw-in metal of various depths and sizes for the 24 mm *f*2.8, the different 28 mm and the 35 mm *f*2 lenses. Each lens has its own hood, usually stored in the lens case; the applicable lens details are marked on the hood.

(c) A special case is the shallow 49–72 mm adapter ring which also serves as a hood for the 18 mm lens.

(d) Deeper screw-in hoods are provided for the 37–70 mm zoom lens and for the 85 and 100 mm lenses (the same hood fits both of these).

(e) Clip-on metal hoods fit the 35 mm *f*2.8, 50 mm *f*1.8 and *f*1.4, 55 mm *f*1.2 and 21 mm *f*2 lenses. Again the hoods are marked with the data for the correct lens or lenses.

To fit screw hoods, screw them into the front lens thread. Push clip-on hoods over the outer lens mount and tighten the small clamping screw to secure them in place. To use the built-in hoods of the longer focus lenses, pull the hood forward to its full extent—after removing the lens cap.

The clip-on hoods are designed for fitting on the lens back-to-front when the camera is in its ever-ready case. Once you have pushed the hood reversed over the lens, you can still fit the lens cap—which also holds the hood in position. But you must remove the hood (and put it on the right way round) before you can operate the aperture ring or focusing mount.

The deep rubber hood for the 85 and 100 mm lenses can be folded back over the lens, for instance to accommodate it in the large camera cases without removing the hood. But you cannot in this case fit the lens cap.

Folding the rubber hood back and forth may in time rupture the joint between the rubber and the screw-in mount. A better way is to put the lens cap on the lens and loosely fit the hood reversed over the front. With this arrangement the 85 and 100 mm lenses still fit into the large ever-ready cases. For shooting take off the hood and lens cap and screw the hood normally into the lens front.

There is no point in folding back the shallow rubber hoods—they are too big to fit into ever-ready cases.

Lens caps

All lenses are supplied complete with front and rear caps for protection not only against possible scratches and damage but also against dust and other foreign matter.

The rear cap is the same on all lenses: a plastic cap with bayonet fitting to engage the rear bayonet mounting of the lens.

The front cap on most lenses taking 49 or 55 mm screw filters is a plastic cap with internal spring cheek. To fit the cap on the lens, press in the two keys (to each side of the 'Olympus' name), push the cap over the front of the lens and let go of the keys to grip the inside of the filter thread. Use the specially deep caps provided for the fisheye lenses and certain ultrawide-angle lenses with protruding front glass. The long tele lenses with 72 and 100 mm screw threads take screw-in metal front caps.

Lens mounting adapters

The following are provided for special applications:

The 55–49 mm reducing ring screws into the front of lenses with a 55 mm filter thread and has a protruding front mount with a 51 mm outside diameter—the same as that of lenses with 49 mm screw fitting. This allows for instance the 55 mm *f* 1.2 lens to be retro-mounted on the Auto-bellows or fitted to the Handy copy stand.

The PM-MTob lens mount adapter takes macro lenses with 0.8 × 1/36 inch microscope screw mounts (specifically the 20 and 38 mm Zuiko Macro lenses) for fitting on equipment with a standard OM bayonet mount—primarily the lens standard (front bellows standard) of the Auto-bellows and the PMT-35 bellows as well as on extension tubes. The latter are however used with the macro lenses only in special cases.

The PM-MTob mount is a 6 mm thick plate with the bayonet lens mount on one side, the screw thread on the other and the usual red locating dot and bayonet release catch in the rim. A black milled knob fixed to the rim provides a finger hold for rotating the mount when attaching it to, or removing it from, the bellows lens mount etc.

The Pen F/OM lens mount adapter connects the half-frame Olympus Pen F, FT and FV single-lens reflex cameras to interchangeable lenses and other units of the Olympus OM system. The adapter is an extension tube with an OM bayonet mount at one end and a Pen F bayonet mount at the other. Its length exactly compensates the difference in register (mounting flange/film plane distance) between the OM cameras and the Pen F models. As far as the OM system is concerned, the Pen F—no longer made—is useful for occasions requiring half-frame recording, for instance when making film strips or for microfilming. With appropriate OM system accessories, for instance the Auto-bellows, the camera is connected to the set-up by the bayonet lens mount. This adapter ring does not couple the automatic lens diaphragm with the metering system of Pen F cameras.

Filters

The Olympus range of filters is available in four screw-in sizes covering all OM lenses. The only exception are the fisheye units with built-in filters in a turret.

The full filter range (Chpt. *Tone and colour* and table in Chpt. *Facts and figures*) is available in both 49 mm and 55 mm screw mounts. The 72 mm and 100 mm filters are limited to the No. 1A skylight, L 39 (ultraviolet) and the yellow, orange and red filters. (These are the ones most likely to be needed in for instance telephotography.)

Filters of other makes can also be used provided they have the correct thread (49 × 0.75 mm, 55 × 0.75 mm, 72 × 0.75 mm etc.) and that the thread is precisely cut.

Where a filter and lens hood are used in combination, fit the filter to the lens first and then the hood. That applies also when using a clip-on hood with a screw-in filter; the latter is only accessible with the hood removed.

Use only one filter at a time; superimposing two filters may cause vignetting, especially with the shorter focus lenses.

The 40 cm close-up lens is also available with a 49 mm or 55 mm thread and is fitted in the same way as a filter. When combining a filter and close-up lens, screw the latter into the camera lens first.

COMMON OUTFIT SENSE

Without their comprehensive outfit of accessories, the Olympus OM models would not be significantly more versatile than other single-lens reflexes. On the other hand very few photographers are likely to want—or be able to afford—anything like the whole equipment system. Somewhere between the two extremes is the sensible outfit that makes the most of the Olympus OM features and scope, yet remains manageable.

Obviously building up an outfit is very much a matter of personal inclination and finance. But here are a few ideas on where to start and how to go on past a modest beginning. This applies to all-round photography, not to specific fields calling for sometimes very specialised accessories.

Weight and speed

The minimum you need for picture taking is of course the camera and one lens—apart from the film, those two items you cannot do without. The most versatile standard lens is the 50 mm *f*1.8 or *f*1.4. The extra speed mainly costs money rather than bulk as does the extra versatility of the OM-2 over the OM-1 since the two cameras are identical in size and differ, complete with lens, by a mere 1.5% in weight.

As the OM models are such compact cameras, you are at this point already faced with a decision of how compact you want to keep a growing outfit. In many of the focal lengths between ultrawide-angle and medium tele, Olympus offers a choice of alternative lenses of the same focal length: one is a slightly slower and more compact system, the other is slightly faster and more bulky.

In fact the light-weight ultrawide-angle, wide-angle and standard lenses form units remarkably similar in size and even weight, which facilitates a consistent camera hold with these lenses. Examples are the 50 mm *f*1.8, 35 mm *f*2.8, 28 mm *f*3.5, 24 mm *f*2.8, 21 mm *f*3.5, and even the 16 mm *f*3.5 fisheye. A slightly heavier brigade of high-speed lenses again provides similar dimensions: 24 mm *f*2, 28 mm *f*2, 55 mm *f*1.2 and even 85 mm *f*2 and 100 mm *f*2.8.

Acquisitions beyond a basic minimum are likely to proceed along two lines: lenses and system accessories. There is no rule as to which comes first (another question of personal preference)—you may want a Winder I before any supplementary optics or you may feel the need for alternative focal lengths before considering operational convenience. In addition there are small accessories—filters, eyecup, straps and other odds and ends which you will probably get as you feel the need for them.

The first optical expansion then concerns lenses of additional focal lengths: long focus and wide-angle. And there the embarrassment of choice starts.

Which wide-angle focal length?

As a first wide-angle lens, 28 mm is probably the handiest focal length. Covering about $2\frac{1}{2}\times$ the subject area of the standard 50 mm lens (roughly 60% wider and 60% higher than 50 mm), it is the most useful all-round wide-angle lens.

A 24 mm lens is a useful alternative. It covers about 4 times the picture area (twice the width and twice the height) of 50 mm and is thus in some respects even more versatile. On the other hand with architectural and similar views you get some wide-angle distortion.

In practice I have probably known slightly more occasions when I wished I had the 24 mm while working with the 28 mm than the other way round. But either lens will cover most of your wide-angle and even very wide-angle requirements.

If you aim at two wide-angle lenses, 28 mm and 21 mm make the best focal length combination—28 mm for most wide-angle shots and 21 mm for a few occasions when you need extreme wide angles. The 18 mm ultrawide-angle lens is a more special case and not ideal for general shooting.

On the other hand, I have rarely been satisfied with the 35 mm lenses, either. They cover about 60% more picture area (about 1/3 wider and 1/3 higher) than the standard

50 mm lens—rarely sufficient for wide-angle photography. The 35 mm lens is a more useful in-between stage if you extend your focal length range to two or even three wide-angle lenses. But on its own it tends to be an unsatisfactory half-way stage.

The Zuiko Shift lens with its lateral displacement is particularly useful for architecture, but again a rather specialised lens.

Which tele lenses?

With the tele lens it is probably more sensible to expand in progressive focal length stages. The first stage is thus the 100 mm lens which, with its 2× magnification (compared with 50 mm), covers most needs of portraiture, enlarged landscape views etc. For poor-light photography, theatre and similar fields the extra speed of the 85 mm lens is an asset. And neither of these lenses is any bulkier than the ultra-speed standard lens.

The next step up is either 135 mm or 200 mm. Here I prefer to jump to 200 mm which is already a formidable distance-fetching lens in numerous applications. When you want more image magnification than the 100 mm gives, you will more often want at least twice as much.

Beyond that, acquisition of the long tele lenses becomes a specialist need—none of them is a component of an essential basic outfit!

Fixed or zoom lenses?

Some of the heartsearching over which focal length to choose can be solved with variable-focus or zoom lenses. In theory such a lens of a sufficiently great focal length range could replace most if not all interchangeable lenses of fixed focal length. Something of the kind has already happened in the Super-8 movie field where most cameras have permanently built-in zoom lenses with ratios up to 8:1 and even 10:1. For the Olympus OM cameras that would be equivalent to a focal length range of say 28 to 250 mm. This is not yet feasible for the 24 × 36 mm format because scaling up zoom optical systems from the approx. 4.2 × 5.7 mm Super-8 format would make the resulting lens impossibly complicated, bulky and expensive. (The range would however meet the needs of most photographers.)

So if we look to zoom lenses in place of fixed focal lengths, we have to cover anything more than a limited focal range with at least two if not three zoom systems. In fact they have certain practical advantages as well as drawbacks compared with lenses of fixed focal length. First the advantages:

(a) You carry fewer lenses. To cover a focal length range from say 35 to 250 mm, three zoom lenses can do the job of seven fixed lenses.

(b) You have a continuous focal length range within the zooming limits for precise framing—you are not constrained by fixed focal length steps.

(c) You also change lenses less frequently.

And the drawbacks:

(a) Zoom lenses are a design compromise of largely incompatible requirements: wide zooming range, high optical performance, large aperture, compact construction and—in many minds—reasonable price. So:

(b) Zoom lenses are comparatively slow. You don't get ultra-large apertures of *f* 2 to *f* 1.2.

(c) A zoom lens is bulkier than any one of the focal lengths that it replaces. Hence it's worth getting a zoom lens only if in any case you would be using at least two main focal lengths covered by the zoom (e.g. 85 and 200 mm with the 85–250 mm lens).

(d) It is difficult to design the zoom lens to cover extreme wide angles, so you are likely to need separate ultrawide-angle lenses. The same may apply to specialist tele lenses.

So when is a zoom worthwhile?

The most obvious argument for a zoom is if you would be needing at least two of the major focal lengths covered by the zooming range anyway. For instance if you shoot a lot with 100 mm and 200 mm lenses there is a case for covering the whole field with the 85–250 mm zoom. Similarly, if a lot of your shooting is with the standard lens but you frequently need something just slightly wider or just slightly narrower, the 35–70 mm zoom offers greater flexibility.

But if you need ultra-speed lenses, if you are likely to work with two or three widely different focal lengths (e.g. ultrawide-angle, standard and longish tele), you don't gain much from having a zoom lens. Quite often a useful compromise may be to cover part of your focal length requirements with the zoom lens and the rest with two or three fixed focal lengths.

Second system steps

Interchangeable lenses apart, much of the Olympus OM equipment system caters for increasingly specialised needs, ranging from macrophotography through remote control operation, photomicrography etc. But two items are worth considering from the outset as important parts of the more general outfit.

The first is the Winder 1 or Motor drive 1. Both offer increased shooting convenience at approximately similar bulk (motor drive with Nicad M.15V control pack). With the motor drive you pay a lot for high-speed sequence shooting and extended remote control versatility; in the winder you get motorisation with reasonably rapid sequencing at more economic cost. The problem here is that if you get a winder first and then switch to the motor drive, the winder remains superfluous to the outfit.

The difference is mainly one of specialisation: if you plan to use motorisation features in laboratory and industrial applications, you obviously need the motor drive. But for general fast shooting convenience the winder is adequate most of the time.

A further item worth considering early on is the Quick Auto 310 flash unit, especially if you have the OM-2 camera whose silicon cells automatically control also the flash. The Quick Auto 310 you can acquire in stages—the flash unit first and the bounce grip—if you need it—later.

One consideration in building up any outfit is portability. As the gear increases, it becomes more of a burden to carry—even with the light weight of the Olympus outfit—and impedes rather than aids picture taking. The sensible way to start is therefore with the basic minimum you can get by with, rather than the maximum likely to be needed. Making do with what you have is an excellent way of finding out whether you need additional items badly enough—then you can add them when they really become necessary.

Which holdall case?

If you build up your camera outfit gradually, you may in

that process also outgrow one or two holdall or compartment cases. That is not in itself a bad thing, for a holdall case is not a take-all case. With a bigger outfit you may sometimes want to take the lot, especially on a longer trip. But more often you may want to carry a smaller more basic core of the outfit you have taken, and there a second (or original) smaller case is useful.

Among the Olympus cases my favourite is the compartment case M (medium), partly at least because I prefer soft holdall cases which are lighter and less bulky. You may like to shop around for something slightly larger or slightly smaller, for the holdall or compartment case range on the market is immense and caters for practically every size of outfit. If you are buying a holdall case, take the trouble of taking with you the camera outfit you want to carry in it and try out how well it fits and how conveniently you can get at the camera, lenses or other items.

When buying compartment cases it is better not to buy a size too big for future expansion: carrying a small outfit in a big half-empty case is a nuisance—unless you also take other non-camera items with you.

Holdall or compartment cases are usually tough, but they don't last for ever if you drag them through thick and thin with your camera outfit. On the other hand by the time you have worn out a case you also have a pretty good idea of exactly how you expect the next one to be better.

The outfit for travelling

This is where the two-case idea pays off. The equipment with everything you are likely to need on a long trip goes in a large compartment case which also includes a small holdall bag to carry a more modest outfit. If that bag is a soft one, it becomes easy to stow away in the rest of your luggage.

Taking camera outfits on holiday trips abroad invariably poses the dilemma between what you wish you had not left behind because you need it, and what you wish you had left because anything you carry all day weighs five times as much at the end of it. A rough rule of thumb is to assemble everything you think you might need, including film—then try to reduce the equipment by half and double the amount of film.

It may be wise also to take photocopies of invoices

covering the equipment, as proof for customs checks, when you are returning to your own country, that you have paid duty and whatever taxes are applicable. Sometimes such documentation may also be useful when dealing with customs authorities abroad.

Needless to say, a camera outfit case should be hand luggage on airlines, even if that means that you have to stuff a few other non-photographic items into the case. Airline luggage handlers may be honest, but they are rarely gentle.

Non-photographic items may also form a valuable part of a camera outfit. Mine generally includes at least a pocket tape recorder, small loose leaf notebook plus ball pen and a complete set of spare batteries for every electrically powered item from the camera's exposure meter to the flash or motor drive.

But strictly exclude from the holdall or compartment case all smoking materials and food. Tobacco, crumbs from sandwiches, grease and moisture are particularly bad for precision camera equipment.

Film and security problems

The now widespread X-ray security screening of passengers' hand luggage at airports can ruin unexposed and exposed films. While some security services claim that their X-ray machines are safe for films, experience by photographers has not necessarily confirmed this. Certainly, security screening machines vary in dosage and X-ray intensity but it is safest to assume that all are harmful to film. And irradiation effects are cumulative, so the more X-ray points a film passes—for instance when visiting several countries during a trip—the more ruinous the result.

The following procedures reduce the risk:

(a) Insist on visual inspection, without X-raying, of hand luggage. Some security operators are co-operative, others are not.

(b) Wrap all films in shielding material—either commercially available radiation protection bags or 1 mm thick lead foil. The protection is not fully safe against prolonged X-ray examination, but it helps. If you are worried, use double layers of protective bags or sheeting.

(c) Carry films separately from the rest of the hand

luggage in radiation-shielding bags and show to security staff with a request not to irradiate the film. This is somewhat cumbersome.

(d) If you don't carry too much film, stuff it all in your pockets—preferably in plastic rather than in metal containers. Unload the film in your camera as well—you can put it back later. This is even more inconvenient, but sometimes necessary on airports where security officers are particularly hostile to photographers.

Cleaning the camera—outside

In the course of handling, the camera body accumulates a great deal of dust, grime (your hands don't stay clean all the time you photograph) and possibly scratches and dents. There is little you can do about the latter, but it is worth cleaning off surface grime and dust periodically before it works its way into controls.

For an external clean-up put a lens on the camera and a cap on the lens. Then brush down all the outside, especially corners, edges etc. where dust has collected, with a small semi-stiff and, above all, clean brush. A toothbrush (medium to soft grade) is ideal. The brush at the end of a typewriter eraser is also useful. The idea is to dislodge all loose dust and grit from all the dust traps on the camera exterior. Extend the lens by focusing it on its closest distance and go around the edges of the moving barrel. But do not remove the lens cap—the brush must not get near the glass surface. Nor should it go inside the finder eyepiece.

To clean off deposits of grime, rub the parts concerned with a little water, dry with a handkerchief and repeat if necessary. Very persistent grime may need a little alcohol. But avoid petrol—and never pour any cleaning liquid directly on the camera. Apply it only with a damp (not soaking) cloth.

Camera cleaning—inside

The cleaning aids are a semi-soft long-bristled brush and a small blower—a little rubber ball with a nozzle attached to it.

Open the camera back and carefully brush out any dust, especially from the film chambers, around the transport sprocket and take-up spool. Also brush out dust from the foam plastic seal around the camera back opening, and from the back itself. Then use the blower to blow out any dust that the brush dislodged but didn't take with it. Check also for odd hairs that the brush may have shed; better still use a high-quality brush that does not shed its hairs.

Use the blower also around the film window and the shutter curtains, but do not touch the latter with the brush.

This cleaning routine for the back should be rather more frequent—whenever you change the film if you are at home and can spare the time. For dust that accumulates inside the camera gets carried along on the film and leaves tiny shadows or white spots in the negative image (black on transparencies). On enlarging or projection these dust spots or pinholes become quite noticeable.

If you frequently use the motor drive, remove also the motor drive socket cap in the base plate and blow out (but do not brush out) the gears visible through the opening.

Next remove the lens and with the blower blow out any dust from inside the camera, especially around the inside of the lens mount. You can brush out the inside of the bayonet ring, but be specially careful not to touch the mirror with the brush. Generally it is safer not to use the brush inside the camera front at all.

Cleaning camera optics

For cleaning optical glass surfaces, I have yet to find anything to beat the traditional clean and well-washed (to remove all fluff) cotton handkerchief. I am particularly suspicious of lens cleaning brushes, however soft, because they do not stay clean for long enough. And once you have touched the business end of such a brush with the fingers, it will smear grease and other contamination onto the glass surface every time it takes off a grain of dust.

To remove dust from the glass surface wipe over very gently with the clean handkerchief. And it must be really clean—unfold it before you start so that the handkerchief area that comes into contact with the glass is the one that you haven't touched with your fingers. Wipe off finger-prints or other marks by dabbing them rather than rubbing them off. Check between dabs by looking against the light reflected from the lens coating; when this is completely homogeneous, you have got rid of the print or smear.

Treat the rear glass of the lens in the same way: first dust off loose dust, next gently wipe off smears or other marks and then—still with the handkerchief—wipe clean the metal areas of the bayonet mount.

Finally, remember to wipe any dust off the inside of the lens cap.

The mirror of the camera needs equal care. This is even more delicate than the lens surface. If you have been careless enough to touch the mirror with the fingers, you will need much careful wiping and dabbing to get rid of the marks. If you are not too confident about it, leave them, as an odd fingerprint on the mirror is less noticeable in the screen image than a few scratches. For the same reason, even dust on the mirror or on the screen is a visual nuisance but not a flaw that affects the pictures.

Handle the viewfinder eyepiece the same way as the lens—again with the clean handkerchief. You may have to rub a little more here as the finder eyepiece tends to get coated with smears from eye lashes—especially from women photographers who wear make up.

Two don'ts of lens cleaning:

(a) Never breathe on a lens to wipe off marks. That's fine for spectacles, but not for high-performance camera optics.

(b) Avoid impregnated spectacle cleaning tissue, silicone cloths and lens cleaning fluids. The tissues are again OK for spectacles but what they smear over the glass is not necessarily good for camera lenses. There are safe lens cleaning fluids and people handling lenses in lens factories use them. But there are also those that are harmful (for camera lenses rather than spectacles) and you probably won't know the difference. So better avoid them altogether. Lens cleaning fluids oozing into the lens around the glass rim may also attack the lens cement and cause flaws around the edges.

Similar principles apply when cleaning other OM equipment: dust off external dust with a semi-stiff brush, remove dust in delicate inside areas (that includes bellows, extension tubes, lens adapters) with a soft brush and a blower. Clean optical surfaces (including mirrors, illuminators) with a clean handkerchief.

Admittedly, these are counsels of perfection. You *can* photograph without being so fanatical about it. A small or faint fingerprint on the lens, a bit of dust in the camera won't ruin a good picture, they'll only make it slightly less crisp and clean. It can get by if needed and press photographers often work under worse conditions. But it's nice to feel that one has taken care of the equipment to get best possible performance.

Trouble shooting

The Olympus OM cameras are simple to use—especially with automatic operation—because they are not simple cameras. The sophistication that goes into the mechanical, electrical and optical innards also involves more items that very occasionally appear to go wrong. 'Appear' because it's not only the camera that has to be automatic, but the reaction of the user, too. And if an interlock is meant to stop you from doing something wrong, such as unintentional double exposures, you may also on occasion forget that the reason why you can't take the picture is because that interlock is doing its job. . . .

What follows, then, is a list of various items of Olympus OM operation that might now and again act differently from how you would expect them to act or otherwise appear irregular or puzzling. For convenience they are broadly grouped as viewfinder, metering, releasing and film transport, self-timer and flash problems. Potential problems with the motor drive or winder are covered later (see Chpt. *The motor drive group*).

Finder screen is dark all over: The most stupidly obvious answer is that you have forgotten to remove the lens cap. The finder also stays dark when the mirror on the OM-1 is locked up or if the OM-2 mirror locks up through lack of, or exhausted, battery.

The remedy in most cases is obvious from the causes listed. If that does not appear to cure the trouble, don't be shy to take the camera to an Olympus servicing facility or to consult an expert repairer. You may feel a slight fool if the fault was after all a minor operating error—but not as much a fool as if you caused real damage by trying to force, twist or yank something that was not intended for that treatment.

Microprism or split-image wedge area partially dark: Maximum lens aperture too small for microprism or wedge profile. Often happens when you use a tele lens with the 1–13 or 1–1 screen, in extreme near focusing with a macro lens or when stopping down the lens with the preview key. The microprism spot or its centre may clear in such cases if you keep the eye carefully centred behind the eyepiece. Otherwise focus on the matt area around the microprism spot.

Meter needle does not react at all on switching on meter: The obvious cause is an exhausted battery or batteries, so check by the appropriate battery test procedure. But before you hurry to throw away batteries, check also whether you have put in the cell or cells the right way round and that they are clean. If the meter packs up without warning on the OM-2, remove the cells, thoroughly clean them with a cloth and replace. Getting rid of the insulating effect of chemical deposits from the cell restores good contact.

Battery compartment cap does not fit: If you own an OM-1 and an OM-2 and decided to change batteries on both, you may have switched the very similar looking covers. Only obvious difference is that OM-2 cover has a figure 2 engraved inside it.

ASA dial locks on OM-1: Remember that you must press the small button next to it to rotate the ASA dial.

You cannot reach the ASA value you want to set on the OM-2: To switch from very low to very high ASA settings or vice versa you have to go in two stages: set the highest (or lowest) value you can, then rotate the override knob backwards to make the rest of the ASA range accessible.

Exposure compensation dial won't move to correction wanted: The movement of this dial is limited at the highest and the lowest ASA settings.

Automatic exposures on the OM-2 appear to be much longer than the finder monitoring guide: That is liable to happen when you try out the empty camera. The manual exposure metering and finder monitoring system of the OM-2 is calibrated to indicate the exposure the silicon cells would yield when measuring light reflected from the film. With no film in the camera, the silicon cells measure the black pressure plate and so lengthen exposure time. The exposure will be right when you load the camera.

Appreciably overexposed results with manual metering: You accidentally pressed the preview (stop-down) key on the lens while taking the meter reading. In effect you made a working-aperture reading with full-aperture compensation—having your cake and eating it produced indigestion.

Release button blocked—you cannot release: The obvious cause is failure to advance the film by the winding lever. But failure to operate the lever fully also keeps the release blocked. If you are at the end of the film, see below.

Release button not blocked, but pressing it has no effect: This is the likely condition in the OM-2 when you get mirror lock-up—usually because the battery is exhausted or there is no battery in the camera. In addition to no releasing, the finder is dark and the winding lever blocked.

Winding lever blocked: It obviously always is after you have advanced the film ready for the next shot. But it also remains blocked after mirror lock-up on the OM-2 (see above) and it may block during operation if you have reached the end of the film. In the latter case never force the lever but rewind the film immediately.

Uneven spacing of frames on film with partial overlapping: You accidentally switched the rewind release lever to the rewind position between exposures. The transport system then does not advance the full frame length. The same also happens if you have made deliberate double exposures and then failed to return the rewind release to its normal forward position.

Rewind knob does not rotate during film winding: It won't at the beginning if you haven't taken up the slack in the film cartridge during loading. But don't wait for that—turn the rewind crank until the film is gently tensioned, then check whether the knob rotates during the next film advance. If it doesn't, the film was not attached properly to the take-up spool during loading, or the perforation has torn before both sides of the film have reached the transport sprocket. But the perforation can also tear if you force the winding movement at the end of the film: you can then alternately expose and wind without the rewind knob turning (and without advancing any film).

Rewind knob blocked during rewinding: If you didn't

turn the rewind release lever all the way to the rewind position (lever fully horizontal) it cannot free the transport sprocket to allow rewinding. If the lever is in the proper rewind position and the crank is still blocked, *do not force it*. You may have torn the film (for instance by forcing the transport at the end of the film) and this stops the film from returning into the cartridge. Take the camera into a completely dark room, open the back and feel for any tear in the film. Try to ease the torn part—usually the result of a torn perforation—into the cartridge, wind up some film into the latter, replace the cartridge in the camera back and rewind carefully with the camera open in the dark.

Winding lever remains blocked after an exposure: You have failed to take your finger off the release button. Also let go of the winding lever (especially if it hasn't returned to its starting position) before operating it again. The winding lever also remains blocked if the self-timer has not fully run down after releasing the shutter and so kept the release button partly depressed.

Self-timer does not engage during tensioning: You didn't tension it far enough—pull the lever down till it's at least horizontal.

Self-timer runs down but does not operate shutter: You didn't tension the lever sufficiently (see above) but managed to lock its start lever. Tension by pulling the lever down to at least horizontal.

Self-timer won't start on operating start lever: Same cause as above—self-timer was not sufficiently tensioned.

Self-timer stops during run-down just above horizontal position: You failed to tension the shutter by the winding lever. Pull down the self-timer tensioning lever to at least horizontal again before tensioning the shutter—otherwise the self-timer resumes its travel and immediately trips the shutter.

Electronic flash connected to camera does not fire: Apart from causes related to the flash unit (exhausted battery, poor contact) this occurs on the OM-2 if you have set (or the automatic system has selected) a shutter speed faster than 1/60 second.

Electronic flash fires but has no effect on film: Flash selector switch was accidentally set to FP instead of X.

Half of image missing in flash shot: Liable to occur with

OM-1 if you use electronic flash at 1/125 second or faster.

Only centre of flash shot exposed: Ordinary class M flash bulb of too short duration used instead of FP type.

TECHNIQUE OF THE FILM

All film is loaded into the OM cameras in standard cartridges of 35 mm film—internationally known as the No. 135 cartridge. (The only exception is the 250 film back.) This is also the usual way in which 35 mm film is sold.

The cartridge is light-tight with a velvet-lined slot through which the film emerges. The cartridge can thus be loaded into the camera in daylight (but preferably not bright sunlight). The film unrolls from the cartridge inside the camera when the latter is closed and is rewound into the cartridge before being unloaded. For processing the cartridge is opened and the film removed.

A standard cartridge holds normally 36 or 20 exposures. Some makers also produce 12-exposure cartridges and may market 24-exposure instead of 20-exposure ones. The 36-exposure cartridge contains about 163 cm or 64 inches of film; of this 137 cm or 54 inches is the film length for 36 exposures and the rest is film leader for loading by normal light and the trailer for attachment to the cartridge spool. The actual length is standard within about 1.5 cm or $\frac{1}{2}$ inch of the above value. As with a 24-exposure and smaller cartridge load you still have to pay for the same leader and cartridge itself, the 36-exposure load is obviously the most economical cartridge in terms of cost per exposure.

But don't rely on the full 36 exposures. If you follow the recommended loading procedure with the fairly generous blind exposures at the beginning, the film transport may block when you advance after exposure No. 36. If you process your own films, this doesn't matter as you have enough film for handling after this last shot. But films that are processed by photofinishers—including reversal colour films with processing costs included—may lose this last exposure. For the photofinisher may chop off quite a lot of the film end and use even more for splicing films to run them through automatic processors. And that may encroach on the last exposure on the film.

By all means utilise all the exposures you can on a film. But if the transport stops partway after a shot, treat the previous exposure as probably lost and repeat it as soon as you have changed the film.

Refills and bulk economy

Buying films in standard cartridges is obviously the most convenient way: no fuss for buying and least fuss for loading. If you are particularly cash minded, you can save costs by buying film for the OM camera in one of two other ways: bulk lengths of 5 to 30 metres ($16\frac{1}{2}$ to 100 feet) and darkroom refills. Both are charged into reloadable cartridges before loading into the camera. You also use bulk film for loading the 250-exposure magazines of the 250 film back.

Darkroom refills—also known as a No. 935 packing—were originally produced for a special cassette used in 35 mm cameras. In a few countries this is still the main form in which you obtain 35 mm film. Bulk film is the only form in which certain special materials such as internegative or reversal duplicating films are available.

No. 935 refills and bulk film make film use more economical as you don't have to pay for a new cartirdge every time. In practice you save about 30% in cost with No. 935 darkroom refills and up to 50% with bulk film. You do however need reloadable cartridges with their attendant risks. Apart from special emulsions, bulk film is normally available only in black-and-white—not in the usual colour materials.

Reloadable cartridges

Physically it is possible to load a fresh length of film into a standard cartridge after this has been opened for removing an exposed film. In practice that is risky as a re-closed cartridge may not be light-tight due to damage during opening. More solidly constructed cartridges to stand up to repeated dismantling and re-assembly are however obtainable empty as reloadable cartridges for special materials or bulk film. Apart from the availability of special materials the economics of bulk film reloading has to balance the actual film saving against the reloadable cartridges that have to be bought and the amount of time spent in reloading them plus the risk of scratches, fingermarks etc. in film handling.

Reloadable standard cartridges may be metal or plastic and consist of an outside shell, a lid (or two lids) and a centre spool. The centre spool, with a knob at one end, takes the film which is attached to the core. Inside the hollow core a crossbar engages the forked rewind shaft of the camera. The outer shell has a slot with velvet light-trapping. In more solid metal cartridges both ends of the shell have removable clip-on lids. With these lids removed, the slot spreads open sufficiently to allow the velvet to be cleaned with a fine brush to remove possible dust and grit. Plastic cartridges often have one screw-on lid at one end only; the velvet in the slot is less accessible here.

Partly exposed films

If you routinely use various different films you may sometimes find yourself wanting to use one kind of film while the camera is loaded with a different emulsion. If you have a part-used colour film in the camera but want to make some black-and-white shots (or vice versa) you can fairly easily unload the part-used film and reload it to continue on another occasion.

This is successful if you follow a standard loading procedure, especially for advancing the film to bring both sides of the perforation onto the sprocket wheel and for always making the same number of blind exposures. When you want to change the film for later re-use, note the number of the next exposure on the film counter and rewind the film in the usual way.

However, stop turning the rewind crank before the film end disappears into the cartridge. That point is easy to judge as you can feel the film end leaving the take-up spool. Stop rewinding there, open the camera, remove the film (the trimmed leader will still project from the cartridge at this point) and write the number noted from the frame counter on the emulsion side of the film end. Wind the protruding film leader round the cartridge, emulsion side out, and store in a film container or at least a light-tight box. It helps to enclose a label indicating what is on the film, the date etc.

When reloading proceed exactly as for normal loading, right up to the first exposure. Then set the camera shutter to a fast fixed shutter speed—e.g. 1/1000 second or X depending on model (with manual operation on the OM-2), the lens to its smallest aperture and fit the lens cap. Carry out the next steps in subdued light if possible—an extra safety precaution.

Now alternately release the shutter and advance the film until the frame counter regains the number you had noted and at which you had unloaded the film. Operate the release and transport lever once more (to bring the counter one frame beyond the previous unloading point), switch back to the operating mode that you want to use and continue shooting with that camera and film combination. The release/winder cycles of course advance the film—without fogging—to the point where you unloaded it.

Film types

The main kinds of film you are likely to use are negative colour, reversal colour and negative black-and-white.

On processing, an exposed *negative colour film* shows, compared with the original scene, reversed tones and colours. The tone reversal is a characteristic of any negative-positive process: the more light acts on the film, the darker it gets. So bright subject portions appear dark in the negative and dark subject areas (shadows) light in the negative.

Colours turn into their complementaries: blue sky records in the negative as yellow, green grass as purplish (magenta), red items as blue-green (cyan) and so on. These are dyes formed in the film during processing of a negative silver image which is then removed. Colour negatives are enlarged onto colour paper, where the whole image-forming mechanism and chemistry is reversed once more: the tones return to their correct light/dark relationship and the colours resemble again the hues of the original subject. Hence negative colour film is often labelled colour print film.

On modern colour negative films the complementary colour tones in the negative are not very clearly recognisable as the whole image appears overlaid by an orange-yellow tint. This so-called integral mask functions in a fairly complex way to improve the faithfulness with which the film renders subject colours.

Colour films are processed by commercial large-scale photofinishers (who also make prints) or by professional processing laboratories—who usually yield better results at increased cost. You can also process negative colour films yourself with chemical kits issued by the film makers and independent chemical manufacturers. This is reasonably straightforward, but with some processes requires warming up the solutions to well above room temperature (for instance some 38°C or 100°F) and keeping them accurately at that level.

Reversal colour film yields positive colour transparencies for projection on a screen. It is therefore often labelled *colour transparency* or *colour slide film*. The transparency is produced on the film you exposed in the camera and is therefore unique, though you can have duplicates and enlarged prints made from it. In the transparency the negative and positive image formation take place in succession in the same film during processing, hence the more or less correct tone and colour values in the result.

To look at colour transparencies you need at least a viewer and preferably a projector. This is a little inconvenient, but projected transparencies show a far greater range of luminosities and usually more brilliant colours than a print. The effect is thus more natural.

Many colour slide films are sold inclusive of processing cost. That obliges you to send the films back to the manufacturer or an appointed processing station that returns the finished transparencies without further charge. They usually come back mounted individually in 5 × 5 cm or 2 × 2 inch card or plastic frames, ready for projection. With other types you pay for processing and mounting, and for these films user processing kits are available. But processing colour reversal film is rather more complex than handling colour negative film, involving a longer procedure with more solutions and precise temperature control.

Black-and-white negative film, the classical photographic material, again records images with reversed tonality and yields enlargements of more or less any size. The concept of using a small negative area to produce large prints was at the heart of the evolution of photography on 35 mm wide perforated film. Black-and-white film processing is simple enough for the user. As the chemistry—involving no dye formation—is virtually the same for all black-and-white negative films, there is no need for system-specific processing kits. While manufacturers recommend preferred developing and fixing formulae, many others can be used. Or you can employ commercial photofinishers or higher-quality professional development and printing services.

Film speed

The sensitivity or speed of the film is the most important characteristic for exposure purposes: the more sensitive a film, the less light it needs for a correctly exposed result.

Film speed measurement and specification is unified through most of the world by equivalent national and international standards. Hence in most parts of the world if you buy a film rated at say 80 ASA, that film should yield correctly exposed pictures in a camera whose exposure meter system is set to that film speed figure.

The ASA film speed scale is today the best known and most widely used speed rating system. The system is arithmetic: ASA values are directly proportional to the speed, and hence inversely proportional to the exposure required under given conditions. ASA speed values also run in a prescribed series of one-third step intervals, e.g. 25 – 32 – 40 – 50 – 64 – 80 – 100 – 125 – 160 – 200 – 250 – 320 – 400 – 500 ASA and so on. The standards specifying this film speed scale do not admit intermediate steps between these values. (The values themselves are separated by a factor of cube-root-of-2.) There is thus no such thing as 57 ASA, 75 ASA etc. The film speed scales of the OM cameras carry arithmetic ASA ratings.

ASA stood for American Standards Association—now ANSI (American National Standard Institute); but the ASA designation as a film speed was so familiar worldwide that it survived the Association itself.

DIN speed values are a logarithmic scale still used in central Europe. Here every increase of 3 DIN doubles the film speed (10 DIN increases it ten-fold). The individual DIN steps thus have the same intervals as the prescribed series of ASA values. DIN values are directly convertible to ASA. Though the OM cameras do not carry a DIN film speed scale, the packings of virtually all films rated in DIN also carry equivalent ASA values.

GOST ratings, used in Eastern Europe, are an arithmetical scale similar to ASA. If you use a film of East European origin, scaled in GOST, assume it to be equivalent to the next higher ASA figure. For instance 90 GOST = approx. 100 ASA.

Film speed measurements for negative colour, reversal colour or black-and-white film are based on different criteria but yield equivalent exposures when used in exposure metering systems such as those of the Olympus OM cameras.

Film choice

At first sight, film speed may seem an obvious criterion for choosing films. The faster a film the more versatile it is, for instance in poor light. But other characteristics also count; very high speed is often obtained at the expense of greater image graininess and reduced high detail resolution. Slower films tend to give sharper images and often better colour quality. And a film can be too fast; with extreme-speed film in bright daylight you may be unable to avoid overexposure even with the fastest shutter speed and smallest lens aperture.

So film choice is often a compromise, though rarely a very strenuous one. Among each film type—colour negative, colour transparency and black-and-white—there are all-round materials that offer good useful speed for all outdoor and some indoor shooting (especially with the faster Olympus lenses) combined with highly acceptable overall quality. Colour negative materials of this kind are usually rated at 80 to 100 ASA and often labelled 'something-color II' to distinguish them from earlier film types of coarser grain. The most useful all-round colour slide films are rated at 64–100 ASA and all-round black-and-white films between 100 and 200 ASA.

High-speed films of all three types come at around 400 ASA and still offer an acceptable quality compromise. You would notice the difference in sharpness, graininess and colour saturation if you directly compared the results with those of the all-round films mentioned.

Extreme-speed films (in black-and-white only) show a distinct drop in image quality but these are films you would use to shoot in poorest light conditions where the choice is between no picture and a slightly grainy one of a dramatic or otherwise exceptional situation.

At the other extreme, in good light conditions slow films—colour transparency and black-and-white only—offer specially enhanced image quality that stands up to very high magnification in enlargements and on projection. This is a fine film type to use if you are sure you won't have to cope with indifferent light conditions at short notice.

With reversal colour films you also have the choice between *daylight type* and *artificial light type* film. The colour rendering in a transparency depends on the colour of the exposing light and the film responds sensitively to the difference between white daylight and the rather more yellowish-orange tungsten lighting. The latter would on a daylight type film yield colours with a distinct shift towards orange or red. Artificial light type film is balanced for this excess red (and lack of blue) in tungsten light and there yields results more like what we think the scene looked like.

As the colour quality of electronic flash and nearly all flash bulbs currently available is similar to that of daylight, daylight type reversal colour film will cope with most occasions. Use artificial light type when shooting indoors by lamplight, floodlit buildings at night and in street lighting. (But mercury or sodium vapour lamps yield peculiar results on any colour film.)

Daylight is not constant in colour quality, either and can range from white midday sunlight to warm yellowish when the sun is low or cold bluish for subjects in the shade lit only by blue sky. These variations can be compensated if necessary by filters.

Special materials

Apart from the general-purpose colour and black-and-white films, there exist several 35 mm materials for special applications. Thus colour reversal duplicating and internegative films are used in slide copying, and black-and-white copying and microfilming materials in document copying and similar applications.

First the special colour materials:

Reversal duplicating film is a low-contrast reversal film

for making duplicates from original colour transparencies. It has a comparatively soft gradation to counteract the tendency to contrast enhancement when copying colour transparencies on reversal film. The ideal equipment set-up is the slide copier on the Auto-bellows. Most reversal duplicating film is balanced for tungsten lighting (typically 3200 K). The colour rendering of the original transparency may be modified by placing colour correction filters between the light source and the transparency.

Internegative film is a slow negative colour film of controllable contrast for making negatives from positive colour transparencies. These negatives can then serve for conventional colour enlargements, or for making duplicate transparencies on colour print film. The negatives are again made with the slide copier, effectively by rephotographing the colour transparency at 1:1 scale.

Colour positive film is a material for producing duplicate colour transparencies via internegatives. This is the usual way when large numbers of duplicates are required from one transparency or group of transparencies. Reversal duplicating film is more convenient for single duplicates.

Printing again involves rephotographing, but this time the colour negative goes into the transparency holder of the slide copier and the colour print film in the camera. Colour rendering can be controlled by modifying the light colour with colour printing filters. This slide making procedure (and the film) are however intended more for commercial transparency duplicating services. Those also have access to more sophisticated colour analysers to establish required filtration and colour correction at the printing stage.

The following special black-and-white materials exist as perforated 35 mm film:

Black-and-white reversal film is a camera film for making direct black-and-white transparencies, for instance in film strip production or for making slides as teaching aids. The effective speed of the material is usually around 20 to 50 ASA and it is handled and exposed in the same way as a colour transparency film of a similar speed.

Positive or copying films are slow and usually high-contrast materials usable either for making black-and-white transparencies from negatives or for copying documents, drawings etc. at not too great a reduction. Most such films are blue-sensitive only and can be processed by red darkroom lighting. The films do not normally carry a speed rating as exposures are established by tests. Positives are made by contact printing, by same-size projection printing or by rephotographing, for instance with the slide copier.

Microfilming materials are high-contrast films of specially high resolution and acutance for reduced-size copying of documents. The films may be blue-sensitive or panchromatic and effective film speed varies not only according to the film but also according to the way it is exposed.

Infrared-sensitive film carries an emulsion sensitive to long-wave radiation beyond the red end of the visible spectrum (about 700 nm) up to around 850 nm. The infrared sensitivity of such a film is considerably lower than its speed to visible light. To prevent the latter from overshadowing the infrared effect, the film is always used with a special infrared filter over the camera lens. The lens generally requires refocusing.

Applications of infrared film depend on two properties of such radiation: its reduced scattering by atmospheric haze, etc. and different reflection characteristics of many materials (especially pigments) to infrared and to visible radiation. The reduced atmospheric scatter is utilised in long-distance photography. Views taken on infrared film with an infrared filter over the lens show extremely clear distant detail. Characteristic tone distortions include the dead black rendering of blue skies (which reflect no infrared rays) and the snowy white appearance of foliage due to its high reflectivity to infrared rays.

Differential absorption and reflection characteristics of many materials to infrared can identify such materials or distinguish between different visually similar pigments. This is widely used in forensic photography.

Fluorographic films are blue-sensitive or blue and green-sensitive (orthochromatic) films for photographing images on fluorescent X-ray screens and on cathode ray tubes. The colour sensitivity of the film is matched to the peak spectral emission of the screen phosphor. Similar films are needed for photography with image intensifiers; the camera there records the image on the intensifier tube. Such films have no speed rating (there are no film speed standards for this kind of application) and exposures are based on preliminary trials to establish a suitable correction factor. That allows for the difference in response to the phosphor screen emission by the exposure metering cells and by the film respectively.

Keeping quality of films

The film emulsion is comparatively unstable. It loses speed and changes its sensitometric characteristics during storage. Storage conditions determine how fast this occurs, but it does go on all the time.

To provide a check on slight deterioration under normal conditions, film manufacturers print an expiry date on the film package. This is the limit of the time for which the manufacturer guarantees consistent characteristics of the product. Films of course do not change their properties abruptly at this date but often remain perfectly usable well beyond the expiry date.

The expiry date also gives a clue to the manufacturing date. Slow and medium-speed black-and-white films usually carry an expiry date about 3–4 years after they leave the factory; high-speed films about 2 to $2\frac{1}{2}$ years. With colour films the date is generally 18 months ahead, as the different emulsion layers of the colour material may lose speed at different rates. Hence the colour balance may change noticeably by a date when the loss of speed of a single black-and-white emulsion would not yet be significant.

The deterioration—in colour and speed—varies with different films. But you can assume that a colour film used near the end of its expiry date is about 25–30% slower (one ASA interval on the film speed scale) than when fresh. Colour films used up to 6 months after expiry should generally get double the normal exposure. But if the photographic job is important, use fresh film rather than risk wasting time and effort with stale emulsions.

To avoid inconsistencies from batch-to-batch variations of films, use films of the same emulsion batch only for consistent colour rendering on a job. Generally stock as much film as you are likely to need over 3 to 6 months.

For laboratory use, stock enough film to last for a year, as there consistent characteristics are still more important. In this case store all film in deep freeze conditions. Use up films in the order in which they are bought in.

Storage conditions

Normally store films at between 10° and 20°C (50° and 68°F) and at relative humidity of about 50%. That is what the usual recommendation of a 'cool and dry place' means. Keep the film away from harmful gases and fumes—e.g. ammonia, combustion and exhaust gases containing sulphur (hydrogen sulphide, sulphur dioxide), also solvent vapours, formaldehyde etc. The film containers provide some protection. A tin with a screw cap or a rubber ring or pad is best for more or less hermetic sealing, but this type of container has now largely been displaced by plastic. Foil-sealed packaging is the best protection.

Higher humidity is more harmful to the film than higher temperature. But do not keep films in warm cupboards or near radiators. Open the sealed package only when you are ready to use the film.

Keep films away from X-rays and nuclear radiation—a special hazard in hospitals and scientific laboratories. Such radiation rapidly fogs the film, even when in its normal sealed packing. If there is any risk of radiation exposure, store films in radiation-shielded cabinets. X-ray units used in airport security are also potentially harmful to film.

Refrigeration

Professional and industrial users of colour films often store these refrigerated to reduce deterioration. You can do the same in a domestic refrigerator with suitable precautions:

Store at 5–10°C (40–50°F) if the film is likely to be wanted at fairly short notice. But for long-term keeping (and also infrared film) films may be stored in a deep freeze container at −20°C or thereabouts. Keep films in unopened sealed packages only, to prevent moisture condensation when the film warms up again.

Before use allow cooled or refrigerated films to regain ambient temperature *before the sealed pack is opened.*

Otherwise moisture may condense on the film and cause a variety of image faults. Allow about 6 hours for a film to warm up from deep-freeze storage, 1 to 2 hours from a normal refrigerator. Films warm up quicker in individual rather than multiple packs. Bulk film takes much longer.

Once a film package is opened, do not return it to the refrigerator unless it has first been dried by storage in an air-tight container with silica gel and resealed airtight.

TONE AND COLOUR

We photograph most subjects by approximately white light. This is selectively reflected according to the spectral and overall reflectivity of different parts of the subject, making such parts appear in different colours and different brightnesses. Black-and-white film records such subject detail in tone values depending on corresponding brightnesses and on the film's sensitivity to different colours. In colour film the selective response of the multi-layer system and the dyes generated in processing more or less faithfully reproduce the colour hues of the subject.

In both cases the response of the film can be modified by altering the spectral quality of the light reaching it. The usual photographic way is to place a piece of transparent coloured material—a filter—somewhere between the light source and the film. Filters placed in front of the lens are most convenient to handle and can be small (but must be of high optical quality). Sometimes filters are located in front of the light source, for instance to adjust its colour temperature in macrophotography.

Black-and-white tone control

Filters employed in black-and-white photography are quite strongly coloured. Such a filter preferentially transmits light of its own colour and of neighbouring colours in the spectrum, but holds back light of other colours. An orange filter reasonably freely transmits red, orange and yellow rays, but progressively holds back green, blue and violet. So the light from blue subject portions is reduced more than from orange ones and the former are rendered darker in the final print.

Filter use in black-and-white photography depends on this selective colour control. It becomes necessary because the monochrome rendering of a coloured scene suppresses differences due merely to colour but not to brightness. To take a much-quoted classical case, if you photograph a red rose among green foliage on a medium-speed panchromatic film, the red and green portions reproduce in approximately similar tones of grey. The visual separation due to the colour contrast disappears. We can simulate this missing colour contrast by turning it into a tone contrast—rendering either the green foliage or the red rose lighter or darker than the other.

A similar need for converting colour contrast into black-and-white contrast arises in copying colour originals, photographing postage stamps to show up or suppress coloured post marks against stamp backgrounds of a different colour, in commercial photography, photomicrography of stained specimens etc. The filter in every case lightens (in the final print) subject areas in its own colour and darkens details of other colours. The darkening is progressive, the further in the spectrum the subject colour is removed from the filter colour. Thus while greens are rendered lightest with a green filter, orange to red tones on the one hand and blue to violet on the other get progressively darker.

One of the commonest cases for filter use in black-and-white photography is the yellow or orange filter in outdoor views with blue sky areas. With correct exposure of the foreground the far more luminous sky tends to be overexposed—one reason for the centre weighting in exposure metering. That not only puts the pictorial effect out of balance but also kills the differentiation between blue sky and white clouds. By its selective action on the blue skylight, the yellow or orange filter reduces the sky exposure relative to the foreground and improves cloud detail. At the same time the filter corrects the film's tendency to excessive blue sensitivity.

The effect on the sky is progressively greater with the orange and the red filters, used sometimes pictorially to make e.g. architecture stand out against a deep sky. The selective filter action is however only valid for a blue sky, not for a bright overcast one.

Filter factors and metering

While filters preferentially transmit light of their own colour, they reduce the overall lighting level, and so make extra exposure necessary. This is usually quoted in terms of exposure factors by which the exposure time without a filter has to be multiplied.

The CdS—and especially the silicon—metering cells of the OM cameras reasonably match the spectral sensitivity of the human eye and of modern average films, so the through-the-lens measurement with the filter over the camera lens allows roughly for the exposure increase required with the filter. The manual and monitoring readings with the CdS cell do however tend to underreact slightly to yellow, orange and red filtering. When these filters are on the lens, read off the correct exposure combination for ½ stop overexposure. This does not apply to automatic exposures with the OM-2 where the silicon cell is not affected in the same way by this discrepancy.

With the lighter filters—and the filters used with colour film (see below)—it is convenient to view and focus the image with the filter mounted on the lens. With the deeper filters the image on the screen may become inconveniently dark for focusing—though the filter should not affect the microprism spot. Usually it is more convenient then to focus without the filter and fit the filter immediately before the exposure.

With an infrared filter both focusing and exposure control become impossible through the filter. There focus without the filter and readjust the lens setting to the infrared focusing mark. Measure the exposure in the manual mode—also without filter—basing it on the recommended film speed for the infrared film/filter combination employed.

Are filters necessary?

Not nearly as often as they are used. Normally lenses are designed to yield optimum performance with just the glass elements that they consist of. Any additional element in the optical path, including a filter, tends to impair image performance at the same time as it modifies image tones.

One way in which a filter affects lens performance is that oblique rays may cause a displacement of marginal image points on the film and thus slight image distortion. The risk is greatest with ultrawide-angle lens where filters are best avoided. That is also why the fisheye lenses have filters built-in; there the optical design allows for the permanent presence of a filter element in the light path.

Less important in normal conditions is a focus shift due to the change in the light path through the filter. This shift is about 1 mm in terms of lens/subject distance, but matters in macrophotography. That is why filters are there best used in front of the light source such as the LSD spotlight.

Obviously flaws in filters—fingermarks on the surface, lack of parallelism between the glass surfaces etc.—also affect optical performance. These effects are particularly marked with long-focus and tele lenses. So keep filters clean and be sure you have high-quality filters.

Under most circumstances the image deterioration due to filters is very slight. But it does mean that filters should be used only where they are really necessary. In particular, avoid keeping an ultraviolet filter over the lens all the time. While this does protect the lens against scratches or fingermarks, similar marks on the filter are just as bad for the picture. And you purchase this protection with a permanent slight down-grading of image sharpness.

Filters for colour film

The Skylight filter is an ultraviolet-absorbing filter with a faint amber tint to produce a slightly warmer colour rendering on reversal colour film of outdoor scenes under an overcast sky or lit only by reflected light from the blue sky (hence the name). Such light conditions—i.e. the absence of direct sun—otherwise produce a somewhat cold colour effect. The presence of ultraviolet radiation—for instance in high mountain regions but also nearer large water surfaces that reflect ultraviolet—causes a blue cast on colour reversal films since the blue-responding layer is sensitive to UV. The skylight filter absorbs ultraviolet as well, to eliminate this. A UV filter can be used on its own to cut out UV without the warm-toning effect.

The A4 amber filter is a stronger colour correction filter for more prominent warm effects than the skylight filter. It improves daylight shots in the shade and very dull weather.

The A4 filter is also useful with some types of electronic

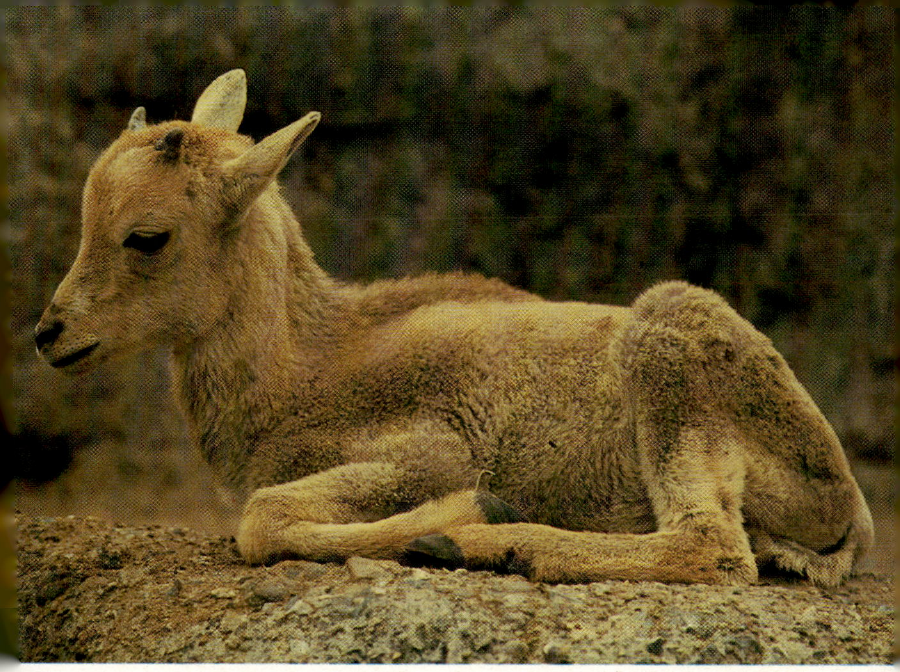

RESTING GOAT
The zoo is the traditional place for peaceful animal shots. With a long-focus lens you do not need to get near but you do need a steady camera. Support it against railings or something similar.

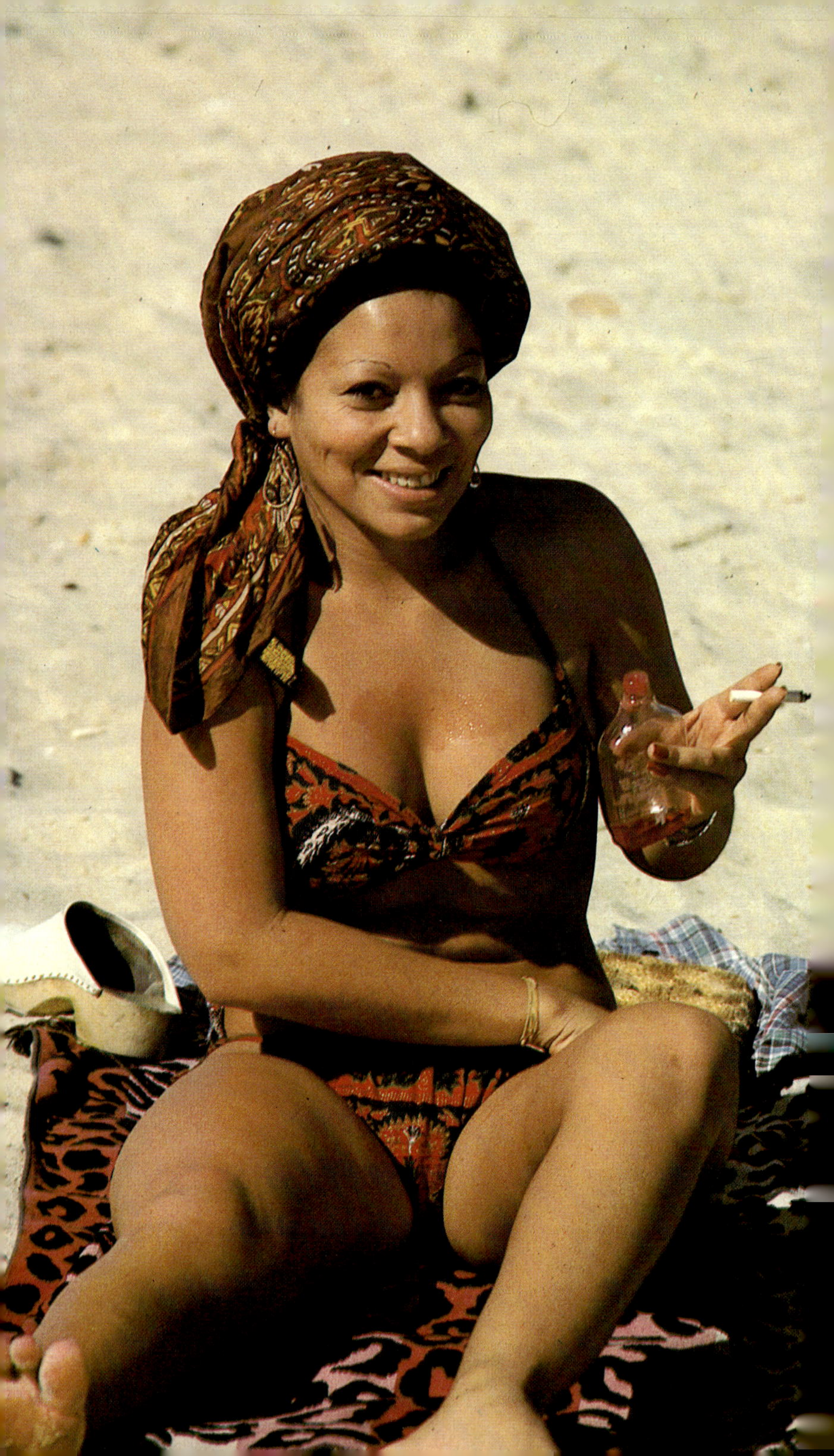

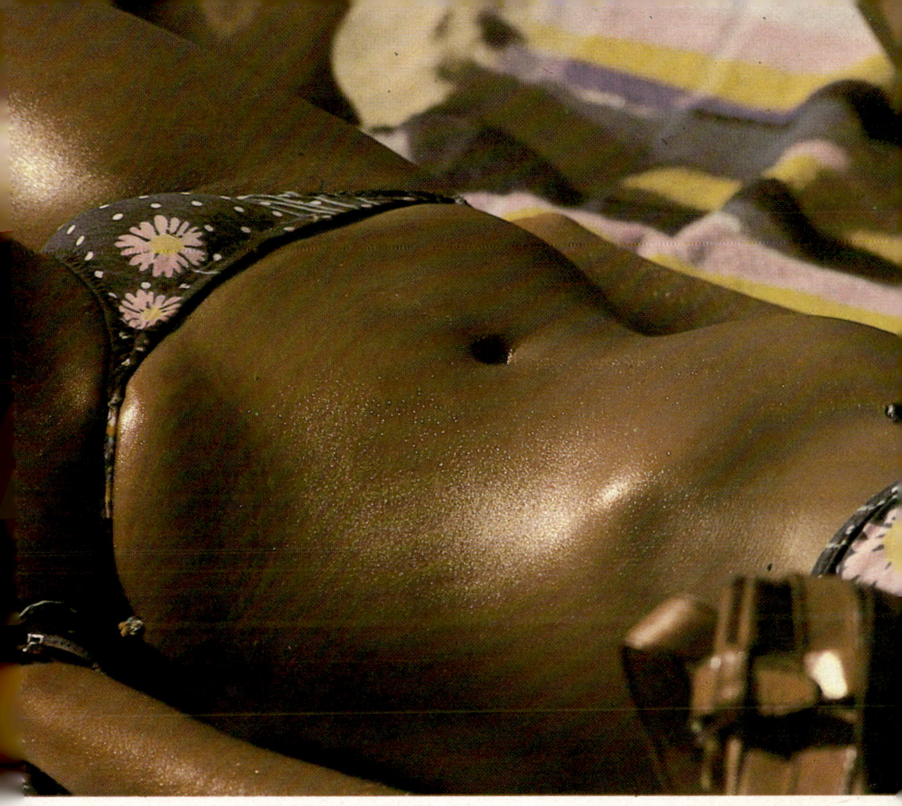

COPACABANA BEACH
Pretty girls on the beach are traditional subjects, too, but you can try less traditional views with the 70-150 zoom lenses. Contrast can be high but pale sand reflects much light into shadows.

AT THE ROYAL BALLET
Plates 4 and 5. Theatre lighting is uneven and often very dim but the colour effects can be impressive. You can even use movement blur for atmosphere. *John Starr.*

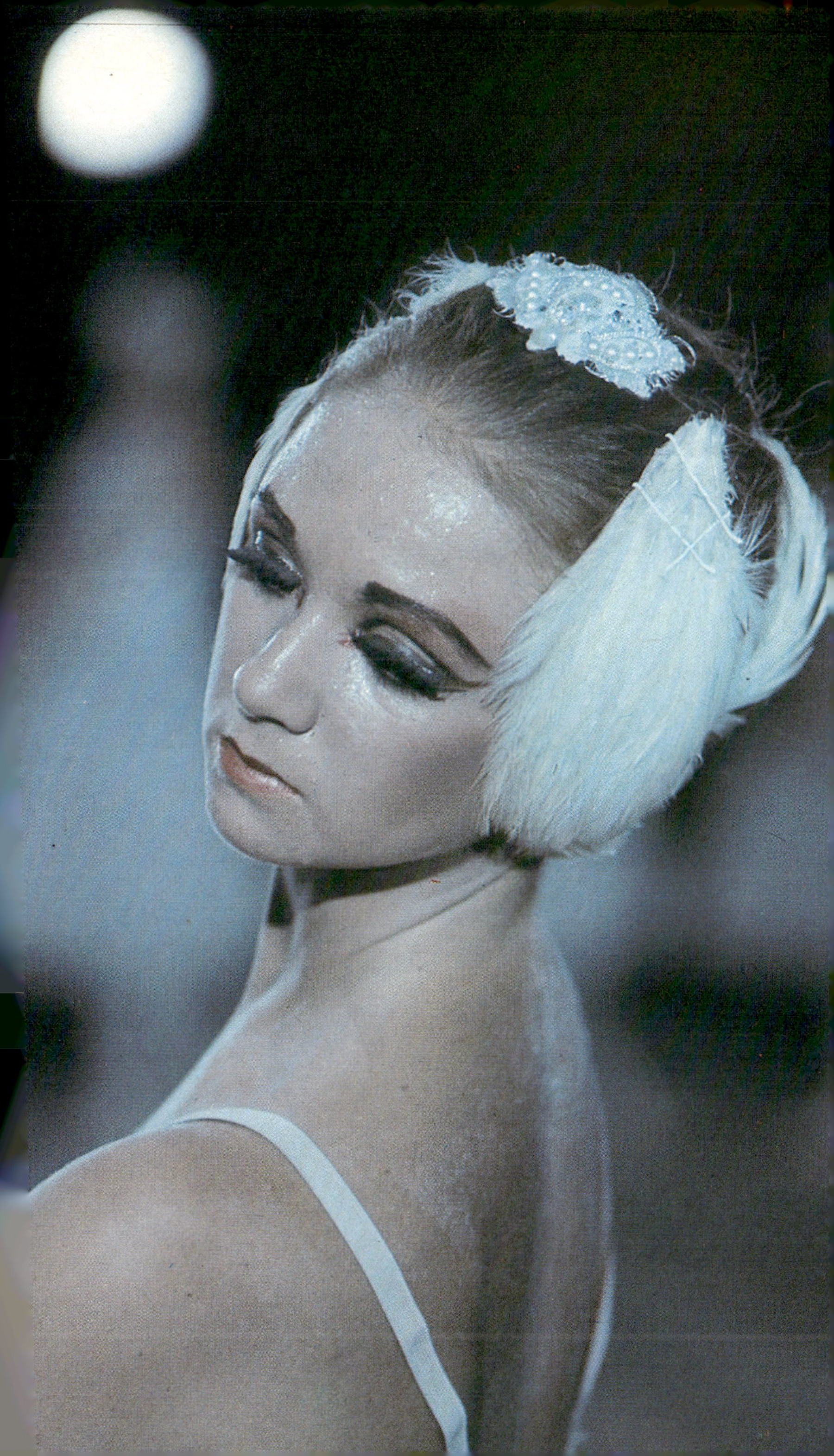

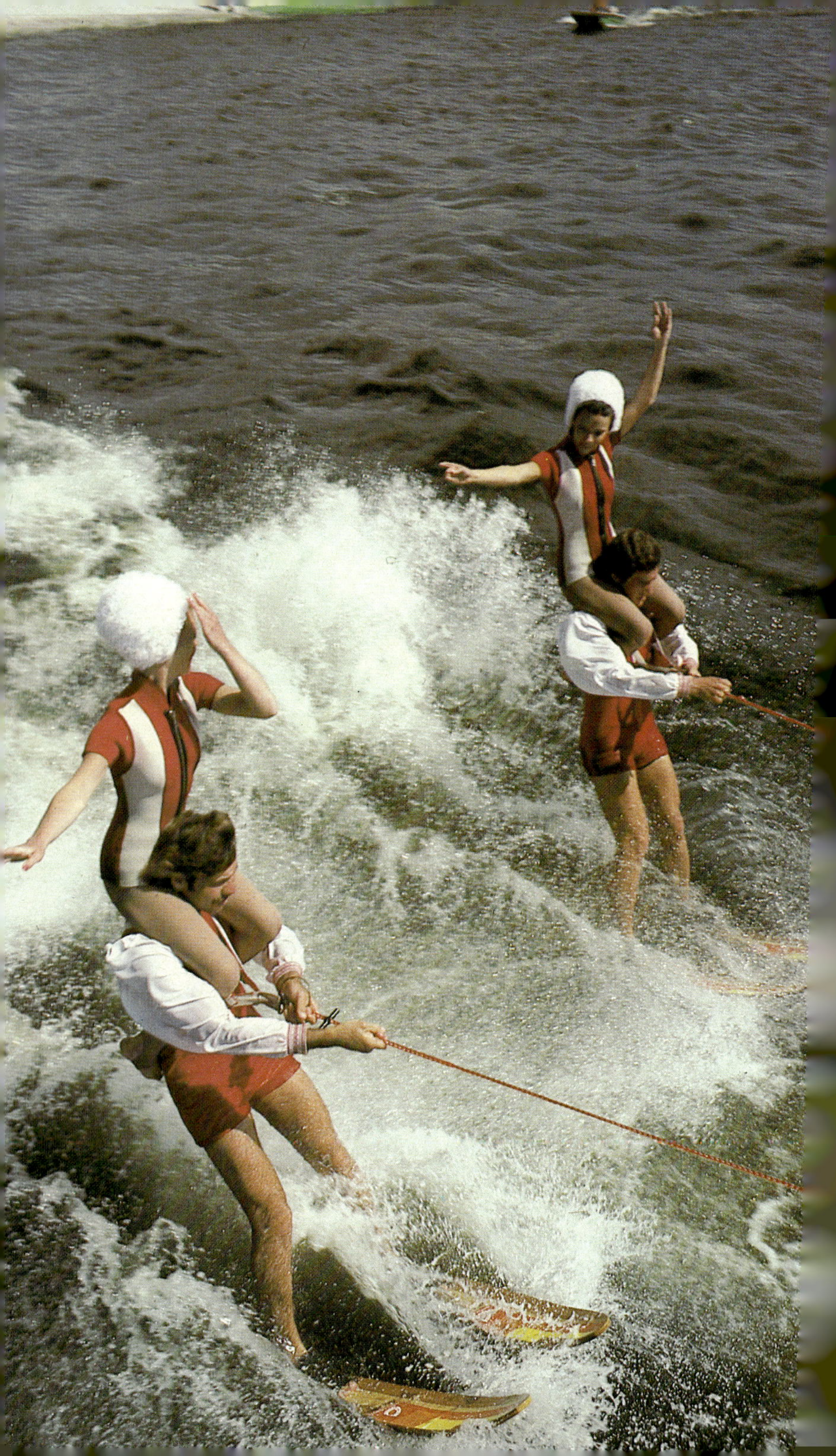

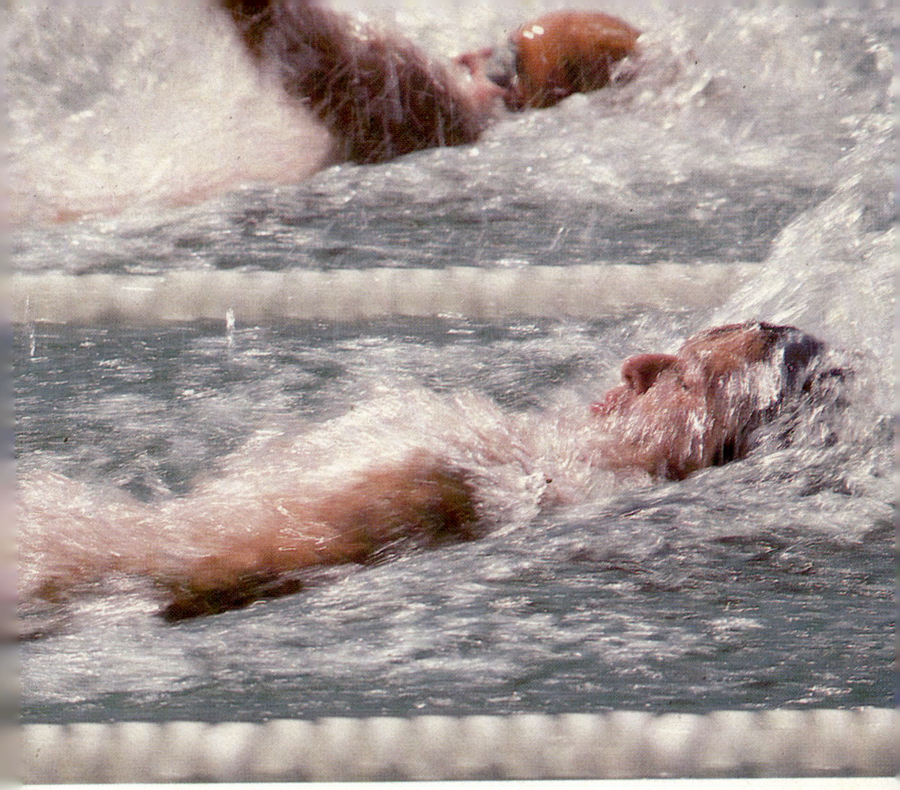

COMPETITIVE SWIMMING, BULGARIA
Above. A longer-focus (in this case, 300 mm) and a slower shutter speed render water with some movement blur, emphasizing the action in the backstroke race.

CYPRESS GARDENS, FLORIDA
Opposite. Fastest shutter speeds—necessary in bright sunshine freeze water to pearl-like spray. Displays are often organised for the photographer. A 35 mm lens pictured these performers.

TABLE TENNIS COLOUR
Plate 8. Three ordinary pocket flashguns fired sequentially provided the strobe effect—two flashes had coloured filters on them—showing Bengtsson in three colours, with three table tennis balls.

ZOOM BURST
Plate 9, top. For a new pictorial approach, zoom the 70-150 mm lens while exposing at $\frac{1}{8}$ or $\frac{1}{4}$ second. The riders coming toward the camera at Mallory Park have become the centre of movement.

SHAPE AND MOVEMENT
Plate 9, bottom: There is little movement in this shot of a custom bike on Daytona Beach; the impression of action comes from the long low shape.

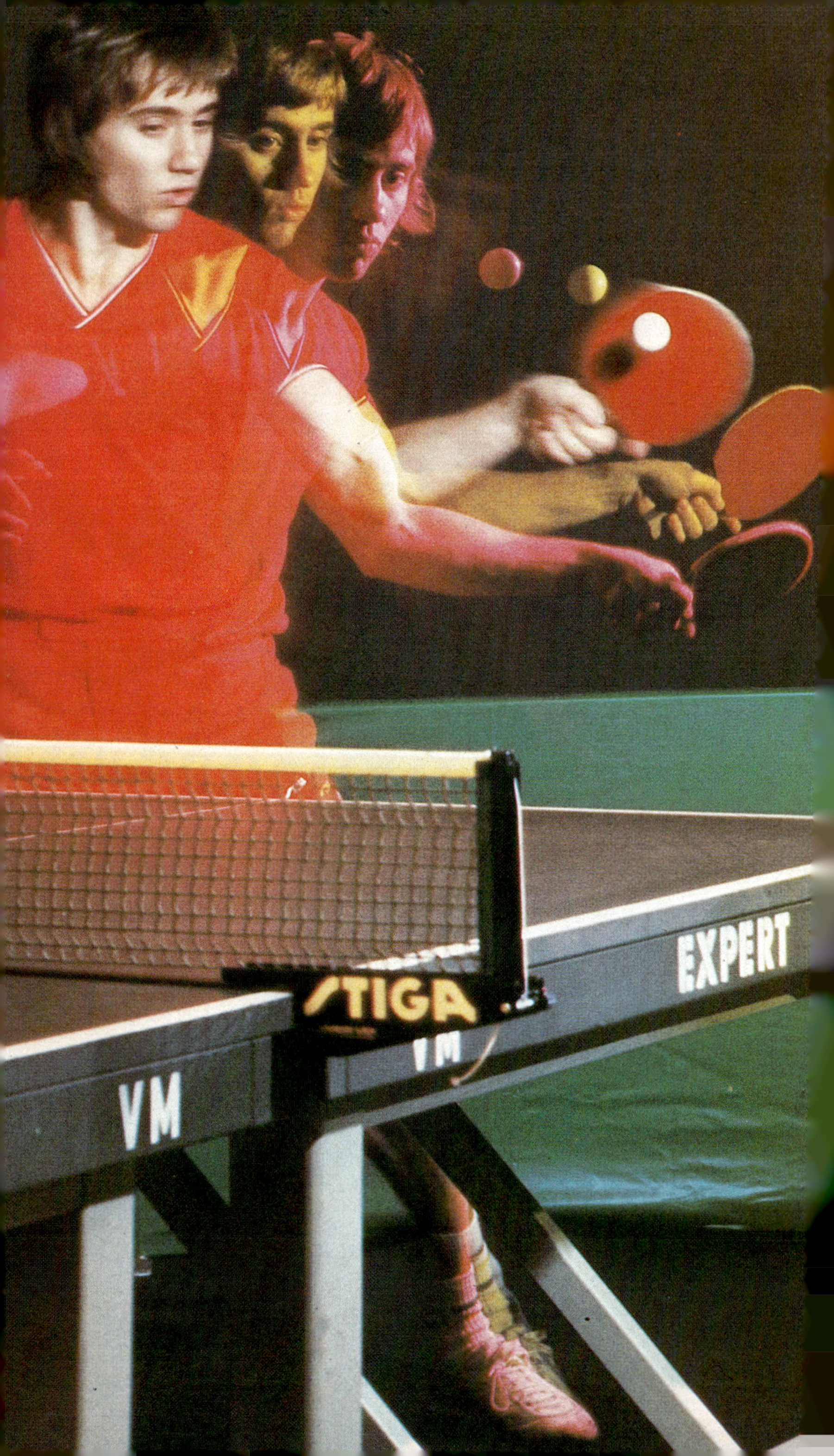
STIGA
EXPERT
VM
VM

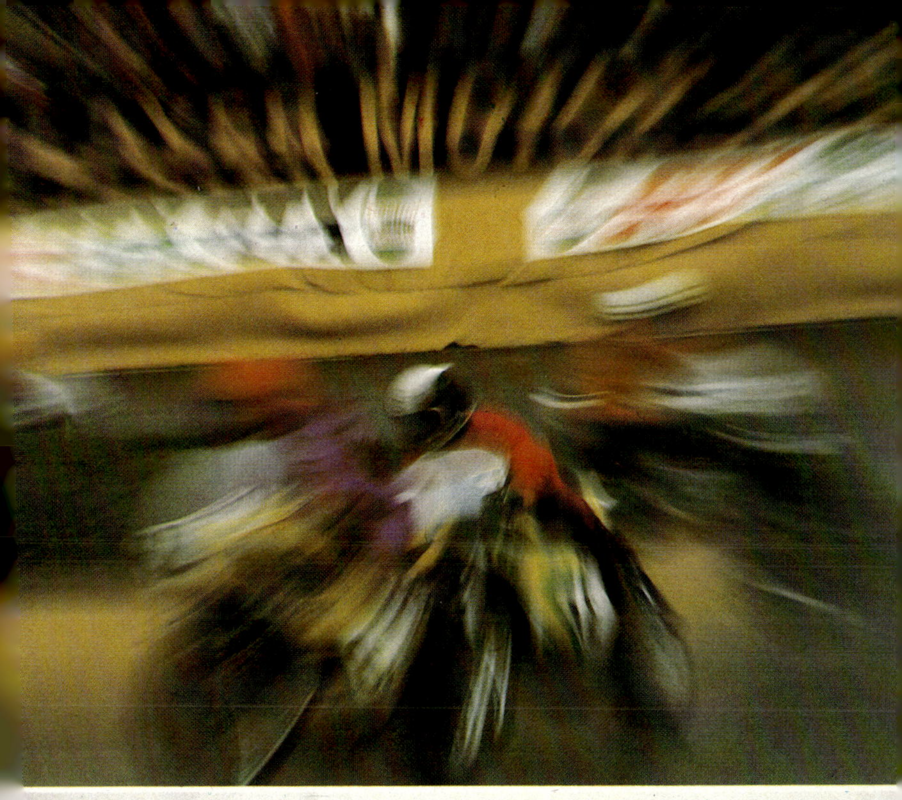

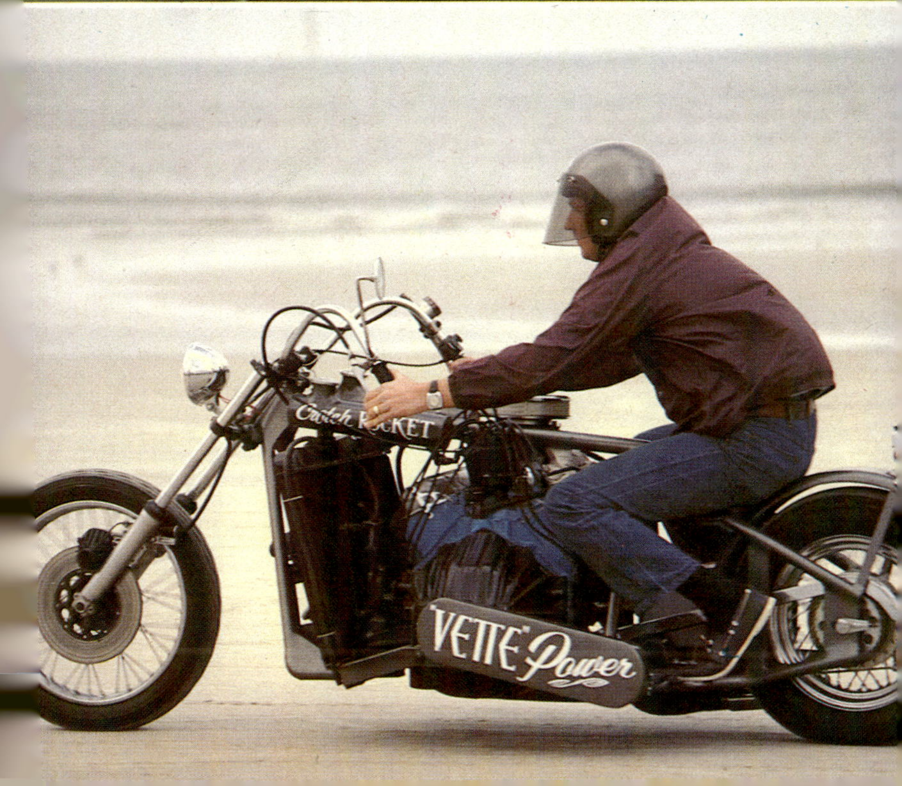
VETTE Power

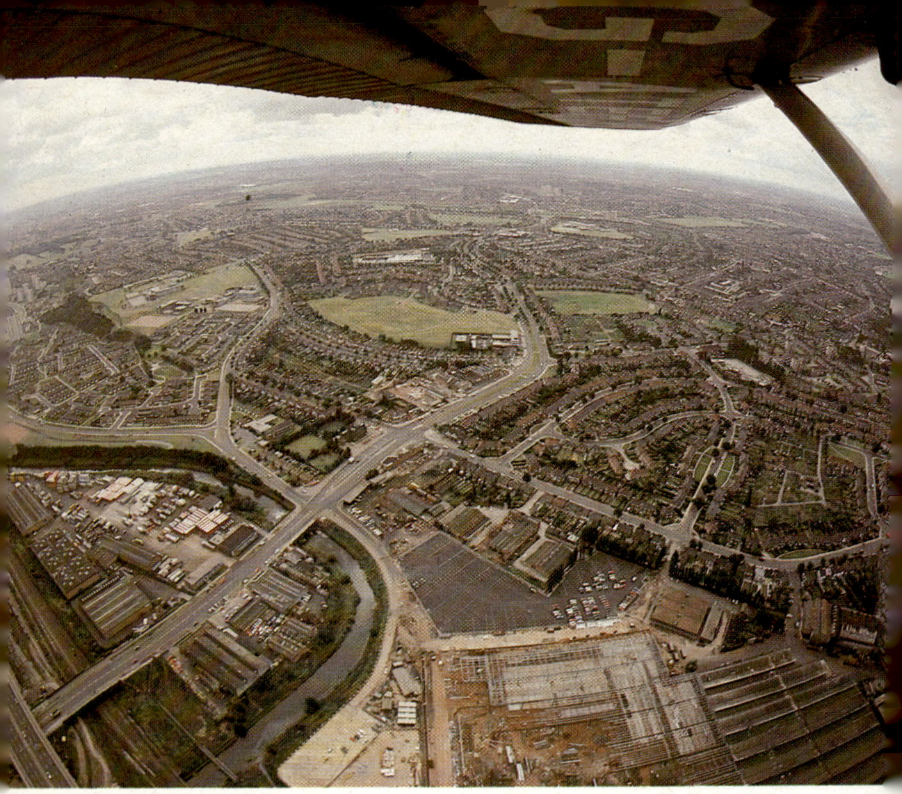

VIEW FROM ABOVE
Above. Aerial shots are often taken with long-focus lenses. This one taken with the 16 mm fisheye makes the horizon curve as if shot from a space capsule—*John Starr.*

LONG FOR FISHING
Opposite, top. Telephoto shots, here with the 400 mm lens, of sunsets are common enough and the pattern and action on the skyline makes this one unusual.

WIDE-ANGLE RUNNER
Opposite, bottom. Fisheye sky views need powerful foreground shapes, here provided by the towering runner following the curved foreground track.

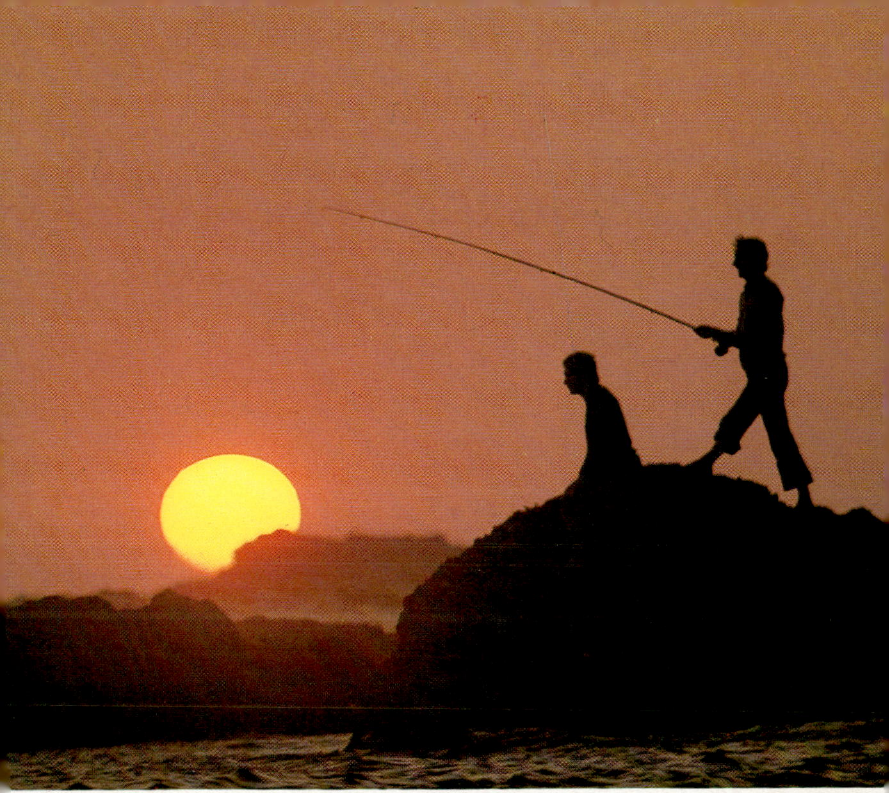

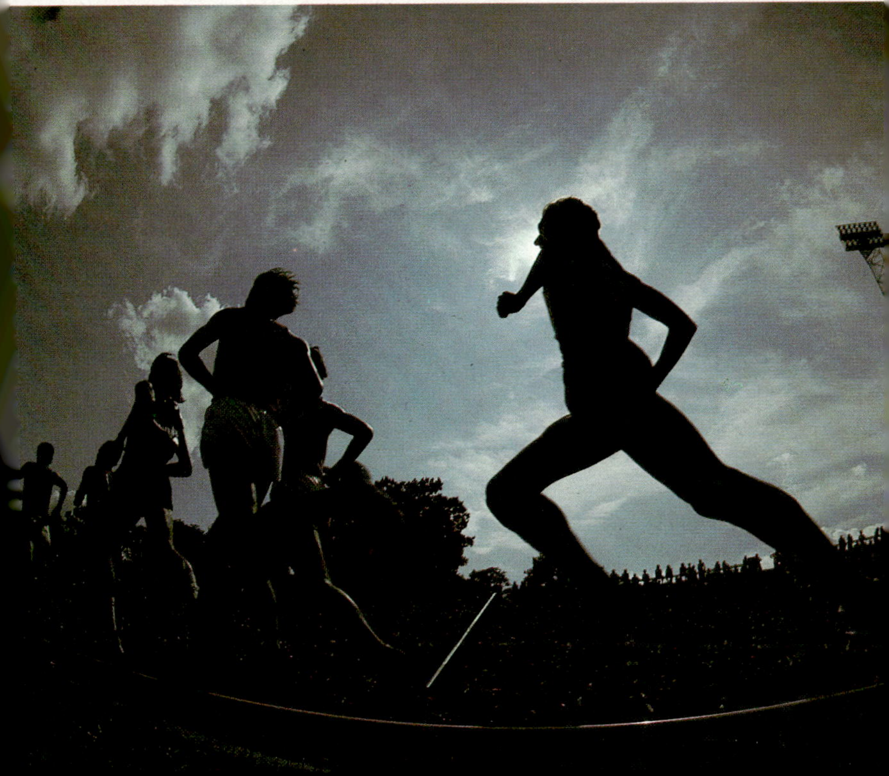

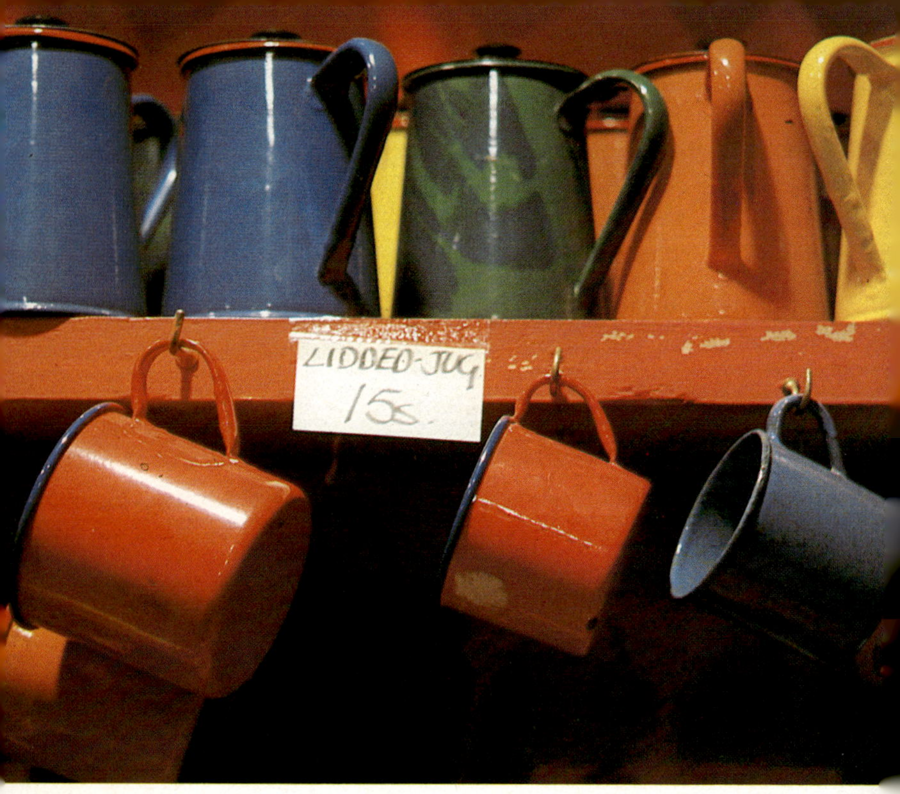

ENAMELWARE
Above. These mugs and jugs in London's Carnaby Street would be expensive to buy but can still be photographed free. This was taken on a sunny day with the 85 mm lens.

LAS VEGAS AT NIGHT
Opposite. The gambling paradise is just a shade more colourful than most city centres at night. The automatic OM-2 produces perfect exposure, hand-held, with the 35 mm lens.

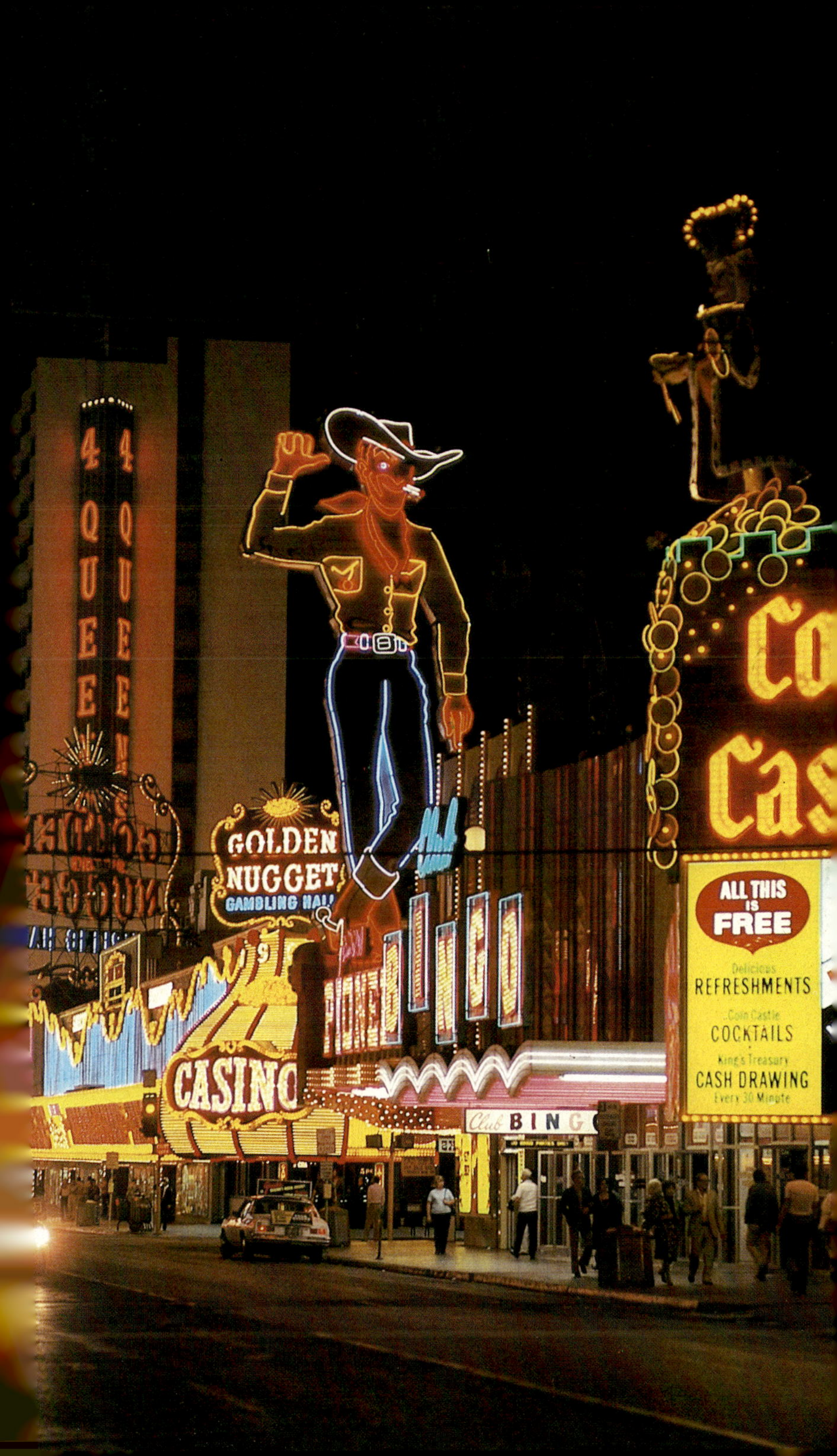
4 QUEENS
4 QUEENS
GOLDEN NUGGET
GAMBLING HALL
BINGO
CASINO
ALL THIS IS FREE
Delicious REFRESHMENTS
Coin Castle COCKTAILS
King's Treasury CASH DRAWING
Every 30 Minute

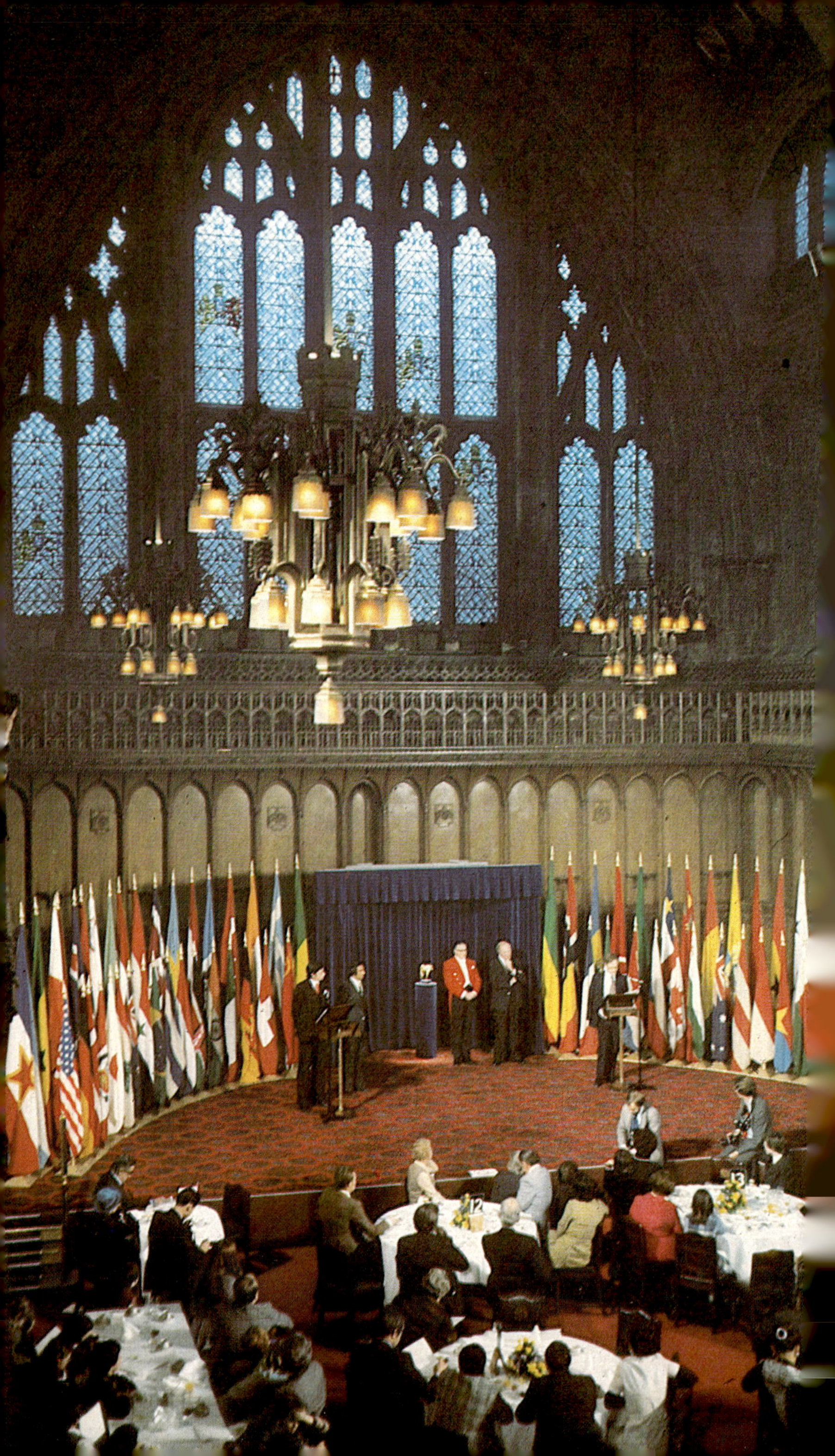

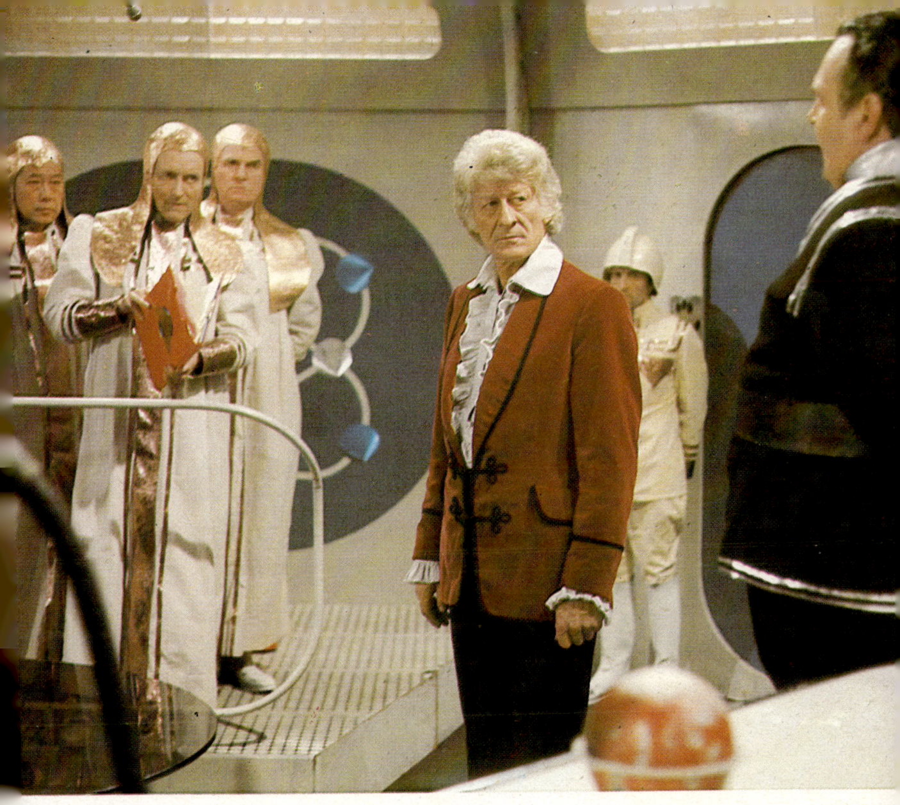

DR. WHO
Above. On a television set, as on the stage, the lights are already there and bright enough for photography if you have artificial light film in the camera. Here the 50 mm lens proved ideal; there is usually plenty of room.

BANQUETING
Opposite. Indoors at night, you need artificial light film. At dusk, the windows still glow blue. This is a 24 mm shot in London's Guildhall.

CONWAY CASTLE
Plate 16. Outdoors exact framing problems are solved with the 70-150 mm lens.

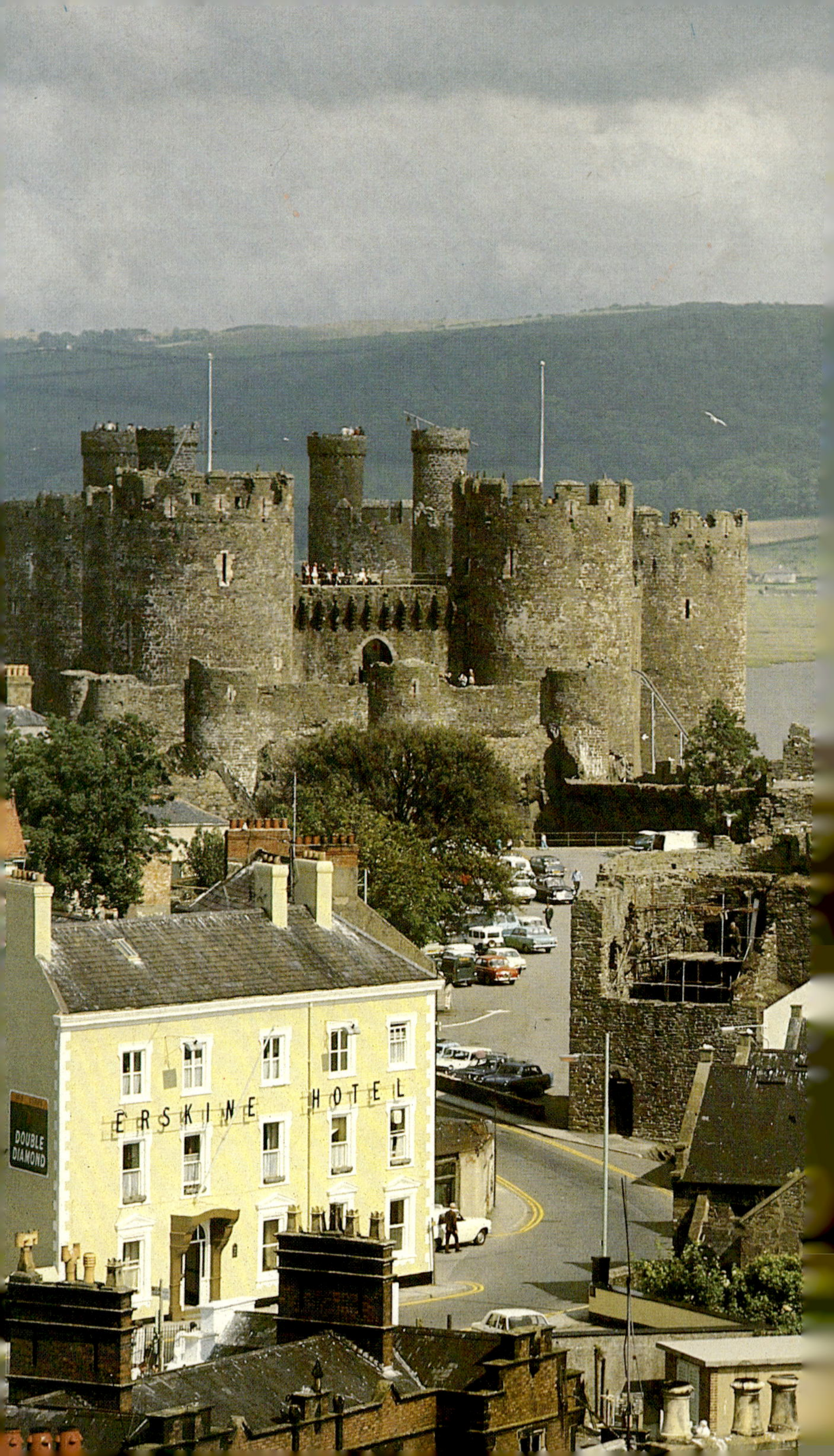

ERSKINE HOTEL
DOUBLE DIAMOND

flash of excessively high equivalent colour temperature and hence blueness.

The B4 filter counteracts excessive warmth of the lighting, for instance in shots taken by late afternoon sun where you want the result to look more like normal daylight. (But the reddish tone is an essential element of sunset photographs.) This filter also brings ordinary household tungsten lighting of 2800 to 2900K up to the colour temperature of 3200 or 3400K for which tungsten and type A colour films are balanced.

There are other colour correction filters, for instance to adapt artificial light type reversal colour film to exposure by daylight and vice versa. This is not an everyday or even a desirable occurrence but a makeshift if you are caught with the wrong kind of colour film in the camera. The colour filter table (see Chpt. *Facts and figures*) sums up the available filters and their effects. With these correction filters the through-the-lens reading of the OM cameras automatically and reliably allows for the light held back by these filters.

Colour light matching

Arising from the specific balance of colour films to the colour temperature of the exposing light is the problem of mixed lighting. If part of a scene is lit by daylight and part by tungsten lighting, the latter will always be more reddish and the former more bluish relative to each other —and no filtering can correct both. This applies equally to reversal and to colour negative film, for in printing a colour negative you can again correct overall colour balance but not local differences.

Unless lighting mismatch is a deliberate colour effect in the picture, light a subject throughout with light sources of matching colour temperature. So fill-in lighting in a daylight scene should come only from electronic flash or blue flash bulbs—not from tungsten lighting. Similarly, in a tungsten-lit set-up avoid using flash bulbs or electronic flash—unless you match their light to the tungsten source by lamp filters.

Neutral density filters

Sometimes the light-reducing ability of a filter is needed without any colour selectivity. The obvious occasion is very bright light conditions when you have a high-speed film in the camera and have difficulty in avoiding over-exposure at the top shutter speed and smallest aperture. Also, with bright subjects it may be difficult to use a large aperture for selective or differential focusing.

Neutral density filters overcome this by cutting down the light entering the lens without affecting its colour. The filters are thus grey in tone. Usual densities are such that they reduce the light to one-half and to one-quarter respectively. Two Olympus filters are available for this. The two filters can also be combined for a reduction of the light to one-eighth, allowing the use of 3 lens stops larger. This is however an emergency measure, for with two filters in front of the lens the unfavourable effects on optical quality are enhanced.

The through-the-lens exposure measurement automatically allows for the light held back by the neutral density filter.

The polarising filter

Under certain circumstances light can undergo changes invisible to the eye but involving the character of light waves. One of these changes is polarisation. Light that is polarised can be held back by a suitably orientated polarising filter. Main causes of polarisation are:

(a) Reflection from the surface of transparent media, for instance glass, plastic, water surfaces, varnish etc.;

(b) Passage through certain crystalline substances (the polarising filter is based on such a crystalline substance); and

(c) Light scatter in specific circumstances—for instance the blue skylight when viewed in certain directions.

When taking pictures of objects with shiny surfaces, reflections and glare can be quite disturbing. For instance when looking into a shop window, reflections of the street often obscure large parts of the display. Placing a polarising filter over the camera lens largely eliminates these reflections—or the glare from shiny table tops, polished furniture, glazed pottery and even coated paper—anything that is not metal. The polarisation is strongest when the light is reflected from the surface at an angle of about 30–35°.

To use the polarising filter for this purpose, mount it

on the camera lens and then rotate the filter while observing the effect through the finder. You will not normally be able to eliminate all reflections but suitable orientation of the filter can cut out the most important ones.

The polarising filter is also useful in close-up photography and product shots of fabrics and other textured material: by rotating the filter you can control the sheen and the underlying pattern in a fabric, or bring out the grain of woodwork often suppressed by reflections from surface polish. Other applications based on suppressing reflections include catch-lights in glass and china, skin detail in medical photography, wax and other layers on leaves and blossoms in botanical photography, glare from printed pages or photographs in copying etc. Often these effects appear greater with longer-focus lenses—largely because in the narrower view a greater proportion of surfaces tend to be near the same reflection angle established as optimum by rotation of the polarising filter.

The second common use of the polarising filter is to darken blue skies in colour photography. This relies on phenomenon (c) above, namely the partial polarisation of scattered blue skylight. This is greatest at right angles to the direction of the sun, i.e. towards the horizon when the sun is more or less overhead and towards the south or north when it is in the west or east. This is the only way of rendering skies darker in colour photographs without changing the colour value. The polarising filter also cuts some of the haze in distant views. In such outdoor shots the filter again subdues reflections from various shiny surfaces—for instance roofs, foliage etc.—increasing the colour saturation of such areas. Landscape shots in colour on a dull day can gain brilliance that way.

Polarisation by passage through substances has more complex applications, mainly in macrophotography and photomicrography. The idea there is to use two polarising filters, one between the subject and the light source and the other between the subject and the camera lens, oriented so that between them they cut out most of the light. Certain substances placed between such so-called crossed polarising filters modify polarisation and produce brilliant colour patterns. Obvious subjects are thin transparent crystalline layers that are colourless by normal lighting but take on multicoloured hues between crossed polarisers. On a larger scale, sheets of plastic—again colourless—stretched and overlaid in various ways yield similarly abstract colour patterns that have sometimes been exploited as an art form in their own right.

Trick filters for colour effects

Elaborate trick effects are obtainable in colour also by using single and multiple split filters. These may be light to medium yellow, green, blue, purple etc. A uniform filter of any such colour would of course tint the whole picture in its own hue (on colour reversal film) or in a complementary tone (in a negative).

There are however also filters where only half the glass is coloured while the other half is clear, with an abrupt or a shaded transition. A single such filter could for instance keep a foreground in a colour shot in its natural colours and overlay the background with the filter tint (or vice versa).

Still more elaborate effects are possible by combining two split filters at an angle. For instance with a yellow and a pale blue filter you could have segments that are clear, yellow, green and blue. By rotating the filters against each other the segments can be of different size. Appropriate orientation in front of the lenses can be used to select what parts of a view should be overlaid with which colour.

Obviously this is experimental photography, but half the fun is trying out the different effects. The finder image is a good guide, but note that the slightest alteration in camera direction may significantly shift subject portions from one colour segment to another. Hence a firm permanent camera support such as a tripod is advisable.

In principle the same drawbacks of multiple filter use apply as mentioned before. But here you can forget about them—this type of picture depends on its colour effects and not its detail definition.

FLASH EQUIPMENT

The most convenient and the most widely used artificial light source for photography is flash. It provides the light in packages of predictable intensity with easily portable equipment. Flash gear is portable because it has to produce an intense light for only a fraction of a second during the exposure, and not continuously.

The most versatile current flash source is electronic flash which in a discharge tube can produce many thousands of intense flashes. Electronic flash units accommodate the circuitry and power source—usually small batteries—needed for this in the comparatively compact housing of the unit.

An alternative flash source is the flash bulb which produces its light by a chemical combustion of fine metal wire sealed inside a glass bulb. Flash bulbs—more usually in multiple assemblies such as flash cubes—are even more portable but good for only one flash per bulb. They need a holder with a battery-powered firing circuit.

For flash photography, the flash is usually fired by a contact built into the camera shutter, so that you get the flash exactly when the shutter is open during an instantaneous exposure. It is this synchronisation contact which makes the electrical link between the flash unit and the camera via the accessory shoe or a synchro cord essential. This is a mechanisation of the method of opening the camera shutter, firing the flash and closing the shutter again. (Such open flash operation is still used for certain subjects.)

The synchronising system of the camera has to allow for the different firing characteristics—delay and duration—of flash sources and for the piecemeal manner in which the focal plane shutter exposes different parts of the image in succession.

Electronic flash takes a fraction of a millisecond to reach its full intensity and rarely lasts much longer than 1 or 2 milliseconds (1/1000 to 1/500 second). The sensible way of synchronising this with the shutter is to close the firing circuit as soon as the first shutter blind has fully uncovered the film. This is X-synchronisation.

To be able to expose the whole of the image, an X-synchronised flash must be used at a shutter speed that fully uncovers the film—i.e. 1/60 second or longer with the Olympus OM cameras. For at say 1/125 second, the second shutter blind has already moved halfway across the film by the time the first blind has reached the end of its travel and triggered the flash. That way, half the picture would be unexposed.

Flash bulbs with their chemical combustion take about 10 to 20 milliseconds to build up to a useful light output. If they were fired in the same way as electronic flash, the exposure time would have to be longer still to allow for this firing delay and you couldn't synchronise flash bulbs at times shorter than 1/15 second. This long exposure time is also needed because the flash builds up to a peak and then decays in brightness; the shutter must remain open during the whole of this time, otherwise different parts of the picture are unevenly exposed.

For focal plane shutter use, special flash bulbs are available that yield a uniform light output over a longer period (about 1/50 to 1/30 second) while the shutter runs down—i.e. while the slit travels across the film plane. These bulbs can be used at fast shutter speeds. Here however the flash must be fired before the shutter opens, so that it reaches its full brightness as soon as the shutter slit starts to move across the film, and stays at that brightness during the shutter movement. This is known as FP synchronisation.

You can select the synchronisation required by the collar surrounding the flash socket on the OM cameras. Setting this so that the red mark points to the blue X selects X-synchronisation; setting it to the black FP selects FP synchronisation for type FP (focal plane) bulbs. The red mark is not very clear, but at the X setting the selector lever (the two serrated grips on the collar) appears vertical and at the FP setting it appears inclined—obvious at a glance.

FLASH EQUIPMENT GROUP

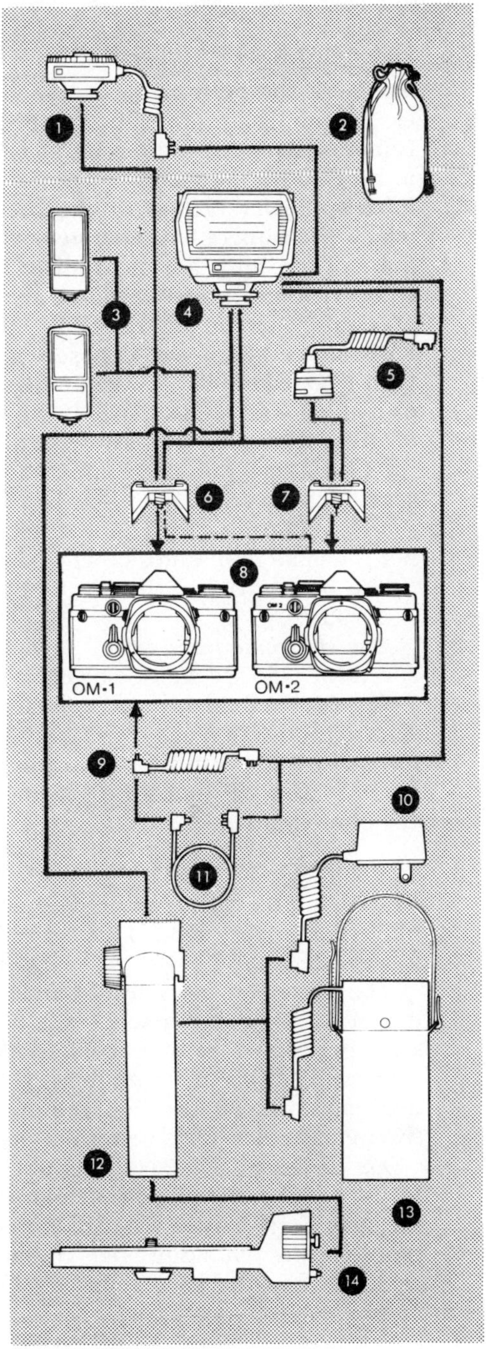

This group system chart shows how the flash accessories link up with the OM cameras. The flash group is centred around the Quick Auto 310 unit; the same connections apply for the Quick Auto 300, except that the Auto cord (item 5) becomes pointless. The chart illustrates the following items.

1. Remote sensor.
2. Lens pouch 200, also a convenient protective container for the Quick Auto 310 or 300 flash units.
3. PS 200 flash units, Olympus's version of straightforward simple pocket flash units.
4. Quick Auto 310 flash unit.
5. Auto cord, 0.6 metre long.
6. Accessory shoe 1, fits OM-1 or OM-2 cameras.
7. Accessory shoe 2, fits only OM-2.
8. OM-1 and OM-2 camera bodies.
9. Synchro cord, 0.6 metre long.
10. F.AC adapter.
11. Synchro cord, 5 metres long.
12. Grip part of Bounce grip.
13. 315 volt power pack.
14. Bracket section of Bounce grip.

Synchro safety circuit

To mark the permissible X-synchronisation speeds for electronic flash, the shutter speed ring on the OM cameras has the speed figures at 1/60 and slower marked in blue. With automatic operation of the OM-2 you are however never certain of the precise shutter speed at which the camera will operate—with too short an automatic time and X-synchronised electronic flash this could yield only partly exposed shots.

A safety circuit in the OM-2 therefore cuts out the flash altogether if the exposure time becomes shorter than 1/60 second. This operates equally for automatically or manually set shutter speeds. So if you want to be sure of firing an electronic flash (e.g. fill-in) in daylight with the OM-2, use it in the manual mode and with a shutter speed of 1/30 or longer.

FP synchronisation is not suitable for electronic flash nor for small flash bulbs other than the FP type; the flash would be over before the shutter begins to open.

To sum up:

Use electronic flash with X-synchronisation at shutter speeds of 1/60 second or slower;

Use most normal flash bulbs (including flash cubes) with X-synchronisation at 1/15 second or longer;

Use FP bulbs with FP synchronisation at 1/30 to 1/1000 second. (But FP bulbs are gradually disappearing from the photo market.)

Accessory shoes

The Olympus OM-1 and OM-2 cameras do not have a built-in accessory shoe. This is a separate item and exists in two versions:

The Accessory shoe 1 has a single centre contact in the top of the shoe and a screw shaft with internal contact screwing down into a corresponding socket in the camera. The shoe fits both the OM-1 and the OM-2, but does not provide the link required by the OM-2 for through-the-lens flash metering.

The Accessory shoe 2 is similar, but has a second contact in front of the first one, in the black area in the middle of the shoe. In its underside the shoe has a second small pin that engages an additional contact inside the OM-2 camera when the shoe is fitted. This model is marked

SHOE 2 at the back (above the toothed wheel). Because of the protruding second pin this shoe cannot be fitted to the OM-1. The Accessory shoe 2 is essential for through-the-lens flash metering with the OM-2 and QA 310.

To fit the accessory shoe, remove the small black plastic plug from the screw-in socket in the top of the pentaprism just above the finder eyepiece. Place the shoe over the prism housing so that the screw shaft with the contact engages the threaded socket on the camera, and turn the toothed wheel protruding at the rear of the shoe in the direction FIX to screw the shoe firmly into the camera. (The screw shaft has a left-handed thread.) When mounting the Accessory shoe 2 on the OM-2 make sure also that the thin second pin correctly goes into the small hole just behind the threaded fixing hole.

To remove the shoe, turn the securing wheel to the left to unscrew, and lift off. Again take care not to bend the smaller rear pin on the Accessory shoe 2. Close the opening on the camera top with the black plastic plug. Unfortunately the latter easily gets lost, when on the camera. If necessary, close the opening with a small piece of adhesive tape—less elegant, but better than allowing dust to get into the hole.

Mounting a flash unit directly on the camera is simplest but does put some strain on the accessory shoe. You may have some 400 grams in weight taken by a hollow screw stud 3 mm in diameter. So when you use the flash unit on the camera, fit and handle it carefully—and remove as soon as possible. A better way and safer way, better also for lighting, is to use a flash bracket such as the Bounce grip (see below). It makes the camera with flash a little bulkier but is more convenient to handle. And there is less risk of the accessory shoe mounting being torn out of the camera if you knock the flash against something—or even dash it against someone in a crowd.

The Quick Auto 310

This electronic flash unit with photocell-controlled flash duration for automatic (computer) flashing fits the accessory shoe of the OM cameras or of the bounce flash grip (see below), providing a variety of operating options. Maximum power dissipation is 54 watt-seconds with approx. 2200 beam candle-power seconds output.

With a film speed of 100 ASA this is equivalent to a metric guide number of 34.

With automatic operation the Quick Auto 310 uses a so-called energy-saving series-thyristor circuit that stores any residual energy not used during a flash. Under certain conditions that permits very short recycling times, i.e. the unit is ready to flash again almost instantly after an exposure.

The whole unit is 73 × 80 × 105 mm large overall (2.9 × 3.15 × 4.1 inches) and weighs about 420 grams (14.8 ounces) with batteries. When mounted on the camera it protrudes about 70 mm (2.8 inches) above the accessory shoe and the flash reflector is about 46 mm (1.8 inches) in front of the camera's lens mounting flange. The flash reflector is still a few mm in front of the 50 mm *f* 1.8 or *f* 1.4 standard lens. When mounted on the camera, the 25 × 54 mm (1 × 2.1 inch) reflector area is horizontal and the flash reasonably covers a horizontal angle of 80° and vertical angle of 50°, or—with reasonably accurate aiming of the flash—the view of the 28 mm wide-angle lens.

QA 310 features and controls

The sensor cell at the front of the unit responds to the light reflected from the subject during the flash and in the automatic mode controls the flash duration for the exposure.

The foot fits the camera's accessory shoe. To attach the unit, push it into the shoe from behind, then turn the large black plastic wheel to the right to secure the unit in the shoe. The foot carries three contacts: one at the side, to contact the lateral rails of the shoe, and two in the base for the synchronising centre contact (hot-shoe contact) and for the front TTL metering contact. The hot shoe contact is a standard feature on most current electronic flash units, the TTL contact is unique to the OM-2. Before removing the unit from the camera shoe always turn the black locking wheel fully to the left. (It has a left-handed screw thread.)

The external power socket at the front of the foot links up with a supply plug of the AC adapter, the bounce grip or 315 volt power pack. The connecting cord has a flat right-angle plug that fits into the power socket only one

ACCESSORY SHOES

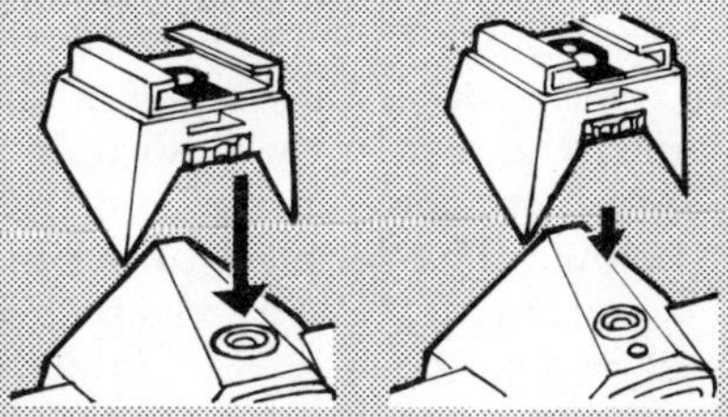

Fit accessory shoe 1 on OM-1 *(left)* or shoe 2 on OM-2 *(right).* Shoe 1 also fits OM-2, but shoe 2 does not fit OM-1.

QUICK AUTO 310

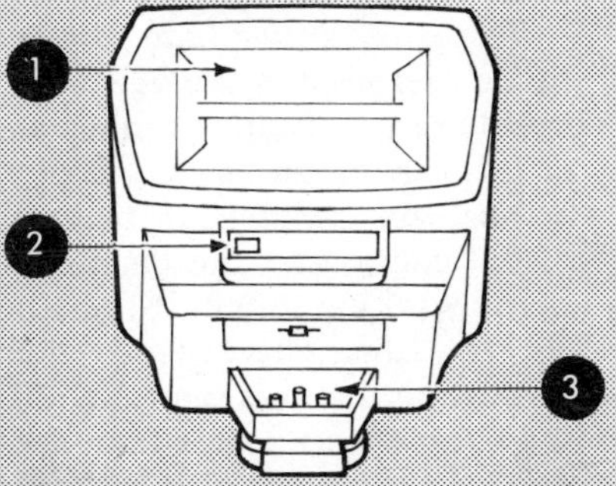

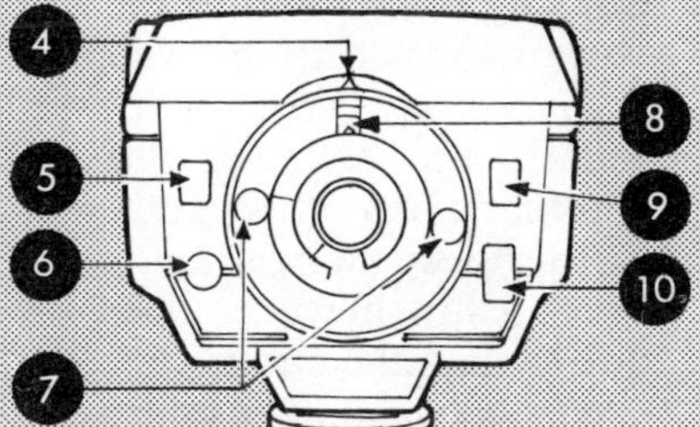

The features and controls of this flash unit are:

1. Reflector.
2. Normal auto sensor window.
3. External power socket.
4. TTL index setting.
5. Auto check lamp.
6. Test and manual firing button.
7. Grips for rotating ASA dial.
8. ASA window.
9. Ready/charge lamp.
10. On/off switch.
11. Synchro cord socket.
12. Locking knob.
13. Battery chamber cover.
14. Hot shoe contact.
15. TTL auto contact.

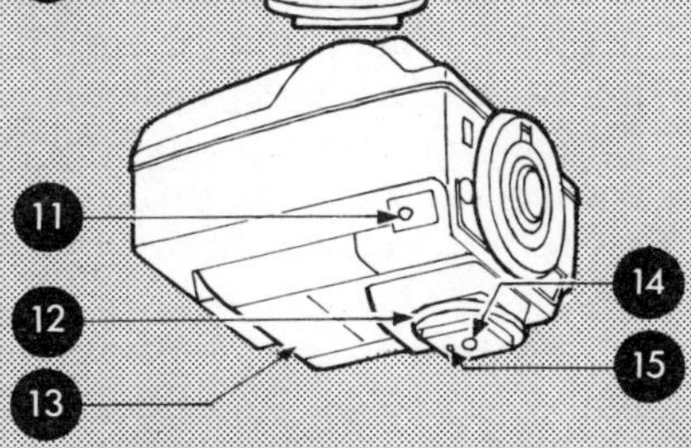

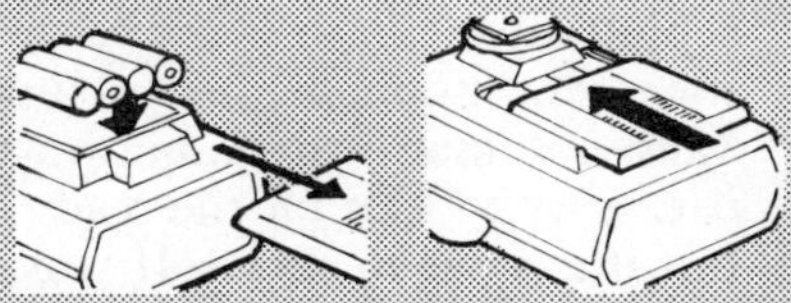

To fit batteries, remove the battery chamber cover *(left),* insert the batteries and slide on the cover *(right).*

way round: when you look at the flash unit from behind, the cable of the plug emerges at the left.

The synchro cord socket at the left (seen from behind) near the rear of the flash unit takes the various Synchro and Auto cords or the cord from the Remote sensor (see below). The socket fittings involve a 3 mm coaxial plug and a flat pin. The coaxial plug is extra long, and the plugs of normal flash leads do not reach far enough to make contact—you can use only Olympus's own synchro or other cords.

The main setting dial (control dial) sets the operating mode, serves for the ASA setting and indicates guide numbers or distance ranges as required. The functions of this dial are described in more detail below.

The auto check lamp to the left of the main dial is a visual check that the flash exposure is within the automatic working range. If the automatic flash exposure was correct, this check lamp flickers for a few seconds, indicating that less than the full flash power was used, i.e. the subject was nearer than the far limit of the automatic working range. It also flickers on firing the flash at the LOW manual setting (which also involves reducing the flash output). If the auto check lamp does not flicker after a flash, the flash has discharged its full energy; with automatic operation this means that the subject was further away than the far limit of the automatic range. The check lamp however does still flicker if the subject is nearer than the automatic near limit.

The test button just below the auto check lamp is a manual firing button for open flash and any other triggering of the flash independently of the hot shoe or synchro contact. The test button fires the flash in whatever mode was set on the main dial—except that in the TTL auto mode (see below) the test button operates as if the flash were set to MANUAL HI.

The ready/charge lamp to the right of the main dial lights up when the power capacitors of the unit are charged ready for operation. The time the lamp takes to relight after a flash is the recycling time and depends on the operating mode, power supply, state of batteries etc. With automatic operation at close range it is not always necessary to wait for the ready or charge lamp to relight, but it is safer to do so. If you flash before the lamp has lit up again and the auto check lamp flickers after the flash, the exposure was correct even though the ready/charge lamp did not relight.

The power switch to the right of the main dial, below the charge lamp, switches the batteries of the QA 310 itself into the charging circuit. When the QA 310 is not connected to any external supply, this switch simply switches on the unit. With the bounce grip, AC adapter etc. connected, switching the power switch to ON adds the power of the unit's own batteries to reduce the recharging or recycling time.

Inserting batteries

When used on its own, the Quick Auto 310 takes four size AA dry batteries of 1.5 volts each. Preferably use alkali batteries which offer the greatest flash capacity: Olympus claims that a set of fresh alkali batteries gives around 120 flashes at full-power operation. With automatic operation this may be increased; if however you keep the flash unit switched on for extended periods between flashes, you get fewer flashes per battery set. Ordinary leak-proof cells can be used as a standby, though the flash capacity is far lower and in any case uncertain. *Do not use rechargeable nickel-cadmium cells;* their lower internal resistance may in certain switching situations lead to high surge currents that can damage transistors in the flash unit.

To fit the batteries, switch the unit off (pull down the power switch at the rear) and slide off the black battery compartment cover in the base—pull forward as shown by the embossed black arrow. Insert the four cells in the +/− orientation shown, then replace the battery compartment cover and push home against the foot.

Change batteries when recycling times become excessive—more than about 30 seconds—or if the unit fails to charge up when switched on.

The ASA setting

In all three modes the main dial provides certain distance and/or aperture indications which in turn depend on the correct setting for the ASA speed of the film in the camera.

To set the ASA speed rotate the transparent plastic top

of the control dial by the two ribbed spots provided as finger holds. Hold the serrated rim of the dial stationary. Movement of this top carries with it a black segment underneath with a cut-out window. Next to the window the segment is marked ASA in orange (ignore the other markings in white and orange for the moment). Adjust the plastic top so that the required ASA speed value appears opposite the small bright marker protruding into the window.

Operating modes

The QA 310 flash unit is one of the most versatile of its kind in terms of operating modes. These modes are selected on the control dial which as a result appears a little complex at first sight. Three main positions for the dial line up the large white arrow head on it with a mark at the top, a group of marks at the bottom right and another group at the bottom left. These define the operating modes:

(a) TTL auto where the flash is controlled entirely by the OM-2's internal silicon cells;

(b) Normal automatic operation with the flash controlled by its sensor cell;

(c) Manual with a choice of two fixed flash power level outputs.

The operating mode should not be confused with alternative flash/camera set-ups. Thus all three of these modes are available with the QA 310 mounted directly in the accessory shoe of the OM-2 camera. Variations arise when the flash is not mounted on the camera (e.g. in the bounce grip) or is used in different other ways. Those concern largely the placement of the flash unit and the way it is linked to the camera; they may work with some or all of the operating modes, but they do not change these modes.

TTL auto operation

In this mode, unique to the Olympus OM-2 camera with Quick Auto 310 flash unit, the SBC metering system of the OM-2 is directly linked with the flash duration control.

The two silicon cells in the usual way measure the light reflected from the film and terminate the flash of the

QUICK AUTO 310
MODES

Fit the 310 into the accessory shoe by pushing in from the back and tightening the screw wheel *(left)*.

Set the ASA speed by rotating the transparent top against the rim of the control dial *(right)*.

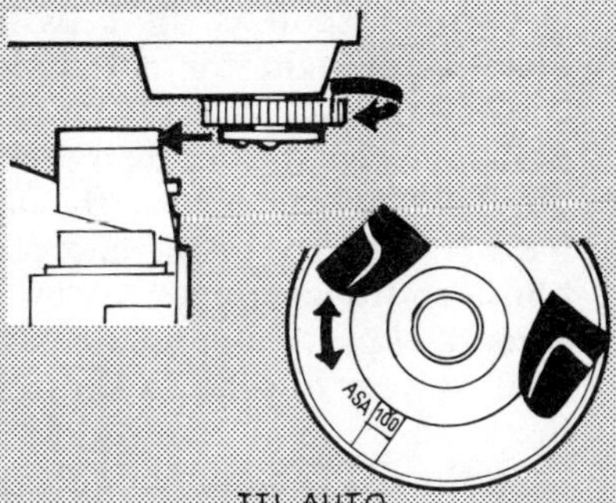

Dial setting in TTL AUTO mode:

1. White arrowhead mark.
2. ASA window.
3. Coloured *f*-No. range symbols.
4. Distance scale (working ranges).

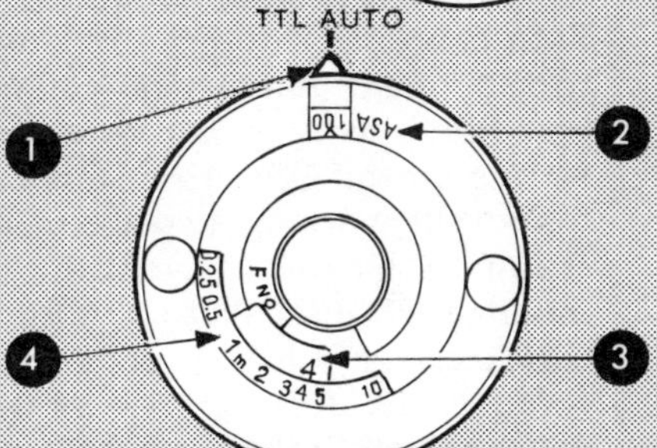

Normal auto setting:

1. Arrowhead mark.
5. Auto distance range.
6. *f*-No. indication.
7. Auto setting symbols.

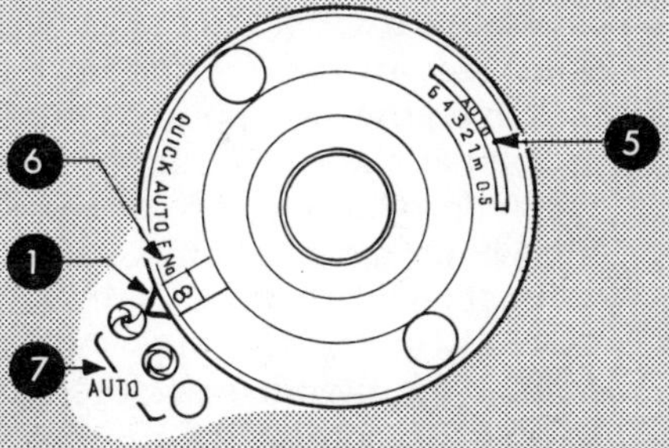

Manual setting of control dial:

1. White arrowhead.
4. Distance scale.
8. Manual *f*-No. scale.
9. Manual HI and LOW indications.
10. Guide number indication.

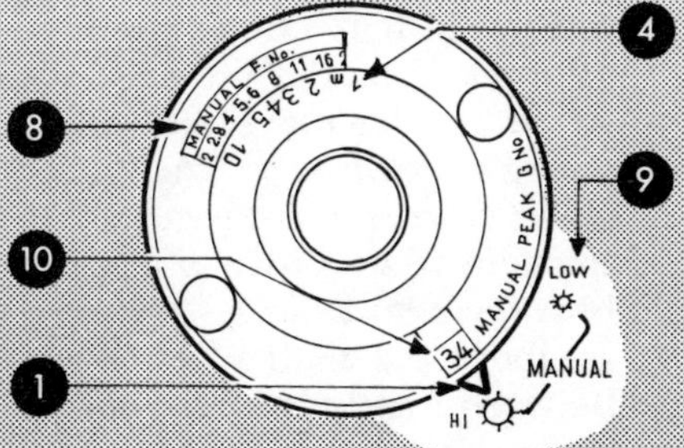

QA 310 as soon as the cells have recorded a sufficient quantity of light for correct exposure. After that, the SBC system also releases the second shutter blind. As the flash is always shorter than the shutter exposure time, this does not interfere with the flash itself. Moreover, the flash is triggered at the end of the run-down of the first blind, so the opening time of the shutter is at least 1/60 second. If prevailing light conditions cause the automatic SBC system to select a shorter time, the flash does not fire at all.

In the TTL auto mode the camera thus measures the flash exposure through the lens. Further, this exposure measurement automatically allows for the lens aperture and film speed, as set *on the camera*. The film speed setting on the QA 310 in this case is purely informative to indicate working distance ranges on the control dial.

For automatic through-the-lens operation therefore mount the Quick Auto 310 on the Olympus OM-2 via the Accessory shoe 2 (or connect the flash to the shoe through the Auto cord—see below), set the camera's meter switch to AUTO and the synchronising selector to X. Then turn the control dial on the flash unit to bring its white arrow head to the white index line at the top, marked TTL AUTO. On the camera select the lens aperture you want to use (as for normal automatic operation), switch on the flash power (power switch to ON) and shoot as soon as the charge light on the flash comes on. If the system produced a correct exposure, the auto check lamp flickers for a second or two after the shot.

That is all there is to it. If you set the ASA speed correctly on the QA 310, you can also read off the automatic working range at different apertures—or select an aperture according to the distance range you want to cover. For example with a film speed setting of 100 ASA, the lower half of the dial shows a distance scale and different coloured segments next to it with *f*-numbers. At *f*4 you have a green segment extending from about 6 metres down to 0.7 metre, at *f*2 it is an orange segment going from some 12 metres to 1.4 metres, at *f*8 a red segment from 3 metres down to 0.35 metre and at *f*16 a blue segment from 1.5 metres down to what can be taken as about 0.2 metre. So if your subject is likely to be between 1 and 2 metres you can use *f*4, *f*5.6 or *f*8.

With this shooting mode check also the automatically selected shutter speed in the camera's viewfinder. The needle should be in the blue speed range of 1/30 second or slower. That makes sure that you are not too near 1/60 second where the automatic cut-out system would stop the flash from firing at all.

A few more points on the TTL auto mode:

(a) Don't set the meter selector switch on the camera to MANUAL. That way the flash is not controlled automatically but you get a full-power flash at most shutter speed settings. (At 1/60 second you get a reduced-power flash.)

(b) The TTL auto mode is inoperative if the flash is not linked to the camera through the Accessory shoe 2. For instance you don't have TTL auto operation if you plug an ordinary synchro cord from the flash to the camera's flash socket—or from the bounce grip into the camera's flash socket.

(c) The same happens if the flash unit is mounted on the OM-1 or on either camera with the Accessory shoe 1. The control dial in the TTL AUTO position again yields a full-power manual flash.

(d) If you pull the QA 310 unit out of the accessory shoe while switched on and set to TTL AUTO, you get a low power flash—this is normal and is nothing to worry about.

The TTL auto mode is suitable for all general photography with the flash on or off the camera (in the latter case linked with the Auto cord—see below), for bounce flash and even close-up photography. In fact the TTL auto mode is the only one that permits accurate close-up flash exposure since the internal SBC sensors in the OM-2 camera measure the subject brightness, allowing automatically for any close-up anomalies in illumination levels. The one application that automatic through-the-lens flash metering is not suitable for is fill-in lighting in daylight (see *Flash and daylight*, below).

Normal auto operation

This is the method of automatic flash control where the sensor cell built into the Quick Auto 310 controls the flash duration. (The cell of the Remote sensor—see below—does the same.) It is the operational mode to use with the OM-1 camera (and indeed with any other camera) or with the OM-2 when for any reason coupling through

O.W.—O

the Accessory shoe 2 is not possible (shoe 2 not available, Auto cord not available for off-camera flash). There is no point in selecting the normal auto mode when you can mount the QA 310 on the OM-2 via the Accessory shoe 2 —the internal SBC system of the OM-2 controls exposure more accurately than the sensor on the QA 310.

In this mode, the sensor cell cumulatively registers the light of the flash reflected from the subject while a comparator circuit compares this with a preset quantity equivalent to correct exposure. When this latter amount is reached, a switching system instantly switches off the flash discharge through the tube, thus prematurely terminating the flash. The reaction time of the silicon cells used is extremely short—they can cut down the flash duration to as little as 1/40,000 second. This is the principle of so-called computer flash operation, perfected to a particularly sophisticated degree in the TTL auto mode described above where the camera's internal silicon cells take over the role of the sensor.

The flash duration obtained depends partly on the subject reflectivity, but above all on the distance. With near subjects the flash duration becomes very short, with more distant ones it is longer. The maximum distance range with automatic operation extends from 0.5 to 8 metres; within this range subjects of average reflectivity are correctly exposed. At 8 metres (26 feet) away the full power of the flash is discharged and it lasts 1/1000 second. At greater distances no more light can be produced and such subjects are underexposed. At the other end of the scale, the flash duration cannot become shorter than 1/40,000 second for subjects nearer than 0.5 metre and such subjects are overexposed.

At different working apertures—selected by different settings on the control dial (see below)—the automatic range becomes shorter.

For normal automatic operation turn the control dial to bring its white arrow head to one of the three AUTO engagement positions at the bottom left. With the OM-1 the meter switch setting is immaterial, but switch on the meter if you want to check the required exposure for prevailing daylight conditions. With the OM-2 either use MANUAL (and a shutter speed of 1/60 second or slower) or turn the meter switch to AUTO or OFF to combine automatic exposure control for the prevailing light conditions with automatic flash control. The flash in this case does not terminate the exposure time of a subject in poor ambient light.

For the correct flash exposure be sure you have first set the control dial to the correct ASA speed. Immediately below the ASA window there appears an aperture number in white—opposite the white indication QUICK AUTO F NO. Set this aperture on the lens, connect the flash to the camera's synchronising outlet (shoe or coaxial flash socket) and shoot. As with TTL auto operation, the flash exposure is correct if the auto check lamp flickers after the shot.

A window at the top right of the control dial carries a row of distances marked in white below the indication AUTO. If the subject is in the indicated distance range, your exposure is likely to be correct.

There are three AUTO settings which switch the sensitivity of the sensor cell, associated with three apertures, depending on the film speed setting. For instance at 100 ASA, the full aperture setting (lowest of the three engagement positions) is *f*4, the medium aperture setting *f*5.6 and the small aperture setting *f*8.

The MANUAL meter setting on the OM-2, with 1/60 second or longer, is preferable to the AUTO setting. With the latter, check that the shutter speed is in the blue range (1/30 second or slower) on the monitoring scale in the finder. The system works equally in the OFF position but this is pointless as you have no check on whether the shutter speed will be long enough for flash firing.

Auto pre-exposure check

In the normal auto mode, you can use the test button and auto check lamp for a preliminary check of correct exposure.

Point the camera at a subject, focus, etc. and set on the control dial the lens aperture you propose to use on the camera. Now press the red button. If the auto check lamp flickers, your exposure is in the correct range. If the auto check lamp does not flicker, and you had selected a small-aperture auto setting, switch to the medium or full-aperture setting (turn control dial anti-clockwise through 1 or 2 small clicks) then try again. If the auto check lamp still does not flicker, you need to go closer to the subject.

Normal auto operation is suitable for all the same occasions as TTL auto operation, including off-camera shooting and bounce flash operation in conjunction with the Remote sensor. It is less suitable for close-ups and much less so for ultra-close-ups since it becomes difficult to arrange the sensor so that it covers the exact subject field taken by the lens.

Manual operation

The Quick Auto 310 has two MANUAL settings of full power and quarter power respectively. There is however no other control of the flash output and for correct exposure you have to match the lens aperture used to the flash/subject distance by the usual guide number method. That is, you divide the flash distance into the guide number specified for the flash to obtain the correct aperture.

In the manual mode the QA 310 however indicates both the guide number and corresponding aperture/distance combinations.

For full-power manual operation turn the control dial to bring its white arrowhead opposite the large sun symbol marked HI to the right of the dial on the back of the unit. If the ASA film speed is correctly set, underneath it the window will show the guide number (in metres) next to the indication MANUAL PEAK G NO. For instance with the film speed set to 100 ASA, the guide number appearing in the window is 34. At the same time a segment window near the top left of the dial shows an aperture scale of white figures on black (marked MANUAL F NO) and opposite it distances in metres. For a manual exposure setting you thus establish a subject distance—e.g. by focusing and reading off the distance on the lens's focusing scale—and set the corresponding aperture. Thus the subject at 2 metres would need *f* 16. (For feet convert distances to metres first—multiply by 0.3.)

For the quarter-power setting turn the dial to bring the white arrowhead to the small sun symbol marked LOW. The guide numbers are now halved, as are the distances for the various apertures (or the *f*-numbers for given distances).

The manual mode is primarily useful for daylight fill-in flash with the OM-1 and OM-2, the latter with the meter switch at MANUAL.

Flash cords

When the Quick Auto 310 flash is not mounted in the camera's accessory shoe, it has to be connected to the camera by a suitable synchro cord for synchronisation with the shutter. This applies to variations of off-camera flash, operations with the bounce flash grip (see below) etc.

Olympus offers several such cords:

The Auto cord 0.6 m is a coiled extension cord with an Olympus synchro plug (coaxial male plug plus flat pin) at one end and a double-contact foot for the Accessory shoe 2 at the other. The 0.6 metre (2 foot) length is a nominal one of convenient extension; the cord can extend up to twice as long, though that tends to strain the coiling.

The primary purpose of the Auto cord 0.6 m is to connect an off-camera QA 310 (for instance when used for bounce flashing in the bounce flash grip or for close-ups) with the Accessory shoe 2 on the OM-2 for TTL auto operation.

Push the foot into the Accessory shoe 2 on the OM-2 camera with the lettering TTL AUTO CORD facing to the front (you can only push it in this way round). Plug the other end into the synchro socket at the side of the flash unit. Set the meter switch on the OM-2 to AUTO, and shoot as for TTL auto operation described above.

When the auto cord is used and the meter switch of the OM-2 is set to MANUAL—or if you connect the foot of the auto cord to the Accessory shoe 1—the QA 310 always operates in the full-power manual mode—again irrespective of the control dial setting. One exception is at 1/60 second setting of the OM-2 (meter switched to MANUAL): the QA 310 here yields a very weak almost spurious flash, normally useless for exposure purposes.

The Synchro cord 0.6 m looks similar to the auto cord but instead of the foot for the Accessory shoe 2 has a single coaxial male plug to fit the camera's flash socket. This links the QA 310 with the OM-1, or with the OM-2 for manual mode operation of the flash off the camera. Note that when the flash unit is in the camera's accessory shoe, connecting the Synchro cord 0.6 m as well stops the unit from firing altogether during an exposure. Hence you can use only one camera/flash link at a time.

The Synchro cord 5 m is a straight flash cable of 5 metres (16½ feet) length to link the QA 310 with the camera in the same way as the Synchro cord 0.6 m. It again permits both manual and normal operation (not TTL auto) for subject set-ups where the flash has to be at some distance from the camera—for instance for local fill-in lighting. With automatic long distance operation the sensor on the flash controls the duration according to the flash/subject (and not camera/subject) distance.

The Remote sensor

This unit duplicates the sensor cell and part of the control dial of the Quick Auto 310. It facilitates automatic exposure control with off-camera flash in conjunction with the OM-1—for instance bounce flashing with the bounce grip. The sensor clips into the accessory shoe and measures the light reflected towards the camera irrespective of the position or direction of the flash. This is useful also for close-up photography—but not macro where through-the-lens metering with the SBC system of the OM-2 is the only reliable flash automation system.

The Remote sensor is normally superfluous with the QA 310 on the OM-2—it would there be analogous to clipping an external exposure meter onto a camera with through-the-lens metering. For the silicon cells measuring the light reflected from the film carry out the flash duration control function of the Remote sensor more efficiently than the latter would do on its own.

To use the Remote sensor, push it into the camera's accessory shoe. The sensor cell must of course face forward. Plug the other end of the cord into the synchro socket at the side of the QA 310. This automatically cuts out the built-in sensor circuit of the QA 310 together with its control dial; the corresponding elements of the remote sensor take over. The position of the control dial on the flash is thus irrelevant. The sensor cord is a coiled type similar to the 0.6 m synchro and auto cords (see above); 0.6 to 0.9 metre (2–3 feet) is the maximum feasible distance between the flash and the Remote sensor.

For automatic operation set the ASA speed as on the dial of the QA 310 and turn the dial to bring its white

REMOTE SENSOR

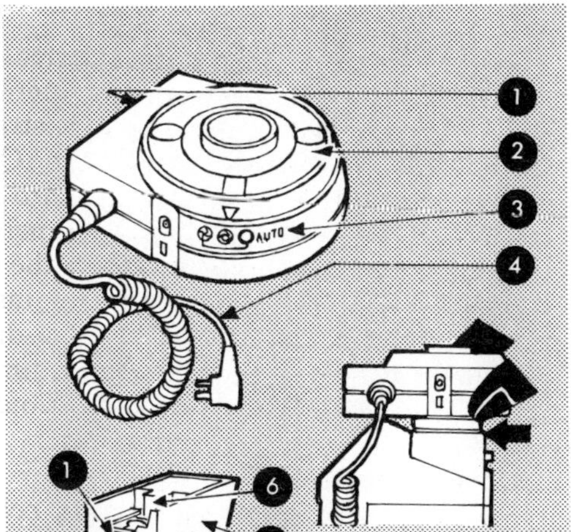

1. Sensor cell.
2. Control dial.
3. Auto aperture settings.
4. Cord and plug.

Fit the sensor by pushing it into the camera's accessory shoe, then connect to synchro cord socket on flash.

BOUNCE GRIP

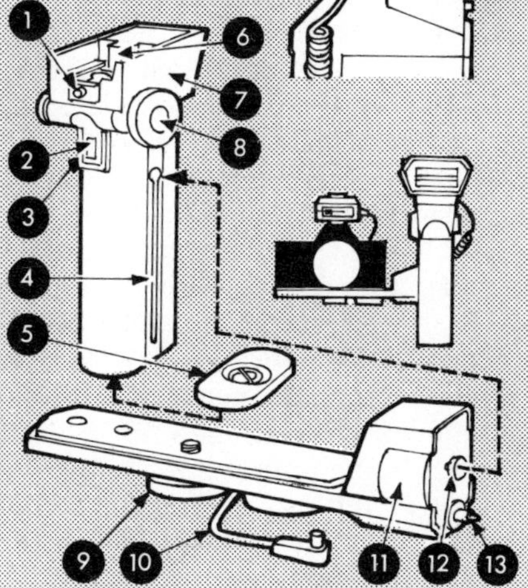

1. Foot release.
2. Power switch.
3. External power socket.
4. Bracket mount and guide groove.
5. Battery chamber cover.
6. Power plug.
7. Swivelling head.
8. Head clamp.
9. Tripod screw.
10. Built-in cord.
11. Bracket clamp.
12. Mounting pin.
13. Contact pin.

BASIC FLASH COMBINATIONS

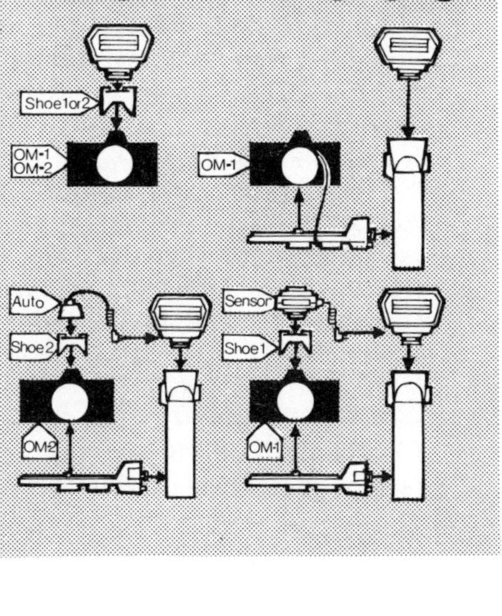

Auto 310 on the OM-1 with the shoe 1 or OM-2 with the shoe 2 *(left)*. Bounce grip mounting with the OM-1 *(right)* and built-in cord.

For automation *(left)* the Auto cord 0.6 links the 310 to the OM-2 via the accessory shoe 2.

The equivalent for the OM-1 is the remote sensor plug fed into the accessory shoe 1, *(right)*.

arrow head to one of the three AUTO positions for full, medium or small aperture. The window below the ASA figure, marked QUICK AUTO F NO indicates the required aperture setting on the lens while a distance scale near the rim of the dial shows the available automatic range. With bounce flashing remember that the working distance range has to allow for the total travelling distance of the flash to the reflecting ceiling or wall and from there to the subject. However, here the sensor automatically allows also for reflecting surfaces of different reflectivities.

The sensor acceptance angle is about 20°—the same as that of the built-in sensor on the QA 310—and is approximately equivalent to the horizontal angle of the 100 mm lens (or the appropriate focal length setting of zoom lenses covering this focal length).

The sensor also has a manual setting, but only at full flash power. To select this, turn the dial to bring its arrow head to the large sun symbol marked MANUAL HI. The dial then shows the guide number and an aperture and a distance scale as with manual operation directly on the flash unit (see above). The purpose of the manual setting on the Remote sensor is to save you the bother of disconnecting the sensor for occasional shots with manual control (for instance fill-in flash outdoors). If you need more elaborate manual control, including the reduced-power setting, unplug the Remote sensor plug from the QA 310. The control dial of the latter then resumes its normal function.

The side of the Remote sensor carries a synchro socket similar to that on the QA 310. This takes the Synchro cord 0.6 m and allows the Remote sensor to be used on cameras without hot shoe. Obviously this particular combination is unnecessary with Olympus OM models.

Certain plugging operations of the various cords into the QA 310, the camera or the accessory shoe fire the flash if the unit is charged up. This is harmless, but of course wastes some battery energy. So preferably connect up the various units before switching on the flash power.

The Bounce grip

When a flash unit is used off the camera, it is convenient to mount it on a bracket with a handle or grip and a connecting rail to fix to the camera. The OM Bounce grip combines these functions with those of a battery case for an additional power supply and various mounting adjustments. In providing these features the Bounce grip is comparatively bulky; the grip part is 165 mm (6.5 inches) high without the flash unit and the overall length of the bracket section when mounted on the grip is some 215 mm (8.1 inches). This size however also allows the flash to be mounted some distance above and to one side of the camera lens. The complete Bounce grip without batteries weighs 380 grams (13.4 ounces).

The Bounce grip is in two parts for more convenient storage and carrying—but both parts are always used together: the grip unit itself and the bracket. The grip is also a battery case taking four size C batteries which increase the flash capacity of the QA 310. According to Olympus, a set of fresh size C alkali cells gives up to 350 full-power flashes on the QA 310. The power is fed to the flash unit through a small 3-pin plug built into the front of the top section to engage the external power socket on the QA 310 as the latter slides into the accessory shoe of the grip. A further external power socket is provided in the side of the grip to connect the F.AC mains adapter or 315 volt power pack.

The top section tilts through 75° upward and 15° downward for bounce flash in the first case and close-up flash in the second.

A rachet engages the tilting section at $7\frac{1}{2}$° intervals; the horizontal position has an extra strong engagement point. The large milled knob at the side of the top section locks the head in any selected tilt position.

The synchronising connection of the flash unit to the camera goes either through one of the synchro or auto cords that plugs directly into the synchro socket of the QA 310 or through the centre contact of the hot shoe and a simple synchro cord built into the bracket. Having a standard accessory shoe with centre contact on the Bounce grip means that you can mount other flash units on it—provided the contact foot is high enough to reach the shoe in the recessed Bounce grip top—and benefit from the adjustability of the grip. But in practice the grip is an accessory of the Quick Auto 310 (or 300—see below), not the other way round.

The synchro contact link from the grip to the bracket goes through a contact strip inside a groove of the bracket mount and a contact pin on the bracket itself. The pin rides on the contact strip inside the groove and so keeps contact at the different positions of the bracket on the grip. On the bracket the synchro cord sits in a groove out of the way when not in use.

When attached to the grip, the bracket can move up and down along its mount through some 65 mm (2.5 inches) for a greater or lesser distance between the flash and the camera. The grip further carries a captive tripod screw which can be switched to one of four mounting holes at different distances from the end of the bracket. One purpose is to provide optimum alternative mountings for cameras other than the Olympus OM; but they also permit mounting the OM at different horizontal distances from the flash. With all these mounting combinations the minimum separation between the flash reflector and lens centres is about 130 mm (5.1 inches), the maximum separation about 220 mm (8.8 inches).

Finally the bracket has a tripod bush for mounting the whole camera, Bounce grip and flash assembly on a tripod.

Assembly

To attach the bracket section to the grip itself, turn the milled clamping screw on the bracket to extend fully the mounting pin on the bracket base. Place the bracket with its face against the side of the grip to fit the mounting pin into the large hole at the end of the slot. Push down along the slot so that the latter engages the mounting pin. If the bracket is stiff to push down, ease it sideways a little. Set the bracket at the desired point on the grip and tighten the milled clamping screw to hold it in place.

To insert the QA 310 in the top of the grip, turn the locking wheel above the foot of the 310 against the FIX arrow, guide the foot into the accessory shoe on the bracket (at the same time depressing the small bright pin at the back of the shoe) and push forward to engage. Turn the locking wheel of the 310 in the FIX direction to secure.

Fit batteries in the grip if required (see below, *Power supplies*).

The normal attachment point for the camera is the innermost hole of the bracket. Normally the tripod screw is already located in that hole. To fit the OM camera, screw the tripod screw through this hole into the camera's tripod bush. To complete the synchronising circuit, either:

(a) For automatic operation with the OM-2 plug the Auto cord 0.6 m into the synchro cord socket on the QA 310 and fit the foot of the cord into the Accessory shoe 2 on the OM-2; or

(b) For bounce flash and accurate automatic operation with the OM-1 fit the Remote sensor in the accessory shoe of the camera and plug its lead into the synchro socket on the QA 310; or

(c) For manual operation or automatic control with the built-in sensor of the QA 310 unhitch the built-in synchronising cord of the bracket from its groove in the base and plug into the camera's coaxial flash socket. Set the switch of the latter to X.

You get the same result by plugging the Synchro cord 0.6 m (not auto cord) into the camera's flash socket and the synchro cord outlet of the QA 310.

Do not plug the built-in bracket cord into the camera when anything is plugged into the flash unit's synchro cord outlet (Auto cord 0.6 m or Remote sensor) as the flash will not then fire.

To dismantle the unit, *first unplug all cords*. Unscrew the tripod screw and remove the camera. To remove the QA 310 from the grip, release the locking wheel of the 310 foot (turn against the FIX direction), pull down the small chrome stud just behind the accessory shoe and ease the flash unit out of the shoe while gently pulling it backwards. During this operation have the tilt movement of the head firmly clamped. Slack off the milled clamping nut on the bracket and slide the latter up to the top of the guiding groove on the grip section; the bracket then comes off the grip.

Power supplies

The basic power supply for the Quick Auto 310 comes from the size AA batteries that fit into the base of the unit. There are also the following further options:

(a) Size C batteries housed in the grip section of the Bounce grip.

(b) The F.AC adapter to operate from the normal mains supply (house current).

(c) A 315 volt high-tension power pack (see below).

The various sources can be combined—for instance the internal batteries of the 310 with (a) and/or either (b) or (c). Similarly you can rely on (a) or (b) or (c) only. The sole impossible combination is (b) and (c)—because these connect to the QA 310 or Bounce grip through an external power socket and the units only have one such socket.

To fit batteries in the hand grip, turn the chrome lock in the base (use a coin) to position OPEN. Lift off the base and insert four size C alkali batteries in the orientation marked on a label just inside the battery chamber. If you hold the grip so that the connecting groove is at the top, the left-hand batteries should slide into the chamber with their top (+) contact facing you, the two right-hand batteries with their base (− pole) facing you.

As with the Quick Auto 310, *do not use rechargeable nickel-cadmium batteries*. Their lower internal resistance could under certain circumstances permit excessive current surges that might be harmful to the control circuits of the QA 310.

Replace the battery chamber cover (the baseplate of the grip section) with the red dot in the base lined up with the red dot just inside the open chamber. (The cover does not go on if wrongly oriented.) Secure by turning the slotted disc in the base to LOCK.

When the QA 310 is mounted on the grip and you have batteries in both the flash unit and the grip, you can control which you use by the two power switches. Turning the switch on the flash unit to ON connects the internal batteries to the charging circuit. Moving the switch on the grip to ON connects the batteries on the grip to the circuit. In the ON position of both these switches a red area is visible below the switch.

If the flash unit switch is OFF but the grip switch ON, only the batteries of the latter feed the charging circuit of the flash unit. If both switches are ON, the flash is fed from both sets of batteries which shortens recycling.

The F.AC adapter

This unit plugs into a suitable mains supply socket and directly powers the QA 310 flash. For this, plug the 3-pin female plug at the other end of the lead into the external power socket on the QA 310 or of the Bounce grip—when the flash unit is mounted on the grip. Once the lead is plugged in, the unit begins to charge up irrespective of the position of any switches. The F.AC adapter has no switch of its own.

The recycling time of the flash with the F.AC adapter is about 10 seconds; you can decrease this by also switching on the power switches of the flash unit itself and/or the Bounce grip.

The F.AC adapter is useful when you use the flash at a fairly fixed location within easy reach of a mains socket. And of course you use no battery power (there is no need even to have batteries in the flash unit or Bounce grip). The 190 mm (7.5 inches) length of the lead does not however give you much mobility.

The adapter itself is a housing about 50 × 42 × 67 mm (1.95 × 1.7 × 2.6 inches) large with contact pins for the mains socket in the underside. The top carries the input data, e.g. AC 240 V, 50/60 Hz for supplies of up to 240 volts. You may need an adapter for the plug fitting. Alternative models exist with different plug-in pins (flat US, round European) and for different input voltages.

The 315 volt power pack

This portable external power source is mainly intended for news reporters and other professional photographers requiring very fast recycling times with a high flash capacity irrespective of cost. The power pack consists of a 315 volt layer battery in a battery holder, housed in turn in a leather case. The unit is 47 × 83 × 180 mm (1.9 × 3.3 × 7.1 inches) large and weighs 390 grams (13.8 ounces) without battery. One battery yields over 500 flashes at full power—more than four times the capacity claimed for a set of size AA alkaline batteries. But the 315 volt pack is not a cheap power supply, as replacement batteries cost about four to five times as much as the 16 size AA cells that match them in capacity. For photographers needing almost instant recycling this is however still worth it; with the 315 volt power pack the QA 310 recycles in $\frac{1}{2}$ to $1\frac{1}{2}$ seconds with full power flashing—and of course very much faster when only part of the energy is used in one of the automatic modes.

To fit a battery in the pack, remove the battery holder from the leather case, turn the power switch to OFF and push in the 315 volt layer battery correctly lined up with the marked + and – terminal contacts. Return the holder to the leather case and plug the plug of the connecting cord into the external power socket on the QA 310 or the Bounce grip. The spiral connecting cord is 1.5 metres (5 feet) long—sufficient when you carry the power pack over one shoulder.

For operation turn the power switch—accessible through the side of the carrying case—to ON, wait for the ready/charge light to light up and shoot in the operating mode selected before. To save battery power, turn the switch to OFF when the flash is not being used. You can combine the power of the 315 volt pack with the internal batteries of the Bounce grip and/or QA 310 to shorten the recycling time further, though in practice there seems little point in that.

Fast-repeating flashing at full power puts considerable thermal strain on the flash tube and circuit, and the QA 310 becomes warm. With the 315 V power pack therefore do not fire more than 10 rapidly consecutive flashes at full power; after that allow the unit to cool down for at least 1 minute. The power pack is thus not a unit for high-speed sequencing with the motor drive.

This does not apply where fast recycling is obtained by reducing the flash power during automatic or TTL auto operation. With the 315 volt power pack you are not however sure how much of the power is used on automatic operation and the unit may still be overloaded. The safest procedure in that case is to rely on charging by the alkali cells only in the QA 310 itself or in the Bounce grip—or work with the F.AC adapter. With these units you are sure that the flash recycles quickly only if the previous flash used little of the available energy.

The Quick Auto 300

This is a discontinued predecessor of the Quick Auto 310 with all the same features and identical operation except for the TTL auto control. The operating modes available are therefore:

(a) normal automatic at three alternative aperture settings, and

(b) manual with full and with quarter power.

The control dial on this model therefore turns only between the small-aperture AUTO and the LOW MANUAL settings, engaging at each of the marked positions. At each of these settings the windows show appropriate *f*-numbers, automatic distance ranges, peak guide numbers, manual *f*-number and distance combinations exactly as on the Quick Auto 310. The handling, mounting on the Bounce grip or camera and power options are the same as on the 310, as are the dimensions and weight.

Several points arise in practical applications:

(a) When mounted on the OM-2, the QA 300 operates exactly as the QA 310 in the normal automatic and manual modes. There is thus no link to or control by the internal SBC metering system of the camera. It is immaterial whether on the OM-2 you use the Accessory shoe 2 or 1. The silicon cells however meter the light in the film plane for the existing lighting level independently of the flash.

(b) For off-camera automatic operation the most efficient way is the Remote sensor mounted in the camera's accessory shoe. This operates in the same way with the OM-2 and OM-1. Preferably set the OM-2 to manual metering; if the meter switch remains at AUTO or OFF and the prevailing light is strong enough to select a shutter speed faster than 1/60 second, the flash will not fire at all.

(c) For off-camera manual operation the flash may be linked to the camera either via one of the synchro cords or with the built-in cord of the Bounce grip. Do not use the Auto cord with the QA 300; that always fires the flash at full manual power irrespective of the control dial setting.

(d) When using the Quick Auto 300 in the normal automatic mode on the OM-2 camera, set the meter switch of the latter always to MANUAL.

Other flashes

The OM cameras operate also with other electronic flash units as well as with holders for flash bulbs or flash cubes. When these are fitted by a shoe with centre contact, the Accessory shoe 1 or 2 provides the direct synchronising link. Otherwise synchronise with the synchro cable of the unit plugged into the camera's flash socket. The versatility and usefulness of such flash units is determined by their features and may include manual flashing at one or more power levels and/or normal automatic operation with a built-in or even external sensor cell. Such other units may offer the advantage of compactness, usually with smaller light output. This is often adequate for near subjects and a pocket electronic flash is convenient to carry.

Two units in this category from Olympus are the PS 200 and the PS 200 Quick. They are specially compact units of low power and simple operation; their features are comparable with many other makes of pocket electronic flashes of similar specifications.

The Olympus PS 200 is the more compact model of the two with overall dimensions 31 × 55 × 64 mm (1.2 × 2.2 × 2.5 inches) and weighs 75 grams (2.6 ounces) without batteries. The unit takes two 1.5 volt size AA batteries and is claimed to yield up to 200 flashes with fresh alkali batteries. The recycling time is 7 seconds and the guide number is 14 (metres) or 45 (feet) for 100 ASA film.

The Olympus PS 200 Quick is similar to the PS 200 in light output but recycles in only 2–3 seconds. To achieve this, the PS 200 Quick is powered by four size AA batteries of 1.5 volts and is accordingly slightly larger (32 × 71 × 73 mm or 1.3 × 2.8 × 2.9 inches) and weighs 95 grams (3.4 ounces) without batteries.

Flash lighting applications

A flash mounted directly on the camera yields rather flat frontal lighting. This is accepted as a necessary evil in press, feature and similar fields of photography where you need maximum light on a subject with minimum fuss. You get improved modelling by mounting the flash on a bracket such as the Bounce grip that holds it a few inches to one side and if necessary above the camera.

The most effective way of soft illumination with flash is by reflected light from the ceiling or walls. For ceiling reflection with subjects around 6 feet (2 metres) away tilt the Quick Auto unit fully upwards on the Bounce grip. Turn it up through lesser angles for more distant subjects to spread the reflected light evenly. For bouncing sideways from a wall hold the camera as for upright

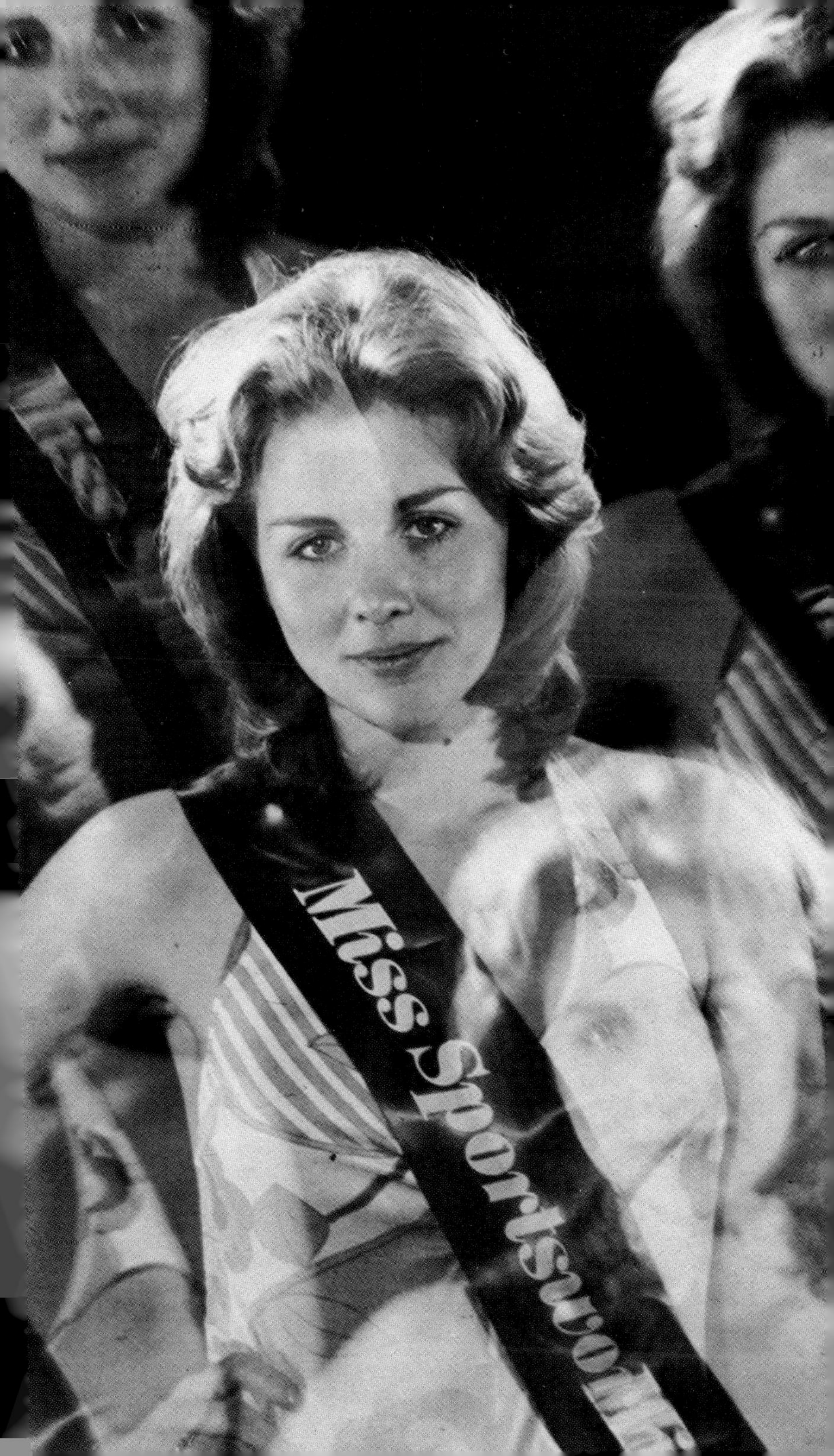
Miss Sportswom

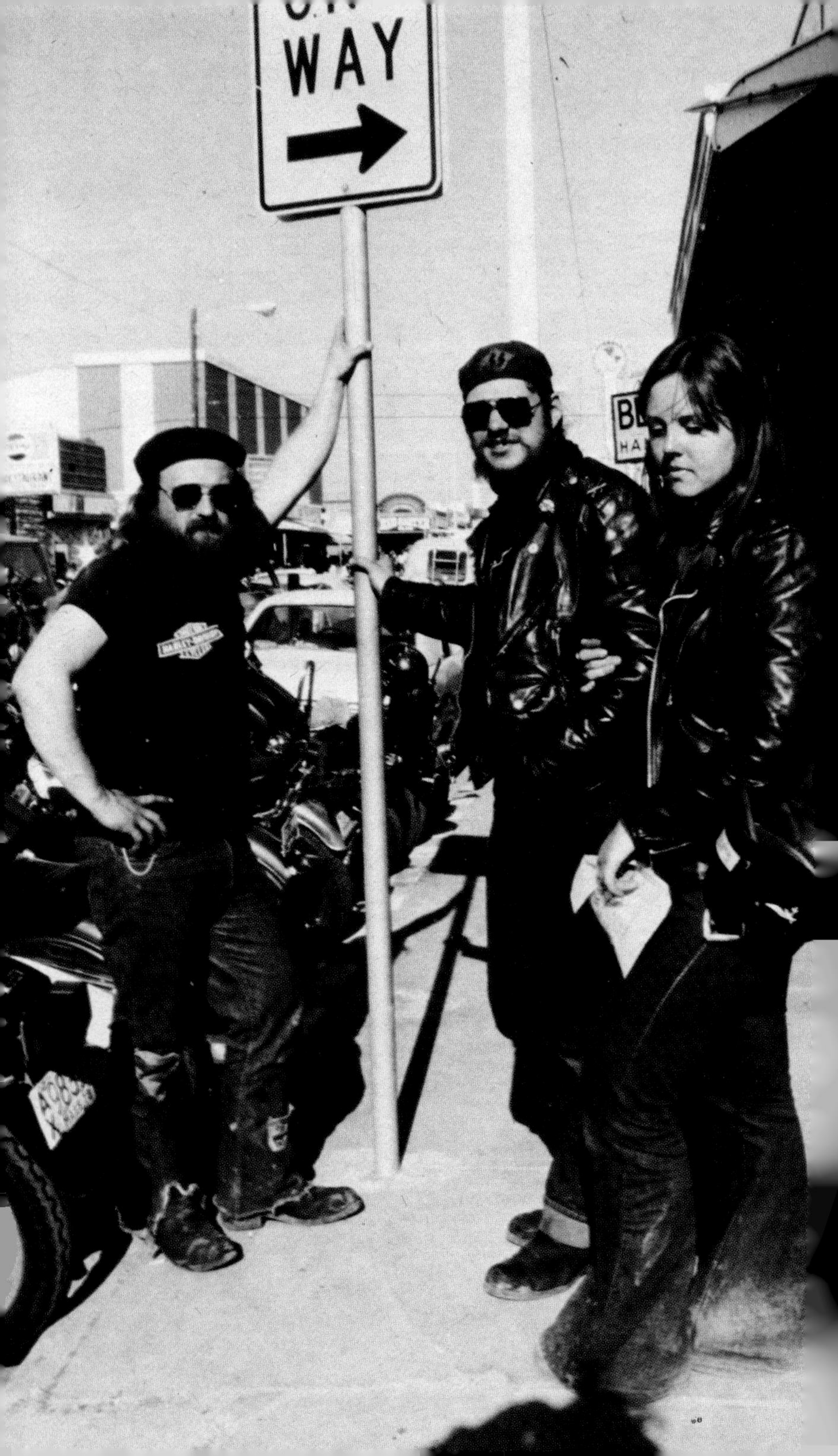
WAY

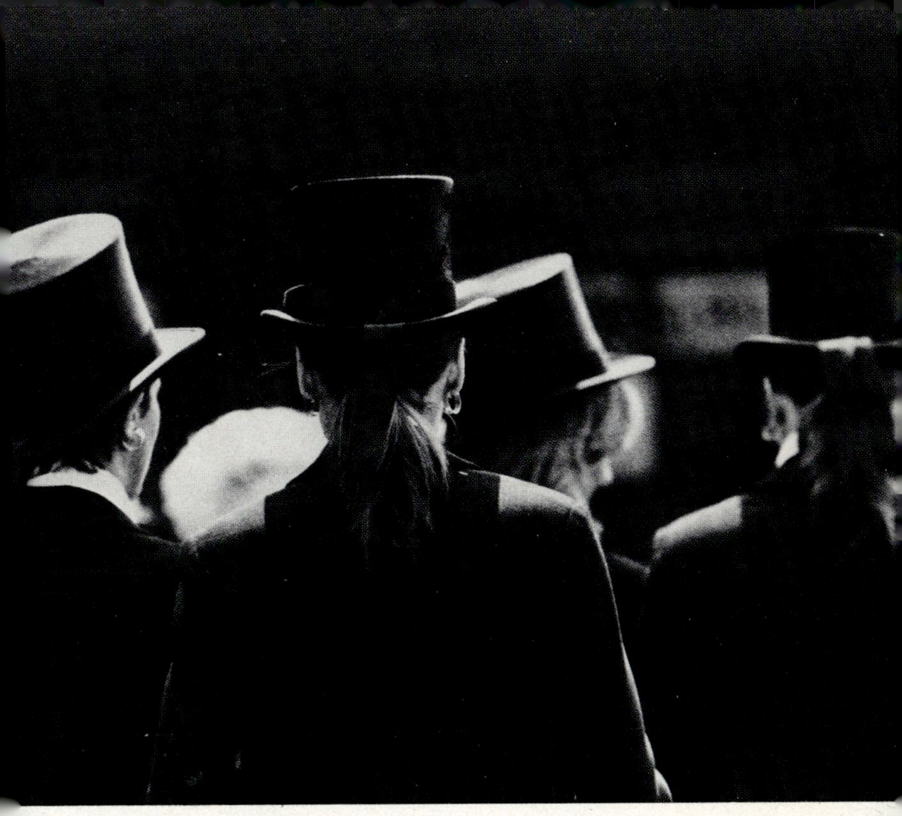

HATS
Above. Shooting against the light with a 200 mm lens turns these Derby-goer's hats into an almost abstract pattern.

HELL'S ANGELS
Opposite. The 18 mm wide-angle lens with its coverage of a lot of subject area from nearby, is popular for conveying sprawling atmosphere.

DOUBLE AND MORE
Plate 1. Facetted prism attachments in front of the lenses (preferably use the standard lens) yield multiple images repeated around the central image. The multi-images show up best against a dark ground. (From a colour transparency).

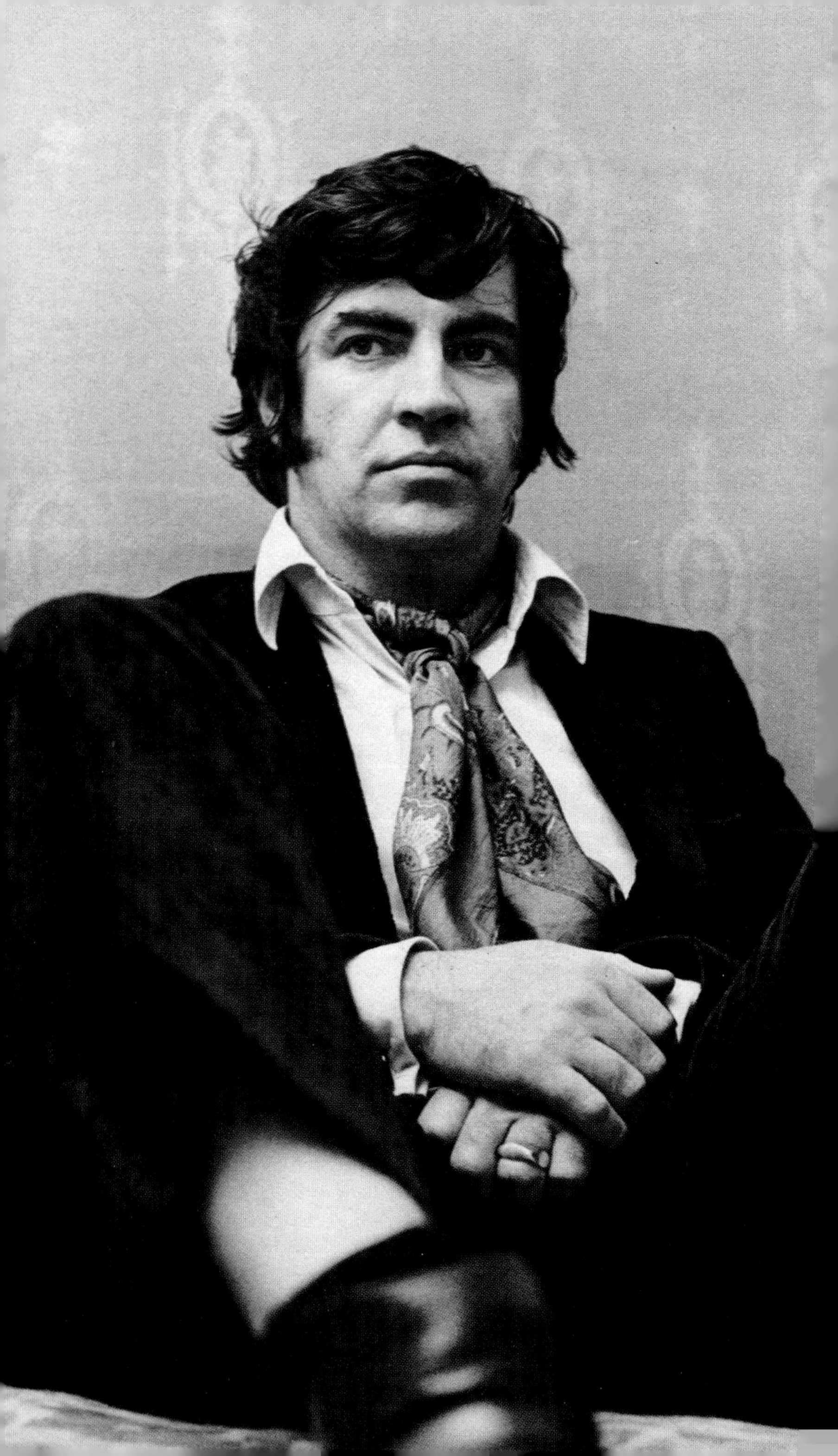

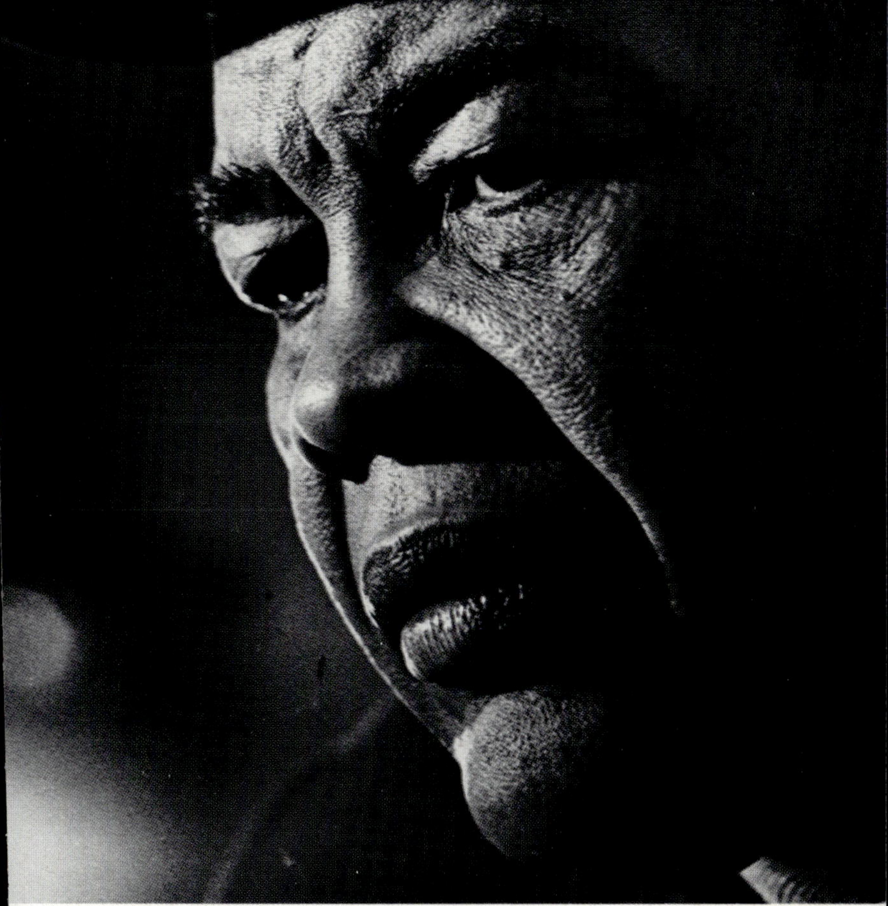

BOXER

Above. Strong side and backlighting was used here to accentuate former champion, Joe Louis' face. The 85 mm lens restricts the depth of field to just facial detail.

BACKSTAGE

Opposite. A large lens aperture and hence one of the fast standard lenses was needed to make the most of the natural light in the dressing room. Careful positioning of Alan Bates ensured sufficient light reflection into shadow areas.

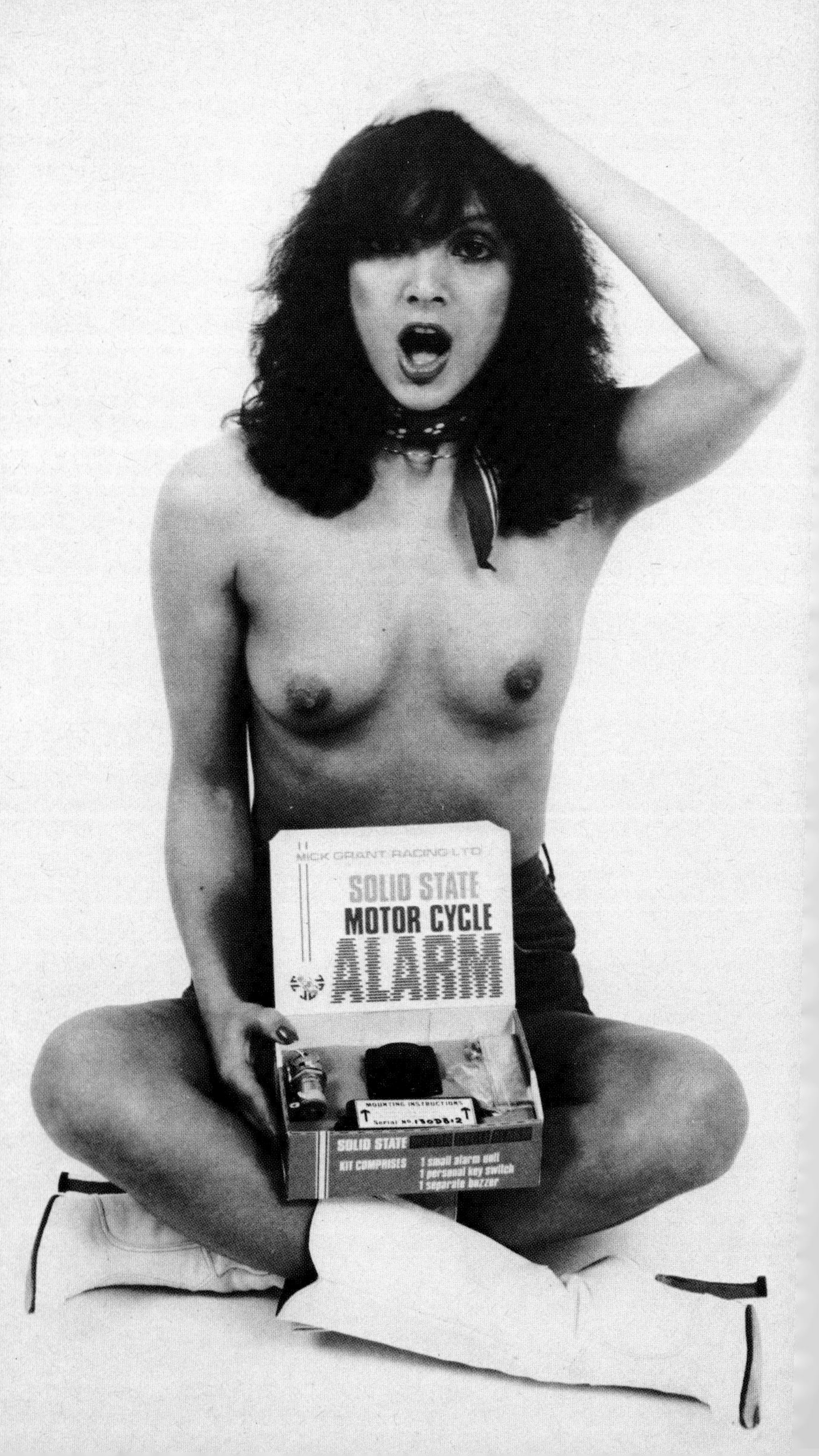
MICK GRANT RACING LTD
SOLID STATE
MOTOR CYCLE
ALARM
MOUNTING INSTRUCTIONS
SOLID STATE
KIT COMPRISES
1 small alarm unit
1 personal key switch
1 separate buzzer

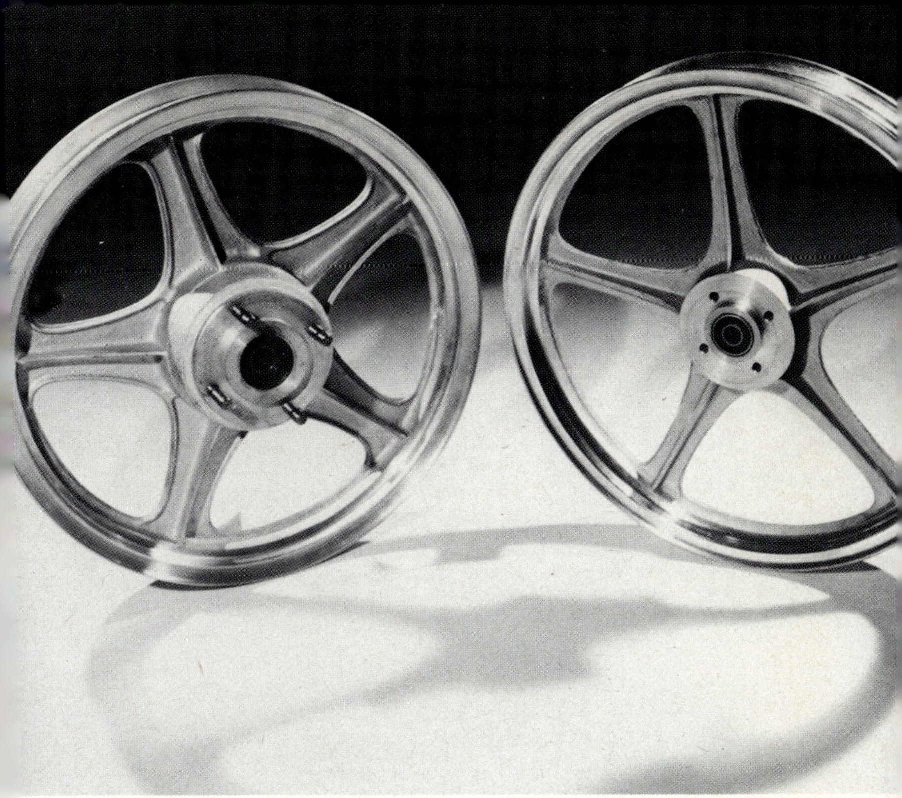

WHEELS
Above. Commercial product shots call for careful lighting balance: the picture must show every modulated detail of the subject texture. The 100 mm lens allowed a far enough viewpoint for natural perspective yet filled the frame with the subject.

ALARM
Opposite. Flash in the studio provides fairly stark general light to put over the slightly phoney alarm of the model.

SECRETARY
Plate 8. The 85 or 100 mm lens is often ideal for studio advertising shots. The rest is a matter of trying poses and shooting pictures to give the client a selection of posture and expressions.

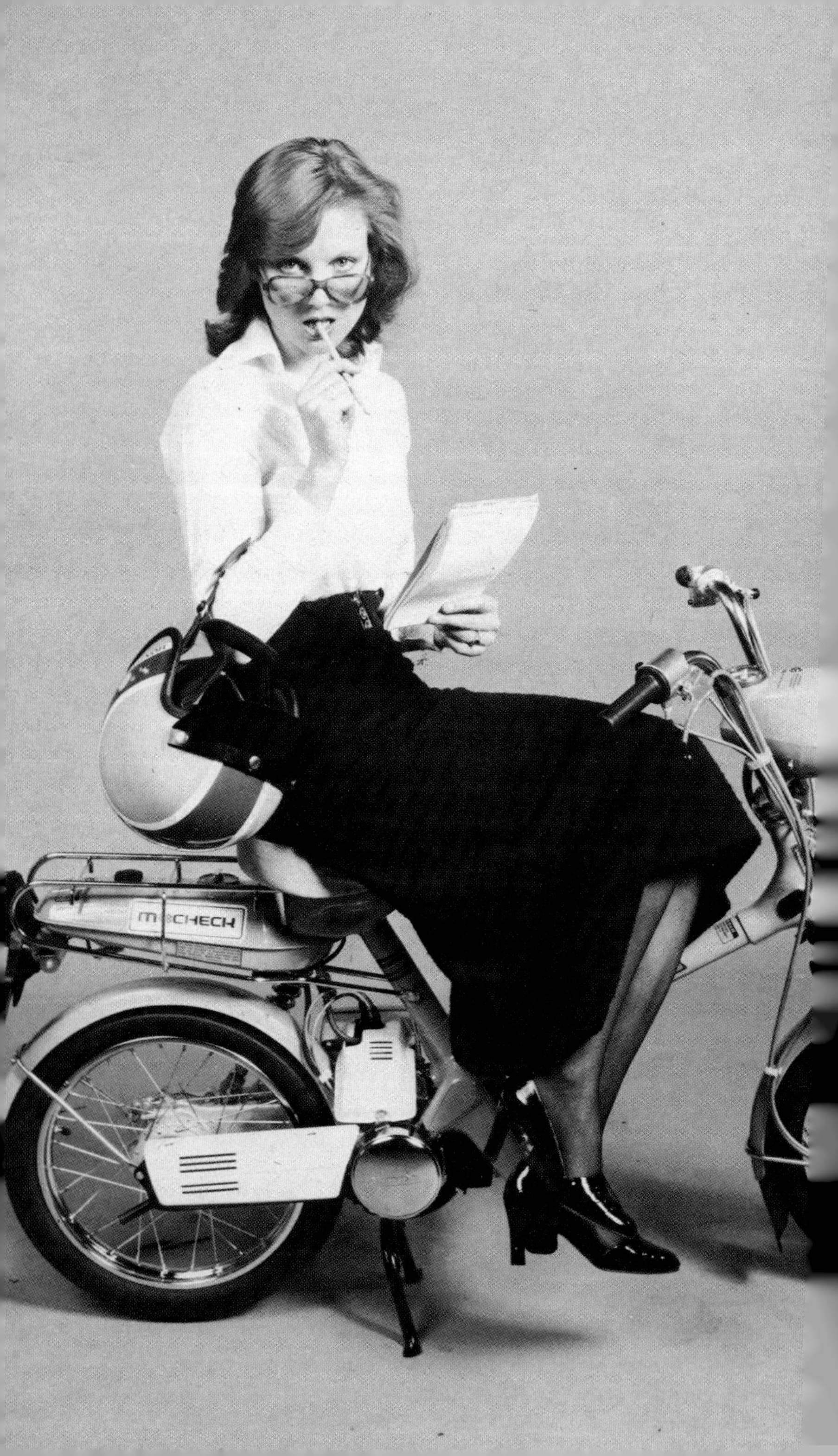

views; the tilted flash now points to the side. (With horizontal format shots detach the grip from the bracket and point it separately at the wall.)

For near subjects the flash and lens axis have to converge for optimum lighting. Slack off the tripod screw and turn the camera slightly on the Bounce grip for horizontal convergence. Use the downward tilt of the head on the grip for vertical convergence. A 15° down tilt of the flash with the camera bracket at the bottom of the grip converges the flash and lens axis on a subject about 56 cm (22 inches) away. For still nearer subjects move the camera bracket nearer the top of the grip or point the flash on its own in the required direction.

With these ways of pointing the flash, ensure correct exposures by:

(a) Using the Auto cord to link the OM-2 to the Quick Auto 310, the latter being set to TTL AUTO, or

(b) Mounting the Remote sensor on the camera and connecting it to the Quick Auto via the Synchro cord. (This is with the OM-1, and indeed any camera other than the OM-2.)

The near metering limit of a computer flash such as the Quick Auto is around 25 cm (10 inches) even at the smallest aperture. To avoid overexposure, mount a layer or two of thin tracing or tissue paper over the flash reflector. Two layers roughly halve the near distance limit.

At close range the flash duration of the QA units in the AUTO modes also becomes extremely short—between 1/20,000 and 1/40,000 second. This permits sharp pictures of quite fast moving near items such as insects etc.

Flash and daylight

Flash can be useful auxiliary lighting for difficult contrasty subjects, for instance brilliant back lighting by daylight. Flash here acts as fill-in lighting to bridge the excessive brightness range while retaining the atmosphere of the daylight set-up. Typical applications are backlit pictures of people where we have to cover a sunlit halo rim around the head as well as the part of a face in shadow; or indoor views with a window and a sunlit view outside.

Correct fill-in flash use depends on balancing the daylight intensity and the flash-illuminated shadows to an approximate 2:1 intensity ratio for colour shots on negative film, or 4:1 for more dramatic black-and-white shots or colour transparencies. Here is how you do it with the QA 310 (or any other computer flash unit, including the QA 300) mounted in the camera's accessory shoe or the Bounce grip:

Measure the required aperture for a 1/60 second shutter speed for the daylit parts of the subject, without allowing for the dark shadows. Set this aperture in the camera (with the meter switch of the OM-2 at MANUAL). On the flash select an AUTO setting with an aperture one stop larger (for a 2:1 highlight shadow ratio) or two stops larger (4:1 ratio) than you have set on the camera. For example, with *f* 8 on the camera, use an AUTO setting on the flash that would call for *f* 5.6 or *f* 4. If you shoot with these settings, the flash brings the required fill-in lighting into the shadows but automatically underexposes them to avoid competing excessively with the daylit parts.

Note that you are here using the OM-2 in the *manual* mode. This is easier than the automatic mode which in this case introduces complications. For the same reason avoid using the QA 310 in the TTL auto mode for fill-in flash.

If you want an equal flash/daylight balance—shadows as light as highlights, for instance for indoors views with the window—proceed as above but select a computer flash setting for the same aperture as you have set on the camera. With reversal colour film reduce the exposure by one-third to one-half lens stop to avoid slight over-exposure.

A non-automatic flash unit can also be used for this filling in. Here divide the guide number of the flash/subject distance to obtain an aperture, and then set 1 or 2 stops smaller on the camera. Establish the required shutter speed (not faster than 1/60 second for electronic units) for this aperture, with the camera in manual mode.

THE MOTOR DRIVE GROUP

An unusual aspect of the OM equipment system is the sophisticated equipment for motorised, remote-controlled and programmed photography. The concept is based on the very compact motor drive with a range of alternative power sources and remote control connections including interval timing. A simple motor wind attachment is also available. Finally, motorised and remote-controlled photography makes sense especially with an enlarged film capacity—the 250 exposure film back which in turn forms a self-contained mini-system of its own.

The motor drive group thus naturally divides into four related but reasonably independent subsections. For optimum clarity the equipment is therefore described in terms of these subsections as follows:

Winder 1 covers the simple motorised winder for speeded-up camera operation.

Motor drive 1 covers the drive itself, the various power sources, connecting and relay cords and the M.AC control box.

250 film back 1 covers the 250 exposure bulk film back with its film magazines and loader.

Remote control and unmanned photography covers more general points of motorisation, including those applying to all the drive units and combinations.

Winder 1

The Winder 1 is a motor unit that attaches to Olympus OM cameras (other than the very earliest OM-1 models) and runs the whole exposure cycle on pressing a button. You can with reasonably skilled manipulation even shoot sequences at up to 2 frames per second, though the winder is primarily intended as an electric release and winding unit. These functions can also operate by remote control, for instance for unmanned photography.

The Winder 1 consists of a base section about 127 mm

long, 34 mm high and 36 mm deep (5 × 1.3 × 1.4 inches) with a hand grip protruding about 28 mm (1.1 inches) in front and 100 mm (4 inches) high. When the unit is fitted on the camera, it is mainly the 34 mm extra height that counts. Complete with batteries the Winder I weighs about 390 grams (13.8 ounces).

The Winder I carries various elements in its top surface to link with the camera (this surface mates with the camera baseplate):

At the left in the top (when looking at the winder from behind so that the lettering is upright) is a pair of ball contacts that couple with the contact in the camera bottom. They are in turn linked with the shutter and close the film transport circuit of the winder as soon as the shutter is closed (but prevent movement of the film during an exposure). A little to the right, in the rear of the winder, is a pair of contacts for coupling with the transport system of the 250 film back (see below).

Near the centre of the base is a $\frac{1}{4}$ inch tripod screw turned by the chrome milled knob set in the front of the winder. This screws the winder to the camera.

Further to the right are two mechanical items for coupling with the camera through the latter's motor coupling section: the shutter release coupling pin and the film transport claw. The coupling pin triggers the shutter release via a lever inside the camera base. The transport claw engages a driving wheel also inside the camera base and linked with the transport movement.

Further to the right, next to the hand grip, a steel pin protrudes about 5 mm from the winder platform. This is a guide pin that engages a corresponding guide hole in the camera base (next to the camera's battery chamber) for accurate location of the winder on the camera.

Finally, at the right-hand end a gear wheel protrudes into a cut-out and is coupled with the film transport claw. This wheel serves for mechanical linking to the 250 film back. Normally a swivelling cover protects the gear wheel. Always keep this cover closed except when you use the winder with the 250 film back.

The hand grip part carries on top a release button—actually a relay switch—to trigger the release and transport sequence. Next to it is a 2.5 mm jack socket to take a remote control cord with switch or other remote control

MOTOR DRIVE GROUP

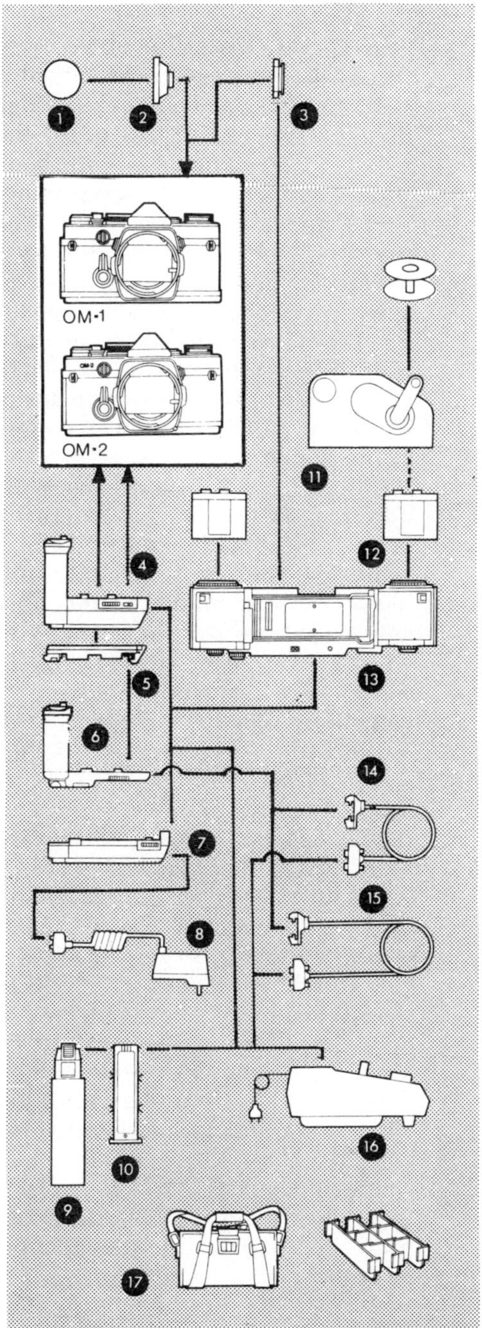

This group system chart shows how the motor drive and its accessories link up with the OM cameras. The chart illustrates the following items.

1, 2, 3. Eyecoupler, needed to take the eyecup when used with the 250 film back, and dioptric correction lenses.

4. Winder 1.
5. Battery holder for Winder 1.
6. Motor drive 1.
7. M.15V nickel-cadmium control pack 1.
8. Charger 1 for above.
9. M.18V control grip 1.
10. M.18V battery holder 1 for above.
11. 250 film loader with large spool.
12. 250 film magazine for film back.
13. 250 film back 1.
14. Relay cord, 1.2 m.
15. Relay cord, 10 m.
16. M.AC control box.
17. Compartment case L with special partitioned inserts for motor drive group equipment.

gear. Closing such a switch has the same effect as pressing the release button.

In the base the winder carries a tripod bush for mounting the whole camera assembly on a tripod, and at the end a sliding latch. This releases the battery holder which then slides out of the lower section of the winder. The underside of the grip section carries a rotary switch with two positions OFF and SINGLE. To switch on the winder for operation, lift the milled knob and return it to bring SINGLE opposite the white index mark. The ring engages in two other positions: opposite the OFF setting is an unmarked one which is also off and opposite the SINGLE setting an unmarked position again switches the unit on. To avoid confusion however, use only the marked settings of the switch.

The centre of this rotary switch carries an external power jack to connect external power supplies (see below). Next to the switch dial is a small carrying strap eyelet. If you use the camera predominantly with the winder, it is worth disengaging the camera strap with its split ring from the right-hand strap eyelet (next to the winder lever) and re-attaching it to the eyelet on the winder. But if you use the camera without the winder, you have to transfer the strap back again.

Attaching to the camera

Before fitting the Winder I to the camera, check that the switch dial is set to OFF. If it is not, pull up and turn to OFF. Make this a basic rule whenever fitting the winder to or removing it from the camera and also whenever you plug in any remote control unit. It prevents inadvertent camera operation during fitting—that can even happen on plugging in without pressing the release. If the switch dial is at ON, contacting the camera base could cause the winder motor to whirr continuously until the coupling elements engage with some force—not very good for the coupling.

With a coin, turn the motor drive socket cap in the camera base anticlockwise (index dot on cap against index dot on camera) and remove to uncover the camera coupling elements in the base. Store this socket cap inside the winder: Remove the battery holder and push the socket cap—with its bayonet fittings facing up—into the recess just inside the winder base. If the camera has a

WINDER 1

The components and controls are:

1. 250 film back coupling contacts.
2. Camera coupling contacts.
3. Clamping screw.
4. Release button.
5. Remote control jack.
6. External power jack.
7. Film advance claw.
8. Shutter release coupling pin.
9. 250 film back coupling gear.
10. Guide pin.
11. Strap eyelet.
12. Battery holder lock.
13. Switch dial.
14. Tripod bush.
15. Battery holder.

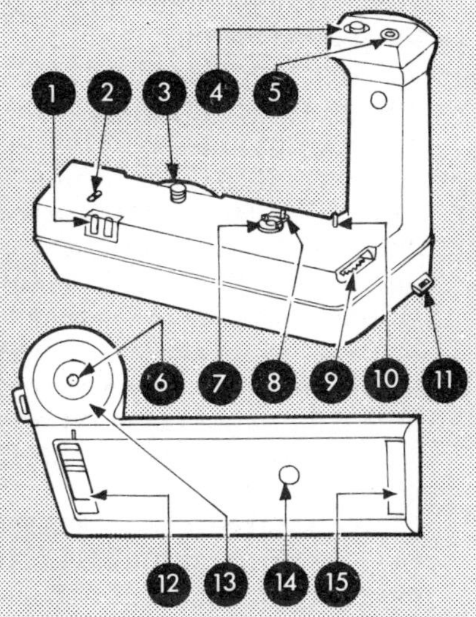

Before fitting the camera, open the battery holder *(left)*, remove the motor drive socket cap from the camera *(right)*.

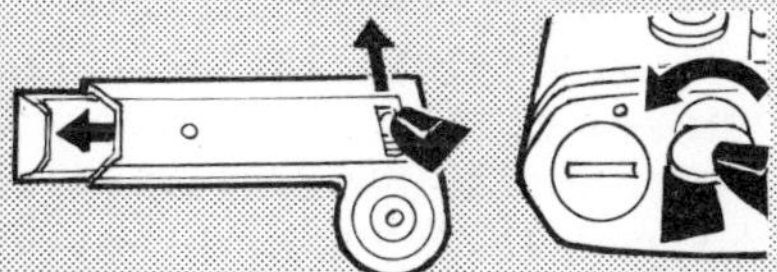

Store the cap inside the winder's battery chamber *(left)*. Load the battery holder with four size AA batteries *(right)*.

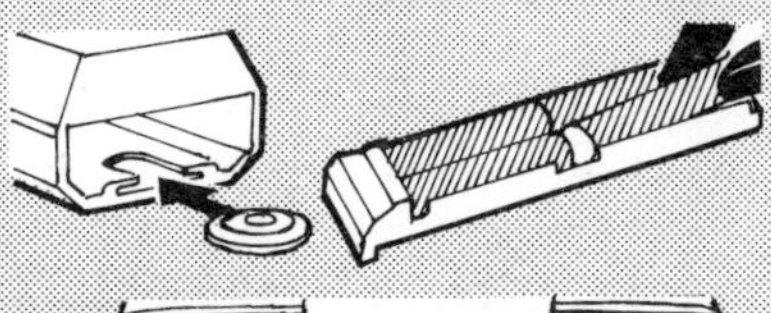

When attaching the winder to the camera line up the guide pin with the guide pin hole first, then screw the clamping screw into the tripod bush.

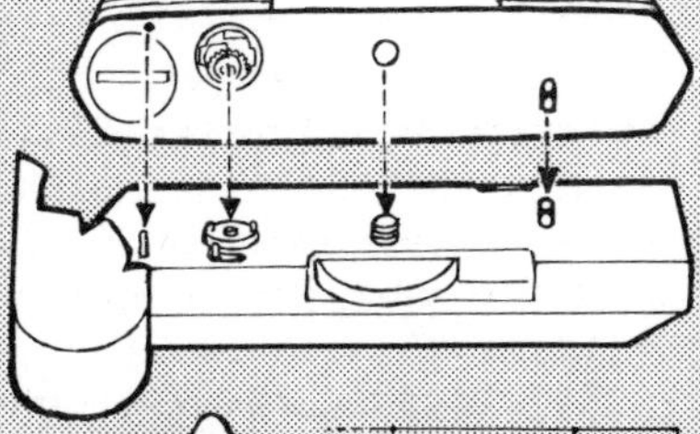

External sources up to 6 volts with coaxial plug (note polarity), plug into the external power jack *(left)*. Several cameras with winder can be linked via remote control leads connected in parallel *(right)*.

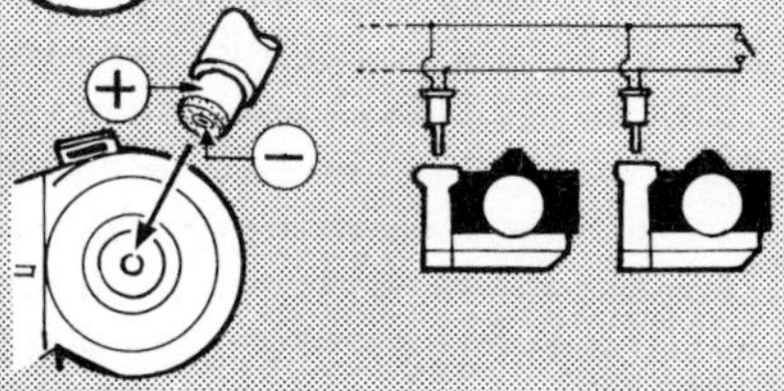

strap fitted, fold the split ring upwards flat against the camera body so that the front right-hand camera edge is unobstructed from the strap eyelet down to the baseplate.

Now attach the winder: First engage the guide pin into the guide hole in the camera base, next to the battery chamber cover. Then locate the fixing screw against the tripod bush and turn the screw clockwise (as seen from underneath) till the winder is firmly attached to the camera base. It must be completely in contact with the camera base from end to end.

When the winder is correctly fitted, the right-hand carrying strap eyelet on the camera should press against the small plastic stud at the rear of the winder hand grip. (That's why you have to move a carrying strap with split ring out of the way.)

Provided the winder is charged with batteries, it is now ready for operation: with the dial switch at ON, pressing the release button triggers the camera release and advances the film.

To remove the winder from the camera, turn the milled clamping screw anticlockwise (as seen from the camera base) until it disengages from the tripod bush. Then lift the camera off the winder, retrieve the motor drive socket cap from inside the winder's battery compartment and replace on the camera. Put the cap in position with its index dot facing the dot in the camera base. Turn clockwise with your fingernail or a coin to secure. When correctly fitted, the slot in the motor drive socket cap is parallel with the baseplate edge.

Power supplies

The winder is normally powered by four size AA batteries —either alkali or rechargeable nickel-cadmium—in the battery holder. One set of fresh alkali batteries lasts for up to fifty 36-exposure films; nickel-cadmium cells have about one-third that capacity per charge.

To fit or change batteries, push the battery holder latch in the winder base—next to the switch dial—in the direction of its arrow. The battery holder then springs partway out of the base at the other side and can be fully pulled out. Insert the four AA cells into the spaces in the holder, with the +/− orientation as marked inside the plastic holder. (The winder won't work if the batteries are inserted the wrong way round.) Push back the battery holder into the winder base from the side. It only goes in one way round, with the flat surface of the battery holder facing up towards the camera.

The battery holder is quite an inexpensive unit also available separately. You can thus take one or two spare battery holders complete with extra batteries with you if you use the winder a lot. To change batteries, release the battery holder by pressing the latch, pull out and replace by the second holder with new batteries. That takes just a couple of seconds.

The M.6V power pack 1 is an external pocketable power unit for the Winder 1, similar in principle to the battery holder (but not insertable in the Winder 1), complete with a 1.2 metre (4 feet) lead and plug to fit the external power jack of the winder. The power pack end of the lead plugs into a battery terminal on the battery holder. The latter is carried inside a plastic case. If you keep this in your pocket, the winder remains efficiently operative even in very cold weather. The battery holder itself of the M.6V power pack takes four size AA batteries, exactly as the internal battery holder of the Winder 1.

Other alternative power supplies also plug into the same external power jack of the winder.

Winder operation

To switch the winder on, lift the switch dial in the base of the grip and turn it from OFF to SINGLE.

The normal operating mode is single exposures, i.e. every time you press the release button the winder releases the shutter and immediately afterwards advances the film. For every fresh release cycle you must however let go of the button and press it again.

Steady releasing is of course still vital with the winder but is easier as you are pressing a switch and nothing else. You can find the exact release point by listening carefully when you press the button with winder switched off. A faint click indicates the point when the switch closes. If you press the winder release to nearly that point, very slight extra pressure closes the switch.

You may feel a slight 'kick' of the camera during winder operation. This is due to the transport motor, not the release action, and occurs after the exposure where it causes no camera shake. For single shots the winder is an aid to smoother releasing. In rapid sequence shooting however the kick may affect subsequent exposures with too slow a shutter speed. It will incidentally cause vibration much more in a camera mounted on a flimsy tripod than one held in the hand—which damps the movement.

The camera hold with the winder is often more comfortable—at any rate for people with big hands. Hold the camera/winder combination in much the same way as the camera on its own, but keep the index finger on the winder release and the right thumb on the camera back. The left hand supports the camera and the winder from underneath; there is now more room for tucking the ring finger and little finger underneath the winder base.

With the winder on the camera (and even switched on) you can still operate the mechanical release button and winding lever in the normal way. Pressing the winder release after pressing the camera release only winds on the film by the motor. A next pressure on the winder release then takes a further picture and advances the film. (After electrical triggering the winder always advances the film as well.)

Winder sequencing

The Winder 1 is not primarily intended for rapid sequence shooting. Nevertheless it is capable of cycling at up to about $2\frac{1}{2}$ frames per second. There are two ways:

One depends on skilful pressing and releasing of the winder release. With a little practice you can shoot at quite fast rates up to about 2 pictures a second. For fastest cycling find the pressure point of the winder release (you hear a faint click on pressing the button with the winder switched off). By pressing the release to just below, and letting go to just above, this pressure point, it is possible to keep shooting at quite a steady rate. Use a fast shutter speed—the winder cannot cycle the transport until the shutter is closed and this rhythmic pressing and releasing does tend to shake the camera a little.

An even simpler way of continuous cycling with the winder at $2\frac{1}{2}$ frames per second is to make contact between the negative pole of the remote release socket and the camera body. For instance, connect a short length of wire to the negative pole (longer tongue) of a 2.5 mm jack plug,

plug the latter into the remote control jack and touch the other end of the wire to any metal part of the camera. That can be the chrome (but not the black) camera top, the outer rails of the accessory shoe, carrying strap eyelet etc. As long as the contact is maintained, the camera continues to cycle. Convenient also if you have a chrome-topped camera is to place a small office paper clip over the 2.5 mm jack plug (without anything wired up to it), plug the jack into the remote socket and adjust the paper clip so that it touches the neighbouring camera top. The clip is fairly easy to swing back and forth to switch the sequencing on and off.

Olympus do not guarantee that this 'unofficial' method works every time—it does seem to operate with all the winders I have handled.

Various other ways may suggest themselves, but don't stick paper clips or other objects *into* the remote socket—this can not only damage the socket but if the contacts are short-circuited you cannot trigger the winder until you break the circuit again.

When sequencing in this way, keep an eye on the end of the film to avoid film perforation damage.

Motor drive 1

Similar in application to the Winder 1, the Motor drive 1 is a more versatile unit that automatically runs the exposure and transport cycle on pressing a button. It has two operating modes, for single exposures and for sequences at up to 4 to 5 frames per second. The Motor drive 1 is always used in conjunction with a control unit which also provides the power supply—the M.18V control grip, the M.15V control pack or the M.AC control box, described in more detail below. These may be linked with the motor drive via remote relay cords.

The Motor drive 1 consists of a base section 116 mm long, 30 mm wide and at its deepest about 15 mm deep (4.6 × 1.2 × 0.6 inches), with a hand grip protruding about 32 mm (1.26 inches) in front and about 82 mm (3.2 inches) high. With the compactest control unit—the M.15V control pack—the overall depth becomes about 38 mm (1.58 inches) and the overall length some 127 mm (5 inches). When the unit is fitted on the camera, the assembly thus becomes some 38 mm higher. The motor drive with M.15V control pack closely resembles the Winder 1 in dimensions and shape but the motor drive assembly is slightly heavier at about 490 grams (17.2 ounces) due to the more powerful motor and heavier battery it contains. (The dimensions and weight are different with the M.18V control grip.)

In its top surface—which mates with the camera baseplate—the motor drive carries the same linking elements as the winder:

At the left (when looking at the motor drive from behind so that the lettering is upright) a pair of ball contacts couple with the contact in the camera bottom. These carry back to the motor system the information that the camera shutter has closed at the end of the exposure and the motor can start advancing the film. Near these contacts in the rear of the unit is a contact pair for coupling with the 250 film back (see below).

In the right-hand half of the base are the shutter release coupling pin and below it the film transport claw. These couple with the camera through the opening of the motor drive socket cap. The coupling pin triggers the shutter release and the transport claw engages a driving wheel inside the camera base, linked with the transport movement.

Further to the right, next to the hand grip, is a guide pin protruding about 5 mm from the platform. This engages a corresponding guide hole in the camera base which, in conjunction with a tripod screw going through the motor drive base, ensures accurate location of the drive on the camera.

At the right-hand end a gear wheel protruding into a cut-out is coupled with the film claw. This mechanically links the transport of the 250 film back. Except when this back is used, keep the swivelling cover closed to protect the gear wheel. One further item in the top of the base next to the clamping screw is a circular recess for storing the camera's motor drive socket cap.

The underside of the motor drive carries a tripod bush that serves either to secure the M.15V control pack or for mounting the camera and motor assembly on the tripod when the control grip or a relay cord is used. Next to the tripod bush is the clamping screw which engages the camera's tripod bush to secure the motor drive on the

MOTOR DRIVE 1

The components and controls are:

1. Remote control jack.
2. Gear cover and 250 film back coupling gear.
3. Shutter release button.
4. Film advance claw.
5. Socket cap storage recess.
6. Camera coupling terminals.
7. Guide pin.
8. 250 film back coupling terminals.
9. Hand grip.
10. Shutter release coupling pin.
11. Terminal contact block.
12. Fixing/clamping screw.
13. Red alignment index.

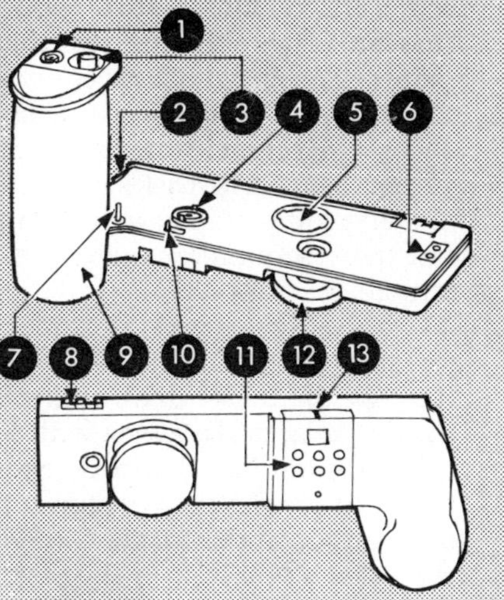

Before fitting the motor drive, remove the socket cap from the OM-1 or OM-2 camera *(left)* and fit it into the storage compartment on the motor drive *(right)*.

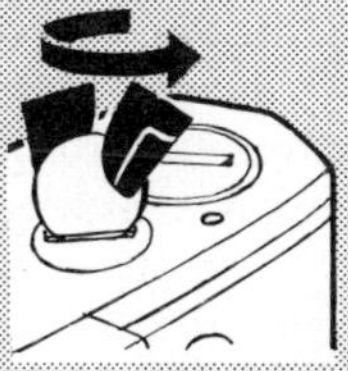

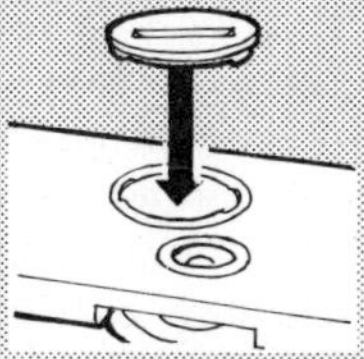

M.15V CONTROL PACK 1

The elements and controls are:

14. Check lamp and button.
15. Clamping screw.
16. Mounting catch.
17. Tripod bush.
18. Alignment index.
19. Mode selector.
20. Strap eyelet.
21. Lock.
22. Release button.
23. Terminal contacts.

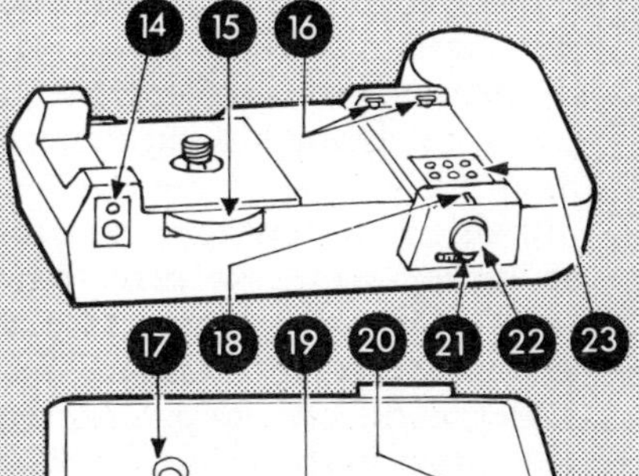

A basic motor drive assembly consists of the camera, motor drive and M.15V control pack.

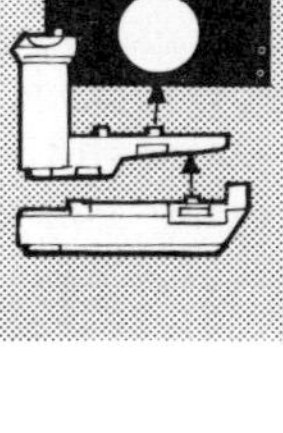

camera. The other feature in the base is a 6-pole terminal that links up with the control unit in use or with the motor drive plug of a relay cord. A feature at the rear of this terminal block is a red index mark, important for correct mating with the corresponding units.

The hand grip part again has the same controls as on the Winder 1: a release button to trigger the release and transport sequence, and a 2.5 mm jack socket to take remote control cords.

Attaching to the camera

Remove the motor drive socket cap in the camera base by turning it anti-clockwise with a coin. This uncovers the camera coupling elements. Store the socket cap in the motor drive socket in the top surface—next to the clamping screw. Fit the socket cap here in the same way as on the camera: place it in the storage socket with the index dot on the cap aligned with the index dot (next to the S of OLYMPUS) on the motor base, then press down and turn clockwise with a coin. That way the cap immediately becomes visible when you remove the motor drive from the camera again, as a reminder to refit the socket cap in the camera. The only other preparation applies if the camera carries a strap: fold the split ring upwards flat against the camera body, so that the front right-hand camera edge is unobstructed all the way down from the strap eyelet.

To attach the motor drive itself, engage first the guide pin in the guide hole in the camera base. Then push the motor drive against the camera base so that the clamping or fixing screw engages the tripod bush. Screw down this screw to secure the drive to the camera. It should be snug against the camera base along its full length. When the drive is correctly fitted, the right-hand carrying strap eyelet on the camera presses against the small plastic stud at the rear of the grip.

In practically every case, that is all you have to worry about when attaching the motor drive. The shutter release coupling pin and film advance claw automatically mesh with the drive elements inside the camera. The release coupling pin is for this purpose in its rest position at the right of the small slot just above the film advance claw. During releasing this pin is pushed to the left

MOTOR DRIVE AND M.15V NI-CD CONTROL PACK

To attach the motor drive to the camera engage the guide pin, then screw down the securing screw *(left)*. To attach the control pack, first line up the red index marks on the pack and motor drive terminals *(right)*.

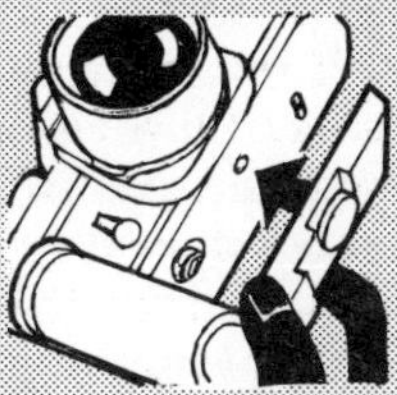

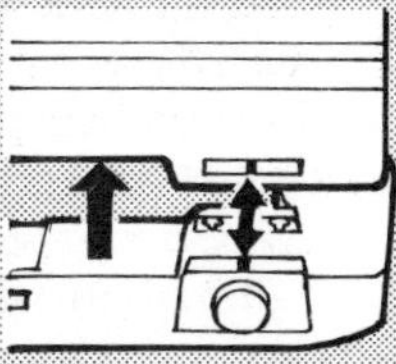

Then clip the control pack to the motor drive and screw tight *(left)*. To check the battery, press the button next to the LED at the rear *(right)*.

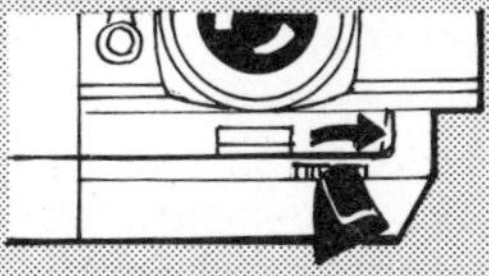

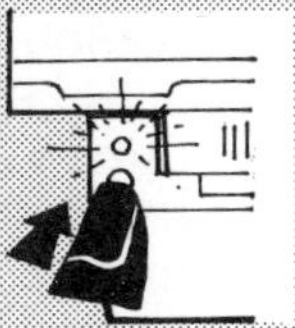

To recharge the control pack plug the DC plug of the charger into the control pack and the charger itself into an AC supply socket.

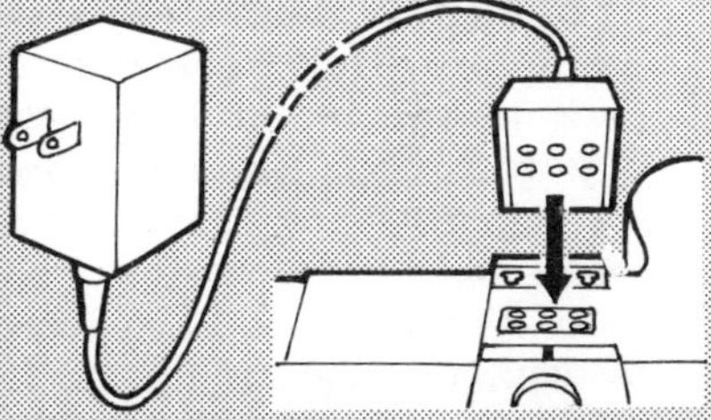

M.18V CONTROL GRIP

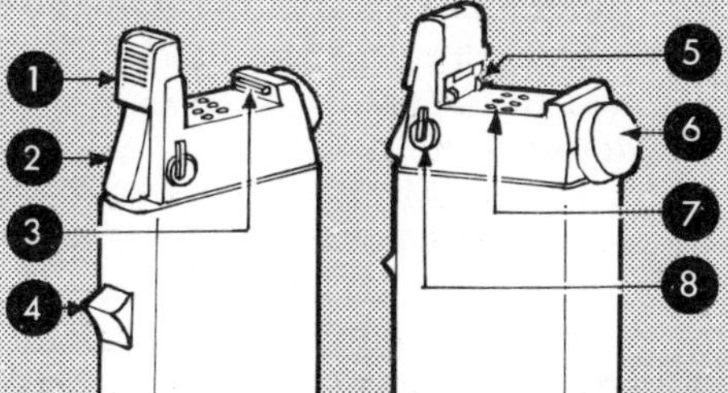

1. Grip release.
2. Release key.
3. Mounting catch.
4. Fingerhold.
5. Grip lock.
6. Mode selector.
7. Terminal contacts.
8. Release lock.
9. Battery holder.
10. Battery holder lock.

To fit the control grip, fit it into the rear of the motor drive terminal block, then swing up the control grip to engage *(left)*. To detach, press the grip release button down and in *(right)*, and swing up the camera.

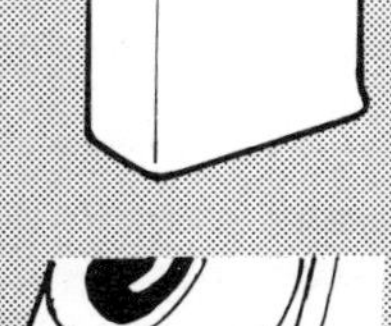

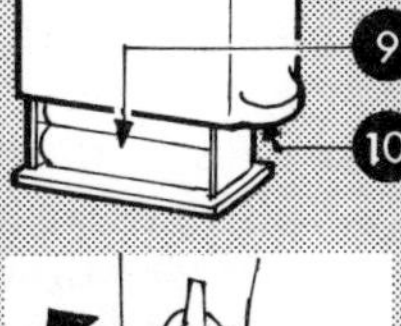

(engaging a lever inside the camera) and immediately returns to its rest position. In exceptional circumstances, for instance power failure in the middle of a release cycle through disengagement of a relay cord plug, it could however happen that the release coupling pin stops in a halfway position. It then fouls the release lever inside the camera (underneath the motor drive socket cap)— i.e. you cannot attach the motor drive. There are two ways of rectifying this condition:

(a) The quickest is to press the release button on the camera and hold it depressed while you attach the motor drive. You lose an exposure that way. The coupling and mechanism return to normal next time the motor drive is energised.

(b) Slightly more involved but without loss of exposure is this procedure: Connect the control grip or control pack to the motor drive, turn the mode selector to SEQUENCE, and place any metal object (e.g. a coin) across the camera coupling terminals on the motor drive. This causes the drive to whirr but also returns the coupling pin to its rest position. Then switch the mode selector back to OFF and attach the motor drive to the camera. Next time you switch on, you will hear a short sharp click—ignore this.

To operate the motor drive you have to attach one of the control units to it, providing usually also the power supply. The control units available are:

(a) The M.15V control pack 1;
(b) The M.18V control grip;
(c) The M.AC control box.

The first two can be attached directly to the motor drive on the camera or linked via a relay cord. The M.AC control box can only be linked by a relay cord (see below).

M.15V control pack 1

This flat power pack attaches to the base of the motor drive, forming a combined unit similar in shape and size to the Winder 1 (see above). The control pack 1 contains a set of 12 permanently built-in, rechargeable nickel-cadmium cells, yielding approx. 15 volts.

The control pack is 129 mm long, 67 mm wide and 35 mm high (5.1 × 2.6 × 1.4 inches) and on its own weighs 260 grams (9.2 ounces).

On the top—the side of the control pack that attaches to the motor drive—it carries a fixing screw that engages the tripod bush of the motor drive, and a block of 6 terminals that mate with the 6 terminal pins on the drive. At the rear of the terminal block the control pack carries a protruding ledge with a red index mark. This serves for alignment when attaching the control pack to the motor drive.

The M.15V control pack carries three controls:

The mode selector switch in the base is a knob with three positions: SINGLE–OFF–SEQUENCE. To select the mode, lift that knob against spring pressure and turn it to the required position.

A release button in the rear, below the red index mark, triggers the motor drive in the same way as the release button on the drive itself. This release on the M.15V control pack is primarily intended for use when the control pack is linked to the camera via a relay cord. A sliding catch underneath the release button locks the latter to prevent accidental operation when the control pack is directly mounted on the camera.

The battery check is also in the rear of the control pack at the left-hand end. It consists of a red LED and a switch button. (See below, *Battery check and charging*.)

Two further features are a tripod bush in the base—to mount the whole camera and motor drive assembly on a tripod—and a carrying strap eyelet in the side next to the mode selector switch.

Attachment and removal

To fit the M.15V control pack to the motor drive, first set the mode selector on the control pack to OFF. Then hook the ledge at the rear of the pack, with the red alignment index, into the recess at the back of the motor drive terminal block, also marked with the red alignment index. Once this ledge is hooked in, push the control pack against the base of the motor drive, so that the mounting catches at the front of the pack engage the two recesses at the front of the motor drive. Finally secure by tightly screwing down the clamping or fixing screw of the control pack into the tripod bush of the drive.

This engagement of the ledge with the red mark into the groove next to a corresponding red mark is the first step in all connections involving plugs with 6-terminal blocks—including the control grip, M.AC control box and all relay cords.

Setting the mode selector to OFF prevents inadvertent tripping of the motor drive while attaching the control pack.

To detach the pack, return the mode selector to OFF (if not already switched off), then unscrew the fixing screw. When this is fully released (you hear repeated clicks as you go on unscrewing) unclip the control pack from the front of the motor drive and finally unhook the rear ledge with the red alignment marks.

Battery check and charging

A fully charged M.15V control pack can, according to Olympus data, provide enough capacity for the motor drive to run up to 40 cartridges of 36-exposure film through the camera. This depends to some extent on frequency of use, as the nickel-cadmium cells are subject to some self-discharge on prolonged storage. Also this capacity drops at low temperatures.

An LED at the back of the unit provides a check on the battery condition. With a fingernail depress the small chrome button at the rear left-hand end of the control pack next to the CHECK indication. If the LED above that lights up, the current reserve of the control pack is sufficient for 10–40 full 36-exposure films. If the LED blinks on and off, you have enough capacity for about 10 films left and if the LED no longer lights up the reserve is less than 10 films. At that point of course you don't know how much you really have left, so recharge the control pack as soon as possible. The voltage drop of nickel-cadmium batteries is very abrupt at the end of the charge, so the power may well give out without much warning—even without any noticeable motor sluggishness in the middle of a roll. The motor then makes a droning sound and you have to recharge the control pack or fit the M.18V control grip as an alternative power supply (see below).

When the motor gives out the first time in this way, you may be able to get a few more exposures out of it—if you have no chance to recharge the pack—by waiting a few minutes and then trying again.

When checking the battery state with the LED, do this before a run with the motor— or about an hour afterwards. Immediately after operating the motor, the LED may blink even with a remaining capacity well over 10 films.

The M.15V Ni-Cd charger 1

A special M.15V charger 1 is needed to recharge the M.15V control pack 1. It consists of a 41 × 49 × 66 mm (1.6 × 1.9 × 2.6 inch) plug with built-in charging circuits and a lead terminating in a power supply plug similar to the terminal block in the base of the motor drive. However here only two of the six pins are fitted. The underside of the charger carries a built-in two-pin plug—alternative versions exist with American type flat pins or European round pins—and four tappings at the bottom of four screw holes recessed into the charger. These are marked 100–115–220–240, representing the voltage of the available mains supply. Check that the voltage screw is in the correct hole for the supply. If it is not, unscrew it (with a crosshead screwdriver) and screw into the correct hole. Some versions made for single-voltage sources do not have this switching screw.

To charge the M.15V control pack 1, plug the power supply plug onto the terminals of the control pack: hook the ledge at the rear of the control pack with the red alignment mark into the recess on the plug with a similar red mark, then push down the plug at the front. Connect the charger itself to a suitable mains supply socket (with a plug adapter if the pins don't fit your socket) and leave connected for about 5 hours. That is sufficient for a full charge—preferably do not leave it ever for longer than 6 hours. In a hurry you can recharge a pack partially: 10 minutes gives enough for a couple of films, 30 minutes enough for 6 to 10 films.

At the end of the period unplug the charger from the mains and the terminal plug from the control pack. To do that pull up the plug end away from the red index mark (the plug carries two small chrome finger pins at this end) and unhook the other end.

In common with other nickel-cadmium batteries, the cells of the M.15V control pack are good for at least 200 recharging cycles—and may well last longer. After that time, the capacity of the control pack per charge may begin to drop. Replacement of nickel-cadmium cells is a repair job for the servicing section of an Olympus agency.

The M.18V control grip 1

This control unit and power pack attaches to the camera/motor drive assembly as a hand grip and takes size AA batteries in a push-in battery holder. It has a trigger-type release key with lock and is overall 32 × 77 × 135 mm (1.3 × 3.0 × 5.3 inches) large. Complete with motor drive, the assembly protrudes 129 mm (5.1 inches) below the camera and about 20 mm (0.8 inch) behind. The M.18V control grip weighs approx. 455 grams (16 ounces) complete with battery holder and batteries. (This can vary slightly depending on the batteries.)

The front of the control grip carries a large release key to operate the motor drive. Next to it in the side is a locking lever—turning the lever with the white line down to horizontal position (marked LOCK) blocks the release action; turning the lever up nearly vertically frees the release key. Just above it is a serrated key serving as a grip release. Pushing that key downwards and then depressing it withdraws two locking claws visible just behind the front part of the grip. These claws normally lock the grip against the motor drive.

The top flat section of the grip carries a terminal block with six terminal points to mate with the terminal block on the motor drive. At the rear there is again a ledge with red alignment index. Behind this in the rear of the hand grip is a mode selector with three positions: SINGLE–OFF–SEQUENCE. The OFF position is marked in orange, the other two in white and you select the mode by turning the knob so that the chosen setting engages opposite a white index mark. This selector does not need raising to turn it.

M.18V battery holder 1

The M.18V control grip takes 12 size AA batteries as the power source. These are housed in the M.18V battery holder—a light-weight plastic carrier that slides into the control grip.

To release the battery holder push the small latch in the base of the grip in the direction of its white arrow. The battery holder, forming part of the baseplate, slides out slightly and can now be fully withdrawn. Insert the 12 batteries in the orientation marked in each compartment. The easiest memory aid is that the minus pole of each battery is against the spring in the compartment (to the right if you look at the holder so that a baseplate faces down) while the plus poles are at the left, against the studs. Thus on each side all poles face in the same direction.

To refit the whole battery holder, slide it into the grip so that the baseplate locks flush against the base. (Sliding the holder in the wrong way round prevents it from closing completely.) If you take a spare M.18V battery holder preloaded with batteries, you can instantly change of the batteries in the grip are exhausted.

For maximum capacity use 1.5 volt alkali batteries. According to Olympus's data, a set of these provides sufficient power to run up to 150 full 36-exposure films through the camera. Alternatively you can use rechargeable nickel-cadmium cells of the same size; here the capacity is about 70 films per full charge. You have to recharge nickel-cadmium cells in a separate charger (not provided by Olympus, but available on the market in various forms).

The choice between the two battery types is in the last resort a question of capacity. As the hand grip offers the greatest shooting reserve with alkali batteries, it makes most sense to use this battery type here. If you want to work with rechargeable cells, the M.15V control pack is specially designed for that purpose. Pricewise, rechargeable nickel-cadmium cells cost about 5 to 6 times as much as alkali batteries, are reusable, but provide less than half the capacity per charge.

With alkali batteries you get some warning of progressive exhaustion: the motor begins to be slightly sluggish and the fastest cycling rate (in the sequence mode) slows down. However when the voltage drops below the level where the motor can perform effectively, it cuts out altogether and you hear a droning noise. This is a signal that the batteries need changing—easy if you carry a spare preloaded M.18V battery holder. But even if you don't, you can often get a few more exposures out of a battery pack if you wait 10 to 15 minutes. With nickel-cadmium cells the exhaustion is more abrupt and you have less warning of impending battery failure.

In cold weather carry the spare battery holder in an inside pocket to keep the batteries reasonably warm—their performance may drop quite radically at low temperature. If the holder is not in use for long periods, preferably remove the batteries as a safety measure against possible leakage.

Attaching to the drive

Before fitting the M.18V control grip to the motor drive, turn the mode selector on the grip to OFF to prevent inadvertent releasing during attachment. Hook the ledge at the rear of the terminal platform—with the red alignment mark—into the groove at the back of the terminal block on the motor, also with the red alignment mark. Then swing the grip forward so that the catches engage at the front. This securely locks the grip against the drive. If you have no film in the camera, set the mode selector to SINGLE and make a couple of blind exposures just to check that the grip is properly seated. (You can't do it if the camera is already loaded—but if you proceed as above, the grip will always engage correctly.)

To remove the grip, turn the locking lever of the release to LOCK and set the mode selector to OFF. On the front of the grip, above the large release key, push the smaller serrated grip release key down and then press in its upper section against the grip itself. This releases the hold claws and the grip now unhinges easily from the motor drive.

This slightly more involved release action is necessary to hold the grip really securely against the motor drive. For with this attachment the fixture carries much more strain than with for instance the M.15V control pack.

When you use the winder with the M.18V control grip, hold the latter in the right hand, with the right index finger on the release key. The left hand operates the focusing and aperture controls. If you wind the camera strap around your right wrist you can push your head forward to steady the camera against your forehead by tension of the neck strap. This is almost a one-handed and virtually a shake-free camera hold, especially with the smooth release with the motor drive.

For upright shots with the M.18V grip support the camera and motor drive in the left hand, operating the lens controls with the thumb and index finger. The right hand steadies the grip.

Relay cords

As an alternative to attaching the M.15V control pack 1 or M.18V control grip 1 directly to the motor drive, you can link the two via a relay cord. This is a 5-conductor cable with 6-terminal contact fittings at each end. One of these is the motor drive plug—a platform with a ledge and red alignment index at one side and a mounting catch at the other. This is similar to the terminal platform of the M.15V control pack. The other end of the cable carries a power supply plug with six sprung pins similar to the terminal block at the base of the motor drive. This plug also has a red index mark next to a groove at one side.

The relay cords are available in two lengths: 1.2 metres (4 feet) and 10 metres (33 feet). They permit two kinds of utilisation:

(a) You can carry the M.15V control pack or M.18V control grip in your pocket (e.g. in cold weather) and only hold the camera and motor drive with the relay cord plugged onto it. That makes the motor drive assembly lighter to hold with just the slight drawback of the cable to your pocket. The 1.2 metre relay cord is the right one for this purpose.

(b) You can set up the camera at one location and control its operation—in single or sequencing mode—from the control pack or grip from another spot. This is more convenient if the camera and motor drive are mounted on a tripod. If you are next to the camera, the 1.2 metre relay cord is sufficient; for greater distances one or two 10-metre cords may be used.

To attach either relay cord to the motor drive, engage the ledge of the terminal platform with its red alignment index in the groove of the terminal block—also with alignment index—at the rear of the motor drive. Push the terminal platform up against the terminal block so that it snaps into place.

To connect the plug to the M.15V control pack 1, hook the groove next to the red alignment mark into the ledge at the rear of the terminal platform on the control pack (again with the red alignment mark) and snap down into the terminal platform to engage the mounting catch at the front. To plug into the M.18V control grip, hook the groove with the red alignment mark into the ledge on the control grip, again with the red alignment mark, and push down the other end against the terminal platform to engage.

As with all connections of the motor drive control units and relay cords, the rule is: first hook the groove of the plug or terminal box section (with protruding pins) into the ledge of the terminal platform (with flat contacts) so that the two red alignment marks line up. Then snap in the other side of the plug or fitting.

To disconnect the cord from the motor drive, push downwards the end of the terminal platform (marked with a white arrowhead) away from its mating terminal block and unhook the ledge with the red alignment mark. To disconnect the plug, pull it up off its engagement at the side of the mounting catch. The plug carries two small chrome finger pins at this end. Then disengage the ledge and groove with the red alignment marks. On the M.18V control grip release the locking keys by the grip release button as when removing the grip directly from the motor drive.

The power plug end of each relay cord (with protruding pins) carries two further sets of internal terminals accessible from the sides. On one side the terminals are marked + and – and *DC 12–16V*. Here you can connect an external power supply of up to 16 volts DC. To make the connection, depress the black button above the aperture in the side, push in the bared wire end of the lead and let go of the button. This clamps the lead in the terminal.

The other side of the plug carries two terminals labelled REMOTE—A and B. These take leads from any remote control switch, radio link, light barrier triggering device etc. The possibilities are described in more detail below *(Electrical remote control)*.

When these external contacts are used, the plug must *always be plugged onto a control unit* (M.15V control pack, M.18V control grip or M.AC control box).

Releasing with the motor drive

With all motor drive combinations mentioned so far—M.15V control pack or M.18V control grip connected

RELAY CORD

1. Motor drive plug.
2. Remote terminals.
3. Finger pins.
4. Red alignment index.
5. Power supply plug.
6. Red index.

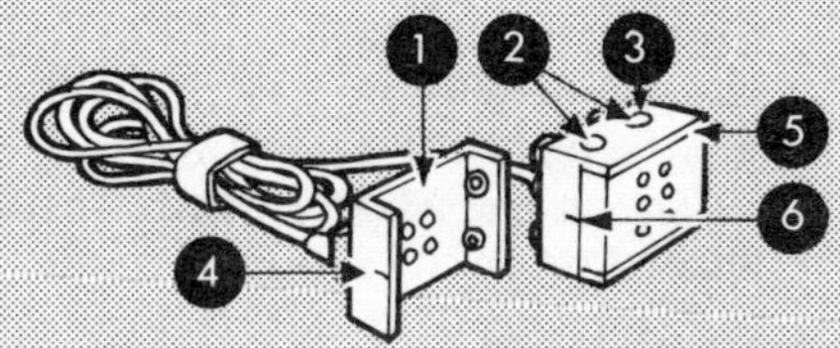

To fit the motor drive plug hook the rear (red index) into the motor drive terminal block and push up *(left).* Align the red index of the plug *(right)* to push into the control grip or pack.

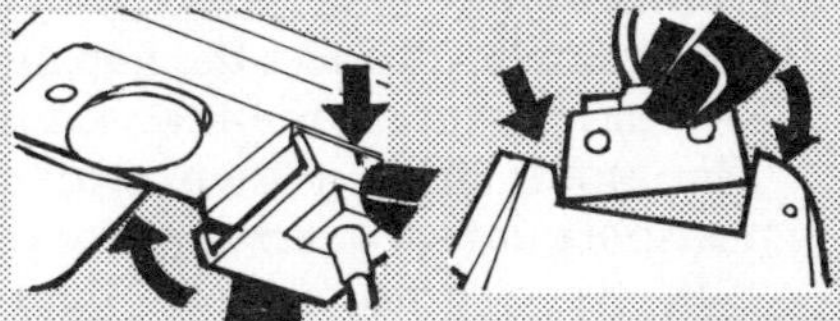

To release the motor drive plug, press down the front and lift off *(left).* Disengage the grip release to free the plug end *(right).*

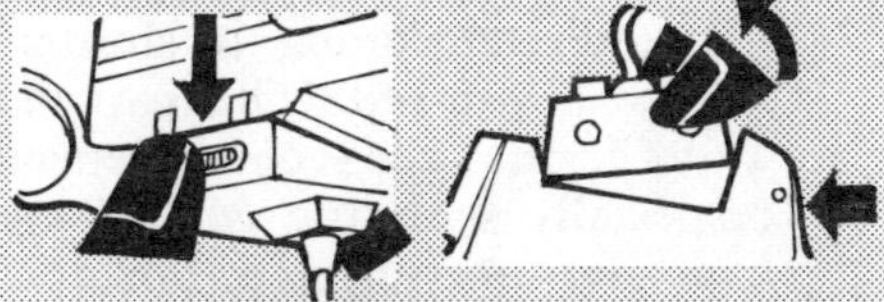

For remote control (or external DC supplies) connect wires into the side terminals of the plug.

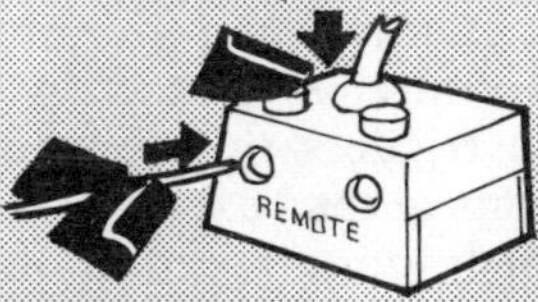

HOLDS WITH WINDER AND MOTOR

For a horizontal hold with the winder or motor drive *(left)* the left hand supports the camera and operates the lens controls, the right holds the grip. The hold is the same with the relay cord *(right).*

For upright holds bring down the left hand and support the camera; the right steadies the camera or motor drive grip.

For horizontal shots with the control grip and motor, the right hand holds the grip and steadies the camera also with the strap. For upright shots, support the camera in the left hand and steady the grip with the right.

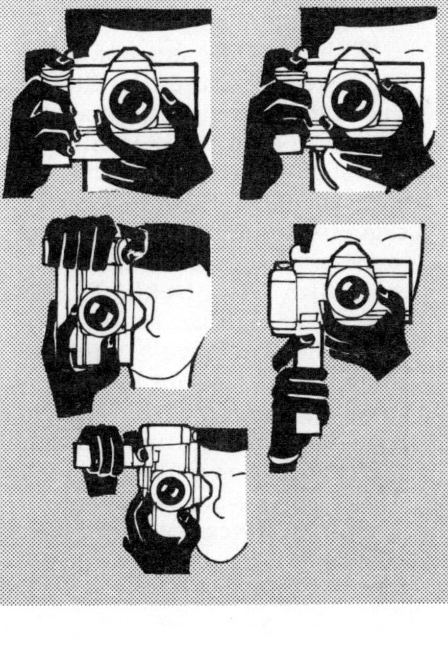

directly to the motor drive or indirectly via a relay cord—the mode selector switch on the control pack or control grip selects the operating mode. Turn this switch dial (lift it on the M.15V control pack) to SINGLE or SEQUENCE according to the required mode.

With single-exposure operation, pressing the appropriate motor drive release (see below) makes one exposure and immediately advances the film and retensions the shutter. You have to press the release afresh for every exposure. The motor drive is then simply an electric release and transport device operating like the winder.

In the sequencing mode, depressing the motor drive release makes a succession of exposures, advancing the film and retensioning the shutter each time, as long as the release is pressed. The sequencing rate may be up to 4 to 5 frames per second, depending on the battery state (especially with the M.18V control grip) and on the exposure time selected. For in every case the film transport cuts in only when the shutter has closed at the end of the exposure. A contact in the camera closes at that point and triggers the transport operation via the two ball contacts in the base of the motor drive. Generally the maximum framing speed is obtainable at shutter speed settings of 1/125 second and faster. The slowing down is negligible at 1/60 second but becomes noticeable at 1/30 second and longer.

With the OM-2 at automatic operation the SBC metering system measures the exposure for every new frame; this can—as with normal through-the-lens metered exposures—run into seconds or even minutes.

A slight increase in the fastest framing rate is possible with the OM-1 by locking the mirror up. Olympus suggests this as one of the uses of the mirror lock-up, but in practice the gain—about 10% faster sequencing—is more than offset by the fact that you lose sight of the subject through the finder.

The motor drive (and winder) can be used at all shutter speeds except B. There you get an indeterminate short exposure since the shutter release coupling pin only triggers the shutter but does not hold it open.

Depending on the control unit connected, the following release options are available:

(a) In every case you can release by the release button

on the motor drive grip. This is most convenient when using the drive with the M.15V pack or when you carry the control unit in your pocket and link it to the drive via a relay cord.

(b) You can release by the release key on the M.18V control grip. This is the most convenient way when using the motor drive with the grip attached. A lock secures this release key against accidental releasing: turn the lever up and the release is free.

This is also the appropriate way of releasing for remote control operation when the control grip is linked to the motor drive via a relay cord (especially the 10 metre cord).

(c) You can release by the release button on the M.15V control pack. This is suitable when the control pack is used as a remote control unit, linked to the motor drive via a relay cord.

In both these cases relay cord operation is also used when the camera and motor drive are mounted on a tripod, when it is obviously less convenient to operate the release directly on the camera. An alternative is however remote control via the remote jack on the grip.

(d) Remote control by closing a switch at the end of a remote control lead plugged into the remote control socket on the grip. Remote control is similarly feasible with leads fitted into the remote terminals on the relay cord plug. (See below, *Electrical remote control.*)

In every case the release works only when the mode selector switch on the control unit used is set to either SINGLE or SEQUENCE.

The M.AC control box

This special control unit provides a number of programming options for motorised camera operation and at the same time powers the operation from an AC mains supply. A built-in transformer and rectifier circuit delivers a smoothed DC output of about 15 volts to power the motor drive. It is connected to the drive by a relay cord. The remote range for automatic unmanned photography, such as instrument dial recording, easily covers the distance spanned by two 10 metre relay cords linked together.

The front of the M.AC control box carries a number of switches and controls:

A pilot lamp marked CHECK lights up when the power is switched on. A needle in the same window deflects whenever the motor drive cycles—a necessary check on the operation of the camera set-up when the control box is some distance away.

The release run switch next to the pilot lamp and check meter selects manual or automatic sequencing in the sequence mode and can also act as a single-release switch.

The mode switch selects single-frame or sequence operation.

The power switch switches the whole control box on and off when operating from the mains supply. The control box can however also operate from an external DC supply plugged into the DC side outlet of the relay cord plug (see below, *External power supplies*).

The intervalometer dial on the lower row selects the sequencing intervals when running in the sequence mode. There are 12 fixed settings: 4, 2 and 1 frames per second are marked in red; 2, 5, 10, 20, 30, 40, 60, 90 and 120 seconds are marked in white. The exact sequencing speed still depends on the shutter speed and also slightly on the supply voltage. The intervals indicate the time between the end of one exposure and the beginning of the next.

The release button at the bottom right triggers the motor drive in the single-frame and the manual sequencing modes.

To operate with the M.AC control box, plug the power lead into a suitable mains supply socket. Connect the motor drive plug of the relay cord to the motor drive on the camera and the power supply plug into the terminal socket on the M.AC control box. As before, always engage the ledge with the red alignment mark into the groove with a similar red alignment mark on the mating plug component, then push home. Turn the release run switch to OFF and the power switch to ON. The check window now lights up and the unit is ready for operation.

M.AC operating modes

The M.AC control box can operate the motor drive in the following modes:

(a) *Single frame shooting.* Set the mode switch to SINGLE. On pressing the release button, the unit then

M.AC CONTROL BOX

1. Fuse holder.
2. Plug terminal.
3. Check meter and pilot lamp.
4. Intervalometer dial.
5. Shutter release key.
6. Release/run switch.
7. Mode switch.
8. Power switch.

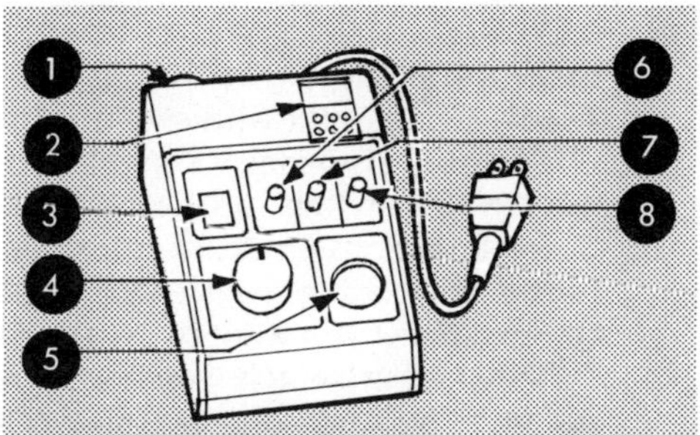

The control box links to the motor drive via a relay cord *(left)*. For single-frame exposures, set switches as shown *(right)*.

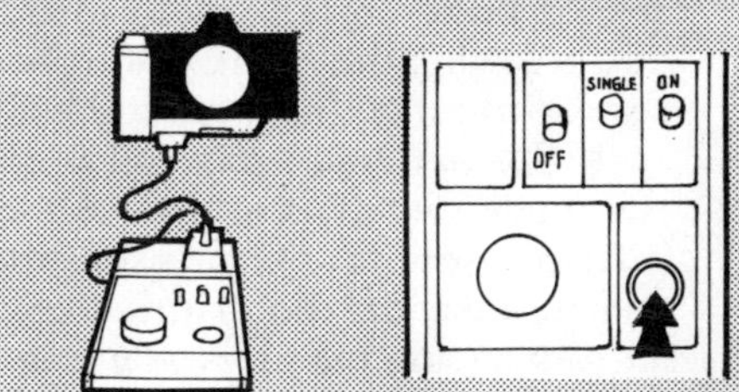

For manually triggered sequencing set intervalometer dial and switches as shown *(left)*, release by pressing key. For automatically triggered sequencing, set switches as shown *(right)*.

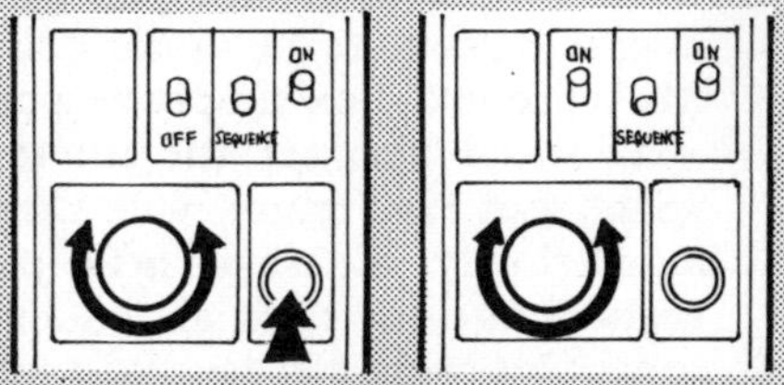

EARLIER MOTOR DRIVE

1. Release key.
2. 250 film back coupling gear and cover.
3. Guide pin.
4. Clamping screw.
5. Camera terminals.
6. Shutter release pin.
7. Film advance claw.
8. 250 film back coupling terminals.

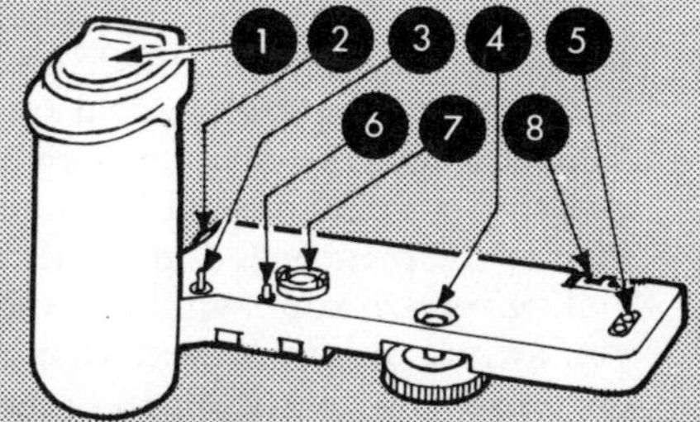

For remote control with the earlier motor drive connect any remote switch through the remote contacts of the relay cord plug.

One way of parking the motor drive socket cap on the earlier model is to tape it to the back of the grip with adhesive linen tape.

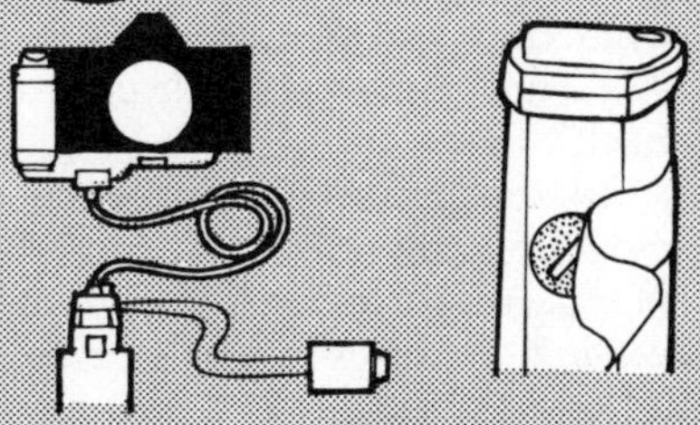

makes a single exposure. At the same time the check needle swings out to indicate that the motor has responded.

You can also make a single exposure by moving the release run switch to ON and back to OFF again. Do not however keep the release run switch at ON, otherwise the motor drive cannot be energised for the next exposure, for instance if you want to use the release button next.

With these switch positions—release run at OFF and mode at SINGLE, you can also release by operating the release button on the motor drive itself. This is handy if you are using the M.AC control box only as an AC power supply for shooting with the hand-held camera.

(b) *Manual sequencing*. Set the release switch to OFF and the mode switch to SEQUENCE. Set the intervalometer to 4 frames/second. On pressing the release button on the control box, the motor drive keeps releasing the shutter and advancing the film as long as the button is depressed. In this mode you can equally sequence by pressing the release button on the motor drive itself—again using the M.AC control box simply as a power supply.

You can also set the intervalometer to a different value, but the motor will then cycle correspondingly more slowly. There is little point in setting a slower cycling rate for manual sequencing unless particularly consistent cycling at say 1 second, 2 second, 5 second etc. intervals is wanted. (But then automatic sequence operation is more convenient.)

(c) *Automatic sequencing*. For this set the release run switch to OFF and the mode switch to SEQUENCE. Select the required cycling interval on the intervalometer dial. Start the cycling sequence by moving the release run switch from OFF to ON. The motor drive now cycles on its own at the preselected intervals.

The release run switch should always be at OFF when you switch on the power. If the release run switch is at ON while you switch on the power, the motor drive will cycle once and then stop. To restart the automatic cycling sequence, move the release run switch to OFF and then back to ON.

In the automatic sequence mode the intervalometer overrides the release button both on the control box and on the motor drive itself. You cannot trigger exposures during the intervals by pressing the release—other than by the mechanical release button of the camera.

If you do that, the motor advances the film at the next cycling point but then interrupts the sequence. To restart the sequence, turn the release run switch to OFF and then to ON again.

To terminate a release sequence move the release run switch from ON back to OFF or move the mode switch from SEQUENCE to SINGLE. If the release run switch is at OFF but the mode switch at SEQUENCE, pressing the release button on the control box or motor drive returns you to manual sequencing as in mode (b) above. If the release run switch is at ON and the mode switch at SINGLE, no further operation is possible.

For sequencing at intervals other than those marked on the intervalometer dial (intermediate or longer) connect a timing switch to the motor drive via the remote control jack or the remote outlet on the relay cord plug. Then operate the AC control box in the single-exposure mode (a) above.

At the end of operations unplug the control box from the mains supply. To disconnect the power supply plug of the relay cord, pull up at the front by the finger pins on the plug, then unhook the rear ledge.

The PM-CBTL intervalometer

This is a rather more elaborate control unit than the M.AC control box, has been demonstrated in prototype form and is made to special order only. Briefly, the intervalometer extends the M.AC cycling operations to over 4-day intervals, can run for altogether 999 exposures and controls light sources for time lapse photography and regular recording as well as the motor-driven camera. In addition, the PM-CBTL keeps count—by LED displays—of the number of exposures made and of the progress of timing intervals.

The unit built into a 315 × 290 × 115 mm (12.4 × 11.4 × 4.5 inch) case is fed from the A.C. mains supply and in turn feeds two lamp circuits and the motor drive—via a relay cord and terminal socket—or a Winder I via a DIN socket and lead. It can also trigger a flash unit. The controls are:

(a) A frame counter to preselect the number of frames to be exposed in automatic sequence, up to 999, on a mechanical 3-digit dial. A 3-digit LED indicates the number of frames actually exposed; the sequencing stops when this number of frames equals the preset number.

(b) A time selector to preset intervals from 0.1 to 99.9 in seconds, minutes or hours. Exposures take place at these intervals (subject to exposure time requirements at the shortest intervals) while a 3-digit LED display counts down the time until the next exposure. With sufficiently long intervals this countdown also allows you to reload the camera at leisure if the film is finished, in time for the next exposure cycle.

(c) A light selector. This switches on lamps in time for each exposure, to avoid the inconvenience of keeping lamps burning continuously. A prelighting selector switches on the lamps up to 30 seconds before required, for instance to cope with lighting systems that need stabilisation when first lit.

(d) Various switches switch on the power, select synchronised or continuous lighting, start or stop the timing sequence etc.

A supplementary unit for the intervalometer is the PM-CBTLAD repeat adapter. This programming unit can repeat a time lapse photography cycle set up on the PM-CBTL up to 99 times. Again readouts indicate the number of frames exposed, the number of cycles completed and the time intervals selected. In theory, the combined outfit could keep a camera set-up going for months on an automatic recording project.

Earlier Motor drive 1

An earlier version of the Motor drive 1 differs from the current model in two visible respects:

(a) In place of the small release button and remote control jack sockets, the grip carries only a large release key and no remote outlet. For remote releasing with this motor drive, connect to one of its control units (control pack or grip) via a relay cord and attach the leads of a remote control switch to the remote outlets A and B of the relay cord (see above).

(b) The older motor drive has no storage socket for the camera's motor drive socket cap. You thus have to keep the socket cap in a pocket or whatever else is available and hope that you won't lose it.

If you should ever lose the motor drive socket cap, cut a piece of thin card the same size as the socket cap to cover the opening and tape to the camera base with a short piece of black adhesive tape. Don't use the tape without the card; adhesive—or dust picked up by it—could otherwise get into the inside of the camera.

You can also park the socket cap on the earlier motor drive 1 with a piece of adhesive linen tape (not cellulose tape) 19 mm (¾ inch) wide and about twice as long. Keep this taped to the back of the motor drive grip between the base and the small protruding stud that bears against the camera's carrying strap eyelet. When you remove the socket cap from the camera, peel back about half this tape from the side of the grip, put down the socket cap (slotted side up) and pull the tape over it to hold the cap in position.

250 Film back 1

Various applications of unmanned photography, especially recording things at regular intervals over long periods, need a greater film reserve than the normal 36-exposure cartridge. And in sequence photography you get through 36 exposures in a matter of seconds. The 250 film back 1 provides this increased shooting capacity with up to 250 exposures on a 10 metre (33 feet) bulk length of film.

Basically the film back is an alternative camera back replacing the regular back, but carries two magazine chambers for the bulk film magazines. This makes the back somewhat large—it is 272 mm (10.7 inches) long, 85 mm (3.4 inches) high and 63 mm (2.5 inches) deep. Apart from the length, none of the other dimensions protrudes beyond the outside dimensions of the camera with motor drive. Complete with magazines and film, the 250 film back 1 adds about 880 grams (31 ounces) to the weight of the camera assembly. (This allows also for the normal camera back it replaces.)

The 250 film back is invariably used with either the motor drive or the winder. It is an accessory to the motor unit, rather than the other way round. The motor coupling is needed to turn the spool of the take-up magazine in the back—without the drive you would have to wind up slack film by turning the magazine spool knob after every exposure. So even if you want to shoot manually, you still need the drive or winder attached to the camera.

Operating the release and camera winding lever is a little more awkward as the manual film transport is heavier. In this case the winding lever also turns the take-up spool of the magazine via the motor drive coupling in the camera base and via the coupling gear of the motor drive itself engaging the coupling gear wheel on the 250 film back.

250 Film back features

The controls and features of the 250 film back 1 are concerned with camera attachment, motor drive coupling and management of the film in the magazines.

The magazine chambers, protruding at the side of the film back, take the 250 film magazines. These are closed, once inside the back, by the large knobs on top of each magazine chamber. The knobs turn through half a turn and are marked with arrow heads and the lettering CLOSE and OPEN REAR COVER. Note that these markings refer to the rear cover. At CLOSE, the magazines are open; at OPEN, they are closed. Only in the latter position can the 250 film back be removed from the camera. In the CLOSE position an additional camera hold or tongue moves out of the top of the left-hand magazine for maximum camera security. The CLOSE position of the right-hand knob locks the camera clamping plate and the back opening key.

A film type indicator surrounds the left-hand magazine opening knob. This is a reminder only and has no mechanical or control function.

The frame counter surrounds the right-hand magazine opening knob and carries numbers (in intervals of 10) from 0 to 250. Intermediate positions are marked for alternate exposures by dots—i.e. to indicate exposures No. 2, 4, 6, 8 and so on.

Set the frame counter to the number of exposures you have loaded in the magazine. During operation the counter then runs backwards to 0. At 0 a switch cuts out the motor drive—important in unmanned photography and useful for presetting a given number of exposures for a sequence. The switch cuts in again if you move the dial past 0 to a position where the chrome stud is opposite the index line at the back.

If the film is finished (and has left the spool of the feed magazine) the frame counter—linked with a special

250 FILM BACK 1

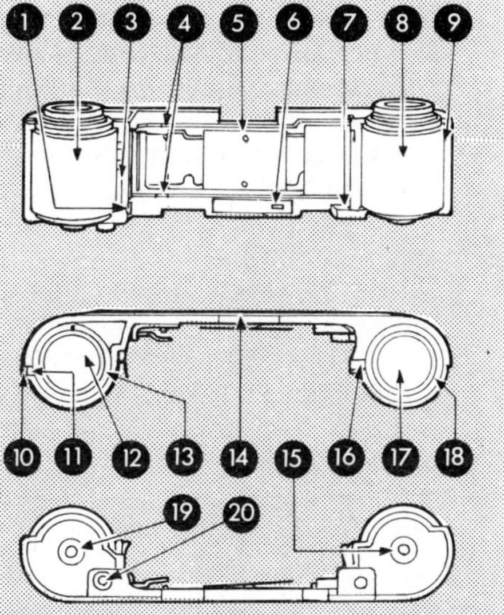

1. Motor drive coupling gear.
2. Right-hand magazine chamber (i.e. at right-hand camera end as seen from behind).
3. Camera clamping plate.
4. Camera set groove.
5. Film pressure plate.
6. Motor drive coupling terminal.
7. Camera stage.
8. Left-hand magazine chamber.
9. Rear cover catch.
10. Lock key.
11. Lock key plate.
12. Right-hand magazine opening knob.
13. Frame counter.
14. Rear cover.
15, 19. Spool knobs.
16. Camera holder.
17. Left-hand magazine opening knob.
18. Film type indicator.
20. Camera clamping knob.

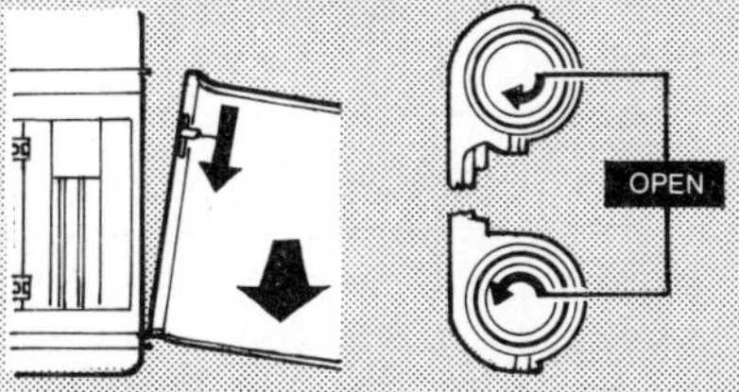

To fit the 250 film back, remove the normal camera back *(left)*. On the film back turn both magazine chamber opening knobs to REAR COVER OPEN *(right)*.

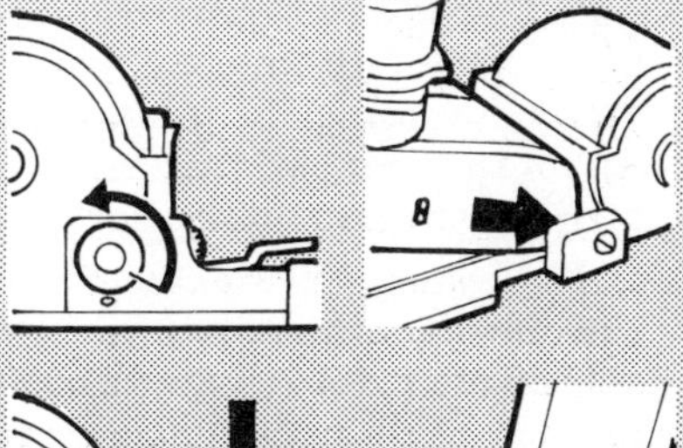

Unclamp the camera clamping knob *(left)* and insert the left-hand end of the camera on to the camera stage *(right)*.

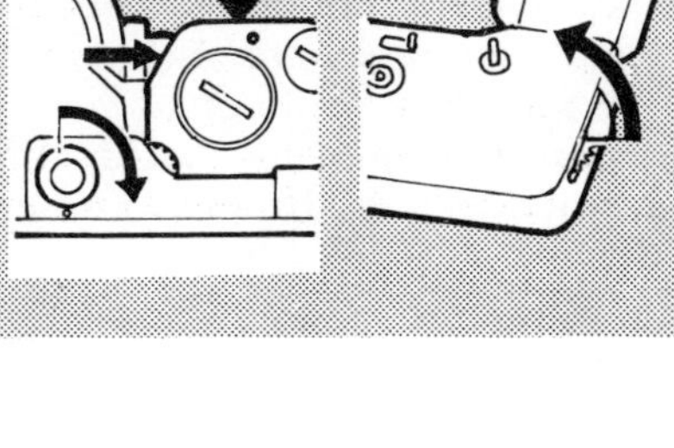

Push the camera in position at the right end and clamp *(left)*. Before attaching the motor drive, open the gear cover at the side *(right)*.

sprocket wheel in the rear of the film back—stops moving. So watch the frame counter during sequencing.

The white index is wider than the dots marking alternate exposures; get used to reading off the exposure number by the position of the dots relative to the one or other edge of the index line.

The camera clamp knob in the base operates a clamping plate that swings forward once the camera is in position, and holds down the right-hand end firmly against the back. The clamp plate is open when the arrow head on the knob, next to CLAMP, is opposite the white dot in the base. You can unlock the clamp plate only when the right-hand magazine opening knob is in the OPEN position. You can close the clamp plate if the magazine opening knob is already at CLOSE, but then it stays locked.

A spool knob in the base of each magazine chamber holds the magazines in place. The knob pulls out to release the magazine. It also engages the magazine spool by a friction coupling for taking up slack in the film.

The rear cover lock is a sprung latch in the right-hand end of the 250 film back. When the right-hand magazine opening knob is in the CLOSE position, meaning that the magazine is open, a key plate moves over this latch so that the back cannot be opened.

The rear cover is like an extended camera back with pressure plate and three film guide rollers. It presses the film against the frame counter sprocket, the camera's transport sprocket and guides the film at the left-hand end. The 38 × 51 mm pressure plate is somewhat shorter than that of the normal camera back. The rear cover detaches completely; it hooks into a recess at the left-hand end of the unit and then engages the latch at the right. It carries a small handling button near the right-hand end.

The motor drive coupling elements are a coupling gear wheel below the camera clamp plate near the right-hand magazine chamber, and a pair of coupling terminals in the rear. The coupling gear engages a similar gear at the end of the motor drive or winder. That drives the take-up magazine spool which has to take up the film pushed forward by the transport sprocket. The motor drive coupling terminal is linked with the switch built into the frame counter. It opens a switching arrangement inside the motor and puts the latter out of action when the counter reaches 0.

Attachment to the camera

While the 250 film back is used in conjunction with the motor drive or winder, you can assemble them in either order. On the principle of building up an assembly by successively attaching smaller pieces rather than big ones, I find it more convenient to fit the camera on the 250 film back on its own and attach the motor drive or winder afterwards. If you proceed in this sequence, however, be sure that the motor drive switch is at OFF—otherwise there is a slight risk of contact damage if you earth the motor contacts to the camera body. Better still, attach the motor drive without the control pack or control grip and fit the latter afterwards. Attaching the motor drive to the 250 film back and then mounting the combination on the camera gets over this difficulty, but is more cumbersome.

The camera strap tends to impede fitting of the 250 film back and the motor drive so, if you don't really need it, remove it from the eyelets, together with the split rings.

The fitting procedure is not difficult, but does require a number of steps that must be carried out in the right order:

1. Turn the magazine opening knobs above both magazine chambers to OPEN (i.e. magazines closed). The OPEN marking next to the arrow head must be opposite the broad white index at the rear of the film back.

2. In the base of the film back turn the camera clamp knob anti-clockwise to bring the arrow head next to CLAMP opposite the large white dot.

3. On the camera remove the normal back by opening it and pressing down the small pin in the hinge; unhook the back and remove.

4. Place the rewind crank end of the camera against the left-hand recess of the film back. The camera base-plate should rest flush against the small projection of the film back at the bottom—the camera stage. If you are fitting the camera together with its strap, hold the split ring in the strap eyelet upright to prevent it from being clamped between the camera and the film back. (A cut-out in the retaining ledge clears the carrying strap ring.)

5. Push down the other end of the camera firmly

against the film back and turn the clamping knob clockwise. This swings the clamp plate in against the side of the camera to hold it firm. Keep the camera strap (if used) clear of the clamp plate. If the plate does not engage smoothly, check that the camera is correctly aligned. The end of the baseplate (just past the battery chamber cover) must be flush with the upper inside wall of the small compartment housing the motor drive coupling gear.

6. Now attach the winder or motor drive in the normal way as described before. However before fitting it, fully open the coupling gear cover at the hand grip end of the drive or winder. If you neglect this, the motor can still be attached to the camera but it does not then couple with the take-up magazine spool, causing various troubles (failure to advance the film, torn perforations etc.) during shooting. When attaching the motor or winder again keep the carrying strap and split ring out of the way.

7. Once the motor drive or winder is in position, check the action by operating the drive or the camera's film transport lever. The spool knob in the right-hand magazine chamber base (the one nearer to the clamp knob) should rotate. This only signifies that the motor drive coupling gear of the 250 film back has correctly meshed with the corresponding gear on the motor drive or winder.

If you attach the camera with the motor drive already mounted on it, the procedure is much the same except that correct alignment of the camera may be very slightly trickier. Again be sure to open the coupling gear cover on the motor and check correct meshing by rotation of the right-hand spool knob in the base of the magazine chamber as above.

Detaching the film back

This is largely the reverse of the fitting procedure. You can detach the back with or without film in it—in the former case the film length between the magazines is of course fogged.

1. Turn the magazine opening knobs of both magazine chambers to OPEN.

2. Turn the clamping knob in the base of the film back anti-clockwise so that the arrow head is opposite the white dot. (Preferably have the camera lying on its back while doing this.)

3. Raise up the end of the camera body next to the clamp knob, then disengage the other end.

4. Refit the normal camera back by pushing down the hinge release pin, hooking in the bottom pin of the hinge, lining up the other end with the top hinge and letting go of the release pin so that the upper part of the hinge also engages.

If the film back you have removed from the camera contains film, this will be visible across the front of the pressure plate. Do not move this film or pull at it.

250 film magazines

These light-tight containers for loading film into and unloading it from the 250 film back fulfil largely the same function as the standard cartridge in the normal OM camera. The film here runs from one magazine into another, without rewinding (impractical with a 250-exposure film length) and the magazines have no velvet light trap. Instead the film runs in a light trapping channel when the magazine is closed, and freely from spool to spool when the magazines are open in the back.

A film magazine consists of an inner shell, an outer shell and a spool. The latter has approx. 53 mm (2.1 inch) flanges and a centre core with two slots for attaching the film. The inner shell and outer shell both have an approx. 26 mm wide opening—the film runs in and out through this without hindrance when the openings are superimposed. The inner shell carries a couple of buttons; a flat-topped one which merely facilitates manipulation and a round-topped one that lifts a spring latch to allow the shells to be turned against each other.

When a magazine is closed, the two chrome buttons are opposite the opening of the outer shell. To open it from this position, press the round-topped chrome button and rotate the outer shell—with the button depressed—in either direction through 180°. Turn by the serrated rim of the inner shell if necessary. At this point the two slots are superimposed and the inner shell can be withdrawn from the outer one. You then have the three parts mentioned above: inner and outer shells and centre spool.

To assemble, place the spool in the inner shell, and the outer shell over the inner shell with the two slots superimposed. Press down the inner shell into the outer shell and rotate to bring the two chrome buttons opposite the slot of the outer shell. At this point the magazine is closed and the spring latch in the side engaged. The closing direction is important if—as is usually the case—you have a film attached to or wound up on the centre spool. If the magazine is used as a supply magazine, i.e. holds a full spool of film, the film should emerge anti-clockwise from the magazine (as seen from above) and you turn the inner shell clockwise to close it. If the magazine serves as a take-up magazine with the film only hooked onto the spool, it enters the magazine anti-clockwise and you close the magazine also anti-clockwise. This is to free the film run when you open the magazines inside the 250 film back—we'll come back to that again.

Loading magazines

The 250 film magazine takes up to 10 metres of film, loaded from bulk film which is available in various lengths and packings. Before actually loading a magazine with film, practise assembling it—especially as a feed magazine—until you can do it by touch. For you will have to do this in the dark. It is also worth investing in one short bulk length (e.g. 5 metres) and wasting it to practise the loading and unloading operations.

To load a magazine:

1. Dismantle the empty magazine into the inner and outer shell and spool. Place these items where you can easily find them in the dark, for instance inside a medium sized flat open box. From here on proceed in total darkness (except during the trial runs).

2. Cut 10 metres of film from your bulk length—or a shorter length if you do not need the full 250 exposures.

3. Taper the end of the film so that at least 2 or 3 cm (or an inch) of it is not more than 2 cm or $\frac{3}{4}$ inch wide.

4. Push this leader into the slot of the spool with the emulsion side of the film facing the spool core. *Do not fold in the film to make a hook.* That could cause trouble when the film comes off the supply spool—as it has to at the end of the film.

5. Wind film onto the spool with its emulsion side in. Hold the film only by the edges, never touch the film surface or back. The 250 film loader (see below) greatly

250 FILM MAGAZINE

1. Inner shell.
2. Spool.
3. Outer shell.
4. Fixed flat button on inner shell.
5. Round headed push button (sprung).
6. Film slot on spool.
7. Film cutter on outer shell.
8. Index mark.

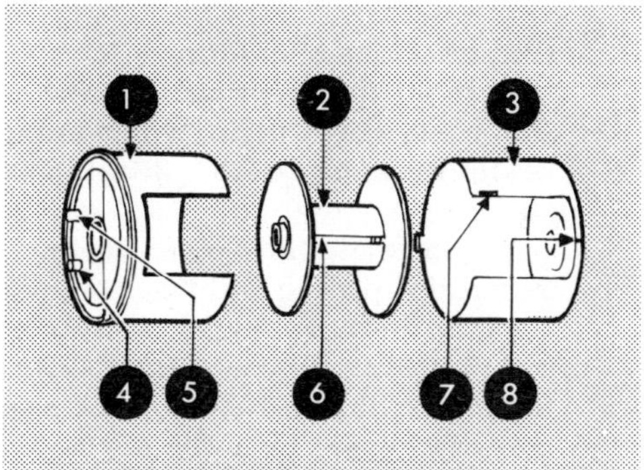

To open the magazine, press the push button and turn the inner shell before removing *(left)*. Attach the film to the spool *(right)*.

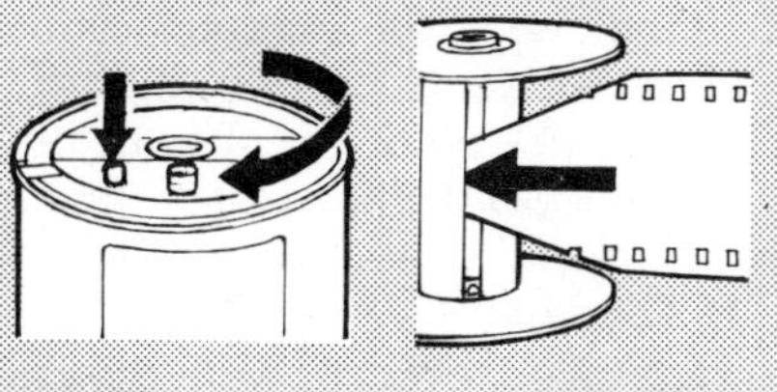

With film wound on the spool assemble this with the magazine shells *(left)* and close the magazine, *(right)*.

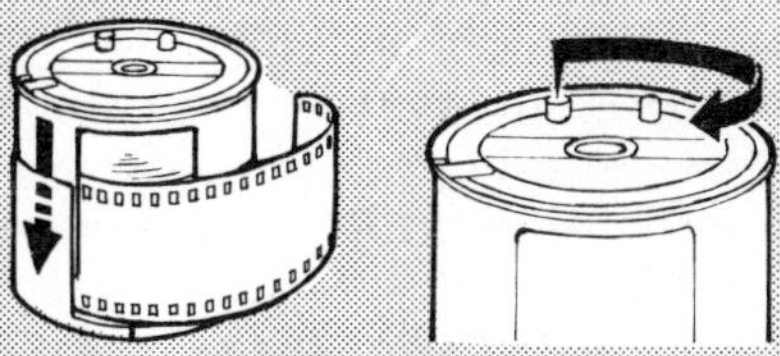

Open the back lock *(left)* and remove the back cover *(right)*.

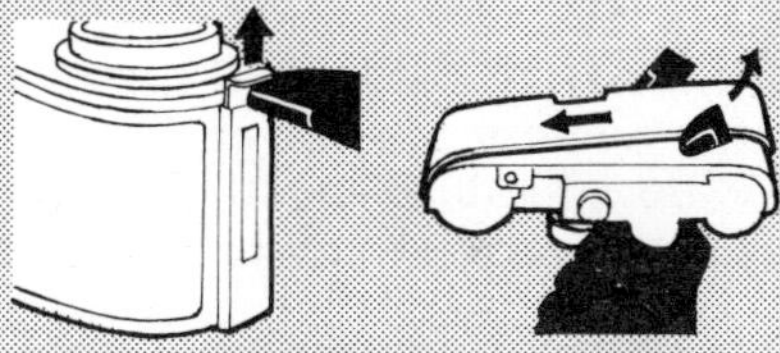

Insert the film, attached also to the take-up magazine, in the two chambers of the open back.

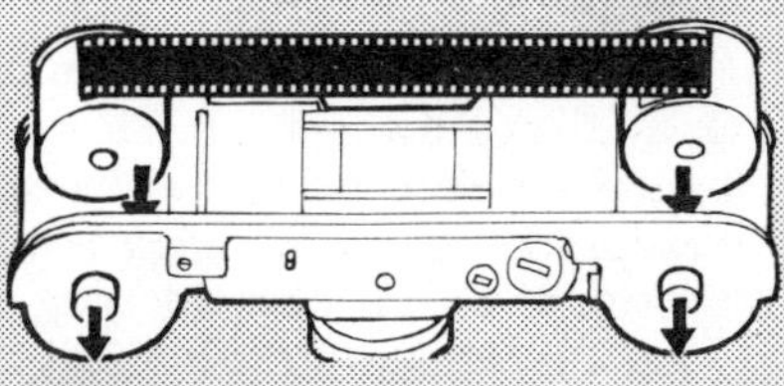

After replacing the back cover, turn both locking knobs to CLOSE *(left)* and set the frame counter *(right)*.

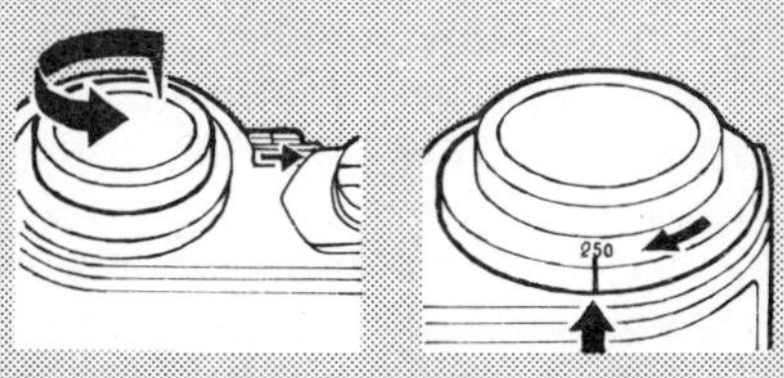

simplifies this operation.

6. Hold the inner shell in the left hand and place the spool into it with the right hand, so that the film comes off upwards away from you through the opening of the shell.

7. Leave at least 10 cm or 4 inches of film protruding from this opening and place the outer shell over the inner shell, with the openings lined up.

8. Looking down on the magazine from above (top of inner shell), the film now emerges from the openings anti-clockwise. Turn the inner shell clockwise to engage. This closes the magazine and you have the film leader protruding from the channel between the two shells. From this point on continue in ordinary light.

9. Trim the protruding film end in the same way as the other end, but this time fold in about 2 cm ($\frac{3}{4}$ inch) to form a hook.

Preparing the take-up magazine

This logically continues the sequence of loading the magazine but you can do it at any later time when you are ready to insert the magazine in the film back. You need no darkroom.

10. Dismantle the second magazine which will serve as a take-up magazine.

11. Hook the folded-over end of the film into the slot of the take-up spool, with the emulsion side inwards.

12. Wind up about 3 or 4 turns of film on the take-up spool to make sure that it is anchored securely. If necessary pull more film from the supply magazine—but do not open the latter.

13. Place the spool in the inner shell so that the latter faces the same way as the inner shell of the supply magazine. So if you hold the inner shell in the left hand and the spool in the right, the film must come down towards you out of the opening of the inner shell.

14. Place the outer shell over the inner shell, with the openings superimposed.

15. Depress the rounded button of the take-up magazine and turn the inner shell anti-clockwise to close it.

16. If you place the two magazines on the table in front of you, with the lettering on the inner shell upright, the

film should now emerge anti-clockwise from the supply magazine at the left and run also anti-clockwise into the take-up magazine at the right.

Insertion in the film back

17. On the 250 film back, mounted on the camera as described (see above, *Attachment to the camera*), turn the magazine opening knobs at each side to OPEN.

18. Lift the rear cover latch at the right-hand side of the film back (as seen from behind) to release the back cover. Lift this cover completely off the back.

19. Fully pull out the spool knobs below each magazine chamber.

20. Insert the supply magazine into the left-hand chamber (while holding the take-up magazine in the other hand). Check that the magazine is correctly located: The red dot at the bottom of the outer shell opening must be lined up with the white line inside the left-hand magazine chamber. Also, the two chrome knobs of the inner shell must fit into the cut-out in the circular plate that forms the extension of the magazine opening knobs inside the chamber.

21. Insert the take-up magazine in the right-hand chamber in the same way, again making sure that it is correctly lodged.

22. Fully push in the spool knobs below each magazine chamber. Turn the knobs slightly if necessary to engage the crossbar of the spools. The knobs must lie in contact with the bottom of the magazine chambers.

23. Turn the right-hand spool knob to the right to take up any slack in the film. This is linked to the internal fork by a friction drive which winds up slack but does not easily pull out film from the supply magazine.

24. Check that the film runs straight from magazine to magazine and especially that it engages the right-hand sprockets on both sides. Those are the frame counter sprockets of the 250 film back—not the camera transport sprocket.

25. Hook in the rear cover at the left of the 250 film back. Then push home at the right to engage the latch.

26. Turn the magazine opening knob of the right-hand chamber clockwise to CLOSE. The knob must turn smoothly; if it does not, turn back to OPEN and check that

the back is properly closed. If the knob still does not rotate easily, re-open the back and check that the magazine is correctly located in its chamber as described above.

27. Turn the magazine knob of the left-hand magazine chamber to CLOSE. This also must turn smoothly—if it doesn't, the left-hand magazine was not correctly located.

Setting the magazine knobs to CLOSE opens the magazines inside the camera so that the film then runs without hindrance through the aligned openings.

28. Advance the film by about 6 frames to check operation. You can do this by the motor drive or winder or even with the manual winding lever of the camera, releasing the shutter between each winding movement. (Set the OM-2 to MANUAL and a fast shutter speed.) During the film advance, the spool knob in the base of the right-hand (take-up) magazine chamber must rotate, and so must the frame counter underneath the right-hand magazine opening knob. Note however that (a) this frame counter moves very slowly—one dot division for every two frames—and (b) the motor drive or winder will not operate if the frame counter is at 0. If you are using the camera's normal winding lever, it is more convenient to advance the film by short multiple rather than by long single strokes. *The camera's own frame counter does not move from S.*

29. Set the frame counter to the number of exposures you have loaded in the supply spool. For reckoning numbers of exposures from film length see below, *The 250 film loader*. Set also the film type indicator below the left-hand magazine opening knob in the same way. Check that you have not moved the magazine opening knobs from the CLOSE position during this manoeuvre.

Loading the 250 film back off the camera

It is possible to load the 250 film back without having it on the camera. This is less convenient as you cannot check the film advance and proper operation, nor must you open the magazines (and hence close the magazine opening knobs) except in the dark. However, if the camera is in use with its normal back (or the Recordata back) or if you are working with two 250 film backs, here is the loading procedure.

Prepare the film magazines, remove the rear cover and

insert the magazines, then take up the slack exactly as when loading on the camera. Replace the rear cover and make sure that the latch is securely engaged. Do not however open the magazines (i.e. set the knobs to CLOSE) in normal light. Instead take the back into a completely dark room. Check the operation of each magazine knob, making sure that the magazines are correctly located and the rear cover properly closed. Turn the magazine knobs back to OPEN again before re-emerging into the light. The back is now ready for attachment to the camera.

After attaching the back to the camera, turn the magazine knobs to CLOSE. Make the six blind exposures to check operation and advance the fogged stretch of film between the magazines into the take-up magazine. Then set the frame counter, film type indicator etc. ready for shooting.

The 250 film loader

To load film with the 250 loader, take apart a 250 magazine and fit the spool on the friction-driven take-up shaft next to the sprocket. The remaining operations need total darkness.

1. Mount the supply spool of bulk film on the feed shaft, i.e. the one at the extreme right when you look at the side of the board with the sprocket. Such spools generally have an 8.5 mm or $\frac{5}{16}$ inch square hole which fits easily over the feed shaft if you slightly depress the split shaft while mounting the spool on it.

For bulk film on a core use the large spool supplied with the loader as a supply spool. Unscrew one end flange by turning it clockwise as you look at the flange face-on while holding the other flange tightly. (Only one flange unscrews.) Place the film over the spool core and replace the flange. Then mount this spool on the feed shaft. In either case the film must run off the supply spool at the top towards the sprocket.

2. Swing back the film holding bracket off the sprocket against the stop screw.

3. With a pair of scissors taper the film end coming off the supply spool as described above (see *Loading magazines*).

4. Lead the film off the top of the supply spool over the sprocket and push it into one of the two slots of the maga-

zine spool. *Do not however fold the film back on itself;* this tongue must only curve around the spool core without being actually hooked into the slot.

5. Check that the film perforations engage the sprocket along both edges, then fold down the film holding bracket onto the film. It now presses down and holds the film in contact with the sprocket.

6. Turn the magazine spool anti-clockwise, i.e. in the direction of winding in the film emulsion inwards, to take in any slack.

7. Set the number of exposures you want to load. Pull the crank on the gear side of the board outward on its shaft and turn anti-clockwise so that the arrow head at the centre of the crank shaft points to the number of exposures you want on the scale along the crank rim. (Preset this accurately before switching off the light.) The arrow head pointer and the marks for 0, 50, 100, 150, 200 and 250 are marked with luminous paint and so are visible even in the dark. As a guide in the dark to which dot is which, the markings for 250 and 0 are closer together than any of the others. The right-hand dot of the two close-spaced ones is then the 0 setting, the next one clockwise the setting for 50 frames and so on.

8. Now turn the crank slowly to wind the film from the supply spool onto the magazine spool. When using a bulk film spool supplied with the film, keep the left hand gently in contact with the spool flange to slow it down while winding. This is not needed with the large feed spool supplied with the loader, as this spool engages the friction brake shaft and so is automatically slowed down by friction.

Do not turn too fast, as that can tear film perforations and disengage the film retaining bracket from the sprocket. While winding check by touch that the bracket is still securely down on the sprocket.

9. Continue winding the crank until you suddenly feel it going much harder. This signals the braking mechanism; you can turn the crank by one more turn after which it locks.

10. With a pair of scissors cut the film between the sprocket and the supply spool.

11. Fold open the film holder bracket, remove the magazine spool with the wound-on film and load into the

250 FILM LOADER

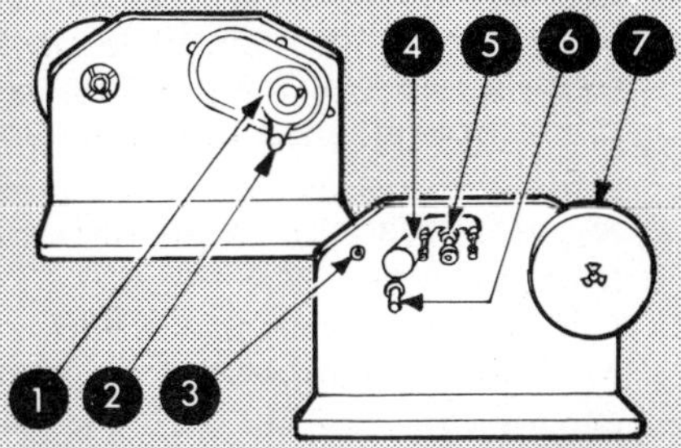

1. Exposure scale plate and index.
2. Hand crank and exposure scale.
3. Stop screw for film holder bracket.
4. Film holder bracket.
5. Sprocket.
6. Magazine spool shaft.
7. Supply spool on feed shaft.

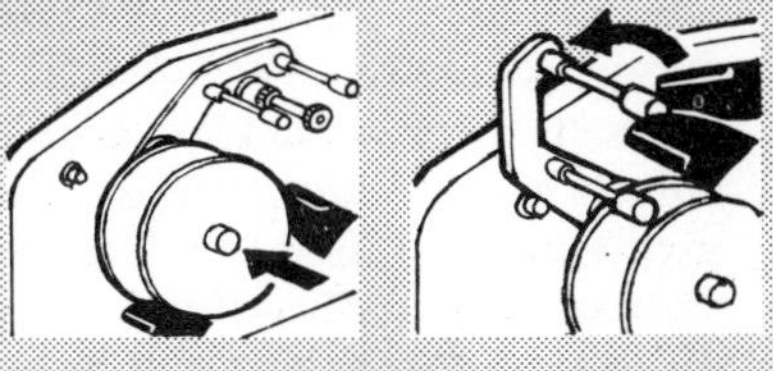

Place the magazine spool on its take-up shaft *(left)* and swing open the film holder bracket *(right)*.

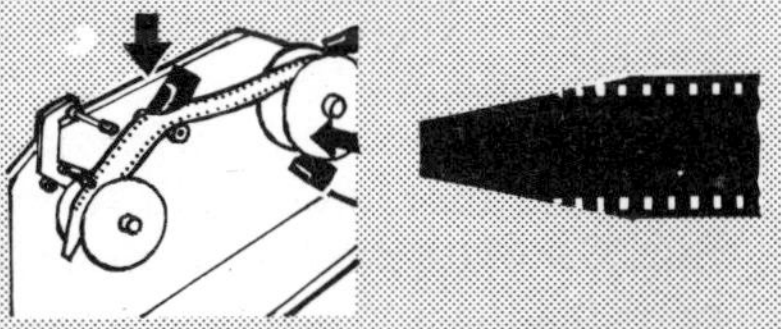

Fit the supply spool on the supply shaft and lead the film end to the magazine spool *(left)*. The end should be suitably tapered *(right)*.

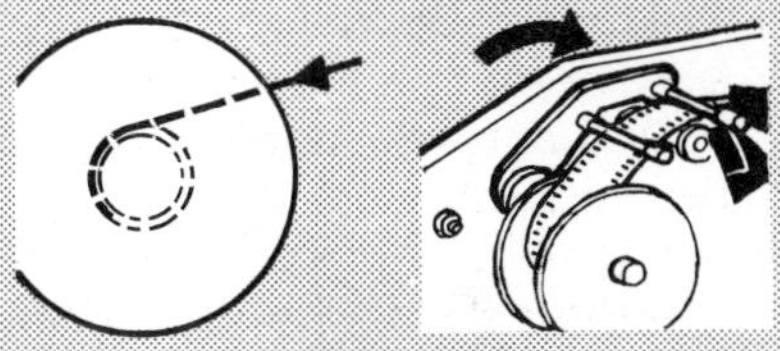

In the spool the film must run straight into the slot *(left)* without being hooked back. Then swing down the film holder bracket *(right)*.

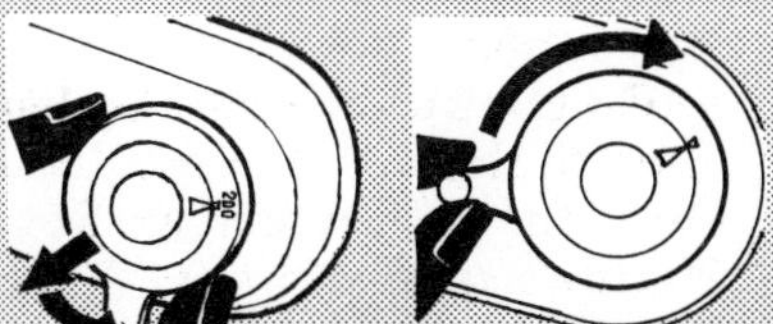

Set the number of frames to be wound *(left)*, then gently turn the crank to wind up the film *(right)*.

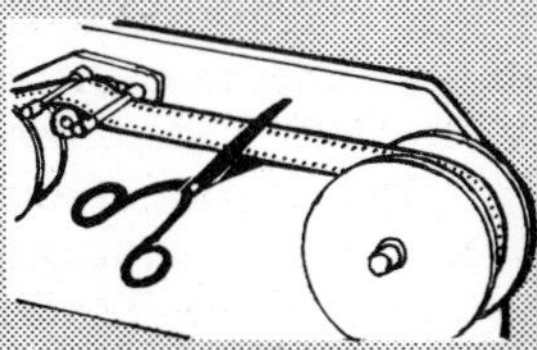

Once the transport has locked, cut the film off between the sprocket and supply spool.

magazine as described before.

12. Carefully rewrap the supply spool of film light-tight before switching on the light. If you have started a 100-foot bulk length from a core, the remaining film can remain on the loader's supply spool. (But you may need an additional supply spool if you next want to spool a different film type.)

The full 250-exposure load of the magazine amounts to about 10 metres (33 feet) of film, including allowance for a leader and trailer for loading in the camera. Thus one 30-metre or 100-foot bulk length yields three 250-exposure loads. A 17-metre bulk length yields a full 250-exposure load and a small 175-exposure length (or a couple of 220-shot lengths) while a 5-metre bulk length yields about 118 exposures. Naturally you can load any shorter length you want.

The automatic winding lock after presetting the crank counts the film length in terms of actual number of frames passing the sprocket, without allowance for any leader or trailer. Add at least another 10 frames for those. You can also meter a film accurately by counting the number of turns of the crank. Each crank turn is equivalent to $2\frac{1}{2}$ standard 24 × 36 mm film frames, or four turns of the crank advance 10 frames. To avoid being disturbed by the automatic lock, preset the counter to 250 before you start if you want to measure film by counting crank revolutions.

Measuring out 36-exposure lengths

The 250 film loader can also measure out film lengths for 36 exposures for loading into reloadable cartridges. In total darkness proceed as follows:

1. Fit the bulk film spool to the feed shaft of the loader (or fit the film core on the large feed spool and place this on the feed shaft).

2. Open the film hold lever.

3. Run the film from the feed spool over the sprocket, through the magazine spool take-up shaft (with no spool on it) and let it hang down to the base of the film loader.

4. Close the film holder onto the sprocket.

5. Set the film scale on the loader to exactly 40.

6. Turn the crank to wind up film on the take-up shaft until the crank locks. Then cut off the film to the right of

UNLOADING

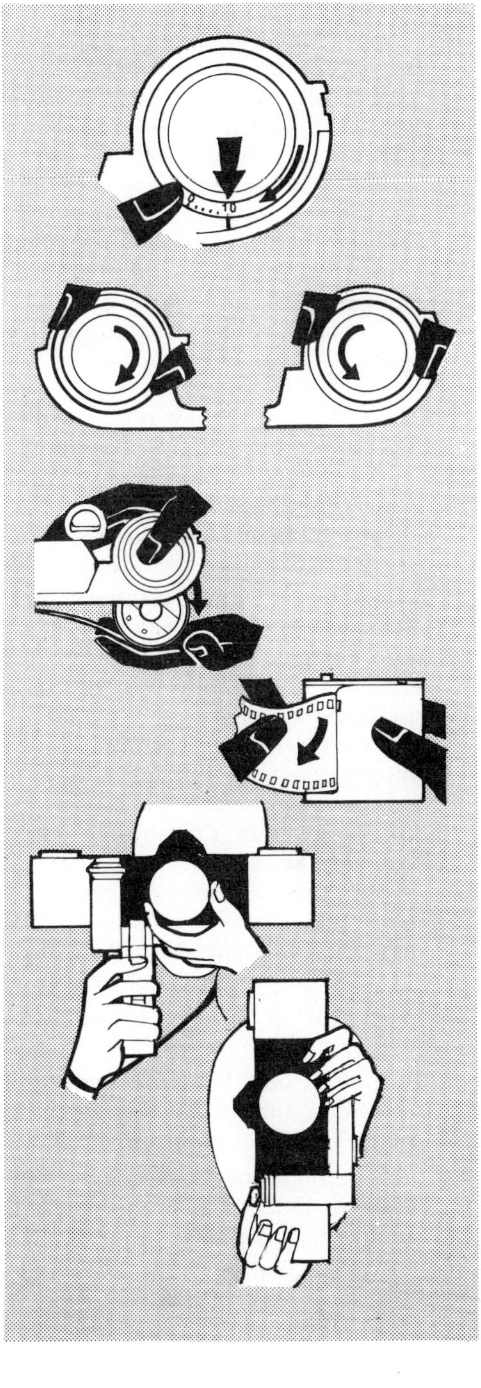

At film end, set back the frame counter to wind up last frames, then open the magazine chamber knobs.

Remove magazine from camera.

To cut film, tear it against film cutter in magazine lip *(right)*.

250 BACK HOLDS

The M.18V control grip with motor drive provides most convenient hold *(left)*. For upright shots with winder, support camera assembly in right hand.

Adopt the upright format hold with 250 film back and winder (or motor drive and M.15V control pack); right-hand magazine chamber in palm of right hand, index finger on drive release button and other fingers around front of magazine chamber. Left hand presses on camera front with index finger to push whole camera against forehead. The other fingers of the left hand operate controls.

the sprocket, open the film hold lever and remove the film from the shaft.

The film winds up very loosely so there is little risk of damage. Keep a check on the turns of the crank; the full 36-exposure load needs 16 turns. (If the crank locks sooner, you did not set it to exactly 40 on the scale.) Also let the film hang down through the take-up shaft slot to at least the wooden base of the loader—if the film hangs shorter, it may not wind up around the shaft and spill all over the table or even the floor.

Finally load the reloadable cartridge in the normal way.

Unloading

With no need for rewinding, removal of the exposed film is comparatively simple. Generally the signal of the film end is that the motor drive or winder stops advancing the film. This happens when the frame counter reaches 0. If you had originally set it for the number of exposures loaded in the magazine, this then is the point for unloading:

1. Turn the frame counter back to about 10 on its scale, set the shutter to a fast speed (at MANUAL with the OM-2) and advance the film by 6 frames. That winds the last exposed frame fully into the take-up magazine and so prevents fogging.

During this step the film end may come off the supply magazine spool. The importance of not hooking the film on this spool (see above, *Loading magazines*) is that a hook could catch in the shutter curtains and jam or even damage the camera.

You can also carry out the step of advancing 6 frames with the manual winding lever of the camera—in that case there is no need to set the frame counter to 10.

2. Turn both magazine opening knobs to OPEN.

3. Pull up the latch of the back cover and remove the cover.

4. Pull out the spool knob of the take-up magazine chamber, turn the whole assembly over, and allow the magazine to drop out. Shake slightly if necessary.

The magazine may or may not have film protruding from it. If there is film protruding, take care not to pull film out of the take-up magazine again—that might fog the last exposures.

Magazine management

Obviously you need at least two complete 250 magazines to operate with the 250 film back, as the film always runs from a feed to a take-up magazine. For efficient handling you should however have at least three magazines. For once you have unloaded a film, that magazine is out of action until you have removed the film for processing—not always convenient if you are away from your own darkroom. With the third magazine you can take an additional film load for reloading the camera immediately. The previous feed magazine now becomes the take-up magazine.

For more film, you obviously need more magazines. Extra magazines are also useful if you propose to switch films without cutting off an exposed section; there you need at least two spare magazines.

Beyond that, magazine management becomes a matter of the amount of film you are likely to need for a run or series of runs. If you carry a number of spare magazines with film, remember to mark on each a film type and number of exposures. On an exposed magazine mark also the fact that it is exposed, together with any other identifying data you may need. To tell apart an exposed from an unexposed magazine, look at the way in which the film enters or leaves the magazine slot. When you look down on the top of the magazine (with the lettering and white film marking panel) the film emerges anti-clockwise from the slot if it is a feed magazine and clockwise if it is a take-up magazine.

Switching films

As the 250 film back I does not permit rewinding of the film, the usual method of switching part-exposed films by rewinding is out of the question. The only feasible way of switching film in this case is to remove the film as it is, change over, and carry on shooting later on when returning to the original film.

This is easiest if you use the alternative film in normal 36-exposure cartridges without the 250 film back. In that case, make six blind exposures (release and advance the film six times) to move the last exposure safely into the take-up magazine. Then turn the magazine opening knobs of both magazine chambers to OPEN (to close the magazines) and remove the whole 250 film back from the camera. Fit the normal camera back, load with the alternative film you propose to use and continue shooting.

Put away the 250 film back carefully and especially do not shift the film that appears in front of the pressure plate. Also, of course, do not turn either magazine knob to CLOSE, which would open the magazine.

When refitting a 250 film back to continue shooting, proceed in the same way as for normal attachment, again paying special attention to keeping the motor drive coupling gear cover open. After turning the magazine chamber knobs to CLOSE, advance the film by about five frames and at the same time check that the spool knob of the right-hand magazine chamber rotates. Then continue shooting normally. The frame counter indicates the correct number of exposures made, including the blind exposures inevitably lost when removing and refitting the 250 film back.

If you want to switch to another bulk film to be used in the 250 film back, you'll have to unload the film from the back itself. In this case make again six blind exposures to clear the exposed film from the back into the take-up magazine, turn the magazine opening knobs to OPEN and open the rear cover. Put the camera with the 250 film back with its back down on a table and pull out the spool knobs of both magazine chambers. Slightly lift the camera and tap both chambers so that the magazines drop out of the open back.

Alternatively, pull up the spool knob of the right-hand chamber and remove the magazine as when unloading normally, then repeat the same with the left-hand chamber. In doing this, take special care not to pull film out of either magazine again. Pulling film out of the take-up magazine may bring out and fog the last exposures; pulling more out of the feed magazine simply wastes film.

Store the two magazines while maintaining the film length between them. Note also on the feed magazine the number of frames already exposed, as read off the frame counter on the 250 film back.

When reloading the magazines to continue shooting, proceed in the same way as for normal loading on the camera, again taking care not to pull any film out of the take-up magazine. Once the two magazines are installed in the open back, take up any slack of film between them by rotating the spool knob of the take-up magazine (not of the feed magazine). Close the rear cover and lock by turning the magazine knobs to CLOSE. Set the frame counter beneath the right-hand magazine opening knob to the number of frames noted on unloading. (Note down the number in pencil on the white panel on top of the magazine.) Advance the film again by at least six frames to bring an unexposed and unfogged piece of film into the camera gate. Then continue shooting.

This operation obviously needs an extra pair of magazines for the second film. If frequent film changing from one kind of 250-exposure film load to another is a routine necessity, it may even be worth getting a second 250 film back: it is quicker to change the backs than to load and unload magazines from a back. And the 250 film back automatically keeps the magazines separated by the correct film length without risk of pulling film out of either magazine.

Removing part-exposed films

Where there is no special need for maintaining the full film length or continuity between the film before and after changing, it is much more convenient just to unload the part-exposed section of the film. The occasion for that may arise fairly frequently if you are handling film in 250-exposure lengths, as you may not always want to wait for the full 10 metres of film before getting it processed. The procedure is as follows:

1. Make six blind exposures to advance the last exposed film sections safely into the take-up magazine.

2. Turn the magazine opening knobs of both chambers to OPEN.

3. Remove the rear cover of the 250 film back.

4. Pull out the left-hand spool knob, turn over the film back and let the left-hand magazine drop out.

5. On the right-hand magazine, which is still in the back, press down the right-hand lip of the magazine opening with the film cutter. Pull up the film towards you against the cutter to tear it off. The exposed film is now fully inside the right-hand (take-up) magazine while a leader still protrudes from the left-hand or supply magazine.

6. Remove the right-hand magazine from the camera back by pulling out the right-hand spool knob and let that magazine drop out. This part of the film is then ready for processing. Mark on the magazine also the film length (number of exposed frames as read off the film counter)—both to know how many exposures you have made and the film length you have to load into a tank.

In calculating this film length divide the number of exposures by 8 to get the length of the film in feet. Add another $2\frac{1}{4}$ feet to allow the leader and trailer—film lost in loading and unloading. For metres divide the number of exposures by 26.25 (26 is near enough) and add 0.7 metres for the beginning and end of the film.

7. Reshape the film leader for attachment to a new magazine centre spool. Note also on the supply magazine the number of frames remaining before removal from the camera. When reloading this film, set the frame counter to about 12 frames less than this number after you have advanced the beginning of the film ready for the first exposure.

250 Film back operation

Picture taking with the 250 film back is largely the same as with the Winder 1 or Motor drive 1. The 250 film back does not noticeably slow down cycling in the sequencing mode of the drive.

Much of the time, especially for unmanned photography, the 250 film back is used for single exposures at regular or irregular intervals and the sequencing feature of the motor drive is not really needed. But the remote control and especially remote-power facilities (e.g. shooting at regular intervals with the M.AC control box) make the motor drive more versatile here than the winder. And as the motor or winder is essential with the 250 film back, the obvious way of releasing and film transport is by motor power. If necessary—or if the batteries are exhausted—you can still operate the camera manually by pressing its release button and working the winding lever. But even here the motor drive or winder must be mounted on the camera/250 film back assembly. It transmits the transport operation from the winding lever via the motor drive coupling gear to the take-up magazine to spool the film.

For sequencing, the frame counter is a useful way of preselecting the number of frames to be exposed in a sequence. Set the counter to that number by turning it in either direction. When the camera runs in sequence mode it then stops automatically as the counter reaches 0.

When working in this way however keep a separate note of the number of exposures made during each run so as to avoid running out of film at the end of the supply. Best of all, keep this record in terms of remaining exposures. By the time a few sequences have reduced this remaining capacity to say 75 frames, you know you cannot set the counter to say 90 frames for the next run. For the only indication that the film is finished is a slightly less noisy transport and the fact that the frame counter stops turning—neither of which is noticeable from a remote control position in unmanned photography.

The eyecup can be used with the 250 film back, only when fitted via the eyecoupler (see Chpt. *Focusing screens and finder accessories*). The rear cover of the 250 film back protrudes behind the normal camera back, impeding attachment of the eyecup with or without its dioptric correction lenses. The Varimagni finder can be attached directly (it has a cut-away to clear the extra thickness of the 250 film back). Remove the eyecup or Varimagni finder before opening or removing the 250 film back from the camera.

A final point: operate the camera only when the magazine opening knobs *are both in the* CLOSE *position.* Otherwise the magazines are closed which increases the friction on the film running through the light trapping channels. At the best that leads to scratches on the film, at the worst the drive may chop up the film perforations instead of moving the film on. Almost the only obvious sign of running with the magazines closed is apparently laborious operation. So carefully check the position of the OPEN/CLOSE knobs before every exposure sequence.

Remote control and unmanned photography

By connecting the motor drive to its power source (control grip, control pack or M.AC control box etc.) via one of the relay cords you can operate the camera with motor drive from up to 10 metres or 33 feet away. Provided that the power source delivers at least 15 to 16 volts (in other words not too exhausted batteries) you can also link a couple of 10 metre relay cords together for still greater range. More than that is inadvisable—the voltage drop in the long cable connection may reduce reliability. (It also slows up sequencing, but then you would rarely need high-speed sequence shooting at long range.) With these arrangements the power supply unit is also the switching control which provides additional security—you can switch off the whole system at the control end.

With other remote systems listed below only the triggering of the release and transport cycle is remotely controlled. The power source is directly connected to the motor drive and must be switched on or off at the camera. On the other hand these methods also work with the Winder 1. They are all based on the 2.5 mm jack socket in the top of the motor drive or winder hand grip, next to the release button. This provides the following possibilities:

(a) *Simple remote triggering* with the remote control cord of the winder or with other remote control switches used for tape recorders, 8 mm movie cameras etc. All these consist of a 2-wire lead with a 2.5 mm jack at one end and a switch at the other. You can even make up a cord of this kind yourself from a suitable lead, jack and switch. For the latter preferably use a press button switch—the kind that closes the circuit on pressing it and opens on releasing—rather than a sliding switch needing separate actions for opening and closing. (With the winder or with single-frame operation with the motor drive the circuit must be opened after triggering before you can release by closing it again.) In view of the triggering circuit involved, the remote control lead can be quite long—hundreds of feet with normal lighting flex.

(b) *Indirect remote triggering* can use the same 2.5 mm jack fitting with the lead connected to suitable triggering devices: trip wires, step-on contacts etc. for wildlife photography (possibly with an electronic flash connected to the camera), light barrier or acoustic signals, a radio-controlled relay for wireless releasing and so on. In every case the remote triggering lead must end in a switch or switching circuit that is capable of closing and carrying about 5 to 10 milliamps.

(c) *Programmed operation* is possible in the same way by connecting the remote control lead to a timer that closes a contact at a predetermined time or at presettable intervals. The M.AC control box for the motor drive includes timer functions but the maximum interval is 2 minutes. Besides, this is not usable with the winder.

(d) *Multiple camera control.* If you have several OM cameras with winders or motor drive attached, you can trigger them together. For this, operate each camera via remote control lead with 2.5 mm jack and connect together all the negative wires of the leads on the one hand and all the positive ones on the other. For triggering the cameras, short circuit these two groups of leads or wire them through a switch.

With the older motor drive (no 2.5 mm jack socket in the grip), use the 1.2 metre relay cord between the motor drive and any of the power sources and insert bared lead ends of the remote control line into the A and B remote sockets on the power supply plug of the cord.

Non-motorised remote releasing

The winder or motor drive are of course the ideal way of remotely controlling the camera. A couple of more primitive ways exist when you have neither of these motorised items at hand.

Long cable releases are available in runs up to about 6 metres or 20 feet. However, with the friction of the cable inside its sheath, such long lengths need rather more force to operate. The weight of the cable makes additional support for it necessary, especially to prevent transmitting vibration.

Pneumatic releases consist of a thin plastic tube connected to a rubber ball at one end and to a mechanism operating a short cable release at the other. Compressing the rubber ball causes the cable release adapter to depress its plunger, so releasing the camera to which it is connected. Pneumatic releases can run to lengths of around 20 to 25 metres or 65 to 80 feet. The plastic tubing is much lighter and easier to place than an extra long cable release.

Long cable releases and pneumatic releases tend to get 'mushy' in action the longer they are, because of elasticity and strength in the cable or compression of the air in the pneumatic system. The shutter is thus released with some delay—up to about a second—after you have started pressing. And with both these remote releases you must of course go back to the camera after each exposure to advance the film.

External power supplies

The Winder 1 can be used with batteries in the slide-in battery holder or with external power supplies. These must have a correctly wired coaxial power plug, with the centre pole negative and the outer one positive. Such plugs are widely used for external powering of tape recorders and similar equipment. The supply should be 6 volts and capable of yielding about 500 milliamps. The voltage can be less with sources capable of higher currents—e.g. 3 nickel-cadmium cells yielding about 4 volts are just adequate. Also usable are certain mains adapters for tape recorders if they have a 6 volt output, a correctly wired plug and can deliver at least 250 milliamps. This is rather near the lower limit and the Winder 1 gets a little sluggish (but is still operational) with this type of supply.

The main purpose of an external power supply is to provide an extra power reserve but still remain conveniently portable. I have made up a battery pack with four size C cells in an inexpensive plastic battery holder (obtainable from most electronics shops) and carrying a 3 foot lead with a coaxial power plug as described above. It takes four alkali cells (Mn 1400 or equivalent) and is particularly useful in cold weather when batteries get less efficient. This home-made reserve pack sits in an inside pocket and I only have to plug the lead into the external power jack. (That disconnects the internal batteries of the winder.) But you can equally carry two or three normal battery holders in an inside warm pocket and fit them into the winder just for shooting.

The M.6V power pack for the winder serves the same purpose—but with the capacity limited to its 4 AA cells.

The Motor drive 1 not only has alternative power units (control grip, control pack, M.AC control box) but can also be fed from an external power supply. That should be a DC source of not less than 12 and not more than 16 volts capable of delivering a current of at least 500 milliamps. A motor car accumulator would thus serve excellently, so would a mains adapter with a smoothed DC output of 12 to 16 volts (that is built into the M.AC control box, anyway).

The external power source is always connected through one of the relay cords. That must be used in conjunction with one of the control units (control grip, control pack or M.AC control box) even if these are not themselves connected to any power source. The control unit, e.g. M.18V control grip, is essential for its switching circuit. But if you are using an external power source, it is immaterial whether there are batteries in the control grip or not.

The external source to be connected needs to have bare-ended output wires of approx. 2 mm maximum thickness. Attach these to the plus and minus terminals on the relay cord plug (i.e. the outlets at the side marked + and − above DC, 12–16V). Attach the wires singly by depressing the black button above the terminal outlet, pushing the wire fully into the opening and letting go of the black button again. Be sure that the wires from the current source are connected in their correct polarity.

In a motor car, the cigarette lighter is a useful point to link up with the car's electrical system. Plugs to fit the cigarette lighter socket are available for this purpose.

For operation, switch the mode selector switch on the control grip or pack to SINGLE or SEQUENCE as required. Then shoot by pressing the release on the motor drive itself. To change the mode you must however go back to the control unit.

If you are using the M.AC control box as a switching point for the relay cord plug, the position of the power switch becomes irrelevant, nor need the control box be connected to the mains supply. The release run switch should however be at OFF and the mode switch at SINGLE or SEQUENCE as required. When the mode switch is set to SEQUENCE, the sequencing rate on pressing the release on the motor drive itself is that selected on the intervalometer.

Hence the M.AC control box can control the camera for unmanned photography even without an AC supply. Just connect a suitable DC supply to the +/− outlets on the relay cord plug while this is plugged into the M.AC box. Apart from the fact that the power switch is inoperative, all the functions of the control box for single shooting and sequencing with the intervalometer operate in exactly the same way as described before.

This is useful for sophisticated remote-controlled photography in locations where no AC mains supply of the correct voltage is available.

Film management

Loading and unloading of the camera with the winder or motor drive attached follows exactly the same procedure as without any motor unit. After loading the camera with film when the motor drive or winder is already mounted, make the first blind exposures by hand and not by motorised releasing.

Olympus recommends loading the camera with film *after* attaching a motor unit, largely because of risk of possible light leakage through the motor drive socket cap when this is removed from the camera for attaching the motor drive. Actually this is almost over-cautious, as the risk of light leakage during attachment and removal of the motor or winder to the camera is negligible. My own trials under various conditions produced no sign of leakage. That's just as well, for there are sure to be occasions when you have a camera already loaded with film and you decide that you want to shoot with the winder or motor. But a sensible precaution is to attach or detach the drive unit in the shade rather than in bright sunlight—as you would for loading or unloading the film. Also, replace the motor drive socket cap on the camera as soon as you have removed the drive or winder—not just for light leakage reasons but because of the risk of dust and grit entering the camera mechanism.

More serious is a need to keep an eye and an ear open for the film end. For in sequence photography especially it is easy to run through a whole film in no time: at say 4 frames/second a 36-exposure film takes 9 seconds to run right through. It is then that problems can start.

At the end of the film the usual 'click-whirr' sound of the release/transport sequence changes to just the repeated clicks or a rapid loud chattering. This is due to the film perforations stopping the transport sprocket in the camera from moving. When you hear this, *stop shooting immediately*. For if you go on—particularly at the SEQUENCE setting—the repeated attack of the transport sprocket very quickly tears out the film perforations and all subsequent exposures take place on the last frame of the film behind the film window. If you are unlucky, the motor may even tear the film end off the cartridge spool—though this is rare. But the perforations tear quite easily, so after you have unloaded the film, carefully check the inside of the camera for any bits of film debris—i.e. the shreds of film torn out between neighbouring perforations. These shreds can cause trouble if they lodge between the film window and shutter blinds.

Perforations may tear in this way equally with the winder or the motor drive if you try to go on shooting after the first film end signal. Worse still is the possibility of tearing of the film edge together with the perforations. On rewinding, this tear in the edge usually fails to run smoothly back into the cartridge—instead, the film tears right across or jams. You then have to salvage the rest of the shredded film by unloading in total darkness.

With the 250 film back most of these problems disappear. Even at the fastest sequencing rate of 4–5 frames per second the camera could run for a full minute on this film load. And as the film detaches itself from the feed spool at the end, you are unlikely to have perforation tearing problems, either.

Actually the film management problem becomes one of power management. In terms of power consumption (and allowing for the extra load on the drive), a 250-exposure load is equivalent to about ten to fifteen 36-exposure cartridges. Thus if you choose to use nickel-cadmium batteries in the Winder 1, a set of fully charged batteries will just last out a 250-exposure magazine. If you are near the end of the capacity of the M.15V control pack on the motor drive, the motor may well pack up in the middle of a run. With the 250 film back therefore be sure to have a fully charged or fresh power source (nickel-cadmium or alkali batteries respectively) and don't run batteries down to their capacity limit. You can always utilise the remaining battery capacity of alkali batteries in motorised photography without the 250 film back. Alternatively, use an appropriate external power source (see above) or the M.AC control box.

However, even with the greater film reserve of the 250 back, sensible management is important. You can easily lose track if you do not set the frame counter to the correct number of frames as soon as you load the magazines into the film back. Keep a record of the number of frames exposed if you use the frame counter as a sequence control (see above, *250 film back operation*). At the end of the film, if the frame counter was not correctly set, the camera and drive or winder combination will continue cycling even if the film is finished. At that point the frame counter with the 250 film back stops turning and the operating noise gets slightly smoother. But that is not very noticeable from a remote control position in unmanned photography. You could then find yourself exposing picture after picture on the film back's pressure plate. For the film end leaves the supply spool and you do not have the automatic cut-out (and shut-down) of the motor drive or winder as at the end of a normal film without the 250 film back.

Motorisation with other systems

The motor drive and winder, with or without the 250 film back, can of course be used with a number of other equipment groups for specific applications ranging from macrophotography through photomicrography, endoscopy and others.

The motor drive can also be combined with flash units via the Bounce grip. With the winder or with the motor drive and M.15V control pack, attach the Bounce grip in the normal way, as when using the grip directly on the camera. Keep the unit as low down on the grip as possible because the extra thickness of the winder or motor drive brings the flash nearer the level of the lens axis.

With the motor drive and M.18V control grip (or a relay cord), relocate the tripod screw of the bracket unit in the extreme end hole and use this to attach to the camera. If you want to use the combination on a tripod, use one of the centre tapped holes of the bracket unit.

Similar combinations are possible with the motor drive or winder plus the 250 film back. Again, mount the bracket unit with the tripod screw in the end hole. This is necessary even with the winder or M.15V control pack as you need space for the supply magazine chamber between the camera and the Bounce grip.

Further possibilities involve the motor drive or winder

etc. with macro and micro equipment. Here the camera, drive and film assembly are mounted on the bellows, microscope or other optical unit via OM mount adapters. The problems then involve clearing the optical units with the extended bulk of the assembly, and rigidity to take the weight. For both conditions the ideal combination is the motor drive on the camera without either control grip or control pack. Link the drive to these units via one of the relay cords. That way the drive freely clears all parts of bellows, rail, knobs etc. during adjustment. Mount the motor drive on the camera before attaching the latter to the bellows. (You can fix the drive to the camera when already on the bellows—provided the rear standard is at the rear end of the rail—but this is less convenient.)

The Winder 1 is more restrictive as the rear bellows standard must remain at the back end of the rail. The base of the winder protrudes too far away from the camera base to clear the rail. For focusing you then have to rely on the movement of the front standard and movement of the whole rail only.

The weight of the assembly—for instance over 1.6 kg or $3\frac{1}{2}$ lbs of the camera with 250 film back and motor drive—places extra strain on the adjustments of the macro equipment. With the Auto-bellows or the PMT-35 unit lock the bellows adjustments securely. For photomicrography a set-up that supports the camera independently of the microscope—for instance with the PM-PSS stand—is preferable.

Motor and winder trouble shooting

The motor drive and winder may give rise to problems that are caused partly by the versatile applications and partly by the fact that optimum operation of the motorised units depends on the film having not always predictable values of tensile strength, toughness, friction resistance when passing through the velvet-lined cartridge slot, etc.

Unless otherwise indicated, the points below refer to both the Winder 1 and the Motor Drive 1 used with their normal power units (M.18V control grip or M.15V control pack in the case of the motor drive).

Motor drive cannot be attached: Very occasionally the motor drive (but not the winder) encounters an obstacle inside the coupling elements under the camera's motor drive socket cap. This may be due to a displaced release coupling pin. Rectify by connecting a control unit to the drive, switching on and short circuiting the camera coupling contacts with a coin.

Motor drive or winder starts whizzing on attachment to camera: The mode selector or switch dial was switched on and the camera coupling contacts got short circuited (by simultaneously touching the metal part of the camera body) while you also pressed the release. Immediately set the switch of the mode selector etc. to OFF. Always attach the motor drive or winder with the unit switched off.

After attachment to camera, switching on winder or drive causes a short jerk or click: That's normal—the drive and camera mesh after the condition just described.

Motor drive or winder triggers release cycle on attachment to camera: Again the switch or mode selector dial was left switched on (SINGLE or SEQUENCE position).

Motor or winder triggers release sequence on plugging in a remote control unit: The act of plugging in can trigger a release cycle if the motor or winder switch was on even with remote control switched off. No harm done—beyond wasting an exposure.

Motor drive (with M.15V control pack) cycles unexpectedly: You accidentally pressed the release button at the rear of the M.15V control pack while the drive was switched on. The release button on the M.15V control pack is used normally when the latter serves as a remote control unit via one of the relay cords.

Motor or winder cycles in sequence mode without pressure on release: Accidental electrical contact between outer terminal or remote control jack and metal parts of the camera.

Motor drive or winder only advances the film, without releasing: You had pressed the manual release button of the camera. On its next triggering, the motor drive first advances the film for the next shot.

Drive or winder only releases shutter without advancing film: Can arise on mirror lock-up or with OM-2, or if the film is literally on the last exposure and the winder is stopped from advancing the film. Or there may be a fault in the internal camera contacts.

Motor drive fails to reach maximum framing rate in sequence mode: The camera was set to a slow shutter speed (or the through-the-lens metering system of the OM-2 selected a slow speed). The framing rate also drops slightly as the battery gets near exhaustion. But the motor cuts out altogether before the battery voltage gets too low.

Erratic operation: Intermittent stopping and starting etc. can be due to dirty camera coupling contacts, e.g. through grease or dust or other grit that has entered the camera's motor drive socket cap.

Motor drive or winder fails in cold weather: Battery power drops at low temperatures. Keep battery holder, control pack etc. separately in a warm pocket and attach to drive only just before use. Sometimes it helps to advance the first frame manually and then use the motor.

Motor or winder stops with low hum or droning noise: Exhausted batteries. Switch off mode selector or switch and replace batteries. This cut-out operates when the battery voltage has dropped just below a preset operating level. When the batteries are completely dead (or no batteries fitted) you won't of course get the droning noise either.

Winder or motor stops with or without a chattering sound: The film is finished. Stop operating the winder or motor immediately and rewind the film.

Torn perforations near film end or film tears on rewinding: Direct result of continuing winder or motor operation when the film is finished, as above.

No motor drive operation with M.AC control box: Provided no other motor drive troubles are involved check the power supply and fuse. When power switch is set to ON, pilot lamp should light.

Motor runs on connecting relay cord to motor drive or M.AC control box: M.AC power switch was set to ON. When connecting the relay cord, always have the power switched off.

Motor cycles on turning M.AC power switch to ON: Release run switch was set to ON. It should be at OFF—like the power switch—when connecting the power switch to the motor drive.

In sequence mode of M.AC control box, motor stops after one exposure: Power switch was switched on after release run switch. For sequencing, switch on power switch before release run switch (that's what the red numbering 1 and 2 signifies). Turn release run switch to OFF and then back to ON again—sequencing will continue.

In single-exposure mode of M.AC box, pressing release takes one picture but no more: Release run switch left in ON position. Release run switch must be OFF for repeated single-frame exposures, otherwise release system is blocked.

Remote control units fail to operate: Motor drive not connected to a power unit (control grip, control pack or M.AC control box).

250 film back difficult to attach to camera: Check possible interference by carrying strap. Also check that both magazine opening knobs are in the OPEN position.

Magazine opening knobs hard to close: Don't force. Magazines are incorrectly seated in back.

Rear cover of 250 film back won't open: Magazine opening knobs in CLOSE position—turn both knobs to OPEN.

Frame counter does not move at beginning of film: Coupling gear cover of motor drive or winder not opened. (Right-hand spool knob won't turn, either.) Remove winder or drive from camera/film back combination, open coupling gear cover and re-attach.

Camera clamping plate will not unclamp: Right-hand magazine opening knob left in CLOSE position. Turn to OPEN to release movement of clamp plate.

Frame counter stops moving: End of film has left feed magazine and passed beyond film transport sprocket.

Chattering noise by motor drive or winder: Frame end was hooked onto feed spool core (instead of being simply pushed into the spool slot) and on detachment got caught in shutter blind or jammed in the shutter. Open 250 film back, carefully disengage film and check that winder or motor correctly operates camera and shutter.

Motor drive or winder stops completely: Frame counter has reached 0.

Torn film perforations and failure to advance film: Can arise with the 250 film back if you try to operate with the magazines closed (magazine chamber knobs in REAR COVER OPEN position).

CLOSE-UP AND MACRO TECHNIQUE

Close-up photography is taken to cover subjects nearer than the near focusing limit of the camera lens. With the standard 50 mm lenses of the Olympus OM this limit is usually around 0.45 metre or $1\frac{1}{2}$ feet. At this distance objects are reproduced near 1/7 natural size on the film (1:7 reduction or 0.15 × magnification). With most wide angle, standard and medium long focus lenses the near focusing limit—though not the same in every case—yields an image scale between 1:6 and 1:8 (the 50 mm macro lens is an exception) and higher magnifications need accessory equipment. The purpose of this is:

(a) To extend the focusing range of the lens by supplementary lenses or extension units (tubes, bellows);

(b) To provide a more solid camera support that facilitates precise distance setting which is critical at close range. Such supports include various stands with or without lighting accessories to illuminate close-up subjects, especially at high magnifications;

(c) To utilise special lenses of improved near range correction.

Near photography can be considered as covering two ranges of broadly different reproduction scales and equipment involved: close-up photography at magnifications smaller than 1 × or 1:1, and macrophotography proper with magnifications above 1 ×. The latter involves the more elaborate accessories ranging from focusing aids to special stands. All close-up and macro accessories are described in detail in the subsequent equipment chapters, here we deal with more general principles of equipment selection for the job and with differences in technique at close range.

Macro lenses

Specially designated macro lenses are corrected for best performance at certain close-up ranges between—depending on the focal length of the lens—1 × and 12 × magnification. These are thus the ideal lenses to use for routine macrophotography, for instance in medical, scientific and other laboratories, where optimum image quality is vital. The 50 mm macro lens with an extended focusing range to 1:2 scale (0.5 ×) is also corrected for close-up photography to this limit and can be used for higher magnifications.

The macro lenses of the OM system are designed for four slightly overlapping ranges:

(a) From infinity to about 1.5 × natural size on the film: 50 mm.

(b) From 0.5 to a little over 2 × : 80 mm.

(c) From about 2 × to 6 × : 38 mm.

(d) From about 4.5 to 12.5 × (larger still on the PMT-35): 20 mm.

This scheme not only allows for the special close-up correction of these lenses but also for the fact that at low magnifications a longer focus lens needs a greater subject/camera distance which makes the set-up less convenient.

In close-up and macrophotography it is the image scale that counts, hence the subject distance is a secondary point to be considered in terms of the convenience of the set-up. For as far as the picture is concerned, for instance a 2 × macro shot of a butterfly's wing looks much the same with the 80 mm macro lens taken from about 8.5 cm away as it does with the 38 mm lens from perhaps 4.5 cm, but in nature the creature may be easier to approach less closely for the purpose with the 80 mm.

Subject distance, however, still affects perspective even in close-ups. Even if the distance of nearer and further portions varies by only a cm, from 5 to 6 cm away this can make a noticeable difference. So if you have the choice of say the 50 mm and 80 mm macro lenses at magnifications between 0.5 × and 1 ×, choose the 80 mm lens if you can. That also provides more elbow room between the lens and subject for lighting etc.

Above about 1.5 × magnification, perspective ceases to play any significant part in lens choice, as the available depth of field becomes too limited to cover any useful subject extension in depth.

MACRO RANGES

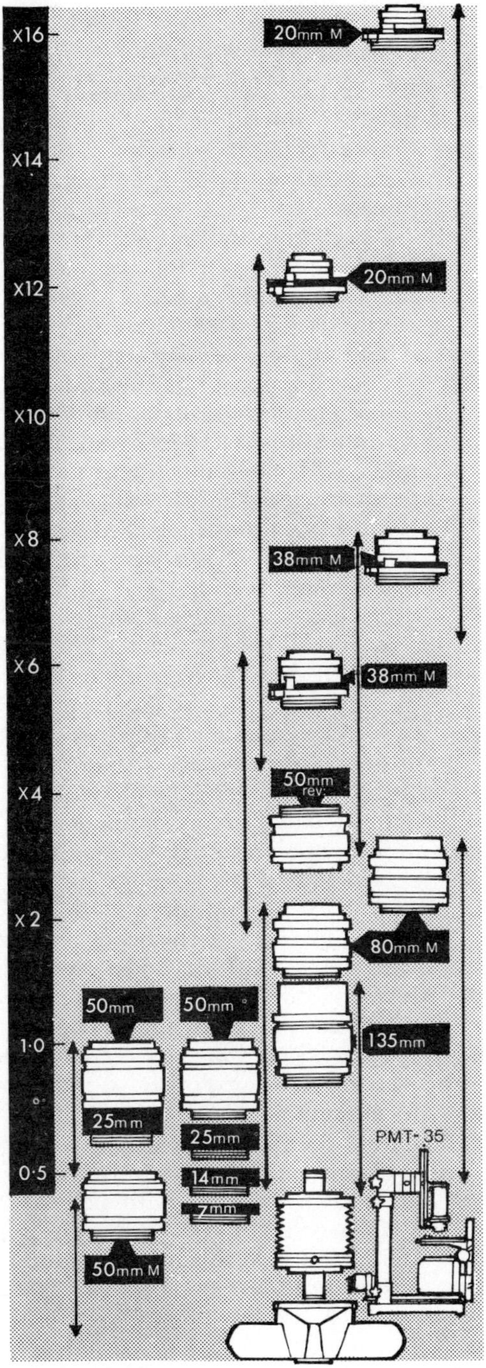

The Olympus OM system covers the full range of macro magnifications with comparatively few lenses. These are all macro lenses (marked M in the focal length indications here). The double-headed arrows indicate the macro range available with each lens. Standard lenses indicate possible, but not preferred 'combinations'.

The left hand column indicates the scales reachable with the 50 mm macro lens directly on the camera and with a 25 mm extension tube. The second column shows the available range with a standard 50 mm lens and extension tubes. The third column covers the ranges obtainable with the Auto Bellows and the fourth column the ranges with the PMT-35 outfit.

Choice of equipment combinations

The actual items of close-up equipment described in detail in the subsequent equipment chapters comprise numerous alternatives for various applications. How do we assemble the most suitable combination for a given purpose?

Apart from the lens—chosen primarily for the scale of reproduction wanted—we have to consider extension units to permit sufficiently close focusing, the focusing device itself and a suitable support for the camera set-up. These are again determined to a great extent by the scale of reproduction to be covered.

For low magnifications up to 0.5× (1:2 reduction) the 50 mm Auto-Macro lens is ideal, as it covers this focusing range with the built-in lens mount and most of the time permits hand-held shooting.

Other 50 mm lenses used with the supplementary lens or extension tubes cover part of this near range up to 0.5× magnification. The same applies to some of the other lenses combined with extension tubes.

A special case is that of low magnifications with long focus lenses, achieved with the aid of extension tubes. The purpose here is not so much getting large image scales but to avoid having to go too close to the subject for it.

For medium macro magnifications between 0.5 and 2× the 80 mm macro lens used with the Auto-bellows as an extension and focusing unit is ideal.

Two other alternatives for a range between 0.5 and 1× magnification are the 50 mm Auto-Macro lens with 25 mm extension tube, and the medium long focus lenses up to 135 mm with the bellows. For the 50 mm macro lens with extension tube, focus by the lens mount or by the focusing rail and stage; support the camera in both cases on the copy stand or a table tripod.

From about same-size reproduction upwards the 50 mm Auto-Macro lens, other 50 mm lenses and certain other focal lengths can be used with the bellows. In this case mount the camera on a firm stand, preferably the VST-1.

For magnifications between 2 and 6× the ideal lens is the 38 mm macro unit with bellows and mounted on the VST-1 or PMT-35 stand. (The copy stand is no longer rigid enough at this magnification range.)

For a range from about 5 to 12× magnification use the

MACRO EQUIPMENT COMBINATIONS

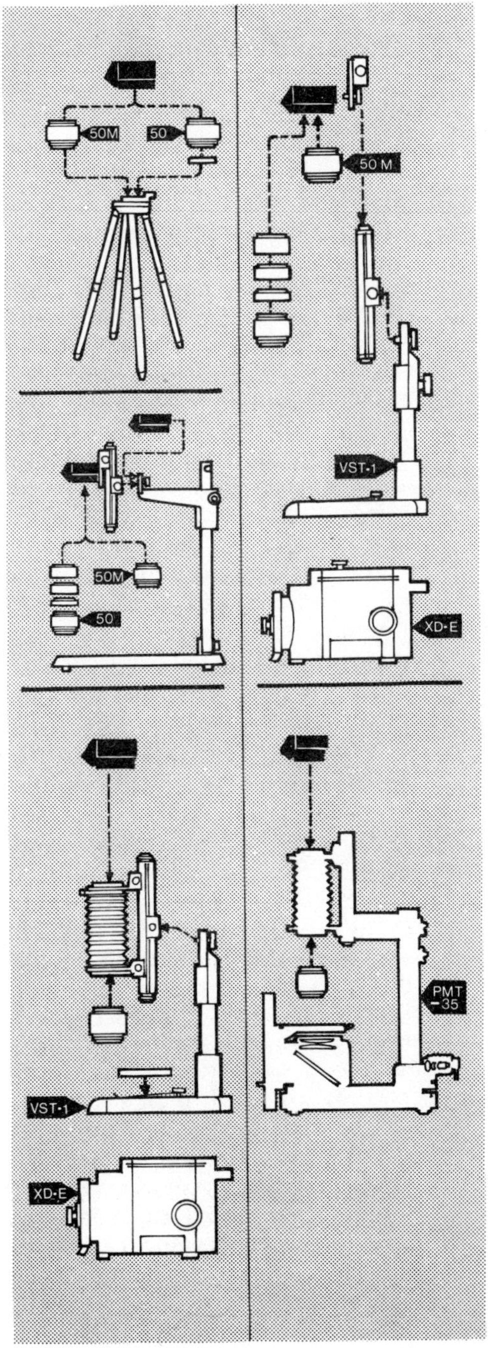

The simplest close-up combination *(upper left)*: cameras with 50 mm macro lens or with standard lens and supplementary lens, on tripod or handy copy stand.

Steadier support: copy stand with camera body direct or via focusing stage and rail *(lower left)*, plus macro lens or standard lens with extension tubes.

More rigid copy stand with greater lighting scope: VST-1 stand *(upper right)* with or without the X-DE transilluminator, focusing stage and focusing rail plus a macro lens or other lens with extension tubes.

A more versatile mode for higher magnifications: VST-1 with Auto bellows *(bottom left)* and macro lenses.

The most sophisticated specialised macrophoto unit: PMT-35 outfit *(bottom right)*.

same set-up but with the 20 mm macro lens.

The table of recommended close-up/macro combinations (see Chpt. *Facts and figures*) sums up main useful set-ups along these lines.

All close-up and macro set-ups can be combined with the motor drive and the 250-exposure film back.

Squaring up with a mirror

For copying and close-ups of flat originals, all-over sharpness depends a lot on setting up the camera so that its axis is exactly at right-angles to the plane of the original being copied. A useful aid is a mirror. It should be flat and unmounted, so that the front surface is strictly parallel with any surface on which you place the mirror. A high-quality plate glass mirror (but not in a frame) is suitable; so is the PM-ELCS centering mirror. On the mirror surface draw a circle about 10 mm in diameter approximately in the centre, using a solvent-based fine felt pen (as employed for writing on glass or china). Then use the mirror as follows:

Mount the camera on the copy stand and place the mirror on the original being copied on top of the baseboard (or on the table when using the table clamp). Move the mirror into the middle of the field of view and focus the camera lens on the circle in the mirror centre. In the mirror you will also see a somewhat blurred reflected image of the camera lens. Adjust the mirror position so that its circle appears exactly centred in the lens's reflection in the mirror.

Now check the location of the centre spot of the camera's focusing screen with respect to the mirror circle. If the central focusing screen spot is also concentric with the mirror circle and the lens reflection, the camera is correctly squared up to the subject plane. If the central focusing screen spot is not centred over the mirror circle and lens reflection, adjust the camera direction to get this spot centred. To check their concentric alignment, you may have to move the focus setting of the lens to see the circle and the lens reflection reasonably sharp alternately.

A lateral camera correction is fairly easy; just swing the camera stand about the tripod screw with which it is fixed to the copy stand camera platform. Longitudinal centering is more difficult as you cannot twist the camera platform up or down. But tightening the holding screw in the camera platform can noticeably affect centering.

This squaring up procedure, while particularly useful for copying, works equally with other camera supports, for instance a tripod with ball-and-socket or pan-tilt head to point the camera down on the floor. The felt pen circle easily wipes off the mirror afterwards.

Close-up focusing

Unlike subjects at medium to far distances, close-up shots are best focused by adjusting the distance between the subject and the whole camera assembly and not by altering the lens extension. This is because (a) movement of the lens at around same-size reproduction involves only very gradual sharpness change and is therefore inexact, and (b) because in macrophotography we normally aim at a specific reproduction scale and changing the lens/film plane distance changes the scale.

The correct procedure is therefore first to select the lens extension according to the wanted image scale. Go by the scales on the Auto-bellows rail (for certain lenses), on the PMT-35 bellows rail, by the scale on the Auto-Macro lens mount or by the appropriate tables for close-up scales of reproduction (see Chpt. *Facts and figures*).

With bellows units then tightly clamp the front and rear (lens and camera) standards. When using lenses on extension tubes, preferably set the lens to either infinity or its nearest setting; this reduces the risk of accidentally upsetting a pre-selected scale.

This is a convenience rule rather than an optical law; intermediate focusing mount settings are of course usable but you will risk changing the focused setting while you handle the lens for other purposes, e.g. stopping down. If you always make it a rule to use the lenses at infinity or the close limit, it is easy to check instantly whether the lens is at its correct extreme setting all the time. With the extension tubes the magnification differences between the infinity and closest focus mount settings are not that great, anyway. And if you use a lens on the bellows, it is simpler to restrict your variables by using only the bellows adjustment and leaving the lens at the infinity setting.

This does not quite apply to the 50 mm Auto-Macro lens whose extreme focusing range is part of its reason of being. But when using this lens on the bellows always keep it focused at the closest setting to benefit from the near focusing range correction. (This applies also when the lens is retro-mounted.)

Finally, fine focus by adjusting the camera/subject distance: turn the focusing knob of the tripod block on the bellows or the focusing rail, turn the focusing knob of the focusing stage or adjust the subject stage on the PMT-35 outfit. With the copy stand the fine adjustment of the arm can also serve for fine focusing, but the focusing rail and stage are more precise.

Near focusing by lens adjustment remains the suitable way with the Auto-Macro lens mentioned above and when using the Handy copy stand as there the subject distance is fixed. Another exception is focusing by the zoom adjustment of zoom lenses when used with extension tubes.

Once the image is sharply focused, also clamp the focusing knob or adjustment. With the camera pointing vertically downwards, the camera assembly may otherwise move down on the bellows or focusing rail under its own weight.

Screen selection and aerial focusing

In the close-up range up to about 0.5 × (1:2 reduction) the microprism screens (especially 1–2), the fine grain matt (1–8) and wedge (1–13) screens are adequate. At larger scales, microprism spots and rangefinder wedges rapidly become useless owing to the relatively small effective aperture while the grain even of the fine-grained screens tends to be disturbing. Here aerial focusing on the clear centre spot of the macro screens (1–11, 1–12) is more convenient. The sharp image plane is then sufficiently localised even on a clear screen to permit accurate sharpness adjustment of this so-called aerial image. This method is suitable mainly for magnifications above about 3 ×, i.e. with the bellows.

When sharply focused, the image is located in the plane of the crosshair graticule marks of the screen and you must therefore focus your eye accurately on these marks. This requires the Varimagni finder with its focusing eyepiece. For high-magnification macro-photography you usually have the camera set up vertically on a stand

(VST-1 or PMT-35) so you need the Varimagni finder for convenient horizontal viewing, anyway.

Focus the eyepiece of the Varimagni finder unit until the hairline graticule of the screen appears clear and sharp. These crosshairs are actually pairs of fine lines, 0.05 mm apart, intruding into the centre circle from the two sides, top and bottom. When the Varimagni is correctly focused, you should clearly see the two separate lines of each pair. With the combined camera and Varimagni finder magnification ($5\frac{1}{2}\times$ at the normal Varimagni setting) the visual depth of field is small enough so that you see the image sharply only if it is correctly focused in the plane of the graticule marks. So adjust the camera focus until this image appears at maximum sharpness. The lens must of course be at full aperture during focusing.

As a check move the eye slightly to and fro sideways behind the eyepiece: at the sharp focus setting the image detail must not shift relative to the graticule lines. If it does, this slight image parallax means that the image projected by the camera lens is not exactly in the correct graticule plane. Adjust the camera focus (not the Varimagni eyepiece focus) accordingly. By switching the Varimagni to 2.5× magnification (11× overall) you get a still better check of the aerial image sharpness, though at the cost of not seeing the whole picture area.

Close-up depth of field

Following familiar depth of field trends the depth of the sharp zone in close-up and macrophotography shrinks very drastically as the image scale increases. In this range the depth depends mainly on the magnification (and lens aperture) but not on the focal length of the lens. Also the depth is virtually evenly distributed in front of and behind the subject plane; it is thus usual to quote total depth of field as the zone of sharpness from the nearest to the furthest subject point. The plane of maximum sharpness is in the middle of this zone.

At high magnifications the effective depth becomes a small fraction of a mm—this explains the need not only for extreme focusing accuracy but also for a very rigid camera support to avoid slightest variations in the subject distance. A close-up depth of field table (see Chpt. *Facts and figures*) lists the available depth at different scales of reproduction.

Moreover, the gain in depth of field by stopping down is limited in macrophotography by the magnification. This is due to diffraction of the light going through small lens openings. This diffraction, resulting from the wave nature of light, reduces definition—i.e. increases the circle of confusion or unsharpness limit. In effect, part of the depth of field gained on stopping down is at the expense of overall definition: we are obliged to relax our standards of tolerable unsharpness.

The same close-up depth of field table therefore also indicates limiting apertures beyond which the lens should not be stopped down at various macro magnifications. Thus above about 7 or 8 ×, the 20 and 38 mm macro lenses should only be used at full aperture—and even there some definition loss is involved at the highest magnifications. (That is the point where photomicrography through a microscope gives better pictures with more information content less degraded by diffraction effects.)

Two practical aspects provide some relief to these problems. The first and obvious one when you have to work at magnifications where diffraction effects become significant, is to take the picture at a lower magnification (when shooting on negative material) and enlarge it more afterwards. This is contrary to normal 35 mm photographic practice, but in this particular case yields often as good if not better results in terms of definition.

The second point is that practice is not quite as stringent as theory. At high magnifications, macro subjects show much more detail than we normally see on everyday observation, even through a magnifying glass. So the macro image appears fascinating through its wealth of detail and some definition loss may not be as obvious as it would in normal photography. That is also why the close-up depth of field table still gives values for apertures that are strictly speaking beyond the limiting aperture on theoretical considerations.

Checking the image scale

As image scale has come into close-up and macro considerations such a lot, just how do we find the exact scale of reproduction? The scale on the bellows gives an approximate idea. For an accurate value at low magnifications (reductions below 1.0 ×) place a ruler in the subject field so that the mm scale cuts across the central circle of the focusing screen. Measure the number of mm divisions that the ruler takes up within this central circle and divide by the diameter of the circle itself. The latter is 4 mm with most screens (including the 1–11 macro screen) or 8 mm with some screens (1–4 and the clear macro screen 1–12). If for instance the part of the ruler within the central circle is 16 mm and you are using a screen with a 4 mm circle, the magnification is 4/16 = 0.25 ×.

At higher magnifications it may be more convenient to measure the length that the ruler takes up across the whole screen width. Then divide that into the width of the screen frame on the OM camera, i.e. 35 mm. E.g. if the ruler scale visible on the screen extends from 12 mm to 87 mm, the length of the object space covered on the screen is 75 mm and the magnification 35/75 = 0.47 × or just over a 1:2 reduction.

At high magnifications with the VST-1 macrophoto stand or the PMT-35 macro outfit place a stage micrometer on the stage plate in place of the subject. This is a glass slide with a mm scale in 0.1 and/or 0.01 mm divisions. Again check how many divisions occupy the central screen circle and divide this length into the diameter of that circle (4 mm or 8 mm) to get the magnification. At very high magnifications it may be more accurate to measure the length of the scale micrometer within the width of the image on the screen and divide that into 35.

A special method with the FM mechanical stage is to line up a distinctive subject point with the left-hand and the right-hand edge of the screen frame, in turn using the Vernier adjustment of the FM stage. Then divide the exact displacement measured on the Vernier scale into the 35 mm of the screen frame width.

With a ruler or stage micrometer temporarily in place of the subject for checking the image scale, the focus setting may not be exactly the same for the subject and for the mm scale. In that case refocus only by moving the whole camera assembly and not by altering the lens extension (e.g. with the focusing mount or bellows), otherwise you also change the magnification.

Close-up lighting

Lighting of close-up items is simplified by the fact that illumination is easier to control over a smaller subject area. This applies especially to artificial light—though that may get more complicated in the extreme macro ranges.

For outdoor nature and similar close-up subjects you can often take the light as it is. If you specialise in nature close-ups, make a habit of carrying a fill-in reflector—an A4 size card (21 × 29 cm or around 8 × 12 inches) white on one side and covered with tinfoil on the other. It works wonders with directing light into deep shadow areas, especially in sunlight. The tinfoil-covered side gives more directional lighting.

If you use flash for filling in, diffuse the flash light by one or more layers of tissue paper placed over the reflector; at close range the flash is often too powerful anyway. As exact aiming of the flash can appreciably affect the exposure, use either the Quick Auto 310 unit for internal metering with the OM-2 (the ideal combination) or the Remote sensor on the OM-1. Flash is also better diffused if you are using it on its own. At close range use the flash with the bounce grip to permit separate aiming of the flash to overcome lighting parallax problems.

With many close-up subjects—for instance pathological specimens, engineering parts or catalogue illustrations and various product shots—even lighting is desirable to show up all detail without heavy shadows. This is best achieved with the gooseneck lamps of the Olympus lighting set used on their own or in conjunction with the normal copy stand. A small spotlight is often useful to pick out details of special interest or importance in the subject.

Transparency copying

Transparency originals (including negatives) to be copied cover large formats (for instance radiographs) down to miniature. The slide copier is particularly useful for the latter.

Place larger transparency originals on a suitable trans-illuminator and arrange the camera above it, pointing down (e.g. on the copy stand) with a suitable lens and extension tube—the necessary combination for the reproduction scale involved. The simplest transillumination unit is a light box—essentially a box with a diffuser illuminated from behind by tungsten or other lamps, as in X-ray illuminators, transparency display boxes etc. Any light source will serve for black-and-white transparency copying. For colour you need a source yielding a continuous spectrum, e.g. tungsten lighting or certain kinds of fluorescent tubes. This lighting must be matched to the balance of the colour film you are using, e.g. with filters (see Chpt. *Facts and figures*).

These units are easily placed on the baseboard of the copy stand while the camera points down from above—or even on the table if you use the table clamp to hold the copy stand arm. Another convenient source is the exposure unit of an office copier, especially if you can mount the camera above it with the Handy copy stand or even the VST-1 macro stand. An overhead projector makes an excellent light box for copying large transparencies used for overhead projection.

Light boxes and especially the exposure units of office copiers are suitable for large or small transparencies. Smaller roll film or sheet colour transparencies up to 10 × 12.5 or even 13 × 18 cm can be arranged on a glass stage supported above a sheet of clean white paper or card. This is then lit by suitable lamps—the gooseneck lamps of the copy stand lighting set or a pair of LSD 2 micro spotlights—to form a bright background for the transparency.

With all these arrangements mask off the area surrounding the transparency on the light box or stage with black paper or card to prevent direct light from reaching the camera lens. That would not only reduce the contrast of the reproduction but also falsify exposures.

Lighting for the slide copier

The built-in diffuser of the slide copier makes it usable with a wider range of light sources:

(a) *Daylight :* Point the hand-held slide copier assembly (copier plus camera on focusing bellows with lens or camera on focusing rail and stage with extension tubes plus lens) at the sky for both focusing and exposure. When duplicating colour slides, point at a white cloudy sky area rather than blue sky or directly at the sun. Alternatively point at a brightly lit white area (whitewashed wall or a large sheet of white card or paper set up outdoors). If such an area is sufficiently evenly lit you can do without the diffuser in the slide copier to permit shorter exposures.

(b) *Simple lamp:* The slide copier can stand horizontally on a table; place a desk lamp in a reflector a foot or so behind the diffuser of the slide/film holder. Mount the Varimagni finder on the camera for convenient viewing and focusing.

(c) *On a light box:* An upright light box or slide display cabinet can replace the desk lamp in the above arrangement. If the light of the box is sufficiently diffused, you can remove the built-in diffuser of the slide copier. Alternatively, the slide copier can stand upright directly on a horizontal light box or exposure unit of an office copier. Again the built-in diffuser of the slide copier may not be needed. The VST-1 macro stand makes a convenient support for holding the slide copier and camera assembly above a light box.

(d) *On the copy stand:* Mount the camera and slide copier assembly on the arm of the copy stand, pointing downwards, and arrange a suitable light source underneath. This can be a light box, a gooseneck lamp or an LSD micro spotlight pointing upwards and focused to an even spot covering the slide copier's diffuser.

(e) *Electronic flash:* Instead of a normal lamp place an electronic flash unit behind the diffuser of the slide copier. With the Quick Auto 310 connected to the accessory shoe 2 of the OM-2 the latter even controls the exposure automatically. The flash reflector should be about 0.3 metre or a foot from the diffuser.

Particularly convenient is a set-up on the copy stand with the QA 310 lying on the baseboard. Fit the flash on the Bounce grip; that way you can lay it down on the baseboard with the flash pointing reasonably straight up.

Macro lighting

The lighting requirements for macro subjects photographed at larger than natural size (usually with the camera on the bellows or extension tubes and mounted on the VST-1 macro stand or the PMT-35 outfit) differ

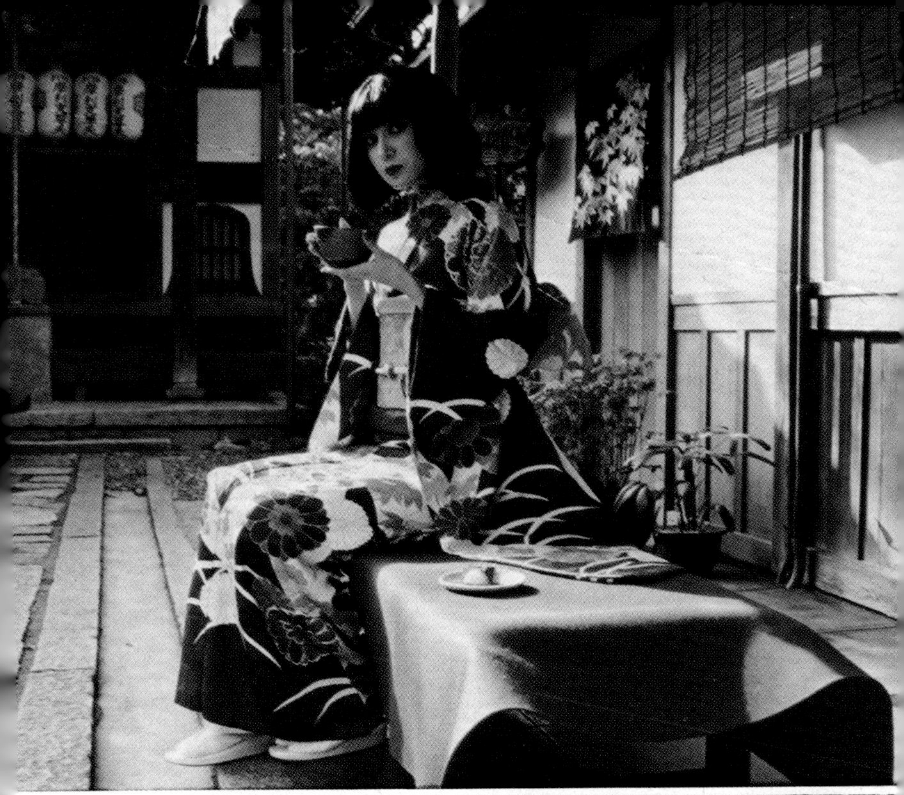
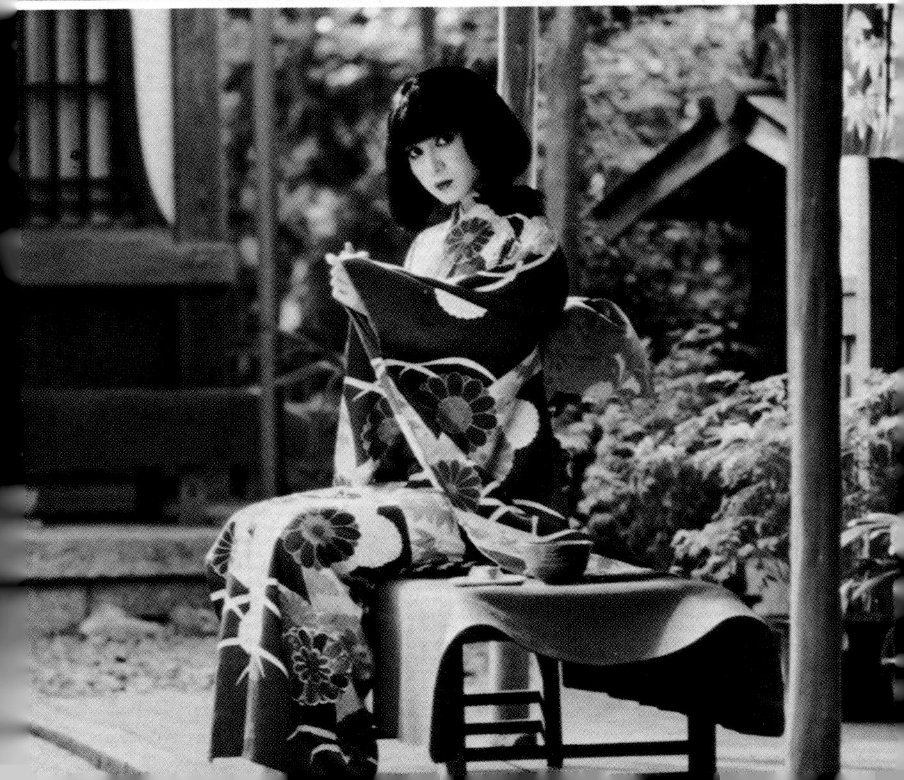

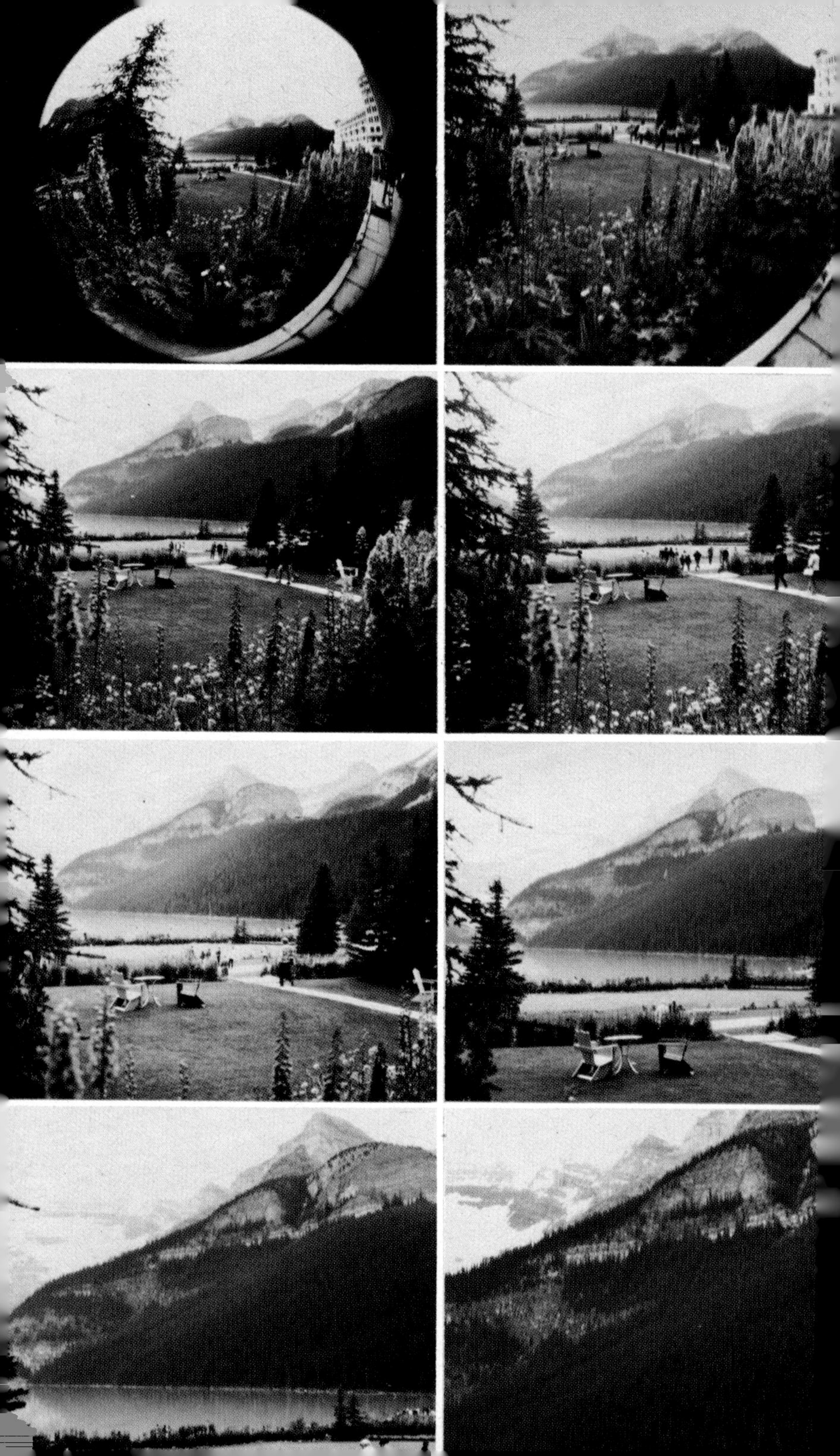

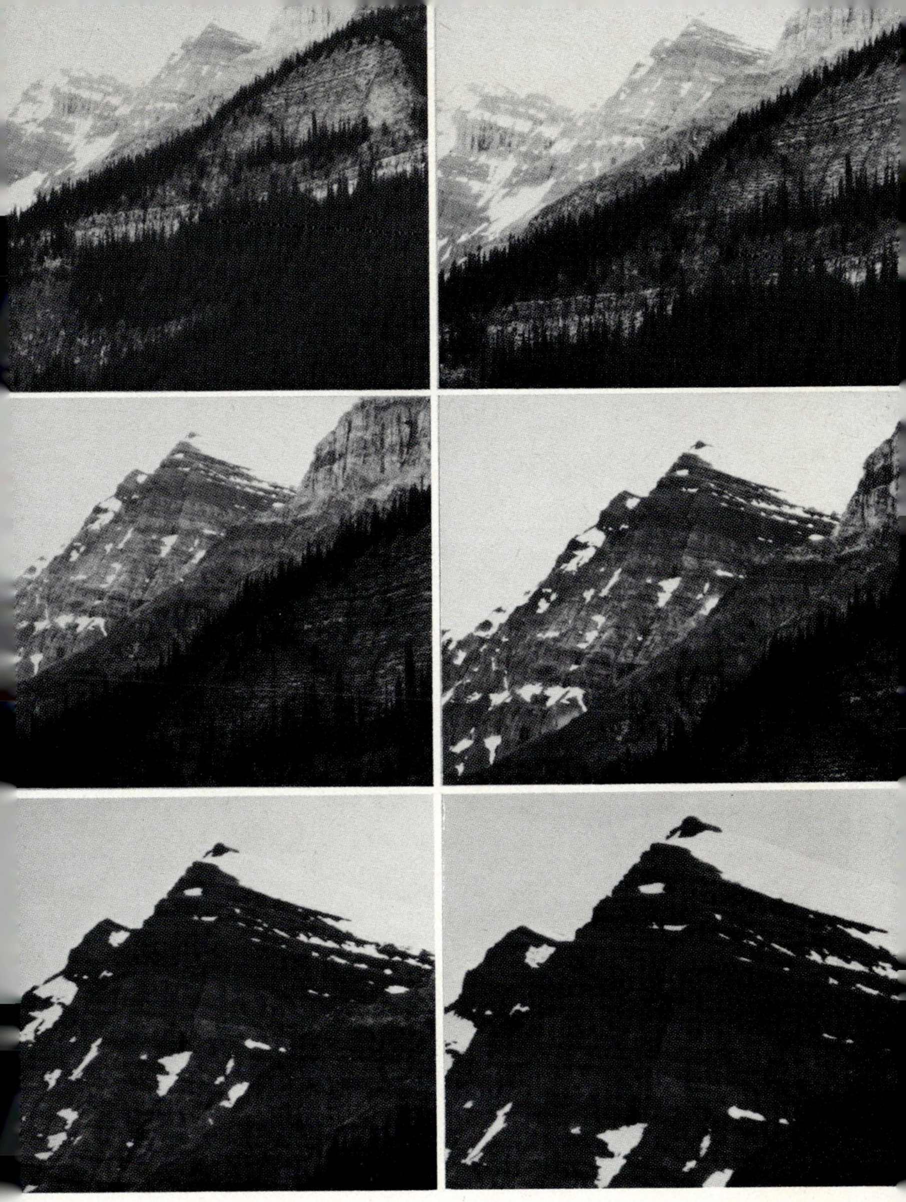

LENS COVERAGE

From the same position, subject size is governed by the focal length of the lens you use.

Above, left to right, top to bottom. 135 mm, 200 mm, 300 mm, 400 mm, 600 mm, 1000 mm.

Opposite, left to right, top to bottom. 8 mm and 16 mm fisheye, 21 mm, 24 mm, 28 mm, 35 mm, 50 mm, 85 mm.

PERSPECTIVE

Plate 1. Changing lenses and position to keep your main subject the same size alters the background. *Top* 35 mm, *bottom* 200 mm.

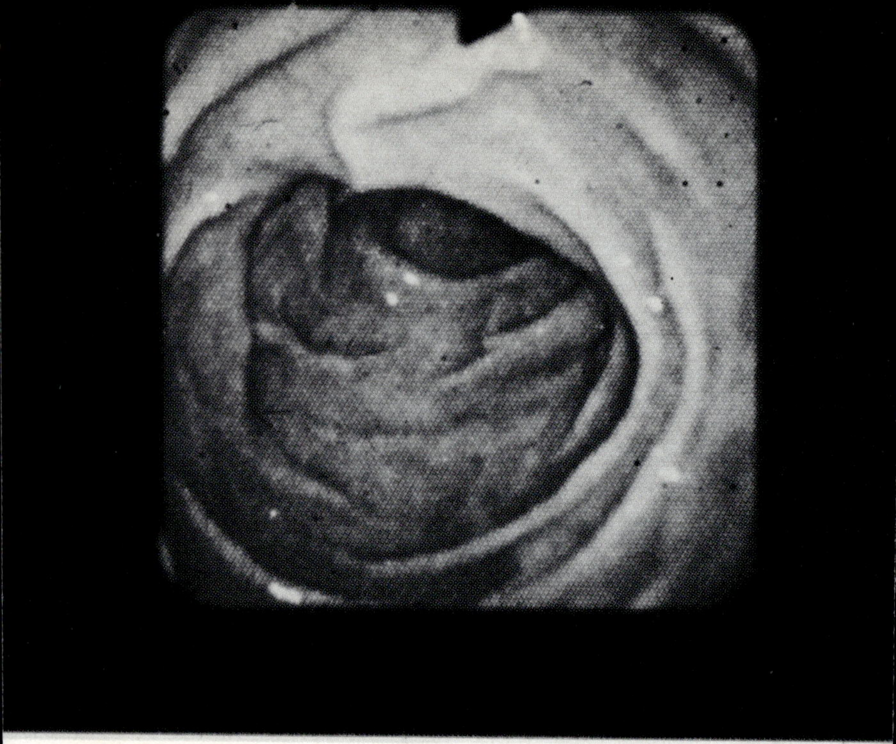

INSIDE VIEW
The OM-mount endoscope adapter allows you to photograph directly through an endoscope. The grain pattern is due to the fibre optics.

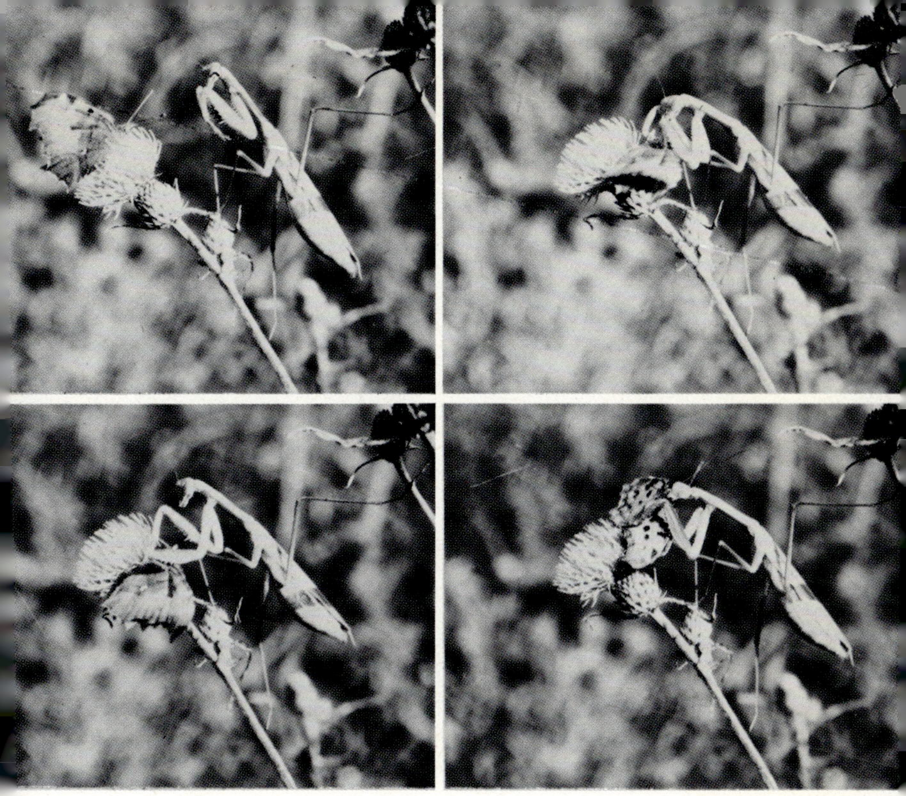

FEEDING TIME
Above. With the 50 mm *f*3.5 macro lens you can approach insects—such as this Praying Mantis having a meal. The Motor Drive shoots sequences even with remote releasing.

DEVELOPING EGGS
Plate 6. Photomicrographs taken through the PM 10A adapter mounted on a BHA microscope with x 40 objective and x 3.3 eyepiece reveal the mysteries of developing sea urchin eggs.

MICROSCOPE SLIDE
Plate 7, top. A biological transverse section of the gullet tissue of a bullfrog presents little problem. A x 40 objective provides the right magnification without recourse to an eyepiece. This stained section was photographed on colour film, matched of course to the light source.

MACRO SHOT
Plate 7, bottom. Close-up of part of a stamp—reproduced here about 20 x natural size—taken with the 20 mm *f*3.5 macro lens on the bellows.

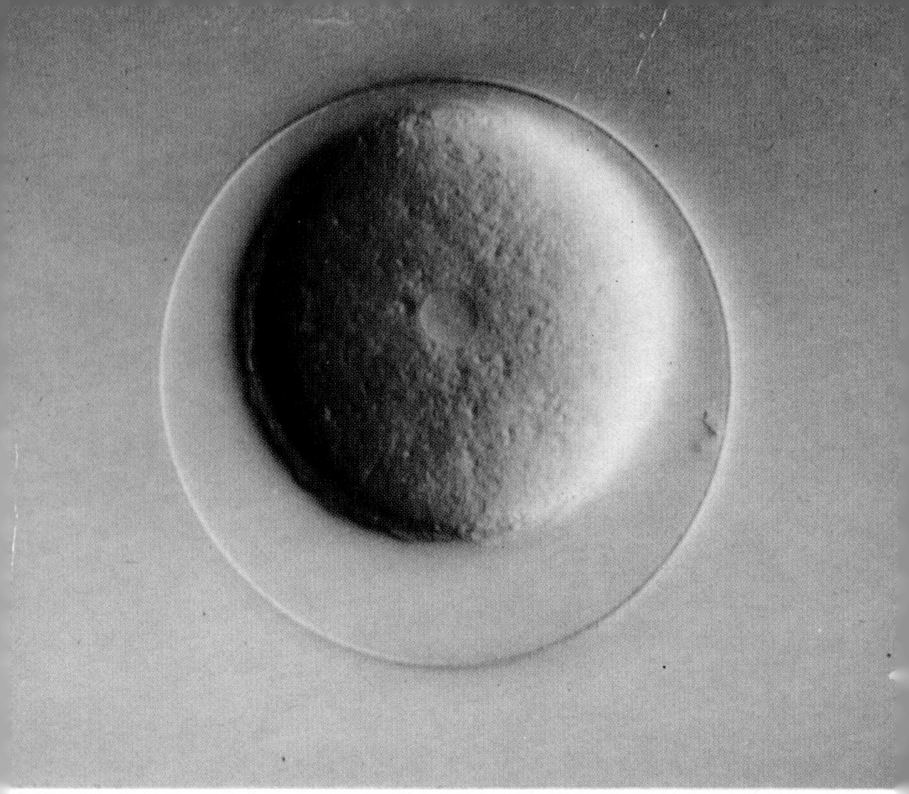
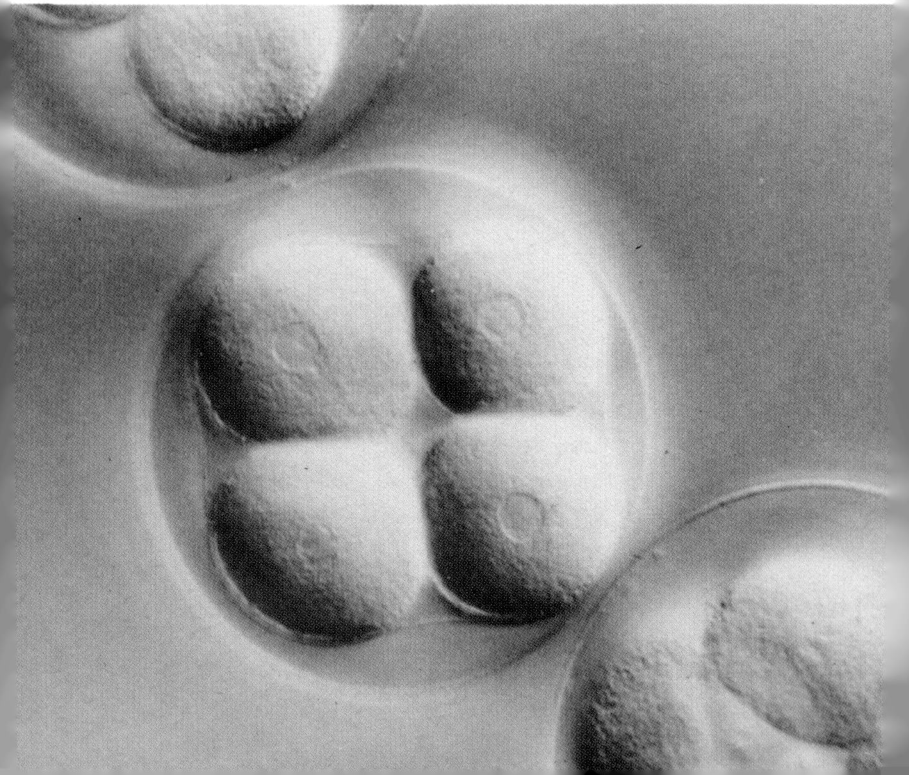

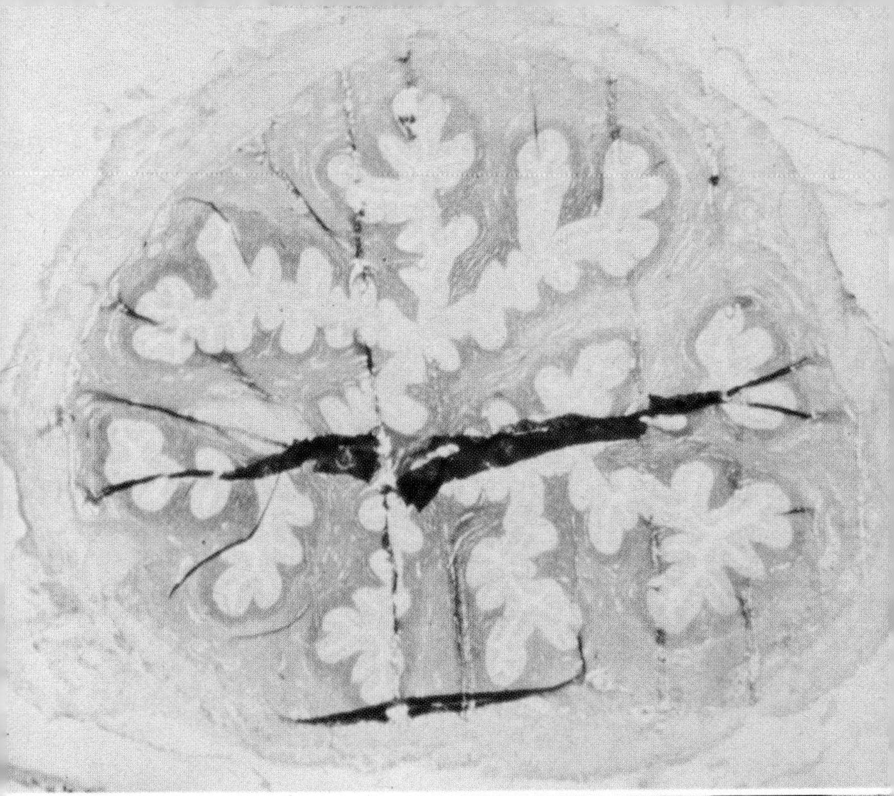

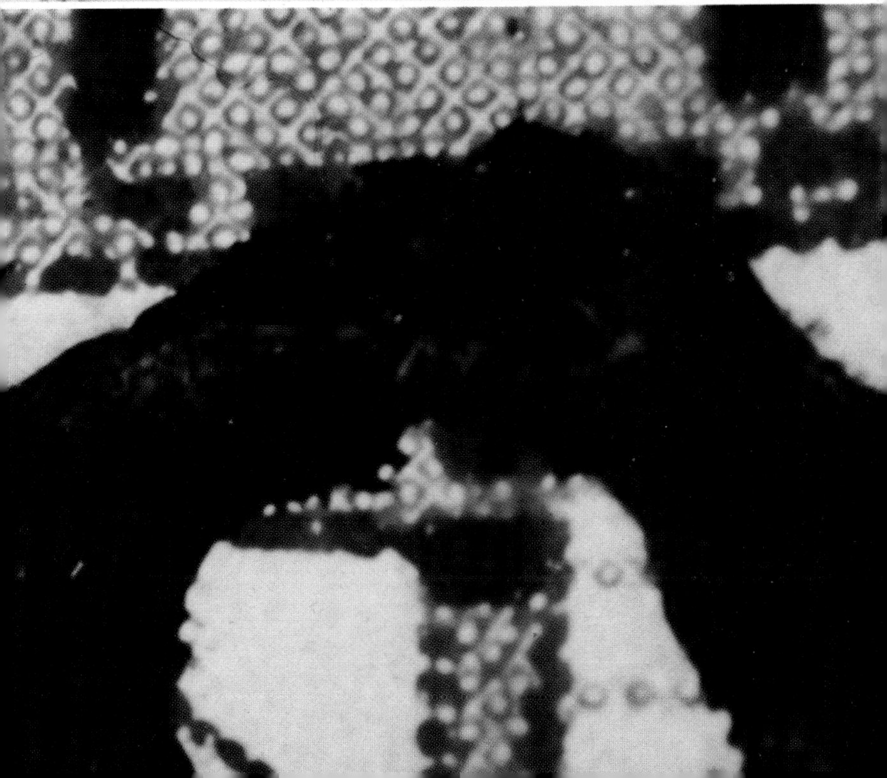

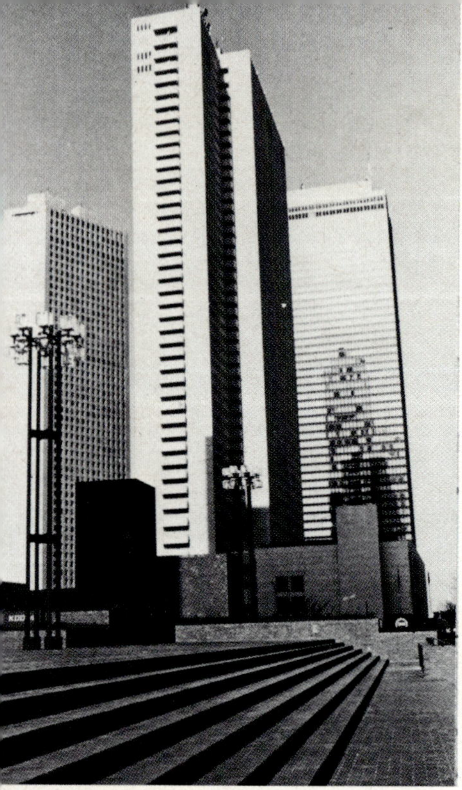

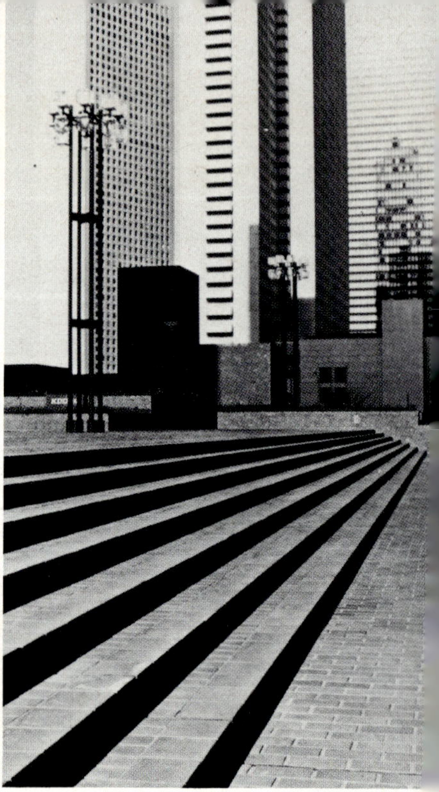

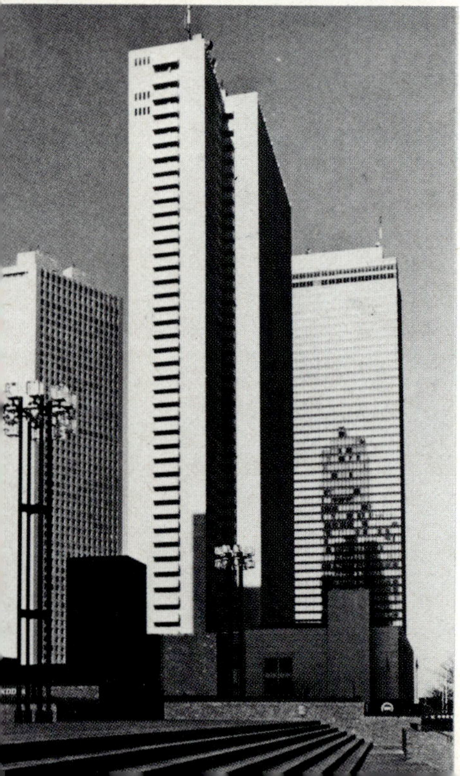

SELECTIVE WIDE ANGLE
Tilting the camera up when you photograph high buildings (*top left*) makes the structures appear to lean over; if you hold the camera straight (*above*) you may not get the top in and you include too much foreground. With the 35 mm *f*2.8 PC Zuiko you can shift the lens to include the whole building without converging verticals and without excessive foreground (*bottom left*).

All pictures in this section courtesy Olympus Optical Co.

somewhat from those of smaller-scale close-ups. For at higher magnifications even illumination by artificial light or specific lighting effects requires more specialised accessories. The lighting set-ups described below thus involve the selection of the following equipment: the VST-1 macro stand, the Auto-bellows assembly or the focusing rail with the focusing slide and extension tubes, stage plates and/or the FM mechanical stage, LSD micro spotlights, the X-DE transilluminator base, the TE-II transformer, incident illuminator mirror housings, PM-ELCS centering mirror, Lieberkühn reflectors and the PMT-35 macrophoto outfit. We are here concerned with how they are used in practice; the detailed handling of the various equipment items is described in the next chapters.

Normal reflected light

At magnifications around 1 to 2×, especially with the 80 mm macro lens, there is sufficient space between the lens and subject to use the gooseneck lamp holders of the Olympus lighting set. With reflector spotlights, they provide reasonably directional general illumination. Alternatively one or two PM-LSD 2 illuminators provide more concentrated lighting.

The LSD or LSD 2 illuminators are equally useful for low-angle oblique lighting, for instance to bring out the relief texture in coins and similar objects even at the highest magnifications. The small spot lamps of the LSD illuminators can here be brought near enough to the subject stage for sufficiently intense lighting.

Flash units such as the Quick Auto 310 (or 300) can provide the same kind of general lighting at lower magnifications as the gooseneck lamps or a broad-beam LSD illuminator. You will however need—at least temporarily—an additional lamp to illuminate the object during setting up and focusing. With the QA 310 the OM-2 can control the flash exposure automatically by the built-in camera metering circuit. At the macro scales we are concerned with here that is not usually possible with other electronic flash units.

With all macro set-ups check the lighting effect carefully through the viewfinder. With normal incident lighting watch especially for glare reflected into the lens from subject surfaces. In most cases you can reduce such glare by slight re-adjustment of the lighting angle. Highlights on shiny objects can be toned down by a correctly orientated polarising filter over the camera lens. That often also kills any characteristic surface sheen. To retain a hint of surface modelling, the coaxial front light systems with the incident illuminator mirror boxes or Lieberkühn reflectors (see below) are more useful.

Coaxial incident illumination

At higher magnifications with the macro lenses the space between the lens and subject is usually too small to introduce direct front lighting. Here the PM-EL mirror housings can be used to reflect light from the LSD illuminators down in the lens axis onto the subject.

The coaxial lighting set-ups are generally used with the camera on the bellows and the VST-1 stand or on the PMT-35 unit. These units are here used with the black/white stage plate. Use the white side for setting up the lighting and switch to the black side if the subject is to appear against a dark background. The FM mechanical stage can also be used in conjunction with the 20 mm macro lens. But it may obstruct the PM-EL mirror housing from getting sufficiently close at the higher magnifications with the other macro lenses.

Coaxial lighting with a spot lamp beam is different in character from diffused lighting at lower magnifications (which is flat), also from low-angle spot lighting (which picks out surface texture) and also from shadowless lighting with the Lieberkühn reflectors (which is again soft and suppresses surface texture). Coaxial lighting picks out highlights and surface patterning, as much of the light from the subject is reflected back along the lens axis. It thus differentiates strongly between more reflective and less reflective surface detail. This differentiation by highlights thus differs also from the texture emphasis by shadows with low angle oblique lighting.

Setting up and centering

Correct incident axial illumination depends on correct setting up and centering of the camera and lamp. Mount the camera and selected lens on the bellows in the usual way and attach the appropriate PM-EL mirror housing to the front of the lens. The most convenient way with the VST-1 macro stand (or copy stand) is to have the field lens window of the mirror housing face to the left or the right. With the PMT-35 outfit turn the field lens window to the rear (past the column) and set up an LSD lamp there.

As a first stage in setting up, place the subject on the stage plate, light it obliquely (to make it visible) and adjust the camera and bellows to the image scale you want. Set up the LSD illuminator so that it points horizontally and is in line with the centre of the field lens window on the mirror housing. Have the lamp as near the camera set-up as possible—that makes accurate alignment easier. Adjust the lamp direction so that the beam points squarely at the mirror housing opening. If you are using the white stage plate (or a plain white paper laid over the stage plate) the lamp should now project an evenly illuminated rectangle onto the stage plate. If the lamp is correctly centred, this rectangle should also appear regular with no more than a slight but even curvature around its four edges.

Ideally, you should re-adjust the lamp height when you change the magnification. With the 20 and 38 mm macro lenses the change in subject/lens distance is not very great between the highest and lowest magnification. Here the evenness of illumination will not in practice vary much if you leave the lamp at the same height for moderate changes in image scale.

With the 50 mm and 80 mm macro lenses this coaxial lighting set-up with the PM-EL 80 mirror housing only works at magnifications of 1 × or higher. With the VST-1 macro stand you will usually have to set up the lamp in front of the arrangement and not at the side to ensure that the illuminated field covers the subject field taken in on the film. To go beyond 1 × with the 50 mm lens, mount this with the front bellows standard reversed and attach the mirror housing to the rear side of the front standard. This gives more space between the mirror housing and the subject for magnifications up to 1.6 ×. With normal mounting of the macro lens the mirror housing prevents a closer approach to the subject beyond a 1:1 scale. The 80 mm macro lens is thus more versatile for this application.

At lower magnifications you can no longer get a large enough light spot projected on the subject to cover the full field of the lens. There it is better (and by now feasible) to use one of the LSD illuminators shining straight down on the subject area from a direction close to the camera axis.

Transillumination

Transparent or translucent objects may be lit from underneath. Most convenient with larger objects is a light box, as for transparency copying (see above). For smaller items photographed at 1:1 scale or larger, the X-DE transilluminator base provides the necessary illumination.

Set up the X-DE base and VST-1 macro stand on top of it. The built-in lighting of the X-DE base is simplest to use with the white back of the cylindrical reflector, but needs fairly long exposures and is suitable only for black-and-white photography. (You can compensate for low colour temperature only by filters over the camera lens.) Do not use the cylindrical reflector; this is intended for visual observation only when the X-DE base forms a substage base for a microscope. (The lighting with the cylindrical reflector is far too uneven for even black-and-white photography.)

With the lamp switched on, adjust the reflector laterally (by its pivots in the holding fork) and turn it by the knob in the X-DE base to centre the illumination in the plane of the transparent stage plate.

For colour photography—and also more intense lighting—remove the light source of the X-DE base and set up the LSD lamp behind it. This then shines through the opening left by the X-DE lamp to strike the white surface of the built-in reflector. With the LSD spotlight you can also modify the light quality with the lamp filters to match the colour balance of daylight or tungsten-type colour film.

Illumination is particularly even with the PMT-35. Its transilluminator with the built-in and supplementary condenser lenses evenly covers subject fields up to virtually the 95 mm substage iris diaphragm diameter. And this requires minimum lamp adjustment throughout the range.

Shadowless illumination with the Lieberkühn reflectors

This is suitable for high-magnification macrophotography with the 38 and 20 mm macro lenses, i.e. at magnifications from about 2 × upwards. The Lieberkühn reflectors direct soft diffused light onto the subject—the most effective way at the short lens/subject distances involved. In addition to the Lieberkühn reflectors this requires the shade stage plate with black or white centre disc on the VST-1 macro stand and X-DE transilluminator base plus the LSD illuminator. The same set-up is also possible with the PMT-35 macrophoto unit, shade stage plate and Lieberkühn reflectors.

When using the VST-1 stand with the appropriate bellows assembly mounted on it (camera, bellows, 20 or 38 mm lens in the PM-MTob mount) remove the built-in lamp holder from the X-DE transilluminator base and fit the plane reflector (PM-ELCS centering mirror). Mount the VST-1 stand with the camera assembly on top of the X-DE base. Insert the shade stage plate with the black or white centre disc (depending on the subject). Clip the appropriate Lieberkühn reflector over the lens. Line up the bellows on the VST-1 stand so that the lens is accurately centred above the centre disc of the shade stage plate. Locate the subject on this disc. Arrange the LSD illuminator, with the lamp centred and focused for a parallel beam, about 15 cm or 6 inches behind the X-DE base so that the beam projects through the lamp holder opening in the rear of the X-DE.

The centre disc shields the lens from the direct light beam while allowing the light to pass round it for reflection from the Lieberkühn. Even the white centre disc is sufficiently opaque not to pass direct light into the lens.

Do not use this lighting technique with objects substantially larger than the centre discs of the stage plate. Otherwise the object may obstruct part of the light to the Lieberkühn reflector, so making the lighting uneven. There ring lighting or light tents are better.

Carefully wipe off any fingermarks etc. (which might just show up in the picture—especially with the black centre disc) before inserting the centre discs in the stage plate.

Adjust the lamp position and the X-DE mirror so that the light beam is centered on the mirror. Place the subject on the centre disc of the stage plate and adjust the bellows assembly for the magnification you want and for approximately sharp focus. Focus the beam of the LSD illuminator so that on reflection upwards through the shade stage plate it just fills the area of the Lieberkühn reflector. You can check this from the front of the set-up by watching the reflection of the Lieberkühn in the surface of the stage plate. At the correct setting this reflected image of the Lieberkühn should appear evenly illuminated, with the shadow of the centre disc centered in the reflected image of the Lieberkühn. At this setting the centre disc and subject also appear at their brightest—particularly noticeable with the white centre disc. You may have to adjust both the lamp focus and the mirror angle in the X-DE base to obtain this correct illumination. Also, the lens axis must be accurately centered over the shade plate centre disc. The iris diaphragm of the LSD spotlight should of course be fully open.

Adjust the final magnification and exact focus of the camera and bellows, then recheck the illumination once more and re-adjust if necessary. At this stage only the slightest refocusing of the lamp should be necessary. Then proceed with taking the picture.

The procedure is simpler with the PMT-35 outfit used with the shade stage plate and Lieberkühn reflectors, as the light beam from the illuminator is there centered and focused via the fixed mirror of the illuminator. You only have to fit the stage plate with centre disc, the lens and appropriate Lieberkühn reflector. Do *not* use the supplementary condenser (normally needed with the 20 mm or 38 mm macro lens). Slightly extend the lamp socket from the lamphouse for an even beam spread.

SMALL-SCALE CLOSE-UP EQUIPMENT

For greater clarity the description of close-up and macro equipment in the next two chapters is broken down into two groups covering related equipment systems, either used together much of the time or of closely associated application. The first—in this chapter—deals with basic close-up equipment:

Simple near focusing aids cover the close-up lenses, extension tubes, the focusing rail and stage as simple means of convenient camera/subject distance adjustment.

The Auto-bellows is the principal macrofocusing gear with the macro lenses.

The slide copier and its accessories, generally used with the bellows, permit direct copying of 35 mm and some other transparencies.

The copy stand system covers stands and supports for close-up photography just below the near focusing limit of a normal lens—the copy stand, table clamp, lighting set and Handy copy stand.

The following chapter will deal with more sophisticated and specialised macrophotography accessories:

The macro stand system involves more elaborate supports for large-scale macrophotography: the VST-1 stand and its accessories, the stage plates and stages and the transilluminator base.

The macro lighting system encompasses the LSD miniature spotlights with their filters and transformer, the PM-EL mirror housings for coaxial lighting (with accessories) and the Lieberkühn reflector system for shadowless illumination.

The PMT-35 macro outfit is a comprehensive specialist equipment system for routine macrophotography with all the features of the bellows, macro stand and macro lighting systems.

The close-up lens

With some exceptions, most of the lenses for the OM cameras focus down to a closest distance that yields an image scale between 0.1 and 0.17× on the film. Certain macro lenses have an extended close-up focusing range or are designated for use with the Auto-bellows for macrophotography. For straightforward close-up shots with the standard and a few other lenses, rather simpler and less expensive aids available are the close-up lens and the extension tubes.

The close-up lens is a 2.5 dioptre (40 cm focal length) meniscus lens that screws into the front of the camera lens. It effectively shortens the focal length of the latter so that with a given extension of the focusing mount the lens can focus on nearer distances for larger reproduction scales.

There are two versions, with a 49 mm screw-in mount and with a 55 mm mount. The former fits the standard 50 mm lenses and a number of other lenses. The 55 mm diameter lens fits the 55 mm *f* 1.2 lens and certain other large-aperture long focus lenses. The front of the close-up lens carries a screw thread identical to the lens's own thread to take filters etc. When using filters with close-up lenses, always screw the close-up lens into the camera lens first and the filter into the close-up lens—not the other way round.

With any camera lens that takes the Olympus close-up lens, the subject distance with the camera lens set to infinity becomes just under 40 cm. The scale of reproduction depends on the focal length of the camera lens, as does the subject distance and scale with the camera lens at its near focusing limit.

The close-up lens is primarily intended for use with the 50 and 55 mm standard lenses (including the macro lens). It can also be used with a few other lenses, for instance the 100 mm *f* 2.8. Further, the close-up lens can be combined with the extension tubes (see below). The table of close-up ranges with close-up lens and extension tubes (see Chpt. *Facts and figures*) gives relevant subject distance and image scale data. These are mainly a guide to the selection of the best combination for different close-up ranges; the exact subject distance is of course established by focusing on the screen.

MACROPHOTOGRAPHY EQUIPMENT GROUP

This group system chart shows how the various close-up and macro accessories hang together.

5. Extension tubes.
7. Photomicro H adapter.
8. Lighting set.
9. PMT-35 outfit.
10. Copy stand.
11. Table clamp to take column of copy stand.
12. Auto bellows.
13. Focusing stage.
14. Cable releases.
15. Focusing rail.
16. PM-MTob lens mount.

17, 18. 38 mm and 20 mm macro lenses.

19. 50 mm macro and standard lenses.

20, 23. Lieberkühn reflectors.

21, 27. Close-up lenses.

22. 55-49 mm step-down adapter ring.

24, 25, 26. PM-EL incident illuminators.

28. VST-1 stand.
29. Stage plate and stages.
30. FM mechanical stage.
31. Handy copy stand.
32. Slide copier.
33. PM-ELCS mirror.
34. X-DE transilluminator.
35. Rollfilm stage.
36. PM-LSD 2 epi-illuminator (micro spotlight).
37. LSD transilluminator.
38. TE-II transformer.
39. Lamp filters.

Also associated with macro or usable from other equipment groups are:

1. Eyecup and eyesight correction lenses.
2. Varimagni finder.
3. Specific focusing screens (No 1-11 and 1-12).
4. Motor drive accessories and 250-exposure back.
6. Recordata back.

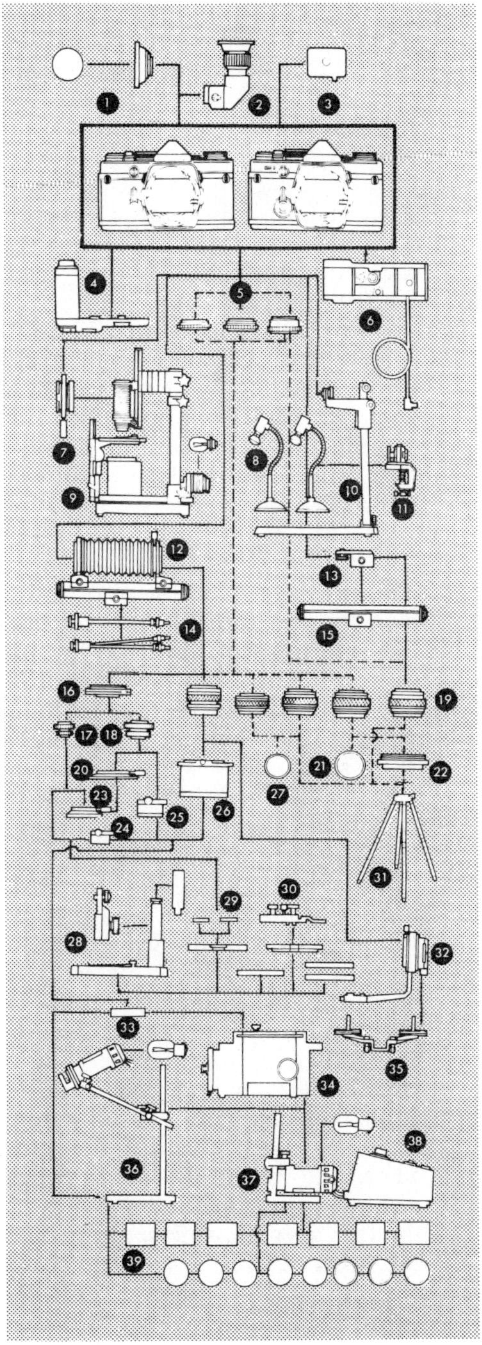

A close-up lens combined with a camera lens covers a greater focusing range than the same camera lens with an extension tube. Also the close-up lens does not interfere with the automatic aperture coupling of the camera lens. On the other hand at reproduction scales above about 0.25 the close-up lens tends slightly to spoil the optical performance of the camera lens at full aperture. Therefore work with at least two stops smaller than the lens's maximum aperture. That may be necessary for depth of field reasons, anyway.

Two close-up lenses may be used in combination on the camera lens. The performance of such a combination is however distinctly inferior to that of the camera lens with an appropriate extension tube or close-up lens plus tube combination. The close-up lens is also used to cover the near range with the Handy copy stand (see below, *Copy stand system*).

Extension tubes

The extension tubes of 7, 14 and 25 mm respectively fit between the camera and the lens to reduce the near focusing limit of the latter by increasing the lens/film distance. The tubes have a rear lens bayonet mount at one side to fit into the camera mount and a front camera mount at the other side to take the lens. The tube length—7, 14 or 25 mm—is the distance between the front and rear flanges and hence the additional lens extension provided. (These lengths are nominal; in fact the three tubes together add up to 47 mm.)

On mounting a tube on the OM camera, a finger protruding from the rear tube mount engages the aperture coupling lever in the camera mount to set the aperture input for the exposure metering to its starting value. A fixed stop inside the front of the extension tube engages the stop-down lever of the lens to stop the latter down to working aperture. Hence with the extension tubes the OM cameras operate only at the working aperture—either with automatic or semi-automatic exposure control.

Fit an extension tube to the camera in the same way as a lens, and then fit the lens in the usual way.

With a lens mounted on an extension tube, focus with the lens aperture ring set to maximum aperture. Setting the aperture ring away from its lowest *f* value directly

EXTENSION TUBES

Features of the extension tubes (front view, *left;* rear view, *right)*:

1. Red locating dot for lens.
2. Lens mounting flange.
3. Locking key.
4. Red locating dot.
5. Engagement finger to set metering system to working aperture measurement.
6. Bayonet camera mount.

Insert the extension tube in the camera's lens mount *(left),* then mount the lens in the front of the tube *(right).*

FOCUSING RAIL AND FOCUSING STAGE

Focusing rail (1-7) and focusing stage (8-12) elements:

1. Rail end screws.
2. Cm scale.
3. Upper rack for focusing stage.
4. Rail clamping knob.
5. Focusing tripod block.
6. Focusing knob acting on lower rack.
7. Rail.
8. Platform.
9. Shift knob of focusing stage.
10. Camera clamping screw.
11. Slideway for focusing rail.
12. Stage clamping knob.

To attach the focusing stage to the rail, unscrew one end, screw and slide the slideway over the rail *(left)* then secure the camera to the platform *(right).*

The movement of the focusing stage on the rail in the focusing block is 180 mm, giving a total of 360 mm, all controlled by rack-and-pinion gearing.

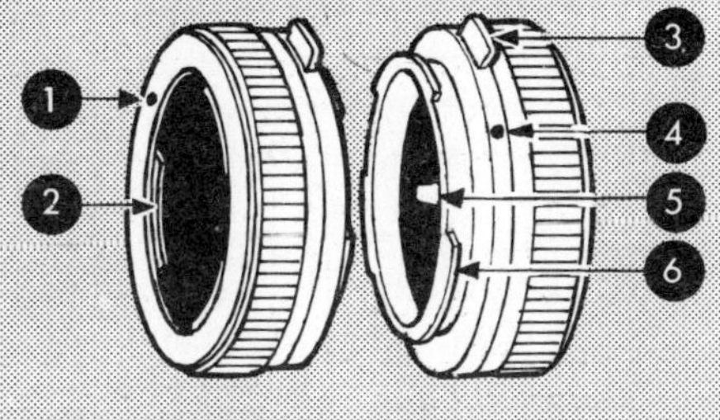

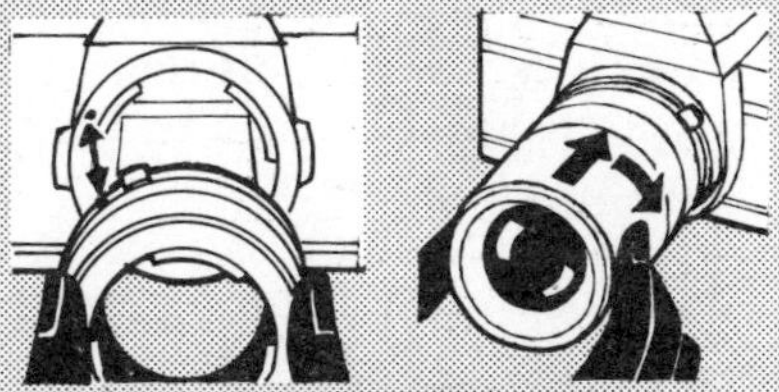

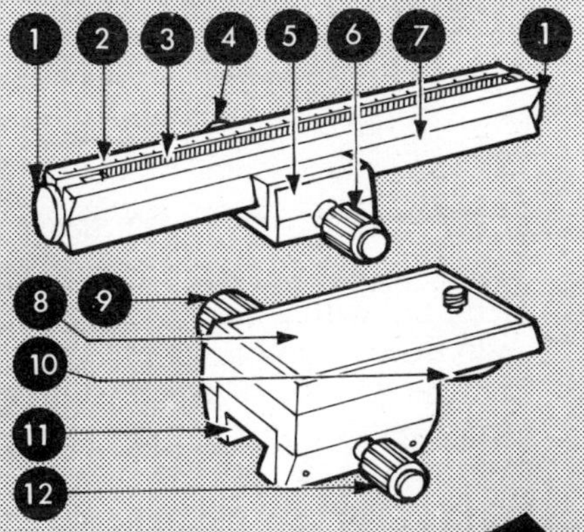

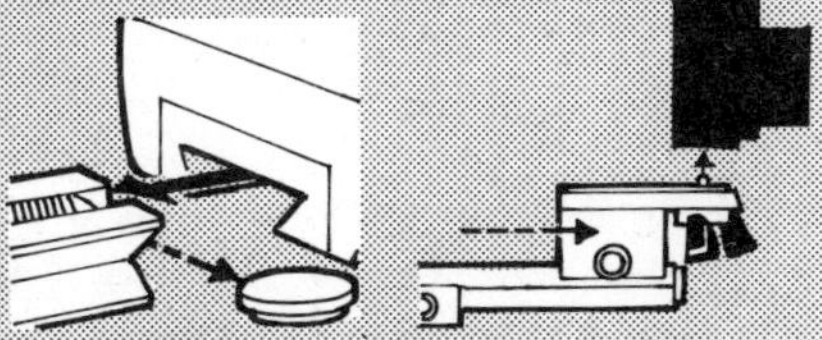

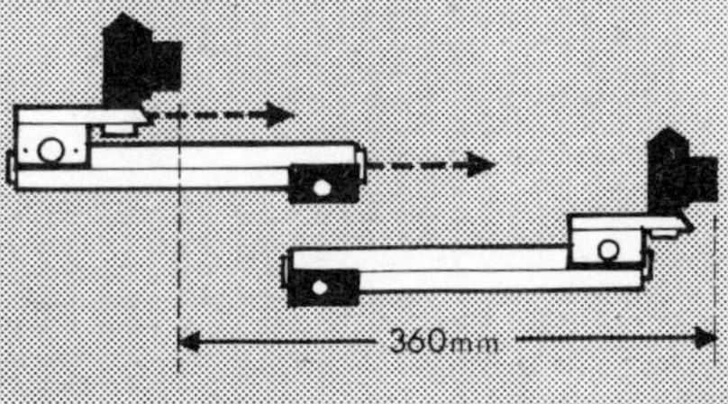

stops down the lens, and not only at the moment of exposure. Stop down only after sharp focusing; for this reason close-ups with extension tubes are best made with the camera mounted on a firm stand (copy stand, macro stand etc.). Focus either with the lens mount or—better still—by adjusting the camera/subject distance with the focusing rail and focusing stage (see below).

To remove the extension tube, first remove the lens in the normal way, then press the release key on the tube (in the same position as the release key on the lens), turn anti-clockwise and lift the tube off the camera mount.

Extension tubes can be used singly or in combination. The maximum extension with the three tubes together is thus 47 mm, which with the standard 50 mm lenses (plus the lens's own focusing movement) permits close-ups to just beyond 1:1 scale. The lens should however be stopped down to about *f* 5.6 or *f* 8 to counteract the lack of lens correction at extreme close range.

With the 50 mm macro lens the 25 mm extension tube alone is enough to extend the near range to 1:1 reproduction.

The focusing rail and stage

The focusing rail is a 230 mm long, precisely machined metal rail with a more or less flat top and bottom surface and cut-in lateral grooves. The top and bottom surfaces each carry a toothed rack. The top surface also has two marked scales: one in mm (with 5 mm interval divisions) from 0 to 230 and the other a series of magnification marks. These are relevant only to the use of the rail with the Auto-bellows (see below). A metal block with a nylon slideway moves along the lower part of the rail, driven by a knob with a pinion that meshes with the bottom rack. This block carries two tripod bushes for mounting on a tripod, or various other stands (e.g. the copy stand, VST-1 macro stand etc.) fitted with tripod screws. With the focusing block so mounted, turning the larger of the two knobs on the block moves the whole rail forward and back. Two screw-in discs, one at each end of the rail, stop the focusing block from running off the rail end.

This focusing rail assembly is identical with the rail and focusing block part of the Auto-bellows, the latter being completed by the lens and camera standards fitted to the upper rail section. The focusing rail cannot be used on its own, but must either form part of the bellows or be used with the focusing stage. The latter is available separately; if you have a bellows, you can remove the lens and camera standards and mount the focusing stage instead.

The focusing stage consists of a block similar to the focusing block of the rail, with the same type of nylon slideway, knob with pinion drive and clamping knob. This block carries a rubber-lined platform overhanging it and—in the overhanging portion—a camera screw to fit the tripod bush of the OM (and other) cameras.

The focusing stage fits over the upper section of the focusing rail and its adjustment knob engages the top rack. With the camera mounted on the platform, the two drive knobs of the pinions can thus move the camera along the focusing rail and the focusing rail in the focusing tripod block. Each of these units has a movement range of 180 mm along the rail; the total combined movement range is thus 360 mm. This is the distance over which the camera can be shifted towards or away from the subject—usually more than adequate for near photography.

The combination of focusing rail and stage is primarily useful for close-up photography with the 50 mm macro lens on its own, or with other lenses and extension tubes and/or the close-up lens. It can be fitted on a vertical set-up (copy stand, macro stand) or equally on a tripod or other support to move the camera assembly towards or away from the subject at any desirable angle. The combination is less recommended for large-scale macrophotography where the Auto-bellows is more flexible. The rail can also serve as a camera holder in photomicrography when lowering the camera—with a micro adapter—onto a microscope.

Assembling the rail and stage combination

To fit the focusing stage on the rail, unscrew one of the end screws and push the slideway of the stage onto the upper rail section. The pinion inside the slideway should then engage the rack of the rail. Replace the rail end screw which now also prevents the focusing stage from going off the rail.

The focusing stage fits over the rail in either orientation. It is usually more convenient to have both adjustment knobs (of the stage and the focusing tripod block) on the same side and both clamping knobs on the other side.

You can however also have the adjustment knobs on opposite sides.

To fit the camera, first mount the lens, extension tubes etc. on it. Move the focusing stage to one extreme of the rail so that the platform overhangs the rail end. That way the camera fixing screw is most easily accessible. Place the camera on the platform, so that the lens protrudes past the platform overhang and secure with the camera screw, screwed into the tripod bush. (If the lens is over the platform, screwing down the camera may lock the lens focusing movement.) Then move the focusing stage back to the centre of the rail.

A starting position with the focusing stage and the focusing block at the centre of the rail provides the greatest movement range in both directions. With a horizontal camera set-up—when the focusing block is mounted on a tripod—this arrangement also starts with the best camera balance.

Adjustment technique

To focus by moving the camera assembly it is generally sufficient to adjust only one of the moving elements. Preferably use the movement of the focusing stage. Keep the tripod focusing block near the centre of the rail and lock by tightening its clamping knob. With a horizontal camera set-up, then slack off the clamping knob of the focusing stage and turn its shift knob to move the stage forward or back. Do this after any focus adjustment of the lens. When the image on the camera's finder screen appears sharpest, lock the clamping knob to secure the camera setting.

With the focusing stage centered on the rail you have about 90 mm of movement each forward and back. If the camera needs to be moved through more than that, use the movement of the focusing tripod block as well. However, a horizontal set-up with the focusing tripod block at one end of the rail and the focusing stage at the other is very unstable. If this is liable to occur, move the whole support carrying the focusing rail assembly and start again with the focusing block and focusing stage roughly centred.

Normally avoid turning either knob unless its movement is fully unclamped. This does not apply when the focusing rail is mounted vertically, for instance on the copy stand or macro stand. There the focusing rail and stage will shift downwards under the weight of the camera. In this case clamp both knobs sufficiently to stop the movement of the assembly under its own weight, but to allow it still to move for focusing. Be sure to clamp the knobs firmly when the best setting is obtained.

With a vertical set-up, balancing problems are far less serious and the focusing block may well end up quite some way away from the focusing stage on the rail.

For very short subject distances move the focusing stage to the front of the rail so that the camera points over the overhanging platform, lock the stage and then focus by adjusting the rail in the focusing block. That way the end of the rail cannot interfere with the subject. (The front of the rail does not however intrude into the field of view with any lens likely to be used for close-up shots.)

The Auto-bellows

The Auto-bellows is the most important close focusing accessory of the Olympus OM system. The 'Auto' designation refers to its built-in provision (when using auto-coupled camera lenses) for full-aperture viewing and stopping down the working aperture immediately before exposure. This involves the twin cable release (see below).

The bellows has a stepless extension range from 36 to 198 mm. This is the separation between the camera's lens mounting flange and the lens's rear mounting surface. When a lens is normally mounted in the camera, this separation is zero, i.e. the camera mounting flange and rear lens mounting surface are in contact. Hence with all camera lenses the focusing range with the bellows starts from a certain near distance and extends to much nearer ones.

The Auto-bellows consists of a rail that moves in a focusing tripod block and in turn carries rigid front and rear standards (also described as the lens mount board and camera body mount boards) to take the lens and OM camera body respectively. The two standards are connected by a bellows fixed to the rear standard but capable of being clipped to (and unclipped from) the front lens standard.

The standards run on a 230 mm long precisely machined metal rail. This has a toothed rack each along a top and a bottom surface, and the standards can be moved back and forth by two pinion drives. The rail in turn moves in the focusing tripod block with another rack-and-pinion drive. This block has two tripod bushes for mounting the rail (and the whole bellows) on a tripod, copy stand, macro stand or other support.

The rail with the focusing tripod block and a pair of screws that fit into each rail end (to prevent the focusing block or the standards from running off the rail) make up a unit identical with the focusing rail (see above). The Auto-bellows is thus convertible to the focusing rail (for use with the focusing stage) on unscrewing the end screws of the rail and pulling off the two standards with the bellows.

Normally the rail is fully assembled with the focusing tripod block fitted to the underside of the rail and the standards to the top side—i.e. the side carrying a mm scale and other markings. When assembling the bellows from their components, unscrew the rail end screws and push the lens standard over the front end of the rail. This is the end with the lower scale numbers—i.e. from 0 (not marked) to 50 and upwards. The bayonet lens mounting flange and the OLYMPUS name should normally face towards the front end of the rail. About 25 mm from this end the rail also carries a white and orange line mark. When pushing the standard over the rail be sure that the clamping knob (the smaller knob on the standard) is slack.

Similarly mount the rear standard with the bellows over the rear end of the rail—where the scale goes beyond 200; there is also an orange $f = 80$ mm marking. The AUTO BELLOWS name in this case must face the end of the rail and the loose bellows extend towards the other standard. Pull the bellows forward so that the round ring fits over the ring protruding from the rear of the front standard. Then clamp in place with the small clamping screw on top of the bellows.

The focusing tripod block on which the bellows rail

AUTO BELLOWS

The components and the controls of the bellows are:

1. Lens, standard.
2. Lens mount.
3. Bellows clamping screw.
4. Bellows.
5. Front standard (lens) shift knob.
6. Stop-down lever.
7. Rail scale.
8. Rear standard (camera) shift knob.
9. Focusing knob.
10. Focusing tripod block.
11. Release lever of camera adapter mount.
12. Camera adapter mount.
13. Rear (camera) standard.
14. Focus and shift clamping knobs.
15. Rail screws.
16. Camera adapter clamping screw.
17. Cable release socket.

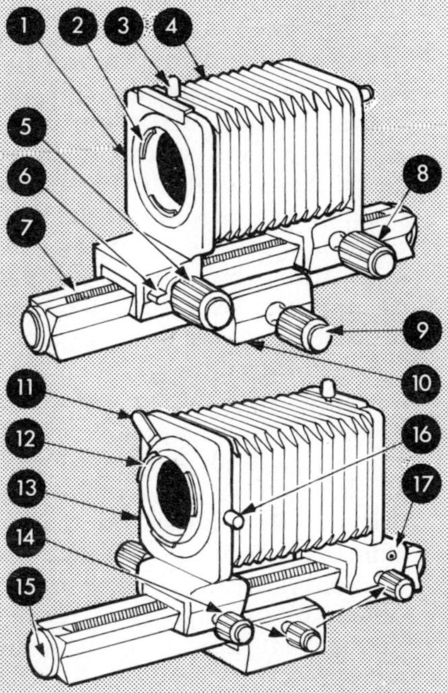

To fit the camera, attach the adapter mount like a lens, then fit it together with the camera into the rear standard *(left)*. To fit macro lenses, screw them into the PM-MTob mount then fit both into the lens mount *(right)*.

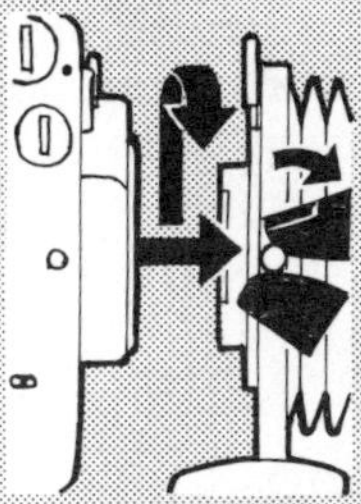

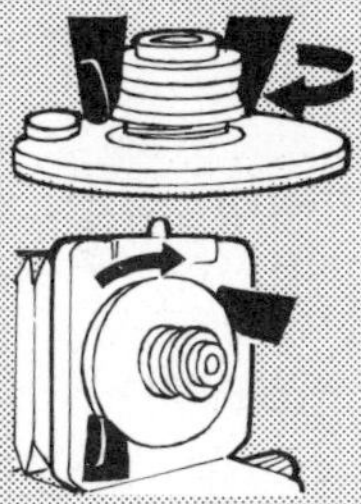

To reverse the lens, remove the lens standard, refit reversed *(left)* and connect bellows to lens front.

Turning the stop-down lever *(right)* stops down auto lenses to their preset aperture.

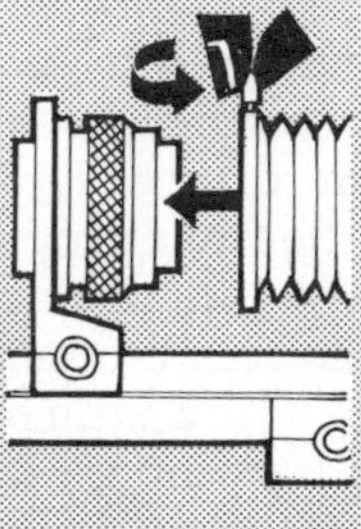

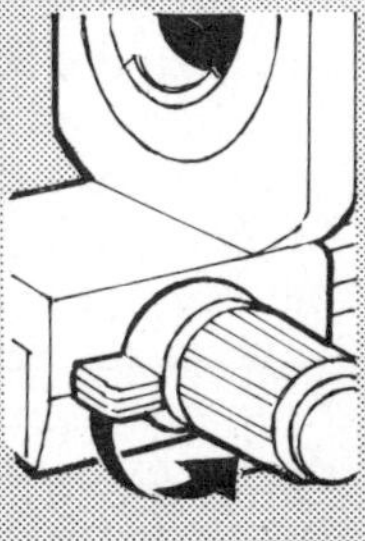

rides can be fitted in one of two ways: so that the large focusing knob is on the same side as the shift drive knobs of the front and rear standards, or so that the focusing knob is on the opposite side. Which way you fit it is a matter of convenience—in particular when the bellows is mounted on the VST-1 macro stand or other set-up. Nor is it any trouble to reverse the focusing tripod block: unscrew one of the end screws of the rail, pull off the block and refit it the other way round. (But the block must always be on the lower rack, i.e. opposite the one carrying the scale.) Refit the end screws to the rail to prevent any of the moving parts from running off it.

When the Auto-bellows is assembled and mounted on a support, with the camera and lens fitted, the drive knob of the focusing tripod block shifts the whole rail and bellows assembly back and forth. This is the correct way of focusing in macrophotography. Movement of the drive or shift knobs on the front and rear standards adjusts the bellows extension to select the scale of reproduction. This depends on the lens employed. For convenient reference to lens extensions on the scale, normally set the front standard to the front of the rail, abutting the rail end screw. Read off the bellows setting on the scale by reading the location of the rear end of the rear standard against the mm scale.

The minimum extension—with the bellows fully compressed—is there about 68 mm on the scale and the maximum extension with the bellows fully extended becomes 230 mm on the scale. The scale values are thus greater by 32 mm than the actual bellows extension (minimum 36 and maximum 198 mm). References in this book to bellows extensions will be to scale values.

Lenses and ranges

For optimum image quality the bellows are intended for use with the 80 mm, 38 mm and 20 mm macro lenses.

With the 80 mm lens the focusing range covers magnifications from about 0.3 to 2.3 × and subject distances (measured from the front of the lens to the subject plane) between 310 and 78 mm or 12.2 and 3.1 inches.

With the 38 mm lens the magnification range extends from just over 1.8 × to a little over 6 ×, with lens/subject distances between 36 and 32 mm (1.8 and 1.26 inches).

With the 20 mm lens the magnification range extends from about 4.5× to a little over 12×, with subject distances between 21 and 18 mm (around 0.7 to 0.8 inch).

The bellows can also be used with 50 mm and certain other lenses. The tables (Chpt. *Facts and figures*) show available and recommended focusing ranges.

Fitting and removing the camera and lens

Slack off the camera mount clamping screw on the rear bellows standard and lift out the camera body mount. This is a bayonet ring similar to a lens mount, with a 10 mm deep tube at the front, carrying a groove all round it. It has a bayonet catch like a lens bayonet mount but this carries a long lever covered with black plastic for easier access to the catch when the camera is mounted on the bellows. The rear of the bayonet ring also carries a protruding stud; this engages the aperture input to the camera's exposure meter, setting it to maximum aperture.

After removing the camera lens, fit the camera body mount in the same way as a lens. To remove the body mount press in the end of the long black lever and turn the mount anti-clockwise, then lift out.

Insert the camera with its body mount into the rear standard opening, line up the camera square with the rear standard and tighten the camera mount clamping screw.

To remove, slack off the clamping screw, withdraw the camera with body mount from the rear bellows standard and detach the body mount from the camera.

Fit any lens other than the 38 mm and 20 mm macro lenses directly into the front of the lens standard—as when fitting a lens in the camera. To fit the 20 and 38 mm macro lenses, screw these first into the PM-MTob mount, then fit the latter into the lens mount of the front standard like a lens. The PM-MTob mount has a red locating dot for correct alignment when mounting.

Retro lens mounting

When the 50 or 55 mm lenses are used on the bellows for magnifications larger than same-size, you get better definition by mounting the lens back-to-front. For this reversed or retro mounting fit the lens into the lens standard in the usual way, then unclip the bellows from the rear standard by slacking off the bellows clamping knob. Unscrew the front rail end screw and pull the lens standard off the bellows rail. Refit it reversed, so that the lens points towards the free bellows end. Refit the rail and screw. Finally attach the clamping ring of the free bellows end to the front lens mount.

On all 50 mm lenses usable in this way, the front mount has the same diameter (51 mm) at the attachment ring at the rear of the lens standard for fitting the bellows. The only exception is the 55 mm $f1.2$ lens with its 57 mm outside mount diameter. Here screw the 55–49 mm adapter ring (these dimensions refer to the screw thread diameter, not the outside mount) into the 55 mm lens; the front mount of this ring then again fits the bellows clamping ring.

Adjusting the extension

The lens/film distance, i.e. the lens extension or bellows length, is one of the main parameters in macrophotography: It determines the image scale. That is one of the reasons why in macro work you first select the lens extension, lock that setting and only then focus by adjusting the lens/subject distance.

It is also important to have repeatable extension settings, for instance to select a given image scale with the aid of the tables (see Chpt. *Facts and figures*). For that reason the bellows rail carries on its top surface a mm scale graduated from 0 to 230 mm. To set a given extension move the front lens standard fully to the front of the bellows rail (the front end should be the one with the low numbers on the scale) to abut the rail end screw. Lock the front standard with the clamping knob (opposite the shift or drive knob). Then move the rear standard so that the rear edge of the white nylon slideway lines up with the required mm setting. Lock the rear standard, too, with the clamping knob.

The mm scale figures are reference values, they are not identical with the actual bellows length. The actual extension (from the front lens mount to the rear camera flange) is 32 mm shorter than the scale distance on the bellows rail.

The image magnification is proportional, however, to the lens extension in front of its infinity position. So every extension increase equal to the focal length of the lens also increases the magnification by 1. For instance if with the 38 mm lens you get a 3 × magnification when the bellows is set to 113 mm, you have to add 38 mm to that to reach 4 × (bellows extended to 113 + 38 = 151 mm).

The bellows rail also carries a number of other markings opposite the mm scale. These are primarily intended for use with the slide copier (see below) but can also serve as quick fixed-scale settings with the 80 mm and 50 mm lenses. For this purpose line up the front of the lens standard with the white/orange mark opposite 25 mm on the scale—instead of with the front rail end. With the 80 mm macro *f*4 lens on the lens standard, move the rear camera standard to the orange 1 × mark for same-size reproduction and to the orange 1.5 × mark for 1.5 × magnification.

With a 50 mm lens (set to infinity) move the rear standard to the white '1 × ' mark (opposite about 110 mm).

Finally, use the white 1.5 × setting for the rear standard with the 50 mm macro lens, retro-mounted on the front standard, the latter being lined up with the front rail end. This gives 1.5 × magnification.

Lens focus settings

When using a camera lens, i.e. with focusing mount, on the bellows, set the lens either to its infinity or to its closest position as follows:

Set any normally mounted (not retro) 50 or 55 mm lens to infinity. (As this arrangement is not recommended for magnifications beyond 1 ×, you gain nothing by focusing on closer distances.)

Set the retro-mounted standard 50 or 55 mm lenses, *other than the 50 mm macro*, also to infinity. Focusing closer here in fact decreases the available bellows extension since it moves the lens backward away from the reverse-mounted lens standard.

Nevertheless, set the retro-mounted 50 mm macro lens to its nearest focus setting. This improves sharpness performance by bringing the internal near-focusing correction into action.

Set longer focus lenses, e.g. 100 or 135 mm, to their nearest focusing distance. This adds about 12 to 15 mm to the available bellows extension.

Focusing

The last adjustment on the Auto-bellows assembly is focusing by adjustment of the lens/subject distance with the large knob of the focusing tripod block. Be sure that the two adjustments of the front and rear standards are also firmly clamped. With vertical camera set-ups the weight of the camera unit, lens etc. can otherwise cause either standard to creep down.

Remember to unlock any movement to be re-adjusted. With the exception of the very last focus adjustment (see below) do not try to turn any knob while its movement is clamped. This puts excessive strain on the gearing and increases the wear on the sliding parts.

Once the focus is exactly right, also clamp the focusing knob. This movement can however itself shift the exact focus setting, especially at high magnifications. There is a trick of locking the clamping knob at the exact setting: while observing the image through the camera finder, hold the focusing knob with one hand and gradually tighten the clamping knob with the other. If this starts shifting the image focus, readjust the focusing knob to correct while tightening the clamping knob. Tighten the latter further and at the same time readjust the focusing knob again if necessary. This will only be a minute adjustment and is the one exception to the general rule of not moving any bellows adjustment while clamped. By alternately tightening the clamping knob and following up the focus as necessary, you end up with the assembly securely locked at the optimum sharpness setting.

Stop-down and releasing

With Zuiko Auto lenses, i.e. where the camera-mounted lens is stopped down to its working aperture by an internal linkage, the lens is open at full aperture when mounted on the lens standard of the Auto-bellows. You can stop down the lens to a preset working aperture by operating the stop-down (preset) lever surrounding the shift knob on the lens standard. This permits checking the depth of field at the working aperture, and also stops down the lens before releasing the camera (with a single cable release screwed into the release button).

For macro lenses without internal aperture coupling

(e.g. the 80, 38 and 20 mm lenses) stop down the lens manually. Depending on the lens, either:

(a) Preset the aperture with the preselector ring and stop down the lens with the stop-down ring (e.g. on the 80 and 38 mm lenses), or

(b) Stop down manually by turning the single aperture ring (e.g. on the 20 mm lens). Again release with a normal cable release screwed into the camera's release button.

The twin cable release

The stop-down mechanism in the front bellows standard for Zuiko Auto lenses can also be operated by a cable release. With the twin cable release you can synchronise this stop-down movement with the camera shutter.

The shorter of the release cables screws into the camera release button. The longer cable with an adjustable nipple screws into the cable release socket in the side of the front bellows standard—next to its clamping knob.

Synchronisation has to ensure that the lens mounted on the front standard is fully stopped down before the shutter is released.

The adjustable cable has at its end a knurled adjustment sleeve, a screw nipple and a knurled lock nut. Before screwing this cable into the socket on the lens standard, screw the lock nut against the knurled adjustment sleeve. Now screw the nipple into the release socket on the bellows standard. Next screw the lock nut down (against the release socket) as far as it will go. This is likely to expose a length of threaded shaft between the lock nut and the knurled adjustment sleeve. Screw down the knurled adjustment sleeve until it almost touches the knurled lock nut.

Screw the other cable release end into the camera's release button. Place the whole bellows assembly horizontally on the table in front of you, remove the lens and observe the coupling lever and stop-down ring inside the mount of the bellows standard. Operate the preset lever to see how far the internal stop-down ring moves, then return the lever to its open-aperture position. Set the camera—unloaded—to a slow shutter speed such as $\frac{1}{2}$ second. (Set the OM-2 to manual operation.)

Tension the camera and press the cable release plunger while observing the stop-down ring inside the bellows standard mount. You will probably see the stop-down lever and ring move through its full path, but pressure on the release plunger will not release the camera shutter. (If it does release the camera shutter, screw down the adjustment sleeve further.)

Now gradually unscrew the knurled adjustment sleeve of the cable end until pressing the release plunger trips the camera shutter *after* the stop-down lever and ring inside the bellows standard mount has reached its end position. The shutter should be released without too much extra pressure on the plunger. Unscrew the adjustment sleeve by a further half turn, then screw up the knurled lock nut against the adjustment sleeve to secure it.

Remount the bellows unit on whatever stand you are using and fit the lens. Now simply expose by pressing the release plunger: this stops down the lens to the working aperture before it triggers the shutter.

With slow shutter speeds always keep the release plunger depressed until the shutter has closed again. Otherwise the lens iris opens during the exposure. For long time exposures lock the plunger in the depressed position by tightening the clamping screw at the side of the twin cable release. Slacking off the screw allows the shutter to close after the exposure time selected on the camera or set by its electronic control (OM-2).

The slide copier

This attachment to the Auto-bellows holds mounted or unmounted 35 mm transparencies at the correct distance for convenient duplication or copying, rigidly connects the camera set-up and transparency and incorporates a diffusing screen for transillumination by various set-ups. It can be used with some of the standard or macro lenses of the OM lens range. A built-in bellows lens hood keeps extraneous light off the transparency being duplicated.

The slide copier takes a roll film stage as an accessory when handling long lengths of uncut film.

The main components are the supporting arm with a tripod screw at one end to fit the focusing tripod block of the Auto-bellows, a magnification indicating scale as an aid to setting up and a slide holder stage. The latter

SLIDE COPIER

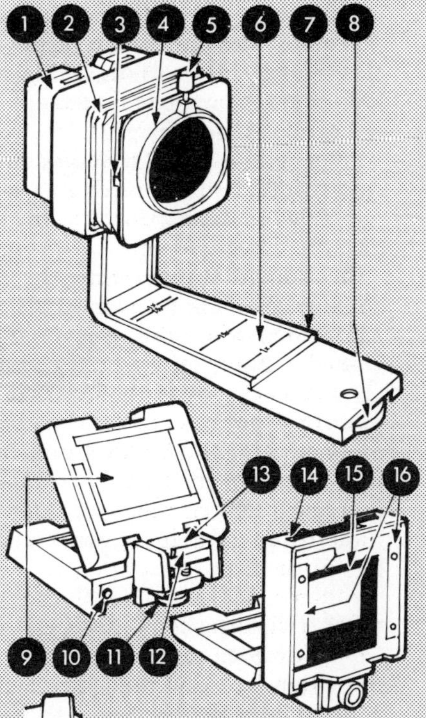

The parts of the slide copier are:

1. Slide and film holder.
2. Bellows.
3. Bellows coupling clips.
4. Bellows panel with lens mount opening.
5. Clamping screw.
6. Magnification panel.
7. Supporting arm.
8. Securing screw.
9. Diffuser.
10. Screw thread for roll film stage.
11. Locking screw.
12. Release.
13. Release key.
14. Slide slot.
15. Slide.
16. Guides.

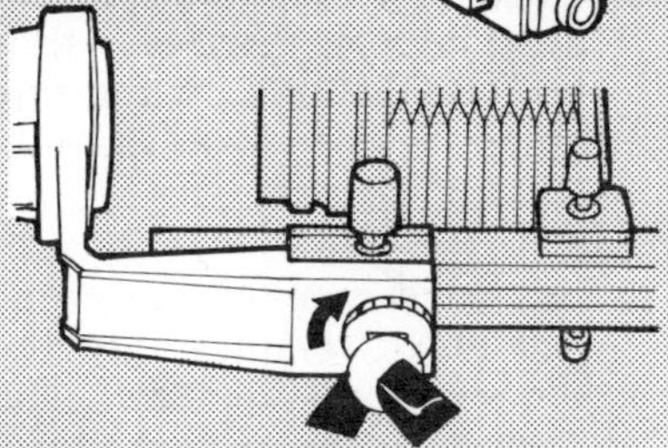

To mount the copier on the bellows, run the focusing tripod block forward and screw the stepped part of the supporting arm into the tripod bush of the block. Fully tighten the securing screw with a coin.

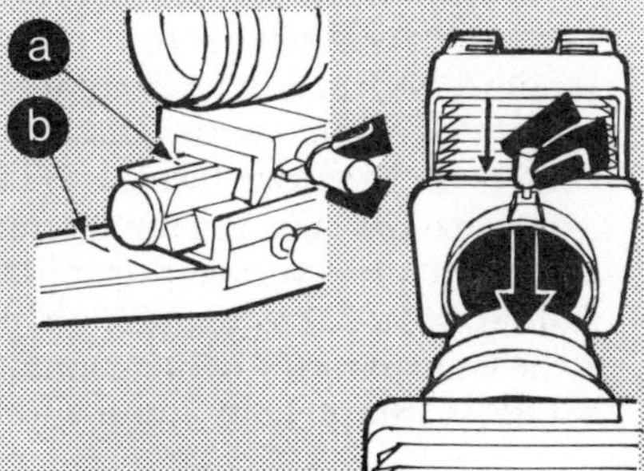

For normal copying *(left)* move the front standard of the bellows to the orange and white index mark (a) and the bellows rail in line with one of the magnification indicator lines (b).

Pull out the bellows panel and clip it to the front lens mount, securing it with the clamping knob *(right)*.

incorporates the bellows connected to a bellows panel that clips into the frame of the stage, and a detachable slide/film holder with the diffusing screen. The slide/film holder can be raised and lowered on guide rails to centre the transparency image.

The slide/film holder takes either:

(a) 24 × 36 mm colour or black-and-white transparencies in standard 5 × 5 cm (2 × 2 inch) slide mounts, or

(b) Negative or positive 35 mm black-and-white or colour film strips or even single films.

The maximum image size is 24 × 36 mm, but you can also copy half frame (18 × 24 mm) onto the full 24 × 36 mm image size of the camera. You can even enlarge 13 × 17 mm No. 110 transparencies in 3 × 3 cm slide mounts if these are fitted in 5 × 5 cm adapter mounts. The slide copier further permits copying by reproducing only part of a transparency image on an enlarged scale, though this of course makes image grain and sharpness loss more visible.

Assembling the copier

First assemble the Auto-bellows and camera so that the front standard is at the lower scale end of the bellows rail and the rear standard is at the upper scale end (200 and beyond on the scale). Mount the slide copier by screwing the supporting arm to the focusing tripod block on the bellows so that the latter is in contact with the stepped end of the arm. Screw together with the tripod screw which goes into the rear tripod bush on the focusing tripod block. Tighten this screw firmly with the aid of a coin in the coin slot. The bellows hood panel of the copier should at this point be fully pushed into the stage frame out of the way.

Fit the lens in the lens mount of the front bellows standard and preset the bellows rail and front standard according to the lens used. Then unclip the bellows panel from the front frame of the slide copier and extend it towards the rail. Fit the opening in the panel over the lens front and secure with the clamping screw. This bellows hood keeps extraneous light away from the front of the transparency being copied.

The 51 mm bellows hood aperture fits the front mount

of the standard 50 mm lenses (except the *f* 1.2), the 50 mm macro lens and the 80 mm Zuiko Macro. When 50 mm lenses are mounted in reverse, clip the bellows hood panel to the ring at the rear of the reversed front bellows standard.

When using the 38 mm macro lens for magnified copying it is sufficient to fit the bellows hood panel loosely over the lens.

Lenses and magnifications

The ideal lens for transparency duplication with the slide copier is the 80 mm Zuiko Macro *f* 4, which covers reproduction from same-size (1:1) up to about 2.3× — more than sufficient for enlarging a 13 × 17 mm transparency to 24 × 36 mm. As this lens is corrected for optimum definition at 1:1 scale, it yields best performance in this range.

A good second-best is the 50 mm Zuiko Auto-Macro *f* 3.5 which, with the slide copier, provides magnification from same-size up to about 4×.

The 50 mm lenses (other than the *f* 1.2) can also be used for same-size copying though with some sacrifice of resolution near the image edges. This becomes worse with magnified copying.

The 38 mm Zuiko Macro *f* 3.5 can with the slide copier handle magnifications between 1.8× and 5× for the rare occasions where this is needed in transparency duplication.

Same-size and magnified copying

Usually you will copy slides or transparencies at same-size, and here the following lenses and settings are applicable—in descending order of preference:

(a) *With the 80 mm macro lens* move the focusing knob on the focusing tripod block to line up the end of the bellows rail with the orange 1× mark on the black panel of the slide copier arm. Lock the focusing knob. Move the front end of the lens standard—by turning the lens shift knob—to the orange/white mark near the front of the bellows rail corresponding to 25 mm on the scale. Turn the camera shift knob on the bellows to line up the rear of the camera standard base (camera body mount board) with the orange 1× mark on the bellows rail scale (just beyond 150 on the scale). Lock the clamping knob of both standards.

(b) *With the 50 mm macro lens* move the bellows rail in the focusing tripod block to line it up with the white 1×/1.5× mark on the slide copier arm. Keep the front standard at the orange/white line mark of the bellows rail and the rear standard to 95 on the scale (bellows fully compressed). Focus the macro lens to 0.3 metre or 12 inches to benefit from the close-up correction (floating elements) of the 50 mm Zuiko Auto-Macro lens.

(c) *With the standard 50 mm lenses* (other than the *f* 1.2) line up the front end of the bellows rail with the white 1×/1.5× mark on the copier arm. Set the lens standard of the bellows to the orange/white mark on the bellows scale and the rear standard to about 110 on the scale (opposite the white 1× mark of this scale). Always keep the standard 50 mm lenses focused at infinity—closer focusing slightly complicates the adjustments with no gain in close-up performance.

Various combinations are possible for magnified transparency copying. The preferable lens is here the 80 mm. For 1.5× magnification line up the front of the bellows rail with the orange 1.5× mark on the copier arm and the rear (camera) standard with the orange 1.5× mark on the bellows scale, just beyond 190. For still higher magnification (up to 2.3×) you can run the rear standard further to the back of the rail. With the 50 mm macro lens at its closest focusing distance with the rear bellows standard at 110 on the scale you can reach a 1.5× magnification. (See also the tables in Chpt. *Facts and figures.*)

Fitting transparencies

Place mounted slides in 5 × 5 cm (2 × 2 inch) frames into the slide slot at the top of the slide/film holder. Insert the slide with the frame opening horizontal, irrespective of the image orientation, since the frame must match the orientation of the film gate in the camera and of the diffusing screen in front of the slide/film holder.

When copying original colour slides made in the camera, the emulsion side of the transparency should face forward, i.e. towards the diffusing screen in the holder.

SLIDE COPIER RANGES

Adjust the front bellows standard and locate the end of the bellows rail—by adjusting the focusing tripod block—according to the lens and magnification required.

A. Same-size reproduction, 80 mm lens: bellows rail to orange 1× mark, front standard to white/orange line mark.

B. Same-size and slightly magnified reproduction with 50 mm lens: bellows rail to white 1×/1.5× marks, front standard to white/orange line mark.

C. 1.5× magnification, 80 mm lens: bellows rail to orange 1.5× line, front standard to orange/white mark.

D. Higher magnifications with 38 or 50 mm lens: front standard to front end of bellows rail, rail end between orange and white 1.5× marks.

E. For higher magnifications reverse 50 mm lens, standard to front of rail, end of rail lined up with white 1×/1.5× marks.

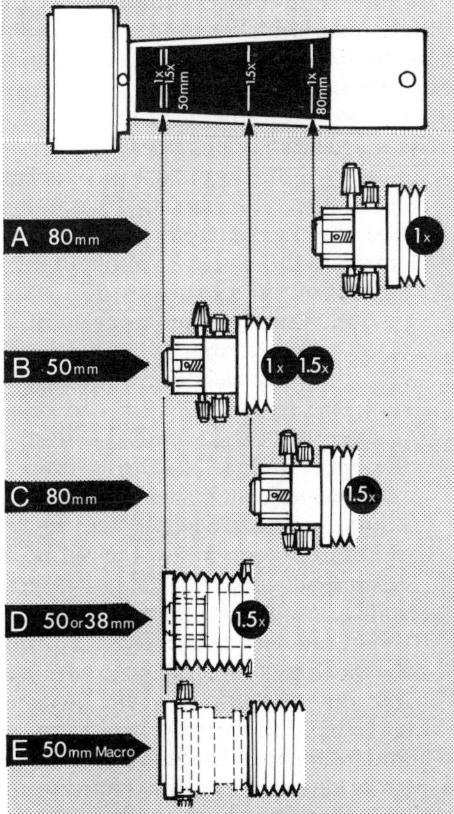

The roll film stage screws into the underside of the slide/film holder *(left)*. To keep long film lengths tidy, roll them up around the centre shaft of the roll film stage plates *(right)*.

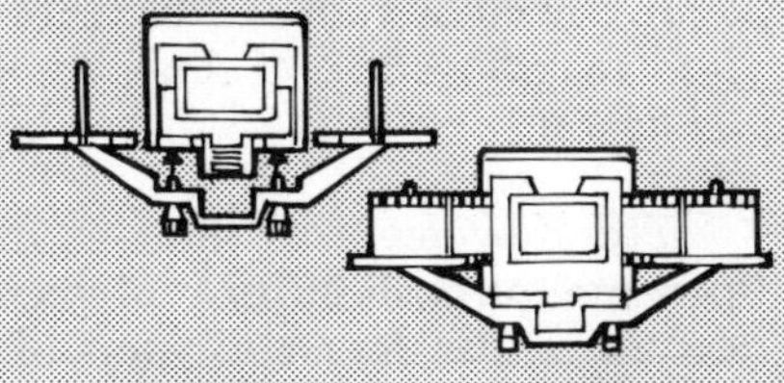

You can also copy slides with the focusing rail and stage mount the 50 mm macro lens set to closest distance, plus the 25 mm extension tube.

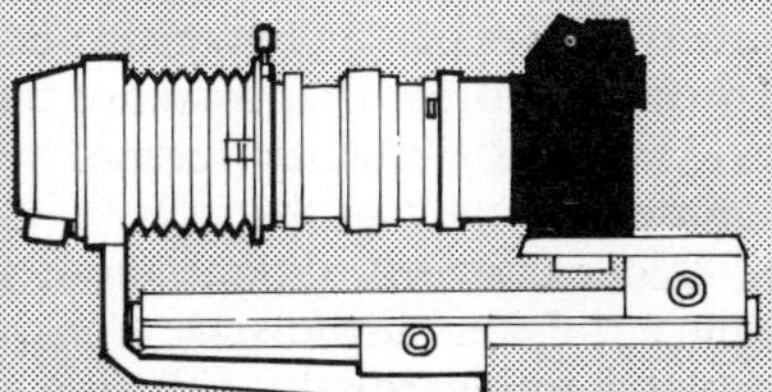

To reproduce commercially duplicated slides, place them in the slide slot with the emulsion side facing the camera lens. In all cases the image on the slide must appear the right way round when you look at it from behind the camera. (The same applies also to film strip transparencies and negatives.)

The slide may be inserted upright (frame opening vertical) if you want to enlarge a central vertical section of the horizontal frame area. With the slide frame opening vertical, the diffuser only illuminates a central square section of the transparency.

Half-frame slides are also inserted with the frame opening horizontal. The slide/film holder takes 3 × 3 cm (No. 110) slides if these are fitted in 5 × 5 cm adapter frames.

To fit film strips pull down the small chrome catch at the bottom of the slide/film holder, just below the black serrated key, so that the hinged film holder frame with diffuser swings open. Place the film on the black ledge below the gate, close the diffuser frame, hold the top against the film holder and press the black key to re-engage the catch. When you press the black key again, the pressure frame slightly lifts to permit horizontal movement of the film to centre an image accurately in a film holder frame.

To secure the pressure frame against opening, screw down the small screw behind the release catch, facing the main frame of the slide copier.

It is usually more convenient to insert films with the holder removed from the copier. To remove the holder, slide it upwards out of its guides. To refit, slide it down over the guides.

The movement of the slide/film holder in its guides permits vertical shifting of the transparency image for centering the part you want, especially with magnified copying. At same-size, the whole slide is correctly centered when the two red dots at the left of the slide holder and copier frame are lined up.

For horizontal centering of film strips move the strip longitudinally in the holder. Horizontal displacement of slides is limited to the lateral clearance between the slide and the size of the slide slot, i.e. about 2 mm. But even this sometimes helps in selective framing.

SLIDE COPIER HANDLING

Insert slides into the slide slot of the slide/film holder *(left)*. For film strips first open the film holder section *(right)*.

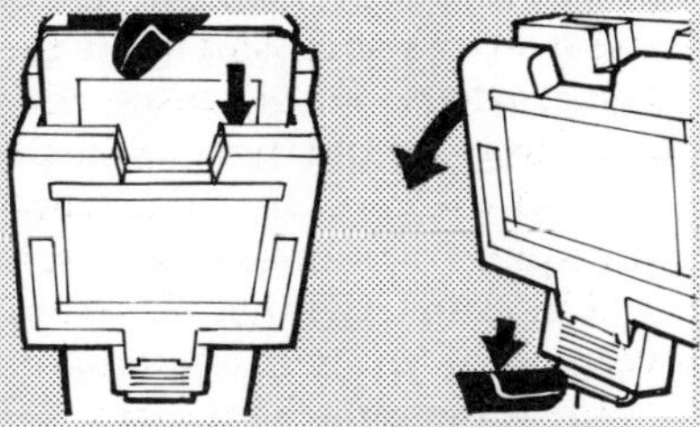

Insert the film by locating it against the bottom ledge *(left)*, then close the holder *(right)*.

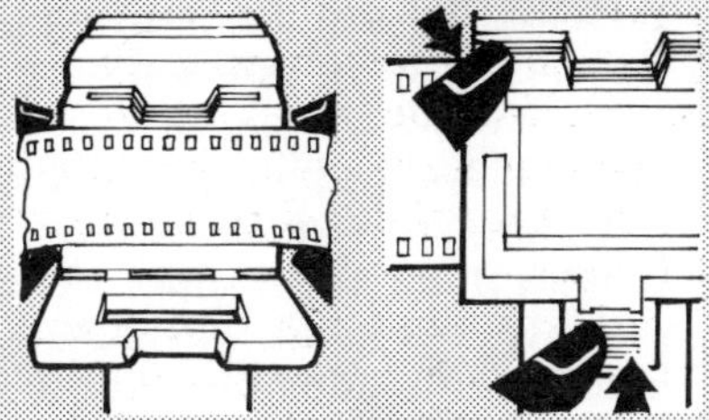

To move a film strip along, press the black key to raise the film holder pressure plate *(left)*; to secure really firmly, screw down the locking screw *(right)*.

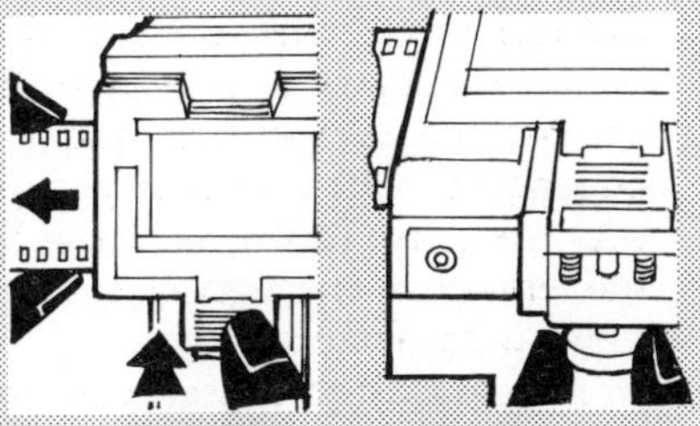

The slide/film holder can move up and down on its guides; when the red dots are lined up, the image frame is centered.

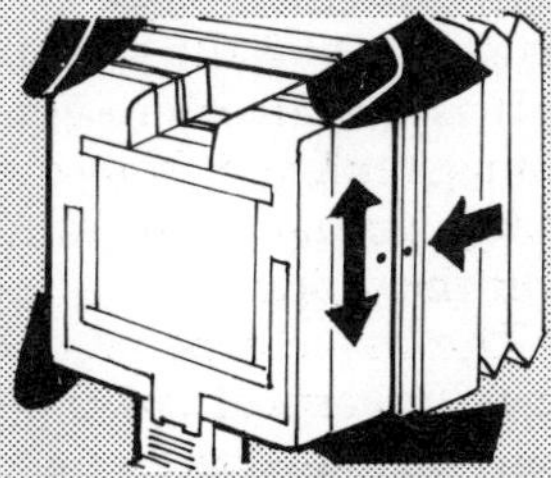

To remove the diffuser *(left)* open the film holder frame first. To replace the diffuser *(right)* drop it into the lower guide and push home.

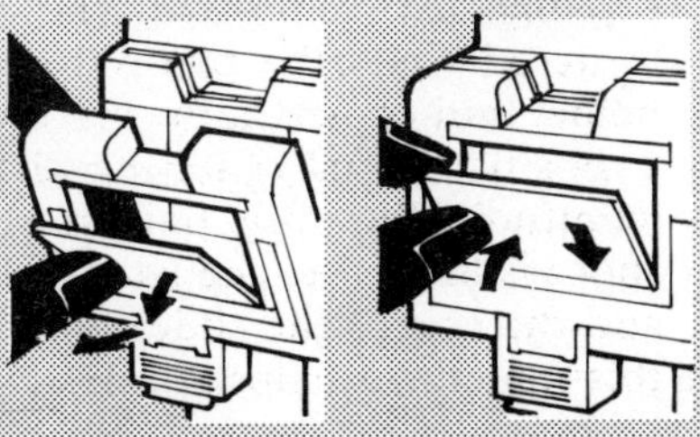

Films inserted in this way may be transparencies or negatives, and cartridge film negatives (No. 126) are handled in the same way. The perforated edge must in this case be at the bottom; the image is then upright.

Proceed in the same way for single 24 × 36 mm transparencies: open the film holder frame, place the transparency on the protruding ledge of the holder, centre behind the window, and close the holder frame.

Strips of No. 110 cartridge film negatives are more difficult. To avoid obscuring part of the picture, place the film strip in position across the middle of the film track, close the pressure frame with the diffuser and then gently move the film against the bottom edge of the closed film slot. This is make-shift at the best, since you cannot reliably hold the frames at either end of a No. 110 negative strip in this way. Also stray light from the diffuser here tends to impair quality on copying.

The roll film stage

When handling longer strips of uncut 35 mm film, the roll film stage holds the rolled up ends of the film neatly in position and out of the way. The stage consists of a bracket with two fixing screws to fit the base of the slide/film holder and a pair of 65 mm circular trays with a centre shaft for the film rolls.

To fit the roll film stage, remove the slide/film holder from the copier and screw the two screws of the stage bracket into the holes underneath the slide/film holder. The arms must protrude forward of the diffuser in the holder. Then introduce the film strip as described above, locate the frame you want in the film holder gate and roll up the excess film on both sides around the centre shafts of the trays. These shafts also keep the film in place when the slide copier is set up pointing downwards on the copy stand etc. Then refit the slide/film holder complete with roll film stage to the front of the copier.

Focusing

The alignment points mentioned before for the end of the bellows rail above the magnification panel of the copier arm are an approximate starting point. The exact position is established by focusing. The exact magnification depends on the lens used and on the bellows extension. So set this first, i.e. the front standard to the orange/white mark (or front of the rail for magnifications) and the rear standard to the settings quoted before. Lock the shift knobs of the front and rear standards with the clamping knob on the other side.

Point the whole bellows and copier assembly—with the transparency in place—at a bright light source. Slack off the rail clamping knob and turn the focusing knob of the tripod block to move the whole rail and camera assembly nearer to or further away from the transparency plane of the copier until the image appears sharpest. When the image is sharp, lock the focusing knob, centre the transparency in the finder by adjusting the slide/film holder, check the lighting and exposure, and expose.

If you want to adjust the magnification, for instance to leave out unwanted material near the image margins, move the camera standard on the bellows rack to a slightly higher setting on the scale, lock again and refocus.

The diffuser

The plastic diffusing panel in the front of the slide/film holder ensures uniform illumination of the transparency with widely varying transillumination. It also absorbs a lot of light and is not needed when you make exposures with the copier pointed at a perfectly evenly lit surface.

To remove the diffuser, open the film holder, hold the diffuser between two fingers, push down and lift out from the front. To replace the diffuser, drop it into the lower guide of the frame (carrying the long leaf spring) from the front, push down and in to engage it in position.

The copy stand system

For close-up photography, and especially copying, the copy stand holds the camera pointing downwards onto a subject plane. It takes the camera with the standard lens or 50 mm macro lens for exposures at subject distances between about 820 and 220 mm (32 and 11 inches), measured from the film plane to the baseboard. With the 50 mm macro lens this covers reductions from 1:14 to 1:2. The distance range can be extended for copying larger originals such as paintings etc. by setting up the copy stand so that the camera points over the edge of the table onto the floor.

The copy stand consists of a 440 × 480 mm (17.3 × 18.9 inch) baseboard of 1 inch thick composition board with plastic covering. The baseboard carries an 800 mm (31.5 inch) column fixed in a column base. The latter is bolted to the baseboard so that the effective area of the latter is 330 × 480 mm (13 × 18.9 inches). The column carries an arm with a camera platform to which the OM (or other) cameras are fixed with a standard tripod screw. The arm incorporates a spring counterweighting system and both fine and coarse height adjustments. The column is also fitted to take two gooseneck lamps of the OM lighting set.

Assembling the copy stand

First decide whether the column is to be mounted so that the arm reaches out over the baseboard or whether the arm should protrude over the back for photography on the floor. Arrange the column holding plate and locking knob accordingly:

(a) For photography on the baseboard unscrew the locking knob and insert the column supporting plate and shaft from the front (the side facing the baseboard) with a knob screwed on at the rear.

(b) If the camera is to point over the baseboard edge, push in the supporting plate from the back and screw on the knob from the side above the baseboard. In that case weight the baseboard with some heavy objects (books etc.) and place it near the edge of the working table or bench.

Pull the column supporting plate as far away from the column base as possible, unscrewing the locking knob to just before the point where it drops off its threaded shaft. Now push the bottom end of the column over the base so that the grooved side of the column slides over one end of the column base and the flat side slides down the rear of the supporting plate. When the column is correctly seated on the base, push the supporting plate against the flat front of the column and tighten the locking knob.

Fit the camera with the lens to be used—generally one of the standard lenses or the 50 mm macro lens. Mount the camera on the camera platform with the tripod screw. For copying flat originals on the baseboard, the camera should point squarely at the original, i.e. with its optical

COPY STAND

1. Lighting arm holder.
2. Arm of lighting unit (separate item).
3. Fine adjustment knob.
4. Camera arm clamping knob (on far side of arm).
5. Column locking knob.
6. Column base.
7. Baseboard.
8. Camera platform.
9. Camera arm.
10. Coarse adjustment plate.
11. Column.
12. Column supporting plate.

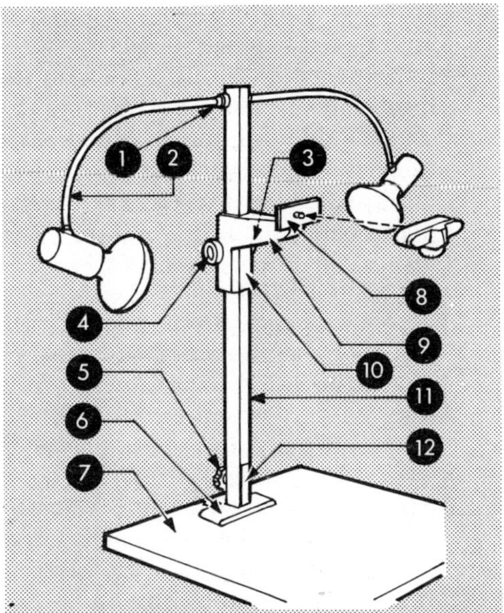

Mount the column with the arm facing inwards for photography on the copy stand baseboard, *(left)* or with the arm facing outwards *(right)* when photographing over the edge of a table. Reverse the locking knob and supporting plate in that case.

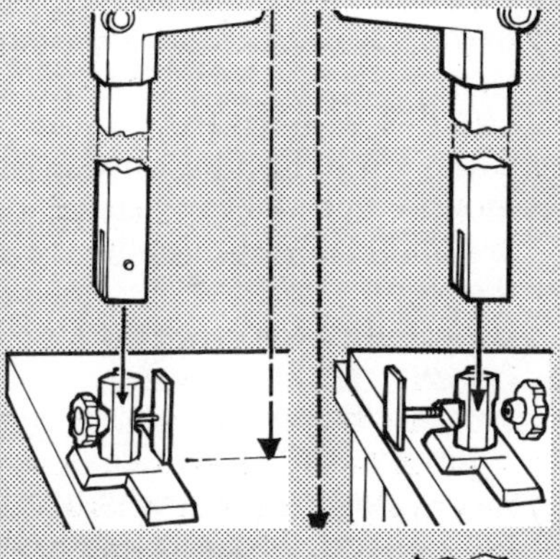

The camera fits on the platform with the tripod screw *(left)*. The camera arm is movable with a coarse adjustment on pressing the large plate in the front, or by fine adjustment of the friction drive knob. The clamping knob (at the other side of the arm) locks both movements.

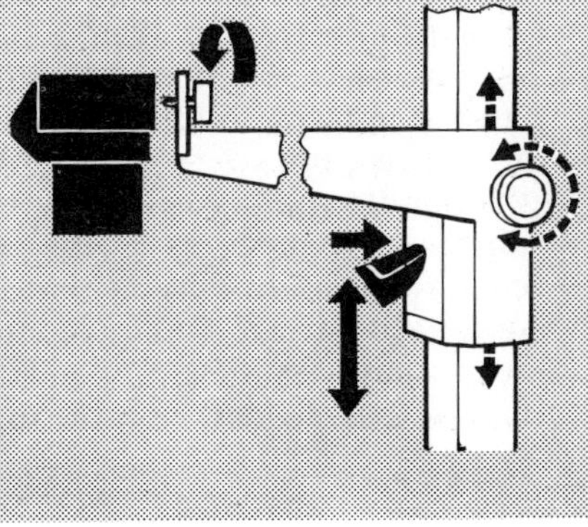

axis exactly at right angles to the subject surface. But for other close-up subjects you don't have to keep the camera pointing vertically downwards; the copy stand is a useful table stand for many oblique close-up shots of small objects. However, with the camera pointing down obliquely, the subject field will generally be outside the baseboard area.

Height adjustment

At the reproduction scales for which the copy stand is used—up to about 0.5 × or 1:2—focus by the lens adjustment and use the movement of the arm up and down on the column to set the camera distance. Press the large plate on the front of the arm to free the movement for coarse adjustment; turn the friction drive knob at the right of the arm for fine adjustment. Both movements are locked by the clamping knob at the left of the arm.

If the copy stand is used for close-ups between 0.5 × and 1 × scale, mount the camera via the focusing rail and focusing stage (see above). That permits fine focusing by fine adjustment of the camera/subject distance.

The table clamp

This is a light-alloy casting similar to the column base mounted on the copy stand, but shaped in the form of a jaw and clamp to support the column and camera arm of the copy stand on normal desks or tables. The table surface then becomes the copying or close-up baseboard. A table top for this purpose should be between 20 and 40 mm thick with a square (not chamfered) edge.

To use the table clamp, fully unscrew the clamping screw, push the clamp with the large plate on top over the table or desk edge and tighten the clamping screw. The column base with locking knob and column supporting plate are identical with the same fittings on the copy stand. So decide whether you want the copy stand arm to face out over the edge of the desk or inwards over the middle and fit the locking knob and column supporting plate accordingly on the column base. Then fit the copy stand column in the same way as for the copy stand itself. All further manipulation is the same as with the copy stand for that is in effect what you now have—except that the desk or table top serves as the baseboard.

TABLE CLAMP

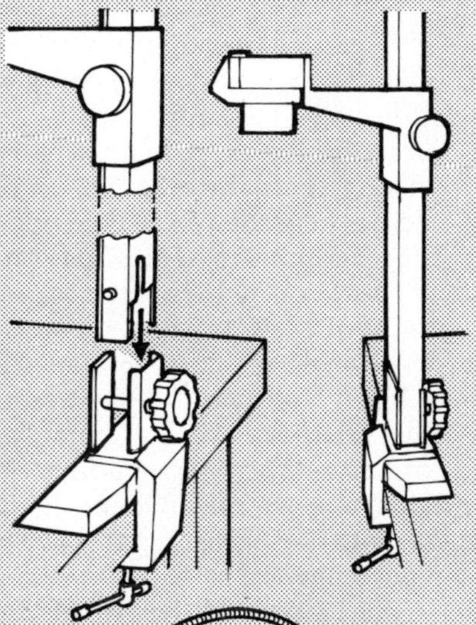

The table clamp carries a column base similar to the copy stand but clamps to the edge of a table or desk. The copy stand column will fit on the column base with the arm supporting the camera above the table surface *(left)* or—with the supporting plate and clamping knob reversed *(right)*—with the camera arm protruding over the table edge.

LIGHTING SET

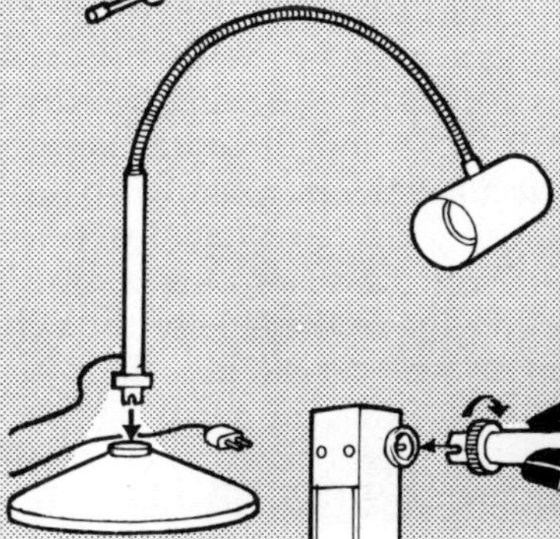

The lighting set consists of a base, a stem with knurled screw-down ring, goose-neck arm and a lamp holder to take screw-based lamps. Preferably use reflector flood lamps.

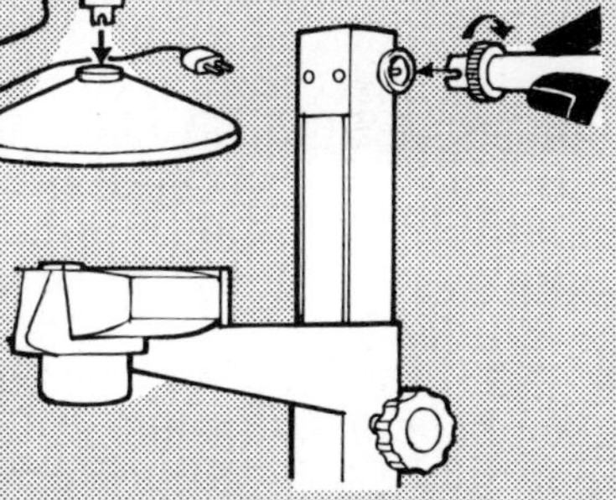

To fit a lamp unit to the copy stand unscrew the cap at the top of the column, place the lighting set stem in position and secure with the milled screw-over ring.

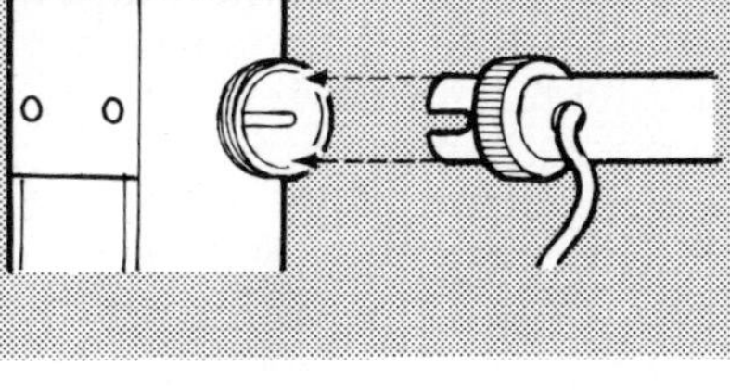

When fitting the lighting set stem, the cut-outs in the stem must engage the cross bar inside the socket.

The lighting set

This pair of lamp holders with a gooseneck arm mounted on a flat base is useful for general lighting of close-up subjects. The lamps can be moved to any height and direction by adjusting the flexible arms. The latter also unscrew from the base and can be fitted into corresponding sockets near the top of the copy stand column for uniform copying lighting of originals on the baseboard.

The lamp holders take standard Edison screw-capped lamps of up to 500 watts. Preferably use integral-reflector floodlamps which give a restricted high-intensity beam of light. Frequently 75 or 100 watt lamps of this type are fully adequate. When lamps have been burning for some time the lamp holder and top of the gooseneck stem is liable to get somewhat hot. So handle with a handkerchief or cloth for adjusting the lamp holder at the end of the flexible arms.

The maximum height of the gooseneck arm is about 57 cm or 22.5 inches; approx. 20 cm of this at the bottom is rigid stem. A milled nut at the bottom of this stem unscrews and allows the stem and arm to be lifted off the circular 21 cm weighted base. When removing the stem lift it gently up while unscrewing the nut.

To fit the lamp units to the copy stand, unscrew the two caps in the side of the column near the top. In each of these sockets introduce the stem of one gooseneck lamp, so that the cut-out of the stem engages the crossbar inside the socket. Then secure by screwing down the milled nut that is captive on the lamp stem. Bend the lamp arms to let both lamps shine down on the baseboard at an angle of about 45° to the camera axis. But for deliberate uneven lighting the lamps can be directed and bent individually.

To refit the lamp units in their bases, unscrew from the copy stand column and insert the lamp stem in the aperture of the circular lamp base, again engaging the cut-out of the stem with the crossbar in the lamp base. Then screw down the milled nut.

When the lamp units are mounted on the copy stand column, run the leads through the wire loop attached to the back of the copy stand arm. The leads are comparatively short (about 70 cm or 27 inches); the best way of connecting them to a supply is to run an extension lead from the mains supply socket to a double socket to take the two plugs near the lighting set-up itself. That avoids multiple trailing cables.

The Handy copy stand

This is a specially compact camera support for close-ups between about 1:10 and 1:2.2 reduction (0.1 to 0.45 × magnification) with the 50 or 55 mm lenses. With the 50 mm macro lens this needs no further close-up aids; with the other lenses the larger scales require a close-up lens or extension tubes.

The Handy copy stand consists of a mount to attach to the lens and a set of four legs that screw into the mount and can be extended to various lengths for four fixed lens/subject plane distances. The Handy copy stand thus supports the camera above the subject—a convenient arrangement for copying documents etc. in libraries. Dismantled, the stand is easy to carry in a briefcase with for instance a small flash unit for simple lighting.

Assembling the legs

Each leg of the copy stand consists of three parts:

A short (129 mm or 5.1 inch) hollow sleeve A with screw stud to screw into the Handy copy stand mount at one end, and an internal thread at the other;

A longer (168 mm or 6.6 inch) hollow sleeve B that screws into the lower end of sleeve A;

A thin solid 310 mm (12.2 inch) leg C with rubber tips at each end. This can screw into the end of sleeve A or sleeve B—in the latter case in two alternative positions.

This combination can yield four different leg lengths for the stand: shortest, short, medium and long. The Handy copy stand data table (see Chpt. *Facts and figures*) shows the scales of reproduction, subject field etc. at these settings with the usable lenses.

In every case screw the short sleeve A of each leg into the copy stand mount first.

After assembling the copy stand mount with the legs at the required length, place it over the subject field to be photographed. Be sure to have a sufficiently large support area for the legs to stand firm. This is larger than the subject area covered; for instance with the long leg extension you need a firm surface of at least 38 × 50 cm

(15 × 20 inches) to support the legs. When copying from books, it may be more convenient to set up the Handy copy stand on a table and slide the book—open at the right page—between the legs. With large documents where you only want to copy part, the Handy copy stand can stand directly on the original.

Lenses and aids

The ideal lens for use with the Handy copy stand is the 50 mm Zuiko Auto-Macro *f* 3.5. This needs no further aids at any of the leg extensions. Simply mount the lens on the camera, slack off the clamping knob protruding from the side of the copy stand mount and place the camera and lens on top of the copy stand mount. The latter has a collar that just fits the 51 mm outside diameter of the 50 mm lenses.

Line up the camera's image frame with the rectangle covered by the legs. As an aid to this locate the red index dot on the lens mount (in the centre of the aperture field scale) with the red dot on the Handy copy stand mount labelled 35 MM SIZE.

The 50 mm *f* 1.8 and 50 mm *f* 1.4 lenses can also be used with the long and medium leg extensions to yield fully acceptable results, especially a couple of stops below maximum aperture. These lenses need additional aids with the short and shortest leg extensions. For the short extension screw the 40 cm close-up lens into the front of the camera lens. With the shortest extension use the 7 + 14 mm extension tubes between the lens and camera. Here however stopping down to about *f* 5.6 is advisable for adequate image quality.

The ultra-speed 55 mm *f* 1.2 lens can also be used with the Handy copy stand. As this has a larger front mount diameter (57 mm), screw the 55–49 mm adapter ring into the front of this lens; this then fits into the collar of the copy stand mount in the same way as the other lenses. (The figures 55–49 mm of this ring refer to the filter screw threads concerned, not the outermost diameters.)

The 55 mm lens also needs a close-up lens with the short leg extension. Use the close-up lens with 55 mm screw mount (the other lenses use the close-up lens with 49 mm mount) and screw the 55–49 mm adapter ring into the front of a close-up lens.

HANDY COPY STAND

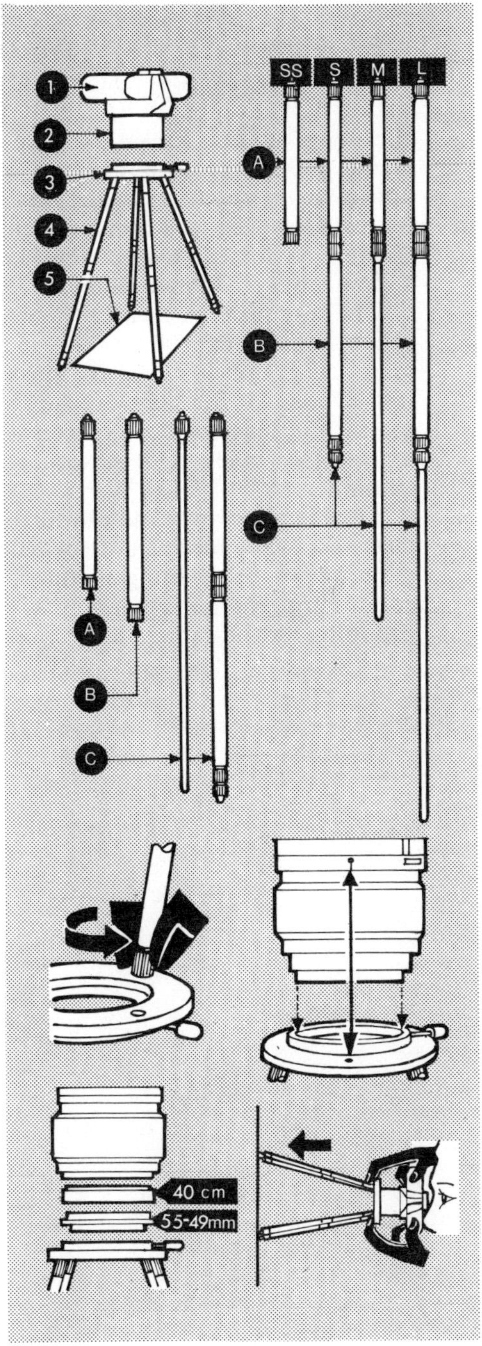

The complete copy stand assembly comprises:

1. Camera.
2. 50 or 55 mm lens.
3. Copy stand mount.
4. Legs.
5. Original being copied.

Each leg consists of three parts: A, B and C. Combined in different ways, these yield various overall lengths to hold the stand at different distances above the subject: very short (SS), short (S), medium (M) and long (L).

After adjusting the right leg length, screw the legs into the mounting ring *(left)*. When attaching to the camera *(right)* line up the red dot "35 mm size" with the red dot on the lens *(right)*.

Screw the close-up lens into the camera lens and then fit the 55–49 mm adapter ring if needed *(left)*. When copying items on a wall, hold the handy copy stand firmly against the camera lens *(right)*.

Handy copy stand handling points

Once the Handy copy stand is assembled and standing on top of an original to be copied, you only have to focus the image on the screen and expose. The Handy copy stand data table (see Chpt. *Facts and figures*) gives approximate focusing scale settings for the different lenses. However, you focus visually on the screen in the usual way, for the legs of the Handy copy stand are a support, not a distance gauge.

The stand is also useful for other small objects photographed in a direct downward view, including items in glass cases, for instance in museums etc. where poor conditions call for long exposures. You may here have to use the legs at shorter extensions if the objects are appreciably below a glass top. Focus visually through the finder.

The Handy copy stand can further support the camera against a wall, for instance when photographing small paintings or other hung pictures. In this case grip the copy stand mount separately to stop the stand from dropping off the camera lens.

LARGE-SCALE MACRO ACCESSORIES

Large-scale macrophotography, especially with the Auto-bellows, calls for a rather more rigid and vibration-resistant support than even the copy stand can provide. The firmness of the set-up must be of the same order as for a laboratory microscope. The specialised macro-photography stands and supports for the OM system are in fact largely the same as those for certain Olympus microscopes. Thus the VST-1 macro stand is a slightly modified form (with a different pillar) of an Olympus microscope stand. The stage plates and stages are accessories of this stand while the X-DE transilluminator base is a microscope substage base. (That's also why the latter has a number of holes that appear to have no purpose in macrophotography set-ups.) The items are here described in their versions for macrophotography.

The VST-1 macro stand

This consists of a heavy cast base with the short sides curved. It carries a 125 mm high pillar at one end and an 80 mm circular hole and a 101 mm recess surrounding the hole, to take various stage plates and stages (see below). The pillar and the hole in the base are so located relative to each other that when you mount an OM camera and lens with either the focusing rail and focusing stage or the Auto-bellows via the macro stand B adapter (see below), the lens axis is exactly centred in the stage plate opening.

The B adapter and extension bar

The VST-1 macro stand is intended for use almost exclusively with the focusing rail and stage or the Auto-bellows. Mounting either of these units needs the macro-photo stand B adapter. This is a carrier with a sleeve that fits over the VST-1 pillar, and a vertical platform with tripod screw to take the focusing tripod block of the focusing rail or bellows unit.

A VST-E extension bar raises the effective height of the B adapter—and hence increases the maximum lens/subject distance—by about 64 mm or 2.5 inches.

Assembly

Place the VST-1 macro stand on a solid flat surface (bench top, desk etc.) or—where used—on the X-DE transilluminator base. Fit the VST-E extension bar if needed. For this, first unscrew the screw cap at the top of the VST-1 pillar and screw the extension bar in place instead.

Fit the B adapter: slack off the locking knob and place the adapter over the pillar. When used with the extension bar, lower the adapter over the pillar until the latter abuts the end of the recess just below the camera screw in the platform. When using the stand without extension bar, fit the B adapter on the pillar so that it sits on the shoulder of the lower wider pillar base.

Mount the focusing tripod block of the Auto-bellows or focusing rail by screwing the camera screw on the B adapter into one of the two tripod bushes of the focusing tripod block. Use the upper bush for maximum stability (focusing block flush with B adapter platform) or the lower bush to permit some sideways tilt.

Finally attach the lens and camera to the bellows or the focusing stage on the rail, fit the stage plate you want and locate the subject on it. Then line up the camera with the centre of the subject field you want to cover. Generally that involves slacking off the locking knob at the rear of the B adapter and rotating this on the VST-1 stand pillar to centre the optical axis. Clamp the knob again to prevent any shift while adjusting the bellows or other focusing settings.

Stage plates and stages

These hold macro subjects on the base of the VST-1 macro stand or the PMT-35 macrophoto outfit for photography by incident or transmitted light. The stage plates drop into the recess of the VST-1 or PMT-35 stage where they can be clamped by a clamping screw. Flat objects—e.g. specimen slides—are held in position by

VST-1 MACRO STAND

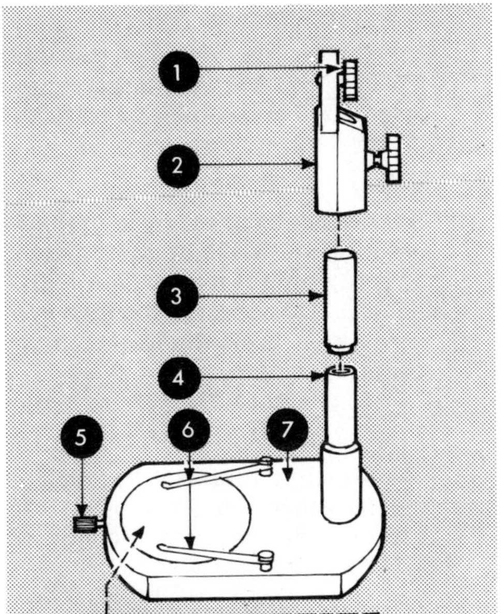

The components of the macro stand are:

1. Camera screw in platform.
2. B adapter.
3. VST-E extension bar.
4. Pillar.
5. Stage plate clamping knob.
6. Stage clips.
7. Base.

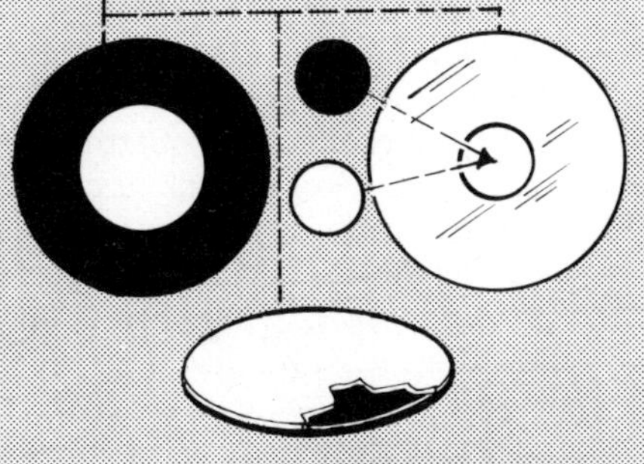

Stage plates fit in the recess of the VST-1 stand and include the stage plate 45 *(left),* black and white stage plate *(centre)* and shade stage plate *(right).*

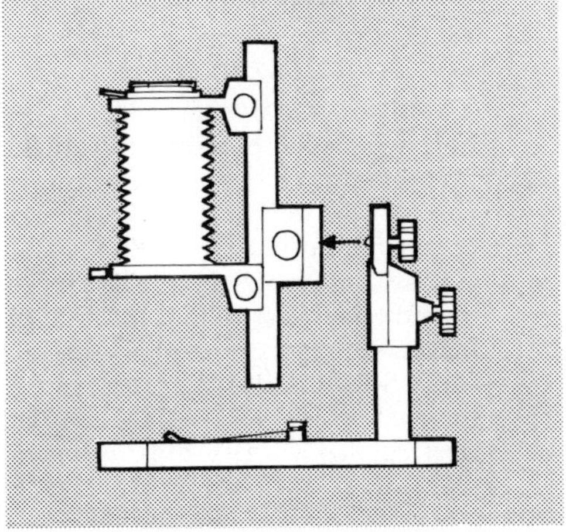

For the complete set-up the B adapter fits over the pillar and takes the focusing tripod block of the focusing rail or bellows.

the stage clips (a pair of swivelling spring clips) of the VST-1 or PMT-35; larger objects simply rest on the stage plate under their own weight.

Glass stage plate

This clear glass plate is 6 mm thick and is used for incident and transmitted light illumination of objects placed on it. It is also useful for incident light photography when the subject is to appear suspended in mid air, possibly against a coloured background that may be placed underneath the glass.

The black/white stage plate

This opaque plastic plate, black on one side and white on the other, carries subjects for incident illumination and provides a neutral or contrasting background.

The shade stage plate

This is similar to the glass stage plate, but transparent plastic with a centre hole of 23 mm diameter and a slightly larger recess surrounding the hole on one side. The recess takes a black or a white disc which blocks light coming from directly underneath. The outside passes light to the Lieberkühn reflectors (see below, *The macro lighting system*) when fitted on the lens for shadowless illumination. The disc diameter also indicates the largest subject area that can be lit by this method, i.e. this is exclusively intended for subjects at larger than 1:1 scale.

The stage plates 45 and 28

The black metal stage plate 45 has a 45 mm clear centre hole which supports larger objects that bridge the hole for transmitted or reflected illumination. The outer black rim reduces the transilluminated area and thus the amount of stray light that can reach the lens.

The stage plate 28 has a 28 mm centre hole but a 120 mm outside diameter with a 100 mm diameter rim protruding below the plate. With this rim, the stage plate 28 fits into the VST-1 or PMT-35 stage like the other stage plates, but the top extends over the top of the stage. This extended part carries a screw hole and two locating holes to take the FM mechanical stage for accurate location of tiny objects (see below).

The FM mechanical stage

The mechanical stage consists of an L-shaped base with an L-carrier that moves up and down by a rack-and-pinion drive. The horizontal bar of the L-carrier has a horizontal slide driven by a worm gear for lateral movement. Two adjustable jaws, one with a spring-loaded finger, are mounted in dovetail guides on this horizontal slide. The left-hand jaw can be clamped in position anywhere along the horizontal arm, the right-hand jaw moves by friction only. The adjustments carry mm scales with Vernier indexes.

The vertical rack-and-pinion movement (forward and aft when the stage is mounted on its stage plate) is 30 mm; the horizontal worm drive movement of the jaws is 52 mm overall. That way you can centre or shift any part of an object clamped between the jaws anywhere within the field of view of the camera. As the FM stage is again primarily intended for macrophotography above a 1:1 scale, the full adjustment range is rarely needed.

The FM mechanical stage is used exclusively with the stage plate 28. To mount the FM stage, place the horizontal section of the lower L member over the three holes in the edge of the stage plate 28 to engage the two pins underneath the FM stage in the two locating holes. Screw down the milled knob in the central threaded hole to fix the FM stage securely to the stage plate 28. This whole assembly can now be mounted on the base of the VST-1 macrophoto stand or the PMT-35 stage and clamped in position. The stage clips of the VST-1 or the PMT-35 are not needed with the mechanical stage—so swing them out of the way.

The FM stage is intended to hold thin flat objects between 1 and 5 mm thick—which can be round, rectangular or irregularly shaped.

To grip small items—smaller than the 28 mm centre opening—move the horizontal adjustment as far to the left as possible (i.e. beyond 90 on the horizontal scale) and the vertical adjustment fully down (above 30). Move the left-hand jaw with the straight upright finger to the right so that its left-hand edge is more or less in line with the small engraved mark above about 63 on the scale. Clamp this jaw in position with the small clamping lever on top (unclamp also before moving it). Slide the right-hand jaw fully up against the left-hand one. Open the large curved finger of the jaw by the small spring lever at the front, drop the coin or object between the left-hand finger and the base of the jaw, then let the right-hand finger close down on it to hold it in place. Now you can move the object held between the jaws up or down and left or right with the micrometer stage controls.

Minute objects (e.g. jewels) can be placed on the black or white disc of the shade stage plate and held in the jaws in the same way.

For larger items, including microscope slides, pull the jaw bases apart and hold the object in place between them and with the sprung finger.

Once the item to be photographed is held in the jaws, turn the vertical and lateral micrometer knobs to centre it in the field of view while looking through the camera viewfinder. Use the Vernier scale for noting the position for future reference or repeat shots. Generally it is sufficient to note the position to the nearest 0.1 mm; note which division on the Vernier scale (the scales marked II or III) lines up exactly with a division on the mm scale. The Vernier scale division then indicates tenths of a mm. For instance if the 0 division of the Vernier scale is somewhere between 21 and 22 mm (vertical scale) and the *second* division on the Vernier scale exactly lines up with a mm line (in this case 25 mm) the actual setting is $21 + 2 \times 0.1 = 21.2$ mm.

To dismantle the FM stage, unscrew the large milled knob on the front and lift the stage off the stage plate 28. The complete stage plate 28 with the FM stage can also be removed from the VST-1 or PMT-35 base on slacking off the clamping screw.

With the PM-EL incident illuminator mirror housings (see below, *The macro lighting system*) use the FM stage only with the 20 mm macro lens and the PM-EL 20 housing. With the 38 mm macro lens the PM-EL 38 housing is too large and its lower surface too close to the subject to clear the thickness of the stage. There is less need of the FM stage with the 80 mm macro lens except at its highest magnification (about $2\times$) on the bellows;

FM MECHANICAL STAGE

The components and controls of the mechanical stage are:

1. Straight-fingered jaw.
2. Clamping lever.
3. Sliding jaw.
4. Sprung holding finger.
5. Lateral slide.
6. Horizontal scale and Vernier.
7. Vertical scale and Vernier.
8. Vertical adjustment knob.
9. Lateral adjustment knob.
10. Fixing knob.

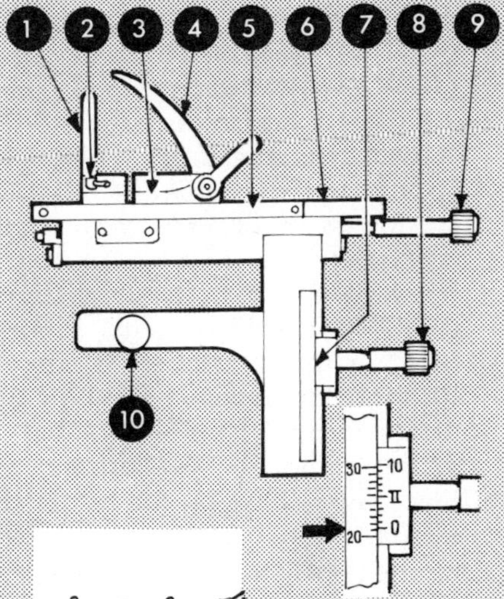

Reading the Vernier scale: here set to 21.2 mm.

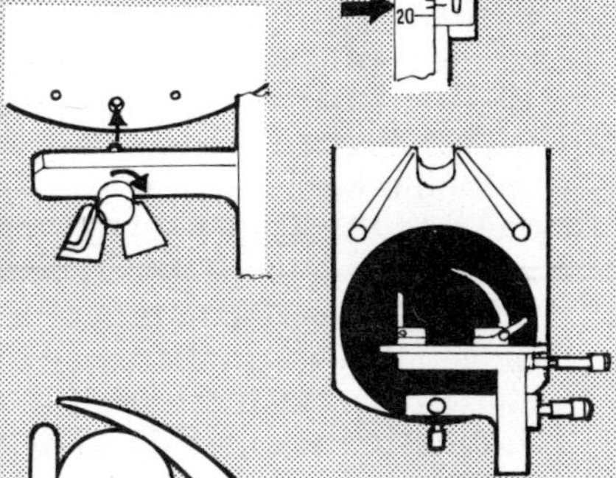

The FM stage screws to the stage plate 28 *(left)*, engaging the locating pins in the locating holes of the stage plate. Then fit the whole assembly in the base of the VST-1 or PMT-35 *(right)*.

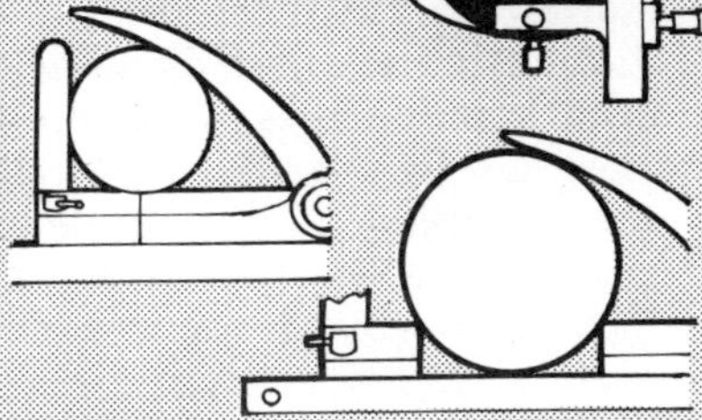

Clamping a small round object, e.g. a coin *(left)* and a large object (up to 70 mm diameter) on the FM stage *(right)*.

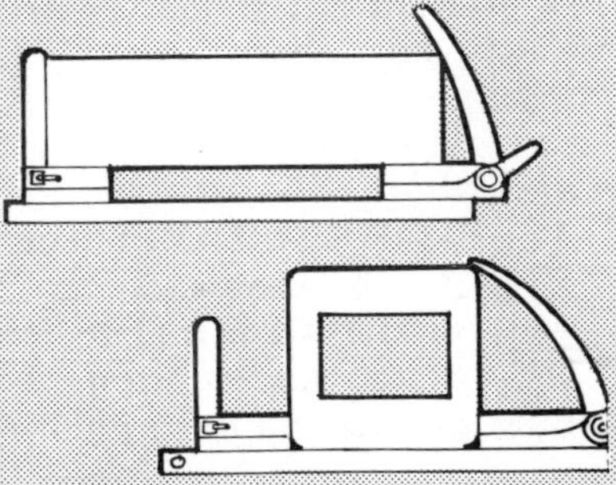

Clamping a microscope slide *(left)* and a larger square slide *(right)*.

the FM stage itself intrudes into the picture at lower magnifications.

The X-DE transilluminator base

This rigid support for the VST-1 macro stand permits transillumination from underneath of subjects placed on appropriate stage plates on the VST-1. It is also used for shadowless lighting in conjunction with the Lieberkühn reflectors.

The X-DE base is a light-alloy casting with a platform to hold the VST-1 stand, a built-in lamp and movable reflector in the bottom section and a pair of hand rests for more comfortable handling of the object on the stage plates, lens adjustments etc.

To set up the X-DE base, place it on a firm table. Place the VST-1 on the recessed platform in the centre, so that the two locating studs at the front of the X-DE engage two corresponding holes in the underside of the VST-1. The curved front edge of the latter is then flush with the front of the X-DE. Then assemble the rest of the unit on the VST-1.

To fit the hand rests, partially unscrew the two large milled screws in the top of the rails, near the back, to each side of the recessed centre platform. Hold the hand rest fully unfolded, hinge underneath and push the metal fixing plate (with the two oblong holes) into the slot in the side of the rails. Move the hand rest forward or back until it fully engages, i.e. the top wooden platform lies close against the side of the rail. Push the hand rest back (in the direction of the milled screw) as far as it will go and screw down the screw. The hand rest is then firmly in position with the top wooden surface flush with the top of the slide rail.

To remove the hand rests slack off the milled screw knobs (up to three turns), slide the hand rest towards the front of the X-DE and pull out from the side.

The lamp and mirror

The X-DE has a built-in lamp and swivelling mirror for simple transillumination of objects placed on the stage plate of the VST-1. The lamp holder is at the rear; simply pull this out from the back. The holder has a built-in push button switch and takes a 20 watt lamp

X-DE BASE

The components of the X-DE transilluminator base are:

1. Lamp holder with switch.
2. Lamp.
3. Lamp holder opening.
4. X-DE base.
5. Retaining screws for hand rests.
6. Hand rests.
7. Reflector control knob.
8. Reflector fork.
9. Reflector.
10. Locating studs for VST-1.

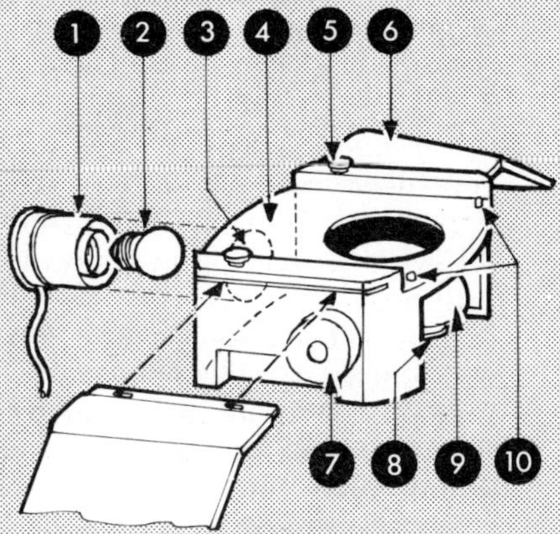

To fit the hand rests, slack off the retaining screw, push the metal plate of the hand rests into the slot and screw down *(left)*.

Place the VST-1 in position to engage the locating studs in the holes in the underside of the VST-1 *(right)*.

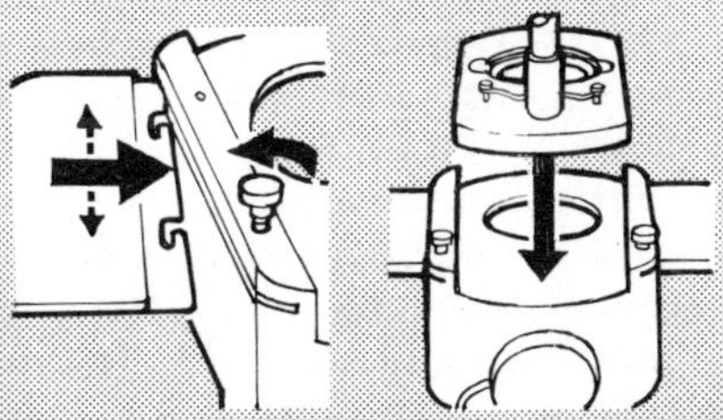

To fit or remove the mirror, push forward against one end of the fork and swing out or in at the other hand.

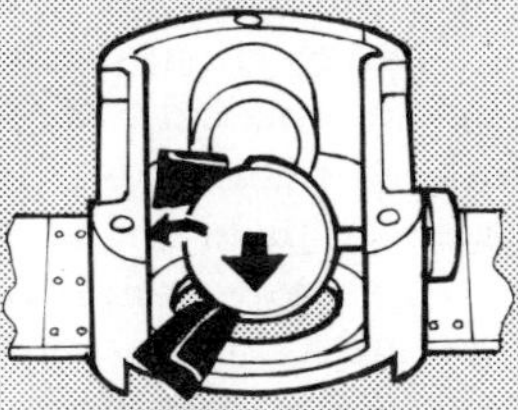

Basic set-up of X-DE base with LSD illuminator for transillumination: remove the lamp holder and locate the LSD at the rear of the X-DE to project on to the reflector and up through the base opening.

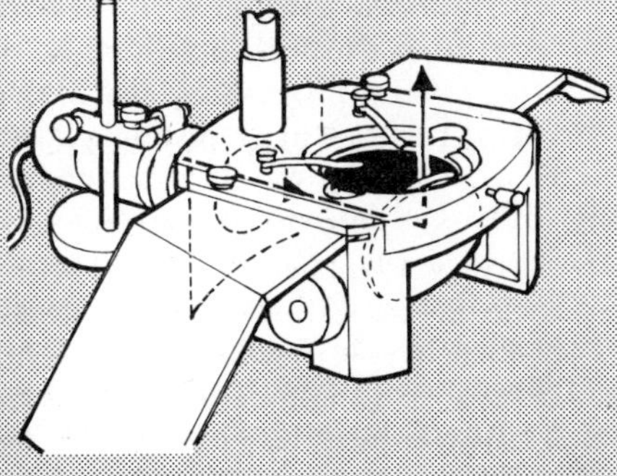

(35 mm diameter spherical bulb) with standard Edison screw (ES 27) cap. To insert the lamp holder, slide it into the spring sleeve inside the circular rear opening of the X-DE.

The mirror in the X-DE base is mounted in a spring fork that swivels about the transverse axis and is controlled by a large knob in the left-hand side of the base. The mirror also swivels sideways in the fork.

The cylindrical mirror side of the reflector directs the light from the built-in lamp onto the subject from underneath. This is however mainly intended for microscope viewing; the light is too uneven for photography. The reverse of the mirror is white plastic for diffused trans-illumination with the LSD spot lamp. When using the latter, remove the lamp holder and set up the LSD lamp behind the X-DE base so that it projects its beam through the lamp holder opening towards the front.

An alternative reflector is the PM-ELCS centering mirror used in conjunction with the incident illuminator mirror housings. This has a plane polished metal surface on one side and a black surface on the other. The plane mirror surface is used for shadowless lighting in conjunction with the LSD illuminator and the Lieberkühn reflectors.

Rotation of the mirror with the fork by the knob in the left-hand side moves the reflected light beam forward or back in the field of view. Swivelling the mirror in the fork—do this from the front by the right-hand mirror edge—adjusts the lateral position of the beam.

To change the reflector, remove the VST-1 stand and turn the X-DE base upside down. (It is usually convenient to fold up the wooden handrests if fitted.) Partly withdraw the lamp holder to keep the lamp out of the way and turn the fork holding the reflector horizontal. Grip the reflector by its edges and pull forward against the front pivot so as to disengage the rear pivot, then lift out. To fit the alternative reflector (or refit the cylindrical mirror) hold it by the edges, engage one of the holes around the reflector circumference in the near pivot of the fork, pull forward against the spring pressure of the fork and let the opposite hole in the rim engage the other pivot. After changing reflectors, wipe off any fingermarks from the surface with a clean handkerchief or lens tissue.

Push back the lamp holder (if used), unfold the hand rests, turn the X-DE base upright again and refit the VST-1 stand and assembly.

The VL-DIA-A transilluminator base

This is a simpler base similar to the X-DE but without built-in lamp. It has a plane mirror and short sheet-metal hand rests. The top of the unit is flat, without side rails to the platform; the hand rests hook into a pair of screw heads at each side and are again level with the top of the VST-1 when fitted. A rod attached to the rim of the reflector protrudes through the opening in the right-hand side for easier lateral reflector adjustment. The back of the base carries a blanking plate. This unscrews to permit transillumination with the LSD lamp from behind, as with the current X-DE base. The VL-DIA-A is now discontinued.

The macro lighting system

Illumination for macrophotography requires considerable light concentration on small areas, yet makes access to the subject difficult as the camera system has to be very near, too. Macro lighting is therefore often based on low-voltage miniature spot-lights such as the LSD illuminators. They provide transillumination in conjunction with the VST-1 macro stand and X-DE transilluminator base, or incident lighting directly on the macrophoto stand base with the PM-EL mirror housings. The spotlights further provide shadowless illumination via Lieberkühn reflectors.

The LSD illuminators

These micro-projection units are miniature spotlights with a 6 volt 30 watt bulb, fed via the TE II transformer. They consist of the spotlight unit itself, a stand and filter holder or combined iris diaphragm and filter holder. Different combinations carry various designations:

The LSD transilluminator carries the spotlight on a solid round 12 cm base with a short (16 cm) column and is equipped with a combined iris diaphragm and filter holder.

The PM-LSD 2 carries the same spotlight on a larger base with tall column (approx. 27 cm high) and an extension column with adjustable fitting. The lamp unit can thus be up to 40 cm above the base for shining down onto the VST-1 (or PMT-35) stage at various angles. The PM-LSD 2 epi-illuminator outfit consists of two such lamps. The spotlights here carry a simple filter holder without iris diaphragm.

In both cases the spotlight is a 13 cm long lamphouse with an adjustable lamp holder at the rear and a condenser lens at the front. The lamp/lens distance is controlled over an 18 mm range by the large knob in the side of the grey housing sleeve. The lamp unit at the rear is removable and carries two knobs on concentric shafts for vertical and horizontal centering of the lamp filament in the optical axis.

Lamp changing

To fit or change the lamp, slack off the black clamping knob at the rear of the grey sleeve and carefully pull out the lamp holder unit. This takes a 6 volt 30 watt bulb of 25 mm diameter and 58 mm overall length (Olympus designation TB-1) with the filament plane at right angles to the lamp axis. The lamp has a small bayonet cap; insert it in the same way as a normal domestic bayonet cap bulb. After fitting the bulb carefully wipe it clean of any fingerprints or grease marks. Then carefully push the whole lamp unit back into the rear of the spotlight housing and clamp with the black clamping screw. It is convenient—but not essential—to have the lamp centering controls arranged at the same side as the spotlight focusing knob.

To centre the lamp in the housing, switch on (after connection to the transformer) and direct the spot squarely at a reasonably light surface about 2 to 3 feet away. Adjust the focusing knob until you see the lamp filament reasonably sharply in the projected spot, surrounded by a diffused halo. Now turn the two centering knobs so that the filament image appears centered in this suffused area of light. This setting of the centering knob should not then need further adjustment until you have to change the lamp.

To focus the spot on the subject, adjust the lamp focusing knob until you see a sharp image of the filament projected on the subject area to be lit. Then turn the knob

LSD ILLUMINATORS

1. Filter holder.
2. Iris scale.
3. Iris control lever.
4. Column and adjustable support.
5. Spot focusing knob.
6. Clamping knob for lamp holder, 7.
8. Base.
9. Clamping screw of iris filter holder.
10, 11. Lamp centering knobs.

The PM-LSD 2 *(left)* is an LSD mounted on a higher stand and with a different filter holder.

Right: lamp location *(top)*; filter location *(centre)*—thick glass and mounted interference filters in rear, thinner glass (rectangular or round) in front compartment.

To remove a round glass without touching the surface *(bottom right),* push up a folded strip of film or thin card through the bottom of the iris filter holder.

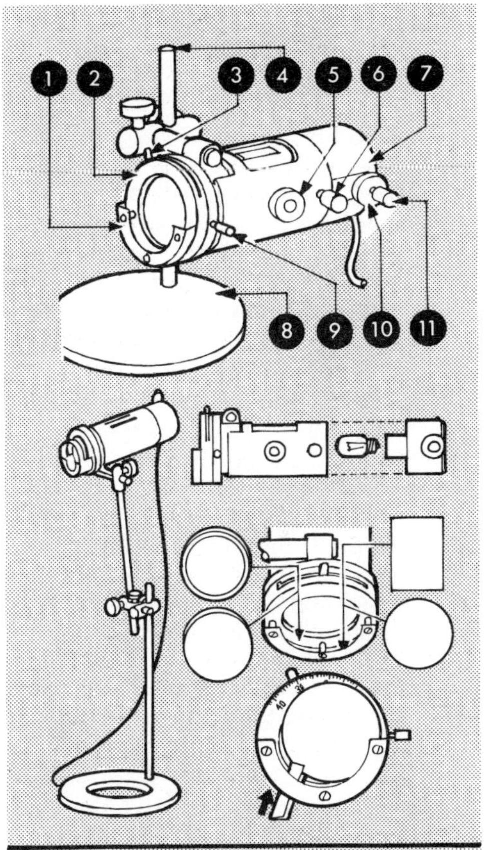

TE-II TRANSFORMER

1. Limit setting dial.
2. Main voltage control knob.
3. Voltmeter.
4. Main switch.
5. Pilot lamp.
6. Scale.
7. Output sockets for LSD lamp.
8. Mains lead.

To preset a voltage *(left),* depress and turn the lower flat knob. To turn the lamp up to power, rotate the main knob *(right)* to its stop.

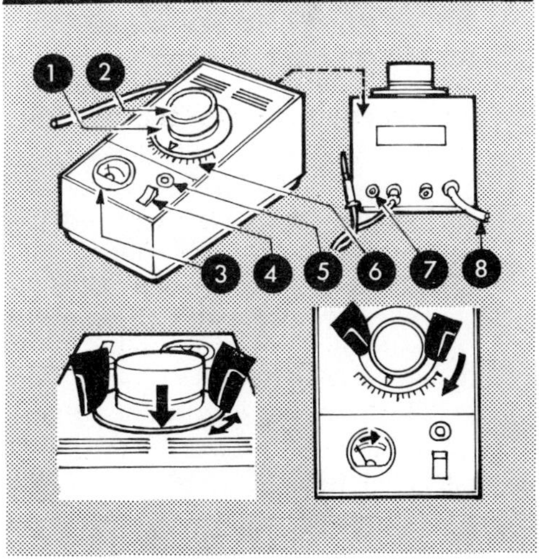

forward (bringing the sliding lamphouse closer to the condenser) until the filament is sufficiently unsharp to produce a reasonably evenly illuminated spot. Turning the knob further enlarges this spot. The actual focusing adjustment here depends on the distance from the spot lamp to the illuminated area. You have the position of maximum spot intensity when the suffused halo of the filament disappears, just before the lit area becomes surrounded by a reddish colour fringe.

Extending the lamphouse backwards increases the suffused area around the filament image and the latter eventually merges into this soft halo. This is not a true spot, for you are catching the beam diverging past its focal point. This lighting can be used for reflected illumination, but is not very even and nearly always has a central hot spot.

At maximum intensity the spot is square (that is the shape of the filament area); on diverging the beam (turning the focus knob to the right) the square becomes round with a reddish colour fringe and has a slightly darker centre spot.

The filter holder and iris

The simple filter holder, forming part of the PM-LSD 2 lamps, fits into the large holding ring at the front of the condenser lens and is secured in position by the chrome clamping screw. To fit filters (circular 45 mm glass or mounted neutral density filters) push them in through the slot at the filter holder rim. To stop filters from dropping out when you turn the lamp in a different direction, re-orient the filter holder—after slacking off the chrome clamping screw—so that the solid part of the holder rim supports the filter from underneath.

The iris filter holder fits on the front of the spot lamp housing in the same way and has a dual semi-circular holder with two filter compartments plus a built-in iris diaphragm. The latter reduces the illuminated field of view when the LSD illuminator is used as a trans-illuminator in conjunction with the X-DE base and the beam focused into the camera lens.

In this arrangement—essentially a standard method of microscope illumination—the iris diaphragm acts as a substage iris.

The 17-leaf iris is adjustable from 41 mm down to 3 mm. The scale on the rim, next to the operating lever, indicates the actual opening diameter in mm at each setting.

As with the plain filter holder of the LSD 2 lamp, you can freely turn the iris filter holder on slacking off the chrome clamping screw, to re-align it with the mm scale on top and to stop filters from dropping out, irrespective of the lamp position.

Lamp filters

To control the light quality and light intensity, the micro spotlights or LSD illuminators for macrophotography and the PM-DL 95 illuminator of the PMT-35 outfit take various lamp filters. They are available as rectangular 45 × 60 mm plain glass filters for the LSD illuminator, 45 mm circular glass for the LSD, PM-LSD 2 and PM-DL 95, or as mounted 45 mm interference filters for the same illuminators. Sets of these filters also form part of the complete PMT-35 outfit and of the EMM-7 photomicrographic exposure meter (see Chpt. *Photomicro equipment*).

The tables (see Chpt. *Facts and figures*) list the filter applications to colour temperature and light intensity control. The following filter types are available:

LB colour temperature compensation filters (circular 45 mm plain glass or 45 × 60 mm rectangular glass): These filters are the blue LB-45, LB-100 and LB-200. The number indicates the approximate negative mired shift.

Monochromatic filters (45 mm circular glass or 45 × 60 mm rectangular): These are the yellow Y-48 and green G-53 for enhanced contrast of certain black-and-white macro shots.

Neutral density filters (circular mounted interference filters) reduce the light intensity of the illuminators without altering the colour temperature.

The neutral density filters are interference filters and use a coating that reflects all light that is not transmitted. This coating is very delicate and is on the inside of the filter disc, protected by a plain filter disc at a slight distance from the coated surface. These interference filters can therefore be safely cleaned—but with care! Preferably however avoid touching any surface of the filter. When cleaning do not press the two discs together.

The LBD interference filter (45 mm circular mounted only) is purplish blue by transmitted light and has a nominal −80 mired shift. In addition to colour temperature compensation, this filter also absorbs some green and so counteracts a residual greenish cast often present in transparencies exposed by blue-filtered tungsten lighting.

The WF diffusing screen (rectangular glass only) diffuses the spotlight beam of the LSD illuminator for general fill-in lighting.

The B 76 heat filter (rectangular glass only) is a blue cobalt glass and fits into the front compartment of the iris filter holder. It filters out part of the heat radiation that might affect delicate specimens during setting up, especially with intense transillumination. Remove the heat filter from the illuminator for the actual exposure.

Fitting filters

Rectangular 45 × 60 mm glass filters only fit the iris filter holder of the LSD illuminator (but the iris holder can be fitted on the PM-LSD 2 in place of the plain filter holder). Place the filter upright into the front compartment of the iris filter holder.

The heat absorbing filter however goes in the rear compartment.

Circular 45 mm all-glass filters are intended for the plain filter holder (normally supplied on the PM-LSD 2 illuminators). Push the filter into the slot of the holder in front of the condenser lens. Circular glass filters can also be used on the iris filter holder and in that case go into the front compartment if they are thin enough (up to 2 mm); thicker all-glass filters go into the rear compartment. When in position on the iris filter holder, these circular filters leave a slight gap near the top of the light opening where white light can emerge. Generally this is negligible; if necessary slightly close down the iris diaphragm (to about 38 on the scale) to cut out this edge light.

The mounted interference filters have a plastic rim with a rebate on one side. They go into the plain filter holder in the same way as glass filters. In the iris filter holder push the mount into the rear filter compartment with the rebate facing forward. The rebate exactly fits the divider between the two filter compartments; this holds the mounted filter correctly centred in front of the condenser.

To keep the filters clean (and to save constant cleaning) handle them by the edges. This is particularly easy with the rectangular filters which are convenient to get hold of in the iris filter holder. Circular filters are trickier to grip once they are in position. A convenient way is to push them up with a narrow strip of film (fold a 2 cm length of scrap 35 mm film in half to form a 10 × 35 mm strip), then grip the edge of the filter to remove it.

The TE-II transformer

The 6 volt micro spotlamp bulbs of the LSD and PM-LSD 2 (also of the PM-DL 95 transilluminator on the PMT-35) are fed from the TE-II transformer. Each illuminator needs its own transformer. But as no macro lighting set-up is likely to use more than two illuminators at a time, a pair of transformers will meet all requirements.

Connect the lamp to the transformer by plugging the two banana plugs into the two sockets at the rear. Always switch on lamps gradually. Before switching on turn the regulator knob on the top fully anti-clockwise (to the left). Switch on the transformer with the on/off switch on the top panel; the red signal lamp immediately above it should light up. Now slowly turn the regulator knob clockwise until the needle on the voltmeter—also on the operating panel—reaches 6 volts. Take about 1–2 seconds over turning the knob. During this operation the lamp fades in to full intensity.

Normally avoid going beyond the 6 volts level. A higher output voltage—up to 10 volts—is permissible for occasional use, for instance to obtain greater light intensity and to increase the colour temperature.

The flat spring loaded knob below the main knob (carrying the white arrow head) serves as a limiting stop to the movement of the regular knob. Depress this and turn to set to the required limit point.

To switch off the lamp, first turn the regulator knob back to zero (anti-clockwise) then switch off the transformer by the on/off switch.

The PM-EL mirror housings

These special light reflecting units attach to the front of Olympus macro lenses to direct light straight at the subject for coaxial illumination. They are useful where there would not otherwise be sufficient room to introduce lamps for incident lighting between the camera set-up and the subject.

The housings are rectangular metal boxes with a partially silvered mirror set at 45° to the main axis. A field lens in one side of the box faces this beam splitter. When mounted in front of the lens, the beam splitter holds back about 30% of the light, reducing the image brightness by the equivalent of half a lens stop. The same beam splitter reflects a light beam coming from the side through the field lens down onto the subject along the optical axis, producing coaxial front illumination. A carefully arranged black mirror in the rear of the mirror housing and the black finish of the inside absorb virtually all light not reflected by the beam splitter, preventing stray light from reaching the camera lens.

The PM-EL mirror housings are used with the concentrated spotlight beam of the LSD illuminators or a similar microscope lamp. There are three mirror housings to match three Olympus macro lenses.

The PM-EL 20 is the smallest of the mirror housings and fits the 21 mm front mount of the 20 mm Zuiko Macro lens. It illuminates an approx. 7 × 10 mm area.

The PM-EL 38 fits the 32 mm front mount of the 38 mm Zuiko Macro lens and with correct lighting alignment illuminates an area of about 16 × 22 mm.

The PM-EL 80 is intended for the 80 mm Zuiko Macro lens but fits any lens with 51 mm front outside mount diameter, including the rear mount of the Auto-bellows front standard. This permits retro-mounting of a 50 mm macro lens (or standard 50 mm lens). The PM-EL 80 then fits on the reversed front bellows standard.

The illuminated subject area with the PM-EL 80 is about 35 × 40 mm at 2 × magnification with the 80 mm lens and even here the corners of the area are not fully covered. At lower magnifications—with greater lens/subject distances—the illuminated area becomes circular and smaller as the condenser Fresnel of the PM-EL 80 causes the LSD spotlamp beam to converge. The

INCIDENT ILLUMINATOR MIRROR HOUSINGS

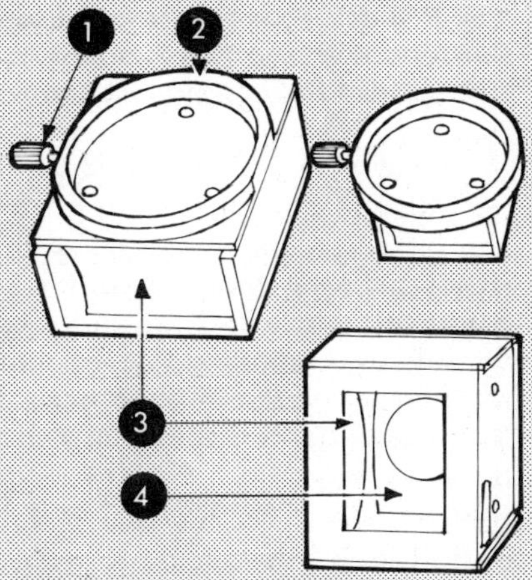

The parts of the PM-EL 38 mirror housing (PM-EL 20, alongside) are:

1. Clamping screw.
2. Clamping collar for lens front.
3. Front condenser lens.
4. Semi-reflecting beam splitter (inside housing).

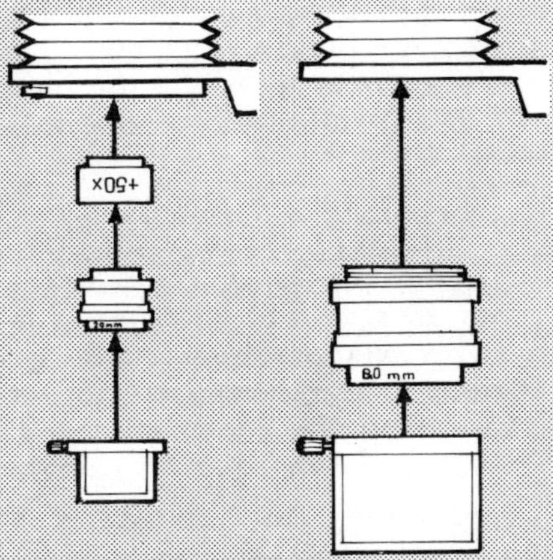

Left: the PM-EL 20 mirror housing goes on the front of the 20 mm macro lens which in turn fits the PM-MTob ring via the +0.5 × adapter ring when used on the PMT-35.

Right: the PM-EL 80 mirror housing fits the front of the 80 mm macro lens.

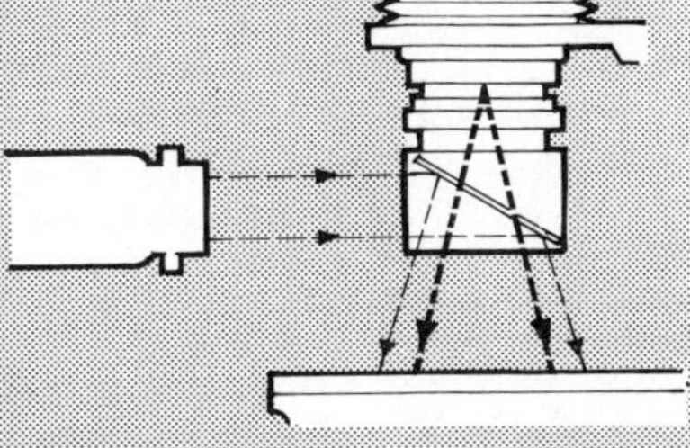

The PM-EL housings depend on reflecting the light from an LSD spotlight downwards on to the subject field while the lens covers the same field through the beamsplitter mirror.

lowest useful magnification for coaxial illumination with the PM-EL 80 is thus 1 ×. At lower magnifications direct lighting with the LSD or LSD 2 illuminators pointing at the subject from beside the camera is more practical.

Fitting and orientation of the mirror housings

Attach the mirror housing to the appropriate lens once the latter is firmly mounted on the Auto-bellows. Run the front bellows standard fully to the end of the rail and raise the whole rail for easy access to the lens. Fit the circular mount of the PM-EL housing over the lens front, orient the condenser window of the housing to the side or front and tighten the clamping screw. Then adjust the bellows extension for the required magnification by moving the rear standard and bring down the bellows rail for focusing.

The orientation of the PM-EL mirror housing depends on the lighting set-up and close-up unit with which it is used. The field illuminated by the reflected light beam is more or less rectangular, and ideally this should be oriented in the same way as the image format in the camera. With the camera on the bellows and pointing vertically downwards, the rectangular illuminated field matches the orientation of the camera's film gate if the condenser window of the PM-EL housing points either forward (towards you as you face the camera set-up) or to the rear. The latter position is fine with the PMT-35 where you can also set up the LSD illuminator behind the unit. It then beams its light forward into the rear facing condenser window of the PM-EL mirror housing. With the PM-EL 20 housing on the 20 mm macro lens, screw the + 0.5 × adapter between the lens and the PM-MTob mount so that the mirror housing is well clear of the end of the bellows rail.

The + 0·5 × adapter ring

This is a 10 mm extension ring threaded to take the 20 or 38 mm macro lens at one end and to screw into the PM-MTob lens mount adapter at the other. Its main function is to extend the front of the 20 mm macro lens away from the front bellows standard of the PMT-35 outfit when the PM-EL 20 mirror housing is used. Without this extension ring, the end of the bellows rail

LIEBERKÜHN REFLECTOR SET-UP

The set-up for Lieberkühn shadowless lighting involves the following items *(left)*:

1. Front of bellows unit.
2. PM-MTob lens holder (for 20 or 38 mm macro lens).
3. 20 or 38 mm macro lens.
4. PM-LM 20 or PM-LM 38 Lieberkühn reflector.
5. Shade stage plate with centre disc.
6. X-DE base and LSD illuminator.

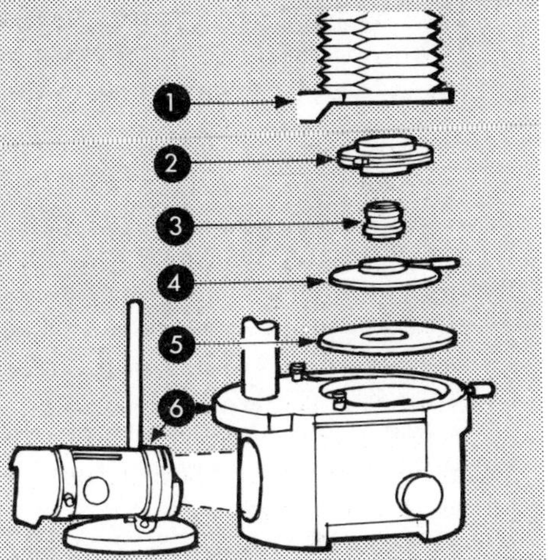

When used with the PMT-35 system, the stage unit and the illuminator of the latter replace the X-DE plus LSD *(right)*.

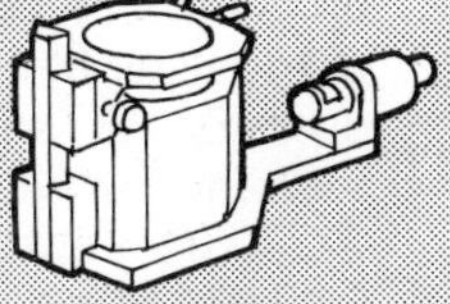

To attach the Lieberkühn reflector to the lens, slack off the clamping screw, place the reflector over the front lens mount and secure with the screw.

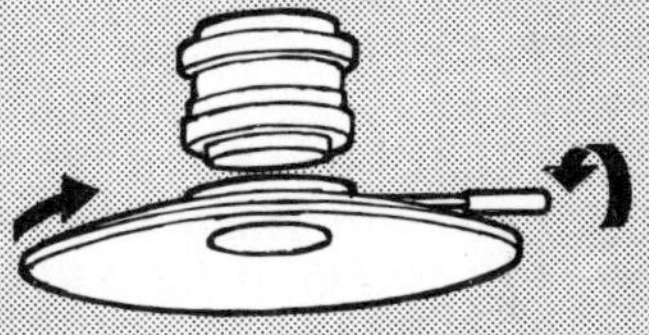

The principle of shadowless Lieberkühn lighting is that a focused beam from the micro spotlight is reflected up by the mirror in the illuminator base towards the Lieberkühn reflector. The opaque centre disc of the shade stage plate keeps direct light out of the lens, while the Lieberkühn reflector directs diffused soft light back onto the subject placed on the centre disc of the shade stage plate.

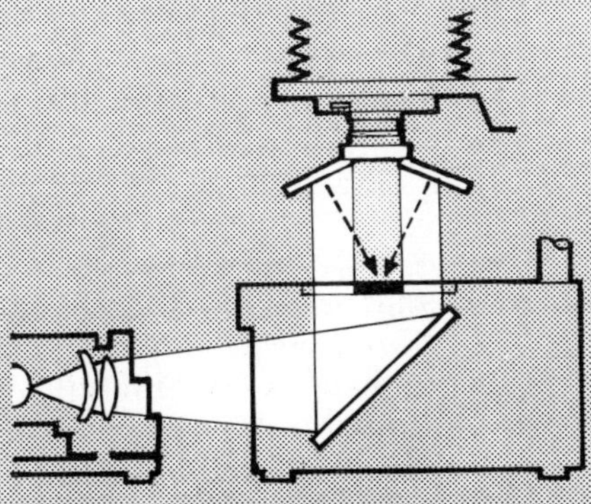

intrudes into the light path between an LSD illuminator and the PM-EL 20 when this faces backwards on the PMT-35. The +0.5× adapter ring goes between the macro lens and the PM-MTob mount on the bellows.

The PM-ELCS centering mirror

This 72 mm diameter disc (6 mm thick) has a polished metal mirror surface on one side and is matt black on the other. It is used as the reflector in the X-DE transilluminator base for shadowless illumination with the Lieberkühn reflectors. It is also a useful aid to centering the LSD spotlight illuminator with the PM-EL mirror housings and for setting up the camera square to the baseboard on the copy stand.

Lieberkühn reflectors

These two shallow dished reflectors clamp onto the front of the 20 mm and 38 mm macro lenses respectively for shadowless illumination. The matt chrome surface picks up light directed towards the lens and reflects soft illumination back to the subject.

The PM-LM 20 *reflector* of 46 mm diameter fits on the front of the 20 mm Zuiko Macro lens and is held by a screw that clamps a spring collar against the front lens mount.

The PL-LM 38 reflector of 68 mm clamps onto the front of the 38 mm Zuiko Macro lens in the same way.

The Lieberkühn reflectors are used in conjunction with the X-DE transilluminator base and the VST-1 macro stand carrying the camera and bellows assembly plus the LSD illuminator and the shade stage plate. The Lieberkühn reflectors are also usable with the PMT-35 macro outfit (see below) and the shade stage plate.

The light from the LSD illuminator is reflected up by the plane mirror in the X-DE base towards the macro lens while the black or white opaque centre of the shade stage plate prevents direct light from reaching the lens. The light beam passing round the outside of this centre disc reaches the Lieberkühn reflector and is reflected downwards on the subject. The set-up works the same way with the PMT-35 and its own illuminator and reflector.

The PMT-35 macrophoto outfit

Useful outfits for macrophotography can be assembled from the Auto-bellows, macro stand and illuminators for high-magnification microphotography, but have to be built up every time from a number of separate units. More convenient for routine macrophotography, for instance pathological, medical, forensic and other scientific applications, is the PMT-35 outfit tailored around a specially rigid stand unit with built-in illuminators and other features but using some standard equipment items already described. The outfit consists of a number of matched components and alternative fittings to form the macro-system:

(a) *The PM-PS35 stand with arm.* This in turn consists of a 320 × 395 mm (12.6 × 15.6 inch) heavy cast alloy base, a 530 mm (20.8 inch) steel column of 46 mm diameter, a supporting collar and an arm with dovetail mount. The base, arm and collar are identical with the same components of the PM-PSS photomicrographic stand which however has a different arm. The base is covered by a rubber mat and carries a screw-in centering pin for locating the illuminator unit; for photomicrography the pin can be screwed in to be flush with the top of the mat.

(b) *The PM-DL95 illuminator.* This in turn consists of the illuminator housing with built-in mirror (sealed dust-proof inside the housing), a 115 mm (4.5 inch) condenser lens, and a vertically adjustable subject stage. The illuminator housing is mounted on a heavy rigid arm that carries a fixed micro spotlamp with a 6 volt, 5 amp compact-filament bulb (TP-1). The latter is similar to, but not interchangeable with, the TB-1 bulb of the LSD.

The subject stage is mounted on an arm that fits into a dovetail guide on the illuminator housing. The stage itself runs up and down the arm by a rack-and-pinion drive with a movement range for the stage—and hence the object plane along the camera axis—of 100 mm or 4 inches. The arm carrying the stage can be raised through a further 70 mm in its dovetail fitting, providing a total adjustment of 170 mm. The stage has a built-in iris diaphragm adjustable from 10 to 95 mm and takes the same stage plates as the VST-1 stand. Similar stage clips are provided, too. The light source, illuminator, stage and camera axis are pre-centered on the PMT-35 so that practically no special setting up is required for transillumination or for shadowless illumination with the Lieberkühn reflectors.

(c) *The TE-II transformer* to feed the lamp of the illuminator. This is the same transformer as employed with the LSD micro spotlights.

(d) *The PM-BD35 bellows unit.* This consists of a dovetail connector, a rail with front and rear bellows standards, connected by bellows, to take the lens and camera respectively. The unit is similar in principle to the Auto-bellows but differs in a number of details. Thus the dovetail connector (with plastic slideway lining) fits onto the PM-PS35 arm at one end and holds the bellows rail at the other. It has however no rack-and-pinion drive and the rail is clamped in position at various points by a clamping knob.

The rail itself is 313 mm long, has the usual end stop screws and carries on its front surface a mm scale. In addition, different colour-coded scales indicate required camera standard settings for different magnifications with the three macro lenses. This side of the rail has a rack extending on it for about 70 mm at its front (bottom) end to mesh with the pinion drive of the lens standard. The latter is similar to the lens standard or lens mount board of the Auto-bellows, but has no stop-down provision (neither lever nor cable release socket), since the PMT-35 is intended exclusively for use with the macro lenses which have no auto-aperture coupling with the camera. The camera standard (camera body mount board) takes the OM camera via a PM-CAMS adapter which is identical with the OM mount photomicro adapter H and almost identical with the camera body mount of the Auto-bellows. The camera standard slides along the rail and is clamped in position by a clamping knob; there is no rack-and-pinion drive.

(e) *The PM-MS35 shutter.* This is a Copal leaf shutter with a 24 mm opening diameter and time settings from 1 to 1/500 second as well as B and T. It is tensioned by a lever and released by a cable release. At the B setting the shutter remains open as long as the release is pressed; at the T setting the shutter opens on the first pressure on the release and remains open until closed again by a

PMT-35 MACRO OUTFIT

1. Shutter.
2. Bellows rail.
3. Bellows.
4. Adapter H for camera back in rear standard.
5. Positioning dot (80 mm (lens).
6. End cap of column.
7. Arm with dovetail.
8. Front bellows standard.
9. Lens.
10. Transmitted light illuminator and stage.
11. Baseboard.
12. Clamping knob of dovetail holder.
13. Clamping knob for bellows rails in dovetail bellows holder.
14. Supporting collar.
15. Lens shift knob of lens standard.
16. Column.
17. Bellows clamping.
18. Positioning mark for mounting lens.
19. Bayonet mount.
20. Rack at front of rail.
21. Clamping knob of H adapter.
22. Magnification scale.
23. Clamping knob for front bellows standard.
24. Stage rail.
25. Stage.
26. Stage clips.
27. Iris diaphragm lever.
28. Stage plate clamping knob.
29. Lamp clamping knob.
30. Lamphouse.
31. Clamping knob of rail adjustment.
32. Stop pin.
33. Rail clamping knob in stage dovetail holder.
34. Stage focusing knob.
35. Stage plate.
36. Condenser built into illuminator base.
37. Filter mount.
38. Auxiliary condenser.

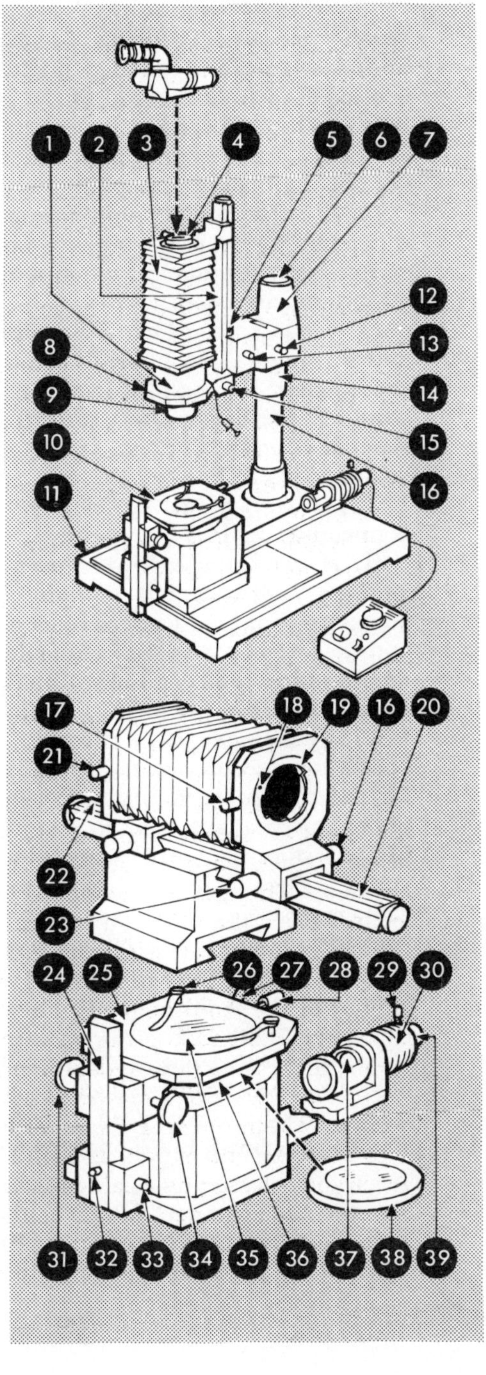

second pressure. It further has a preview lever to open and close the shutter independently of the time setting, a coaxial flash socket and an M/X synchronising lever. The shutter fits between the lens standard and the bellows. A foam plastic mounting connects the shutter to its supporting plate to damp any vibration.

(f) *The PM-MC 38 supplementary condenser* of 72 mm diameter fits over the built-in condenser of the transmitted-light illuminator when working with the 20 and 38 mm macro lenses.

(g) *Three Zuiko Macro lenses:* 20 mm f3.5, 38 mm f3.5 and 80 mm f4. The PMT-35 unit is only usable with these lenses. Though for instance the 50 mm macro lens would fit the bayonet mount of the lens standard, in the absence of any stop-down facility it would be usable only at full aperture.

(h) *A pair of PM-SDM light excluding collars* for connecting the PMT-35 bellows to a microscope.

(j) *A set of circular 45 mm filters:* 45 G-53 (light green), 45 Y-48 (yellow), 45 LB-45 (light blue colour temperature adjusting), mounted interference filters (ND-50, ND-12 and ND-6) and an LBD magenta filter, also for colour temperature control. These filters are the same as the lamp filters for the LSD illuminators. The set of the PMT-35 includes two LB-45 and ND-50 filters each.

(k) *Other accessories.* A PM-MTob lens mount adapter for the 20 and 38 mm macro lenses, a PM-CAMS (or photo-micro adapter H) to take the camera on the rear bellows standard, three stage plates (stage plate 28, 45 and the glass stage plate), spare bulbs, stage clips and a cable release.

Items (e) to (k) are housed in a wooden accessories case with fitted compartments for easy access and storage.

A vinyl dust cover is also provided for the whole PMT-35 set up.

Lighting aids such as the mirror housings for coaxial lighting, Lieberkühn reflectors, micro spotlight, other stage plates etc. can be used with the PMT-35 in the ways already described, but do not form part of the outfit.

Assembling the PMT-35

1. Place the baseboard on a firm working table and slack off the clamping knob of the column base. Insert

ASSEMBLING PMT-35—(1)

Insert the column in the base *(left)* with keyway at side and lock. Fit the collar and arm over the top of the column *(right)*.

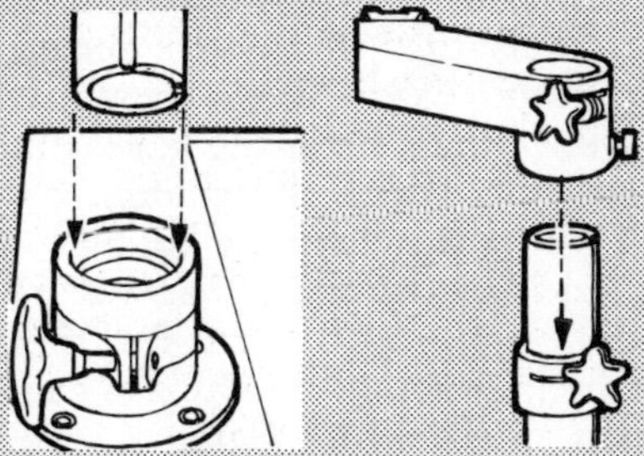

Screw on the cap (1), move the arm to the top of the column and align so that the keyway locking screw (3) engages keyway. Tighten the clamping knob (2) and keyway lock (3). Push up collar and tighten with (4).

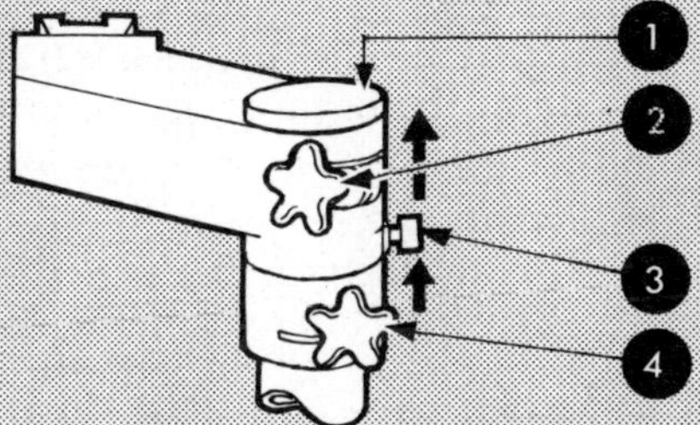

Screw out the centering pin in the baseboard and locate the illuminator base with its locating hole over the pin.

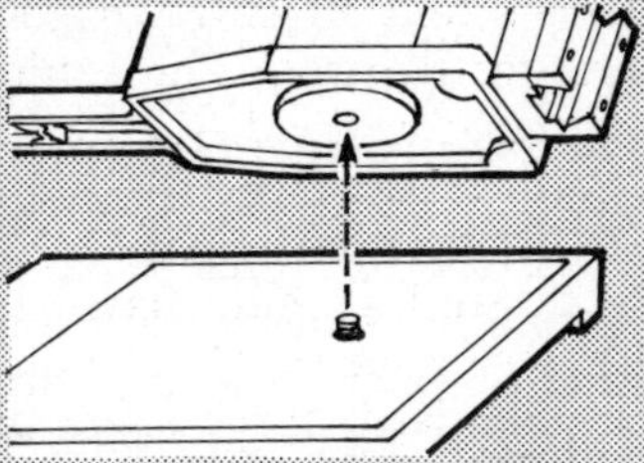

Insert the stage with its rail in the dovetail holder on the illuminator base *(left)*. The stop pin must be unscrewed at this point, then screw it in.

Right: Fit the TP-1 lamp in the lamp socket and insert the latter in the rear of the lamphouse. Clamp tight.

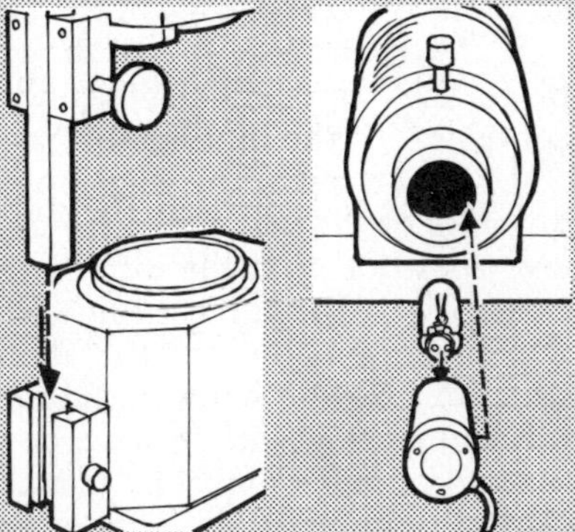

the bottom end of the column (the end with a notch in the rim) so that this notch engages a stop pin inside the column base. When correctly inserted, the keyway groove must be at the left of the base when you face the baseboard with the column base at the far left corner. Tighten the clamping knob.

2. Unscrew the cap at the top of the column and slide the supporting collar for the arm over the column. Clamp it about one-third of the way down from the top.

3. Slack off the clamping knob and the keyway locking screw on the arm and fit the latter—with the smooth side on top (hollowed out section underneath) over the top of the column. The dovetail holder should face forward and the clamping knob to the rear. In this position you can partly screw in the keyway locking screw which will engage in the keyway in the side of the column.

4. Screw back the cap onto the top of the column.

5. Slack off the clamping knob of the supporting collar and move the collar and arm up on the column until stopped by the column cap. In this position firmly clamp the collar and screw the clamping knob of the arm and the keyway locking screw tight.

6. With a coin unscrew the centering pin in the baseboard to its full extent. This precisely locates the illuminator base.

7. Place the illuminator base on the baseboard, with the locating hole underneath the base over the centering pin. Line up the base so that the front (with the dovetail holder for the stage) is parallel with the front edge of the PMT baseboard and the lamp holder arm pointing straight to the rear edge of the baseboard.

8. If you propose to use the 20 or 38 mm macro lens, place the supplementary condenser over the built-in condenser of the illuminator base.

9. On the rail of the stage unscrew the stop pin (three-quarters of the way down from the top) so that its inner end does not protrude into the inside groove of the rail.

10. Insert the subject stage with its rail vertically into the dovetail holder of the illuminator base and let it slide fully down. Screw in the stop pin. This prevents the rail from being withdrawn from the dovetail guide, but the rail remains movable. Clamp it in position with the clamping knob at the side of the dovetail holder. The

ASSEMBLING PMT-35—(2)

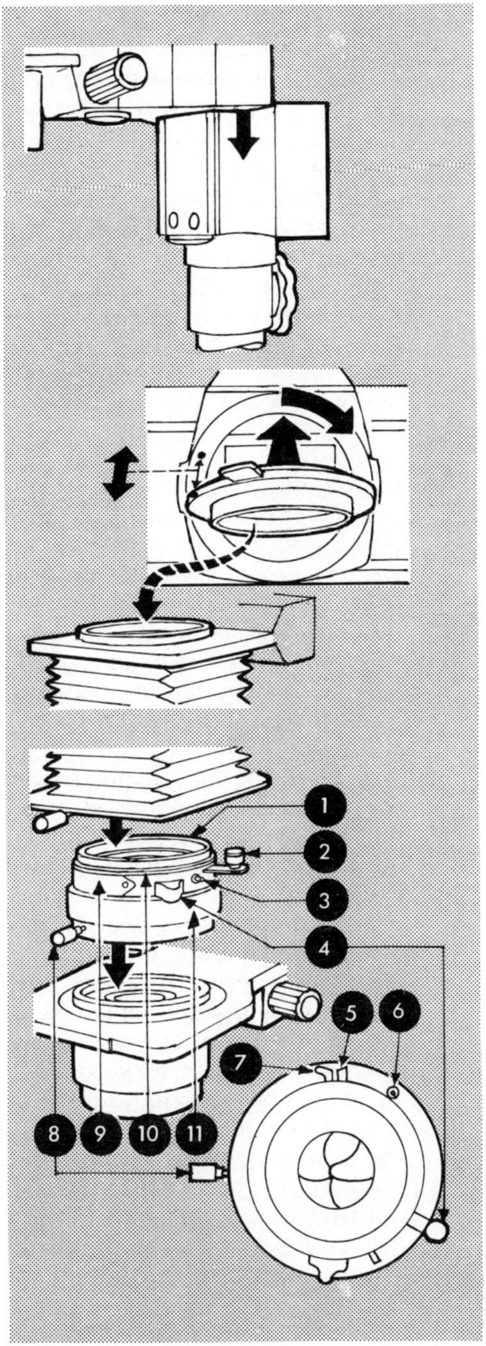

Fit the bellows unit on the dovetail holder of the arm and clamp.

Fit the H adapter ring to the camera, then insert in the rear bellows standard and clamp.

Fit the leaf shutter between the bellows and the lens standard.

1. Bellows mounting ring.
2. Tensioning lever.
3. Flash contact.
4. Opening (preview) lever.
5. Cable release socket.
6. M-X selector lever.
7. Release lever.
8. Clamping screw.
9. Speed scale.
10. Speed setting ring.
11. Vibration-proof mount.

illuminator base may be packed with the stage already inserted in its dovetail guide; in that case check that the stop pin is screwed in before lifting the illuminator unit for placement on the PMT-35 base.

11. Insert a lamp in the lamp socket: line up the red dot on the flange with the left-hand red dot on the lamp socket, press down and turn to bring the red dot opposite the right-hand dot on the socket. Preferably handle the lamp with a handkerchief or cloth; after fitting be sure to wipe the glass bulb carefully to remove all finger marks. If a bulb needs changing, remove it by pressing in the lamp on the socket and turning anti-clockwise to release it from the socket.

12. Slack off the clamping screw on the lamp housing, push in the lamp socket all the way and tighten the clamping screw.

13. Plug the two banana plugs of the lamp lead into the outlet sockets at the rear of the TE-II transformer and plug the mains lead of the transformer into a mains supply socket. Preferably fit an earthed plug to the transformer lead.

14. Mount the bellows unit. Slack off the clamping knob at the side of the bellows dovetail holder (the clamping knob of the free dovetail, not the one holding the rail) and slide this over the dovetail of the main arm. A screw (similar to the bellows rail end screw) is screwed into the bottom of the dovetail fitted on the arm. Check that this is firmly screwed in. Slide down the bellows unit until its dovetail abuts this end screw, then clamp the clamping knob at the side.

15. Slack off the clamping knob on the dovetail holder next to the bellows rail, push the rail fully up on the arm and clamp, ready for the next assembly step.

16. Mount the lens. The 80 mm macro lens fits the bayonet mount of the front standard in the same way as the camera mount. To remove the lens, press the milled key to the right of the red dot and turn the lens anti-clockwise to release it from the mount.

To use the 20 mm or 38 mm macro lenses, screw these first into the PM-MTob adapter mount, then fit the latter to the lens standard by its bayonet mount in the same way as a lens. The black milled button screwed to the edge of the PM-MTob ring facilitates handling. To remove, press the milled key to the right of the black knob and turn the whole mount and lens to the left to disengage.

17. Fit the shutter. Slack off the bellows clamping screw at the left, next to the lens standard, and raise this end of the bellows clear of the standard. On the shutter slack off the clamping screw in the side of the shutter mount and place the shutter over the black ring protruding at the rear of the lens standard. The clamping screw should be at the left so that the small chrome screw inside the shutter mount engages the notch in the attachment ring on the bellows. When properly fitted, the black lever for manual opening and closing of the shutter should be at the front, the chrome tensioning lever at the right and the shutter speed scale at the left. Tighten the clamping screw.

18. Bring down the loose end of the bellows over the ring on top of the shutter and tighten the bellows clamping screw.

19. Attach the camera. Fit the PM-CAMS mounting ring (photomicro adapter H) into the lens bayonet mount of the camera in the same way as a lens: line up the red dot in the rim of the adapter mount with the red dot on the front flange of the camera's bayonet mount, insert the adapter and turn to the right to engage the bayonet lock (the red dot should now be opposite the red index line in front of the shutter speed ring). To remove the adapter mount, press the lever projecting from the ring radially inwards and turn the mount anti-clockwise to disengage. Fitting the mount also programmes the exposure metering system to the light transmission of the set-up.

20. Slack off the clamping screw in the side of the rear standard and insert the camera with the adapter mount. Line up the camera straight with respect to the bellows, then secure by tightening the camera adapter clamping screw. Fit the Varimagni finder to the camera eyepiece.

21. Fit the appropriate stage plate in the object stage according to the macro illumination to be used. Fit appropriate lighting accessories and set up any LSD macro spotlights if needed for additional lighting.

Setting up adjustments

With the three macro lenses from 20 to 80 mm and magnification scales from 0.5 to 16.5 ×, the PMT-35 outfit covers a considerable range of object/lens and lens/film distances which are preset coarsely according to the lens in use. In part this involves different locations of the subject stage which in turn makes some modification of the built-in transillumination system necessary. These modifications are very straightforward and do not interfere with the simplicity and convenience of the prealigned and preset lighting system.

The adjustments are best grouped by the lenses employed:

With the 80 mm macro lens:

(a) Slack off the clamping knob of the bellows rail on the dovetail holder and shift the bellows rail up as far as it will go, so that the yellow dot with the yellow figure 80 on the side of the rail appears just above the arm.

(b) For magnifications between 3× and 1× slack off the clamping knob at the side of the stage dovetail (but do not unscrew the stop pin in the stage rail) and move the stage rail with the whole stage up as far as it will go, then tighten the clamping knob again. For magnifications smaller than 1.0× (down to the 0.37× limit with the 80 mm lens) leave the stage rail in its bottom position.

(c) For magnifications between 0.5× and 0.37× unclamp the clamping screw at the left of the lens standard and turn the lens shift knob to bring the standard up to the top of its rack—with the upper edge of the standard lined up with 100 on the rail scale—and clamp in position. First remember to raise also the rear (camera) standard. This provides the extra lens/subject distance needed at low magnifications.

(d) For magnifications between 3× and 0.75× slack off the clamping screw at the rear of the lamphouse and pull out the lamp socket by about 5 mm. This ensures more even illumination in the subject plane. For magnifications below 0.75× push the lamp socket fully into the lamphouse and clamp.

(e) Magnifications between 0.37× and 0.75× with the 80 mm lens require a short lens/film distance. For this the bellows can be sufficiently compressed only if you remove the diaphragm shutter. At these magnifications the risk of unsharpness through vibration is negligible and you can safely expose with the camera shutter.

PMT-35 SETTINGS AND OPERATING SEQUENCE

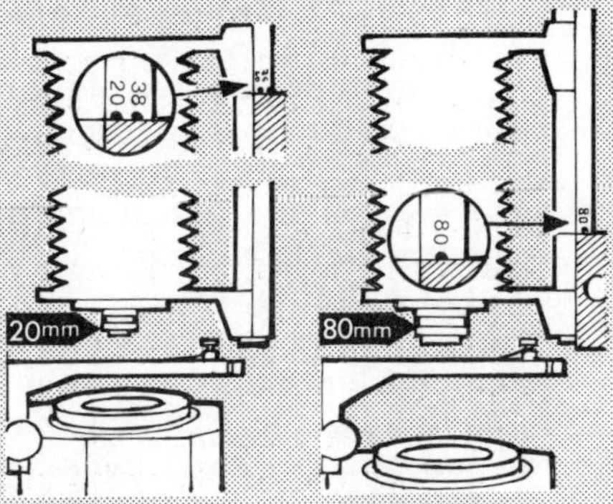

With 20 and 38 mm lenses set the bellows rail to the appropriate markings, subject stage rail in bottom position, and lamp socket fully pushed into lamphouse *(left)*.

With 80 mm lens set bellows rail to top position, stage rail in top position and slightly extend lamp socket in lamphouse *(right)*.

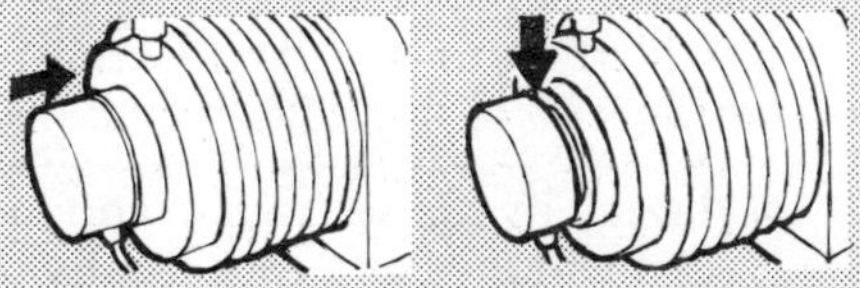

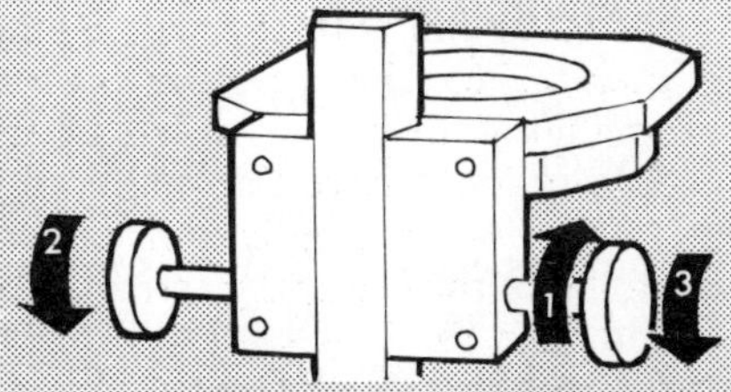

For fine focusing run stage upwards (1) just past sharpest point, clamp with clamping knob (2), then gently turn focusing knob to lower stage to sharpest point (3).

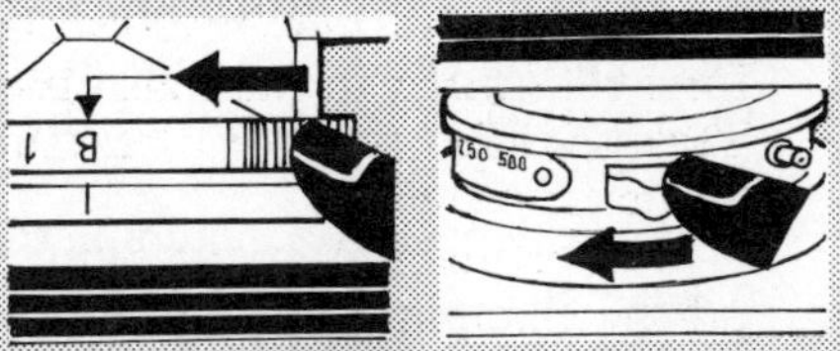

For the exposure set the camera shutter to B *(left)*, then close leaf shutter *(right)*.

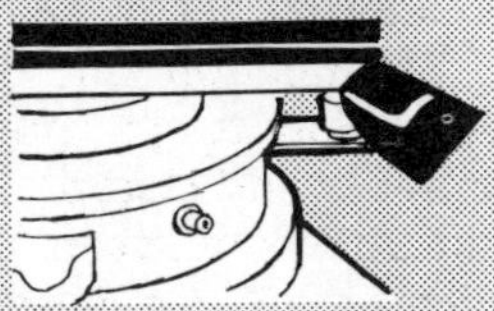

Tension the leaf shutter.

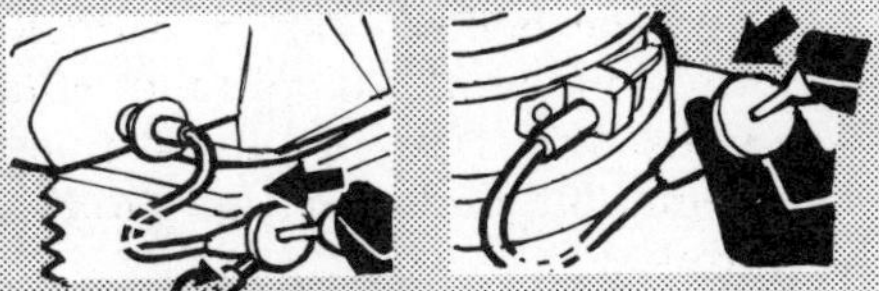

Release first the camera shutter *(left)* then the leaf shutter *(right)*. Finally, close the camera shutter.

With the 38 mm and 20 mm macro lenses (mounted on the PM-MTob adapter):

(a) Lower the stage rail of the object stage to its bottom position on the front dovetail holder.

(b) Place the supplementary condenser over the main condenser on the transilluminator housing. This concentrates the light beam on the smaller subject area covered with these lenses.

(c) Run the subject stage to its bottom position on the rail by the fine adjustment knob.

(d) Release the clamping knob holding the bellows rail and carefully lower the latter on the arm so that the green and blue dots marked 38 and 20 respectively in the side of the rail are flush with the top of the arm. Clamp the rail firmly in this position.

(d) Lower the front lens standard to the extreme end of the rail by the shift knob and lock in position.

(e) Push the lamp socket fully in on the lamphouse and clamp in position.

Lighting adjustment

The techniques of illumination are dealt with in the *Close-up and macro technique* chapter. Here are a few points specific to PMT-35 settings.

The transmitted illumination system of the PMT-35 uses a collector lens and a diffuser in front of the lamp in the lamphouse to produce a light beam that passes through the condenser lens at the top of the illuminator to converge in the pupil of the macro lens. This yields even illumination of the subject field but correct convergence depends on matching the beam to the condenser/macro lens distance. The supplementary condenser lens for the 20 and 38 mm macro lenses increases the convergence to match the shorter condenser/lens distance. The light spot produced in the plane on the stage, for instance when you place a sheet of thin paper on the stage, is uniform over the field covered by the macro lens though it may look less even at the edges outside the camera's field of view.

The size of this field can be reduced by the iris diaphragm built into the stage. To close down this diaphragm move the lever at the left of the stage to the back; to open move it forward, i.e. towards the stage rail.

PMT-35 LIGHT PATH

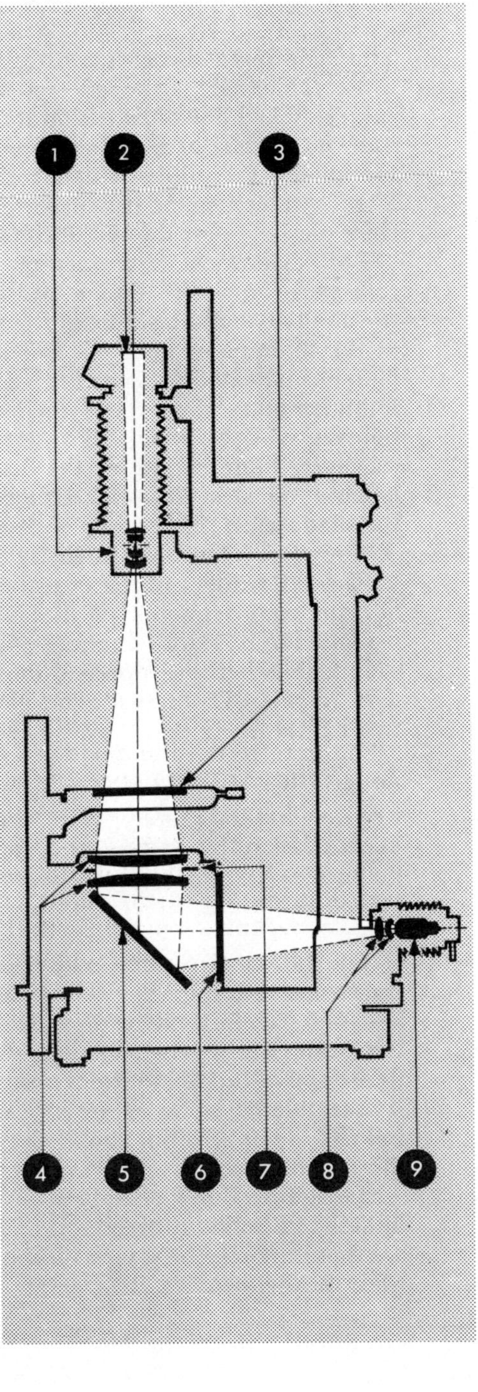

Optical layout of the PMT-35 when set up for transillumination.

1. Camera lens.
2. Film plane.
3. Stage plate in stage (subject plane).
4. Condenser.
5. Mirror.
6. Window in illuminator base.
7. Substage iris diaphragm to limit illuminated area.
8. Collector lens assembly of lamp unit.
9. Lamp.

This set-up is the one employed with the 80 mm lens; with the 20 and 38 mm lenses, the film plane and lens are nearer to the subject plane, and an additional condenser lens is inserted between (3) and (4).

The diaphragm also reduces stray light from outside the subject area that may be reflected back from the lens to the subject. Close down the iris until it just begins to obtrude into the corners of the image seen through the camera's viewfinder, then open it up by about 20% in diameter. You can measure the iris diameter approximately with a ruler placed across the top of the stage.

For shadowless illumination with the Lieberkühn reflectors (only with the 20 and 38 mm lenses) remove the auxiliary condenser from the main condenser on top of the illuminator housing. For here you need a wider light beam to fill the area of the Lieberkühn reflector. Also illumination is improved if the lamp socket in the lamp housing is slightly withdrawn (by about 5 mm). Check the even illumination of the Lieberkühn reflector by looking up at it from underneath the stage, through the shade stage plate.

The light colour and intensity can be modified by the voltage adjustment of the transformer and by filters that fit into compartments of the half-round filter holder trough in front of the lamphouse. The four compartments each take either one mounted interference filter (neutral density or LBD) or two plain glass filters (for instance two LB-45 filters).

Magnification setting

For macrophotography with the PMT-35 select the magnification by setting the camera standard of the bellows by the scale on the bellows rail. Then focus by adjusting the lens/subject distance with the stage focusing knob.

The rail carries three magnification scales—blue for the 20 mm, green for the 38 mm and yellow for the 80 mm lens—and a white extension scale in mm. The magnification scales apply when the lens standard is moved fully to the end of the rail (bottom position when the PMT-35 is assembled). As far as the mm scale is concerned, this rail end is not zero but about + 13 mm. In other words, the 100 mm mark is only 87 mm from the end of the rail. The magnification scales allow for this; the magnification figures indicated on the rail at different mm scale points are therefore not the same as for instance in the scales for the Auto-bellows.

These magnification figures are approximate. For exact magnification check the image scale with a stage micrometer or the FM mechanical stage as described before.

Fine focusing

A large black right-hand knob on the stage carrier raises and lowers the stage for fine focusing adjustment; the knob on the left-hand side locks this adjustment. Provided the whole rail was raised or lowered as described above for the different lens and magnification ranges, the 100 mm fine focusing travel is fully adequate to take care of subject plane shifts when changing the image scale.

Before focusing always check that all other adjustments of the PMT-35—especially the bellows rail, front and rear standards—are securely clamped. The leaf shutter must of course be open: push the black opening lever on the shutter front to the right, towards the coaxial flash socket.

With the left-hand knob of the stage focusing adjustment slack, the stage will travel down the rail under its own weight to the bottom stop. Once you have focused sharply you therefore have to lock the adjustment. The trick lies in doing that without moving the focus setting.

This is a two-handed job: grip the right-hand knob with the right hand and the left-hand knob with the left while observing the image on the camera's screen through the Varimagni finder eyepiece. Start with the stage at the bottom of its travel and slowly turn the right-hand knob towards you to raise the stage until the image appears sharp. Turn very slightly past the sharpest point, hold the right-hand knob tightly and turn the left-hand knob towards you to tighten the movement. Then very gently turn the right-hand knob away from you against the friction of the clamping action until the image is absolutely sharp. If you overshoot the sharpest point, turn the right-hand knob towards you again (without slacking off the left-hand knob) past the sharpest point and then go back again. Check this also with the Varimagni finder set to 2.5 × magnification. Use the 1–11 or 1–12 focusing screen for all macro focusing and check the point of maximum sharpness by moving your head slightly to and fro behind the eyepiece to see whether the hairline images of the screen centre graticule shift with respect to the focused image.

While actually checking the image sharpness at high magnification take your hands off the focusing and locking knobs and do not touch the Varimagni finder eyepiece, either. For any contact with the PMT-35 set-up can induce vibration that upsets the appearance of sharpness in the image.

This procedure of approaching the point of maximum sharpness by raising the stage past it and then going back against the friction of the clamp focusing movement eliminates focusing errors and drift due to the backlash of the rack-and-pinion drive.

Exposure procedure

Determine the required exposure time either with the through-the-lens meter of the camera (in manual mode in the case of the OM-2) or with the EMM-7 exposure meter. After any exposure measurement involving removal of the camera body from the rear bellows standard always recheck the image for maximum sharpness. Measure the exposure with the macro lens stopped down to the aperture to be used. But preferably work at full aperture for maximum resolution.

The exposure is made with the leaf shutter, but the camera shutter must be open for this purpose at the B setting. As two release actions are involved, you need either two single cable releases or a twin cable release. When using two releases at least one must have a time exposure lock, for instance the SR-II release supplied with the PMT-35 outfit. Screw this into the camera's release button and a second cable release into the release socket on the leaf shutter. The sequence of operations is then:

1. Set the camera shutter to B.

2. Close the leaf shutter by moving the black lever on the shutter rim to the left.

3. Tension the leaf shutter by pulling the chrome lever (protruding at the right) towards the back.

4. Press the cable release connected to the camera to open the camera's focal plane shutter and lock it open.

5. Press the other cable release to trigger the leaf shutter, previously set to the required exposure time.

For short time exposures (a few seconds) set the leaf shutter to B and press its cable release; let go after the appropriate time. For long time exposures set the shutter to T and press to open. A second pressure on the release closes the shutter again.

To avoid vibration, correct releasing of the leaf shutter is obviously the most important step. So:

(a) Hold the cable slack, forming a gentle loop between your hand and the PMT-35 leaf shutter.

(b) After opening the camera shutter and before releasing the leaf shutter wait for a few seconds for any vibration to die down.

(c) Stand or sit perfectly still as even walking and movement can be transmitted through the floor and furniture to the PMT-35.

(d) Do not touch any part of the PMT-35 set-up or even the table it is standing on.

(e) If there is heavy traffic passing outside or heavy movement in the building wait for it to die down before releasing the leaf shutter.

PHOTOMICRO EQUIPMENT

In photomicrography the microscope replaces the camera lens. The optical system then consists of the microscope objective which forms a primary image, while the eyepiece magnifies and projects this into the film plane. To adapt the OM cameras to photomicrography we therefore need a suitable coupling unit and an arrangement to support the camera assembly. A sufficiently sturdy microscope can usually support the camera on its own. Failing that, the best alternative is the PM-PSS photomicrographic stand.

A coupling unit specially designed for photomicrography is the OM mount photomicro adapter L (henceforth referred to as the OM-L adapter) which maintains a fixed separation between the microscope eyepiece and the film plane to provide defined magnifications. Alternatives are the manual and automatic exposure bodies (PM-PBM and PM-PBA respectively) with additional control facilities. Further, the stand, arm and bellows of the PMT-35 macro outfit can be used to provide variable microscope/camera distances; the Auto bellows can be used in a similar way with the copy stand.

The OM-L and eyepiece adapters

The OM-L adapter is a tube with an OM bayonet mount at one end and a fitting for eyepiece adapters at the other. The overall length from flange to flange is just over 105 mm. Allowing for the flange/film plane distance of 46 mm on the OM cameras and the protrusion of the microscope eyepiece exit pupil into the OM-L tube, the effective optical eyepiece/film plane distance is about 125 mm.

The OM-L adapter is used with an eyepiece adapter to provide the microscope connection and to hold the eyepiece. FK, P and G adapters are available (types PM-ADF, PM-ADP and PM-ADG respectively) for

PHOTOMICRO SET-UP

The most straightforward set-up for photomicrography with the OM cameras consists of the camera (black) fitted with Varimagni finder (1), eyecoupler, cable release (2) and No. 1–12 screen (6), all mounted on the OM-L adapter (3). This clamps on to the eyepiece adapter (4), holding the eyepiece to connect with the microscope (5).

Right: to assemble eyepiece and adapter, mount the latter on the tube T (a), insert the eyepiece (b) and clamp on the adapter (c). The adapter for the G10 eyepiece *(lower right)* splits to take the eyepiece. Other eyepiece adapters are similar.

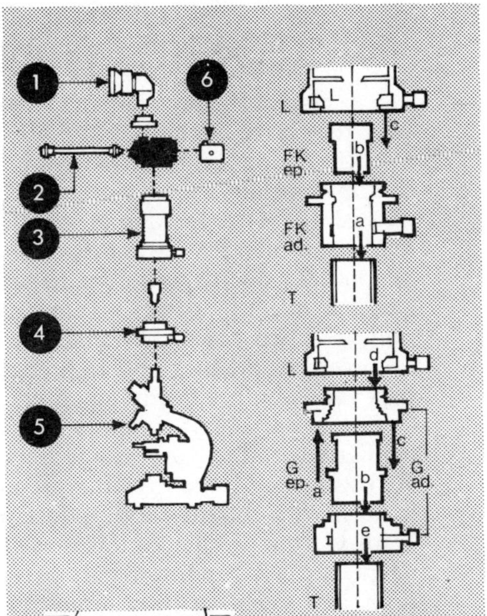

The OM-L adapter attaches to the camera like a lens *(left)*. The PM-PSS stand and the arm provides extra support *(right)*.

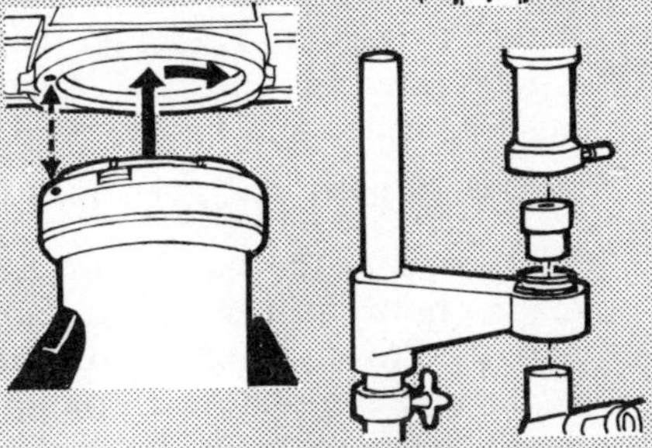

With bellows units use the PM-MTob mount and PM-SDM light excluding collars *(left)*. This is suitable for the PMT-35 outfit *(right)* or the Auto bellows on the copy stand.

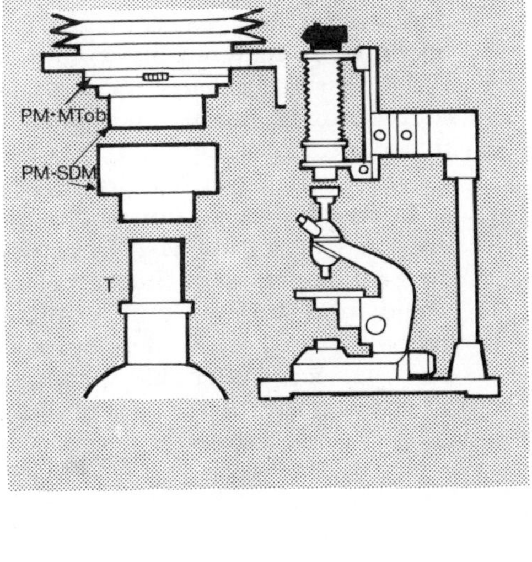

FK, P or G eyepieces. Preferably use FK eyepieces—these are ideally corrected for photomicrography.

To assemble the adapters, mount the FK adapter over the microscope phototube or drawtube. Let it slide over till it stops and clamp with the screw. Then drop in the appropriate FK eyepiece (FK 2.5× to FK 6.7×). Mount the OM-L adapter on the camera—just like a lens—and then place the L adapter over the FK eyepiece adapter. To do this, unscrew the screw knob in the OM-L adapter side till its tip no longer protrudes inside the mount. Then place the flange carrying this screw over the eyepiece adapter and tighten the clamping screw to lock the assembly firmly together.

The P and G 15× and G 20× eyepieces are fitted similarly with the P and G adapters respectively but these are pushed fully over the microscope tube till the adapter is flush with the tube top, before inserting the eyepiece. With G 10× eyepieces unscrew the two parts of the G adapter, place the lower part over the microscope tube, insert the eyepiece then screw the upper part in place. Attach to the OM-L adapter (with camera) and mount the whole assembly on the microscope eyepiece sleeve, pushing it down as far as it will go before clamping.

The PM-PSS stand

The stand is the baseboard and pillar of the PMT-35 macrophoto outfit (see Chpt. *Large-scale macro equipment*) with the PM-10 system arm. The latter carries an opening at the end complete with mounting collar that serves as eyepiece adapter for FK and P eyepieces and has a mounting collar for the OM-L micro adapter. This opening is centered over the baseplate centre. The PM-PSS stand isolates the camera from the microscope, so reducing vibration, especially useful in high-magnification photomicrography. It can be used with all microscopes having a vertical drawtube or vertical phototube.

To assemble the photomicrographic set-up, locate the microscope on the PM-PSS base to bring the phototube under the opening of the supporting arm. Place the light shield tube supplied on the microscope phototube and gently insert the FK photoeyepiece selected. If you use a P eyepiece, insert this without the light shield tube. Then lower the mounting arm over the eyepiece, adjusting the microscope location if necessary. The eyepiece must be perfectly centred in the arm opening and must not touch the arm at any point. Unscrew the clamping screw in the lower flange of the OM-L adapter, place this over the mounting collar on the arm and clamp tight with the screw. The sprung cheek system inside the OM-L accurately centres the adapter over the aperture.

Now gently lower the arm until the fixed diaphragm plate inside the base of the OM-L adapter touches the top of the eyepiece, then raise the arm by about one mm for a minimum clearance. Clamp the arm and raise the clamping collar on the pillar to support the arm, clamping the collar as well. This prevents the arm from creeping down. Finally mount the camera (fitted with the 1-12 focusing screen) at the OM mount end of the adapter.

The PM-PBM and PM-PBA exposure bodies

With the OM-L mount or with bellows systems (see below) the screen of the OM camera serves for focusing and the metering system controls the exposure. The exposure bodies permit both exposure and focus control at a point between the camera and the microscope. This reduces the camera to a film holder and the exposure bodies are indeed parts of the Olympus PM-10 M and PM-10 A photomicrographic systems. These are self-contained, with their own camera bodies and—in one case—remote-controlled film transport. This system however also extends to large-format adapters taking up to 4 × 5 inch Polaroid and other camera backs, roll film adapters etc. The connection between the PM-10 systems and the OM cameras is thus somewhat incidental and even artificial: the exposure bodies are essentially an expensive shutter and focusing system for a camera that already has both. Conversely, with the PM-10 system and the PM-PBA and PM-PBM exposure bodies, the OM cameras serve as little more than expensive film magazines. If you have an OM-2 or OM-1 camera it is much more sensible to use this with the OM-L adapter or bellows. For a particularly versatile and specialised photomicrographic outfit the PM-10 systems with the manual or automatic exposure bodies become more efficient, but then it is worth getting also the camera housings belonging to them. The OM-1 and OM-2 cameras *can* be used with the exposure bodies if you happen to have both at hand. This is therefore only a summary description of these units.

The PM-PBM manual exposure body is a tube with an internal adjustable prism system controlled by a rod (light path selector) protruding from the side. This can divert the light path from the microscope optics in alternative ways: all to a focusing telescope that may be mounted on the front of the unit (selector fully pushed in to white band), 20% to the focusing telescope and 80% to the film plane (selector halfway out—normal exposure position) or all to an exposure and colour temperature measuring port in the side (selector fully out to yellow mark). The body further incorporates a rubber-mounted leaf shutter similar to that of the PMT-35 unit, with speeds from 1 to 1/250 second and B.

An opening at the front of the body takes one of alternative focusing telescope units for direct image observation and focusing; this also indicates the field of view on the film. The side port takes the exposure or colour temperature probe of the EMM-7 exposure meter (see below) to monitor and adjust light quality and to determine the required exposure. This is then set on the leaf shutter.

The PM-PBA automatic exposure body is similar in principle but has an electronically controlled shutter with automatic exposure range from 1/100 second to 32 minutes and built-in colour temperature and exposure probes. The prism system controlled by the light path selector here passes all the light to the focusing telescope, or all the light to the colour temperature meter or splits the light three ways between the film plane (64%), focusing telescope (16%) and exposure measuring photocell (20%). The colour temperature and exposure measurement and the exposing functions are controlled by the PM-CBA automatic exposure control box which combines the measuring functions of the EMM-7 exposure meter with remote control. The same focusing telescopes are used as with the PM-PBM exposure body.

Both exposure bodies need the OM-H photomicrographic adapter and the PM-D35S camera adapter. The PM-D35S ring screws onto the top flange of the exposure body. The OM-H adapter (identical with the camera

MICRO EXPOSURE BODIES

For an exposure body set-up, the camera fitted with cable release (1), is mounted on the exposure body (5) via the OM-H mount (2) and PM-D35S adapter (3). The body takes a focusing telescope (4) and connects to the microscope (7) via the eyepiece adapter (6) holding the eyepiece. Control box PM-CBA (8) plugs in (9) to control exposures.

Upper right: PM-PBA automatic exposure body with camera adapter flange (11), focusing telescope flange (10) and light path selector (12).

Lower right: PM-PBM manual exposure body with shutter (14) and light measuring port (13).

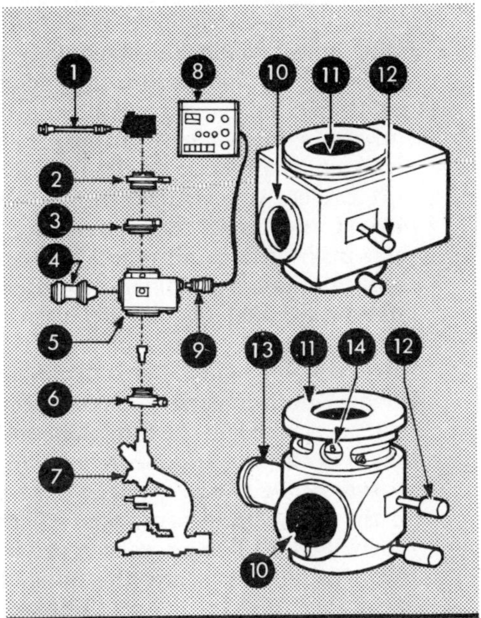

EMM-7 METER

1. CTR index.
2. Meter needle.
3. CT regulator.
4. ASA setting.
5. Direct exposure scale.
6. Index scale.
7. Zero setting screw.
8. Selector switch.
9. Fuse.

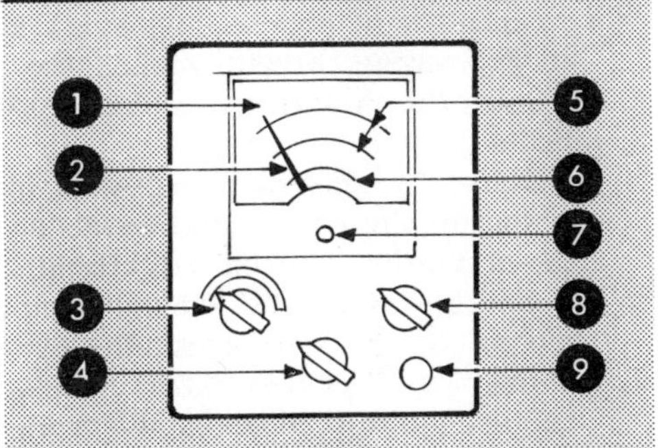

With the PM-PBA housing plug the probe into the exposure metering port *(left)*; with the PMT-35 and bellows fit the probes via the PM-EA adapter.

A makeshift PM-EA adapter can consist of the short rubber tube adapter, a rear lens cap drilled with a 25–26 mm hole, a 25 mm extension tube and the OM-H camera adapter *(right)*.

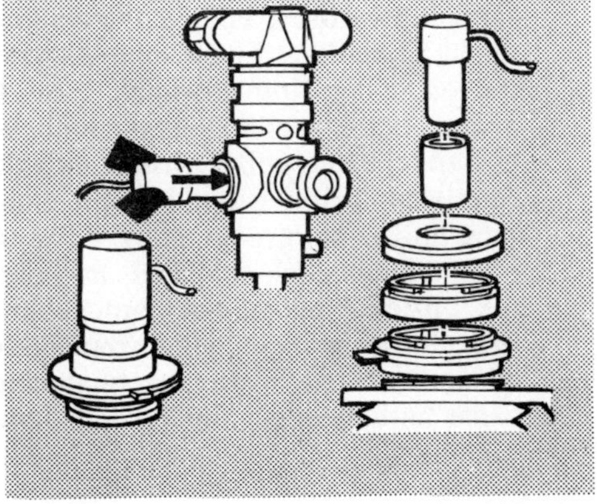

body mount of the Auto bellows, except for a shorter lens release lever) clamps into the PM-D35S. This combination then has the same overall length as the OM-L adapter and the same lower clamping flange for mounting on eyepiece adapters or the PM-PSS arm. When fitting the OM camera it is usually more convenient to mount the OM-H adapter in the camera body first like a lens and then insert the camera and adapter into the PM-D35S ring, aligning and locking it in place with the locking knob on the PM-D35S.

Bellows set-ups

Bellows permit variable separation between the microscope eyepiece and the film plane for additional magnification control (see *Microscope magnification*, below).

Auto bellows and copy stand: Mount the Auto bellows on the copy stand arm, pointing vertically downwards. Fit the PM-MTob adapter in the front bellows standard. Into this adapter screw the upper light-excluding collar of the PM-SDM collar set. This is a 15 mm deep tube of 37 mm diameter, carrying at one end a standard microscope screw thread, fitting the PM-MTob adapter. Mount the camera on the rear (top) of the bellows in the normal way.

Raise the copy stand arm well up and locate the microscope on the copy stand baseboard with the phototube or drawtube centred directly underneath the bellows opening. Attach the lower light-excluding collar to the microscope by lifting out the eyepiece and placing the short narrow section of this collar (25 mm diameter) over the drawtube so that the wider 46 mm diameter section faces upwards. Replace the eyepiece inside the light-excluding collar. The drawtube now carries a 46 mm tube on top, extending upwards. Next lower the copy stand arm to bring the bottom of the bellows—with the upper light excluding collar—right into the lower collar on the microscope drawtube. For the final adjustment use the rack-and-pinion movement of the front bellows standard or of the tripod block. Then carry out any fine alignment of the optical axes of the camera and microscope. If the microscope has a viewing eyepiece as well as a phototube, observe the field alternately through this viewing eyepiece and through the camera's viewfinder. Adjust the microscope position until the two fields are the same. If the microscope has no separate viewing eyepiece, adjust the microscope position until the bottom edge of the light-excluding collar appears precisely centered above the top edge of the lower collar, *when viewed from any direction.* When adjusting the front bellows standard, leave about 1 to 2 mm separation between the flange of the upper collar and the rim of the lower one. This prevents any contact between the two that might transmit vibrations. Securely clamp the copy stand arm, the movement of the focusing tripod block and the front bellows standard. Adjust the bellows extension with the rear standard, then clamp this also.

PMT-35 outfit: The PMT-35, used without the PM-DL 95 illuminator and subject stage, provides an even more rigid camera support than the copy stand and bellows. Lift the illuminator and subject stage off the baseboard and put it aside. With a coin screw in the centering pin so that it is flush with the baseboard. Fully raise the bellows rail as for macrophotography with the 80 mm lens.

Fit the light-excluding collars into the front of the bellows and over the microscope drawtube as described above. With the shift knob on the bellows raise the front standard about halfway up its rack, and clamp.

Place the prepared microscope on the PMT-35 baseboard, centering the optical microscope axis with the centering pin you had screwed back into the base. On the PMT-35 slack off the clamping screw for the bellows rail and carefully lower the rail until the bottom edge of the light-excluding collar screwed into the lens standard is just clear of the top edge of the complementary collar sitting on the microscope drawtube. Fine-adjust the centering and alignment, then lower the front standard by the lens shift knob on the bellows to engage the two light excluding collars as with the Auto-bellows.

Microscope magnification

For visual microscope observation the image through the eyepiece is reckoned to be seen at a visual focusing distance of about 250 mm. The microscope magnification is then calculated by multiplying the objective magnification by the eyepiece magnification.

The magnification on the film will be equal to this

figure if the film plane is 250 mm distant from the eyepiece. This is easy with set-ups involving the Auto bellows or the PMT-35: Allowing for the various component lengths, the eyepiece/film distance is 250 mm if the Auto bellows is set to a lens extension of about 210 mm on the Auto bellows scale. With the PMT-35 the mm scale on the bellows scale effectively starts at 13 mm and the rear camera standard must be set to about 215 mm for a 250 mm eyepiece/film plane distance.

Microscope objectives are calibrated in focal length and magnification for a standard microscope tube length. Usual eyepieces are calibrated by magnification relative to a 250 mm viewing distance (and hence eyepiece/film distance). Eyepiece magnifications may range from 5× to 20×; 10× is the most usual. Thus a 25× objective combined with a 10× eyepiece and a 250 mm film plane distance yields a magnification of 250× on the film. The final magnification in the print (when enlarging from the negative) is then this magnification multiplied by the degree of enlargement.

This is subject to the limitations of 'useful' magnification (see below).

The magnification of the Olympus FK eyepiece is calibrated for a 125 mm eyepiece/film plane distance of the OM-L photomicro adapter or the exposure bodies. The final magnification is then the objective magnification multiplied by the FK eyepiece magnification when using a photomicro set-up with 125 mm eyepiece/film plane distance. When using FK eyepieces with a 250 mm distance, double the magnification figure; when using eyepieces calibrated for the 250 mm distance with the 125 mm OM set-ups, halve the final magnification.

On the Auto bellows you have a 125 mm eyepiece/film plane distance with an 85 mm scale extension e.g. with the lens standard at 0 and the rear camera standard at 85 or front at 25 and rear at 110 mm and so on. On the PMT-35 the rear standard (front standard at end of rail) would have to be just below 100 on the scale—which cannot be reached if the leaf shutter is in position. There it is better even with the FK eyepieces to stick to a 250 mm eyepiece/film plane distance.

To measure the actual magnification for a given microscope setting, replace the subject (i.e. specimen) by a stage micrometer. This is a graticule with a scale graduated in 0.1 and 0.01 mm divisions. In the camera viewfinder count the number of divisions within either the central circle of the screen or across the screen width. Then divide the circle diameter or 35 (the screen width) by the distance on the stage micrometer. For instance if 16 divisions of 0.01 mm (i.e. 0.16 mm) cover the central 8 mm circle of the 1-12 focusing screen, the magnification in the image plane is $8/0.16 = 50\times$.

To show actual dimensions in the image, either:

(a) Calculate the magnification in the final print and mark on it a scale with a fine ruling pin. For instance if the final magnification is $400\times$, a line 4 mm long on the print will represent 0.01 mm in the object.

(b) Or use an eyepiece with a built-in micrometer scale. The graduations of the scale are however relative to the eyepiece only and must be divided by the objective magnification. Thus if the eyepiece micrometer shows 0.1 mm graduations, with a $6\times$ objective, each scale division would then be equivalent to 0.017 mm in the object. However this scale is automatically enlarged with the magnifications involved in the eyepiece/film distance and subsequent print enlargement or transparency projection.

Useful magnification

The resolving power and hence the useful information recalling capacity of a microscope system depends not only on the quality of the lenses but also on factors connected with optical theory, in particular the wavelength of light. In practice, beyond a certain critical magnification (combined objective and eyepiece magnification plus print enlargement) the image gets bigger but does not reveal more detail—so-called (empty) magnification. Below a certain magnification the image produced by the lens contains more detail than the film can resolve. Both the lower and upper magnification limits depend on the wavelength of the image-forming light and on the numerical aperture of the objective lens. This is a light gathering power analogous to *f*-numbers but with higher NA representing more speed. Numerical apertures of microscope objectives range from about 0.1 to 1.4 (higher values only with oil immersion objectives).

Generally objectives of higher magnification also have higher numerical apertures.

In practice useful magnifications in the final print are between about 300 and 1000 times the numerical aperture of the objective lens. Allowing for a convenient viewing distance (about 250 mm) of the enlarged print, it is reasonable to allow a 5 × enlargement of a negative used in a photomicrographic camera set-up with a 250 mm eyepiece/film plane distance. The useful magnification range on the film would therefore be between 60 and 200 times the numerical aperture of the microscope objective. For instance with an objective of NA 0.60 the useful magnification on the film is between about 36 × and 120 ×. This is valid also for colour transparencies to be projected, if we assume that larger projected images would be viewed at proportionally greater distance.

Useful magnification ranges overlap and magnification on the film can be reached by different objective/eyepiece combinations. Higher objective and lower eyepiece magnification yields better resolving power (generally a priority requirement); lower objective and higher eyepiece magnification provides greater depth of field though this is limited anyway.

Focusing and exposure

For set-ups with the OM-L adapter or bellows between the microscope and camera, focus on the 1–12 screen fitted in the camera. You will generally need the Varimagni finder for convenient viewing; be sure to focus the eyepiece for a sharp view of the screen graticule lines. With the exposure bodies use the appropriate focusing telescope, again after careful eyepiece adjustment.

If the microscope has a separate monocular or binocular viewing eyepiece, this can also be used for focusing, subject to correct adjustment. The camera screen or focusing telescope of the micro set-up however tends to be more reliable.

The through-the-lens metering system of the OM-1 and OM-2 cameras in most cases provides reliable exposures. This is subject to exposure corrections for subjects appreciably darker or appreciably lighter than the background. In the first case overexpose by one to two *f*-stops, in the second case underexpose by the same amount. To observe the meter needle you may have to shift the subject temporarily to place a bright view area underneath the meter needle. With the OM-2 this is unnecessary if you do not need to know the exact exposure; the silicon cells look after that. To centre the meter needle between the index marks (OM-1, or OM-2 in manual mode) adjust the light intensity or the shutter speed.

At very low lighting levels the EMM-7 exposure meter (see below) is more sensitive than the CdS cells of the OM cameras in manual mode. The silicon cells of the OM-2 are however still more sensitive, especially in fields such as fluorescence micrography.

With the PM-PBM and PM-PBA exposure bodies the exposure takes place by the internal shutter of the body and not by the camera shutter. The latter must thus be opened first on B with a cable released with lock. For the OM-2 that involves disconnecting the automatic control.

The EMM-7 micro exposure meter

The EMM-7 consists of a measuring instrument with a pointer moving across three graduated scales, control switches to select measuring operations and ranges, and a pair of CdS cell probes for colour temperature and exposure measurement respectively. The outfit is built into a plastic case which also houses three lamp filters (a pair of LB-45 and one LBD), spare fuses and adapters for photomicrographic applications not involving the OM cameras.

The EMM-7 measures colour temperature and exposure for camera set-ups with:

(a) The Auto bellows or PMT-35 bellows linking the camera with a microscope;

(b) The PM-PBM manual exposure body;

(c) The Auto bellows or PMT-35 bellows in macro-photography.

All three systems also involve the use of the OM-H mount adapter (or the almost identical camera body mount supplied with Auto bellows), this being replaced in cases (a) and (c) by the PM-EA adapter for the probes. With the manual exposure body (b) the probe fits in a side port of this body. (The PM-PBA automatic exposure body has its own built-in metering system.)

To open the lid of the EMM-7 housing, slide the yellow clamping peg in the handle slot towards the larger cut-out and lift off the cover with its half of the handle.

The controls on the panel are:

(a) The meter dial with three scales. The outermost '35 (3000)' scale consists of two scales HIGH and LOW with exposure times running from $\frac{1}{2}$ to 1/250 second and from 32 to $\frac{1}{2}$ second respectively. This is the scale for exposure metering with the PM-PBM exposure housing.

The next double scale (again HIGH/LOW) from 4 to 1/30 and from 128 to 4 seconds, labelled L at the left, is for non-OM applications.

Innermost is a linear reference scale calibrated from 0 to 10.

The calibrations of the outer (and middle) scales are exposure times in seconds. The black dot between some of the markings indicates shutter speeds of 1/5, 1/10, 1/25 and 1/50 second.

The left-hand end of the outer scale, just above HIGH, carries an index mark CTR with a yellow and blue arrow pointing to the left and to the right respectively. This is the reference point for colour temperature balancing (see below).

(b) The left-hand knob on the panel moves across an orange and blue scale of dots without numbers, representing colour temperature settings for tungsten and daylight type film respectively. The large dot in the centre of the orange scale is approximately 3200 K, the large dot in the centre of the blue scale approximately 5000 K.

(c) The right-hand four-position switch knob just below the meter dial has settings CTR for colour temperature regulation, HIGH and LOW for exposure metering ranges and OFF.

(d) The centre lower knob on the panel selects ASA speeds for exposure metering.

(e) To the right of the ASA selector is a fuse holder with a standard 20 mm 0.5 amp cartridge fuse.

(f) The colour temperature probe (CT) contains a CdS cell behind four small filter elements, the whole being at the base of a tube which in turn fits into the PM-EA adapter or the metering port of the PA-PBM exposure housing. In the case of the EMM-7 the CT probe has its own plug-in point. The probe is permanently connected to the EMM-7 by leads.

(g) An exposure meter probe (EM) is similar to the CT probe but has no filters in front of its CdS cell. Both probes are normally protected by a soft rubber cap that fits over the end tube.

The selector switch (c) above switches on either of the probes as required.

Probe location and the PM-EA adapter

With the PM-PBM manual exposure body for photomicrography the probe cells plug into the light measuring port of the exposure body.

Where the camera is mounted on the Auto bellows or PMT-35 bellows for photomicrography and macrophotography you need the PM-EA adapter to take the probe. The adapter is a ring with a flange similar to the OM-H mount adapter or the camera adapter of the Auto bellows. But instead of a camera bayonet it carries a narrow tube, open at the end, to take the tube of the CT or EM probes. For all measurements therefore remove the camera with its adapter mounts, fit the PM-EA mount instead in the back of the bellows and plug in the probe. The length of the PM-EA adapter tube locates the probe cell in a position equivalent to the camera's film plane for maximum measuring accuracy.

If you have no PM-EA adapter, here is a simple makeshift. In the centre of a spare plastic rear lens cap drill a 25–26 mm or 1 inch hole. Push the rubber tube adapter (supplied with the EEM-7) into this hole from the outside and then push in the appropriate EEM-7 probe. Mount the whole assembly over the bayonet mounting ring of the OM-H mount adapter of the camera adapter mount of the Auto bellows. Then insert the assembly in the bellows standard in the same way as the PM-EA adapter probe. To place the probe cells in the exact equivalent film plane location, insert a 25 plus a 7 mm extension tube between the H adapter and the drilled probe-carrying rear lens cap. Alternatively, move the rear lens standard back by 30 mm for the exposure and colour temperature readings. (But remember to refocus accurately afterwards.)

Colour temperature regulation

Colour temperature measurement with the EMM-7 is a CT matching operation: you preselect the colour temperature balance of the film and adjust the CT of the lighting by modifying the lamp voltage on the TE-II transformer and by inserting lamp filters until the correct colour temperature is matched. Here is the procedure.

Plug the EEM-7 into the mains supply (check correct voltage) and zero the indicating pointer (by the small plastic screw below the dial) on the CTR index line at the left scale end. Set the left-hand (COLOR TEMP REG) switch to the large dot on the orange (for tungsten type film) or blue (daylight film) scale. This is the film's colour temperature balance which you have to match with the lighting. Move the specimen slide (micro) or subject (macro) out of the way for light colour balancing. Depending on the lighting employed you have to balance the light coming through the transparent stage plate or reflected from the white opaque stage plate; use this (or the white centre of the shade stage plate) even if you are photographing a subject against a black surface.

Fit the CT cell probe into the PM-EA adapter or equivalent and locate in the rear of the bellows. Turn the right-hand switch of the EEM-7 panel from OFF to CTR, fit appropriate lamp filters in the light path and set the lamp voltage approximately (see table in Chpt. *Facts and figures*), then fine adjust until the indicating needle on the EEM-7 dial returns exactly to the CTR index at the left of the scale. Regulating the lamp voltage beyond about 7 volts shortens the lamp life, so it is better to add an extra LB-45 filter instead. Finally replace the subject in the light path or stage, restore the camera, readjust the exact focus and subject location, and proceed with exposure measurement. Colour temperature balancing should always precede exposure measurement as lamp voltage and filter adjustments can appreciably modify the light intensity.

If the colour balance on the photographs is not exactly as you want it, modify the film setting next time. If results are too warm set the CTR adjustment to one of the dots to the right of the large central dot on the orange or blue scale. If results appear too bluish, balance for a lower colour temperature by setting the CTR selector to one or two dots to the left of the centre or reference dot. For routine work it may be worthwhile running a calibration test first with typical subjects and different colour temperature regulation settings. Recheck at intervals after every 10 burning hours of the lamp and when switching film batches.

Exposure measurement

After colour temperature balancing, refocusing and readjusting the subject, plug in the EMM-7, zero the needle and mount the EM probe as described for the CT probe. The subject of course remains in the light path. Turn the ASA speed control switch to the appropriate ASA film speed and the right-hand selector switch from OFF through CTR to HIGH.

Note the needle reading. In photomicrography with the PM-PBM manual exposure housing the reading on the outer (35) scale indicates the actual exposure time required. If the needle indicator is below 1 on the innermost scale turn the right-hand knob to LOW to switch in the more sensitive reading range. (To avoid overloading the measuring instrument, don't switch to the low range unless the high range reading is too low.)

When the EM probe is used in the equivalent film plane of a bellows set-up via the PM-EA adapter (see above), note the readings on the innermost index scale (1 to 10) and obtain the actual exposure required from the table near the end of the *Facts and figures* chapter.

An earlier version of the EMM-7 is the EMM-6 housed in a rectangular instrument case with detachable hinged lid but without integral carrying handle. The instrument differs from the EMM-7 in the control knob layout, in an additional sensitivity switch for different Olympus photomicrographic set-ups and in slightly different calibration of the controls.

Colour control

Photomicrographic specimens, especially biological and botanical ones, are generally stained. Hence correct colour reproduction would at first sight seem less important as the staining falsifies colours that we would normally never see anyway: its purpose is to make detail visible by artificial colour differentiation. It is not vital whether a given stain is recorded on colour film in exactly its correct hue. Correct film/light balance is still important as any overall colour cast reduces the colour differentiation in stained specimens and may mask finer hue graduations altogether; so match the colour of the illumination to the colour temperature for which the film is designed. Check the colour temperature of the light, e.g. with EMM-7 meter, and adjust accordingly with requisite LB and/or LBD lamp filters.

Colour negative film is used less in photomicrography and light/film balancing is less critical. But appreciable unbalance again suppresses finer colour graduations that cannot be regained by filter control in colour printing.

PHOTOTECHNICAL ACCESSORIES

In addition to the well-defined and better known applications of photography with the Olympus OM cameras, the OM system incorporates a few items that are either useful in certain fields of technical photography or provide a connecting link to further photographic applications. Olympus lumps them into a so-called phototechnical group—more a department of useful odds and ends than a coherent subsystem. Its main items are the Recordata backs and OM mount adapters for endoscopic, astronomical and certain other fields of photography.

The Recordata 1 back

This special back, replacing the normal camera back, exposes dates or alphanumeric (letter and figure) codes on the film to identify individual exposures or exposure sequences. The 0.7 mm high figures are printed on the film by a pair of light-emitting diodes located behind a window in the film pressure plate. The figures appear in the bottom right-hand corner of the film frame, about 1 mm above the bottom edge and in a space 4 to 8 mm from the right-hand edge.

The LEDs are triggered by closing a circuit through a synchronising plug, plugged into the camera's flash socket. The system is powered by three silver oxide cells. A selector switch controls the intensity of the imprinting light for different film types. A further LED in the top edge of the back checks operation. The Recordata back circuit includes a safety system to prevent damage through high-voltage discharge if an electronic flash is connected to the camera's hot shoe (wired in parallel with the flash socket).

The Recordata back is 138 mm long, 53 mm high and 28 mm deep; it weighs 95 grams without batteries. At its deepest point—the battery compartment—the Recordata 1 protrudes about 10 mm more beyond the camera back than the normal OM back. This combination therefore does not fit the hard or semi-hard camera cases, but you can carry it in the soft cases.

Fitting on the camera

Open the camera back and remove by depressing the stud in the hinge. Fit the Recordata back in its place by engaging the lower hinge bearing of the camera, depressing the hinge stud, engaging the upper hinge end, and close. Plug the lead from the Recordata back into the flash socket at the side of the mirror housing. If you run the lead underneath the camera baseplate and underneath the strap (if used) and up on the camera front, you can open the Recordata back without unplugging the lead. But don't let the lead run round the camera side where opening the back could strain the lead.

To use the Recordata back together with the motor drive or winder, fit the Recordata after attaching the motor drive. The lead in this case can only run round the camera side, so unplug it before you open the camera back for loading the film.

To remove the Recordata back *always unplug the synchronising lead first*. Then open the back and disengage from the camera in the usual way.

Inserting and testing batteries

The LEDs that imprint the selected data on the film are powered by three 1.5 volt silver oxide button cells of the same kind as used for the OM-2 exposure meter battery. Unless the Recordata is in constant use, a battery set lasts about a year—the current drain is much smaller than in the OM-2 camera, as the LEDs light up for only a fraction of a second at a time.

To fit the cells—with the Recordata on or off the camera—unscrew the slotted screw in the rectangular battery compartment cover and lift the latter. Insert the three cells with their flat sides (carrying the + mark and lettering) facing up in the three recesses and screw down the compartment cover on top.

To check the batteries, without a film in the camera, plug the synchronising lead into the camera's flash socket, tension the camera and release the shutter. The small red LED in the top edge of the back should now

RECORDATA 1 BACK

1. Lead with synchronising plug.
2. Number dial 0–36.
3. Index.
4. Number dial 1–12, 75–84, A-M.
5. Test LED.
6. Film type selector.
7. Battery cover with retaining screw.
8. Battery cell.
9. Screw thread for cover.
10. Cell chamber with terminals.
11. Hinge.

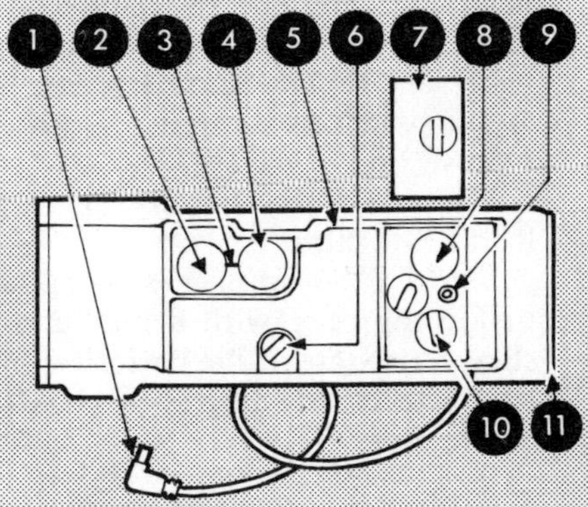

Insert three silver oxide cells in the battery compartment *(left)*. To remove or fit the back, press down the hinge release pin while unhooking or engaging the back *(right)*.

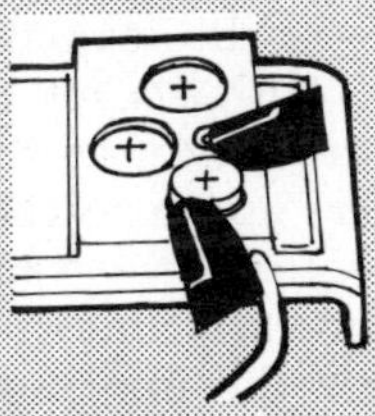

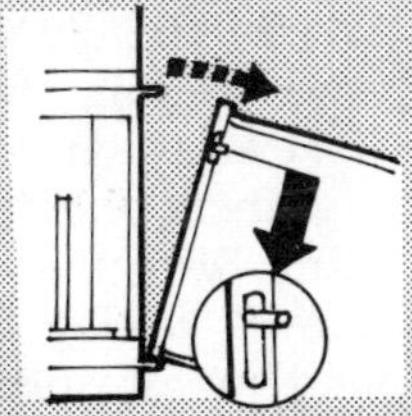

Plug the synchronising lead from the back into the camera's flash socket *(left)*. Release the shutter (before loading the film) and check that the test LED lights up *(right)*.

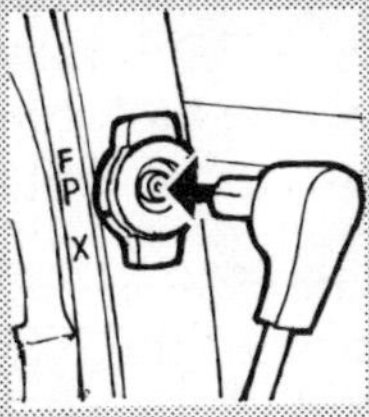

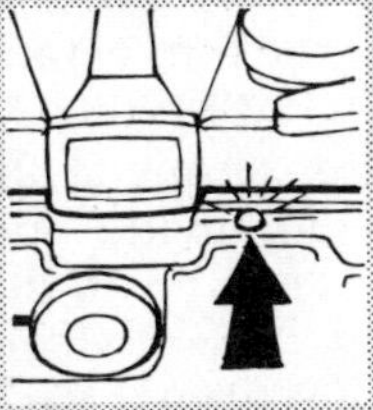

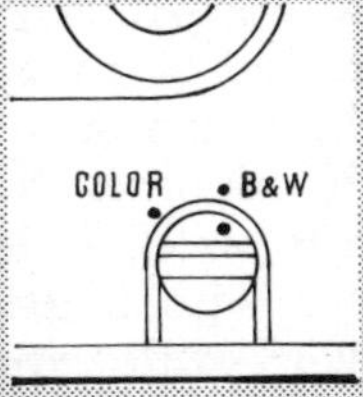

Set the film type selector according to the film loaded *(left)*. Set numbers (0 to 36) on the left-hand dial and letters (A-M) for year numbers on the right-hand dial. Data imprint appears in bottom right-hand corner of the picture (here shown not to scale).

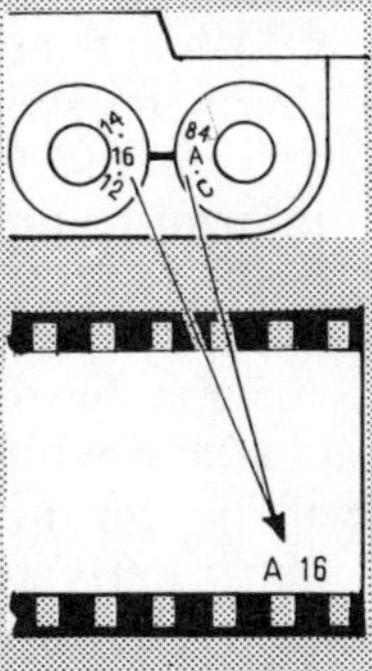

flash. If it does not, the data exposure won't work, either. Check correct battery loading and plug connections; if necessary replace the batteries. With the OM-2 set the meter switch to MANUAL for this check and the shutter to 1/60 second or slower.

Carry out this battery check every time before you load a new film.

The LED also flashes on short-circuiting the contact inside the plug with a pin or other metal object. This shows the state of the batteries, but the test with the plug connected to the flash socket also confirms correct contact of the plug.

Synchronisation and film type settings

With the OM-1 the synchronising switch setting surrounding the flash socket is immaterial. It doesn't matter at what instant during the shutter cycle the data numbers or letters are exposed through the back of the film. With the motor drive at high cycling speeds, select the FP setting for early imprinting, for at high shutter and motor speeds the imprinting may become slightly blurred with the X-setting if the motor starts advancing the film before the LED is fully extinguished.

With the OM-2 the flash contact does not work at the X-setting at shutter speeds faster than 1/60 second. With automatic operation therefore again set the switch to FP to be on the safe side.

For flash shots with the Recordata back you need an electronic flash with centre-contact foot to fit the camera's hot shoe, as the normal contact is already occupied. With the OM-1 remember to set the shutter to 1/60 second or slower and the synchronising switch to X; with the OM-2 and a flash unit other than the Quick Auto 310 set the meter switch to MANUAL. If you use the Quick Auto 310 on the OM-2 with automatic operation, the data imprinting only works with exposures that also trigger the flash.

At the bottom of the Recordata back panel a small chrome button with a red dot can turn to a yellow COLOR or white B & W marking. This adjusts the intensity of the imprinting light for different film types, to allow particularly for the density of the film's anti-halation layer that the light has to penetrate to reach the emulsion.

Generally, colour films have a denser anti-halation layer than black-and-white. So with dense backed colour films set the button to COLOR; with thin-backed emulsions to B & W. Set the film type selector to COLOR also with extra-slow black-and-white document or microfilming material. To get an idea of what dense and thin-backed films look like, hold up the film leader end of a few typical colour and black-and-white films to the light.

Data settings

On the two dials of the Recordata back set the letter/number combination you want to record on the film. The left-hand dial carries numbers from 0 to 36, the right-hand dial numbers from 1 to 12 and from 75 to 84 plus letters from A to M. The right-hand dial figures appear at the left on the film and vice versa. Set each dial so that the required number or letter clicks into position opposite the white index line between the dials. The dials carry dots for intermediate positions between some of the numbers or letters, but such intermediate figures also record on the film.

To use only one dial for imprinting, set the other to a blank position—between 0 and 36 on the left dial or between 12 and 75, 84 and A or M and 1 on the right-hand dial.

The two dials together can indicate year and month (e.g. '78 5' for May 1978), month and day ('9 17' for 17th September) or other letter and number codes to identify exposures for tests, in scientific photography etc.

If you want no data at all while the Recordata back is fitted, unplug the synchronising lead from the camera.

Exposure technique with the Recordata back is the same as with the normal camera back. The figures record white in the print or transparency, black in the negative. To show them up better, preferably keep bright subject portions out of the bottom right-hand corner of the negative. Letters or numbers also show up less distinctly in over-exposed shots.

Remove the batteries when storing the back unused for long periods. Keep the pressure plate and imprinting window clean—but do not clean with any solvent that could attack the tiny numbering images.

The Recordata 2 back

This back closely resembles the Recordata 1 but imprints four letter and number combinations on the film instead of two. The characters are of the same size as in the Recordata 1 and are imprinted by four light-emitting diodes located in the pressure plate.

The figures and the sequence in which they appear on the film is best visualised by looking at the Recordata back upside down. (This also makes the figures appear upside down on the dials, but provides the easiest check.) In this upside-down orientation:

The first dial carries letters from A to Z and figures from 0 to 9. On the dial itself only every other figure or letter is marked, but all—including intermediate ones—register on the film. To set this particular indication, turn the dial to bring the appropriate figure (or interval between figures or letters) opposite the white index line between the first and second dials.

There are also two blanks—with nothing imprinting on the film—between 9 and A and between Z and 0.

The second dial carries numbers from 1 to 15 and from 78 to 98. There are again blanks between 98 and 1 and between 15 and 78. This dial could for instance serve to imprint either month or year dates.

The third dial carries numbers from 0 to 36, with a blank between 36 and 0.

The fourth dial has a similar number sequence to the third dial.

Obviously having four dials provides greater versatility in identification coding: you can code by date, by letters and numbers, by exposure numbers and so on.

Apart from the four dials, the Recordata back 2 differs from the Recordata back 1 in the following respects:

(a) The back takes only two 1.5 volt silver oxide button cells instead of three.

(b) The battery check and signal LED is mounted in the back, next to the first dial (the fourth dial when you look at the back the right way up from the rear) instead of in the top edge.

(c) The selector knob at the bottom of the Recordata back panel has four positions: OFF (for no imprinting—you don't have to set blanks on the dials), 25–160 for low-speed black-and-white film, 200–400 for high-speed black-and-white film (200–400 ASA) and an arrow head for colour film.

The same points for selecting the LED intensities—to match the density of the film's anti-halation backing—apply as for the Recordata 1.

Apart from these points, the two Recordata backs are fitted and operated in the same way.

The endoscope adapter

In medical photography of interior organs and body cavities endoscopes permit access otherwise impossible to a camera. An endoscope consists usually of an ultra-miniature optical system that transfers an image out of the organ being examined. In modern endoscopic cameras it does so with a fibre-optical bundle consisting of up to 20,000 glass fibres (around 1000 fibres per square mm) which provides sufficient information for diagnosis and other medical purposes. Such fibrescopes are equally used in industry to observe and photograph the interior of engine components, pipelines etc. without dismantling them. The fibre bundles may be up to several metres long. Optical systems at the viewing end permit observation or projection into the film plane of a camera. Fibrescopes also incorporate a further light guide to carry illumination to the subject area and may include miniature surgical instruments, also remote-controlled, for biopsies and other on-the-spot operations.

Olympus OM cameras can be linked with such fibrescopes via the OM mount endoscope adapter. Fit the adapter on the camera like a camera lens and plug the lead into the camera's flash outlet at the side of the reflex body. Then line up the fibrescope eyepiece with its orange or red dot opposite the red dot on the adapter, push the latter over the fibrescope eyepiece and turn clockwise to lock. The camera must first be fitted with the 1–9 viewing screen exclusively designed for use with fibrescopes.

The fibrescope yields a 4 × 4 to 9 × 9 mm image on the film, resolving between 30 and 40 line pairs per mm. Exposure is usually controlled by a shutter that opens and closes in the light path of the illuminator supplying the light guide. The camera shutter is normally set to 1/4 second; releasing the shutter triggers the illuminator shutter via the flash synchronising lead of the adapter. Exposures may there range from 1/4 to 1/100 second. With sufficiently intense illumination shorter camera exposure times are possible. Some fibrescopes incorporate a silicon cell to measure light intensity and control the mechanical shutter of the light source.

The synchronising setting on the camera's flash socket X or FP depends on the fibrescope employed.

The astroscope adapter

This connects an OM camera to a telescope for one of two modes of astronomical photography: normal magnification with the telescope objective only or high magnification with the telescope eyepiece as well.

The astroscope adapter consists of six parts which may be combined in various ways:

(a) The camera mount is a 25 mm long tube (flange to flange) with a bayonet mount at one end and a smooth ring with clamping screw at the other. The tube thus fits directly onto the camera like a lens.

(b) The direct focus ring is a chrome tube with a milled rim. At one side it carries a smooth 52 mm (external diameter) tube with an internal 49 mm screw thread to take 49 mm filters. This tube fits inside the camera mount and is clamped in position by the screw. The other side has an external 36.5 × 1 mm thread for attachment to telescope drawtubes or to the magnifying tube (c) below. Items (a) and (b) are used for both astrophotography methods.

(c) A magnifying tube, 64.5 mm long and 51 mm in diameter, carries an internal 36.5 × 1 mm thread at one end and an internal 48 mm thread at the other. The 36.5 mm thread connects this tube to the direct focus ring (b), the 48 mm thread to the eyepiece coupling ring (d) below.

(d) The eyepiece coupling ring carries an external 36.5 × 1 mm thread at one end, an external 48 mm and an internal 36.5 × 1 mm thread at the other. With the external 48 mm thread this ring screws into the tube (c) and the internal 36.5 mm thread takes the eyepiece adapter (e). The external 36.5 mm thread screws into the telescope drawtube.

(e) The eyepiece adapter is a 34.5 mm lamp tube of 24.5 mm internal diameter with a clamping screw to fit

ENDOSCOPE AND FIBRESCOPE ADAPTER

The SM-2S adapter connects OM cameras to endoscopes and fibrescopes. A typical set up involves:

1. Red camera mounting dot on SM 2S adapter.
2. Synchronising lead (to trigger certain light sources).
3. Red locating dot to match with locating dot on fibrescope mount 4.
5. Diopter, focusing etc. ring (depends on fibrescope).
6. Angulation control for bending distal fibrescope end.
7. Light guide to light source.
8. Fibrescope or endoscope tube, inserted in body cavity to be photographed.

ASTROSCOPE ADAPTER

9. Camera mount.
10. Direct focus ring.
11. Magnifying tube.
12. Eyepiece adapter.
13. Eyepiece coupling ring.
14. Reverse ring.

For direct photography the direct focus ring screws into the telescope draw tube (without eyepiece), takes any filters and is linked to the camera via the camera mount.

For high-magnification photography the telescope eyepiece fits into the eyepiece adaptor and coupling ring while the magnifying tube connects these with the camera mount and direct focus ring as before.

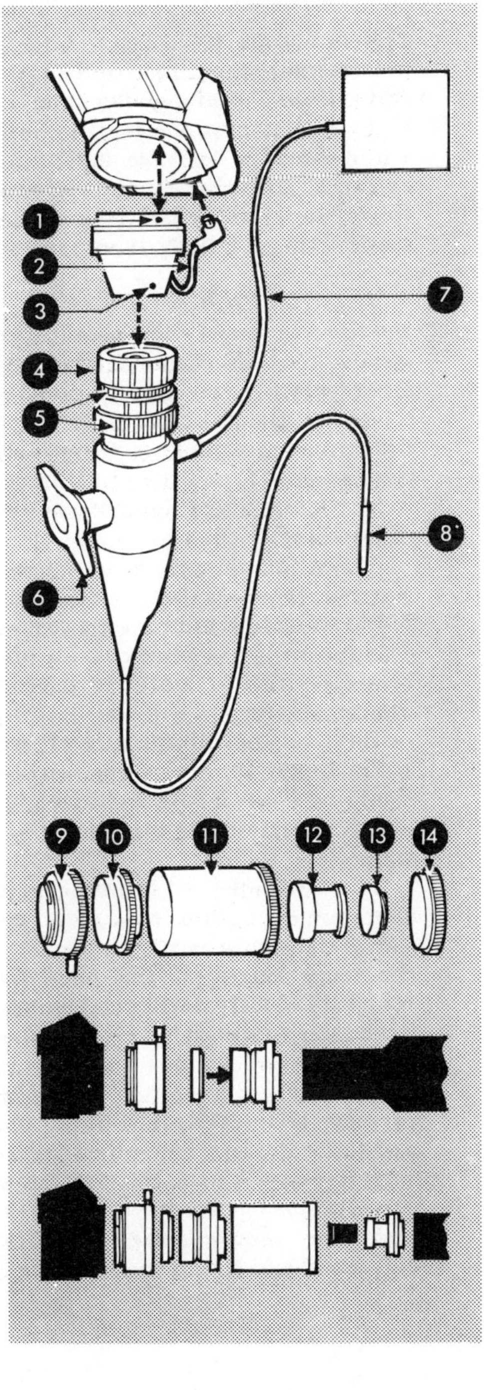

24.5 mm eyepiece tubes. The adapter screws into the internal 36.5 mm thread of the eyepiece coupling ring (d) and is always used together with the latter.

(f) The 40 mm reverse ring carries an internal 36.5 × 1 mm thread at one side and an external 36.5 × 0.5 mm thread at the other. It thus allows the direct focus ring (b) or the eyepiece coupling ring (d) to screw into telescope fittings with a 0.75 mm instead of 1 mm pitch.

Astrophotography set-ups

For direct photography with the telescope objective only remove the eyepiece holder from the telescope drawtube. In its place screw in the direct focus ring (b) if the telescope drawtube has a 36.5 × 1 mm thread. If the drawtube has a 36.5 × 0.5 mm thread, first screw in the reverse ring (f) and then the direct focus ring (b).

Screw any filters (49 mm size) into the internal thread of the direct focus ring.

Attach the camera mount to the Olympus OM body in the same way as a camera lens. The mount has the usual red locating dot and bayonet release catch.

Unscrew the clamping screw on the camera mount so that the screw tip does not protrude inside the smooth mount opening. Then fit the camera with the camera mount over the chrome tube of the direct focus ring and screw down the clamping screw to secure. Until the clamping screw is fully tightened you can turn the camera in any direction for orienting the image in the picture frame.

The direct method is useful for whole images of larger astronomical bodies (sun, moon etc.). The approximate size of the sun or moon on the film is just under 1/100 of the focal length of the telescope objective. Thus a 1000 mm objective will yield an image just under 10 mm large; this is also the size of the image obtained with the 1000 mm tele lens.

For high-magnification astrophotography screw the eyepiece adapter (e) into the eyepiece coupling ring (d) and screw the latter—with or without the reverse adapter ring (f)—into the telescope drawtube from which the eyepiece has been removed. Insert the telescope eyepiece into the eyepiece adapter (which takes 24.5 mm telescope eyepieces) and clamp with the small screw. Into the front

(48 mm thread) of the eyepiece coupling ring screw the magnifying tube so that the eyepiece protrudes inside this tube. Screw the direct focus ring into the other end of the magnifying tube (the 36.5 mm thread) and fit any filters required into the direct focus ring as with direct astrophotography. Finally fit thc camera mount to the camera and attach the camera with the mount to the direct focus ring as described before.

Compared with the direct set-up, the image is magnified by a factor depending on the eyepiece. This factor is very approximately 100 divided by the focal length of the eyepiece in mm. Thus a 9 mm eyepiece yields a 11 × magnification, a 12.5 mm eyepiece an 8 × magnification and so on. These ratios can be further increased by fitting the 25 mm extension tube between the camera mount and the camera. The magnification then becomes approximately equal to 125 divided by the focal length of the eyepiece in mm—e.g. 10 × with a 12.5 mm eyepiece.

Image quality in this set-up depends greatly on the quality of the eyepiece. Olympus recommend Kellner or orthoscopic eyepieces, or—for photographs of the sun—Huygens eyepieces containing no balsam-cemented components.

Points of astrophoto techniques

Obviously photographs through a telescope need a very rigid support for the telescope and camera. The image is focused by the telescope adjustment. Use the No. 1–8 (fine-grain matt) focusing screen. To reduce the risk of vibration during the exposure, release with a cable release or the camera's self-timer.

Different filters may be used for photographs of the sun to show up different surface features; generally special narrow cut filters are required for such techniques. Sun pictures usually have to be exposed at a reduced objective aperture and with high-density grey filters in the light path. For the sun—and under certain circumstances the moon—the through-the-lens metering system of the OM-2 can control correct exposure.

Astronomical photographs of the planets, stars and other fainter celestial bodies require exposures running into minutes or even hours and thus need equatorially mounted telescopes. However, black-and-white emulsions available in 35 mm rarely have suitable reciprocity characteristics for reliable long-time exposures. Hence such exposure times—as also with colour films—have to be determined by trial and error. Colour shots of stars may also need CC filters to compensate for colour shifts caused by reciprocity failure—again determined by trial and error.

FACTS AND FIGURES

BATTERY REQUIREMENTS

Equipment	No. of cells	Volts Each	Volts Total	ASA	Size desig. ANSI	Size desig. IEC	Type	Maker's designations
OM-2 and OM-10 camera	2	1.5	3	–	S-15	–	Silver* oxide	Mallory 10 L 14, Varta 7301, Rayovac RW 42 or 22, National (and Japanese) G-13, UCAR Eveready S-76 or EXP 76
OM-1 camera	1	1.35	1.35	–	M-20	MR-9	Mercury	Mallory PX-625, Eveready EPX-625, Varta 7002, National etc. H-D
Auto-Quick 310 and 300 flash	4	1.5	6	AA	L-40	LR-9	Alkali**	Mallory etc. Mn 1500, Eveready E91, Varta 7244, Japanese AM-3
Bounce flash grip for 310, 300	4	1.5	6	C	L-70	LR-14	Alkali**	Mallory etc. Mn 1400, Eveready E93, Varta 7233, Japanese AM-2
T20 flash	2	1.5	3	AA	L-40	LR-14	Alkali	Mallory etc. Mn 1500, Eveready E91, Varta 7244, Japanese AM-3
or	2	1.25	2.5	AA	K-40	LR-14	NC rechargeable	Varta 500 RS, Saft VR0.5 AA, Eveready CH 500; CF 500
Motor drive 1	12	1.5	18	AA	L-40	LR-14	Alkali	Mallory etc. Mn 1500, Eveready E91, Varta 7244, Japanese AM-3
or	12	1.25	15	AA	K-40	LR-14	NC rechargeable	Varta 500 RS, Saft VR0.5 AA, Eveready CH 500; CF 500
Winder 1	4	1.5	6	AA	L-40	LR-14	Alkali	Mallory etc. Mn 1500 Eveready E91, Varta 7244, Japanese AM-3
or	4	1.25	5	AA	K-40	LR-14	NC rechargeable	Varta 500 RS, Saft VR0.5 AA, Eveready CH 500; CF 500
Recordata 1	3	1.5	4.5	–	S-15	–	Silver* oxide	Mallory 10 L 14, Varta 7301, Rayovac RW 42 or 22, National (Japanese) G-13, UCAR Eveready S-76 or EXP 76
Recordata 2	2	1.5	3	–	S-15	–	Silver oxide*	Mallory 10 L 14, Varta 7301, Rayovac RW 42 or 22, National (Japanese) G-13, UCAR Eveready S-76 or EXP 76

* Do not use mercury cells of same size but lower voltage (1.35 volts).
** Do not use rechargeable nickel-cadmium (NC) cells for this equipment.

Cell types and the number required in OM cameras and other battery-powered equipment. The maker's designations are the type numbers of main manufacturers; often other makers use similar type numbers. Where alkali and rechargeable NC cells are shown as alternatives, the alkali batteries generally have two to three times the capacity of the rechargeable cells. Ordinary zinc-carbon cells of the heavy duty type can be used in place of alkali cells, but have about the same capacity as rechargeable NC cells. Equivalent types of different makes of such zinc-carbon cells are too numerous to list; they are recommended as an emergency measure only.

Characteristics	*Screen types and compatibility codes*												
	1–1	*1–2*	*1–3*	*1–4*	*1–5*	*1–6*	*1–7*	*1–8*	*1–9*	*1–10*	*1–11*	*1–12*	*1–13*
Centre	p	pl	w	m	pw	pl	pe	f	s	m	c+c	c+c	w+p
Centre dia. mm	4	4	4	8	4	4	4	9	23	8	4	8	2.5/5
Outer area (all with Fresnel except*)	m	m	m	m	c	c	c	f	c*	m+g	f	c	m
Lenses and applications													
8 mm fisheye	E	H	E	E	E	–	–	H	–	E	–	–	E
16 mm fisheye	A	D	A	B	E	–	–	–	–	B	–	–	A
18–28 mm	A	B	A	B	E/H	K	–	–	–	A	–	–	A
35 mm shift	B	D	B	A	H	–	–	B	–	X	–	–	B
35 mm other	A	B	A	A	E	H	–	B	–	A	–	–	A
50–55 mm standard	A	B	A	A	E	H	–	B	–	A	–	–	A
85–135 mm tele	A	A	A	A	H	E	–	B	–	A	–	–	A
180 mm, 200 mm *f*4	B	A	A	B	–	E	E	A	–	B	–	–	B
200 mm *f*5	D	A	B	B	–	H	E	A	–	B	–	–	D
300 mm *f*4.5	D	B	B	B	–	H	E	X	–	B	A	–	D
400–600 mm	D	B	D	B	–	–	E	X	–	B	A	–	D
1000	D	D	D	B	–	–	E	X	–	B	A	–	D
35–70 and 75–150 mm zoom	A	A	A	A	K	H	–	B	–	A	–	–	A
85–250 mm zoom	B	A	A	A	–	E	H	B	–	A	–	–	B
Macro													
20 and 38 mm	–	–	–	D	–	–	–	B	–	D	A	X	–
50 mm *f*3.5 (macro range)	A	A	B	B	K	H	–	A	–	B	–	–	A
80 mm	D	B	D	A	–	–	–	A	–	A	X	–	D
Photomicrog.	–	–	–	–	–	–	–	–	–	–	–	X	–
Astrophot.	–	–	–	–	–	–	–	X	–	–	–	–	–
Endoscopic phot.	–	–	–	–	–	–	–	–	X	–	–	–	–

Main characteristics of the 13 screens available for the Olympus OM cameras and their suitability or compatibility with different lenses and applications.

c = Clear screen. c + c = Clear screen centre with crosshair pattern. f = Fine-grained matt surface. g = Grid. m = Standard matt surface. p = Standard microprism pattern. pe = Very low-profile microprism pattern for extra long tele lenses. pl = Low-profile microprism pattern for longer focus and smaller aperture lenses. pw = High-profile microprism pattern for wide-angle and wide-aperture lenses. s = Special condenser lens. w = Wedge range-finder (split-image).

The compatibility codes indicate:

A = Screen compatible with lens or application, yields excellent and convenient focusing image. Meter measurements of screen image indicate correct exposures.

B = Screen compatible with lens or application as A; acceptable rather than best possible screen. Meter measurements of screen images indicate correct exposures.

D = Screen usable, usually subject to vignetting. Microprism or split image pattern blacks out if eye not accurately centred behind finder eyepiece. Meter measurements of screen image indicate correct exposures.

E = Screen compatible with lens or application, yields clear and convenient focusing image but meter measurements of screen image do not indicate correct exposures (OM-1 or manual operation of OM-2) or not possible (with 8 mm fisheye). Despite wrong indication, automatic exposure with OM-2, controlled by silicon cells, is correct.

H = Screen compatible with lens/application as E (incorrect exposure indication of screen image measurements) but not best screen available for the purpose.

K = For emergency use only; screen usable but neither convenient nor yields correct exposure indication.

X = Screen specially designed for this lens/application.

– = Unsuitable screen/lens combination.

No.	*Lens desig.(1)*	*Focal length*	*Max.–Min. aperture*	*Angle of View(2)*			*Nearest focus*	
				Horiz.	*Vert.*	*Diag.*	*Distance (film plane)*	
							m	*ft*
	For use on camera							
1	Auto-Fisheye	8 mm	*f*2.8–22	180°	(circular image)		0.2	0.7
2	Auto-Fisheye	16 mm	*f*3.5–22			180°	0.2	0.7
3	MC Auto-W	18 mm	*f*3.5–16	90°	67°	100°	(4)0.25	0.8
4	G Auto-W	21 mm	*f*3.5–16	81°	59°	92°	0.2	0.7
5	MC Auto-W	21 mm	*f*2–16	81°	59°	92°	(4)0.2	0.7
6	H Auto-W	24 mm	*f*2.8–16	74°	53°	84°	0.25	0.8
7	MC Auto-W	24 mm	*f*2–16	74°	53°	84°	(4)0.25	0.8
8	G Auto-W	28 mm	*f*3.5–16	65°	46°	75°	0.3	1
9	MC Auto-W	28 mm	*f*2–16	65°	46°	75°	(4)0.3	1
10	G Auto-W	35 mm	*f*2.8–16	54°	38°	63°	0.3	1
11	Shift	35 mm	*f*2.8–22	54°	38°	63°(3)	0.3	1
12	MC Auto-W	35 mm	*f*2–16	54°	38°	63°	0.3	1
13	F Auto-S	50 mm	*f*1.8–16	40°	27°	47°	0.45	1.5
14	G Auto-S	50 mm	*f*1.4–16	40°	27°	47°	0.45	1.5
15	Auto-Macro	50 mm	*f*3.5–22	40°	27°	47°	(4)0.23	0.8
16	G Auto-S	55 mm	*f*1.2–16	36°	25°	43°	0.45	1.5
17	Auto-Zoom	35–70 mm	*f*3.6–22	54–29°	38–19°	63–34°	0.8	2.7
18	Auto-Zoom	75–150 mm	*f*4–22	27–14°	18–9°	32–16°	1.6	5.2
19	MC Auto-Zoom	85–250 mm	*f*5–32	24–8.2°	16–5.5°	29–10°	2.0	6.6
20	F Auto-T	85 mm	*f*2–16	24°	16°	29°	(4)0.85	2.8
21	E Auto-T	100 mm	*f*2.8–22	20°	14°	24°	1.0	3.3
22	E Auto-T	135 mm	*f*3.5–22	15°	10°	18°	1.5	4.9
23	E Auto-T	135 mm	*f*2.8–22	15°	10°	18°	1.5	4.9
24	MC Auto-T	180 mm	*f*2.8–32	11°	7.6°	14°	2.0	6.6
25	F Auto-T	200 mm	*f*5–32	10°	6.9°	12°	2.5	8.2
26	E Auto-T	200 mm	*f*4–32	10°	6.9°	12°	2.5	8.2
27	F Auto-T	300 mm	*f*4.5–32	6.9°	4.6°	8.3°	3.5	11.5
28	E Auto-T	400 mm	*f*6.3–32	5.2°	3.4°	6.2°	5	16.4
29	F Auto-T	600 mm	*f*6.5–32	3.4°	2.3°	4.1°	11	36
30	E Auto-T	1000 mm	*f*11–45	2.1°	1.4°	2.5°	30	100
	For use on bellows only							
31	Macro	20 mm	*f*3.5–16	–	–	–	–	–
32	Macro	38 mm	*f*3.5–16	–	–	–	–	–
33	Macro	80 mm	*f*4–22	–	–	–	–	–

Data, setting parameters, construction etc. of lenses announced to date for the Olympus OM cameras. Most lenses are used directly on the camera and many can be used with extension tubes which—in the case of the long focus and tele lenses—also extended the near focusing limit. The macro lenses listed last in the table are usable only in conjunction with the Auto-bellows (or the bellows of the PMT-35 outfit). The 20 and 38 mm macro lenses have to be mounted via the PM-MTob adapter. All lenses with exception of these macro lenses and of the 35 mm shift lens are coupled with the aperture input for full-aperture metering with the OM cameras.

Numbered notes:

(1) All lenses are named Zuiko; this name precedes the codes beginning with 'Auto' but comes after the initial letter code. Thus the full designation of the lens entered as MC Auto-W is MC Zuiko Auto-W. *Auto* in all cases indicates automatic aperture coupling.

OM SYSTEM LENSES

No.	Nearest focus Scale 1:	×	No. of Elements	Groups	Filter mount (screw)	Hood (7)	Length min. (8)	Max. dia. mm	Weight grams
1	–	–	11	7	(5)	–	82	102	640
2	–	–	11	8	(5)	–	31	59	180
3	7.8	0.13	11	9	72 mm(6)	(6)	42	62	250
4	5.8	0.17	7	7	49 mm	49 mm S	31	59	180
5	5.8	0.17	11	9	55 mm	57 mm C	43	60	240
6	6.4	0.16	8	7	49 mm	49 mm S	31	59	180
7	6.4	0.16	10	8	55 mm	55 mm S	48	60	280
8	7.5	0.13	7	7	49 mm	49 mm S	31	59	180
9	7.5	0.13	9	8	49 mm	49 mm S	43	60	250
10	5.8	0.17	7	6	49 mm	51 mm C	33	59	180
11	5.8	0.17	8	7	49 mm	49 mm S	58	68	310
12	5.8	0.17	8	7	55 mm	55 mm S	42	60	240
13	6.7	0.15	6	5	49 mm	51 mm C	31	59	170
14	6.7	0.15	7	6	49 mm	51 mm C	36	60	230
15	2	0.5	5	4	49 mm	B	40	60	200
16	6.4	0.16	7	6	55 mm	57 mm C	47	65	310
17	20–10	0.05–0.10	10	8	55 mm	60 mm S	74	67	400
18	18–8.9	0.06–0.11	15	11	49 mm	BE	115	63	440
19	20–7.2	0.05–0.14	15	11	55 mm	BE	196	70	890
20	6.9	0.14	6	4	49 mm	49 mm S	46	60	260
21	8.1	0.12	5	5	49 mm	49 mm S	48	60	230
22	8.9	0.11	5	4	49 mm	BE	73	60	290
23	8.9	0.11	5	5	55 mm	BE	80	61	360
24	9.7	0.10	5	5	72 mm	BE	124	80	700
25	10	0.10	6	5	49 mm	BE	105	62	380
26	10	0.10	5	4	55 mm	BE	127	67	510
27	9.2	0.11	6	4	72 mm	BE	181	80	1100
28	10	0.10	5	5	72 mm	BE	255	80	1300
29	15	0.07	6	4	100 mm	BE	377	110	2800
30	27	0.04	5	5	100 mm	BE	662	110	4000
31	–	4.3–12.4	4	3	21 mm C	–	20	32	70
32	–	1.8–6.1	5	4	32 mm C	–	28	43	90
33	–	0.3–2.3	6	4	49 mm	–	46	59	200

The letter following this indicates the lens application: W = wide angle, S = standard, T = tele. Initial letters from E to J indicate the number of elements: E = 5, F = 6, G = 7 and so on. MC indicates a multi-coated lens.

(2) At infinity setting.

(3) When the shift is utilised, the lens covers various sections of an image circle amounting to altogether 83°.

(4) Floating elements for close-up performance correction.

(5) Filters built in.

(6) With 49–72 mm step-up ring; this also acts as lens hood.

(7) S = screw-in, C = clamp-on, B = built-in (lens sufficiently recessed not to need hood), BE = built-in extending hood. Filters are all screw-in except for the macro lenses.

(8) Measured from front of lens mount to camera mounting flange, lens set at infinity, i.e. this is the amount by which the lens protrudes from the camera.

FOCUSING ZONES

Lens	*Stop*	*Focus setting*	*Sharp zone (approx.)* metres	feet
Near zones				
28 mm	*f*5.6	6 ft to index	1.5–3	5–10
35 mm	*f*5.6	3 m to index	2–6	7–20
50 mm	*f*4	3 m to index	2.6–3.6	8.5–12
85 mm	*f*8	3 m to index	2.7–3.3	9–11
100 mm	*f*11	3 m to index	2.7–3.3	9–11
Medium zones				
50 mm	*f*4	5 m to index	4–7	13–23
85 mm	*f*8	5 m to index	4.3–6	14–20
100 mm	*f*11	5 m to index	4.3–6	14–20
135 mm	*f*16	10 m to index	7.9–13.6	25–45
Far and extreme zones				
24 mm	*f*5.6	3 m to index	1.5–∞	1.5–∞
28 mm	*f*5.6	6 ft to LH *f*8	2.2–∞	7.2–∞
35 mm	*f*5.6	3 m to LH *f*4/8	3–∞	10–∞
50 mm	*f*8	10 m to index	5–∞	16–∞
85 mm	*f*11	10 m to LH *f*8/16	10–∞	33–∞
100 mm	*f*16	10 m to LH *f*11	8–∞	25–∞
135 mm	*f*16	30 m to index	15–∞	50–∞

The depth of field indicator of the different lenses helps you to select suitable zones of sharpness needed for various subjects. To save time for this however it is also useful to have a few commonly used zones at your fingertips. This table lists a selection of such zones for the lenses most likely to be used in candid snapshooting, sports etc.

The actual zone indicated is approximate, but to know where you are it is useful to have strictly repeatable scale settings. So for these zones set the indicated white metre figure or orange feet value of the distance scale either opposite the red focusing index or to one of the depth of field index lines. Thus '6 ft to index' means that you set the orange 6 on the feet scale opposite the red focusing index. Similarly, '10 m to LH *f*11' means that you set the white 10 on the metre scale opposite the left-hand *f*11 line of the depth of field scale. Occasionally a distance figure has to be set halfway between two depth index lines; e.g. 'LH *f*4/8' means that you set the distance figure in the gap between the left-hand *f*4 and *f*8 index lines.

FILM SPEEDS AND TYPES

ASA	*DIN*	*Film types* — *Black-and-white*	*Colour*
(2–10)	(4–11)	Special copying and	
12	12	extra slow	
16	13		
20	14		
25	15	Extra-fine grain	Slow colour
32	16	films (negative)	reversal film (slides)
40	17		
50	18		
64	19	Fine grain negative,	Medium-speed
80	20	direct reversal films	negative and
100	21		reversal films
125	22		
160	23		
200	24	Medium to high-speed	High-speed
250	25	negative films	reversal films.
320	26		High-speed
400	27		negative films
500	28		
640	29	High to extreme-speed	Forced-processing
800	30	negative films, often	reversal
1000	31	with forced processing	
1250	32		
1600	33		

The ASA speeds listed are those marked on the film speed setting control of the OM cameras (though not necessarily all models cover the full range). Corresponding DIN values—as used in parts of central Europe—are given alongside. Nowadays most films, even if rated in DIN speeds, also carry ASA figures.

When dealing with films of East European origin which may have GOST (Russian standard) film speeds, simply set the OM meter to the next higher ASA value. For instance for 90 GOST film set to 100 ASA.

The table also indicates the general speed range of different black-and-white and colour film types.

FILTERS FOR COLOUR

Filter	*Colour temp. correct.* *Typically* *From K*	*To K*	*Approx. dkM*	*Exposure correct.* *X*	*EV*	*Uses*
UV: L39*	–	–	–	1	0	Absorbs ultraviolet, e.g. in mountain views (daylight film)
Skylight 1A*	–	–	–	1	0	Absorbs ultraviolet, stronger than L39. Outdoor views in shade, dull weather lit by blue skylight. Uncorrected electronic flash with daylight film
Amber filters (lower colour temperature)						
81A	3400	3200	+2	$1\frac{1}{4}$	$-\frac{1}{3}$	Photoflood lighting with type B or K film. Also for stronger effect in same applications as No. 1A
81C or 81D A4*	3800 or 4200	3200 3400	+4 to +5	$1\frac{1}{4}$	$-\frac{1}{3}$	AG1 flash bulbs (clear) with type A film or B or K film
86B			+6.7	2	−1	
85C			+8	2	−1	
85	5500	3400	+11	2	−1	Daylight or blue flash with type A film
85B	5500	3200	+13	2	−1	Daylight or blue flash or electronic flash with type B or K film
Blue filters (raise colour temperature)						
78C or 82A	3200	3400	−2	$1\frac{1}{4}$	$-\frac{1}{3}$	Tungsten (3200K) light with type A film
82C, B4*	2800	3200	−4.5	$1\frac{2}{3}$	$-\frac{2}{3}$	Ordinary tungsten light (2800K) with type B or K film
80D	4200	5500	−5.5	$1\frac{2}{3}$	$-\frac{2}{3}$	AG1 clear flash with daylight film
78B	2800	3400	−6.7	2	−1	Ordinary (2800K) tungsten light with type A reversal film or negative colour film
80C			−8	2	−1	Tungsten light with negative colour films
80B	3400	5500	−11	3	$-1\frac{1}{2}$	Photoflood light with daylight reversal film
80A	3200	5500	−13	4	−2	Tungsten (3200K) light with daylight type reversal film

* Olympus filters

Apart from the UV and skylight filter, the filters listed are colour conversion filters to match different light sources to films of different colour balance. Some filters are also included for correction balancing when copying colour transparencies. The filter numbers—other than the Olympus filters marked with an asterisk (*)—are Wratten, or equivalent designations of other makes using the same numbering system.

FILTER FITTINGS AND AVAILABILITY

Filter size (screw)	1A	L39 (UV)	A4 (81C)	B4 (82C)	Y48 (Y2)	O56 (O2)	R60 (R1)	ND2	ND4	Polarising	Fits (Lenses)
					Availability of Olympus filter types						
55 mm	X	X	X	X	X	X	X	X	X	X	21 mm *f*2 24 mm *f*2 35 mm *f*2 55 mm *f*1.2 *35–70 mm *f*3.6 *85–250 mm *f*5 135 mm *f*2.8 200 mm *f*4
72 mm	X	X	–	–	X	X	X	–	–	–	18 mm *f*3.5 180 mm *f*2.8 300 mm *f*4.5 400 mm *f*6.3
100 mm	X	X	–	–	X	X	X	–	–	–	600 mm *f*6.5 1000 mm *f*11
49 mm	X	X	X	X	X	X	X	X	X	X	All other lenses *except* fisheye (have built-in turret) and 20 and 38 mm macro

X = available filters in size indicated
* Zoom lenses

Olympus filters are available in four sizes which between them cover all lenses of the OM system except the fisheye lenses (which have their own built-in filters) and the 20 and 38 mm macro lenses (not normally used with filters).

The table shows which filters are available in which size. All Olympus filters are available in the 49 and 55 mm sizes.

RECIPROCITY FAILURE CORRECTIONS

Nominal exposure (indicated or calculated)	*Actual exposure required*	*Compensating override on OM-2*
Shorter than ½ sec	As nominal	None
1 sec	1½ sec	+⅓
2 sec	3 sec	+⅔
4 sec	6–9 sec	+⅔ to +1
8 sec	12–20 sec	+⅔ to +1⅓
16 sec	30–65 sec	+1 to +2
30 sec*	100–250 sec	–

* For greater compensation switch to manual exposure control; OM-2 does not reliably time exposures longer than about 45–60 sec.

With longer exposure times the effective film speed drops and exposures need a longer time than the nominal time indicated by calculation or exposure metering. The actual correction for this so-called reciprocity failure varies from film to film, so consult the manufacturer's instruction literature. This table gives a rough guide to the magnitude of corrections to be expected. For automatic exposures with the OM-2 this can be allowed for by appropriate settings of the exposure compensating dial.

(m)						*ASA*	*Speed*			*(ft)*					
25	*32*	*40*	*50*	*64*	*80*	*100*	*125*	*160*	*200*	*250*	*320*	*400*	*500*	*640*	*800*
15	*16*	*17*	*18*	*19*	*20*	*21*	*22*	*23*	*24*	*25*	*26*	*27*	*28*	*29*	*30*
(m)						*DIN*	*Speed*			*(ft)*					
10	11	12	14	16	18	20	22	25	28	**32**	36	40	45	50	56
11	12	14	16	18	20	22	25	28	32	**36**	40	45	50	56	64
12	14	16	18	20	22	25	28	32	36	**40**	45	50	56	64	72
14	16	18	20	22	25	28	32	36	40	**45**	50	56	64	72	80
16	18	20	22	25	28	32	36	40	45	**50**	56	64	72	80	90
18	20	22	25	28	32	36	40	45	50	**56**	64	72	80	90	100
20	22	25	28	32	36	40	45	50	56	**64**	72	80	90	100	110
22	25	28	32	36	40	45	50	56	64	**72**	80	90	100	110	125
25	28	32	36	40	45	50	56	64	72	**80**	90	100	110	125	140
28	32	36	40	45	50	56	64	72	80	**90**	100	110	125	140	160
32	36	40	45	50	56	64	72	80	90	**100**	110	125	140	160	180
36	40	45	50	56	64	72	80	90	100	**110**	125	140	160	180	200
40	45	50	56	64	72	80	90	100	110	**125**	140	160	180	200	225
45	50	56	64	72	80	90	100	110	125	**140**	160	180	200	225	250
50	56	64	72	80	90	100	110	125	140	**160**	180	200	225	250	280
56	64	72	80	90	100	110	125	140	160	**180**	200	225	250	280	320
64	72	80	90	100	110	125	140	160	180	**200**	225	250	280	320	360
72	80	90	100	110	125	140	160	180	200	**225**	250	280	320	360	400
80	90	100	110	125	140	160	180	200	225	**250**	280	320	360	400	450
90	100	110	125	140	160	180	200	225	250	**280**	320	360	400	450	500
100	110	125	140	160	180	200	225	250	280	**320**	360	400	450	500	560
110	125	140	160	180	200	225	250	280	320	**360**	400	450	500	560	640
125	140	160	180	200	225	250	280	320	360	**400**	450	500	560	640	720
140	160	180	200	225	250	280	320	360	400	**450**	500	560	640	720	800
160	180	200	225	250	280	320	360	400	450	**500**	560	640	720	800	900

The table shows equivalent guide numbers at different film speeds and is valid for metric or feet values. To find the equivalent of a known guide number for one speed in a different film speed, look up the known guide number in the appropriate ASA or DIN speed column. From that guide number trace horizontally across to the column of the new film speed value and read off the new guide number there.

All guide numbers follow the preferred guide number sequence recommended in ISO standards and now used by many electronic flash manufacturers in quoting guide numbers.

Example: If the guide number for a given flash is quoted as 32 at 100 ASA, what is the guide number with 250 ASA film? Trace down the 100 ASA column to 32, then trace horizontally across to the 250 ASA column: the new guide number shown there is 50.

The two bold columns in the table—headed *(m)* and *(ft)* at the top—can also serve as a ready reckoner to convert from metric to feet guide numbers or vice versa. To convert a metric guide number to feet, look up the metric value in the left-hand bold *(m)* column and trace across to the right-hand *(ft)* column. To convert from feet to metric, look up the guide number in the *ft* column and trace to the left to the corresponding value in the *m* column.

Example: 36 metric (left-hand column) = 110 in feet (right column). This conversion is approximate but with an average error not exceeding 3%.

QUICK AUTO 310 AND 300 OPERATING MODES

Camera		*Flash connection (2)*	*Uses (3)*	*Mode (4) for selector setting on flash unit*			
Model	*Meter switching (1)*			*TTL AUTO*	*MANUAL High*	*MANUAL Low*	*AUTO*
Quick Auto 310							
OM-2	AUTO	OM-2 shoe	G	A-TTL	MF	MR	A
OM-2	AUTO	AuC	G, B	A-TTL	A-TTL	A-TTL	A-TTL
OM-2	AUTO	SyC		MF	MF	MR	A
OM-2	MANUAL	OM-2 shoe	FI	MF(5)	MF	MR	A
OM-2	MANUAL	AuC	NR	MF(5)	MF	MF	MF
OM-2	MANUAL	SyC	FI	MF	MF	MR	A
OM-1	Any	SyC	G, FI	MF	MF	MR	A
OM-1	Any	ExS	B	Mode as set on remote sensor			
OM-1	Any	OM-1 shoe	G, FI	MF	MF	MR	A
OM-1	Any	AuC	NR	MF	MF	MF	MF
Quick Auto 300							
OM-2 or 1	Any	Shoe	G, FI	–	MF	MR	A
OM-2 or 1	Any	AuC	NR	–	MF	MF	MF
OM-2 or 1	Any	SyC	G, FI	–	MF	MR	A
OM-2 or 1	Any	ExS	B	–	Mode as set on remote sensor		

The Quick Auto flash units operate in different ways according to which camera they are linked with and by what means. This table summarises the combinations and results. The numbered notes below indicate special points and abbreviations used:

(1) With the OM-2 at the AUTO or OFF settings the flash does not fire if the prevailing light causes the automatic system to select a shutter speed of 1/125 second or faster. Nor will the OM-2 trigger the flash at manual settings with such shorter shutter speeds.

(2) The different connections, apart from fitting the flash directly into the camera shoe, are: AuC = Auto synchronising cord (flash off camera or on bounce grip); SyC = normal synchronising cord (with coaxial plug to fit camera socket, or synchronising cord built into bounce grip); ExS = external or remote sensor.

(3) G = general flash photography (preferred combination); B = bounce flash (flash on bounce grip); FI = suitable for fill-in lighting with daylight; NR = not recommended combination (shown only to indicate what happens with it).

(4) The modes indicated are: A-TTL = auto flash with through-the-lens flash control; MF = manual with full power flash; MR = manual with reduced power flash; A = automatic, controlled by built-in sensor of flash or external remote sensor.

(5) Spurious reduced power output if shutter speed is set to 1/60 second.

SELECTING QUICK AUTO 310 AND 300 COMBINATIONS

Flash model	*Camera*		*Flash*		
	Model	*Meter switching*	*Mounting*	*Connection*	*Selector setting*
On-camera automatic: simple, straightforward					
310	OM-2	AUTO	Shoe	Shoe	TTL-AUTO*
310/300	OM-1	Any	Shoe	Shoe	AUTO
300	OM-2	MANUAL	Shoe	Shoe	AUTO
Off-camera automatic: more modelling					
310	OM-2	AUTO	Bounce grip	Auto cord	TTL-AUTO**
310	OM-2	AUTO	Separate	Auto cord	TTL-AUTO**
310/300	OM-1	Any	Bounce grip	Synch cord	AUTO
310/300	OM-1	Any	Separate	Synch cord or remote sensor	AUTO
300	OM-2	MANUAL	Bounce grip	Synch cord	AUTO
300	OM-2	MANUAL	Separate	Remote	AUTO
Bounce flash for soft light					
310	OM-2	AUTO	Bounce grip	Auto cord	TTL-AUTO**
310/300	OM-1	Any	Bounce grip	Remote sensor	AUTO
300	OM-2	MANUAL	Bounce grip	Remote sensor	AUTO
Daylight fill-in (select suitable aperture and/or speed)					
310/300	OM-2	MANUAL	Shoe	Shoe	MANUAL HI
310/300	OM-1	Any	Shoe	Shoe	MANUAL HI
Close-up					
310	OM-2	AUTO	Separate	Auto cord	TTL-AUTO**
310	OM-2	AUTO	Bounce grip (angled)	Auto cord	TTL-AUTO**
310/300	OM-1	Any	Separate or bounce grip (angled)	Remote sensor	AUTO
300	OM-2	MANUAL	Separate or bounce grip (angled)	Remote sensor	AUTO

* Automatic control of flash duration by internal cells of camera.

** In fact auto through-the-lens control takes place irrespective of 310 selector setting when Auto Cord is used and OM-2 set to AUTO (or OFF).

Combinations of camera with flash plus the required mounting, synchronising connection and setting on the selector dial of the flash unit. Where the remote sensor is used, the selector setting applied to the dial on the sensor.

CLOSE-UP TELEPHOTOGRAPHY RANGES

Lens	*Extension tube*	*Focusing range** *m*	*feet*	*Magnification range*
135 mm	None	1.36**	4.5**	0.11**
	7 mm	2.7–0.95	9–3.2	0.05–0.16
	14 mm	1.4–0.75	4.7–2.5	0.10–0.21
180 mm	None	1.93**	6.3**	0.10**
	14 mm	2.5–1.2	8.2–3.9	0.08–0.18
200 mm	None	2.3**	7.5**	0.10**
	14 mm	3.05–1.4	10–4.5	0.07–0.17
300 mm	None	3.1**	10**	0.11**
	14 mm	6.7–2.2	22–7.3	0.05–0.16
	25 mm	3.9–1.8	12.7–6	0.08–0.19
400 mm	None	4.6**	15**	0.10**
	25 mm	6.8–2.8	22–9.4	0.06–0.16
	25 + 14 mm	4.5–2.4	14.8–8	0.10–0.20
600 mm	None	10.5**	35**	0.07**
	25 mm	13.8–5.3	45–17.4	0.04–0.1
	25 + 14 mm	8.6–4.2	28–14	0.07–0.13
1000 mm	None	30**	100**	0.04**
	25 mm	39–15.5	128–51	0.03–0.06
	25 + 14 mm	24.6–12.4	81–41	0.04–0.07
85 mm	None	1.8**	6**	0.05**
(85–250 zoom)	7 mm	1.1–0.73	3.6–2.4	0.08–0.13
	14 mm	0.6–0.48	2.0–1.6	0.16–0.22
250 mm	None	2**	6.6**	0.14**
(85–250 zoom)	7 mm	9.2–1.7	30–5.7	0.03–0.17
	14 mm	4.7–1.5	15.5–5	0.06–0.2
	25 mm	2.75–1.3	9–4.2	0.10–0.24

* Approx. lens/subject distances. ** At near focusing limit of lens

Near focusing limits of tele lenses can be extended for close range telephotography, i.e. medium subject scales at comparatively long subject distances. The table lists the distance ranges and magnification ranges available with long focus and tele lenses combined with extension tubes.

CLOSE-UP ZOOM RANGES

Zoom lens	*Ext. tube*	*Focus setting**	*Zoom distance range** metres*	*feet*	*Magnification range*
35–70 mm	7 mm	∞	0.2–0.75	0.7–2.5	0.2–0.1
	14 mm	∞	0.12–0.4	0.4–1.4	0.4–0.2
75–150 mm	7 mm	∞	0.8–3.4	2.6–11	0.09–0.05
		c.	0.46–0.95	1.5–3.1	0.19–0.19
	14 mm	∞	0.4–1.75	1.3–5.75	0.19–0.09
		c.	0.31–0.7	1.0–2.3	0.23–0.22
	25 mm	∞	0.25–0.95	0.8–3.1	0.33–0.17
		c.	0.18–0.58	0.6–1.9	0.36–0.34
85–250 mm	7 mm	∞	1.1–9.2	3.6–30	0.08–0.03
		c.	0.7–1.7	2.4–5.7	0.17–0.13
	14 mm	∞	0.6–4.7	2.0–15.5	0.16–0.06
		c.	0.5–1.5	1.6–5	0.22–0.2
	25 mm	∞	0.4–2.75	1.3–9	0.3–0.1
		c.	0.3–1.3	1–4.2	0.4–0.35

* Infinity (∞) or closest focus (c.)
** Approx. distance range (lens/subject) covered by zooming from longest to shortest focal length.

By combining zoom lenses with extension tubes you not only bring the near focusing limit nearer but also cover a near subject range at reasonably constant magnification by operating the zoom adjustment rather than the focusing ring. The scale remains particularly constant when the zoom lens is set to its near focusing limit.

The table shows the distance ranges (approximate lens/subject distances) covered by the zooming adjustment with different zoom lenses and extension tube combinations, plus other relevant data. In every case the shortest distance (and the highest magnification) is obtained with the zoom lens at its shortest focus setting.

HAND COPY STAND DATA

Camera lens	*Close up lens or ext. tube*	*Leg extens.*	*Approx. focus scale setting m*	*ft*	*Subject area covered cm*	*in.*	*Reprod. scale 1:*	*x*
Large originals (A4, Foolscap): 38 × 50 cm (15 × 20 inch) support area								
50 mm Macro *f*3.5	None	Long	0.65	2	24.2 × 36.3	9.5 × 14.3	10.2	0.10
50 mm *f*1.8	None	Long	0.65	2	24.2 × 36.3	9.5 × 14.3	10.2	0.10
50 mm *f*1.4	None	Long	0.65	2	24.7 × 37.2	9.7 × 14.7	10.3	0.10
55 mm *f*1.2*	None	Long	0.68	2$\frac{1}{4}$	23.3 × 35.0	9.1 × 13.8	9.75	0.10
Medium originals (Trimmed quarto, larger book): 27 × 36 cm (10.5 × 14 inch) support area								
50 mm Macro *f*3.5	None	Med.	0.50	1.7	17.3 × 26.2	6.8 × 10.3	7.5	0.13
50 mm *f*1.8	None	Med.	0.47	–	17.0 × 25.8	6.7 × 10.2	7.25	0.14
50 mm *f*1.4	None	Med.	0.47	–	17.5 × 26.6	6.9 × 10.5	7.5	0.13
50 mm *f*1.2*	None	Med.	0.50	–	16.9 × 25.6	6.6 × 10.1	7.13	0.14
Smaller originals (Octavo, normal book page): 20 × 28 cm (8 × 11 inch) support area								
50 mm Macro *f*3.5	None	Short	0.40	1.3	12.7 × 19.0	5.0 × 7.4	5.4	0.19
50 mm *f*1.8	49 mm/40 cm	Short	1.15	3$\frac{3}{4}$	12.8 × 19.3	5.1 × 7.6	5.5	0.18
50 mm *f*1.4	49 mm/40 cm	Short	1.15	3$\frac{3}{4}$	13.1 × 19.7	5.1 × 7.7	5.6	0.18
50 mm *f*1.2*	55 mm/40 cm	Short	1.25	4	12.3 × 18.5	4.8 × 7.25	5.25	0.19
Very small: 11 × 15 cm (4.5 × 6 inch) support area								
50 mm Macro *f*3.5	None	Shortest	0.24	9$\frac{3}{4}$ in	5.1 × 7.7	2 × 3	2.25	0.44
50 mm *f*1.8	7 + 14 mm tubes	Shortest	0.9	3	4.8 × 7.3	1.9 × 2.9	2	0.5
50 mm *f*1.4	7 + 14 mm tubes	Shortest	2.5	8	5.3 × 8.1	2.1 × 3.2	2.25	0.44
55 mm *f*1.2*	7 + 14 mm	Shortest	1.50	5	5.4 × 8.3	2.15 × 3.3	2.3	0.43

* With 55/49 mm step-down adapter ring. Where close-up lens is used, screw this into 55 mm lens, and adapter ring into close-up lens

Subject areas covered with different 50 and 55 mm lenses at the three leg extensions of the Handy copy stand. The leg extensions determine the lens/copy distance and the focusing scale settings. The latter are approximate; focus accurately by observing the image in the finder. The lenses are listed in order of preference for optimum quality. Subject areas refer to conditions where the copy stand legs actually stand on the surface being copied—the ideal condition for keeping a page etc. flat. Closer focusing (and hence smaller subject areas) may be involved where a book of finite thickness is placed within the field covered by the legs. Subject areas refer to the field covered by the OM camera finder (and by transparency frames); slightly more is included on the film. The support area in each case is the minimum area required to support the legs safely.

RECOMMENDED CLOSE-UP/MACRO COMBINATIONS

Reprod. scale	*Suitable combinations of*			
	Lens	*Extension unit or accessory*	*Focusing means*	*Minimum camera support*
Preferred combinations				
0–0.5×	50 mm Auto-Macro	None needed	Lens mount, plus possibly focusing rail and stage	Hand held or tripod, copy stand etc.
0.5–2.2× (*3.2×)	80 mm Macro	Bellows	Bellows	Copy stand or VST-1 or PMT-35
1.8–6× (*8×)	38 mm Macro	Bellows	Bellows	VST-1 or PMT-35
4.3–12.4× (*16.6×)	20 mm Macro	Bellows	Bellows	VST-1 or PMT-35
Other feasible combinations				
0–0.5×	Any 50 mm	Tubes and/or supp. lens	Lens mount	Hand held, or tripod, copy stand etc.
	Other lenses	Tubes	Lens mount	As above
0.5–1×	50 mm Auto-Macro	25 mm tube	Lens mount, focusing rail and stage	Copy stand, focusing rail and stage
0.7–1.6×	135 mm	Bellows	Bellows	Copy stand
0.7–2×	100 mm	Bellows	Bellows	Copy stand
0.75–4× (**3×)	50 mm Auto-Macro	Bellows	Bellows	VST-1
1× and over	Other lenses	Bellows	Bellows	Copy stand or VST-1

* Greater maximum magnification possible with PMT-35 system or addition of extension tubes
** Approx. max. magnification with retro-mounted lens

A guide to selecting the appropriate items for different macro set-ups, depending on the scale of reproduction to be covered. The first half of the table (preferred combinations) lists lenses, extension units and focusing means that yield the best results and also indicates the standard of rigidity required in supporting the camera.

The second half of the table shows feasible equipment combinations you can use if for instance you do not have any or all the macro lenses indicated, or if you have to work without a bellows unit.

CLOSE-UP RANGES WITH CLOSE-UP LENS AND EXTENSION TUBES

Lens	*Close-up aid (1)*	*Focusing range (2) mm*	*inches*	*Scale of reprod. Mag. x*	*Red. 1:*
50 mm Macro *f*3.5	None	∞–114	∞–4.5	0–0.5	∞–2
	CL	395–85	15.5–3.3	0.13–0.67	7.7–1.5
	14	200–75	7.9–3	0.29–0.8	3.4–1.25
	14 + CL	130–60	5.1–2.35	0.42–0.9	2.4–1.1
	25	118–64	4.7–2.5	0.57–1.0	1.75–1.0
	25 + CL	89–51	3.5–2.0	0.67–1.14	1.5–0.9
	25 + 14	80–51	3.2–2.0	0.8–1.33	
	25 + 14 + 7	70–48	2.75–1.9	0.93–1.35	
50 mm Standard (3)	None	∞–362	∞–14.75	0–0.15	∞–6.5
	CL	393–188	15.5–7.4	0.13–0.3	7.5–3.4
	7	390–195	15.4–7.7	0.14–0.31	7–3.25
	7 + CL	195–130	7.7–5.15	0.29–0.44	3.5–2.25
	14	204–140	8.0–5.5	0.29–0.43	3.5–2.3
	14 + CL	133–102	5.25–4.0	0.44–0.57	2.25–1.75
	14 + 7	142–110	5.6–4.4	0.44–0.57	2.25–1.75
	14 + 7 + CL	104–84	4.1–3.3	0.57–0.73	1.75–1.4
	25	124–99	4.9–3.9	0.50–0.67	2–1.5
	25 + CL	91–76	3.5–3.0	0.65–0.8	1.55–1.25
	25 + 7	99–85	3.9–3.35	0.67–0.8	1.5–1.25
	25 + 14	86–76	3.4–3	0.8–1.0	
	25 + 14 + 7	76–68	3–2.7	0.95–1.14	
55 mm *f*12	None	∞–349	∞–13.7	0–0.167	∞–6
	CL	394–182	15.5–7.2	0.14–0.31	7–3.25
	7	438–191	17.2–7.5	0.13–0.31	7.75–3.25
	7 + CL	205–127	8.0–5.0	0.29–0.44	3.5–2.25
	14	220–134	8.7–5.25	0.25–0.43	4–2.3
	14 + CL	139–97	5.5–3.95	0.4–0.57	2.5–1.75
	25	124–91	4.9–3.6	0.43–0.62	2.33–1.63
	25 + CL	94–70	3.7–2.75	0.61–0.77	1.65–1.3
	25 + 7	95–76	3.8–3.0	0.59–0.75	1.7–1.33
	25 + 7 + CL	76–63	3.0–2.45	0.87–0.95	1.15–1.08
	25 + 14	78–64	3.1–2.5	0.73–0.89	1.38–1.13
	25 + 14 + 7	66–56	2.6–2.25	0.89–0.98	1.13–1.03
100 mm *f*2.8	CL	390–270	15.3–10.6	0.26–0.43	3.9–2.3
	14	814–470	32–18.5	0.14–0.27	7.1–3.7
	14 + CL	260–212	10.3–8.3	0.43–0.59	2.3–1.7
	25	500–365	19.7–14.4	0.26–0.40	3.9–2.5
	25 + CL	215–187	8.5–7.7	0.61–0.77	1.65–1.3
	25 + 14	355–295	14–11.7	0.42–0.56	2.4–1.8
	25 + 14 + 7	318–274	12.5–0.65	0.49–0.65	2.05–1.55

The close-up lens generally provides a greater focusing range than an extension tube, but the image quality with the latter is better at the higher magnifications. Combinations with the close-up lens at reproduction scales above about 0.3 × require some stopping down to reduce definition loss towards the edge of the field. The same applies also to higher magnifications (above about 0.4 ×) with the extension tubes.

Numbered notes:

(1) CL = close-up lens (40 cm focal length); 7, 14, 25 = length in mm of extension tubes.

(2) Lens-to-subject distances (not lens-to-film plane).

(3) Figures measured for 50 mm *f*1.8; values very similar for 50 mm *f*1.4.

EXTENSION TUBES WITH MACRO LENSES

Lens	*Close-up aid (1)*	*Lens/subject distance (from front lens rim)* *mm*	*inches*	*Scale of reproduction* *Magnif.*	*Red. 1:*
80 mm Macro	25	640	25.0	0.14×	7.25
	25 + 7	393	15.5	0.23×	4.33
	25 + 14	295	11.6	0.36×	2.75
	25 + 14 + 7	238	9.4	0.41×	2.45
	25 + CL	242	9.5	0.36×	2.75
	25 + 7 + CL	195	7.7	0.44×	2.25
	25 + 14 + CL	167	6.5	0.57×	1.75
	25 + 14 + 7 + CL	148	5.8	0.67×	1.5
38 mm Macro (2)	None	71	2.8	0.87×	1.15
	7	62	2.5	1.18×	
	14	56	2.25	1.35×	
	25	51	2.0	1.6×	

The 80 mm and 38 mm macro lenses have no focusing movement and hence yield sharp images with extension tubes and (in the case of the 80 mm lens) the close-up lens only at single fixed distances. In view of the special close-up correction of these lenses, definition performance is however good. The 38 mm macro lens is mounted via the PM-MTob adapter. Still larger scales are possible with further extension tube combinations; here the tube set-up however becomes inconvenient and the bellows should be used. (They are preferable with the macro lenses, anyway.)

Numbered notes:

(1) CL = close-up lens (40 cm focal length); 7, 14, 25 = length in mm of extension tubes.

(2) Mounted via PM-MTob adapter.

Magnif.	*50 mm Macro (N)*		*50 mm Macro (R)*		*80 mm Macro*		*38 mm Macro*		*20 mm Macro*	
	B mm	*L/S mm*	*B mm*	*L/S mm*	*B mm*	*L/S mm*	*B mm*	*L/S mm*	*B mm*	*L/S mm*
0.4×	*		–		79	243	–		–	
0.6×	*		–		**95**	**176**	–		–	
0.8×	74	77	–		**111**	**143**	–		–	
1.0×	84	64	102	62	**127**	**123**	–		–	
1.2×	–		112	53	**143**	**110**	–		–	
1.4×	–		123	47	**159**	**100**	–		–	
1.6×	–		134	42	**175**	**93**	–		–	
1.8×	–		144	38	**191**	**88**	–		–	
2.0×	–		155	35	**207**	**83**	**75**	**44**	–	
2.2×	–		166	33	223	80	**83**	**43**	–	
2.4×	–		177	31	(**)		**90**	**41**	–	
2.6×	–		187	29	(**)		**98**	**40**	–	
2.8×	–		198	28	–		**106**	**39**	–	
3.0×	–		209	26	–		**113**	**38**	–	
3.5×	–		–		–		**132**	**36**	–	
4.0×	–		–		–		**151**	**35**	–	
4.5×	–		–		–		**170**	**34**	**73**	**21**
5.0×	–		–		–		**189**	**33**	**83**	**21**
5.5×	–		–		–		**208**	**32**	**93**	**20**
6.0×	–		–		–		**227**	**32**	**103**	**20**
6.5×	–		–		–		(**)		**113**	**20**
7.0×	–		–		–		(**)		**123**	**20**
8.0×	–		–		–		–		**143**	**19**
9.0×	–		–		–		–		**163**	**19**
10.0×	–		–		–		–		**183**	**19**
12.0×	–		–		–		–		**223**	**18**
Subject/film addition	54 mm		50 mm		60 mm		48 mm		39 mm	

* Magnifications obtainable with lens directly on camera—but minimum bellows extension too long

** Can be reached with bellows and ext. tubes but cumbersome—better use next shorter focal length

Magnifications obtainable with macro lenses used in conjunction with the Auto-bellows. The bold values are preferred ranges.

Higher magnifications are possible with the 80 mm and 38 mm lenses by adding extension tubes to the bellows; in these cases it is however more convenient to switch to the 38 mm and 20 mm lenses respectively.

B in all cases is the location of the rear edge of the rear bellows standard on the scale, when the front standard is pushed fully forward against the rail screw.

L/S is the distance in mm from the front lens mount to the subject plane. The distances give an approximate indication of the amount of space available for lighting etc.

N indicates normal mounting and *R* retro mounting of 50 mm macro lens,

Subject/film addition: The table indicates lens/subject distances. To obtain subject/film distances, add together the bellows extension value (*B*) and the lens/subject distance (*L/S*) for the required magnification, and add to this the subject/film addition shown at the bottom of the appropriate lens column. For example, with the 38 mm macro lens at 3× magnification, the subject/film plane distance is 113 + 38 mm (*B* + *L/S*) plus 48 mm (subject/film addition) = 199 mm.

The figures are also valid for the 20, 38 and 80 mm macro lenses used on the PMT-35 bellows. The setting values on the bellows scale are there however higher by 13 mm (e.g. for the 80 mm macro lens at 1.0× magnification, the bellows scale setting would be 140 mm and not 127 mm) because the PMT-35 bellows scale does not start at zero. To calculate total subject/film distance however use the figures for *B* in this table, not those corrected for the PMT-35 scale. (i.e. the total subject/film distance with the 80 mm macro lens at 1.0× would still be 127 + 123 + 60 mm = 310 mm—*not* 140 + 123 + 60 mm).

Magnif.	*50 mm f1.8(N)*		*50 mm f1.8(R)*		*50 mm f1.4(N)*		*50 mm f1.4(R)*	
	B *mm*	*L/S* *mm*	*B* *mm*	*L/S* *mm*	*B* *mm*	*L/S* *mm*	*B* *mm*	*L/S* *mm*
0.7×	69	92	–		69	82	–	
0.8×	74	83	–		74	73	–	
0.9	79	76	–		79	66	–	
1.0×	85	70	–		85	60	–	
1.2×	–		78	78	–		74	78
1.4×	–		89	72	–		84	72
1.6×	–		99	67	–		95	67
1.8×	–		109	63	–		105	63
2.0×	–		120	61	–		115	60
2.2×	–		130	58	–		126	58
2.4×	–		140	56	–		136	56
2.6×	–		151	55	–		146	54
2.8×	–		161	53	–		157	53
3.0×	–		171	52	–		167	52
3.5×	–		197	49	–		193	49
4.0×	–		223	48	–		219	48
Subject/film addition	45 mm		50 mm		50 mm		50 mm	

* Use 55–49 mm step-down adapter ring on front of reversed lens to couple with bellows

** Data similar with 135 mm *f*2.8 lens but lens/subject distances 28 mm shorter at all settings (*f*3.5 lens is more pronounced telephoto type)

*** Higher magnifications possible with extension tubes but with serious loss of image quality

While the macro lenses are specially corrected for a near focusing range, the other standard lenses and short tele lenses are usable in the near range subject to some limitations. In particular, they need more stopping down for reasonable sharpness over the whole image area.

The standard (50 and 55 mm) lenses should be mounted normally (*N*) at reproduction scales up to 1.0×, or reversed (retro-mounted) for higher magnifications (*R*). These lenses should be set to infinity. The 100 and 135 mm lenses—given here as examples of longer focal length to obtain greater lens/subject distance—are used with the focusing movement set to its closest distance (*C*). With the 50 and 55 mm lenses the bellows can be mounted on the VST-1 stand; use the copy stand or other arrangement for the 100 and 135 mm lenses as the minimum lens/subject distance is here too great for the VST-1.

OTHER LENSES WITH BELLOWS

Magnif.	*55 mm f1.2(N)* B *mm*	*55 mm f1.2(N)* L/S *mm*	*55 mm f1.2(R)** B *mm*	*55 mm f1.2(R)** L/S *mm*	*100 mm f2.8(C)* B *mm*	*100 mm f2.8(C)* L/S *mm*	*135 mm f3.5(C)* B *mm*	*135 mm f3.5(C)* L/S** *mm*
0.7×	72	80	–		88	252	110	362
0.8×	78	70	–		98	234	123	338
0.9×	83	62	–		108	220	136	319
1.0×	89	56	–		118	209	150	304
1.2×	–		–		138	193	177	282
1.4×	–		93	75	158	181	204	265
1.6×	–		104	70	178	172	231	253
1.8×	–		115	66	198	165	(***)	
2.0×	–		126	63	218	159	–	
2.2×	–		137	60	(***)		–	
2.4×	–		149	58	(***)		–	
2.6×	–		160	56	–		–	
2.8×	–		171	55	–		–	
3.0×	–		182	53	–		–	
3.5×	–		211	51	–		–	
4.0×	–		–		–		–	
Subject/film addition	61 mm		50 mm		73 mm		102 mm ($f3.5$) 109 mm ($f2.8$)	

* Use 55–49 mm step-down adapter ring on front of reversed lens to couple with bellows

** Data similar with 135 mm $f2.8$ lens but lens/subject distances 28 mm shorter at all settings ($f3.5$ lens is more pronounced telephoto type)

*** Higher magnification possible with extension tubes but with serious loss of image quality

B is the bellows extension, being the location of the rear standard on the bellows rail scale when the front (lens) standard is moved fully to the front rail end.

L/S is the lens/subject distance (measured from subject plane to front lens mount).

Subject/film addition: The tables indicate lens/subject distances. To obtain subject/film distances, add together the bellows extension value (*B*) and the lens/subject distance (*L/S*) for the required magnification, and add to this the subject/film addition shown at the bottom of the appropriate lens column. For example, with the 50 mm $f1.8$ lens used at 1.0× magnification, add together 85 + 70 (*B* + *L/S*) + 45 mm (subject/film addition) = 200 mm total subject/film plane distance.

SLIDE COPIER LENS AND BELLOWS SETTINGS

Lens	*Mounting*	*Focus setting on lens*	*Alignment of*			*Magnif.*
			Front of bellows rail (mark) on slide copier arm	*Lens standard on bellows rail (front)*	*Camera standard on bellows rail (rear)*	
Same-size copying						
80 mm Macro	Normal	–	1× orange	25 mm (1)	152 mm (2)	1×
50 mm Macro *f*3.5	Normal	0.3 m	1×/1.5× white	25 mm (1)	95 mm (3)	1×
50 mm *f*1.4, *f*1.8, *f*2	Normal	∞	1×/1.5× white	25 mm (1)	108 mm (4)	1×
Magnified copying						
80 mm Macro	Normal	–	1.5× orange	25 mm (1)	192 mm (5)	1.5×
50 mm Macro *f*3.5	Reversed (retro)	0.23 m	1×/1.5× white	0 mm (6)	120 mm (7)	1.5×
50 mm Macro *f*3.5	Normal	0.23 m	1×/1.5× white	25 mm (1)	108–110 mm (4)	1.5×
50 mm* *f*1.4, *f*1.8	Reversed (retro)	∞	1×/1.5× white	0 mm (6)	88 mm	1.5×
80 mm Macro	Normal	–	forward of 1.5× orange	25 mm (1)	230 mm (8)	2×
38 mm Macro	Normal (on PM-MTob)	–	1×/1.5× white	0 mm (6)	80 mm	2×
50 mm*	Reversed (retro)	0.23 m	1×/1.5× white	0 mm (6)	145 mm	2×
80 mm Macro	Normal	–	forward of 1.5× orange	0 mm (6)	230 mm (8)	2.3×
38 mm** Macro	Normal (on PM-MTob)	–	1×/1.5× white	0 mm (6)	115 mm** (7)	3×
50 mm Macro	Reversed (retro)	0.3 m	1×/1.5× white	0 mm (6)	230 mm (8)	3.6×

* Lens needs stopping down to at least *f*8

** Still higher magnifications possible with increased bellows extension but unlikely to be needed

Positions of lens standard and camera standard on the bellows rail and the alignment of the latter against appropriate marks on the slide copier panel, as a starting point in setting up the slide copier for same-size or enlarged reproduction. The magnification is determined by the bellows extension (distance from front of lens standard to rear of camera standard) and by the lens. Alignments of front rail are approximate, preparatory to fine focusing. Combinations marked with (*) yield even overall sharpness only with the lens stopped down to at least *f*8 or even *f*11; with other combinations stop down to *f*5.6.

Enlarged reproduction figures here go beyond the combinations described in the text (Chapt. *Small-scale close-up equipment*).

Lenses are listed in each magnification range in descending order of preference and close-up image quality. Intermediate positions yield intermediate magnifications.

Numbered notes refer to locations of standards on *bellows rail:*

(1) Orange/white line mark. (2) Orange 1× mark. (3) Bellows fully compressed. (4) White 1× mark. (5) Orange 1.5× mark. (6) Extreme front of bellows rail. (7) Near white 1.5× mark. (8) Extreme rear of bellows rail.

PMT-35 SETTINGS

Lens	*Magnif.*	*Coarse adjustment of*		
		Object stage (1)	*Lens standard (2)*	*Illuminator lamp (3)*
Transillumination				
80 mm	3× to 0.9×	Up	Down	Slightly out
	0.75×	Down	Down (4)	Slightly out
	0.5×	Down	Down (5)	In
	0.37×	Down	Up (5)	In
38 mm	8× to 2.9×	Down	Down	In
	2.9× to 1.9×	Down	Down (5)	In
20 mm	16× to 6.2×	Down	Down	In
	6.2× to 4.8×	Down	Down (5)	In
Shadowless lighting with Lieberkühn reflector (no suppl. condenser)				
38 mm	8× to 2.9×	Down	Down	Slightly out
20 mm	16× to 6.2×	Down	Down	Slightly out

Coarse adjustments as initial settings of the object stage and lens standard plus preliminary lamp socket adjustment on the PMT-35 macrophotography unit. The 'down' position of the object stage is the stage rail on the PM-DL 95 illuminator fully lowered on its dovetail guide. The 'up' position has the stage dovetail rail raised in its dovetail holder as far as it will go without unscrewing the stop pin. In both cases the rack-and-pinion fine focusing adjustment of the stage along the rail covers all object positions within the magnification range indicated.

The lens standard is nearly always located at the bottom end of the bellows rail ('down'); the 'up' position implies that the lens standard is raised to the top of its 70 mm long rack. The magnification scale on the bellows rail for the camera standard is in this case not valid. At the lowest magnifications with each lens a sufficiently short bellows extension is only obtainable by removing the leaf shutter at the rear of the lens standard. To retain leaf shutter use in these ranges preferably switch to a longer-focus macro lens.

The lamp socket is normally fully pushed home in the lamphouse; in the cases indicated, pulling the socket out by about 5 mm improves evenness of illumination.

The data for shadowless lighting with the Lieberkühn reflector apply to the supplementary condenser (for 20 and 38 mm macro lens) *removed* from the main condenser.

Numbered notes:

(1) Refers to position of stage rail in front dovetail holder.

(2) Refers to position of lens standard on lower section of bellows rail.

(3) 'Slightly out' means pulling lamp socket about 5 mm out of lamp housing.

(4) Lowest magnification obtainable with shutter in position.

(5) With shutter removed. (With 20 mm and 38 mm lens in this magnification range switch to 38 or 80 mm respectively.)

MAGNIFICATIONS AND SUBJECT FIELDS

Scale of reproduction	*Subject field on 24 × 36 mm film*	
	mm	*inches*
0.1× (1:10)	240 × 360	9.45 × 14.2
0.2× (1:5)	120 × 180	4.7 × 7.1
0.3× (1:3.3)	80 × 120	3.15 × 4.7
0.4× (1:2.5)	60 × 90	2.35 × 3.5
0.5× (1:2)	48 × 72	1.9 × 2.8
0.6× (1:1.67)	40 × 60	1.57 × 2.36
0.7× (1:1.4)	34 × 51	1.35 × 2.02
0.8× (1:1.25)	30 × 45	1.18 × 1.77
0.9× (1:1.1)	26 × 40	1.05 × 1.57
1×	24 × 36	0.94 × 1.42
1.5x	16 × 24	0.63 × 0.94
2×	12 × 18	0.47 × 0.71
2.5×	9.6 × 14.4	0.38 × 0.57
3×	8.0 × 12.0	0.31 × 0.47
3.5×	6.8 × 10.3	0.27 × 0.40
4×	6.0 × 9.0	0.24 × 0.35
4.5×	5.3 × 8.0	0.21 × 0.31
5×	4.8 × 7.2	0.19 × 0.28
6×	4.0 × 6.0	0.16 × 0.24
7×	3.4 × 5.1	0.13 × 0.20
8×	3.0 × 4.5	0.12 × 0.18
10×	2.4 × 3.6	0.09 × 0.14
12×	2.0 × 3.0	0.08 × 0.12
14×	1.7 × 2.5	0.07 × 0.10
16×	1.5 × 2.25	0.06 × 0.09

Size of subject field taken in at different scales of reproduction in close-up macrophotography. The subject fields are based on the full 24 × 36 mm frame recorded on the film; the field on the focusing screen is smaller. Subject fields at intermediate magnifications are proportional. Thus at 0.25× magnification the field would be 96 × 144 mm (or 10 times the field at 2.5×).

CLOSE-UP DEPTH OF FIELD

Magnification	*Limiting aperture*	*Total depth of field (mm) at*					
		f3.5–4	*f5.6*	*f8*	*f11*	*f16*	*f22*
0.1×	–	27	41	59	81	117	162
0.2×	–	7.5	11.1	16	22	32	44
0.3×	–	3.6	5.3	7.6	10.5	15	21
0.4×	–	2.2	3.2	4.6	6.4	9.2	13
0.5×	*f*22	1.5	2.2	3.2	4.4	6.3	8.7
0.6×	*f*22	1.1	1.6	2.3	3.2	4.7	6.5
0.7×	*f*22	0.87	1.3	1.8	2.5	3.7	5.0
0.8×	*f*22	0.71	1.0	1.5	2.0	3.0	4.1
0.9×	*f*16	0.59	0.87	1.2	1.7	2.5	3.4*
1×	*f*16	0.50	0.74	1.1	1.5	2.1	2.9*
1.5×	*f*11	0.28	0.41	0.59	0.81	1.2*	1.6*
2×	*f*11	0.19	0.28	0.40	0.55	0.79*	1.1*
2.5×	*f*11	0.14	0.21	0.30	0.41	0.59*	–
3×	*f*8	0.11	0.16	0.23	0.32*	0.47*	–
3.5×	*f*8	0.092	0.14	0.19	0.27*	0.39*	–
4×	*f*8	0.078	0.12	0.17	0.23*	–	–
4.5×	*f*5.6	0.068	0.10	0.14*	0.20*	–	–
5×	*f*5.6	0.060	0.089	0.13*	–	–	–
6×	*f*5.6	0.050	0.072	0.10*	–	–	–
7×	*f*4	0.041	0.060*	0.086*	–	–	–
8×	*f*4	0.035	0.052*	–	–	–	–
10×	*f*3.5	0.028	0.040*	–	–	–	–
12×	*f*3.5	0.023*	0.033*	–	–	–	–
14×	*f*3.5	0.019*	–	–	–	–	–
16×	*f*3.5	0.017*	–	–	–	–	–

In the close-up and macro ranges, depth of field rapidly decreases and also becomes dependent only on the scale of reproduction.

In addition to listing the theoretically available depth of field at different magnifications and apertures, the table shows the limiting aperture beyond which the lens should not be stopped down at higher magnifications. Otherwise diffraction effects lead to increased unsharpness that masks any gain in depth of field.

The depth values marked (*) indicate depth that would be available in the absence of diffraction; in practice at these limiting settings depth of field is somewhat greater but the standard of sharpness is also inevitably reduced. Where no depth values are given, the lens should not be stopped down to that aperture at the magnification in question.

The values for the limiting aperture and total depth of field are based on an approximate sharpness standard of a 0.03 mm circle of confusion.

LAMP FILTER TYPES AND DESIGNATIONS

Filter type	*45 mm round unmounted (glass)*	*45 mm round mounted (interference)*	*45 × 60 mm rectangular unmounted (glass)*
Monochromatic			
Yellow	45 Y-48	–	60 × 45 Y-48
Green	45 G-53	–	60 × 45 G-53
Heat filter (cobalt glass)	–	–	60 × 45 B-76
Diffuser	–	–	60 × 45 WF
Colour temperature compensating	45 LB-45	–	60 × 45 LB-45
	45 LB-100	–	60 × 45 LB-100
	45 LB-200	–	60 × 45 LB-200
	–	43 LBD W-45	–
Neutral density	–	43 ND-6	–
	–	43 ND-12	–
	–	43 ND-50	–

In conjunction with the LSD and PM-DL 95 micro spotlights the lamp filters modify the light quality and intensity. The monochromatic filters are used primarily as contrast filters in photomicrography and macrophotography, the colour temperature compensating and neutral density filters for colour temperature and intensity control in colour photography. The 45 × 60 mm rectangular filters fit the LSD illuminator, the other filters fit the LSD, PM-LSD 2 and PM-DL 95 illuminators. Colour temperature and neutral density filters can be used in combination. The LSD and LSD-2 illuminators can take two filters at the same time, the PM-DL 95 up to 4 filters.

ND FILTERS FOR MACROPHOTOGRAPHY

Transmission	*No. of ND filters used*			*Effective*	*Exposure factor*	
%	*ND 50*	*ND 12*	*ND 6*	*total density*	*Arith.*	*EV*
50%	1	–	–	0.30	2×	–1
25%	2	–	–	0.60	4×	–2
12%	–	1	–	0.92	8×	–3
6%	–	–	1	1.22	16×	–4
3%	1	–	1	1.52	33×	–5
1.5%	2	–	1	1.82	66×	–6
0.72%	–	1	1	2.14	138×	–7
0.36%	1	1	1	2.44	275×	–8
0.18%	2	1	1	2.74	550×	–9

The number designation of the ND 50, ND 12 and ND 6 filters indicates their percentage transmission—used here to mark the fact that these are lamp filters to reduce the illumination of the LSD and LSD 2 illuminators or the transilluminator of the PMT-35 macro outfit.

The table indicates the transmission, effective density and exposure factors (in arithmetic values and EV) with different ND filter combinations of the PMT-35 outfit. The latter includes two ND 50 and one each ND 12 and ND 6 filters.

LAMP FILTERS FOR COLOUR TEMPERATURE CONTROL

Colour temperature K	*Lamp voltage V*	*Filters*	*Use with*
3200	4.5	LBD + LB 45	Tungsten type (3200K balanced) colour reversal film
	5	LBD	
	6	LB 45	
	7	None	
3400	5	LBD + LB 45	Type A (3400K balanced) colour reversal film
	6	LB 45	
	7.5	None	
4000	6	2× LB 45 or LB 100	Acceptable for negative colour films
	7	LBD	
4500–5000	6	LB 100	Negative colour film or daylight type colour reversal film (warm colours)
	8	2× LB 45	
5500	6	LB 100 + LB 45 or LB 200	Daylight type colour reversal film
	7–8	LBD + LB 45	

The colour temperature of lighting in macrophotography depends on the lamp voltage of the LSD illuminator or PM-LD 95—which can be controlled by the transformer setting and may be modified also by colour temperature compensating filters. The preferred way of matching the colour temperature to the colour film type in use is by checking with the CT (colour temperature) probe of the EMM-7 exposure meter. Lacking such a meter, this table shows approximate colour temperatures obtainable by varying degrees of over-running the lamp of the micro spotlight with or without colour temperature compensating filters. The exact colour temperatures obtained may vary somewhat depending on the age of the lamp.

EMM-7 EXPOSURE SCALE FOR BELLOWS READINGS

Index scale	*Exposure time (sec)*		*Index scale*	*Exposure time (sec)*	
	High	*Low*		*High*	*Low*
1			5		
	1/15	2			1/4
2			6		
	1/30	1		1/250	
3			7		
	1/60				1/8
4		1/2	8		
5	1/125		9		
		1/4			1/15
6			10		

When the EMM-7 exposure meter cell is located in the equivalent film plane (via the PM-EA adapter) exposures are derived by reference to the innermost index scale of the meter. This table shows the actual exposures for different scale readings with the meter switched to its HIGH or LOW range. Note that many of the exposure time settings for the leaf shutter (PMT-35 or PM-PBM housing) or for the camera shutter are between numbered positions on the index scale. As often intermediate exposures are not possible, carry out the final exposure matching with the lens aperture.

INDEX